from the
Which?

THE GOOD FOOD GUIDE
1980

Edited by Christopher Driver

Founded in 1951 by
Raymond Postgate

Consumers' Association and
Hodder & Stoughton

The Good Food Guide 1980 is published by
Consumers' Association and Hodder & Stoughton
on behalf of The Good Food Club Ltd.,
14 Buckingham Street, WC2N 6DS
© The Good Food Club Ltd. 1980

Maps
© The Good Food Club Ltd.

The Good Food Guide is published annually.
This is a new edition, brought up to date
throughout, and with a new Preface. Please do not
rely on an out-of-date Guide. Since many of the
places in the last edition are no longer recommended
(some have closed or changed hands), disappointments
may well result.

Other publications from The Good Food Guide:
The Good Food Guide Dinner Party Book (£4·95)
The Good Cook's Guide (paperback, £3·95)
The Good Food Guide Second Dinner Party Book
(£5·95)

Design by Banks & Miles

Cover design by Tony Garrett

*Typeset, printed and bound in Great Britain by
Hazell Watson & Viney Ltd,
Aylesbury, Buckinghamshire*

CONTENTS

HOW TO USE THE *GUIDE*

CLASSIFICATION Generally speaking, British hotels and restaurants are too diverse for precise classification. Descriptions are indispensable. But over the years, the *Guide* has found that most restaurants and hotels fall naturally into one of the following categories:

Credit This category sets the tone for all entries in the *Guide*. It indicates careful, honest cooking, of whatever national style that is appropriate to the resources of the place. It also embraces wide variations of character and – be it freely admitted – quality. *Guide*-users will know that before they visit a restaurant, they are wise to read all the lines in an entry, and sometimes between them as well. Many different people's thoughts and experiences are represented in what is written, and we therefore like to print as many approvers' names as there is room for (provided the people concerned give their consent on the report forms).

Pass These places are signified by a short description with details printed underneath the text instead of approvers' names. These are hotels and restaurants which are seldom worth seeking out for the sake of their food, drink and service alone, but they are often welcome places to discover, either in a parched terrain or as alternatives to more expensive places. Please remember that we need reports on these places just as badly as we need them on others. This year's pass can be next year's credit – or drop-out.

Italic entries In both these categories, italic type is used to denote a new, newly organised, or otherwise disputable place on which a satisfactory verdict cannot be reached by the time we go to press. We are particularly anxious for reports on these.

DISTINCTION Restaurants and hotels may earn one or more of the following *Good Food Guide* distinctions. The 'pestle', the 'tureen', the 'bottle', the 'glass' – and the value-for-money underlinings – set bench marks for the ambitions of restaurateurs and the judgments of Good Food Club members.

A pestle-and-mortar symbol denotes unusual skill, imagination and energy in a chef or team. Good Food Club members will bestow this label grudgingly. Sound materials, judicious menu-building, and a good technique should be looked for, as well as indefinable, indispensable flair, and more than ordinary reliability.

A tureen is confined to hotels. It signifies at once a well-kept table and a house where it is a pleasure to stay for more than a weekend. This category recognises those hoteliers, especially in parts of the country popular for holidays, who are conspicuous for the trouble they take to please their guests, and whose kitchens can produce – perhaps not every night, but often – a dish or a meal of 'pestle-and-mortar' standard.

A bottle denotes a wine list and service out of the usual run. Here again, it is best to be cautious. Skill is above all shown in the compilation of a well-balanced and annotated list, suitable to the pocket and preferences of discriminating customers, and in cellaring and service. (Service alone can easily subtract pounds from the real value of mature claret or burgundy, and a smoky atmosphere can render the wine almost worthless.) For this distinction to be awarded, a current list must be submitted before the *Guide* goes to press.

A glass symbol picks out places whose resources of skill, space, or capital are not equal to the demands of a 'bottle', but which make a serious effort, in a complicated market, to pick out wines of character, even for the cheaper end of the list. The glass symbol is also sometimes used for places whose wine lists, taken in isolation, might deserve a 'bottle', but which suffer from one or other of the shortcomings discussed in the previous paragraph.

BEER Our criteria for describing the various kinds of beer are outlined on p. 443 of the pub section.

CARAFE WINES The Weights and Measures (Sale of Wine) Order 1976 restricts carafe wines to sealed bottles or open vessels holding one of the following quantities: 25 cl, 50 cl, 75 cl, one litre, 10 fl oz (half a pint), or 20 fl oz. The place must tell you, if you ask, which measure is being used, but in almost all cases where the information has been supplied on our questionnaire we have ourselves specified not only the measure but also the origin or brand.

RESTAURANTS Unless otherwise stated, a restaurant is open all the week and all the year and is licensed. Meal times refer to first and last orders.

Cost of a meal for one
Tdh £5 (meal £7·90)
Alc £7·20 (meal £10·50)

The first **table d'hôte** figure is the cost of a set meal as notified to us by the restaurant in autumn 1979. The first **à la carte** figure is our estimated cost of three middle-priced courses from the menu. The **meal price** (in brackets) in both cases is the food price for one person, with 'extras' (cover and service), plus coffee and half one of the cheapest bottles of wine. Without wine, the cost may well be £2 less. (In oriental or health-food restaurants, we have substituted the kind of food and drink customarily ordered.) 'Service inc' means that an inn's policy is to incorporate any service charge in its food prices. Prices quoted in the text and rubric of details now include VAT.

Value Prices underlined in the left-hand column like this: Tdh D £5·50 (meal £7·25) are those which represent, in our judgment, unusual value for money, taking wine as well as food prices into account. They are not necessarily the cheapest restaurants in the *Guide*. (See list on page 506.)

Children, smoking, music These topics are discussed in the Preface (page 11). Any arrangements for, or exclusions of, children and smokers that are notified to us by proprietors are incorporated either in the text or in the rubric of details at the side. But it is wise to confirm when booking if the answer affects a decision. Silence about music implies no music – to the best of our information.

Access for the disabled ⟨♿⟩ means that doorways are over 33 ins wide and passages 4 ft, and that there are no more than the stated number of steps leading to the restaurant; 'w.c.' means that the lavatories are accessible to wheelchairs – (m) and/or (f). This information has been provided by the restaurants. Please let us know of any inaccuracies.

HOTELS Bed and breakfast and full board prices are those quoted to us by hoteliers; where possible we have given minimum off-season prices for one person sharing a double room and maximum in-season prices for one person in a single room.

Dogs In hotels, 'no dogs in public rooms' may mean that dogs are allowed in bedrooms. Enquire.

Fire cert This phrase (see regulations in the Fire Precautions 'Hotels and Boarding Houses' Order, 1972) means that a hotel was granted a Fire Certificate before we went to press.

GOOD HOTEL GUIDE and CAMPAIGN FOR REAL ALE Hotels whose style and residential amenities are also described in the 1980 *Good Hotel Guide* (an independently edited Consumers' Association publication) have the letters GHG appended to the text. Pubs whose beer also earns an entry in the 1980 *Good Beer Guide* have the letters CAMRA appended to the text. These arrangements are reciprocated by the books in question.

ABBREVIATIONS

a.c.	appellation contrôlée	*Chr*	Christmas	*inc*	inclusive
alc	à la carte	*cl*	centilitre	*L*	lunch
App	approvers	*D*	dinner	*min*	minimum
B&B	bed and breakfast	*d/r*	dining-room	*n.v.*	non-vintage
c.b.	château-bottled	*exc*	except	*p.d.*	per day
Ch.	Château	*fl oz*	fluid ounces	*p.w.*	per week
		HT	high-tea	*res*	residents
				rest	restaurant
				tdh	table d'hôte

TELEPHONE For major cities which have a basic STD code and several all-figure subsidiary exchanges, a dash separates the code from the local number. Thus the telephone number of the Midland Hotel in Manchester is 061-236 3333. For other places listed in the book, the name of the exchange is given, with the formal STD code in brackets. This code will be different when calling from the restaurant's locality.

MAPS Any town or village in which there is a *Guide* entry is printed in black on the maps at the end of the book. 'Credit' recommendations are in bold capitals; 'pass' entries are in small letters; hotels are indicated by a triangle; distinctions have a bolder type and are outlined. A tankard indicates a pub, a glass a wine bar (both in italic type – see map key).

REPORTS Please send in reports as soon as you can during the year, but particularly before September 30, 1980, in time for the next *Guide*. Report forms are at the back of the book. When you have filled them in, send them without a stamp to Freepost, The Good Food Guide, 14 Buckingham Street, London WC2N 6BR, and we will gladly send you more. (Freepost facilities are available only from the United Kingdom.)

THE GOOD HOTEL GUIDE

Consumers' Association and
Hodder & Stoughton £4·95

This year Consumers' Association is publishing for the first time Hilary Rubinstein's *Good Hotel Guide*, which appears simultaneously with the *Good Food Guide*. The two books remain independently edited, from separate sources of information. But Hilary Rubinstein will be very grateful for any reports that Good Food Club members send him about hotels they have stayed in anywhere in Europe, including the British Isles. No stamp is needed for reports to either book if the letters are posted within the United Kingdom, and the addresses are:

The Good Food Guide, Freepost, WC2N 6BR
The Good Hotel Guide, Freepost,
W11 4BR

Reports to the one book will be copied for the benefit of the other *only if the writers so request*.

See also: Preface, page 11; and How to Use the Guide, page 4

DISTINCTIONS

London

Capital Hotel Restaurant, SW3

Carlton Tower Chelsea Room, SW1

Connaught, W1

Le Gavroche, SW1

Lichfields, Richmond

Ma Cuisine, SW3

Oslo Court, NW8

Tante Claire, SW3

Tate Gallery Restaurant, SW1

Vasco and Piero's Pavilion, W1

England

Alresford, Hants
O'Rorkes

Ambleside, Cumbria
Rothay Manor

Bourton-on-the-Water, Glos
Rose Tree

Bray, Berks
Waterside Inn

Burham, Kent
Toastmaster's Inn

Cauldon Lowe, Staffs
Jean-Pierre

Chagford, Devon
Gidleigh Park

Cheltenham, Glos
Food for Thought

Chesterton, Oxon
Kinchs

Chittlehamholt, Devon
Highbullen Hotel

Christchurch, Dorset
Splinters

Cleeve Hill, Glos
Malvern View Hotel

Colyton, Devon
Old Bakehouse

Dartmouth, Devon
Carved Angel

Dedham, Essex
Le Talbooth

East Grinstead, W. Sussex
Gravetye Manor

Fressingfield, Suffolk
Fox and Goose

Gittisham, Devon
Combe House

Glastonbury, Somerset
No 3 Dining Rooms

Grasmere, Cumbria
White Moss House

Gulworthy, Devon
Horn of Plenty

Halesworth, Suffolk
Bassett's

Heald Green, Gtr Manchester
La Bonne Auberge

Helford, Cornwall
Riverside

Henley-in-Arden, Warwicks
Le Filbert Cottage

Hintlesham, Suffolk
Hintlesham Hall

Horton, Northants
French Partridge

Isle of Wight
Peacock Vane

Kenilworth, Warwicks
Restaurant Bosquet

Malvern Wells, Hereford & Worcs
Croque-en-Bouche

Manchester
Midland Hotel

9

Montacute, Somerset   ♟
Milk House

Northleach, Glos   ♔
Old Woolhouse

Oxford, Oxon   🍾
Restaurant Elizabeth

Les Quat' Saisons   ♔

Pool-in-Wharfedale, W. Yorks   ♔ ♟
Pool Court

Poundisford, Somerset   ♟
Well House

Ramsgate, Kent   ♔
Mallet's

Rugby, Warwicks   ♟
Andalucia

St Martin in Meneage, Cornwall   🍲
Boskenna

Shepton Mallet, Somerset   🍾
Bowlish House

South Petherton, Somerset   🍾
Oaklands

Thornbury, Avon   ♟
Thornbury Castle

Tiverton, Devon   ♟
The Lowman

Ullswater, Cumbria   🍲
Sharrow Bay

Uppingham, Leics   ♟
Lake Isle

West Runton, Norfolk   ♟
Mirabelle

Windermere, Cumbria   ♔ 🍲 🍾
Miller Howe

Wye, Kent   ♟
Wife of Bath

Wales

Llandewi Skirrid, Gwent   ♔
Walnut Tree Inn

Llanychaer Bridge, Dyfed   🍲
Penlan Oleu

Swansea, W. Glam   ♟
Drangway

Scotland

Achiltibuie, Highland   🍲 ♟
Summer Isles Hotel

Ballater, Grampian   🍲
Tullich Lodge

Eddleston, Borders   ♟
Cringletie House

Glasgow
Central Hotel
Malmaison Restaurant   🍾

Ubiquitous Chip   ♟

Gullane, Lothian   🍲 🍾
La Potinière

Inverness, Highland   🍲
Dunain Park

Nairn, Highland   🍲
Clifton Hotel

Perth, Tayside   ♟
Timothy's

Uphall, Lothian   ♟
Houstoun House

Channel Islands

Sark   🍲
Aval du Creux

Ireland

Cork, Co Cork   🍲 🍲 🍾
Arbutus Lodge

Dunderry, Co Meath   ♟
Dunderry Lodge

Gorey, Co Wexford   🍲
Marlfield House

Mallow, Co Cork   🍲 🍲 ♟
Longueville House

Oughterard, Co Galway   🍲
Currarevagh House

Shanagarry, Co Cork   🍲 ♟
Ballymaloe House

PREFACE

The eighties on which we are now embarked will be the fourth decade of the *Good Food Guide*'s publication, and it is usual to log yesterday's cross-currents before looking round for the next set of charts. Everyone will have different images of the past thirty years, even in the narrowly focused field of public eating and drinking. But the broad outlines are recognisable: in the fifties, a sense of revival after prolonged austerity, symbolised by what came to be called the '*Good Food Guide* restaurant' and the 'Elizabeth David dinner party'; in the sixties, optimistic spending and a developing mass market for wine, built on subsidised food and other economic illusions which both professionals and amateurs in catering took for the dawning of the millennium; in the seventies, a mounting fear that the accountants were closing in. This last was an anxiety somewhat relieved by the vast sums that foreign visitors have lately been spending in British restaurants and hotels, and also by stimulating changes in diet that could not be attributed entirely to the need for economy (ethnic diversification in the cities, and, everywhere, the restless chopping and whizzing sound of the middle class turning towards healthier food, more casually served).

However, future historians will be more interested in the continuities of the period than in the subdivisions. Raymond Postgate, and the group of friends who helped him, first published the *Guide* in 1951. These were the years in which it became respectable for British men and women with other professional responsibilities to pay attention to the way food was procured, priced and cooked for their own and other people's tables. After all, their only alternative was to put themselves at the mercy of impersonal, mildly distrusted food technologists, retailers, and marketing magicians. With the virtual disappearance of personal service outside a few clubs and colleges, almost everyone now under sixty has spent his adult life in a society where he and his family had to do their own shopping and cooking if they wanted to eat well. No wonder they became at first more frequent, latterly more occasional, but also more discerning customers of restaurants.

The middle class was reconciled to this new system of life-support by its chemists and its engineers. Powders and substitutes, deep freezes and microwave ovens, and other devices have gradually transformed procedures and tastes wherever food is sold for either private or public consumption. Most of these innovations have been greeted in this book with reproof or apprehension, usually justified on the palates of Good Food Club members, who are singularly resistant to uniformity and blandness in what they eat and drink. But when a housewife buys a food processor to bring the classical mousses and sauces of French cuisine within reach of her own time, talent and temperament, she is the child of modernity, as surely as her sister is, who fills her deep freeze with TV dinners. The same contrast and similarity apply to restaurateurs. The choice is between people who are mastering the future and those who are enslaving themselves to it.

The *Good Food Guide* lives by the 10,000 letters that a tiny minority of restaurant customers send annually to this address, so that all of us can share the knowledge of the places in the British Isles where a meal out is a pleasure, not just a convenience. Customers who take this trouble deserve everyone's gratitude, the catering trade's included. Every year I find the experience of reading these letters, for summary and extraction in the pages that follow, by turns absorbing, amusing, humbling, and infuriating, and we shall shortly announce the results of an informal competition we have held to pick out the most perceptive and useful reports we received during 1979. But at another level, the experience is also puzzling. One couple will send to the *Guide* long, loving, and constructively critical accounts of meals they have eaten in the most creative and often costly restaurants to which we are able to direct them. Another couple, if they eat out at all, will go where there are no mysteries beyond steak and scampi, and if they use a restaurant guide at all, ours will not be the one they find most useful. But both couples may have grown up at the same time, perhaps with very similar incomes and educations, if with different expectations, in neighbouring sectors of the same national culture. By what right, it could be objected, does the *Guide* rate the preferences of the one above the other?

This goes to the heart of various assumptions – implicit in the very title – that the *Good Food Guide* has made for thirty years, under Postgate's editorship as under mine. They are worth a moment's thought at the outset of another decade, because *Guide*-users make more useful contributions to this, their annual commentary on the British table, if they have worked out for themselves what they mean by 'good' when they attach the word to 'food'. In short, looking at the whole spectrum of more-or-less-edibles from *haute cuisine* to teenage junk food, what do you dismiss because you happen not to like it, and what are you prepared to call a bad idea, badly executed and unscrupulously priced? (I am reminded that my own mother-in-law is apt to use the phrase 'it's not "good food" ' in offering my family something perfectly wholesome for supper, meaning that it's not what a restaurant would do, and unable to convince herself that the restaurant's version would almost certainly be inferior.)

A further reason for re-examining first principles is that this year for the first time, Consumers' Association is simultaneously publishing the *Good Hotel Guide*, which makes a serious claim to descent from Postgate's original concept of a guide written by its own readers, and is therefore most welcome to the list. The editor, Hilary Rubinstein, explaining his policy in the 1980 edition, makes an interesting attempt to differentiate between the approaches of his book and ours by suggesting that even when you have counted the beds and listed the amenities the all-important atmosphere of a hotel eludes measurement and classification; it matters more to explain why X or Y like staying there and Z does not. Whereas with cooking, merit is more nearly measurable: dishes fail or succeed, and the trained critics among the *Good Food Guide*'s inspectors can tell the difference.

I am not sure that it is as difficult to be certain about hotels or as easy to be certain about meals as this suggests. With food, it is easier to measure close or distant approximation to the goal of excellence if you start, as some do, from the premise that all food is aspiring to the condition of French-ness. Perhaps even in the real, messy world of British catering, value judgments were more clear-cut in 1950. Postgate's circle of friends included a good chef (Philip Harben) and other indignant eaters whose memories and taste-buds told them the qualitative difference between a crisp chip and a recycled mashed potato. The conditions were ripe for a crusade, and it came – as it did again, much later, with the founding of the Campaign for Real Ale. But what kind of crusade have you joined now, when you return the address card interleaved with the bookshop edition of this book, or despatch a report or two on the Freepost forms we supply at the end of the book (with more to be had on request from this office)?

Well, the format, print order, and information content of the *Guide* have swollen beyond recognition from the edition that cost me five shillings as late as 1955 (this was then the price of a standard hotel set lunch). But the principles remain as they are stated on the back cover: no advertising, no free meals, and so on. So does the circle of regular, cherished, knowledgeable correspondents from many different walks of life. This team of voluntary inspectors, though continually refreshed by newcomers, still includes a few who were part of the enterprise at the beginning. So does the spark of democratic devilment, originally struck by the 1950s caterers who thought they knew what Jones would swallow. Thanks to all these influences, the *Good Food Guide* is quite happy to leave the whited sepulchres of the West End restaurant trade to the people who enjoy them, and worry more about doing justice to the talented and conscientious woman in Chuckleton Canonicorum who will serve her guests nothing that she has not cooked herself. Generosity where praise is due and disrespect where it is not are qualities that come easily to the generation that was born with the *Guide*: there is room for both on our report forms, and if you think the discovery of the best and the elimination of the worst can be left to the self-criticism of 'professionals', you have never read either the advertising or the editorial matter in *Caterer and Hotelkeeper*.

But the question about 'good' food remains. With restaurants, it is particularly difficult to keep a sense of qualitative proportion when a meal for two can cost the same as a well-cut suit, and when the price gap between different restaurants of real merit often expresses the income expectations of different nationalities and cultures, rather than taste and protein content alone: compare the Italians and the Chinese on the one hand with the French and the Japanese on the other.

However, in all the arts and crafts, cooking not excepted, it is usually easy to know what is objectively fine when you meet it. This *Guide* edition, for example, will seem thinner to many for want of two places in particular: Crane's in Salisbury and Chez Nico in London. Both restaurants were created by individuals likely to reopen elsewhere, but for the moment it is not invidious to mention them as examples of styles that existed in this country thirty years ago either barely or not at all. The difficulties of judgment, in the absence of precise or universally accepted criteria of quality in a society where some people eat restaurant meals for the sake of the cooking and others for quite different reasons, arise at the margins of this book. It may then be a question of deciding between the 'gourmet experience' that one restaurateur has thawed from Alveston Kitchens' catalogue, and the simple daube or cleanly fried fish that a less – or more? – ambitious competitor has chosen to provide. In such cases, is our notorious self-confidence in adjudication itself justified?

Not always, I am sure. After all, the *Guide* has probably done at least its share in persuading the British bourgeoisie into eating more garlic per capita than the northern French do, and into accepting its lamb and duck as pink as its sirloin. Most of the people who eat for this book prefer their food in these ways, but in the last analysis it is only a preference, not comparable with the educated wine-lover's knowledge that '66 claret is 'better' than Hirondelle, just as Mozart is better than Salieri, and for one or two of the same reasons (complexity, durability . . .)

However, it is also true that most *Guide* entries carry with them another kind of objectivity. In other words, if the book says or implies that Signor Dante's pizza house is better than Signor Petrarco's, this normally means that several people not unfamiliar with pizzas in Britain, Italy, America or all three have committed themselves on paper to this view. That combination of an objective critical process with the collective tastes of a large if self-selected group of people (the Good Food Club's 60,000-plus members) is the whole fun and utility of the *Guide* they buy and use. We who compile it are, more willing than many think to bend our own taste and judgment to accommodate a clear message from members' reports. In these pages, there are a few places which, left to ourselves, we would omit; though there are a good many more that are in because we believe in them, even though we have not really heard enough about them from members at large. But you will not find us putting into the book, simply to fill a large white space on one of our maps, a place that takes excellent raw materials and subtracts goodness from them when it cooks them. I do not have to remind you that in Britain such places are as common in 1980 as they were in 1950 – perhaps more so, relative to the variety of food and drink that this generation of chefs and waiters is in a position to spoil if it so chooses.

For economic and other reasons, it seems unlikely that the British middling classes will ever eat as richly again as some of them have done in the past thirty years. But that does not mean they cannot eat as well, or even better, given the diversity of produce and styles now available to them. The visible popularity of restaurants, and the apparently affluent youth of their customers, suggest that the social catchment has widened, however stringent the financial pressures

15

sensed by individual providers and consumers. I hope it is still true, as a French optimist wrote nearly a century ago, that

> 'The allure, the success of restaurants, and their assurance of perpetual life attended by a steady growth in prosperity, depends on their cooking, whose very roots lie in our desire for variety. Changeable as the generations or the seasons, always adaptable to new forms that fit a diversity of places, people, and occasions, cooking owes no obedience to any fixed rule except the rule of taste. It expresses the eternal present.'
>
> 'L'homme qui dîne', in *La Salle à Manger* (1891).
> I owe the quotation to Jean-Paul Aron's
> *Le mangeur du XIXe siècle* (Paris 1973), p. 316.

EVEN SO, there are undoubtedly plenty of eating places where the cooking pleases but other aspects of the experience do not. No-one expects or seeks disputes about civil liberty as soon as he crosses the threshold of a restaurant. But it is naive to pretend – as many caterers and some customers do – that the genial, yours-to-command atmosphere of a meal out in a public place makes it possible to please all the people all the time. The most frequent sources of irritation or conflict appear to be children, smoking, and music. Other potential areas of disagreement – dogs for example – have faded into the background: I have occasionally seen a dog sitting at, and once on, a restaurant table, but the phrase 'no dogs' is now widespread in the details that accompany *Guide* entries.

Before going further, I should declare my own interests: I have children, who were till recently young enough to be turned away by many places in this book; I dislike tobacco smoke; and I am too fond of good music to be indifferent to the seepage of aural margarine in places where I like to eat or talk. However, it is up to individual proprietors to decide how they should reconcile interests of this kind with others. The starting point is to realise that conflict exists, and that to achieve equitable solutions may require thought and firmness as well as the more ingratiating qualities people expect of caterers.

Take **children**. British people, by and large, are fond of particular children but not of children in general. It is noticeable that Chinese and Italian restaurants, and customers of these nationalities, are usually content to see whole families lunching or dining with young children in tow, while the gentrified British, aiming (as they sometimes say) at 'the atmosphere of a dinner party', often regard children as an

16

intrusion and their tastes an inconvenience. (Of course, the sheer expense of such 'dinner parties' now usually ensures 'adults only', whatever is said.) Somewhere between these stylistic extremes lie innumerable hotels and restaurants that could and should be more receptive than they are to the needs of children and their parents, at least until either or both have proved themselves awkward or disruptive customers. After all, one of the main reasons why the British eat out comparatively seldom by European standards, and are therefore forced to pay through the nose when they do, is that they have not been brought up to it; in other words, they have not learnt as children how to respect the process of cooking and eating in adult company, either at home or in restaurants, and so, when they come to spend money themselves on meals out, they do so either reluctantly or unwisely. This aspect of our culture cannot be reformed overnight, and caterers long-sighted enough to try, with tomorrow's customers in mind, could not expect to reap the benefits themselves. But that is no reason for the national tourist boards, especially, to stand idly by while places they promote or subsidise persist in excluding from their rooms and tables parents who are accompanied by children under fourteen.

Incidentally, in the pages that follow, where children are offered meals at reduced prices, this is indicated in the column at the side of entries. Unusual *attitudes* – whether receptive or discouraging – are often mentioned in the text. Please let us know of your own experiences. But please also be reasonable: some children can wreck any restaurant for others as well as for their parents, and should not be taken until they have learnt better; others, though well behaved, may spread unhappiness in spite of themselves unless their parents have taken care to find out in advance what adaptations of menu and/or price can conveniently be made.

As for **smoking**, it remains obvious from readers' letters that this is a sphere where the mild or (some would claim) intense pleasure of some restaurant customers is bought at the price of genuine distress and annoyance to others. Sometimes one group is in the majority, sometimes the other, but counting heads is not really the point. Air-conditioning helps in some places, but it usually mitigates the nuisance without dissolving it, and there are plenty of places in this book whose atmosphere late on a Saturday night can only be compared with the residual smoking compartments on London tube trains, which even hardened smokers often try to avoid. In other words, smokers in a confined space upset people; non-smokers provoke nobody, and have no counter-attack open to them, except asking their persecutors to desist. The conclusion ought to be obvious, but with honourable exceptions (listed on page 501) restaurateurs and others are reluctant to draw it. One well-known London caterer, though authoritarian enough to withhold from her customers things to eat that she happens not to like herself, rejects all rules about smoking as an infringement of personal liberty, presumably on the grounds that the liberty to kipper other people outweighs the liberty not to be kippered yourself. Indignation expressed by customers in the *Guide* and elsewhere has achieved much in recent years, notably by throwing the worst offenders on to the defensive. But short of a further change in people's habits – which from observation of the young seems unlikely – general restraint must await legislation to ban smoking in a wide range of public places, restaurants included.

Many restaurateurs, including M Albert Roux of Le Gavroche, say when pressed that they would be the first to support this, because it would free them to follow their own personal distaste for smoking without having to look over their shoulders at commercial competitors. But in the meantime, it is worth reporting from my own correspondence that those restaurateurs who have been brave enough to ban pipes, cigars and even cigarettes in their dining-rooms are very seldom criticised for it, even by smokers. The angry customers they have trembled to offend turn out to be tobacco tigers – or else are instantly replaced by new friends. Whereas the places that serve fresh food and fine wines in a haze of foul air not only risk disqualifying themselves from the *Guide*'s highest distinctions, a minor misfortune perhaps; they also attract a strong undercurrent of discontent, voiced by some of their best customers and especially their best customers' wives. This cannot be in their own long-term interests, whatever the current balance sheets say.

At table, recorded **music** is less contentious than smoking, for simple reasons: very few restaurant-goers positively want it; a significant minority feel a positive distaste for it, or at least for the kind to which they are normally exposed; but in the middle there is a vast cohort of people who do not care either way. It would not be fair to ask restaurants to choose meal-time silence (apart from the hum of contented conversation) solely at the behest of professional musicians, among them some of the *Guide*'s most devoted followers, who desire when they dine a refuge from the aural fatigue that is a hazard of their job. But it is entirely fair to insist that the choice made between sound and silence, or between different kinds and qualities of sound, should ordinarily reflect the active wishes of the interested minority, not just the passive indifference of a restaurant's clientele – or service staff. (Waiters who pretend inability to turn the sound tap off on request even in an otherwise empty restaurant stand self-condemned for neglect of their basic function: to gratify paying customers.)

In these connections, one simple remedy is in the customer's hands – short of going elsewhere, which is not always possible. Every time anyone asks in a restaurant whether 'everything is all right, sir?' say (though only if it is true) that the food and drink are fine, but that your pleasure has been curtailed by the cigar at the next table, and by the noise coming out of the wall. The effect may be imperceptible at the time, but multiplied by the tens of thousands who buy and use this book, it will wear a hole in the starchiest shirt-front eventually. It is always worth remembering, as a customer, that restaurant staff do not know what you think until you tell them – and that this applies at least as strongly to what you like as to what you dislike. In this sense, if in no other, silence is the enemy of good cooking and good eating.

Christopher Driver

RESTAURANT 'HOUSE' CLARETS

by Edmund Penning-Rowsell

Last year the *Guide* published the results of a tasting of twenty cheap branded wines commonly found as the 'house' or 'carafe' wine on the lists of restaurants figuring in its pages. These results were disappointing, so we have now followed this up with a tasting of what, traditionally, has been the wine most commonly acceptable to that still rather small section of the British public that draws corks at least once a week – claret.

For this tradition we do not have to look back to the marriage of Henry Plantagenet to Eleanor of Aquitaine, but rather attribute it to the exceptional variety in quality and price of red wines in France's largest fine-wine area, and the ease of its transport by sea from the Gironde to the Thames, the Solent and the Severn. Cheaper than burgundy, superior in general to the Loire reds, and more accessible than those of the Rhône, claret has always been the cheapest wine of some distinction available here. Consequently, every traditional wine merchant has found it necessary to offer a 'house claret' and supply it not only to private customers but to restaurants, clubs and institutions where wine is provided.

Accordingly, we sought out a selection of basic *appellation contrôlée* red Bordeaux from traditional wine merchants, who ought to know how to select them, and who supply restaurants that wish to list as their house red something better than *ordinaires* of varying origin. We bought clarets from such firms as Averys, Berry Bros and the Malmaison Wine Club (which supplies the wines for British Transport Hotels); and to provide a comparison we bought a red *vin de table* from another old-established City of London wine merchant, Corney and Barrow, although it was not bottled by them but by Lebègue. This firm, as experts in French postal codes could discover from close examination of the label, is established in St Emilion, but there is no claim that the wine in question is from Bordeaux.

It must be admitted at once that in selecting a 'house claret' British merchants have a problem. In France basic Bordeaux Rouge and Bordeaux Rouge Supérieur – the difference is only one of slightly higher alcoholic strength, though this may give added character to the wine – are nearly all consumed within a year of the vintage. They form the Sunday *déjeuner* wine of many French families, particularly in Paris and in the north of France. They are deep-coloured, rather raw wines, yet with a touch of 'class' that distinguishes them from the everyday '*Onze*' or '*Douze Degrés*' in litre bottles. However, few of us who drink claret in Britain are attuned to such wines, and we look for something rather rounder, more mature-tasting and less aggressive. Yet to hold down the price the merchants here cannot afford to keep such basic wines very long, especially not at current interest rates.

Unfortunately, in the circumstances, a great deal depends on the bottle-age of these wines, which can round out and improve quite remarkably after a year in bottle if the quality is reasonable, and will be notably better even after six months. An alternative device, increasingly used for such wines, is to produce them by the *macération carbonique* process, by which the grapes are put into a closed vat, covered with CO_2, and the juice expressed by the weight of grapes. Thereafter the wine is fermented in the normal way, but the result is non-tannic, fast-maturing wine that lacks the character of traditionally made wines. Originating, as far as France is concerned, in the Rhône, and also practised in the Beaujolais region, *macération carbonique* is being used more and more in the lesser areas of the Gironde. How many of the wines that we sampled were made by this process could not be known, although we suspected that some were; and for wines of this kind, why not?

Apart from myself, the tasting team of eight men and women consisted of the Editor, the Chief Inspector, and other wine drinkers no more 'expert' than thousands of the critical customers who frequent the restaurants in this *Guide*.

Nine wines had been selected for sampling, but unfortunately one of them was distinctly volatile, indeed vinegary. This was Findlater's Selected Claret, an AC Côtes de Bourg, selling in a 70-cl bottle for £2·75 – an above-average price that the origin might have justified. As bad bottles may come from the most reputable of sources, we tried a second but this was no better. (However, the wine provided a useful object lesson in the importance of that often derided procedure, tasting at table. None of us found it drinkable, but by no means all of us, experienced drinkers included, became suspicious on the basis of a sniff alone.)

So we were left with seven clarets and the single *vin de table rouge*, and these we rated from 5 ('very good') down to 1 ('very poor'). Of course our rating was in terms of the level of quality expected, and not that of classed-growths. Some intermediate 'half-marks' were given, and this was partly attributable to the fact that several wines were found better or less good the second time round, and were given an improved rating, although all had been opened well in advance of the tasting.

	AVERAGE (OUT OF 5)
Vin de Table Rouge 12°, Corney and Barrow Ltd. bottled by Lebègue 73 cl £1·84	2·86
Good Ordinary Claret, Berry Bros & Rudd Ltd. AC Bordeaux 70 cl £2·47	2·92
Bordeaux Rouge AC, Christopher's 70 cl £2·24	2·78
Bordeaux Supérieur AC, Averys 70 cl £2·40	2·92
College Claret '78, Dolamore AC Bordeaux Supérieur 73 cl £2·42	3·00
Bordeaux Supérieur AC, Malmaison Wine Club (BTH) Selected by William Bolter, shipped and bottled by Paul Faugerois, Floirac 75 cl £2·30	3·97
Médoc AC, Harvey's 70 cl £2·64	4·11
Marquis de Ville, El Vino AC Côtes de Bourg, VSR 70 cl £2·35	2·61
Findlater's Selected Claret, Findlater Mackie Todd & Co, Ltd. AC Côtes de Bourg 70 cl £2·75	—

On the whole, the results were disappointing this year too, though one must make allowance for the absence of food, for the initial hardness of most young claret makes it difficult to taste on its own, and tannin is mollified by food. However, like was more or less being compared with like. Only two wines were given the 'very good' (5) rating by any tasters: the Malmaison Wine Club Bordeaux Supérieur bottled in Bordeaux (two tasters) and Harvey's Médoc (one taster). The latter was also given a 'good' (4 or 4½) mark by six of the tasters, leaving it with the highest mark (an average of 4.11) on the list. The BTH claret attracted 4 'goods', and came second overall, with an average of 3·97. As can be seen from the table all the others came a long way behind. Only three of the other half-dozen wines rated 'good' (4) average rating, although Dolamore's College Claret '78 (the only wine with a vintage on the label) secured this rating from three of the tasters, but was let down by the low evaluations of some of the others. So although third in the rank order, its average was exactly 3 ('acceptable'). El Vino's Marquis de Ville picked up a couple of 'goods', but otherwise achieved the lowest rating (an average of 2·61 being 'poor'), and the only other 'good' was given by one taster to Averys Bordeaux Supérieur, which was generally reckoned as no more than 'acceptable' and averaged

2·92, exactly the same as Berry Bros Good Ordinary Claret, for which the level of marking was more uniform. Half the tasters put Christopher's Bordeaux Rouge in the 2 ('poor') class, and it scored marginally less well than Corney and Barrow's 12° Vin de Table Rouge. This was markedly the least expensive wine. Otherwise the differences in price were slight, although all but two were in bottles containing 70 cl, whereas the BTH wine contained 75 cl – the size to be enforced by the EEC, and already compulsory for exports to North America – and Dolamore's 73 cl, hitherto the normal size for red and white Bordeaux bottled at source.

In theory, Harvey's Médoc should have been the best wine, as the appellation is a superior one compared to the others, and it was satisfactory that its 'class' was confirmed. One comment was 'fair colour, good wine with some style and flavour of Médoc.' Another was 'pleasant – round, well-balanced, decent length; tastes like Médoc', and a third 'fruity on nose, well-built and might keep well.'

Nearly everyone commented on the deep colour – generally a good sign – of the Malmaison Bordeaux Supérieur, and its fruitiness was liked, although its youth was commented on, and one taster wrote: 'I wouldn't know what it would turn into, but I'd sooner wait till it does.' By that time, in all probability, it will all have been consumed!

As the voting showed, opinions were more divided about Dolamore's College Claret, which was last year's 'yard-stick' wine among the *ordinaires*, and had then shown very well. Indeed one of this year's tasters expressed the view that he had remembered better from this source in the past. It was generally noted as very light in colour – possibly a *macération carbonique* wine – but having a real claret flavour, although one taster detected 'gooseberry'! Several felt that it needed more age, which is almost certainly true of a year-old '78 claret of any quality. The Averys and Berrys wines that tied for fourth place produced similarly varying opinions. Of the former, although one taster stated that this was the first wine 'with any real weight and length' (the wines were tasted in the order shown in the table), the general view was that it was light in colour, sharp and short; but one taster thought it would repay keeping and had 'a touch of class'. The Berrys Good Ordinary Claret was considered rather too ordinary, even slightly woody, by one taster, and most noted its light colour, liked the nose and either found it 'pleasant' or disappointing compared with the bouquet. Others found it sharp or short.

Although the greater amount of colour of Christopher's Bordeaux Rouge was noted, it was generally thought lacking in flavour and character. One found the nose 'chemical', to another the taste was 'mouldy', but others more generously accepted it as a very light claret.

El Vino's ennobled Bourg had few supporters, and even the taster who marked it 'good' and noted its 'characteristic Bourg nose and flavour' found it 'slightly sour', which was a fairly general reaction.

Finally, although three of the tasters put Corney and Barrow's Vin de Table Rouge in the 'poor' class, others liked it more; rather a negative wine, but for its somewhat indeterminate status not a bad one.

What conclusions can readers and restaurant clients deduce from this tasting? First, of course, that tastes vary according not only to experience but to what the drinker looks for in a wine. The more sophisticated the taster the more critical he or she is likely to be, whatever allowances are being made. But this applies also to food and almost everything else where quality is a consideration.

Secondly, the claret drinker must not expect too much from these mostly basic red Bordeaux. At the same time the slightly higher appellation of Bordeaux Supérieur and the definitely higher Médoc one seemed to be reflected in quality.

Thirdly, better value for money may be found in table wines that conscientious and skilful merchants have selected from other less expensive regions of France. Exploration of these must await another year.

The usual *caveat* about the vagaries of bottling must be entered. Apart from the unfortunate Findlater wine, a second bottle of the Berrys claret was opened, following some variations in opinion, but there was no marked difference.

Finally, the fact that several of the wines tasted better when they had been opened for an hour or more demonstrates that this does pay off, and emphasises the point that in most cases the wine should be the *first* not the last thing ordered and brought to table in a restaurant. This will give it a chance to breathe and soften the asperities of youth. No doubt to ask for the wine to be decanted would be better still, but with the house wine, generally the cheapest on the list, that might take a touch of bravado seldom found among British restaurant patrons.

Vintage Chart

This year the 1–7 vintage rates, intended to be helpful but in no way claimed to be infallible, have been amplified by brief notes on every vintage likely to be found on a restaurant list. It does not go back further than 1967. Those prepared to lay out their money on earlier vintages are likely to be sufficiently aware of what they are ordering not to need notes, although the earlier years are included in the chart itself for the historical record.

As usual, a warning must be given against expecting an even level of quality throughout an area, especially if it is one covering a great extent of country, such as the Rhône and the Rhine. For quite small distances, the differences in quality may be marked. For example, it is generally agreed that in 1971 the St Emilions and Pomerols were superior to the Médocs; in 1976 the reverse was probably true.

Finally, a rating must be related to the age of the wine. It would almost certainly be a mistake to open the much-esteemed 1975 classed-growth Médocs in the expectation of finding them ready to drink, just as it is foolish to count on such rarities as the 1953s still being at their best.

YEAR	BORDEAUX CLARET	BORDEAUX SAUTERNES	BURGUNDY RED	BURGUNDY WHITE	LOIRE WHITE	RHONE RED	GERMANY	ENGLAND
1955	5	5	5	5	4	5	4	—
1956	1	—	—	—	—	—	—	—
1957	2	3	4	4	—	5	2	—
1958	3	4	—	—	—	—	—	—
1959	6	6	6	5	6	6	6–7	—
1960	3	2	—	—	—	3	2	—
1961	7	4	6	5	4	7	4	—
1962	4	4	3–4	7	—	5	3	—
1963	1	—	—	—	—	—	—	—
1964	4–5	3	5	5	4	5	5	—
1965	1	—	—	—	—	—	—	—
1966	5–6	4	6	6	4	5	4	—
1967	3–4	7	3–4	4	3	5	3	—
1968	1–2	—	—	—	—	—	—	—
1969	2	3	5	5	5	5	6	—
1970	6*	5	4	4	6	5	4	5
1971	4–5	6	6	6	5	6	7	6
1972	2*	2*	5	3–4	3	6–7*	3	—
1973	3–4	3*	3–4	6	6	3*	4	5
1974	4	1*	3	3	3	3*	3	2
1975	6*	6*	2*	4	6–7	3–4*	7	3
1976	6*	5*	6*	6*	6	6*	7*	4
1977	3*	—	2	3	2	4	3	2
1978	—	—	6*	6*	4	7*	3	5
1979	—	—	4†	—	—	—	—	—

7 = very good
1 = poor
* = recommended for future rather than current drinking
† = Beaujolais only

Rhine and moselle have been combined since in no case do they differ by more than half a point.

In port and champagne, vintages are declared in good years only. The best include:
Port: 1945, 1948, 1955, 1958, 1960, 1963*, 1966, 1967*, 1970*, 1975*, 1977*
Champagne: 1966, 1969, 1970, 1971, 1973, 1975

VINTAGE REPORT

Claret

1977. A very poor summer was followed by a fine autumn. The wines were usually green and unripe, though some were reasonably soft. Most were bottled early. Not much should be expected of them, nor much paid for them.

1976. Although the summer was very fine indeed, the weather at the vintage was unsettled and quality varies. The *petits châteaux* often lack colour, fruit and body, and are for early drinking; but the finer wines will certainly take time to develop. They should not be opened yet.

1975. Most of the wines of this much-acclaimed vintage are still very tannic and backward, and are far from ready to drink. There may be some exceptions among the *petits châteaux*, but they should be approached with caution and enquiry on any wine list.

1974. In general these wines of a prolific vintage lack charm, owing to bad weather at vintage time. So far they seem hard and 'ungrateful', although in Bordeaux they are usually thought to have greater prospects of development than the 1973s. The St Emilions and Pomerols are rounder than the Médocs or Graves. Inexpensive at source, they have been widely bought for restaurant drinking in both France and Britain. Enquire about any particular wine before ordering.

1973. Yet another 'vintage of the century' was diluted by poor weather at the vintage. The crop was a record for Bordeaux and, made in the middle of the slump, the wines were inexpensive. Although light, many have turned out most attractive for drinking now, and, with the usual *caveat* about variable quality, are probably the best bet for restaurant drinking. But they should not be too expensive, even well into the classed-growth hierarchy.

1972. Hard, unripe, acid wines, and generally the worst vintage since 1968. But some have lost some of their aggressiveness, and there are those who find a few now drinkable. Unless recommended by a restaurant-owner or *sommelier* on whom one can rely, they are best left alone.

1971. These wines have developed much more quickly than anticipated, and many of even the leading growths are very near their peak, the *petits châteaux* more so. They lack some body and fruit, but most make very agreeable drinking now. A good vintage to order in a restaurant, but not to pay astronomic prices for, as some well-known names produced disappointing wine.

1970. The lesser wines of this vintage now make very agreeable drinking, but the finer are still very backward and closed-up, therefore disappointing to drink now and, probably, for several years to come. Certainly a very fine year, but on the whole it needs keeping.

1969. Originally over-praised and over-priced, these wines have turned out thin and lacking in body, fruit and character. A few Pomerols and St Emilions made acceptable wines, but generally these are not bottles on which to spend one's money.

1968. Whatever virtue there was in a handful of the clarets of this vintage has now departed.

1967. Apart from a few leading growths most of the wines of this vintage are now showing their age, although remaining agreeable, easy-to-drink clarets, and still retaining some character and distinction. A vintage to drink now, but not one to expect too much from.

White Bordeaux

1978. Successful dry wines in a small crop, but not much is expected of the Sauternes.

1977. Although in a poor year dry white Bordeaux often fares better than the red, the lack of sun produced 'skinny', green wines.

1976. An excellent crop of dry wines, and a fair one of the sweet, but neither as good as the previous year.

1975. A very fine year both in the Graves and Sauternes, which made probably their best wines of the decade.

1974. An undistinguished vintage throughout the white wine districts, with the Sauternes particularly disappointing.

1973. All but the small band of top quality white Graves are likely now to be past their best, while the poor weather at the vintage spoiled the prospects of the Sauternes.

1972. No better in their way than the red wines: unripe and green.

1971. An excellent year in all parts of the white wine districts. The '71 Sauternes are very good, and probably more lively and with more character than the '70s.

1970. A fine, relatively plentiful year, with successful wines everywhere.

Red Burgundy

1978. Nothing but Beaujolais is likely to appear on restaurant lists in 1980. While much promoted, it was not, however, a classic Beaujolais vintage, as 1976 was, for the *cru* wines – Moulin-à-Vent, Fleurie, etc. – lack the body and the backing for real distinction. They should still drink well in 1980, but are not worth extravagant prices.

1977. A very poor year throughout the red wine region. After a miserable summer the wines lacked fruit.

1976. A very fine year, but, in contrast to Bordeaux, the wines are big and backward, with a considerable amount of tannin. They are predicted as requiring years to come round – after the 1978s, some suggest. A very fine year for *cru* Beaujolais.

1975. A disappointing year with rather thin wines.

1974. Some quite good burgundies were produced this year, but it depended almost entirely on the skill and careful selection of the individual growers. Before ordering any that may be found on a restaurant list the wine waiter's advice should be sought – and quickly evaluated.

1973. This big vintage, as everywhere, produced light wines. Coming from a good source they can still make amiable drinking – light in colour and soft on the palate – provided that they are not over-chaptalised (sweetened).

1972. This vintage suffered in reputation from the poor quality of the over-priced clarets; but in fact some fine big fruity red burgundies were produced that year. The best have some time to go, but are certainly drinkable and worth looking at.

1971. Deliciously well-balanced wines, neither too big nor too light. Caution is needed as some were affected by hail, and a decayed '*goût de grêle*' resulted. But generally an excellent vintage for current drinking.

1970. A big vintage, which in its time produced agreeable, early-maturing wines, but these have now generally disappeared, and only the exceptional bottle remains.

White Burgundy

1978. An excellent vintage whose only failing was its high prices from Chablis in the north to the Côte Chalonnaise in the south, though the value for money was more evident in this latter area. The Côte d'Or wines are certainly not ready for drinking in 1980, though the lesser Chablis should be.

1977. A poor, thin, mean year, though there was some acceptable Chablis.

1976. The last vintage to date of quality that is now drinkable, and the best year since 1973. Fine wines with excellent bouquet and plenty of body, but perhaps lacking a little acidity and so a bit short of liveliness. This may be a phase in their maturing.

1975. Better in whites than reds, and some agreeable wines were made, but they lacked 'guts', and developed fast. To be drunk without further delay.

1974. Acceptable if not very distinguished when they were young, but now generally past their best, and in any case probably all consumed.

1973. An exceptionally fine year which perhaps has yet to be equalled. Beautifully balanced wines. The lesser varieties will certainly be ready to be drunk up, but the more important single-vineyard Côte d'Or whites still have plenty to sustain them.

1972. The acidity and immaturity that affected this vintage everywhere in France outside Burgundy made these wines rather firm and 'ungrateful', but by no means bad. However they have nothing more to give.

1971. The finer wines of this excellent vintage are still à point, although they will scarcely improve, and the lesser ones may well have had their time. It would be wise now to restrict choice to wines bottled in France as these usually keep best.

1970. Never considered a great vintage in Burgundy, the best of these wines can still be found, surprisingly, in possession of all their faculties. But any to hand that were bottled in Britain are likely to be well past their best.

Loire

1978. Generalisations about the vineyards that intermittently line France's longest river are even more difficult to provide than elsewhere; but, broadly, 1978 was an acceptable year, and much superior to 1977. However, coming after the latter disappointing, small vintage, prices were elevated to levels that implied a quality higher than the reality. A good year in Muscadet.

1977. With the possible exception of Muscadet, where some acceptable wines were made, elsewhere the Loires, red and white, were green and raw, made from grapes not fully ripe.

1976. A very successful year throughout the region. The whites are now probably at their best, since few, except the finer sweet varieties in the Coteaux du Layon, are keepers.

1975. A fine, fruity vintage in which excellent wines were made throughout the long valley, especially the sweet types, but they should now be drunk.

For what may be called historical reasons the quality of earlier vintages is listed in the Vintage Chart, but as few wines before 1975 are likely to be found in restaurants any more detailed comment is valueless. They will probably be past their best anyway. Muscadet is generally drunk young, at least by the French

Rhône

1978. This was an exceptional year, with wines of very deep colour and full of fruit: big-bodied. But in consequence they are wines that will take time to develop, with the top qualities needing years. Châteauneuf-du-Pape and Côtes-du-Rhône made by the *macération carbonique* method, resulting in light, largely non-tannic wines, will mature much more quickly, but these are still in the minority. Very fine in whites too.

1977. A lighter than normal vintage, but generally superior to the burgundies. The whites are thought to be better than the reds.

1976. Another exceptional year, being compared with the classic '61s, though not so powerful and big. The lesser reds, such as Côtes-du-Rhône, and the whites should drink well in 1980.

1975. Generally regarded as a disappointing year, with the wines lacking body. The whites were often more successful, but generally white Rhônes are not for keeping. Acceptable wines at the Hermitage-Côte-Rôtie level.

1974. A better vintage than further north, with the more southerly wines, including Châteauneuf-du-Pape. more successful than the others. Not a great year, but one of at least acceptable quality for some years yet. A good year for whites, but they may well be now past their best.

1973. In this case the northern Rhône wines were much superior to the southern; particularly good in Hermitage and Côte-Rôtie. Otherwise the very large crop resulted in reduced quality.

1972. A very fine year in some parts, though the leading wines are still too backward to drink at anything like their best. More variable in the Côtes-du-Rhône, and considered disappointing in Côte-Rôtie.

1971. Another fine vintage, but thought to be rather more supple than the succeeding '72s. The top wines still need keeping, but any of the excellent whites, if still to be found, should doubtless be drunk.

1970. A successful vintage, showing its best at ten years old, but probably hard to find now.

Germany

1978. Possibly an even poorer vintage than 1977, with wines lacking both character and fruit. Little if any wine of qualities higher than QBA (Qualitätswein bestimmte Anbaugebiete) made.

1977. A rather thin poor year, generally lacking in balance, but wines from the most distinguished estates, particularly on the Mosel, succeeded in making some QBA wines that had fruit as well as acidity.

1976. An outstanding vintage. The finer wines are by no means ready, while the quality was so good that the lesser wines were notable for their relative scarcity.

1975. A very fine year, although now the palm is usually awarded to 1976. The wines are slightly less full and luscious, but this may be a recommendation to some. Again there was a shortage of wines of Kabinett quality and below, since the fine summer brought an abnormal proportion to the higher levels of Spätlese and Auslese.

1974. A poor year without distinction, though slightly better than 1973.

1973. The record size of this crop militated against quality and the wines were of little distinction.

1972. A poor year in which the grapes did not ripen.

1971. An outstandingly good year, and the finer wines are now ready for drinking, particularly in the Mosel and Rheingau. The 'small' wines will all have been drunk, and rightly.

1970. A very useful year in its time but now past its best.

England

England may be a small country, but its wine production, though tiny, is scattered in a way that makes a cursory summing-up almost meaningless. For 1977, for example, I have been given ratings as variable as 5 and 2: the former a very respectable marking, the latter distinctly poor. On the other hand, 1978 was much better, possibly with a rating of 5, but the crop was small. It is generally agreed that 1976 was the best recent vintage in England – and Wales – but there were also some very agreeable '75s. Earlier years, though recorded in the Vintage Chart, are there only for the benefit of viticultural archivists.

Closures and changes of management

Readers who notice the disappearance of a restaurant or hotel from the *Guide's* pages often ask why. For obvious reasons, we cannot tell them about individual cases. But it has been found helpful to list here places that have been dropped for reasons unconnected with inspectors' verdicts and other members' comments or silences: for instance, closure, fires, and material changes in management or kitchen team that took place too late for adequate investigation.

London
Chez François, N21
Chez Nico, SE22
Le Connaisseur, NW11
La Fringale, SW10
La Grenouille, SW11
Light of India, W6
Peking House, W2
William F's, SW10

England
Badwell Ash, Suffolk
Singing Chef
Bilbrook, Somerset
Dragon House Hotel
Blockley, Glos
Lower Brook House
Borrowdale, Cumbria
Leathes Head House
Brighton, E. Sussex
Lawrence
Claughton, Lancs
Old Rectory
Colchester, Essex
Wm Scragg's
Coningsby, Lincs
Ratty's
Great Dunmow, Essex
Starr
Halland, E. Sussex
Halland Motel & Old Forge Restaurant
Hastings, E. Sussex
The Mitre
Hertford, Herts
Maison Carton
Hungerford, Berks
Thompson's
Hythe, Kent
Gambrinos
Lymington, Hants
Limpets
Marlborough, Wilts
Pharoah and Clarke's
Norwich, Norfolk
Bistro Beano
Plush, Dorset
Brace of Pheasants

Southport, Merseyside
Le Coq Hardi
Southwold, Suffolk
Dutch Barn
Sutton Bingham, Somerset
Sutton Bingham Manor
Teignmouth, Devon
Churchill's
Thetford, Norfolk
Anchor Hotel
Tonbridge, Kent
A la Bonne Franquette
Torquay, Devon
Fanny's Dining Room
John Dory
Woolverton, Somerset
Woolverton House
Worthing, W. Sussex
The Paragon

Wales
Solva, Dyfed
Old Pharmacy
Three Cocks, Powys
Three Cocks Hotel

Scotland
Corsock, Dumfries & Galloway
Glaisters Lodge
Crinan, Strathclyde
Crinan Hotel
Cupar, Fife
Timothy's
Galashiels, Borders
Redgauntlet
Overscaig, Highland
Overscaig Hotel
Portpatrick, Dumfries & Galloway
Knockinaam Lodge

Channel Islands
Jersey, Gorey Pier
The Moorings
Jersey, St Peter
Greenhill Country Hotel

Republic of Ireland
Cahirciveen, Co Kerry
Murray's Seafood Restaurant
Dun Laoghaire, Co Dublin
Digby's

GREATER LONDON

AJIMURA   Map 15

51-53 Shelton Street,
W.C.2
01-240 0178

Susumi Okada aspires to fresh and authentic food
'just like a good provincial restaurant's in Japan.'
Certainly the leisurely air and simple, almost Nordic,
decor are light-years away from Tokyo neuroses. The
prices, sadly, are metropolitan but protein which is
fresh and tender enough to serve raw never comes
cheap (and on Mondays may not come at all). Risk
sashimi (slivers of raw mackerel, lemon sole and
salmon, perhaps, with horseradish, from £3·70), as
well as tempura (vegetables, prawns or fruit, mostly
crisply fried in batter), hiya yakko (chilled bean curd
with ginger and spring onion, 50p), lemon sole with
salted sea-urchin ('fine old Roman flavour', 70p) and
soba (buckwheat) noodles in broth, either hot or cold.
Novices might prefer to have a set meal and some
gentle instruction: various 'dinners' from £3·60 for
grilled mackerel (with hors d'oeuvre, soup, rice, fruit
and tea). Drink tea, saké (£1 for a tiny *tokkuri*),
French house wine (£3·22) or even 'Calpis, taste of
the first love', 35p.

Closed Sun; Sat L;
public hols
Must book D
Meals 12–2.30, 6–11

Tdh L £3·45 (meal £5·30),
D from £3·60 (meal £5·45)
Alc £5 (meal £7)

Service 10%
Seats 50 (parties 15)
No dogs
Access, Am Ex, Barclay

ALONSO'S   Map 16

32 Queenstown Road,
S.W.8
01-720 5986

Closed Sun; Sat L;
Apr 4 & 6; Dec 25 & 26
Must book
Meals 12.30–2.30,
7.30–11.30

Tdh L £4·60 (meal £9·95),
D from £8·05 (meal from
£11·70)

Seats 80
No dogs
Am Ex, Diners

Alonso Galvez has extended his habitat and Habitat
into the shop next door, but give or take a few
reservations about details, quality and value in his
Spanish cavern do not seem to have suffered. 'The
garlic bread is soggy, but it was soggy last year too.'
The style is all his own, and, as an inspector says,
one would not wish to meet his *outré* sweet-savoury
mixtures every week: besides, the brisk waiters
themselves may induce indigestion if the champagne
and Camembert soup, the seafood pancake with
Pernod and lobster sauce, the avocado and tomato
salad with sour cream and honey, and the fillet steak
with smoked salmon fail to do so. Still, though no
sensible person will expect three- or four-course
dinners with a dozen choices of main dish and almost
as many in the peripherals to be uniformly good,
everyone reports something nice: 'Pâté de foie with a
slightly marmalady sauce, followed by superb ajillo',
'succulent prawns, then guinea-fowl with fresh herbs
and green peppercorns, then lovely bitter-chocolate
sauce with ice-cream', 'three fish mousses wrapped in
smoked salmon, entrecôte with paprika and walnut

cream, and apple brûlée or petit pot de crème with Tia María.' Vegetables are more hit-and-miss, either side of *al dente*. The wine list has not been submitted, but look first at the Marqués de Riscals at about £5: big French names hardly suit the food even if purses are deep enough for them. Recorded music. No children under five.

App: D. G. Poole, David Potter, Nancy Taylor, Roy Mathias, D.A.S., Jane Winston, M.E., and others

---

L'AMICO Map 16

Dean Bradley House, 44 Horseferry Road, S.W.1 01-222 4680

One regular thinks Gino Tecchia (late of Locket's, *q.v.*) is dazzled by his division-bell distance from Westminster and 'charges £2 a head more than the food deserves.' Another still recognises the Old Russia's decor. But hung-over Russian loyalties are the stuff of Whitehall these days, and do not distract politicos from their tagliatelle with cream and ham (£1·75), 'good pea soup with crisp croûtons', scaloppine San Carlo (with peppers and mushrooms, £3·75), 'crisp and dry' courgettes in batter, and the rest. 'Poor cheesecake; good coffee.' Veronello is £3·55; other better Italian wines under £5.

Closed Sat; Sun; public hols	Alc £7·90 (meal £12)	Seats 80 (parties 28) Air-conditioning
Must book L Meals 12–2.45, 6.30–11	Service 12½% Cover 50p	No dogs Access, Am Ex, Barclay, Diners, Euro

---

LES AMOUREUX Map 13

156 Merton Hall Road, S.W.19 01-543 0567

Closed L; Sun; Aug; most public hols Must book D only, 7.30–10

Alc £5·80 (meal £8·70)

Service 10% Cover 30p Seats 48 ⅙ rest Access, Am Ex, Barclay

The divisions and draperies of the capacious room 'make it rather like eating in a grand French double bed', which seems appropriate enough to the restaurant Nigel Thomson and Angela Scott-Forbes conceived for Wimbledon doubles. Mr Thomson's food ideas – with the day's changes expressed in the handwritten menus – are also enterprising, though the thorns among the roses in reports suggest that he sometimes loses nerve in the execution: 'underseasoned pork in calvados and tasteless whiting in Provençal sauce'; 'dull and unsubtle mustard dressing for cauliflower.' However, another visitor was much better pleased by 'garlicky and strong' ratatouille with merguez and by veal in tarragon sauce well combined with red cabbage. A test meal, too, found hot coquilles of soft herring roes and avocado (£1·40) 'delicately cooked if you like the idea', crêpe of smoked haddock and spinach competent, and chicken breast with fresh ginger 'rather light on the ginger but not a bad dish.' Noodles with cream and mushrooms, vegetables, apple tart, coffee cream choux buns, and 'rather too sweet and smooth' cheesecake are also mentioned. Civet de lièvre (£3·50) and crème brûlée (£1) are other favourites. Cheeses are well varied, and one can surely protest if they are 'so sparingly served that a mouse wouldn't suffer indigestion.' Keen young girls serve under Angela's eye. The Fitou, Corbières, Limoux and other southern French wines under £5 are probably the best choices. Smoking and recorded music may both irritate some.

Recipe in Second Dinner Party Book: crème brûlée

App: Peter Casey, F. J. Darry, M.J.M.

ANARKALI   Map 13

303–305 King Street, W.6
01-748 1760 *and* 6911

One grumble against waning service in the late evening but, on the whole, King Street competition means extra effort and contented diners. Rafique is still in the kitchen, so 'spicy and creamy' moghlai chicken and lamb remain pleasures. Start with onion bhaji and expect 'subtle' methi gosht, good tandoori chicken ('with uninspired greenery'), tasty chicken korma (though prawn korma was too sweet) and 'salty sag'. Do they still serve kerala and niramish? Lager, and wine (£4·40 the litre). Sitar records.

Closed L Dec 25 & 26
Must book D & weekends
Meals 12–2.45, 6–11.45

Alc £4·75 (meal £5·70)

Seats 80 (parties 20)

No dogs
Access, Am Ex, Barclay, Diners

ANNA'S PLACE   Map 12

90 Mildmay Park, N.1
01-249 9379

Closed L; Sun; Mon;
3 weeks Easter; Aug;
3 weeks Chr; public hols
(exc May 5 & 26)
Must book
D only, 7–10.15

Alc £8·50 (meal £12·25)

Cover 35p
Seats 35
No dogs

Anna Hegarty has moved her restaurant and family, including her brother Eric Norrgren who cooks, to the Newington Green frontier of her N1 territory, where there is a little more room for cooking, dining, and living all at the same address. From the dark outside, the scene behind the shop window 'must recall a television opera' – Capriccio, perhaps, except for the Scandinavian (but not stark) decor. The food, though it includes Swedish classics such as the 'gravlax matured in a huge hand-carved trough', mixes nationalities as easily as opera casts do. One visitor therefore misses a sense of house style, but the whole is knit together by Anna's own warmly personal descriptions of what is being offered: Camembert frit with 'splendid deep-fried parsley and not-too-sweet gooseberry jam' and Chabichou grillé avec crème aigre, 'a whole goat's cheese the size of a night-light, gently browned, and set off by a sour-cream sauce flecked with chives.' (Guess which is the first course, which the third . . .) Lövbif (£4·05) – a steak beaten wafer-thin, like Italian carpaccio, and flash-fried – can be had either with Café de Paris butter or a traditional egg yolk in shell; filet de veau Maxim has 'a superb cream and wine sauce with mushrooms added at the last moment'; suprême de turbot au vin de Pouilly (£4·50) is a speciality; and vegetables are normally original and

33

admirable – 'not the tough and caramelised onions that came with *lövbif*, but the ingeniously fried *klyft potatis* (30p) and white cabbage (60p) steamed with cloves and orange juice and rind. Bread, butter, patisserie and coffee are also mentioned favourably. French-bottled house wines are £2·95 and there are other good choices from Laytons. In general, the quality for the price sets a high standard for 1980's first London restaurant opening. More reports, please.

Recipe in *Second Dinner Party Book*: Camembert frit

ARIRANG Map 15

31–32 Poland Street, W.1
01-437 6633 *and* 9662

Closed Sun; Apr 6 & 7;
Dec 25, 26 & 31; Jan 1
Must book
Open noon–11 p.m.
(L 12–3)

Tdh L from £2
(meal from £2·60),
D £7 (meal £8·10)
Alc £5 (meal £6·70)

Service 10%
Seats 65 (parties 35)
♿ rest
Air-conditioning
No dogs
Access, Am Ex, Barclay,
Diners

The functional ceiling pipes would suit a play set in a boiler-room (say, Henry Livings' *Eh*?) but the Wees have made the room into a grey-green Korean grotto, served by waitresses, 'gaudy as peacocks, strict as Jean Brodie.' You are reminded, as a guest puts it, that 'Seoul is a very expensive city', and sesame oil is the key to most tastes, but experienced orientalists find bul kal bee (spare ribs, £2·90), chilli-hot ojingo pokum (squid with green pepper in a thick red sauce, £3·50) and thak thoree tang (braised chicken) 'addictively delicious', while the raw shredded beef ball with fresh pear and a sweetish sauce remains 'the best new idea for many moons.' Shikumchee is a useful cold spinach side dish perhaps preferable to kosaree (marinated bracken shoots, 'rather khaki and chewy, but a great saving on the hill farm subsidy if the British could get the taste too'). The set meals are praised by some, criticised for cynicism or want of balance by others. Avoid neng myun (cold noodle soup, with pointless additions), and the Hyde Park branch too, by the account of a test meal there.

App: Joan Ellis, Rita Piepe, C.P.D., Nova Whyte, A.H., and others

---

ARK Map 13

122 Palace Gardens
Terrace, W.8
01-229 4024

This one-storey wooden hut looks too frail to survive the deluge but it has lasted eighteen years and members have spared their wrath this year. A bistro's strength is a short, simple menu; here, gazpacho, mussels, 'smoky taramosalata', 'meaty' sea bream with fennel ('prettily served but for missing a bone plate', £2·35) and calf's liver win praise. Vegetables have been lukewarm, crab mousse bland, and moussaka out of sorts. French house wine is £2·85 the litre. Friendly service. 'Doubtless Noah's was crowded and dim, but surely not tobacco-smoky.'

Closed Sun L; public hols
(D May 5 & 26, Aug 25,
Jan 1); Dec 24
Must book

Meals 12–3, 6.30–11.30

Alc L £4·45 (meal £6·75),
D £5·50 (meal £7·90)

Seats 60
♿ rest (1 step)
Am Ex, Barclay

ARLECCHINO　Map 13

8 Hillgate Street, W.8
01-229 2027 *and* 727 6292

No hint of the buffoon in this harlequinade with a patched history, lately in favour for its easy ambience and alert cooking. Mozzarella impannata, mushrooms in garlic, mussels marinara, breaded lamb cutlets, sole Véronique ('no flour in the sauce') and mange-tout peas impress this year's reporters. 'Uninspired' salad and made-up sweets 'with less flair than fresh figs'. Enforced intimacy from darkness and crowded tables. House Chianti is £2·90 for 72 cl. Taped music.

Closed Apr 6 & 7; Dec 25 & 26 Must book D Meals 12–3, 6–11.30	Alc £5·30 (meal £9·05) Cover 50p Seats 48	🔊 rest Air-conditioning Access, Am Ex, Barclay, Diners

AVEROF　Map 15

86 Cleveland Street, W.1
01-387 2375

'An endearing, family-run taverna, light-years away from the histrionics further south.' Cheerful service of competent hummus, wine-soaked or spiced sausages, various kebabs ('try the Averof special: pork, sausages and dolmades, £2·10'), flavourful souvla or keftedes ('slender, light, mint-flavoured rissoles', £2·10) with salad or rice. Skip the sweets and settle instead for strong 'Greek' coffee and a glass of Filfar, a Cypriot liqueur tasting of orange peel (50p). Good list of Greek-Cypriot wines, mostly £3·50. Recorded music.

Closed Sun; public hols Must book Meals 12–3, 6–10.45	Alc (min £3·50) £3·90 (meal £6·80) Cover 20p	Seats 40 Air-conditioning Access, Am Ex, Diners

AZIZ　Map 13

116 King Street, W.6
01-748 1826

Closed Dec 25 & 26
Must book D
Meals 12–2.45, 6–11.45

Alc £4·60 (meal £5·55)

Seats 52
🔊 rest
No dogs
Am Ex, Barclay, Diners

'Too much creamy sauce with a whole chicken'; 'chicken Kashmir was meant for a regiment.' With such faint quibbles is this civilised little place praised in plain tales from Hammersmith, 'the curry capital of London'. Too much it may be, but of a good thing. 'Fragrant chicken tikka, onion bhajia and reshmee kebab came hot and delicious' is typical praise for first courses. Though one report remarks that main dishes, apart from chicken tandoori (£2·20 for half), were 'a little oily and indistinct' and another wonders about a 'ubiquitous sauce', few faults are noted in 'tender' lamb Madras, 'carefully spiced' chicken or lamb dhansak (£3), prawn patia 'with flavour' and Bangalore phal lamb (£2), an 'extra hot speciality of Mr Aziz'. 'Service helpful' – sometimes over-zealous. There are wines and lager. Recorded sitar music. No children under five. Dress tidily.

App: D. Robson, P. & H. Holmes, C.J.R., and others

35

BAGATELLE   Map 13

5 Langton Street, S.W.10
01-351 4185

Closed Apr 4, 6 & 7;
Dec 24–26
Must book
Meals 12–2.30, 7–11.30

Alc £8·60 (meal £13)

Cover 50p
Seats 60
♿ rest (1 step)
Access, Am Ex, Barclay,
Diners, Euro

The original is in the Bois de Boulogne, though
worldly readers may wonder whether King's Road is
wise to invite comparison with the *16ᵉ arrondissement*.
Messrs Chiesa and Marrocco feed the illusion of *rus
in urbe* with pots of plants, sprays of flowers and a
sizeable garden, but urbanity filters back in the shape
of bentwood chairs, fringed lamps, marbled wallpaper,
and, not least, the cooking of Alain Lolom and Michel
Bastide. An inspector returned to make sure the
Lyonnaise potatoes were done properly and to renew
an acquaintance with the cheeseboard (£1·20), as
good an advertisement for French goats as any in
London. Gigot d'agneau (£4·40) was more than an
overdue gesture of goodwill from a Frenchman to
English lamb: 'Came pink so I couldn't expect it hot,
though mild chervil sauce needn't have been tepid.
The lettuce wrap and subtle use of garlic and thyme
were nice touches.' Helpings of roasts may be modest
but 'two thick slices of a coarse, pink terrine de
canard au poivre vert (£1·70) with delicious bread
made me pray they'd hold back on the lamb.'
Vegetables are simple and crisp but World's Enders
have overlooked the sweets. Last year's *Guide* warning
on the poor value of wine by the glass has been
noted, perhaps: while a bottle of the French house
wine is now up to £4·40, a 6 oz glass costs much the
same (£1). A live lutenist is engaged at weekends:
who's for *daurade*?

App: D.B., G.P., A.M.

BALZAC BISTRO   Map 13

2 Wood Lane, W.12
01-743 6787

'Businesslike at lunch-time, romantic in the evening'
(BBC customers in both moods?), Lorenzo Vucciol's
unfussy bistro, 'like a cross between a junk shop and
a railway waiting-room', still pleases. Two set menus,
the cheaper slightly more limited in choice, might
offer 'bubblingly hot' champignons farcis, crêpe de
fromage (or de poisson), boeuf bourguignonne, carré
d'agneau ('lovely baby lamb cooked *rose* as desired'),
poulet aux crevettes, faisan en cocotte, cassoulet
maison, or lotte provençale, all with competently
cooked vegetables. Finish, perhaps, with 'smooth and
creamy' crème caramel. 'Quietly efficient' service.
French house wine £2·95 for 72 cl. No pipes. French
recorded music.

Closed Sun; Sat L;
public hols; Dec 23–Jan 6
Must book
Meals 12.30–2.30, 7–11

Tdh £4·95 & £6·95
(meal £7·70 & £10)

Service 12½%

Cover 35p
Seats 55 (parties 30)
No dogs
Access, Am Ex, Barclay,
Diners

BANGKOK   Map 14

9 Bute Street, S.W.7
01-584 8529

The Bunnags' 'hot and crowded' Thai restaurant flew our solitary flag for South-East Asian cooking for so long that it is easy to overlook now that there are alternatives. But at a test meal beef with ginger and mushrooms (£2) was delicious, and Thai rice noodle (£1·40) 'deftly cooked with a spicy undertone.' Chicken crab soup and chicken chilli ('very hot') are also praised, and 'satay beef was tender.' Fried chicken with garlic (£2) may be tried too ('the whole place smelled of it'). But bland or tepid dishes are noted by some. Wines from £2·85; 'dear beer.'

Closed Sun; Dec 24;
public hols (exc May 5 &
Jan 1)
Must book D

Meals 12.30–2.10,
6.30–10.55

Alc (min £3·15) £4·50
(meal £5·50)

Service 10%
Seats 60
No dogs

BEOTYS   Map 15

79 St Martin's Lane,
W.C.2
01-836 8768

After 35 years the same family is still serving pre- or post-theatre suppers and business lunches for regulars. Most prefer the Greek-Cypriot dishes ('they're cheaper too'): 'the best taramasalata eaten outside Greece and my own home' (£1·05), dolmadakia 'a little dull but acceptable', 'quite delightful' kalamarakia (£1·15), moussaka 'always dependable' (£2·30), and souvlakia marred only slightly for a purist who prefers rigani to coriander. 'Greek peasant salad' may have a vinegary dressing. End with sticky pastries or fruit salad, or be content with the Turkish delight served with the coffee. Greek-Cypriot house wines, £2·75 for 70 cl; retsina (£3·40). 'Service has real grace', though one visitor finds it gruff.

Closed Sun; Dec 24;
public hols (exc May 5)
Must book
Meals 12–2.30, 5.30–11.30

Alc £5·85 (meal £8·45)

Cover 80p
Children's helpings
Seats 100

  rest (1 step)
Air-conditioning
No dogs
Access, Am Ex, Barclay,
Diners, Euro

BLOOMERS BRASSERIE   Map 13

94 Church Road, S.W.13
01-748 0393

Closed Mon L;
Dec 25 & 26; Dec 31 L
Must book D
Meals 12.30–2.30, 7–11
(11.30 weekends)

Tdh Sun L £4·55
(meal £8·15)

Bloomers, an inspector thought, could refer either to the mildly naughty Victorian photographs or to the *plume de ma tante* menu French. But the actual environment, cooking, staff supervision, 'and even the pianist' were all most agreeable surprises, and well worth the long wait. 'I could have eaten the sizzling champignons provençale (stuffed with crab-meat and breadcrumbs, in garlicky butter, £1·25) for all three courses, but for the rival claims of canard au citron vert (£3·75), which I'd love to be able to do as crisply, and the wallow in dark, rich chocolate sauce with

Alc £9·30 (meal £13·30)

Service 10%
Cover 50p
Children's helpings
(under 10)
Seats 60
⚹ rest (1 step)
No dogs
Access, Am Ex, Barclays,
Diners, Euro

unusually light cream-filled profiteroles.' M. J. Lester's repertoire in the kitchen further includes filet de porc farci en croûte (£3·25) foie de veau au Cointreau (£4·55) and friture de laitances sauce moutarde. Generous lapin provençale, crisp noisette potatoes, and *al dente* cauliflower are also reported. So is croque-monsieur as a lunchtime bar snack. Tarte aux pommes or pot au chocolat are other possible sweets, and coffee is Cafetière. Pasquier-Desvignes table wines are £3·70, and Loires or Riojas look the best value after that, with a glance at a '71 Barsac (Ch. Ménota, c.b., £5·70) for pudding, perhaps. Jean-Pierre in the bar also mixes insidious tropical fruit cocktails at £2 or so.

App: Christopher & Caroline Neame, A.A.B.C., D.W., and others

---

BLOOM'S   Map 12

90 Whitechapel High
Street, E.1
01-247 6001 *and* 6835

Closed Fri D; Sat;
Jewish hols; Dec 25
Open 11.30–9.30
(Fri 11.30–2 [winter],
11.30–3 [summer])

Alc £4·40 (meal £5·20)

Children's helpings
Seats 150
⚹ rest (1 step)
Air-conditioning
Unlicensed

There is 'no main chef' and no main customer in democratic Bloom's, where the jocular waiters rule and you are treated like a (slightly stupid) human being whether you are an East End momma in black satin or a rubberneck from Toronto. For one former admirer, the actual tastes of the boiled gefilte fish, chopped herring, salt beef and veal dumplings fell off in August, but though a test meal found the tongue and the braised sweetbreads (£2·40) on the bland side, the 'very yellow and good' kneidlach soup with light matzo dumplings, and the latkes, restored faith. Lockshen pudding is a perpetual favourite. Drink lemon tea, or ask them to send out to the pub next door. No dogs. Take-away counter. Car park. Telephone to enquire about Jewish holiday closures.

App: R.H., J.A., A.G.H., P. Diamond

LA BOURSE PLATE   Map 12

78 Leadenhall Street,
E.C.3
01-623 5159

'The empty purse' is roughly the meaning, though it is the Bon Accueil Italians who claim here '*cuisine et vins de France*'. Cooking when tested was sadly approximate to the hopes cherished for crêpe aux fruits de mer and wild duck paysanne. But mushrooms fried with butter and garlic, medallions of pork in a 'rather glutinous' sweet sauce, and ratatouille pass muster for half-full purses in the deprived City. The cheaper set meal is the more inventive. 'A pity the sweets are not confined to just one or two good ones.' The house red is Fleur de Bourgade at £3·80.

Closed D; Sat; Sun;
most public hols
Must book
L only, 12–3

Tdh £9·60 & £11·50
(meal £11·50 & £13·40)

Service inc

Seats 80
⚹ rest
Access, Am Ex, Barclay,
Diners

LE BRESSAN   Map 13

14 Wrights Lane, W.8
01-937 8525

Closed Sun; Sat;
public hols
Must book D
Meals 12.15–2, 7.15–11.30

Alc £11·85 (meal £17·80)

Service 15%
Cover 70p
Seats 50 (parties 30)
No dogs
Access, Am Ex, Barclay,
Diners

François Bessonnard has run Le Bressan – 'a pretty pastiche of *fin-de-siècle* French, with pleats, tassels, candelabra and apricot suede walls' – for ten years now, and for most of them a once-bitten twice-shy wariness has marked inspectors' reports. Recent accounts have been much warmer, and perhaps the French customers *Michelin* sends encourage Paul Raclot and the staff to give of their best – though even so 'the delicate white wine sauce with mousseline de sole had broken, there were grimaces when I asked for my salmon trout to be taken off the bone, carré d'agneau en croûte was *bien cuit*, and the périgourdine sauce with it was too thick.' The more surprise that a normally even more severe judge was so impressed later with 'soft and buttery scrambled eggs with a heap of tiny fresh girolles' (£2·70) and ris de veau en croûte sauce périgourdine (£4·80) – 'a drawstring bag of fragile pastry hiding very tender and creamy sweetbreads. The sauce was indeed too thick to be classic, but the flavours were rich and well-married.' Oeufs en meurette, fish pâté, coquilles St Jacques beurre blanc (a £4·10 main course which you might be able to share as a first course), 'succulently combined petite marmite de la mer', and the speciality poulet de Bresse crème et morilles ('a marvellous taste of that gastronomic region', £5·50) are also warmly praised. Sometimes they do not time pommes dauphine or dauphinoise quite right: 'the choux paste could be tasted in the former.' They keep good cheeses – 'a sliver of Chaource in fine condition' – and take trouble with sweets too, to judge by their soufflé glacé Grand Marnier, lychee water-ice, and pêche Aurore (£1·80). Wines from £5 or so are not greedily priced by London French standards: Alsace Riesling les Murailles and Ch. de la Rivière '67, a Côte de Fronsac, were under £8 in 1979. No pipes. No children under twelve. 'The maître d'hotel made sensible suggestions about the rich menu.' Recorded music.

App: H. Berger, Alberto Portugheis, B. A. Boucher, M. S. Raschid, R. J. Woodward, A.H., A.W.M.

BRINKLEY'S   Map 14

47 Hollywood Road,
S.W.10
01-351 1683

Closed L; Sun; Dec 24;
public hols
Must book
D only, 7.30–11.30

John Brinkley and his chef Antony Worrall-Thompson are both fairly recent graduates of catering schools (Ealing and Westminster respectively), backed by Mr Brinkley's mother, a consultant radiotherapist. They may be excused a faint didacticism in their nouvelle cuisine touches: 'a warm salad of avocado and goose liver' (£1·65) and 'grilled breast of duck served pink with raspberry vinegar sauce and a trio of vegetable purees' (£4·45). (Perhaps one should eat these in

Alc £8·50 (meal £12·85)

Service 12½%
Cover 50p
Seats 55 (parties 24)
♿ rest (1 step)
Air-conditioning
Access, Am Ex, Barclay,
Diners

summer in the pretty sheltered courtyard rather than inside by candlelight, where there is little chance of seeing them.) The air of suave competence – and the cellarful of good claret – are two surprises, and inspectors and others report good crudités with dips, 'rather disappointing' fried mushrooms, and mackerel fillets in cider and sour cream, 'delicious salmon in a fresh sorrel sauce', and 'excellent poussin à l'estragon and fried liver with avocado and bacon, with pleasantly undercooked vegetables', including new potatoes in oatmeal, butter and garlic. Apart from 'Dr Brinkley's chocolate bombe', presumably therapeutic, sweets are agreeably fruity, with red fruits in Crème de Cassis and yoghourt with fresh blackcurrants, blackberries and honey praised. Wines begin at £3·85 with Cuvée Vercherre Rhônes, and clarets below or just over £10 include Ch. Batailley '73, Ch. Ducru-Beaucaillou '69, and Ch. Troplong-Mondot '70, all château-bottled. 'Mixed' recorded music. More reports, please.

BUBB'S   Map 12

329 Central Markets,
E.C.1
01-236 2435

Closed Sat; Sun; Aug;
public hols
Must book
Meals 12.15–2, 7.30–9.30

Alc £7·05 (meal £10·15)

Service 12%
Seats 36 (parties 10)
No dogs
Access, Barclay, Diners

From the ground floor's deserted cafe or vestibule, 'with a drunken notice pointing upstairs', you would deduce a restaurant either lately arrived or on the point of departure. But Peter and Catherine Bubb are in their fifth *Guide* year now, and their first chef, Francis Bureau, is still in the kitchen. Apart from an unpremeditated May holiday, and sporadic doubts – surprising at the gates of Smithfield – about the basic quality of kidneys or a steak, the initial delight at finding an honourable French restaurant convenient to St Paul's and Fleet Street remains: no wonder a member says it would be 'ideal for an outing with your bank manager or (the next step up?) your tax inspector.' Mr Bureau's favourite dishes are lotte bretonne (£3·80), croustade de St Jacques au beurre blanc (£4·15), ris de veau normande (£3·95) and timbale de cailles au cidre (£4·15): interesting choices that show off his skill as a *saucier*. Others also mention among first courses crêpe moscovite (with shrimps and cheese), 'excellent sardines', 'generous mussels', and leeks vinaigrette 'not on the menu but sensibly proposed when something light was requested.' 'Very fine salmon trout', 'really good steaks, béarnaise and au poivre' – and even tripe – are also remembered. For sweet try Mont Blanc or cassis sorbet, perhaps, or take cheese. 'With such food the house wine at £3·40 seemed poor', but the provenance of these and other bottles has not been communicated this year. Acceptable French-bottled Brouilly was £8·30 in 1979, but the marcs on the shelf may be the most distinctive liquors here. Kirs are made very dry.

App: John Stevenson, J. D. Corbluth, W.D., J. R. Tyrie, G. E. Bennett, and others

BUMBLES Map 16

16 Buckingham Palace
Road, S.W.1
01-828 2903

Handy for Victoria and the Palace but cooking stumbles and service rumbles, especially in the newly extended basement. Detailed descriptions on the long, inventive menu assist new arrivals; the kitchen's facility, however, is disputed. Ayes for cold lettuce soup, courgettes in wine and almonds, 'tender pork fillet with apple, prune and redcurrant jelly' (£3·40), kidneys in champagne with saffron rice, mushrooms stuffed with prawns and grilled with Stilton, and crisp salads. Noes to 'harsh' sauce with good roast gammon, 'floury' celery soup and 'penitential' coffee. Valbois (Gironde) £3·25 a bottle; few half-bottles. 'Facile' recorded music.

Closed Sun; Sat L;
Dec 24 D; public hols
Must book
Meals 12–2.15,
6 (6.30 Sat)–10.30

Alc (min £3·50) £7·50
(meal £10·65)

Service 10% (Sat)
Children's helpings
(under 12)

Seats 72 (parties 16)
 ⌖ rest (1 step)
Air-conditioning
Access, Am Ex, Barclay,
Diners

BUNNY'S Map 12

7 Pond Street, N.W.3
01-435 1541

Closed L (exc Sun); Mon;
Apr 4; Dec 26
Must book D
Meals 12–3 (Sun),
7–11.15

Tdh Sun L £4·95
(meal £7·75)
Alc £7·55 (meal £10·60)

Cover 40p D
Children's helpings
(Sun L under 12)
Seats 45
Am Ex, Barclay

Royal Free doctors have found a new burrow in Sue Winston's spacious basement nearby, decorated in modish salmon and spinach, and lucky in its chimney-piece feature. Although it is early days yet, a member who writes libellously about the Guide's *previous Hampstead choices praises Keith Shudall's changing menu here, and his skill with a deep-fried mushroom pâté sandwich, veal stuffed with spinach, and poussin in a good mushroom and bacon sauce. An exacting inspector concurs, after 'a superior version of petite fondue bourguignonne, with a nutty taste of Gruyère, and fresh basil in the tomato sauce.' Truite soufflée à la pistache (£2·80) was also very competently done, 'and the vermouth cream sauce was poured round, not over.' 'Moist and tender' carré d'agneau on a bed of fresh ratatouille (£7 for two) is also mentioned. 'Green peppercorn and brandy sauce for pink breast of duck tasted too strongly peppery, salty, and "brown", as though over-reduced.' 'Salade verte was unmistakably English.' Good sweets have included 'orange-liqueur-laden chocolate mousse' and 'light, moist banana cake'. Coffee is strong. The house Hérault red at £3·20 was in ferment at a test meal but 'adequate' at a later date. On the rather limited list, Muscadet or minor young claret is about £5. 'Earl Grey tea is served in leaf form – a pleasant refinement.' The girls who serve, 'though in Hampstead you would not expect a uniform style', are friendly and well supervised. Recorded classical music. More reports, please.*

IL CAMINO Map 3

282 Burlington Road,
New Malden, Surrey
01-942 1932

Shrewd restaurant-chasers whom duty or pleasure takes
to this dormitory suburb say that Paolo and Danilo are
running a small and cosy place with 'most of the usual
Italian clichés' but also 'a touch of loving care'
with their salami (£1·85), scampi zingara with cream
and pimentos (£4·15), duck à l'orange, even, and
courgettes in batter. 'A liquorous zabaglione' cost £1.
Pinot Grigio white or Chianti Classico are £4·40.
Recorded music. More reports, please.

Closed Sun D; Sat L; public hols	Tdh L from £3 (meal £5·05)	Seats 45 Air-conditioning
Must book	Alc £7·20 (meal £10·55)	No dogs
Meals 12–2.30, 7–11		Access, Am Ex, Barclay,
	Cover 35p	Diners

CANALETTO Map 12

451 Edgware Road, W.2
01-262 7027

Smart Italian place with a mirrored wall and mutable
pictures on a Little Venice corner. Voluble service and
the handsome cold table both bemuse guests briefly, but
persevere and you may find 'light and delicate'
cannelloni (£1·65), spaghetti al aglio e olio (£1·55),
seafood salad (£1·70), 'pink and tender' fegato al burro
(£3·20) and 'carré d'agnello'. Sauces are hit-or-miss,
whitebait may be bendy, kidneys tough and vegetables
'soggy'. Zabaglione 'whipped up in a copper bowl with
minimum fuss and maximum Marsala.' Casual service
of unusual Italian wines; house Monica or Nuragus is
£3·50 for 75 cl. More reports, please, of this place and
their new one in Uxbridge Road, Hatch End.

Closed Sun; Sat L; most public hols	Alc £8·50 (meal £12·50)	Air-conditioning No dogs
Must book	Cover 55p	Access, Am Ex, Barclay,
Meals 12.30–2.30, 7–11	Seats 60 (parties 40)	Diners, Euro
	🔲 rest	

♣ CAPITAL HOTEL RESTAURANT Map 14

Basil Street, S.W.3
01-589 5171

Must book
Meals 12.30–2, 6.30–10.30

Alc £13·80 (meal £18·15)

Service inc
Cover 50p
Seats 30 (parties 22)
Air-conditioning
Car park

There are doubtless foreigners who see no more of
London than the few steps from David Levin's baby
grand hotel to Harrods and back again. Though a
social psychologist might pity them, a hedonist
could only envy. The resources of Brian Turner's à la
carte menu in the aeroplane-age restaurant might be
quickly exhausted by a customer rich or foolish
enough to eat every meal of the week there, but it
would be a shame to spend the flight home thinking
of what might have been, and there are at least five
first courses worth trying: the coeur d'artichaut farci
à la Nissarda (compare it with the version at
Langan's, q.v., where it is cooked by Mr Turner's

No dogs in public rooms
Access, Am Ex, Barclay,
Diners, Euro
60 rooms (all with bath)
Room only, £28·75–£40·25
Breakfast from £2·50

predecessor), the 'crispest and lightest' tartelettes aux poireaux (the leeks in a cream sauce, not a quiche custard), and perhaps the terrine de pigeons sauce cresson (£2·58), or gravadlax, or the famously pretty mousseline de coquilles St Jacques à la crème d'oursins. The kitchen's favourite main dishes are the navarin de fruits de mer au Champagne (£8·33), entrecôte sautée aux morilles, and carré d'agneau persillé aux herbes de Provence (£15·87 for two – the jagged prices are explained by Mr Levin's desire to show on his menu the effect of VAT and service charges, as though both were attributable to government action). But quenelles de brochet and médaillons de veau aux fines herbes are praised too, and an inspector who risked tournedos Rossini was taken aback by 'one of the most virtuous sauces it has been my good luck to meet.' Mange-tout peas and haricot verts are crunchily done, though if you want your lamb *saignant* you will have to ask. The only problem with meals here is knowing how to round them off. They keep normally excellent cheeses, offer (between courses) a remarkable sorbet à la Fine Champagne (£1·52) and brew 'superb strong coffee', but the trolley sweets at a test meal 'looked like advertisements for shaving soap, and cheesecake tasted that way too.' Chefs are not obliged to be their own *pâtissiers*, and many customers may rest content with the petits fours, but 'a daily fruit tart ought not to be beyond a kitchen that makes such fine pastry.' Service is generally punctilious. The wines are excellent, though the claret prices may terrify. With Chx. Cantemerle and Meyney '67, c.b., at £18·52, some may care to drink the house white, or Chardonnay Blanc from California (£11·57), followed by '76 or '78 Beaujolais or, better, Auxey-Duresses '73, Duc de Magenta, 'ready to drink and lovely at £12·23.'

App: David Charlesworth, David Wooff,
A. B. Stenhouse, A. C. Palmer, and others

CARLO'S PLACE   Map 13

855 Fulham Road, S.W.6
01-736 4507

Closed L; Sun; Mon;
public hols (exc Jan 1);
1 week Easter;
July 26–Aug 23; 1 week
Chr (exc Dec 31)
Must book
D only, 7–11

Alc £7·70 (meal £10·10)

Service inc

Stay away if you have an octopus phobia, because the central stove and tentacular pipes may remind you. But Carlo's grip on customers and the *Guide* has not loosened since his partner Malcolm MacDonald took over the cooking. 'Mild, creamy and delicious' fish soup, crunchy avocado salad, and seafood cocktail 'grilled with cheese but keeping the taste of its ingredients' are mentioned among first courses. For main course, daily specials will be gabbled by the waiters along with the printed ones, but one visitor thinks some of them might as well be printed – which would enable them to explain that the meat in the duck pie is minced. Sweetbreads, 'hearty' beef in red wine, and carré d'agneau au poivre (£4·65) are other

Cover 40p
Children's helpings
Seats 48 (parties 14)
Air-conditioning

possibilities. The confection of meringue, cream and grapes is worth trying if you have room, and a mint ice-cream is offered sometimes. Espigou or Solitaire wines are £3·20.

App: Michael Copp, M.E., and others

🍲 **CARLTON TOWER CHELSEA ROOM** Map 14

Cadoga.n Place, S.W.1
01-235 5411

Closed Apr 7; Jan 1
Must book
Meals 12.30–2.45, 7–11

Alc £17·75 (meal £21·20)

Service inc
Seats 50
🔽 rest; w.c.
Air-conditioning
Car park
No dogs
Access, Am Ex, Barclay, Diners, Euro
296 rooms (all with bath)
Room only, £42–£78·20
Breakfast from £2·90
Fire cert

This handsome and spacious hotel dining-room with a tree-top view – 'a very comfortable place on a hot London summer day' – came to life in 1977, when Bernard Gaume moved into the kitchen and Jean Quéro into the restaurant. They are still there, and thoroughly into the rhythm of the place, touring France together once a year in search of new gustatory sensations. Several members in 1979 placed it among the elect, and the opinion was confirmed by a test meal that embraced – *le mot juste* – four major dishes: feuilleté d'asperges beurre blanc au cerfeuil (£4), salade de ris de veau aux truffes noires (£5·50), gratin de sole et langoustines aux pistils de safran (£7·50), and saumon d'Ecosse en papillote (£6·50). 'Perhaps on mature reflection the prize went to the exquisite puff pastry coffin made for the asparagus, and the heavenly beurre blanc that was poured round (never over, here), but the fat fresh scampi, with a cream sauce the colour of a Buddhist's robe, ran it very close, and the other two dishes would have been hailed with acclamation in most restaurants.' A later menu is commending instead yet other *trouvailles*, the salade nouvelle with raw spinach and goose liver tossed in butter, the fricassée de turbot et homard aux concombres (£8·95), and filet d'agneau au basilic et tomate (£8·05). Crab soup with rouille and breast of duck with chanterelles are other notions. *A vous, mes camarades.* Vegetables – not to mention 'crisp, clean and puffy' pommes soufflées, just to prove they can do them as well as the Connaught (*q.v.*) – are cooked to match. 'Gratin de fraises (£2·90) was too creamy for me': if you contemplate it, perhaps just take a first course and no main dish. But one connoisseur of hotels still managed three such courses, finishing with a pastry of fraises des bois and crème pâtissière. The service is becoming more used to administering such food. Wines begin with Loire or Beaujolais at £6·70 a litre, and there is an important list of *premier-cru* claret. Under £10, you could do much worse than the Georges Duboeuf or Paul Bocuse '78 white or red Beaujolais (in the plural). A pianist plays at night. Wear a jacket and tie. The Rib Room downstairs is worth a thought if you have a yearning for beef in Chicago style and quantity.

App: Paul Bass, John Stevenson, Peter Thomson, H.R., A.H., and others

CARRIER'S   Map 12

2 Camden Passage, N.1
01-226 5353

Closed Sun; public hols;
Apr 5
Must book
Meals 12.30–2.30,
7.30–11.30

Tdh L from £12·50
(meal £17·20), D from
£14·05 (meal £19)

Service 12½%
Seats 82 (parties 25)
Air-conditioning
Am Ex card

Robert Carrier's initial venture in Islington is a famous and in its own idiosyncratic taste a pretty restaurant, 'in the style of a 19th-century French inn', says Jacqueline Cottee, who has directed it for years. The great man's dishes – some of them great, some not – are cooked by Gunther Schlender and Terence Boyce, and dished, all too often, by anonymous hands. Two Englishmen of substance on separate occasions speak of having the feeling we were being done a favour' by being fed at over £20 a head. However, most members are content, and report delight at their (four-course) set meals: 'elegantly served and subtly flavoured pâté de brochet with a wedge of spinach in the centre, original and delicious watercress and wild mushroom soup, well-trimmed and pink baby lamb chops with herb butter, indifferent vegetables, and sublime orange and Grand Marnier mousse.' Vegetable antipasto in agrodolce 'tasted pleasingly fresh and crunchy', 'prettily marbled ballotine of chicken and sweetbreads tasted genuinely French, though the green sauce with it did not', and creamy Amaretti soufflé, strawberries Romanoff, and red fruit in alcohol amounted to a pudding person's dream.' 'Pappy pink trout in lettuce packets, accompanied by musty rice and virtually unseasoned courgettes' sounds like the year's worst great dish, but even that meal was redeemed by 'sublime Roquefort quiche, a trembly custard on very crisp buttery pastry', and by another eggy masterpiece for pudding, oeufs à la neige 'equal to the Gavroche's' (*q.v.*). Rillettes d'anguille fumée aux petits légumes and sauté d'agneau aux flageolets are other favourites. Wines, from £3·30 for Provencal, are well chosen, with Pouilly Blanc Fumé '78 (Michel Redde), Gigondas '75 (Roger Meffre) and Ch. Broustet '71 in the £9–£10 range. But advice and service should be better.

App: Christopher Forman, V. Westerman, M.C.,
John Rowlands, C.P.D., and others

CARROLL'S   Map 15

32 Great Windmill Street,
W.1
01-437 7383

Admire boxing photos by the back counter at the crowded tables of Mark Segal's salt beef and lemon tea cafe. David Haron has taken over the kitchen and members find latkes and gefilte fish crisper. Tongue and beef (£2) remain tender, juicy bargains. New green pickles (20p), caraway rye and chraine (beetroot horseradish) are other pleasures, and 'lockshen pudding and lemon pancakes are at least lemony.' No dogs. Unlicensed. Bring your own wine.

Closed Sept 20; Dec 25
Open noon–11.30 p.m.

Alc £3·65 (meal £4·30)

Seats 30
Air-conditioning

CERVANTES   Map 3

105 Brighton Road,
Coulsdon, Surrey
01-660 0907 *and* 3721

Closed Sun; L Dec 26 &
Jan 1
Must book
Meals 12.30–2.30, 7–11
(12 weekends)

Tdh £4·95 (meal £8·60)
Alc £6·90 (meal £11·25)

Service 12½%
Cover 45p
Seats 100 (parties 40)
♿ rest
No dogs
Access, Am Ex, Barclay,
Diners

Tony Lopez and his chef Manuel Fidalgo have had their ups and downs in this two-floor Franco-Spanish restaurant, but one regular visitor is grateful 'not just for one meal but for five years of brighter Coulsdon.' We still hear little of the set meals, which may or may not be good value. But à la carte, there are contented consumers of 'mushrooms in garlic butter, seafood crêpes (£1·70), and excellent scallops, zarzuela for main course, and fresh peaches for dessert.' For one couple, school visiting nearby has been relieved by oeufs Rossini, chicken Wellington and 'for the housemaster a magnificent veal chop on a wooden platter' (£4·50). Another couple, though, argued about the paella, he liking it, she calling it 'greasy and tasteless'. Happily they could agree that the prawns in chilli and garlic were good, that baked eggs should have soft yolks, that lemon mousse was nicely astringent, and that fresh peach tart was spoilt by a coating of very sweet jam. 'French bread was stale and hard, coffee good, and the crystallised fruits with it most welcome.' However, when all faults coincide, as they sometimes do, dear and dismal meals are reported. Paul Bouchard table wines are £3·90, and there is a note in favour of Navarra Clarete (£4·80 in 1979). Recorded music – live with optional dancing downstairs at weekends. 'My only real complaint is that Tony rides the till and the hi-fi like a cowboy.'

App: E.B., Joyce & John Levi, Joan Clowes, M.S., B.J.W., and others

CHAGLAYAN KEBAB HOUSE   Map 12

85 Brent Street, N.W.4
01-202 8575

Closed Sun L; Apr 4,
6 & 7; Dec 24–26; Jan 1
Must book D & weekends
Meals 12–2.30, 6–12

Alc £4·50 (meal £7·30)

Seats 40
♿ rest (1 step); w.c.
No dogs
Access, Am Ex, Barclay,
Diners, Euro

Ata Chaglayan's father's restaurant of the same name opened in Nicosia in 1928, and here too, within hailing distance of the Hendon Odeon, 'we have eaten regularly since 1974 and never had a meal that was other than well-cooked and presented.' The rope macramé ceiling may surprise you, but the hors d'oeuvre, tahini, mancha (spinach, yoghourt and onion, £1·04) and aubergines Imam Bayeldi are reassuring ('do ayatollahs swoon?' a member asks wistfully). Kleftiko (£2·90) is Mr Chaglayan's speciality, but karisik kebab with spicy lamb sausage (£4), chelik kebab, chicken Chaglayan and, for that matter, 'large, correctly cooked steaks' are worth ordering. Sweets surpass the usual Levantine factory sort (kadayif, harem delight and others at 83p), and 'rahat loukoum was the real thing, as was the coffee.' Retsina is £4, Bellapais white or Villa Doluca red £4·60, and ouzo or raki 50p a glass. Recorded music.

App: David de Saxe, W. G. White, C.P.D., M. F. Cullis

CHANTERELLE Map 14

119 Old Brompton Road,
S.W.7
01-373 5522

Lighter and airier under new management with 'high-class bistro cooking at lower-middle prices.' At a test meal, poached egg, red wine and kidney ('duller than it sounds', £1·10) was the only hot first course, apart from celery broth and pumpkin and shrimp soup, but cream cheese and watercress mousse was skilful, and oeuf mollet with sorrel 'a fine special'. 'Chicken with raisin and almond stuffing a good try with a dull bird, jugged venison fair (£3·80), vegetables fresh and hot.' Rich chocolate sweets. French Ecusson house wines, £3·25 a bottle. Young waiters inclined to bustle.

Closed Dec 24–26
Must book
Meals 12–2.30, 7–12

Tdh L £3·50 (meal £5·75)

Alc (min £3·50) £7
(meal £10·60)

Service 12½%
Cover 40p D

Children's helpings
(under 10)
Seats 40
♿ rest (1 step)
Access, Am Ex, Barclay,
Diners

CHAOPRAYA Map 15

22 St Christopher's Place,
W.1
01-486 0777

Shy Thai place on two floors ('tropical ground floor preferable to torrid basement') offering delicately spiced food 'with a flavour of its own'. Praise for satay served with 'a lovely spicy-hot peanut sauce', crisp wun-tun with a sweet-and-sour sauce, chicken cooked with cashews and peppers, beef curry 'flavourful as well as hot', and steamed mackerel with sour plums and vegetables. Simpler menu at lunch-time. Set meals from about £4·90. Wines from £2·60 a half-bottle. 'They pop beer cans at your table as if they were champagne corks.' Thai music.

Closed Sun; public hols
Meals 12–3, 6.30–11

Tdh from £4·90
(meal from £5·40)

Alc £6·05 (meal £6·70)

Service 10%

Seats 120
No dogs
Access, Diners

See p. 110 for London pubs and wine bars.

The Guide News Supplement will be sent out as usual, in June, to everyone who buys the book directly from Consumers' Association and to all bookshop purchasers who return the card interleaved with their copy. Let us know of any changes that affect entries in the book, or of any new places you think should be looked at.

Inspections are carried out anonymously. Persons who pretend to be able to secure, arrange or prevent an entry in the Guide are impostors and their names or descriptions should be reported to us.

Bed and breakfast prices have been quoted to us by hoteliers; where possible, we have given minimum off-season prices for one person sharing a double room and maximum in-season prices for one person in a single room.

CHARING CROSS HOTEL
BETJEMAN RESTAURANT Map 15

Strand, W.C.2
01-839 7282

Betjemania's in season
At this BTH hotel:
Read his verse; admire (with reason)
Barry's dining-room as well.
Daily, Chef's 'executive luncheon'
Feeds the rising men from Cheam;
A la carte at night, you munch on
Till the tum runs out of steam:
Steak Diane, and sole Walewska
('£7·85, you say?');
Wash them down with Avelsbacher
(£10·15: 'the firm will pay').
Vegetables are best forgotten;
Chocolate mousse will not be missed.
Coffee's decent; cloths are cotton;
Wines good value. Pianist.

Closed Sun; public hols
Meals 12.30–2.15, 6–9.15

Tdh L £6·25 & £7·25
(meal £10·10 & £10·50),
D (pre-theatre) £7·25
(meal £10·50)

Alc £13·20 (meal £17·85)

Service inc
Seats 120 (parties 120)
&. rest
No dogs in public rooms

Access, Am Ex, Barclay,
Diners, Euro
207 rooms (129 with bath,
78 with shower)
B&B £27·50
Fire cert

CHATEAUBRIAND Map 12

48 Belsize Lane, N.W.3
01-435 4882

The fillet steak is the draw, of course, but some think
there are even better dishes on this well-appointed
restaurant's conservative menu. Carré d'agneau and
filet Diane (£4·75) are good of their kind; bain
d'épinards aux crevettes, 'shrimps sandwiched between
good spinach and thick cheese' (£1), and stuffed
mushrooms are more exhilarating. Fish soup 'was
more a *fumet*', and filet piémontaise has displeased,
but deep-fried aubergines 'are the best of good
vegetables.' Apart from oranges in a zesty Grand
Marnier syrup, sweets seem avoidable. Good house
burgundy is £4·40 a bottle. Friendly, unhurried
service. No music except for what drifts up from the
bistro below. No dogs.

Closed L; Sun; Apr 6;
Dec 24–26; Jan 1
Must book

D only, 7–12

Alc £6·80 (meal £10·35)

Cover 50p
Seats 35
Access, Am Ex, Barclay,
Diners

See p. 508 for the restaurant-goer's legal rights, and p. 510 for information on
hygiene in restaurants.

Prices of meals underlined are those which we consider represent unusual value for
money. They are not necessarily the cheapest places in the Guide, or in the locality.

LE CHEF   Map 12

41 Connaught Street, W.2
01-262 5945

Closed Sun; Mon; Sat L;
Dec 24; public hols
Must book
Meals 12.30–2.30, 7–11.30
(Sat 11)

Tdh L £5·75 (meal £7·75),
D £6·75 (meal £8·85)
Alc £6·95 (meal £10·15)

Service 10%
Cover 25p
Children's helpings
Seats 44
No dogs
Access card

Alan and June King, who have run this *restaurant du quartier* with a few pavement tables for almost ten years now, live next door: it is their life, and it shows in the quality maintained and the fair price charged for cooking that one would mostly be happy to find in a Paris equivalent. True, there is one 'dear at any price' outburst from an inspector who hit an off-night for a celebration, and one or two murmurs that the decor needs a fresh eye. In a test lunch, both croque-monsieur and the crust for strawberry tart lacked all crunch. But in the set meals, 'fish soup always seems freshly made from whatever is to hand, and the rouille and trimmings are excellent', 'poulet basquaise with rice and prawns tasted home-made and original', 'couscous was filling and honest and so was the orange-flavoured daube', 'rôti de porc was meltingly tender, and braised courgettes kept their shape and flavour.' Rognons dijonnaise (£2·85, if à la carte) had 'a good dun sauce, not flour-thickened, for tender kidneys.' The cheeses are an unfailing joy – 'runny Brie, good Explorateur, intriguing Rouy from Burgundy, and garlicky Gaperon from the Auvergne.' The fruit tarts (90p) are usually the best sweet choice, though 'profiteroles had a very good dark sauce.' French Costières du Gard table wines are £2·30, and thereafter consider 'strong-willed' Ch. l'Archevesque (Fronsac) '70 if it is still there, or Ch. Millet '71 (a red Graves) in the £5–£6 range. Don't be surprised if you need a shoe horn to get into your place. Recorded *chansonniers*.

App: E. Davies, Carol Steiger, Michael Copp, D.B., Gerald Froyd, Paul Gambaccini, and others

CHEZ MOI   Map 13

3 Addison Avenue, W.11
01-603 8267

Closed L; Sun;
last 3 weeks Aug;
3 weeks from Chr;
public hols
Must book
D only, 7.30–11.30

Alc £9 (meal £13·20)

Cover 50p
Seats 54 (parties 16)
Air-conditioning

There is no entry to Addison Avenue from Holland Park Avenue – but after a dozen years most customers must know how to find this *restaurant (trop) intime*, run by the triumvirate of Roland Peacock, Colin Smith and Richard Walton, with Mr Walton in the kitchen. He is a skilful chef, which makes the character of the place – and the sparse reports – a puzzle, until you realise that by the owners' own confession, the favourite dishes tend to be something with smoked salmon in it, followed by the carré d'agneau either stuffed with garlic and mint, or diablé (£5·75). In other words, there is an element of unfulfilled potential, vividly realised by inspectors who started with the brochette de coquilles St Jacques sauce mousseline (£2·85) and the oeuf à la pomme d'amour (£1·45) – 'a delightful conceit with a runny egg yolk under a cap of Parmesan inside a large skinned tomato, mounted on a croissant-like base.'

Then there was the saddle of hare, 'deliciously high and red, with truffle scraps and a marked taste of madeira in the sauce: we demanded a spoon, to the waiter's pleasure.' Vegetables too had refreshingly 'separate' tastes: minute, crunchy mange-tout peas with shreds of onion, red cabbage strongly spiced with cumin. It is a shame that another report in the same month describes the same hare as 'tough and overcooked', with no regrets from the staff. Crêpe de palourdes Chez Moi with mushrooms and grapes in a cream champagne sauce (£1·70) and cervelle de veau frite with a green peppercorn Chantilly (£3·60) are other interesting ideas – though not in the same person's dinner, naturally. Meals tend to fade after the main course: 'Cheese biscuits were stale, and the cherry brandy or crème de menthe ice-creams are not masterpieces.' But 'the petit pot au chocolat is one of the best in London.' The French red and white table wines are £4·40 and domaine-bottled Muscadet £4·80. Too many of the clarets in 1979 were '72; Ch. Palmer '71, c.b., is £13·60.

App: Henry Fawcett, C.P. & M.E.D., Maurice Hall, V. Westerman

CHUEN-CHENG-KU   Map 15

17–23 Wardour Street, W.1
01-437 1398

Closed Dec 26
Meals 11 a.m.–10.45 p.m.

Tdh D from £3·30
(meal from £3·95)
Alc (min £3·30) £5·25
(meal £6·10)

Service 10%
Seats 600
&. rest
No dogs

The Au family's long-lived (for Chinatown) warren of rooms still wins members' affections on goal average, as it were, though a November dim-sum lunch for an inspectorial team drew so many rude adjectives – 'greasy', 'lukewarm', 'tainted', 'stale' – along with temperate praise for prawn cheung-fun and steamed spare ribs with black-bean sauce, that a large question-mark hangs over this department (sad when regulars delight so much in the char siu buns, chicken and glutinous rice in lotus leaves, prawn dumplings, coconut tart and others). A visitor shrewd enough to eat at tea-time with the place full of Chinese did better. The menu is itself irresistible – especially the 'miscellaneous' section with its 'deep-fried giant bowels' (£2·15) and 'fried chicken blood with ginger and spring onion' (£2·15), and though we lack reports of these, 'half a braised duck with fish lips, and fried oysters with crispy pork, were beautifully cooked and presented.' The eel dishes are also notable, crab with ginger and spring onion is 'incredibly tasty, though messier than the Battle of Waterloo', and a soup noodle dish with liver, squid, Chinese mushrooms and greens 'makes a meal on its own.' House suggestions include Chinese-style steak with onions and tomato sauce (£2·50). Portuguese Vinho Verde is £3·10 if you want to augment the mediocre tea. 'Fried New Year's cake can only be had at (Chinese) New Year: how stupid of me to ask.' Service varies, but 'one of the younger and happier waiters said he would do us a meal for about £12, and though his choices were unadventurous, the tastes were distinct.'

App: David & Jane Copeland, Barnaby Marder, P. Diamond, P.G., W. B. O'Neill, and others

---

COLOMBINA Map 15

4 Duke of York Street, S.W.1
01-930 8279

In this block, *bien-pensants* buy their cheese, borrow their books, bank with Coutts, and buy lunch at the double from a trio of Italian brothers. Mozzarella and orange salad, green fettuccine with cheese and herbs, 'variable but usually hot and meaty lasagne', 'spicy calamari Santa Lucia' and mediocre vegetables are in the year's bag; try too, they say, medaglioni con peperoni (£2·15), and fegato burro e salvia, or lunchtime specials. Zeal and custom may flag at night. Sangiovese and Trebbiano are £2·90. 'They commended a superior Italian white wine by telling me it was made of grapes.' Espresso coffee. Recorded music.

Closed Sun;
most public hols
Must book L
Meals 12–3, 6–11.30

Alc £5·35 (meal £8·30)

Cover 35p D

Seats 90
♿ rest
Access, Am Ex, Barclay, Diners

♿ ✎ ⑩ CONNAUGHT HOTEL Map 15

Carlos Place, W.1
01-499 7070

Closed (Grill Room)
weekends & public hols
Must book
Meals 12.30–1.30, 6.30–10

Tdh (Rest) from £10·65
(meal from £15)
Alc (Grill Room; min £5)
£15·10 (meal £20)

Service 15%
Seats (Rest) 80 (parties 20),
(Grill Room) 35
♿ rest (3 steps)
No dogs
Access, Euro
89 rooms (all with bath)
Prices on application
Fire cert

La Serenissima – the old phrase for Venice, in whose great hotels Mr Zago, the Connaught's present manager, spent much of his working life – will stand for this decorous Mayfair house too. Little ruffles its elegance, unless it be an Englishman approaching in jeans or an American expecting 24-hour room service, and nothing expresses the British aristocracy's talent for adaptation better than the presence here of a 'new wave' French chef, Michel Bourdin, who has astonished his own compatriots by persuading his conservative WASP clientele to contemplate their lamb and duck in the pink. You may eat with Widmerpool in the handsomely panelled Restaurant or with Margot Metroland in the smaller and less inviting (but more smoothly served) Grill Room. The former is table d'hôte, the latter à la carte, but the kitchen is the same, and the prices comparable. The menu is a bizarre but usually successful marriage of native tradition and foreign invention: braised oxtail, 'gigot de Kent' or steak, kidney and mushroom pie, preceded by salade d'avocats et langoustines au cerfeuil, or petit hâtelet du pêcheur grillé sauce Mireille, or the justly famous croustade d'oeufs de caille Maintenon. Every now and then there are odd lapses – 'a disgusting mint sauce' – but members' and inspectors' comments are generally reassuring: 'terrine de coquilles St Jacques was rich, delicate and delicious', 'pâté de turbot sauce pudeur had been transformed since a mediocre version I remember some years back', 'salmon trout was perfectly poached, and the sauce verte a dream.' The fragile balloons called pommes soufflées are as good as ever, and the purées of sprouts, celeriac and chestnuts served with lamb at a test meal were well judged (more than could be said for the 'game sauce' that did duty for the desired natural juices). Thereafter, one is well advised to become a patriot again and swear fealty to the bread-and-butter pudding, though 'mille-feuille aux fraises des bois had a nice taste of the fruit', and tarte caramélisée aux deux fruits beurre de Paris is one of M Bourdin's specialities at £2·35. (Main-course set pieces such as sole Jubilee and noisettes d'agneau Edward VII at £9 or so must be ordered in advance.) Breakfasts are very fine. The bottle distinction is earned as much by the wine service as by the list itself, which is patchy, especially if you want a half-bottle of serious white wine before one of the big clarets (Ch. Pichon-Longueville '66, £18·25). If the budget will stretch to it, one solution might be a half-bottle of the many distinguished champagnes (Pol Roger '73, at £8·25, say). The ports (from £32 to £90 for a half-bottle of Martinez '27) are unrivalled in bottle, mediocre by the glass – 'how short-sighted not to offer a good tawny.' No pipes. (GHG)

App: V.R., David Charlesworth, R. J. von Witt, Susan Kellerman, David Wooff, and others

LA CROISETTE   Map 13

168 Ifield Road, S.W.10
01-373 3694

Closed Mon; Tue L
Must book
Meals 12.30–2.30, 8–11.30

Tdh £12 (meal £16·40)

Service 15%
Seats 35
No dogs
Am Ex card

'There are strong overtones of "civilisation ends at Calais",' but French customers as well as French waiters are a good sign, and British natives are graciously allowed into Albert Bracci and Pierre Martin's fishy feasts at prices justifiable for the quality and quantity. 'The plateau de fruits de mer nearly defeated us and entirely defeated the next table.' 'We tackled a particularly splendid crab.' A complimentary Kir and a few prawns and canapés precede first courses: 'big fat mussels in garlic and parsley butter, or sliced coquilles St Jacques au safran'; then (at a test meal) well-cooked and filleted filet de rouget Bercy, and St Pierre with a good niçoise sauce of tomato, garlic, black and green olives. Others say their sauces for sea bass and bream also 'allowed admirable fish to speak for itself.' Potatoes, tomates provençale, and salad or a puree of leeks make good accompaniments. The pastry for the sweet tarts is less good than the fruit it supports. Coffee is adequate. Service responds best if addressed in its own tongue. Drink the house Estandon or Métaireau Muscadet. Recorded music, 'avoidable at the garden tables in summer.'

App: David Charlesworth, M.E., L. & R.D., W.A.W.

CURRY HOUSE   Map 12

756 Finchley Road,
N.W.11
01-458 6163

Tiny – but vocal – place in Temple Fortune, dropped last time after criticism. A test meal this time, after further nominations, succeeded with onion bhajia, lamb korma, chicken piaza, pilau rice and paratha, but fell off with reshmee kebab and dry brinjal. Mr Ghose would counter by suggesting his chef's rogan gosht and methi gosht (both £1·55) and moon biriani (£2·60). Effusive service. Some wines.

Closed Dec 25 & 26
Must book D & weekends
Meals 12–3, 6–12

Alc £3·35 (meal £4·35)

Seats 44

 ⅊ rest; w.c.
No dogs
Am Ex, Barclay, Diners

CYPRIANA KEBAB HOUSE   Map 15

11 Rathbone Street, W.1
01-636 1057

'An undemanding place to eat,' inspectors say, for the Soterious are known quantities for the usual Cypriot range of hummus and taramosalata, dolmades (£2), moussaka, and kleftiko (£2, including salad and potatoes). 'Afelia was over-fried, and coffee gritty, but salads and sweets fresh enough.' Troodos wine £3 or by the glass. Olives and chillies come if you order ouzo.

Closed Sun; Sat L;
2–3 weeks summer;
public hols (exc
Dec 25, 26 & Jan 1)

Must book
Meals 12–2.30, 6–11.30

Alc £3·45 (meal £5·90)

Seats 50
 ⅊ rest (3 steps)
No dogs
Barclay, Diners

DAPHNE'S   Map 14

112 Draycott Avenue,
S.W.3
01-589 4257 *and* 584 6883

Closed L; Sun; Dec 24;
public hols
Must book
D only, 7.30–12

Alc £8·45 (meal £13·15)

Cover 75p
Seats 60 (parties 18)
 ⅊ rest (1 step)
Air-conditioning
Access, Am Ex, Barclay,
Diners, Euro

Daphne long ago took root in Chelsea, and her conservative menu and loyal chef still earn good opinions for Messrs Tennant and Ponticelli (the latter is now part-owner as well as manager). Pierre Brebbia's *plats du jour* are 'chalked on a blackboard, for all the world like a bistro' though a glance at the bill will tell you it is not. Game has its seasons, and autumn sees a run on wild duck in armagnac, médaillons de chevreuil with chestnut puree, good roast woodcock (£5·50) and 'roast hare thickly sliced and well blended with pepper and cognac sauce.' Members normally wary of first courses built on smoked salmon or avocado cheerfully risk salmon mousse fumé, and avocado Madras, 'a giant pear with shrimps in a curried mayonnaise.' Soupe de cresson (95p) was 'rather insipid' but artichokes in soup or vinaigrette may be a more stimulating start (and they offer crudités with sherry). 'Turbot Dugléré was delightful' and 'the meat for filet de boeuf béarnaise and carré d'agneau paloise were of the highest quality and enhanced by their sauces.' One diner could have done with fewer vegetables 'or more of the quality of the steamed new potatoes and crisp bean sprouts'.

Profiteroles are praised all round and £2·15 'is not too much for a chocolate soufflé.' Coffee is liked generally too. The house Bordeaux is thought good value at £4; we have not seen this year's list, but 'Echézeaux '71 at £9·50 even survived a zealous waiter's attempt to pour it from a cradle without drawing the cork first.' Service as a whole is good.

App: M.E., Mr & Mrs D. R. Linnell, A. M. Sterry, H.W., David Wooff, J.C.

DIWANA BHEL POORI HOUSE   Map 12

(1) 121 Drummond Street, N.W.1
01-387 5556
(2) 50 Westbourne Grove, W.2
01-221 0721

Closed (1) Dec 25 L
(2) Thur; Dec 25 L
Open (1) noon–11 p.m.
(2) 12–3, 6–11

Tdh £1·75 (meal £2·20)

Alc meal £2·70

Seats 50
No dogs
Unlicensed
Access, Barclay, Diners

'Food for the masses' is Sharad Patel's business at these two suitably basic Gujerati vegetarian restaurants, the first hard by Euston and the second near enough to Paddington. At peak periods it is evident that London's teeming millions agree with his prescription – and prices. Considering the demand, standards are remarkably even, whether you take the thali (a tray with little dishes of rice, dhal, varying vegetable curries, deep-fried bhajias, puffy puris, and sweet, £1·95), or whether you choose individually: dahi vada (black-pea fritters with a mustardy sauce, 50p), crisp samosas with a chilli and tomato dip, or bhel poori and dahi poori specials with their 'delightfully complex flavours and textures', fresh coriander usually dominant, and green chilli, lemon and fenugreek somewhere. The crisp pancakes ('de luxe dosa, 75p') are another speciality. Shrikhand – a stiff cream with lemon and cardamom – is everyone's favourite sweet, on the thali or separately (45p). 'Kashmiri falooda, in a glass with straws supplied, could be imitated by Italians with Campari, soft ice-cream and spaghettini, if you can imagine.'

App: J. R. Hughes-Lewis, R. A. Bailey, A.H., Dr & Mrs S. I. Cohen, Dr M. Bhatia, and others

---

DOWN BY THE RIVERSIDE   Map 13

Canbury Gardens,
Lower Ham Road,
Kingston, Surrey
01-549 3059 *and* 546 6562

Closed L Sat & Sun;
Dec 23–Jan 7
Must book D
Meals 11–2.30, 7.30–11

Alc £5·95 (meal £9·35)

Cover 35p
Seats 48
&. rest (1 step)

Down by the riverside – next to a boat house in a park – George W. Baron v. Heye is stirring 'fish soup, hot and tasty', or Stilton and onion ditto, followed perhaps by pork on a bed of sauerkraut or duck in blackberry sauce (£2·75) – 'unexpectedly good,' says a doctor rightly sceptical of restaurant ducks. 'Capability Brown Stilton pear' (£1·10) is another opening idea that works. An inspector wondered about the future of an ambitious menu combined with the kind of view that disarms criticism, in summer at least. But she found the restaurant pretty, the service relaxing, and the cooking sincere and dexterous. The rillettes de caneton, stuffed trout (£2·15), pigeon à la paysanne (£3·10), and tender lamb chops Lucullus enveloped in pastry (£3·20) were all very competent, and the vegetables in

No dogs
Access, Am Ex, Diners

*the party's communal dish 'admirably done'. 'Caroline's
chocolate pudding' was the best of the sweets, though
profiteroles with chocolate sauce make a sound
alternative. Paul Beaudet's red and white table wines
are acceptable at £3·50, and there are others. Recorded
music. Tables on the terrace. More reports, please.*

DRAGON GATE   Map 15

7 Gerrard Street, W.1
01-734 5154

Closed Dec 25 & 26
Must book D
Open noon–11.15 p.m.

Alc £5·90 (meal £6·70)

Service 10%
Seats 80 (parties 40)
♿ rest
Unlicensed
Am Ex, Diners

'For those who like spicy hot Szechuan Chinese food,
this is the place,' says a member who enjoyed 'a
plateful of large prawns in red thickened chilli sauce
with chopped chives and about three cloves of garlic –
exquisite.' 'My favourite here remains the aubergine
with a brown fish sauce tasting nicely of soy, sesame
and ginger', then perhaps 'messy chunks of grey tripe
with Szechuan pepper', and more delicate sweet-and-
sour fish (£2·80) with 'lotus nuts like stray fish eyes
for decor. It vastly excelled the glacé fruit and plum
jam versions of a sweet-and-sour sauce.' Smoked
duck, double-cooked pork, and mixed vegetables are
other good dishes. If your mouth needs soothing, try
almond curds. Do not expect to be soothed by the
staff, who smoke and may seem brusquely ungrateful
for your custom, nor by what you may deduce about
hygiene from the state of the basement (on two
separate visits). 'They would prefer you to go to their
posh new place, Jubilee Dragon.' You might prefer to
stay here.

*App: A. Taylor, S.L., S.B., R. A. Hutson,
Abigail Fawcett, and others*

DRURY LANE HOTEL
MAUDIE'S RESTAURANT   Map 15

10 Drury Lane, W.C.2
01-836 6666

The real Maudie Littlehampton's comments on the
service would be worth hearing, and the case for a
visit rests on the terrace where you may have a snack
(fetch your own drink from the bar) after shopping in
Covent Garden; and on the Italianate cold buffet
indoors ('serve yourself and go back for more'). From
the *carte*, some good and some unspeakable dishes
have been reported. 'Adgestone '77 and Crozes-
Hermitage '76 were good buys in the £5 range.' Lager,
and bottled beers. 'I sometimes wonder why London
hotels bother to employ people rather than just throw
the doors open.'

Closed Dec 24–29
Meals 12.30–2.30, 6–9.30

Tdh buffet L from £5
(meal £8·40),
L from £7 (meal £10·60),
D £8 (meal £11·70)

Children's helpings
Seats 90 (parties 80)
♿ rest (3 steps)
Air-conditioning

No dogs in d/r
Access, Am Ex, Barclay,
Diners, Euro
130 rooms (all with bath)
Prices on application

EATONS   Map 14

49 Elizabeth Street, S.W.1
01-730 0074

Closed Sat; Sun;
public hols
Must book
Meals 12–2, 7–11

Alc £7·40 (meal £10·40)

Service inc
Cover 35p
Seats 40
♿ rest
Access, Am Ex, Diners,
Euro

The impressive feature of Pope and Vagts' inviting little restaurant near Victoria is the number of people reporting regular visits and consistent high standards at fair prices. Space is at a premium, says a member quoting Belloc's 'they spoke of their affairs in loud and strident voices.' But this does not interfere with pleasure in Santosh Bakshi's cooking, and in service 'that never seems to have to ask who's having what.' Favourite dishes of the chef this year include melon, prawn and avocado salad with sour cream, followed perhaps by éminces de veau lyonnaise (£4·40), escalope of pork filled with red cabbage and raisins, and cold poached salmon trout with mayonnaise, cucumber and tarragon. Others also describe the ever-popular smoked salmon blinis and soused herring with sour cream, 'very good chicken Kiev', carré d'agneau, and boeuf Stroganoff, all with vegetables lightly and accurately cooked – 'that includes rice, French beans, cauliflower and courgettes.' 'Coquilles aux fruits de mer (£4·50) was full of prawns, shrimps, scallops and turbot.' The sweet pastry for strawberry tart is admired, as is the coffee. Red burgundy or white Tarn wines are a modest £4 a litre, Loire Sauvignon '78, £4·95, and Ch. Millet '71, £7·76. Recorded light music. You may now take your dog (if miniature): a retrograde step, many will think. 'One of the owners, thinly clad for a cold night, himself went out to flag down a taxi for us.'

App: P. & L. M. Luscombe, Peggy Ravenshaw, A.S., Robert Gomme, C. A. Grundy, and others

EFES KEBAB HOUSE   Map 15

80 Great Titchfield Street,
W.1
01-636 1953

Closed Sun; public hols
Must book
Open noon–11.30

Alc (min £2·50) £5
(meal £7·60)

Seats 50
Access, Am Ex, Barclay,
Euro

Efes is also express, at least at lunch-time, but people anxious to earn a living rather than spend one do not mind that, and are grateful for the sprightly cooking at this Turkish place, at a modest price for central London. Cold first courses include 'nutty-tasting' hummus, dressed beans, peppers stuffed with rice, nuts and raisins, and more comprehensive hors d'oeuvre. A traveller records 'better spitted lamb than any of us remember from the Middle East.' Salads are good 'and the green garnishes of meat courses were just as fresh.' 'Lovely sickly baklava' is praised, but fruit may be the best ending, with Turkish coffee. We have not been shown menu or wine list this year, but people speak well of the Buzbag or Gunesi Turkish wines. Vigorous ethnic music on record. 'The proprietor and waiters seemed genuinely pleased that we had enjoyed our meal.'

App: C. K. Knapper, A.J.R.S., I.W., John Rowlands, Michael Copp, and others

L'EPICURE   Map 15

28 Frith Street, W.1
01-437 2829 *and* 734 2667

Closed Sun; Sat L;
3 weeks from July 28;
Dec 24; public hols
Must book
Meals 12–2.30, 6–11.15

Alc £8·10 (meal £12·35)

Cover 60p
Seats 50 (parties 20)
♿ rest (1 step)
No dogs
Access, Am Ex, Barclay,
Diners, Euro

Though something of a curate's egg, like much else in the old Soho, even the retirement of Harry the head waiter/sommelier after 27 years does not seem to have upset the rhythm of Mr Tarr's restaurant and its Greek chefs. You find the place by the flaring gas jet outside and the flaring lamp within, and dishes people have liked include the shrimp crêpe flambée to start (£1·80), sweetbreads, escalope de veau either maison or Parmesan, and pigeon en cocotte. The kitchen would add mushrooms Dordogne (£1·45), seafood tartlets, and steak maison (£5·45). 'Grenouilles were tasteless and tough, and there was more cream than sauce with suprême de volaille sous cloche.' 'But mange-tout peas were crunchy, and the sauté potatoes were the best-cooked I have had in ages.' 'Bananes flambées afterwards were more like an orange toffee sauce with banana flavour, tangy and caramelly.' Crêpes Suzette and the coffee are also praised. The fumes in the restaurant may make it wiser to drink Crozes-Hermitage '76 in the £6 range than Ch. Giscours '73 at £9·75, but the cellar is a sound one. Retsina is £4·75.

App: Alan Sayer, P. Findlater, Anne Hardy, J. Freebairn, J. W. Moss-Norbury, and others

L'ETOILE   Map 15

30 Charlotte Street, W.1
01-636 7189 *and* 1496

Closed Sat; Sun;
public hols
Must book
Meals 12.30–2.30, 6.30–10

Alc £12·20 (meal £17·05)

Service 12½%
Cover 60p
Seats 50 (parties 15)
No dogs
Am Ex, Diners

'A sanctuary', one member calls Chris Vavlides' restaurant, looking over his shoulder at his fan club rather than nursing fears of Turks with knives. Another says, 'It is not a restaurant I would normally desecrate with business entertaining' but it is probably just as well for the balance sheet that others, lunchers particularly, do not suffer from similar scruples. This means eating between the Scylla of the spirit lamp and the Charybdis of customers' cigars: a pity, for Jorge Ribeiro's turbot or (better) loup de mer monégasque, and the famous cellar, are too good for the setting, in spite of the linen, the roses, and the evocative purple-ink menu. Other good hors d'oeuvre on the trolley include the dressed crab, 'nicely oily and gently savoury, if greedily priced', stuffed aubergine (£2·10), and 'chunky gelatinous salade de pieds de porc with onions and lightly blanched celery.' Nothing is ever quite as good thereafter, and vegetables at a test meal were 'a massacre' ('just how do they achieve croquette potatoes with that gummy texture, no taste of potato, and excess nutmeg? – well, I can guess'). Brains would have been better without sage crumbled on top, but others have reported fair petit poussin en cocotte, pintade rôti, and filet mignon de chevreuil (£5·25). The kitchen adds ris de veau braisé champignons and rognons de

57

veau au vin rouge (£3·60). 'Why didn't they take a couple of fresh asparagus spears from the trolley for médaillons de veau princesse instead of using half a dozen nasty tinned ones?' Sweets are better than you fear, and richer than you think prudent: play safe with seasonal fresh peaches in orange and lemon syrup rather than set sail for the coronary coast with marron meringue. Coffee was 'stewed but strong' when tried. The wine waiting is 'manic' but not vandalistic. The carafes of unknown origin are £3·50, but £10 buys Ch. Troplong-Mondot '67, for instance. Halves of Ch. Doisy-Védrines '70 for pudding are £4·30.

App: Hilda Woolf, H.L.P., R. J. Mullis, P.G., Erica Swift, and others

FINGALS   Map 13

690 Fulham Road, S.W.6
01-736 1195

'Not for purists or bankers on certainty in food and drink.' Richard Johnston and Tina Boland are still there, but the evening chef is new since last time. The minute front room and conservatory have an amiably freakish air. On good days, expect 'lovely crab soufflé (£1·10), smoked haddock in cream cheese sauce, and deep-fried mushrooms', worthy sea-trout en croûte (£3·75) and chicken savoyarde, and more debatable sweets. 'Pretty, chirpy', ill-preened waitresses. Lunchtime salads and plats du jour. Finatello red or Terral white wines £2·70. Music live or recorded. A few tables in the garden.

Closed Sat; Sun (exc L in winter); 2 weeks Aug; Dec 25–Jan 1; public hols Must book D	Meals 12.30–2.30, 8–11.30 Alc L £3·35 (meal £5·55), D £6 (meal £9·25)	Cover 50p D Children's helpings Seats 50 (parties 20) ♿ rest Barclaycard

FOGAREIRO   Map 12

16 Hendon Lane, N.3
01-346 0315

Closed Sun; Dec 24; public hols (exc May 5 & 26)
Must book D
Meals 12–2.30, 7–11.30

Tdh L £4·95 (meal £8·75)
Alc £7·40 (meal £11·45)

Cover 65p
Seats 80
♿ rest
Air-conditioning
No dogs

Augusto Costa's fish-fancying, Portuguese-plus restaurant, a step up the road from the Guide's birthplace, was one of 1978/9's popular and critical successes. The usual penalty of queues, cramped tables, and bad air has been paid (but there is to be an extension). However, although George Ing took over the kitchen last spring, no serious stutters in the cooking have been noted, unless it be a 'lukewarm, not very tasty brill with cucumber and paprika, garnished with dull creamed potatoes.' August visitors report 'large and succulent grilled sardines' and 'the best halibut dishes (maison, and Bréval) that I can recall'. 'I was given a superb sole in wine with prawns and saffron, and a handsome mixed salad with an oily dressing.' The seafood pancake, too, is a revelation after Soho versions. Fish soups should also be tried. Meat dishes are less distinguished, even the speciality

Access, Am Ex, Barclay,
Diners, Euro

juliana preta e branca (beef and veal with peppers).
Fresh fruit or strawberry flan is probably the best
conclusion. At the start, there are agreeable crudités.
Note that when the menu says 'vegetables 75p' it
means per portion: if you want a selection, order
separately and trade later. There are some fairly
priced clarets and white burgundies but try rather
some of the Portuguese whites under £5, such as
Bucelas Velho and Branco Seco. Portuguese records.

*App: Ron Salmon, J. P. Read, P. Flatter, Roy Mathias,
Ivor Hall, R.M., R. N. Howgego, M.F.C., and others*

FOOD FOR THOUGHT   Map 15

31 Neal Street, W.C.2
01-836 0239

'What a beanfeast!' says one member, and the
expression is literal for Siriporn Duncan and Jan
Fullerton's vegetarian cooking. Characters from *Mrs
Weber's Diary* trip down the street but are perhaps too
old for the queues and sit-up-close that lead to nut
roast with mushroom sauce, lasagne, and soya bean
Stroganoff (all 85p, or 60p for a smaller helping).
'Potato and fennel soup was bland and I'd have done
better with a single salad than a mixture with quiche'
(£1·35). Self-service – and take-away too. No-smoking
section. Bring your own drink without corkage.

Closed Sat; Sun;
public hols
No bookings
Open 12–8

Alc £2·40 (meal £2·60)

Service inc
Children's helpings
Seats 40

Air-conditioning
No dogs
Unlicensed
Access, Am Ex, Barclay,
Euro

GANPATH   Map 12

372 Gray's Inn Road,
W.C.1
01-278 1938

Closed Sun; most public
hols
Must book D
Meals 12–3, 6–10.15
(10.45 Fri & Sat)

Alc (min £1) £3·50

(meal £4·50)

Service 10%
Seats 40
♿ rest
No dogs
Access card

'You would easily miss it but for the *Guide*, a step
away from King's Cross', but Mr Ramalingam's
gentle management and forceful South Indian cooking
(try his rasam soup, 30p) is 'as good as Diwana's and
not confined to vegetarian dishes', say some assiduous
experimenters. 'Delicious green bananas, uppuma,
bhuna gosht, iddly (rice cakes) with sambar sauce
(£1·05), and lemon rice,' says one girl now lost to
Colorado. Another member finds the masala dosai
(70p) 'very light and crisp, with a chilli-hot filling',
prefers among the fried items the vadai to the rather
similar aloo bonda, and was pleasantly surprised by
'juicy prawns with chilli-red dry onions', and spinach
lamb well flavoured with cardamom. But beans and
coconut needs the bite of fresh beans. 'Delicious onion
bhajias; endearing service.' 'They serve lassi, of
course: in Letchworth when I ask they bring lychees
instead.' Almond cake too. Indian records 'sometimes'.

*App: Yvonne Williams, Philippa Hayward,
Brenda Jeeves, M. M. Silver, C.P. & M.E.D.*

GATAMELATA   Map 13

343 Kensington High
Street, W.8
01-603 3613

Closed Sun; Sat L; Dec 24;
public hols
Must book D
Meals 12–2.45, 7–11.30

Tdh £5·45 (meal £8·05)
Alc £7·05 (meal £11·15)

Service 12½%
Seats 40
Air-conditioning
No dogs
Access, Am Ex, Barclay,
Diners

'A well-prepared set meal for £5·45, served willingly
on a busy Saturday night, seemed like a miracle in
west London in 1979,' growls one Paddington bear
amiably, and others on the whole agree about
Giuseppe Dilema's cooking for Mr Carraro's 'tunnel-
like' place. Experience must tell you which are the
hot, chilly or unrestful seats, and the hors d'oeuvre
praised last time seem more variable in quality now,
'but funghi with venison pâté united taste and
freshness.' In the set meal, lasagne was 'cheesy and
meaty', chicken pancake 'formidable' and piccata
of veal 'well flavoured with herbs and garlic.' The
couple who were unlucky with the hors d'oeuvre
did much better later with 'splendid' sole, trout with
almonds and 'heavy but home-made' profiteroles.
'Lamb cutlets in rosemary and wine sauce have looked
and tasted delicious on two occasions.' 'Pollo Valentina
was exquisite, vegetables mushy.' Calf's liver with
sage, roasted quails with grapes, venison in Guinness,
and kitchen-made pasta are suggested too. 'Sound'
Valpolicella or Soave are £3·45 a litre. 'Coffee jugs
tend to leak rather than pour.' 'No dogs, they say,
but a customer was admitted with hers. I almost
prefer cigars.'

*App: Shirley Winn, G. R. Webster-Gardiner,
Michael Copp, W. Frankland, I. H. D. Johnston*

♥ LE GAVROCHE   Map 14

61–63 Lower Sloane Street,
S.W.1
01-730 2820 *and* 5983

Closed L; Sun;
public hols
Must book
D only, 7–12

Alc £17·75 (meal £26·70)

Service 15%
Cover £1·20
Seats 47
♿ rest
Am Ex, Diners

For the first time in many years, the Roux brothers'
hard-core Parisian, orchidaceous restaurant for the
déclassé rich sets a problem. At the outset, '*un peu
d'histoire*'. In Postgate's time, the Gavroche always
drew mixed reports, and was actually dropped in the
year of his death. But every year since 1973 professional
inspection has endorsed the general judgment (and
the owners' own expressed opinion) by awarding the
highest honours. (See also Bray, Waterside, in case
anyone imagines that MM Roux's rooted objection
to the *Guide*'s methods affects our opinions of the
food.) 'Yes, the place *is* full of oblivious Americans
and arrogant Frenchmen, but they are more interesting
to listen to, between courses at the jammed tables,
than your typical reticent, non-smoking Londoner.
This time the next table was discussing breasts at the
top of its voice.' Even Britons, though, are prepared
to pay the bill for 'superb service and advice, leading
to many dishes that can fairly be called heavenly',
above all the feuilleté pastry for bécasse Néné (a rich
and gamey first course) or its sweet counterparts, such
as 'the tarte Tatin, which came the size of a dinner
plate but which my stepmother and I were miraculously
inspired to consume between us.' The highly decorated

fish or other mousses shown when you sit down, soufflés suissesses (a cheesy equivalent to oeufs à la neige), the duck that gives you a Lévi-Straussian experience of the raw and the cooked in successive stages, and the dazzling, delicate sorbets ('my favourite is the kiwi-fruit') are other triumphs. 'Petit poussin sarthoise (boned and stuffed with chicken mousse, in a very rich calvados and cream sauce, £9·50, with vegetables) was classically Norman.' However, price and professionalism together are unforgiving masters. Never mind the occasions when the two-stage duck misfires, or displeases people unused to the style. Never mind a few grumbles about poor salads. But it is different when a former admirer receives deficient staff advice, pays £9·50 for clumsily salted oeufs brouillés au caviar and thick, boring soupe aux moules ('the memory of Chez Nico's saffron-delicate mussel soup was still with me'), has noisettes d'agneau aux racines (£10·50, with salade de mâche aux noix included) cooked well past the requested *saignant*, notes the weary taste of his partner's vegetables, and finishes with poached peach (£4·20), served in a cafe-model coupe which left no room for the champagne syrup to be poured over. 'A spell at the drawing-board would do no harm.' The restaurant's former sommelier has opened his own place in Wales (the Crown at Whitebrook: 'not yet ready,' thinks an inspector). But the new man knows and is helpful about the vast list, at least if it is a question of deciding between Ch. La Lagune '73 at £18·50 or Ch. Chasse-Spleen '72, both c.b., at £14·50: who, after all, is to be the guide between *premier cru* clarets at £100 or so (the '61s), £200 or so (the '45s), and the in-between price-tags MM Roux affix to First World War Musigny or Pommard?

App: Paul Gambaccini, Adam Mount, C.P.D., C.S., and others

GAY HUSSAR   Map 15

2 Greek Street, W.1
01-437 0973

Closed Sun; public hols
Must book
Meals 12.30–2, 5.30–11.30

Tdh L £5·50 (meal £8·75)
Alc £7·40 (meal £10·85)

Cover 35p
Children's helpings
(under 8)
Seats 35 (parties 10)
⑤ rest (1 step)

No Protection of Information bill will turn off the leaks as long as Victor Sassie's banquettes exist to slide Official Secrets along – but better do the deal at lunch when the place is crowded, and the set meal keeps the price within bounds. Better not do it, though, straight after return from a mission to Budapest where, says one man, 'the cold wild cherry soup bears no resemblance to cherry yoghourt and the gulyas is designed for Magyars, not milquetoasts.' All the same, in this long-lived, long-loved place, there are good things, 'and it was interesting to note that fish salad à la carte was identical in size and content to that on the set menu.' Fish soup, smoked goose pâté, and bean soup are other possible first courses, followed perhaps by hortobagyi pancake with spinach,

Air-conditioning
No dogs

'surprisingly crisp' (for Soho) roast duck, Serbian chicken with 'lots of paprika, green pepper, sour cream and yellow Bosnian barley', stuffed cabbage, or 'a ragout of liver with caraway.' Ponty gerinc (roast saddle of carp, £4·50) and serpenyos rostelyos (paprika braised steak, £5·75) are other dishes to consider à la carte at night. Cheese and lemon dumplings with plum sauce, if you have a Central European appetite, and blackcurrant sorbet if you do not, are possible sweets. Fruit tarts tend to be dry: at a test meal 'the glaze on the Dobostorte was beginning to cloud over, which surely takes a day or two to achieve?' Decadents may begin with a Puszta (peach brandy and Tokay) cocktail at £1·45. Drink thereafter is difficult apart from the adequate Hungarian Riesling at £2·30 for 50 cl, because their Hungarian reds are mostly sweet, but £12 is not a bad price for Ch. Giscours '66, c.b., and if you fancy prolonging, or at least assuaging, existence with Tokay Aszu Essenz at upwards of £30, it is there.

App: by too many members to list

GEETA   Map 12

59 Willesden Lane,
N.W.6
01-624 1713

Closed Dec 25 & 26
Must book weekends
Meals 12–2.45, 6–10.45
(11.45 weekends)

Alc (min £1) £2·90

(meal £3·90)

Seats 40
&. rest
No dogs

M. V. Nair, who has 'cooked for Ravi Shankar and George Harrison' but more importantly for the Vijay restaurant down the road, is chef at this small, light, neat place with 'well-supervised service'. His speciality is South Indian vegetarian cooking, with some meat dishes of which he is also proud: chicken curry in coconut milk (£1·70) and bhuna gosht. But it may be better, and is certainly very economical, to eat 'thin and crisp masala dosai with a spicy, not stodgy filling and coconut chutney' (80p), avial and sambar (80p each), lemon or coconut rice, 'beautiful puffy puris', 'lovely fudgy ladoo which they may let you take away', and 'salted lassi to drink since lager is 70p a pint.' Recorded music is threatened.

App: David de Saxe, P.S., J.C., and others

GINO'S   Map 13

15–17 Hill Rise,
Richmond, Surrey
01-940 3002

Closed Mon; public hols
Must book weekends
Meals 12.30–2.30 (3 Sun),
6.30–11.30 (Fri & Sat 7–12)

Tdh L from £4·50
(meal from £6·75),
D £6 (meal £8·40)

The Italian genius for creating an environment that encourages appetite is well expressed in the Santins' open-plan room in green, white and pine, with plants, Welsh dresser plate displays, and a handsome view of the Thames. At a test meal, the impression was momentarily clouded by stale bread and foil-packeted butter, but sunned again by 'a small mountain of fresh mussels in a well-blended tomato, chilli and garlic sauce', and spare ribs in a sauce that sounded the same but packed a quite different punch. Most people, though, start with Andrea Zaccaria's pasta, which at its best is very delicate: 'cannelloni was superb'; 'the waiters are

Alc £6·30 (meal £9·80)

Service 10%
Cover 45p alc
Seats 80 (parties 40)
No dogs
Access, Am Ex, Barclay,
Diners

instructed to let two diners share two pasta dishes, so we could both enjoy spaghetti alle vongole with clams on the half-shell, and also the creamy, mushroomy tagliolini Gino.' King prawns in butter and garlic, tender scaloppine al marsala, discreetly sauced turbot and sole, and lightly cooked, deftly served vegetables are also mentioned. A member needing to ask for entrecôte without salt and salad without dressing had his prescription met. The test meal fell off somewhat at the sweet stage, but others report good sweet crespelle (chocolate pancakes), chocolate gateau, and cheesecake. The Settesoli white house wine is £3·60 and good. Other prices have not been sent, but Corvo di Salaparuta is in the £5 range. More reports, please.

LA GIRALDA   Map 3

66 Pinner Green,
Pinner, Middlesex
(Rickmansworth Road
between Cuckoo Hill and
Elm Park Road)
01-868 3429

Closed Dec 25
Must book
Meals 12–2.30, 6–10.30

Tdh L £3 (meal £5),
D £5 (meal £7·20)
Alc L (min £3)
£4·10 (meal £6·25)

Service 10%
Seats 90 (parties 40)
⟨&⟩ rest; w.c.
Air-conditioning
No dogs
Access, Am Ex, Barclay,
Diners

So many restaurants have bad systems or no system at all that it seems harsh to come down on a previously admired place whose system (for delivering vaguely Spanish food and splendidly Spanish wine at modest prices to large numbers of people) is becoming its own downfall. But an evenly divided file and a highly critical inspection report (for the second year running) cannot be gainsaid. The restaurant (in an unpromising shopping parade) is crowded and noisy, and fair enough at the price. The service is cheerful-casual, 'acrobatic by necessity', and only occasionally snappish. At the test meal (second-sitting dinner), pancake with beef and herbs in tomato and cheese sauce was quite good, and entrecôte Santa Cruz cooked rare as requested. But too much else bore out other visitors' reports of 'cool, pedestrian and flavourless dishes.' 'Pollo ajillo, "chicken fried in olive oil with lots of garlic", was nothing like its description or one's Spanish memories', gazpacho was vinegary and watery, and the palmiers served with ice-cream a disgrace to whoever baked them. The wines are so distinguished and moderately priced that they are now a grave mismatch with the food: anyone who goes there to enjoy himself (or herself) with an unrivalled collection of Riojas and other regions, listed in Spanish (but quite well understood by the senior staff) is going to want something more dependably good (and preferably Spanish) to eat. Live guitar music at night. Progress reports, please.

The Guide News Supplement will be sent out as usual, in June, to everyone who buys the book directly from Consumers' Association and to all bookshop purchasers who return the card interleaved with their copy. Let us know of any changes that affect entries in the book, or of any new places you think should be looked at.

See p. 508 for the restaurant-goer's legal rights, and p. 510 for information on hygiene in restaurants.

IL GIRASOLE   Map 14

126 Fulham Road S.W.3
01-370 6656

Closed Mon; Dec 31;
public hols
Must book D & weekends
Meals 12.15–3, 7–11

Alc (min £3) £6·30
(meal £9·50)

Cover 40p
Seats 60
&. rest (1 step)
No dogs
Am Ex, Barclay, Diners

The food is far better – if dearer – than average Italian 'if you interpret the menu and consult the staff,' says one regular firm enough to make a fuss with Armando when something miscarries in this sunstruck restaurant. 'I have never had good soup, but the pasta is authentic, and the tomato and cream sauce for tagliatelle Positano delightful.' Peppery gamberoni nerone, or the 'very oily and nice' hors d'oeuvre from the impressive cold table are good too if price does not signify, and the same is true of 'carré d'agnello Persiano' or nodino alla Sassi. Fish-lovers may be directed to scampi e calamari fritti, or scampi Portofino in a cream and brandy sauce, or the day's dish 'which might even be sole cooked with banana.' 'Veal helpings are rather small.' Wines and prices have not been notified to us this year. Some tables outside. It is imperative to check the bill and specify closely what you want in both food and drink: too many guests are too frenetic or lordly to do so, and the waiters are sometimes as casual with their sums as they are with their shirts.

App: D. Westoby, P.M., V. G. Saunders, M.E., and others

GOURMET RENDEZVOUS   Map 12

263 Finchley Road, N.W.3
01-435 0755

The optimistic overheard comment 'you can eat kosher here' may account for a certain blandness that belies Mr Tsui's Szechuan ambitions, and prawns with crispy rice 'failed utterly' at a test meal. But most people approve the pork with pickled cabbage, baked crab with ginger and spring onion, 'over-sweet but capable' beef in yellow-bean sauce, quick-fried fresh prawns, deep-fried beef with chilli, and Pekinese duck or grilled dumplings. 'They made our very young children welcome at Sunday lunch', and toffee apples were 'light and crisp'. Good tea, too. Wines. Recorded music.

Closed Dec 25 & 26
Must book D
Meals 12–2.30, 5.30–12

Tdh D £4·40 (meal £5·10)
Alc £3·60 (meal £4·25)

Service 10%

Seats 46
No dogs
Access, Am Ex, Barclay, Diners

See p. 110 for London pubs and wine bars.

Unless otherwise stated, a restaurant is open all week and all year and is licensed.

Numbers are given for private parties only if they can be accommodated in a room separate from the main dining-room; when there are several such rooms, the capacity of the largest is given. Some restaurants will take party bookings at times when they are normally closed.

GRAHAME'S SEA FARE   Map 15

38 Poland Street, W.1
01-437 0975 *and* 3788

'Ideal for solitary males: regulars sit at communal tables and address the waitresses by name.' But Robert de Haan's Mittel-Europa fish restaurant by the side door of the Oxford Circus Marks & Spencer pleases others too who like gefilte fish or chopped herring, followed by 'very fresh and moist, if rather darkly fried' cutlet of haddock (£2·50) or whole plaice, perhaps with latkes, sweet-and-sour cucumber, or apple and celery salad. Drink lemon tea, or one of the few white wines they keep. 'They very politely asked a party of pensioners who came in if they had read the menu prices first.'

Closed Sun; Mon D;
public hols (exc Apr 4 L);
Sept 19, 20 & 28;
Dec 24 D
Meals 12–2.45, 5.30–8.45

Alc £5·65 (meal £9·95)

Cover 35p D & Sat

Seats 78
♿ rest
No dogs

GRANARY   Map 15

39 Albemarle Street, W.1
01-493 2978

The strength of Jon Shah's up-and-downstairs daytime utility is that his partner Margaret McDonald cooks. Though meat sometimes suffers from the warming oven, regular and critical visitors admire avocado with prawns in curry cream sauce on spinach (£1·30), pork and plums (or prunes), beef burgundy, salad (try the niçoise version), and puddings, 'especially fruit salads or Pavlovas'; others add strawberry japonaise, gâteau progrès or crème brûlée. Unnamed plonk is 55p a glass. 'Staff seem to care.' Recorded classical music. 'A pity they shut a little too early for theatre-goers.'

Closed Sun; Sat D;
public hols; 1st 2 weeks
Aug
Open 10–6.50
(10–2.30 Sat), L 12–2.30

Alc L (min £1) £2·85
(meal £3·65)

Service inc

Seats 98
♿ rest (1 step)
Air-conditioning
No dogs

THE GRANGE   Map 15

39 King Street, W.C.2
01-240 2939

Closed Sun; Sat L;
Dec 24 D; public hols
Must book
Meals 12.30–2.30, 7.30
(6.45 Sat)–11.30

Tdh from £8·50
(meal £9·35)

The Communist Party of Great Britain and the new-poor bourgeoisie rub shoulders in this Covent Garden cul-de-sac, and the latter's eye for a bargain takes them time and again to Geoffrey Sharp's long-running, vegetable-proud, uncertainly served restaurant, 'presided over by Victorian frumps in gilt frames.' The pricing policy demands a keen eye, a logical mind and a good memory (for they will offer you a sweet even if you initially opted for two courses). But a musician 'did not hesitate to abandon Götz Friedrich's Covent Garden *Idomeneo* in the middle'

Seats 65
♿ rest
Air-conditioning
Am Ex card

in favour of Jurgens Boldt's scrubbed crudités with various dips, fried collops of fennel with tartare sauce, smoked haddock flan, lamb Shrewsbury, and beef Wellington. Other dishes warmly praised include 'unexpected' terrine of spring vegetables, cream soups (avocado with watercress, and artichoke), mussels in curry, devilled turkey kebabs, spiced sausages, steak and kidney pie, 'juicy lamb cutlets in pastry', 'roast veal and stuffing in which I lost count of the herbs', 'buttery new potatoes in their skins, young turnips à la crème, lightly cooked broccoli and other good vegetables.' Occasional miscarriages in the early part of the year do not erase the favourable overall impression. 'Budino di ricotta was a dense, downright Tuscan concoction of ricotta, cream, dried fruit and chocolate': blackberry and apple pie (in February) was 'downright British, and just as good.' Rhubarb, orange and ginger fool, crème brûlée and brandy-snaps are other pleasures, though 'flak jackets should be worn by your neighbours for the last two items.' The French house wines, of which a half-bottle is included in the set meal prices, are sound, c.b., and others can be had instead at a surcharge (£5·95 for Ch. Branaire, c.b., '73). Pipes are discouraged.

App: P. G. Urben, Eileen Mitchell, Roy Mathias, P.S.A.W., Pat & Jeremy Temple, H. B. Cardwell, J.R.T., and many others

GREEN JADE   Map 12

29–31 Porchester Road, W.2
01-229 7221
Closed Dec 25 & 26
Open noon–11.30 p.m.

Tdh L £1·30, D from £4·10
Alc meal about £4·60

Seats 50
No dogs
Access, Am Ex, Barclay

In spite of the ominously long menu offering both Peking and Canton cooking in a 'splendidly garish little place near Paddington', various members and a critical inspector ate very well both ways in the autumn of 1979: 'nine dishes in the £6·75 banquet, including not very grand hors d'oeuvre but crisp, hot and aromatic dumplings, crunchy sweet-sour pork, vegetables very al dente even to the lettuce, and very fresh and iodiny quick-fried prawns.' Hot-and-sour beef, bird's nest with fillet steak and 'expertly de-fatted' Cantonese duck are also praised, along with unobtrusive service whose suggestions should be heeded. 'Hotter food would be appreciated.' Some exotic spirituous drinks (£1). More reports, please.

We rewrite every entry each year, and depend on fresh, detailed reports to confirm the old, as well as to include the new. The further from London you are, the more important this is.

Bed and breakfast prices have been quoted to us by hoteliers; where possible, we have given minimum off-season prices for one person sharing a double room and maximum in-season prices for one person in a single room.

If we know that a restaurant has music, of whatever sort, we say so.

GURKHAS TANDOORI RESTAURANT   Map 15

23 Warren Street, W.1
01-388 1640

The kukris on the wall (balanced by Botticelli's *Birth of Venus*) are the setting for the Manandhars' Nepalese and tandoori dishes. Both are good, and are served with 'smiles and firmness'. Nan keema (65p) was puffy and fragrantly spiced, channa masala (90p) and tandoori tikka masala (£1·80) very good versions, mountain specialities such as bhutuwa (fried) chicken livers, shak su ka (minced beef, tomato and egg, £1·70), and the 'sour, clinging' potato pickle (aloo kerao ko achar, 90p) are well worth a try. Tiny place, slow delivery: 'I'd have liked the nans first and the rest hotter later.' No dogs.

Closed Dec 25 & 26
Must book
Meals 12–2.45, 6–11.45

Alc £3·10 (meal £4·15)

Service 10%

Seats 32
Access, Am Ex, Barclay, Diners

LES HALLES   Map 12

57 Theobald's Road,
W.C.1
01-242 6761

Closed Sun; Sat L;
Mon D; Dec 25
Must book L
Meals 12–2.30, 7–10.30

Alc £7·40 (meal £10·70)

Service 15%
Seats 55
♿ rest
Access, Am Ex, Barclay,
Diners

Mr Conrad, of the Language School next door, has made an effective translation of a Paris brasserie – marble table-tops, plants, black and white photos, and ebullient typography – for the lawyers and journalists who frequent this district. True, the best dishes have been those that give the chef Robert Magnaud the least trouble: 'onion soups, excellent Brie and herb-coated goat cheese', and espresso coffee. But though M Magnaud could profitably learn elsewhere how to make fish soups and sauces, or fry aubergines, simpler poulet à l'estragon or faux-filet dijonnaise are praised. Jambon persillé (£1) and canard sauvage sauce grand veneur (£4·25) are also promising. 'Crème viennoise was delicious.' The Domaine de Massignan red wine is fairly priced here at £3. Air-conditioning. No dogs. More reports, please.

HARD ROCK CAFE   Map 15

150 Old Park Lane, W.1
01-629 0382

Even a disc jockey reports earache inside Mr Nallamilli's 'funky roadside diner', though people outside are 'not queuing for their health but for the best hamburgers and French fries we expect to find in London.' An inspector also liked the club sandwich: 'plenty of chicken breast, crunchy and tasty bacon, and lettuce as crisp as celery.' Steaks and (in winter) chili con carne too. Apple pie and cheesecake or hot fudge sundae if you still have an appetite. American beers. The system and formula are simple: the secret must be the control of quality and balance sheet alike.

Closed Dec 23–26
No bookings
Open noon–12.30 a.m.

Alc £3·45 (meal £5·75)

Seats 125

♿ rest
No dogs

HATHAWAYS   Map 13

13 Battersea Rise, S.W.11
01-228 3384

Closed L; Sun;
2 weeks Aug; public hols
(exc Apr 4)
Must book
D only, 7–10.30

Alc £5·75 (meal £9·05)

Service 10%
(parties over 10)
Cover 50p
Seats 34
♿ rest
Air-conditioning
No dogs
Access, Am Ex, Barclay,
Diners

Recipes in *Second Dinner
Party Book:* Eliza Acton's
salmon pudding;
tourtiere québecoise;
cheese and vegetable
chowder

The main thing about Carl and Kathie Scheiding's homely, cramped, rather busily served restaurant is that it is very difficult to dislike, especially if you start with a south Londoner's surprise that it exists. 'My guest said she felt as if she had gone to the kitchen, sat down, opened a cookery book at a page she fancied, and miraculously found the dish in front of her.' Others too speak of 'coming home' for Kathie's fish or vegetable and cheese chowders, 'the former full of squid, prawns and white fish', the latter 'like her chili con carne, fit for a freezing winter.' Admirers also describe pheasant and hazelnut or vegetable pâtés 'light in texture, positive in flavour', fish puddings and pies, 'melting salmon quiche' (90p), 'melodiously herbed hare casserole', 'crisp and tender boned duck leg with a dark and fruity stuffing tasting of the liver', chicken Neptune 'generously stuffed with crab-meat and served with prawn sauce on a bed of rice' (£3·60), and 'carefully roast guinea-fowl with a beautifully made orange sauce.' 'An overpowering Alsace pork dish' is also mentioned, and Sauerbraten is a speciality (£3·85). Vegetables and sweets, relatively speaking, may be a disappointment: 'Why do they still serve a salad at the beginning?'; and 'bananas baked in rum were nice but some of the "made" puddings are on the heavy side for this menu, especially since abundant Turkish delight comes with coffee.' But the bread is good. The Spanish house wines are £3·05 and 'they unwisely stress claret names over claret years' (though Ch. Grand-Puy-Lacoste '71 is a defensible £10·50). They welcome children in the early evening only.

App: V. G. Saunders, Neil Fairlamb, Michael Mansky, David Potter, F. & D.N., Margaret Noble, and others

HOLY COW   Map 13

38 Kensington Church
Street, W.8
01-937 2005

People got off on the wrong foot with last year's wrong address (apologies) and not all are sure that 'tepid or salty' Indian dishes were worth finding. But late autumn inspection found 'outstanding' chicken Begum Behar in a thick, reddish creamy sauce with 'rather sweet' spices (£3·35), and good meat in rogan gosht. 'Aloo chat was tamarind-sour, tarka dhal bland by contrast, and gajar ka halwa first-rate, with strong cardamom flavour.' 'Hesitant' or 'persuasive' service; ill-chosen music; fair comfort. Wines and beers.

Closed Dec 25
Must book D & weekends
Meals 12–2.45, 6–11.45

Tdh L from £3·75
(meal £5·25)
Alc £5·65 (meal £8·60)

Cover 40p alc

Seats 85
No dogs
Access, Am Ex, Barclay,
Diners, Euro

HUNG FOO   Map 13

6–8 West Hill, S.W.18
01-870 0177 *and* 874 2500

Closed Sun; Dec 25 & 26
Must book D
Meals 12–2.30, 6–12

Tdh D from £4·85
(meal £5·40)
Alc £5·35 (meal £5·90)

Service inc
Seats 90 (parties 40)
⑤ rest (2 steps)
No dogs
Am Ex, Diners

'Three doors from Wandsworth police station' is Mr Keung's monitory direction. *Guide*-readers, solid citizens all, will be more afraid of the South Circular parking, but still pleased to find this lately extended, 'rather subfusc and western-looking' Pekinese place. Service has yet to gather pace again and, for the enlarged numbers, table plate warmers would be a good idea, and more absorbent paper napkins too. But the cooking, admirers say, deserves better than last year's 'pass' category, notably the Peking soup (70p), 'quick-fried three delicious' ('enormous prawns, chicken and pork in a delicate ginger sauce', £2·30) and 'ambrosial' deep-fried shredded beef in chilli sauce (£2·75); and – adds an inspector – Chinese fried stuffed mushrooms (£3·20): 'slivers of pork inserted in large mushrooms, the whole encased in dumpling dough, and topped with transparent rounds of garlic and ginger – bliss.' Sesame prawns, Szechuan cabbage, grilled dumplings, and toffee apples were also good at a test meal: however, crab-meat and asparagus was poor, and duck with pineapple tasted well but was full of bone chips. Prices have risen sharply with the re-fit, and quantities may have declined. Recorded Chinese music. There are wines from £3·50.

App: Sue Duke, D.W., T. M. S. Tosswill,
Ellis Blackmore

JASON'S   Map 16

50 Battersea Park Road,
S.W.11
01-622 6998

'There's a jolly thing at the back of the bar called Jason's Fleecing Board,' reports an inspector who enjoyed dinner at this simple and dark – but neatly served – family restaurant where Michael, in the kitchen, specialises in meze, shashlik, moussaka and kleftiko. At a test meal, tender kalamares in red wine and lemon (£1·10) and the 'intensely flavoured' kleftiko with well-cooked rice were better than the kebabs, salad, pitta and baklava. 'It is well worth paying the 20p extra for Castel Danielis red at £3·50,' says a wine critic. Greek recorded music.

Closed L; Sun; Dec 24;
public hols (exc Apr 4)
Must book
D only, 6.30–12

Tdh £4 (meal £6·75)
Alc £4·10 (meal £6·85)

Cover 15p

Seats 55 (parties 32)
⑤ rest
No dogs

The Guide accepts no advertising. Nor does it allow restaurateurs to use its name on brochures, menus, or in any form of advertisement. If you see any instances of this, please report them to us.

For the explanation of ⑤, denoting accessibility for the disabled, see 'How to use the Guide', p. 4.

JOE ALLEN   Map 15

13 Exeter Street, W.C.2
01-836 0651

'Take junk food seriously,' counsels a London American. Richard Polo, manager here, has seen his cellar and bar ride the curve of a convivial trend, and 'though entrees are catastrophic the burgers are good.' The burgers ('coolish if rare') are called chopped steak (£2·90, including vegetables) on the blackboard menu, but others put in words for 'crisp fresh Stilton salad with an oily dressing' (£1·35), the crisp'n'dry Henry's fried chicken (£2·95), rare steaks, and 'decadent but fresh' banana cream pie (90p). Drink Bloody Marys, whisky sours, house Soave and Valpolicella (£3·45), and don't attempt three courses. Expect piano or juke-box.

Closed Dec 25
Must book
Meals noon–1 a.m.
(midnight Sun)

Alc £3·65 (meal £6·30)

Seats 128
Air-conditioning

JONATHAN'S   Map 13

71 Blythe Road, W.14
01-602 2758 and 603 0070

Closed Sun; Mon; Sat L;
Dec 25 & 26
Must book
Meals 12–2, 7–10.45

Alc £7·40 (meal £10·90)

Service 10%
Cover 50p
Seats 40
No dogs
Access, Am Ex, Barclay,
Diners, Euro

Jonathan and Janet Keyne, whose civilised basement (ring the bell) is handy for the unpromising Olympia district, have been better appreciated this year by regular visitors (professional cooks included) than they were by more cursory critics when they opened. True, their desire to make a 'relaxing and fairly priced place that they would like to eat in themselves' has left their chef José Santillan cooking mostly variations on familiar restaurant dishes. But exacting visitors did not mind because their chicken and shellfish pancakes, tarte aux champignons (£1·45), noisettes d'agneau à l'estragon, 'pink and tender' boeuf Wellington (£4·50) and, more remarkably, the pommes lyonnaise, were so deftly done. Hot avocado with crab and quenelles de brochet (£2·90) are among other successes. Profiteroles are praised too. The house red and white table wines are £3, Corney & Barrow's £3·40, and Ch. de Barbe '75, £5·95. Recorded classical music. More reports, please.

JOY KING LAU   Map 15

3 Leicester Street, W.C.2
01-437 1132

Must book D
Open 11 a.m.–11.30 p.m.
(Sun 10 a.m.–10 p.m.)
Tdh from £3·80
(meal £3·60)
Alc £3·90 (meal £4·40)

Norman Han's palace of Cantonese varieties had more PR push than most Chinese restaurant debuts, but it still took a year for inspection reports to warm up to the point where the accolade 'as good as Manchester', could be conferred. Even now, dim-sum are not their strong point – 'nothing was hot enough except the char siu bun, and the siu mai were old, cool, and glued together.' *Autres plats, autres moeurs*, for fried lettuce with Chinese mushrooms (£2·80) had 'a captivating smoky flavour and lettuce that stayed crisp even in its gravy', fried chicken blood

Service 12½%
Seats 200 (parties 60)
⅙ rest
No dogs
Am Ex, Diners

with ginger and spring onion (£2·40) produced 'a gorgeously different gravy for those nuggets of wobbly carmine custard', and eel with fresh garlic was a further contrast. Another inspector was impressed with delicately cooked rice, and found the prawns baked with chilli and salt, cold roast duck, and braised brisket – 'like a good farmhouse stew with dashes of soy and ginger' – well up to the best of the genre. This only touches the fringe of the vast repertoire. For a sweet, try egg tart. There are wines.

App: M. F. Cullis, O. MacPherson, N.F.J., Abigail Fawcett, D.B., and others

JUSTIN DE BLANK   Map 15

54 Duke Street, W.1
01-629 3174

Justin de Blank himself is flying high (his hotel at Shipdham in Norfolk opened in 1979) and his croissants even higher with royal custom, but the more credit to the natural merit of the self-service food now cooked here by Elizabeth Crossfield for Oxford Street shoppers and slaves: notably, cold lettuce and mint soup, tasty fish-cakes, 'very light smoked haddock vol-au-vents', good shepherd's pie, 'variable roast meat seldom quite hot enough', turkey Florentine, good fresh cheeses, sweet Indonesian fruit and nut rice, and fruit brûlée (£1). Wines from £1·60 for 50 cl of ordinaire; English Kelsale '77, £5·25.

Closed Sun; Sat D;
public hols
Open 9–3.30, 4.30–9.30
(L 12–3.30, D 6–9.30)

Alc £3·90 (meal £5·80)

Seats 60 (parties 14)

Air-conditioning
No dogs

KERZENSTUBERL   Map 15

9 St Christopher's Place,
W.1
01-486 8103 *and* 3196

There is an old saying that you have to be feeling very strong to go to hospital, and one man feels exactly the same about Herbert and Ilse and their earnest Austrian desire to please: 'The accordion and the singing gave us a headache, though the food was good.' Mixed verdict after a test meal: 'hot and tasty' deep-fried mushrooms in a good crumb coating, fair pork cutlet serbische Art, poor steak in burgundy, and nice apricot pancakes. Klaus Stange also suggests Bauernschmaus (£5·65) or Kessel goulash (£3·30). Austrian Blauer Burgunder or Riesling a stiff £2·95 for 50 cl. Cramped dancing space. No dogs.

Closed Sun; Sat L;
public hols; mid-Aug to
mid-Sept
Must book
Meals 12–2.15, 6–11

Alc £9·10 (meal £12·85)

Service inc
Cover L 65p, D 75p
Children's helpings

Seats 48
⅙ rest (2 steps)
Air-conditioning
Access, Am Ex, Barclay,
Diners, Euro

KEW RENDEZVOUS   Map 13

110 Kew Road,
Richmond, Surrey
01-940 1334 *and* 948 4343

Closed public hols
Must book D & weekends
Meals 12–2.30, 6–11.30

Tdh from £6
Alc meal £5·85

Service 15%
Seats 120 (parties 20)
 ⅃ rest (1 step)
Air-conditioning
No dogs
Access, Am Ex, Barclay,
Diners

Perhaps the new mortgage rates on the elegantly
designed Richmond building justify the service charge,
perhaps not – but even those who find the waiters
lackadaisical and the helpings less than lavish are
content with Mr Wong's delicate hand with quick-fried
lamb, garlic and spring onions, and aromatic
crispy lamb with 'lovely wafts of aniseed', 'crunchy
green beans with garlic and soy as a seasonal
vegetable', and 'gentle' grilled prawns Peking-style.
'Mixed fish is less gentle, being solid with garlic, but
none the worse for it.' Dried seaweed and scallops for
a start, deep-fried shredded beef with chilli, spare ribs,
chicken with cashews or walnuts in yellow-bean sauce,
and the toffee apples are also praised, but avoid
sweet-sour pork and other conventionals. No wine
prices supplied this year.

*App: V. Westerman, J. S. & F. Waters, L.S.H.,
M.J.F., Ian Prowse, and others*

KOLOSSI GRILL   Map 12

56–58 Rosebery Avenue,
E.C.1
01-278 5758

*The name and the chef remain the same, but a change
of owner in mid-1979 makes more reports desirable on
this useful Cypriot place whose family atmosphere
'may overpower' towards the end of meal-times. But
the artichoke and broad bean salad, 'succulent and
crunchy spare ribs' (sirinjiahi, £2·45) 'hottish'
Armenian lachmado (minced meat on pitta bread),
and mixed kebabs suit local regulars and strays from
Sadlers Wells. Wines from £2·85.*

Closed Sun; public hols
Meals 12–3, 5–11
(Fri & Sat 12)

Alc £3·30 (meal £5·65)

Service inc

Seats 52
 ⅃ rest
No dogs

KOWLOON   Map 15

21 Gerrard Street, W.1
01-437 1694

Arrive sharp at noon or an hour later at this Chinese
bakery with cafe and restaurant attached. The trays
of buns will then be hot from the oven, at their most
appetising: point to char siu pau ('slightly sweet yeast
dough, with a filling of barbecued pork and hoisin
sauce, 30p to take away') or any of the equally light
and interesting sweet buns or wobbly egg tarts. Sit
down to try soup noodles, a huge bowl of fragrant
broth, tender noodles and generous slices of duck or
barbecued pork (£1·30). Expect dictatorial service,
though the chef in the window is cheerful.

Must book
Open noon–midnight

Tdh L £2·60 (meal £3)
Alc from £1·90
(meal £2·25)

Service 10%
Seats 150
Access card

LANGAN'S BRASSERIE   Map 15

Stratton Street, W.1
01-493 6437

Closed Sun; Sat L;
Dec 24 D; Dec 25 & 26;
public hols
Must book
Meals 12.30–2.45, 7–11.45
(Sat 8–12.45)

Alc £9·35 (meal £13·45)

Service 12½%
Cover 75p
Seats 70 & 140
 rest (1 step)
Air-conditioning
Am Ex, Diners

Peter Langan, Michael Caine and Richard Shepherd, whose faces drawn by Patrick Procktor surmount the purple-ink menu, own and operate this capacious, casual, picture-hung room opposite the Ritz. It has made itself indispensable, if no longer cheap – and indeed, *le patron mange (et boit) ici*. Mr Shepherd is a fine chef but there is no need to consider him wasted since the menu goes beyond the usual brasserie repertoire. Artichaut farci à la Nissarda has gone from 90p to £1·95 in a year but remains delightful, stuffed with duxelles, coated with lemony hollandaise, and served *tiède* 'for maximum pleasure in all three elements.' Another inspector hails the 'wet but floaty' texture of his quenelles de saumon. Soufflé aux épinards sauce d'anchois (£1·50) is another speciality, and among meat dishes, rare fillet of beef, en croûte or not, and carré d'agneau rôti aux herbes de Provence (£4·75) are well worth considering, though in a brasserie you may feel more comfortable with the bratwurst and a well-dressed hot potato salad (£2·75), a tranche of very fresh turbot, or 'underdone and very tender calf's liver'. The sweet tart pastry is variable but 'they do use lovely fresh strawberries or blackberries.' Crème brûlée (£1·10) and glace aux noix sauce caramel are other suggestions. The Achilles' heel is the service, though it can be amusing if you do not mind having to repeat yourself rather often – 'our own Manuel approached saying "feesh", exactly like Tolkien's Gollum.' The first-floor Venetian room (also by Patrick Procktor) opened too late in 1979 for discussion here. The house wines at £3 are reasonable, and Chianti Classico '73 or Muscadet '78 are under £5. Jazz sometimes.

App: Christine Stewart, G. E. Bennett, G. Rowing, V. Westerman, David Charlesworth, and many others

LEBANESE RESTAURANT   Map 12

60 Edgware Road, W.2
01-723 9130 *and* 262 9585

Mona Haddad's comfortable, Arab-beset place with bamboo walls and pale turquoise linen has not caught the British love of hot plates and paced courses, and the crudités and olives at the start, lentil-based moujadara 'like hummus with different spices', and deep-fried savoury pastries, or rissoles (sambousek, kibbeh mikhee or falaffa) convey a promise that mixed grill, stuffed lamb (£3·50) and shish Taouk or kafta Dejaj (chicken dishes) cannot always fulfil. Levantine sweets and wines, but ordinaire is French at £3·50.

Open 12.30–11.30

Alc (min £1) £7
(meal £11·60)

Seats 70
Air-conditioning
Car park

No dogs
Access, Am Ex, Barclay,
Diners

LEE HO FOOK   Map 12

New College Parade,
Finchley Road, N.W.3
01-722 9552

Must book D
Open noon–11.30 p.m.

Alc £4·50 (meal £4·95)

Service 10%
Seats 120
Access, Am Ex, Barclay

'Lots of loyal Soho customers are just waiting to be fed
nearer their home ground,' thinks the inspector who
commends this new branch of the Gerrard Street Lee
Ho Fook. Some of the familiar faults of Cantonese food
in London survive: 'rice was reheated in coolish lumps,
and there were no plate-warmers.' Chicken à la
Kamwah was also 'a boring dish with packet ham.'
But beef steak (£2·80) had 'a lovely "hot" sauce with
fermented black beans and chunks of green pepper',
steamed bass with ginger and onion (£3·50) tasted
'very fresh and good', and a couple who chatted up
the waiters (who, 'if they came from the parent place,
must have been to charm school in the interim')
were given 'lots of tender fresh eel, whole sweet garlic
cloves, and nicely crisped belly of pork' from the
untranslated list of dishes in Chinese characters.
'Greens should have been seasoned.' Shark's fin soup
is one of Chen Yuk's favourites, it seems. There are
wines. More reports, please, especially of the
lunchtime dim-sum, as yet unrecorded.

LEITH'S   Map 12

92 Kensington Park Road,
W.11
01-229 4481

Closed L; Dec 24–26
Must book
D only, 7.30–12

Tdh £14 (meal £16·40)

Service inc
Seats 95 (parties 30)
♿ rest (2 steps)
Air-conditioning
No dogs
Access, Am Ex, Barclay,
Diners

It seems logical that the owner of a restaurant which
makes much of its hors d'oeuvre and pudding
trolleys, wheeled to and fro by the staff, should
graduate to advising British Rail. Otherwise, stability
is Prue Leith's forte, and Max Markarian is still in
the kitchen. True, no sooner was the Editor quoted
in print last September with a remark to this effect
than a couple of people reported uniformly depressing
meals. An inspector, sent up the train to tap the
wheels, found most tastes ringing true, though apart
from the fish pâtés, curried cucumber à la crème, and
raw spinach with walnuts among the cold first courses,
and one or two of the sweets, there was little that
cookery school students could not have achieved, and
possibly had. However, this system does allow the
chef to concentrate on main dishes, with just a couple
of hot first and third courses. Besides, if you
contemplate Leith's fruit-and-nut-crisp duckling (a
whole one for two), and the copious al dente
vegetables from Leith's farm, you are wise to go easy
at the start. They now do nouvelle cuisine fish dishes,
such as steamed turbot with shredded courgettes, and
reports praise excellent deep-fried devilled sardines
followed by rack of lamb or stuffed poussin, with
ginger syllabub at the end. 'Recipes range from
classical French to the directors' own creations' – the
latter meaning Mr Reynaud's juniper hare, perhaps,
which works admirably at home too. At a test meal,
soufflé à l'orange et au citron proved excellently light
and tangy, 'though clotted cream seemed superfluous.'
The waiters tend to stumble over each other (or you),

and fine wine is a risk, what with smoking, 'two chipped glasses in succession', and the price of it. Beaune Clos du Roi '71 (Jouard) proved excellent, even at £18. There are a few clarets still in single figures, and the house Côtes du Rhône '76 or Georges Duboeuf white table wine is under £5 ('why no half-bottles of it?'). The north Kensington house is cleverly designed in the stark '60s manner, and the chairs swivel.

Recipe in *Second Dinner Party Book:* Mr Reynaud's juniper hare

App: Gillian & Bruce Boucher, Ron Salmon, P.G., Mary & Rodney Milne-Day, M.E., W.J.M., and others

---

LEMON TREE   Map 13

8 High Street, S.W.19
01-947 6477

Michele d'Aversa's pipeclayed Wimbledon place with vivid prints has a new chef since last year's doubts. Apart from maladroit service and some cool food, a late autumn test held out more hope – crunchy vegetables, and a tart-sweet balance of black cherries and sherry in médaillons de veau (£3·95). 'Try mousse de crevettes and curried soft roes (£1·05) as first courses, then poulet orientale, and chocolate and orange mousse' (90p), but the noisettes d'agneau speciality may be 'too fussy and fatty for the price'. 'White Trebbiano is better than red Sangiovese at £3·15': pay £1·50 more for Chianti Classico?

Closed Mon; Dec 25 & 26; Jan 1 Must book D Meals 12–2.15, 7–11	Tdh L £3 (meal £5·85) Alc £6·65 (meal £9·85) Cover 35p	Seats 55 (parties 25) ❺ rest; w.c. No dogs Access, Am Ex, Diners

---

✍ LICHFIELD'S   Map 13

Lichfield Terrace,
Sheen Road,
Richmond, Surrey
(near Lichfield Gardens)
01-940 5236

Closed Sat L; Sun D;
Apr 6 & 7; May 26;
Aug 25; Dec 25
Must book D
Meals 12.30–2.30, 7–11

Alc £10·90 (meal £15·50)

Cover 75p
Seats 40
❺ rest
No dogs
Access, Am Ex, Barclay

'The best meal I have had outside London for many years,' says a Surrey man firm about his geography, and there is no lack of yes votes from other quarters. Behind the red awning and decorously spaced tables Stephen Bull is now doing his own cooking, from a short and controllable à la carte menu that changes often. 'I wish my clients would eat more fish,' he says. People who have eaten his scallop quenelles (£3·25), coquilles St Jacques, brioche stuffed with sole, and grilled brill with Escoffier's walnut and horseradish sauce are inclined to suggest that he should change his clients. But that will come as more serious admirers of a serious young man's cooking find the place. A test meal, though not flawless, began well with the butter, the bread, and the miniature cheese gougères served as you contemplate menu and wine list. Crudités with bagna cauda and hummus (£2) flew strong taste signals – cumin in the hummus, garlic and anchovy in the bagna cauda, 'sublime with broccoli and beans'. Gigot à la crème d'ail (£4·25), with an equally pungent

75

sauce for a pink and juicy *tranche* of lamb, and a
separate boat of madeira-flavoured gravy, was
marred only by poor, old-tasting gratin dauphinoise
potatoes among several admirable vegetables. Others
report, among much else, 'a superb broth for moules
à la normande, a thin, slightly moist crust for quiche
au Roquefort. strips of breast of duck wonderfully
combined with fresh figs poached in claret', 'fillet of
beef with Stilton and horseradish sauce and a
celeriac puree', and the much-admired roast duck
with lime compote (£6). A wisely limited range of
good French and English cheeses is offered, and
puddings have included 'spicy' cold ginger soufflé, 'not
oversweet' marc de champagne sorbet, 'hot gâteau de
Pithiviers with rum-flavoured cream' and 'boozy St
Emilion au chocolat with that nicely broken texture
you get when it is properly made.' (Hot walnut pie,
though, was 'too dry and unsuitable for the end of a
rich meal.') The coffee is espresso. The house red and
white Rioja is £3·50; Ch. Giscours '71, c.b., and
Auxey-Duresses '66 (Ponnelle) £10 or so. Service is
quiet and good, 'even when we arrived *en déshabillé*
after a walk in Richmond Park.' 'But they pollute
their own food by touting cigars – early in the
evening too.'

App: by too many members to list

LITTLE AKROPOLIS   Map 15

10 Charlotte Street, W.1
01-636 8198

Closed Sun; Sat L;
3 weeks Aug;
public hols (exc Jan 1)
Must book
Meals 12–2.30, 6–10.30

Alc (min £4·60) £6·85
(meal £10·45)

Seats 32 (parties 25)
▣ rest (1 step); w.c.
No dogs
Access, Am Ex, Barclay,
Diners, Euro

Apart from one or two minor eccentricities – 'they
regularly confuse the words *chambrer* and *flamber*,'
say wine-drinkers – the Ktoris' florally inviting Cypriot
restaurant remains more popular than ever after its
sixth successive *Guide* entry. It has the old Soho
'feel', with good linen, a genial host, and careful
cooking of the Levantine classics: stuffed aubergine
and vine leaves, 'very fresh and lemony' taramosalata,
good avgolemono soup, ('even good tomato soup,'
adds an inspector), and herby kleftiko in a glass-lidded
dish with rice. (A member who grumbled of bone
splinters was told 'the chef gets carried away with the
chopper', and ate his meal very quietly after that.)
Chicken and scampi pilaffs, charcoal-grilled lamb
chops, moussaka 'with an almost soufflé-like top', and
'if you want a change, steak Diane' are also
recommended, and it is worth £1 to try the rose-petal
jam pancakes. Greek coffee and loukoum are
excellent, and 'though Castel Danielis is the same
price as Demestica (£4·50) it is a much more
convincing red wine.' Recorded Greek music.

*App: J. W. Moss-Norbury, G. J. Dykes, M.M.,
Nicholas Avery, M.M-S., Julian Corbluth,
J. B. Curtiss, and others*

LOCKETS   Map 16

Marsham Court,
Marsham Street, S.W.1
01-834 9552

'Gluttons at noon and abstinent at night,' said Misson of the English in 1719. Midday gluttons in this soberly set Berkmann restaurant are brought up short by the Westminster division bell, but mostly enjoy Rafael Mulling's idea of English dishes ('very good soused herring', Stilton soup, boiled beef in strong ale, or lamb Shrewsbury). Vegetables have been well cooked this year, and 'fresh fruit brûlée was exquisite.' Wines are admirable (half-bottles included), from the Georges Duboeuf Beaujolais and burgundy in the £6 range to major clarets (Ch. Malescot-St-Exupéry '61, £24). They 'try to divide the restaurant into smoking and non-smoking.'

Closed Sat; Sun;
public hols; Dec 31 D
Must book L
Meals 12.15–2.45, 6.30–11

Tdh D £6·50 (meal £10·10)

Alc £10·05 (meal £14)

Cover 55p
Children's helpings
(under 6)

Seats 100 (parties 30)
 ♿ rest
Air-conditioning
No dogs
Access, Am Ex, Barclay,
Diners, Euro

LOK HO FOOK   Map 15

4 Gerrard Street, W.1
01-437 8961

Must book
Open noon–midnight

Alc £7·40 (meal £8·40)

Service 10%
Seats 100 (parties 50)
Air-conditioning
No dogs
Access, Am Ex, Barclay,
Diners

An awkwardly joined pair of shops ('difficult work-flow for the red-jacketed service') make a new Cantonese place that pleased some critical Sinophiles in 1979, whether for dim-sum or main dishes. Menu translations into French as well as English also suggest serious ambition. Dim-sum successes include cheung fun 'with fresh chopped prawns instead of little dried ones in it', 'fragrant stuffing mushroom', 'unusually fresh and moist' char siu pau (pork-stuffed steamed bun) and spare ribs with plenty of garlicky broth. Main meals at different times of the year have yielded 'fragile and really delicious' sweet-and-sour wun-tun, batter-fried scallops, and seaweed with shredded duck as first courses for a party; then fried milk Tai Leung 'like smooth white scrambled egg with ham on crispy noodles' (£3·50) contrasted with 'fresh and sharp-tasting bitter melon with duck and black-bean sauce' (£2·50), generous crab with garlic and ginger, a good version of monk's vegetables, and (from the Chinese list at the back of the menu) crispy tripe with pickled cabbage, which 'the waiter thought would be too strong for English taste, explaining that the English cooked tripe once and threw away the water while the Chinese put it through four processes and (by implication) discard nothing.' Recorded music.

App: P. Wright, C. & C. Tillyard, A.H., J.A., and others

See p. 110 for London pubs and wine bars.

LOON FUNG Map 15

37–38 Gerrard Street, W.1
01-437 5429 *and* 5034

'Not a pretty place' by current Chinatown standards – though large and comfortable – and the printed *carte* is not the best of it, but their supermarket along the road is reassuring, and the dim-sum too if you try paper-wrapped prawns, prawn cheung-fun, and pork pudding with Chinese mushroom, 'with good tea'. Otherwise, get the waiter to translate the pink card with Chinese characters above the dish prices, for the dearest (eel and pork casserole) is 'fragrant, colourful, and lovingly cooked'. Chinese family Sunday lunch is also quite an experience.

Closed Dec 25
Open noon–11.30 p.m.

Alc £4·95 (meal £5·45)

Seats 200
No dogs

✔ MA CUISINE Map 14

113 Walton Street, S.W.3
01-584 7585

Closed Sat; Sun;
July 15–Aug 15;
public hols
Must book
Meals 12.30–2, 7.30–11

Alc £8·80 (meal £13·50)

Cover 60p
Seats 30
⟨⟩ rest; w.c.
Am Ex, Diners

'My choice for a dream lunch. Somehow the setting and service suggests this rather than dinner,' says one would-be regular, and the opinion is confirmed by another account of an evening with 'nightmare service, and a table neighbour's cigar casually extended over my plate.' The intimacy of Guy Mouilleron's restaurant – a favourite place for Belgravians who like to make or break their affairs with maximum éclat – is not his fault, but some other features are. A test meal in 1979 detected, along with ample evidence of the owner's skill, signs of strain: 'fridge-tainted butter, near-cold vegetables, and a taste to the stuffed goose-neck that made me wonder whose goose it had belonged to.' Perhaps too much rather than too little is attempted, given a style that presumes daily marketing and sprightly tastes, as in the same meal's panache de poissons Ma Cuisine (£5·10) with 'all the fish firm, the turbot sweetest.' 'A fresh crispness to the wine-pickled vegetables', 'paté d'anguilles à la mousse cresson just as good as the *Guide* says', 'subtle and delicate mousseline de St Jacques' and 'perfectly cooked noisettes d'agneau pastourelle' are also reassuring messages. Oeuf Vert Galant (£1·40), filet de truite Ninotte (£4·20) and the much-admired ballotine de volaille Lucien Tendret, the chicken married to an unctuous lobster sauce (£4·75), are the *patron*'s own nominations, and a critical diner notes that tournedos béarnaise 'though unexpectedly surrounded by pastry, was very fine, and properly hung for once.' *Desserts*, too, are often *du jour*, and a member tiring of the mousse brûlée, light though it is, was charmed by peach clafoutis – 'a sensible eggy modification of the original.' Home-made chocolates no longer arrive with coffee, unless by whim. Wines are dear on the whole, but 'punchy, mellow, yet dry' Savennières Clos du Paradis '77 or Ch. Meyney '73 may still be undercutting £10.

There are some, this year, who would award the pestle without the mortar, or the mortar without the pestle, 'but in the end, which of us would decline an invitation to eat here?'

App: A. F. Meath-Evans, Bruce and Gillian Boucher, E. L. F., Steven and Ruth Curston, R.B.J., J.R., P.G., and others

---

MANDARIN Map 12

---

33 Craven Road, W.2
01-723 8744

But for the convenience of seven-day, till-midnight opening near Paddington, and quite lively Pekinese cooking, dubious smells and grudged linen would rule this place out, inspectors say. In context, though, 'juicily prawned toasts fried in clean oil', 'very hot' fried dumplings, and competent hot-and-sour soup, egg-fried rice, Szechuan chicken, crispy duck and other regional classics were a pleasant surprise. Australian house wine is £3·50. Recorded Chinese music. More reports, please on this and the related Peking House (in the '79 Guide), which reopened after a fire just as we went to press.

Closed Dec 25 & 26	Tdh from £3·50	Seats 45
Must book Sat	Alc meal about £4·50	No dogs
Meals 12–2.30, 6–12		Am Ex, Barclay, Diners
	Service 10%	

MANDARIN Map 12

279c Finchley Road, N.W.3
01-794 6119

Mr Koh cooks for his son's restaurant, with two girls to serve, and though the Szechuan flavours are a little nervous 'he let go at a test meal on a mixture of squid, scallops, various fungi and bamboo root in a stinging clear sauce with no sugar.' Fried seaweed with dried fish (£1·30) was also 'crisp and delicious'. Szechuan hot crispy beef with vegetables (£2) was less impressive, but jin jiang chicken with pancakes (£2) had 'a nice beany taste to the sauce, strong on sesame oil.' Quick-fried prawns with cashew nuts is another suggestion. 'Poor rice and fresh greens; good tea and toffee apples.' Wines from £3·05.

Closed Sun L;	Meals 12–2.30, 6–11.30	Service 10%
Apr 4, 6 & 7; Dec 24–26		Seats 46
Must book weekends	Alc (min £1·50) £4·40	No dogs
	(meal £5·15)	

PLEASE keep sending in reports, as soon as possible after each meal. The cut-off date for the 1981 Guide is September 30, 1980, but reports are even more useful earlier in the year, especially for the remoter areas and new places. Late autumn reports can also affect corrections at proof stage.

Unless otherwise stated, a restaurant is open all week and all year and is licensed.

MANDEER Map 15

21 Hanway Place, W.1
01-323 0660 *and* 0651

The cooking in this civilised basement with pictures and soft Indian music, near Tottenham Court Road tube, had recovered its Gujerati elan when tried in 1979. If you are hungry take the thali (£3·95) which brings hot spiced bhajias or pakoras with dips, rice, dhal and raita, vegetable and bean curries, puffy puris and lemony, cardamomy shrikhand for sweet. A la carte, don't miss masala dosai, vadi and onion ('almost persuades you it is meat-based', £1·25), patra ('a curious Swiss-roll of advi leaves and spiced gram flour', 95p), and dhal vada (lentil fritters). Other sweets are also worth a try. Drink lassi or lager.

Closed Sun; public hols	Tdh from £3·95	Seats 75 (parties 100)
Must book weekends	Alc from £3·30	No dogs
Meals 12–3, 6–10.30		Access, Am Ex, Diners,
	Service 10%	Euro

MANZI'S Map 15

1–2 Leicester Street, W.C.2
01-437 4864

Lapses do occur, and even upstairs in the Cabin Room the setting falls short of London's posher fish places. But both upstairs and down, most people favour the Italianate cooking of 'minestrone and its fish equivalent', whitebait, skate in black butter, or fried with good chips, and 'light cheesy sauce for lobster thermidor'. 'Salads are good too, and at least the butter packets are unsalted Normandy.' Strawberry tart is the usual sweet. The French house white wine is clean, and there are sound Italians under £4. No children under five. 'Acceptable' bed and breakfast.

Closed Sun L;	Service 12½%	Access, Am Ex, Barclay,
Dec 25 & 26; Dec 31 L	Cover 40p (Cabin Room)	Diners, Euro
Must book	Seats 70 & 45	14 rooms (12 with shower)
Meals 12–2.45, 5.30–11.40	🔊 rest (ground floor;	B&B £8·50
	2 steps)	Fire cert
Alc £7·05 (meal £10·40)	No dogs	

MATA HARI Map 12

34 Eversholt Street, N.W.1
01-388 0131

Closed Mon; Dec 25 & 26;
Jan 1
Must book D
Meals 12–3, 6–11.30
(12 Fri & Sat)

Tdh L £5,
D from £6·50

Mr Lim's spacious, comfortable and for the most part cordially served Indonesian restaurant opposite the east entrance to Euston has settled down and chosen its clientele – misguidedly, say many lovers of food in this style who reject tired rijsttaffel, stringy beef, and lunchtime pop ('in the late evening there is a band you can twitch to'). However, an inspector found the £5 business lunch (including chicken leg, fish steak and egg in the main course) good value, and diners also report excellent squid, and mild curried lamb in coconut sauce. Most people begin meals with saté

Alc (min Fri & Sat after 8.30 £5) meal about £6·35

Service 15%
Cover 30p
Seats 100 (parties 70)
 rest (1 step)
Access, Am Ex, Diners

(£1·20), and Mr Romli's other favourite dishes include fried prawns (£3·30) and kelia kyam (a chicken dish, £2·20). 'Rice should have been fresher and tastier, and hot plates used.' Stowells wines from £3·10, or lager. Air-conditioning. No dogs.

App: Ian Waitt, E. Jenkins, D. J. Dee, T. H. Nash, J.L., H. D. Rose, and others

---

MAXIM Map 13

153–155 Northfield Avenue, W.13
01-567 1719

Closed Dec 25 & 26
Must book D
Meals 12–2.30, 6–11.30
(12 Fri & Sat)

Tdh from £3·60
(meal from £4·30)
Alc (min D £2) £4
(meal £5·20)

Service 10%
Seats 120 (parties 40)
 rest
Air-conditioning
No dogs
Access, Am Ex, Diners

Mrs Chow (who cooks, with 25 years' experience) and Tony clearly did not waste their three months' closure. Returned customers in the autumn found a spacious room, attractively designed menus, and efficient table-warmers along with good dishes both table d'hôte and à la carte: 'delicious fried crab-meat with egg and black fungus', and three delicacies with spring onion (£1·90) or with crispy rice. Peking crispy duck (£2·80 the quarter) and sesame-seed prawn toasts are also suggested by the Chows and praised by customers; Pekinese hors d'oeuvre are 'a picture', and fried three vegetables (£1·20) appear among other interesting leguminous dishes. Shangtung spring chicken (£2·50), garlicky chicken with cashew nuts, and 'delectable toffee apples and bananas', are mentioned too. At 24 hours' notice and £11, a whole roast wind-dried duck can be served. Wines from £2·90, but drink tea.

App: John Carne, Anna Dickie, H.C., M.R., T. Dickie, Elaine Lee, and others

---

MELATI Map 15

31 Peter Street, W.1
01-437 2011

Closed Sun; Apr 7;
May 26; Aug 25;
Dec 25 & 26; Jan 1
Must book D
Meals 12–2.30, 6–11.30

Tdh D £5 (meal £5·50)
Alc £3·30 (meal £4·05)

Seats 30
No dogs

Michael Ting and Margaret Ong run this diminutive new Indonesian place in the Wardour Street blue-movie hinterland, and their partner Sjamsir Alamsjah cooks. English is spoken and the menu translated: a set dinner for two (not yet reported on) is also offered, but at lunch-time Singapore laksa (rice vermicelli in spicy coconut soup with prawns, fish balls and vegetables, £1·30) – or other dishes of the kind – makes a soothing meal by itself, preceded perhaps by chicken satay, though the satay's mild sweet sauce was not the best feature at a test meal. Note that when other dishes say 'spicy' they mean 'hot', and a side dish, sambal blachan, was 'fiercely Roman in its rotted saltiness'. But sambal goreng terong (aubergine done with chilli, oil, and the little dried fish called bilis, 75p) was 'riveting', and for gentler classics of the region, try beef rendang (£1·30) and the salad called rojak (£1·10). Sweets are in full technicolour: the starch-based ones are an acquired taste but avocado or papaya bases sound more promising, and Berwick Street's fruit market is but a step away. Wines from £2·80, and lager. Soupy Singapore music. More reports, please.

MONTE GRAPPA   Map 12

339 Gray's Inn Road,
W.C.1
01-837 6370

Perhaps Italian families use King's Cross rather than other termini – but at any rate, Celts and Anglo-Saxons who find themselves in the same predicament report 'cannelloni hot and rich and far above the national norm', served by Mrs Novi's amiable shirt-sleeved waiters. Whitebait and pizzas approved too. 'Traffic roars past but I was too relieved to notice it.' Belloni wines. Note the flexible evening hours, convenient for Night Scotsmen. More reports, please.

Must book D
Open 11 a.m.–midnight
(L 12–3.30)

Tdh L from £1·95
(meal £4·30)

Alc £6·15 (meal £8·95)

Service 10%
Children's helpings
(under 6)
Seats 120 (parties 70)

♻ rest
Air-conditioning
No dogs
Access, Am Ex, Barclay,
Diners

MONTPELIANO   Map 14

13 Montpelier Street,
S.W.7
01-589 0032

Closed Sun; public hols;
Dec 24
Must book
Meals 12.30–3, 7–12
(Sat 7.30–12)

Alc £7·70 (meal £11·65)

Cover 50p
Children's helpings
(under 10)
Seats 75 (parties 25)
♻ rest (2 steps)

Pietro cooks and Claudio manages at this Italian restaurant for the Italians. At least, one critical member who likes Italian food 'and therefore shuns it in London' is prepared to except this place which enabled him to start with radicchio 'coated with the Piedmontese sauce of olive oil, anchovies, garlic and walnuts, and warmed under the grill' (£1·95). Crudités with the same sauce are equally good, and there followed two similarly typical but more delicate dishes: sweetbreads wrapped in prosciutto and done in butter, and brains crumbed and gently fried. Better leave the mixed fish salad to Venetians or Neapolitans who know better than to allow preserved mussels into it, but the clams with another member's spaghetti (£1·95) were a different matter, and fettuccine Montpeliano with 'plenty of cream and cheese' is also 'delightful', as is the veal dish that bears the name of the house (£4·60). Bollito misto might be a dish worth trying here. Salad may be better than vegetables. 'The sweet pancake laced with Tia Maria and covered with Amaretti was heavenly.' Valpolicella or Soave are £3·45, and a member was pleased to find white Tocai '77 and red Carema in the £5–£7 range. 'No large dogs.' There is rather more space with the open roof and plants downstairs if you prefer talking to eavesdropping.

App: P. B. & F. H. Wells, M. J. Cleave, B. A. Boucher, D. Westoby, D.B., Alf Erickson, Nicholas Avery, and others

---

'Meal' indicates the cost of a meal for one, including food, coffee, a half-bottle of one of the cheapest wines listed, cover, service, and VAT (see 'How to use the Guide', p. 4).

MR BUNBURY'S   Map 3

1154 London Road,
S.W.16
01-764 3939

Ken Williams' mirrors-and-marble bistro takes its name rather than its style from Wilde, and the service is welcoming rather than highly skilled. 'The meat in Bunbury pie (£2·90) should have been better trimmed.' But this, seafood à la maison and filet chasseur are suggested, and perhaps it was just a day's oddity that had over-salted onion soup and virtually unsalted vegetables in the same meal. The few sweets include cabinet pudding (95p). House Bordeaux is £3; a member praises the white. Recorded music.

Closed Sun; Mon L; Sat L; public hols
Must book weekends
Meals 12–2, 7–11

Alc £7·05 (meal £9·80)

Children's helpings (under 10)

Seats 40
♿ rest (1 step); w.c.
No dogs
Access, Barclay

M'SIEUR FROG   Map 12

31a Essex Road, N.1
01-226 3495

Closed L; Sun; 3 or 4 weeks Aug; Dec 24; public hols (exc Apr 4)
Must book
D only, 7–11.30

Alc £7·30 (meal £10·30)

Service 10%
Seats 51
No dogs

The Frog may be about to spawn, Howard Rawlinson says, but probably not by the time these words appear, and it enters its fifth *Guide* year secure in the affections of the kind of Islingtonians who take the *Guardian* at home and read the *Times* in the office. The garlic on their breath may ensure that no one reads over their shoulders after Gerard Samy's grenouilles, cassoulet and aïoli with 'crisp, young and fresh crudités'; 'the cassoulet, though honestly declared to contain chicken rather than confit d'oie, was outstandingly good.' Fresh haddock, 'nicely underdone gigot bretonne', and beef fillet with Roquefort are other dishes that have been carefully cooked – 'not too rich, and not those huge gluttonous plates that destroy appetite.' A May visitor was not pleased to find mediocre tomato sauce for squid duplicated later with potatoes. 'We ended with chocolate and raisin cake as on many previous occasions.' The *patron*, whose brother-in-law is sous-chef, keeps his interest in both food and clientele and has a new partner now to help prepare for Master Frog (will he surface somewhere in Ballspondia?). Espigou table wines are £3·25. Beyond that, 'Petit Chablis was not worth £9 or so, but the Nuits Villages '76 (Jaffelin) was.' Recorded music, usually drowned by all those incisive voices.

App: Nina Kark, John Banks, Leslie Valentine, M.Q., and others

The Guide News Supplement will be sent out as usual, in June, to everyone who buys the book directly from Consumers' Association and to all bookshop purchasers who return the card interleaved with their copy. Let us know of any changes that affect entries in the book, or of any new places you think should be looked at.

MUNBHAVE   Map 3

305 London Road,
Croydon, Surrey
01-689 6331

Closed Mon; L Sat & Sun;
Dec 25 & 26
Must book D
Meals 12–2, 6–11

Tdh L £1·75 (meal £2·95),
D £4 (meal £5·80)
Alc (min D £2) £4·15
(meal £5·30)

Seats 40
No dogs
Access, Am Ex, Barclay,
Diners

'A fish pond and a fountain make a pleasant change from flock wallpaper', and the Tanks' new restaurant has brought Gujerati vegetarian cooking to the needy district within range of Croydon's Fairfield Halls. A member who ate here enthusiastically several times in 1979 recommends for robust appetites the de luxe thali (£3·80), which brings tastes of delicious dhal, basmati rice, curried mung beans, vegetable curry, farshan (fermented rice made into a cornbread-like cake and topped with sesame and mustard seeds), lemony-sweet shrikhand (a cardamom-flavoured curd), chapatis and puris. Other specialities include the samosas and kachori pastries, served very hot, masala dosai ('a beanshoot pancake filled with spiced vegetables and served with apple and green mint sauce', £2), and 'crunchy-chewy bhelpuri salad (60p) with a hot and sweet dressing.' Gulab jamun at a test meal was also well made. Skip coffee; drink lager or tropical fruit juices. Recorded Indian music. More reports, please.

NEW FRIENDS   Map 3

53 West India Dock Road,
E.14
01-987 1139 and 3440

Closed Dec 24 D;
Dec 25 & 26
Must book
Meals 12–3, 6–11
(11.30 Thur & Sat)

Tdh L £3·50 (meal £3·85),
D £5·50 (meal £6·05)
Alc £4·75 (meal £5·20)

Seats 55
Access, Am Ex, Barclay,
Diners

George Cheung split off from the old Good Friends in 1978, and inspectors unsentimental about London's Cantonese pioneers hailed in 1979 'favourite stuffed mushrooms', 'delicate whole mullet with mushrooms and ginger', 'well-balanced prawns Chinese-style' (£1·80) and 'outstanding' crackling pork with meaty eels and chopped garlic. Prawn toasts, pancake rolls, Chinese vegetables and soups are praised too. Other specialities to try include 'special chicken with mayonnaise sauce' (£1·95) and Kupar chicken with crispy rice (£2·80). Wines from £3. 'Hawksmoor churches and the street names of famous East End rumbles punctuate the long journey from the Bank to this strip of shops near council houses and derelict wharves.' No dogs. More reports, please.

NICK'S   Map 13

88 Ifield Road, S.W.10
01-352 5641

Closed Mon; Apr 4;
Aug 3–25; Dec 25 & 26
Mus: book D
Meals 12.45–2, 7.15–11.15

Tdh L £5·50 & £7
(meal £8·55 & £10·25),
D £6·50 & £8
(meal £9·70 & £11·40)

It was a simple matter to drop the 'Diner' from the late Nick Clarke's old place to accommodate the Earl of Avon (Nick to his friends) and Malcolm Johnson. Well, a man is never so harmlessly occupied as when he is cooking, and diplomacy's loss is gastronomy's gain, according to a comfortable majority of those who have tasted these sensibly composed and priced set meals over the past two years. True, there is a minority of radicals who have taken against the cooking or the dining-room management, but a test meal showed promise, with true tastes of tarragon in potted shrimps and veal kidneys, and of asparagus in a mousse.

Service 15%
Seats 55 (parties 20)
Access, Am Ex, Barclay,
Diners, Euro

Vegetables, too, were carefully cooked, but scallop soup needed a fishier flavour, and mocha soufflé, though it tasted well, had separated. 'If you chose cheese you were asked which you wanted, not offered the board.' Nick Avon and Philip Delia between them are proudest of their oeufs aumale, crab pancake and mousse of smoked trout among first courses; and then of medallions of veal in white wine or devilled chicken – 'the sauce chutney-sweet, but quite agreeable,' reports an admirer. Game is also a speciality. The wines from Berry Bros and others begin with French table wine at £4·40. Four out of twenty bottles on the list are Taittinger champagnes, which seems disproportionate. Ch. Beau Rivage '71 and Ch. Fonbadet '72 were under £7 in 1979. Recorded music. More reports, please.

NONTAS Map 12

16 Camden High Street,
N.W.1
01-387 4579

'Crowded, noisy and jolly', this little Greek taverna pleases for the most part with filling meze ('a bite of various dishes', £3·75) and other tasty first courses: 'highly seasoned hummus', 'hot and tender fried squid' (65p). Kebabs are popular too: arnishio (lamb, £1·75) or psari ('four huge chunks of firm fish', £1·55) with rice and salad. Or try moussaka or gemista ('stuffed marrows, onions and vine leaves', £1·45). Yoghourt and honey – or 'fresh, soft Turkish delight, nearly as good as in Istanbul' – are the safest sweets. Greek-Cypriot wines from £2·30. 'Soft Greek' recorded music.

Closed Sun; public hols
Must book D

Meals 12–2.45, 6–11.45

Alc £3·20 (meal £5·05)

Seats 50
No dogs
Access, Diners

OSCAR'S BRASSERIE Map 12

5–8 Temple Chambers,
Temple Avenue, E.C.4
01-353 6272

'The best people one could wish for' is the Skeltons' verdict on their customers, mainly lawyers, reporters and insurance brokers 'from the wig and pen no-man's-land'. This welcome comes with generous helpings of fresh materials, often well cooked. Praise for 'sizzling snails in garlic butter', sole maison with a 'spicy and sharp fresh tomato sauce' (£3), and 'pink and tender' but gas-fired rib of beef, both with lightly cooked but undersalted vegetables (65p). 'A pity they take less trouble with potatoes.' Peach Melba is a fresh peach in summer. Fair wine prices: Ch. Guionne '73 (Côtes du Bourg) £6·35.

Closed Sat; Sun;
Aug 18–31; Dec 25–Jan 5;
public hols
Must book

Meals 12–2.30, 6–10

Alc £6·65 (meal £9·90)

Cover 25p
Seats 40
Access, Am Ex, Barclay,
Diners

If we know that a restaurant has music, of whatever sort, we say so.

Prince Albert Road,
N.W.8
01-722 8795

Closed Sun; Mon; Sat L;
Apr 4; Dec 26
Must book D
Meals 12.30–2, 6.30–10.30

Alc £9·55 (meal £14·20)

Cover 60p
Seats 80
♿ rest (4 steps)
Air-conditioning
No dogs

'A sensitive sociologist would be interested in this
Balkan family restaurant' at the foot of a block of
flats, and if the Katnics are catnip to the St John's
Wood diaspora, it is because their temple of
gastronomy, unlike French counterparts, is conceived
as a fun palace, where momma can actually enjoy her
birthday, from June's florid introductions of Rajko's
ways with duck and salmon, to 'the first, second, and
third world troupe of waiters pirouetting between the
crowded tables.' 'We sweated profusely even before
we saw the bill', and you will need considerate table
neighbours if you are to enjoy the fine wines kept
(although the Katnics now try to stop people smoking
cigars till those nearby have finished their main course).
With these caveats, only misanthropes will fail to
succumb. By the most severe standards, Rajko Katnic
invents too much and perfects too little. 'For instance,
crab La Rochelle came with an inappropriate red
cabbage salad, and the tarragon sauce for the veal
and cray-fish roly-poly idea (veal San Stefan) soaks
into the pastry quickly and baffles the flavours.' But
when everything comes off the result can be superb:
'red and succulent spring salmon very handsome in a
yellowish, slightly tart sorrel sauce', 'unbeatably crisp
and juicy duck Bosnaka (£5·75) with morello cherry
sauce', and 'marinated lamb with cracked wheat on a
bed of spinach, served with mange-tout peas and
potato cakes.' The onion hors d'oeuvre (stuffed with
bass and salmon) is another *coup de théâtre*, and this
year we are also offered salmon trout Mama Zoma
(£11 for two) and roast lamb Licko Solo (£5·75):
speculation should force the dinar up a few notches
on the foreign exchange market. One man grumbles
that a flakily fresh Apfelstrudel was the only
interesting item on the sweets trolley, but others have
been happy enough by this stage with berries in
slivovitz or 'water-melon spiked with strawberries, a
promise of summer in a cold May.' The wine list
(from French white or Yugoslav Cabernet at £4·30)
has 300 bins and many treasures, half-bottles
included. Members' cellar notes include 'Puligny-
Montrachet Les Combettes (Jacques Prieur) '75,
heavily fragrant, superb colour, rich gelatinous tears
on the glass' and 'Ch. Bel-Orme '61, lovely raspberry
nose, slightly less follow-through, but a classy claret
from a great year, decanted without fuss.' Comparable
wines (for these have gone now) would cost about £40
the pair. The '75 clarets are rounded off, incidentally,
by a double magnum of Ch. Margaux '61 at £380.

App: Edward Hugo, Roy Mathias, Julian Corbluth,
A.H., Irene Hepburn, M.M., A.A. & F.M., R.J.M.,
and others

OSTERIA LARIANA   Map 15

49 Frith Street, W.1
01-734 5183

'Fine for a quick pre-theatre meal', with pasta, wine and coffee delivered generally with speed and good humour. Others praise Giovanni Dalmasso's simple little place for its 'crisp and non-rubbery fried squid', 'hot minestrone', trout meunière, bistecca Lariana (£3·05), 'correctly prepared piccata alla limone', and moist 'knot-free' calf's liver with sage, served with crisp and fresh salads. 'Generous' strawberry ice-cream and decent fruit salad. Various wines, from £2·90 the bottle. Recorded music. No recent reports of the modestly priced set lunch.

Closed Sun; last 3 weeks Aug; public hols Must book L Meals 12–3, 6–11.15	Tdh L £2·10 (meal £3·55) Alc £5·65 (meal £7·75) Service inc	Cover 30p D Seats 30 No dogs

OVEN D'OR   Map 3

4a Crescent Way,
Orpington, Kent
Farnborough (0689) 52170

Closed Sun; Mon; Sat L;
Aug 4–27; 1st week Jan;
public hols (exc Dec 25 L)
Must book D
Meals 12.30–2, 7–10

Tdh D £10·80
(meal £14·40)
Alc £8·40 (meal £12·30)

Service 12½%
Seats 30 (parties 11 & 15)
No dogs
Access, Am Ex, Barclay,
Diners, Euro

The gilded oven of Janice and Alain Grenier and the gilded youth of Orpington meet in this upstairs room while others spend their small change on ready-plated dishes in Le Troquet downstairs. The bills have raised a few eyebrows in commuterland, but Kunihiko Ohno's cooking justifies a premium, by accounts of his hot pâté in puff pastry with madeira sauce (£2·40) followed by suprême de volaille aux langoustines (£4·45) or roast crab with herbs and cream sauce (£4·25) – 'the first time I have been offered roast crab outside a Chinese restaurant but I hope not the last.' Crêpes Edouard VII ('stuffed with smoked salmon in a delicate curry sauce'), tournedos in a Meaux mustard sauce, and for sweet a light mousse brûlée (90p) or 'exotic' sablé aux poires (£1·65) have also delighted visitors. Coulibiac de saumon and entrecôte canaille further suggest the chef's interest in fish and marked flavours alike. Note that the choiceless set 'menu du gourmet', on which we would welcome reports, is normally for two or more people. Several of the house wines (from £5·05) are from the Roussillon district; prices for the classic areas are rather off-putting, with occasional exceptions: £17·25 for Ch. Pichon-Longueville '62. Cigar-smokers are discouraged until late in the evening. Recorded music.

App: J. R. M. Lees, J.B., F.L.H., Brian Pickering, E. A. M. Graham, and others

Entries for places with distinctions carry symbols (pestle, tureen, bottle, glass). Credits are fully written entries, with approvers' names below the text. Passes are telegraphic entries (useful in the area) with details under the text. Provisional entries are in italics (see 'How to use the Guide', p. 4).

LE PALME Map 12

46 Market Place, N.W.11
01-458 8170 *and* 7305

The chef changed as we went to press, but there was plenty of praise in 1979 for this Garden Suburb Italian place with 'scatty service but a touch of style' as well as an inviting central hors d'oeuvre table, good whitebait, pasta, gamberini allo spiedo (in garlic and fresh herb butter), rosticciata, and scaloppine con carciofini. 'Avoid sweets but take the coffee.' 'Tuscan white wine good value at £2·30.' Recorded music. More reports, please.

Closed Mon; Dec 24–26;
Jan 1
Must book D & weekends
Meals 12–2.30, 6.30–11.15

Alc £6·10 (meal £9)

Service 12½%
Cover 35p

Seats 45
♿ rest
Access, Am Ex, Barclay,
Diners

PAVILION see VASCO AND PIERO'S PAVILION

PILGRIMS Map 12

175 Archway Road, N.6
01-340 3344

'Homely, competent and touched with imagination' is one inspector's account of this shopfront on the juggernauts' Hill Difficulty. Roy Pilgrim (who cooks) and Reg Fuller have improved their room since last year's first entry. 'Sauces are not their forte', but steak au poivre (£3·20) and rack of lamb were pinkly and juicily done, vegetables tasted natural, and turkey and walnut pie (£2) is still liked. Chocolate pot was 'orangey', and apple and blackberry pie 'had a nice taste of clove.' 'Very Hib' service. Poor wines: drink the Roi de France at £3·90 rather than the cheapest. No children under ten. Recorded music.

Closed L; Sun; Mon;
Dec 25, 26 & 31; Jan 1
Must book
D only, 7–10.45

Alc £4·95 (meal £7·95)

Service 10%
Cover 30p

Children's helpings
Seats 45 (parties 20)
No dogs

PIZZA EXPRESS Map 15

10 Dean Street, W.1
01-437 9595

Pizza Express is a chain with over a dozen London outlets and it is perhaps arbitrary to pick this one, apart from its special hours licence and live jazz downstairs every night except Monday. But the setting is at once bright and relaxing, prices fair, and pizzas sound by London standards: marinara (£1), American (with 'plenty of peperoni sausage, good Mozzarella and tomato', £1·25) and the others. Spanish red wine was £2·75 in 1979, 'and tolerable, like the coffee.' Peter Boizot's paperback (80p) tells customers how they made his money for him.

Closed Dec 25

Open noon–midnight

Alc meal about £3·55

PIZZA HOUSE Map 15

54–56 Goodge Street, W.1
01-636 9590

'Real dough in a real oven' makes a change from many London pizzas, say inspectors back from an Italian holiday falling happily on the ham (£1·50), mushroom, quattro stagioni (£1·65), and con salsiccia varieties on successive visits. 'It took me an hour to work through it,' says someone else. Fair pasta and salads, and espresso coffee, but the pizzas are the thing. 'Zuppa inglese reminded me of those Tudor gardens where they had artificially coloured earths.' 'Eat early or expect a queue.' Lively service and setting. 'Drinkable' Tuscan red wine at £1·85 for 50 cl.

Closed Sun; public hols
Meals 12–3, 6–11

Alc £3·40 (meal £6)

Seats 148
No dogs

POISSONNERIE DE L'AVENUE Map 14

82 Sloane Avenue, S.W.3
01-589 2457 *and* 5774

Closed Sun; Dec 24;
public hols
Must book D
Meals 12.15–2.45, 7–11.30

Alc £9·90 (meal £12·60)

Service 12½%
Cover 60p
Seats 80 (parties 26 L)
Air-conditioning
Access, Am Ex, Barclay,
Diners, Euro

'More space seems to mean less room' chez Peter Rosignoli. 'Oppressive service', 'aggressive smoking', and too many very poor dishes reported from the middle of the year also indicate the strains of controlling a fish restaurant that does not charge an ocean. Yet the potential is high, for even some of those who complain about this or that element in their evening also signal 'delicately flavoured raw mushrooms', 'delicious clams with fresh herbs and garlic butter', 'moules au vin blanc so good that my wife had a second helping instead of her second course', 'bouillabaisse with North Sea fish but an admirable fumet', and 'nicely poached salmon trout'. Paupiettes de mulet à l'angevine and bar bonne femme are two more of Messrs Tomassi and Roses' favourite dishes. 'How can the same kitchen produce the lobster soup – perhaps it doesn't?' The French table wines are £3·85 and beyond that the Sauvignon or Sancerre are reasonable buys – but pot-luck, since with continental insouciance Mr Rosignoli's list denies his customers vintages. Only small dogs allowed. Dress smartly. Pavement tables in summer. Please continue to report, because the issue was finely balanced this time.

App: Leslie Valentine, M.E., D. R. & A. J. Linnell, Sean Magee, Anthony & Rita Piepe, and others

POON'S & CO Map 15

27 Lisle Street, W.C.2
01-437 1528

Closed Sun; Dec 24–26
Must book D & weekends
Open noon–11.30

'Something about the old Poon's draws me like a magnet,' says a member who is sometimes puzzled by himself 'given the claustrophobia, the shared glass-topped tables, and the diabolical steps to the now labelled loos.' Even the food is not always hot enough. But the wind-dried meats that are the

Tdh from £2·60
(meal £2·85)
Alc (min £1·05) £3·85
(meal £4·20)

Seats 40 (parties 20)
No dogs
Unlicensed

(winter-month) speciality of the place, fried chicken with Chinese mushrooms, 'sweet-and-sour crispy wun-tun in a fruity, offaly sauce', beef with green peppers and black beans, stewed eel with bean curd, pork and vegetable soup and other dishes compel loyalties. It is happily many months since an inspector reported 'oily batter, dubious tasting prawns, and sweet cornfloury sauce for whiting.' Mix B-B-Q (£1·95) and stewed crab with ginger and spring onion (£2·85) are suggested, and if you have an adventurous party and can order in advance, says Shirley Poon, consider also kam ling duck in three courses, deep-fried fresh milk and stuffed Chinese mushrooms. Unlicensed, but plenty of hot tea.

App: W. B. O'Neill, Paul Gambaccini, P.S.A.W., H.W., and others

---

LA POULE AU POT   Map 14

231 Ebury Street, S.W.1
01-730 7763

The style is urban French farmhouse, with 'lacy cloths and open fires.' Too many customers are content to accept second-best, which may mean 'good sole served cool in a heavy cheese sauce', 'overdone gigot and heavy, lardy apple tart'. Still, 'the quiche pastry is much better', crudités, and poule au pot (£3·85) are ever-popular, and lemon mousse is a possible sweet. The set lunch under £5 is also welcome. French table wines are 'served in magnum and charged at 65p the gill.' Recorded classical music.

Closed Sun; Dec 24 & 31;
public hols
Must book
Meals 12.30–2.30, 7–11.15

Tdh L £4·55 (meal £7·70)
Alc £8·70 (meal £12·55)

Service 12½%

Seats 40 (parties 18)
♿ rest (1 step)
No dogs
Access, Am Ex, Barclay

PRINCE OF INDIA   Map 13

75 The Broadway, S.W.19
01-542 8834

Abdul Quddus in the kitchen is sometimes let down by the service in this 'small, narrow, red and green' restaurant, by the 'loudly wailing Indian music' or by Wimbledonian demand for sweetened curries, but at a test meal the samosas and onion bhajias were crisp, mushroom bhaji 'piquant and lightly cooked', and prawn korma (with coconut, paprika and tamarind, £1·65) excellent. Lamb dopiaza and keema methi tasted authentic, and chicken dhansak and lamb pasanda may be worth trying. 'Tandoori chicken was over-charred, though, and jelabis stale.' Drink lager.

Closed Dec 25 & 26
Must book D & weekends
Meals 12–2.45, 6–11.30

Alc £3·30 (meal £4·40)

Service 10%
Children's helpings
(under 12)

Seats 56 (parties 30)
No dogs
Access, Am Ex, Barclay, Diners

PROVANS   Map 14

306b Fulham Road,
S.W.10
01-352 7343

Closed L; 1st 3 weeks Aug;
Dec 24–26
Must book
D only, 7–12

Tdh £7·50 (meal £10·50)
Alc £8·10 (meal £12·50)

Service 12½%
Cover 60p alc
Seats 40
Access, Am Ex, Barclay,
Diners, Euro

Members fell out of love with Fergus Provan's restaurant four years ago, but have responded to a recent face-lift which has exchanged the old railway-coach effect for a 'penicillin and peach Edwardian boudoir'. The owner and Gerry Smith in the kitchen offer both à la carte and set four-course dinners. The set meal from a wide repertoire – perhaps cold carrot and thyme soup, hot tomato soufflé, guinea-fowl in calvados and cream, and pudding – has so far been less reported on than the individual dishes, such as 'delicious chilled salmon and sorrel soup', 'timbale of broccoli, a sweet fresh green mould bathed in saffron-coloured sauce Choron', moist and crisply fried calves' sweet-breads, and other things. Kitchen favourites include mussel and saffron tart (£1·80), hot mousse of sea bass hollandaise (£2), soufflé of crab (£5) and pheasant and green grape pie in season. Not everything succeeds – 'rice was glutinous, and pistachio ice-cream tasted mostly of almond essence.' Other cold sweets may be more fallible than simple apple and prune pie. Chocolates arrive with coffee. Marcel Amance table wines are £3·65, and on an enlarged list, Saumur or Apremont are £5 or so, Ch. Cantemerle '67, £8·20, and Ch. Meyney '66, £9·90. More reports, please.

AU PROVENCAL   Map 16

295 Railton Road, S.E.24
01-274 9163

Closed L; Sun; Dec 24;
public hols
Must book weekends
D only, 7–10.30

Tdh (8 or more) £5·50
(meal £8·10)
Alc £5·70 (meal £8·70)

Cover 30p
Children's helpings
Seats 50
♿ rest
No dogs
Access card

Trevor Keith, restaurateur and operator of the Wine & Dine Gourmet Club, has been one of the great irrepressibles of south London eating for many years, and it did not take members long to unearth him and his chef Dermot Jones (another remembered hand from Battersea) near a busy road junction by Herne Hill station entrance. The district has embraced them with open arms, it seems, and never mind the garlic breath from the 'superb aïoli with crudités' and 'rusty red fish soup with rouille'. An inspector also liked most of the main dishes a party ordered, especially the generous pigeon casserole 'with chunks of braised steak too, presumably on purpose.' The coq au vin 'claimed to be a maize-fed bird from France.' Other ideas include home-made quenelles (£3·40), porchetta (stuffed with apple, and done in calvados sauce) and boned stuffed duck with Grand Marnier sauce (£4·20). As one would expect of the style, most of the effort goes into earlier courses, but at a test meal the Grand Marnier ices were 'soft and creamy in texture and liquorous in taste.' The seven-course French regional dinners served to Club members on intermittent Sundays, with special wines included in the price, have yet to be reported on. The ordinary wine list is interesting and not over-priced, with several French table wines just over £3, and Givry '73 (Pigneret), £5·95. More reports, please.

QUINCY'S Map 12

675 Finchley Road, N.W.2
01-794 8499

Michael Folkard, and perhaps his waiters, are theatre refugees with a womb-like place in the Child's Hill sector of Finchley Road. After five years in and out of the *Guide*, fair prices and honest cooking from a short but varied menu please people again this year. At a test meal, first courses were best (pipérade aux oeufs and 'delicious mustard mayonnaise for sardines'), trifle worst. In between, lamb Stroganoff (£3·70), beef in Guinness (£3·85), and crusty pies or lamb's liver sautéed with parsley and caper gravy, sound good. Provencal red and white at £3·85 are wiser than the £2·95 plonk. Classical records. No dogs.

Closed L; Sun; Apr 7; May 26; Aug 25; Dec 26 Must book D only, 7–11.15	Alc £5·65 (meal £8·80) Service 10% Cover 45p	Seats 32 rest Air-conditioning Am Ex, Barclay

RAMA SITA   Map 13

6 Clarendon Road, W.11
01-727 9359

Closed Sun; Apr 7 L;
Aug 15–31; Dec 25 & 26
Must book
Meals 12–2.30, 6–11

Alc (min £3·50) £5·90
(meal £7·50)

Service 10%
Cover 40p
Seats 41 (parties 18)
No dogs
Access, Am Ex, Barclay,
Diners, Euro

Chelas of Ali Ashraf and his Provencal wife in Chez Danali, Hemel Hempstead, a decade ago have now turned up on his doorstep in Holland Park where he practises, he says, 'a kind of Indian *nouvelle cuisine*' at French rather than Indian prices, in a room decorated with murals depicting the tale of Rama and Sita. 'He is still the exquisitely polite autocrat, but his famous opening "Might I suggest?" means that you would be both rude and foolish to ignore.' Whether or not the tastes go back to the Moguls or are the fruits of a gustatory marriage between Mysore and Marseilles, a test meal confirmed other people's pleasure in the expensive but delicate first courses ('tikka murgh tasting nicely of almonds and cardamom, bright red langoustines with lemon and ginger, butter nan') and shakouti ('tender lamb in a dark rich sauce tasting of coconut and cardamom with a vinegary kick', £2·65). Badami gosht, murgh da Gama, and langoustine Niroupa are other delights a French-woman notifies, along with muttar paneer (with home-made goat cheese) or samé coco (haricots with coconut and garlic) for vegetarians. Several other reports sound like the old vodka advertisements ('Indian sweets used to baffle me until I encountered Sita surprise'). However, 'malpoua may have left the kitchen as a crunchy cake but was a soggy pair of failed fritters by the time it reached me in a pool of anise-flavoured Cointreau syrup.' Besides, a January lunch was lamentable by normal London Indian standards, apart from the sweet ras malai, so eat critically. French table wines are £3·65, Provencal £1 more.

App: Richard Mabey, Nurul Islam, M. W. Warwick, M. & N. Hull, Christine Duncan, A.H., and others

RED LION CHINESE Map 13

18 Red Lion Street,
Richmond, Surrey
01-940 2371 *and* 948 1961

The Chens have outlasted Mr Young's chain as Richmond's Pekinese representative here – but prices have risen to match, and regulars and others think that rice (70p) and mixed vegetables (£1·40) should be better cooked at this level. Still, grand hors d'oeuvre (£2), hot-and-sour soup, and the house's suggested chicken and almonds in yellow-bean sauce, and aromatic and crispy Peking duck, from a comparatively short *carte* or set meals, are dependable enough. 'Toffee banana was mean in quantity and I think we were charged for tea refills: Richmond's water rates must be exorbitant.' Recorded music.

Closed Dec 25 & 26
Must book D & weekends
Meals 12–2.15, 6–11.15

Tdh from £3
(meal from £3·70)

Alc £5·85 (meal £6·80)

Service 10%
Seats 44 (parties 40)

♿ rest
Air-conditioning
No dogs
Access, Barclay, Diners

THE REFECTORY Map 13

6 Church Walk,
Richmond, Surrey
01-940 6264

Closed Mon; D Sun–Wed;
public hols (exc Jan 1);
2 weeks spring & autumn
Must book D & weekends
Meals 12–2 (Sun 12 &
1.30), 7.30–8.45

Tdh D £6·25 (meal £8·50)
Alc (min L 75p, D £5·50),
£4·50 (meal £6·85)

Children's helpings
Seats 50
♿ rest (1 step)
No dogs

Recipe in *Second Dinner
Party Book:* jugged beef
with orange

English cooking of any quality is so uncommon in Greater London (outside private homes, of course) that Mary Kingsley's 'parsonage-style' kitchen in the shadow of the parish church may be over-valued. But members report 'a festive, almost Christmassy atmosphere' and forgive a (diminishing) tendency to undersalt. 'We found the first courses best: a light and creamy crab mousse, and seafood flan with good pastry, minced shellfish and a cheesy topping.' Main courses are casseroles for the most part, which is more sensible than mistimed roasts, and veal in lemon, beef with orange, and spicy lamb with apricots are among those mentioned. 'Four vegetables were all well cooked and liberally helped (from dishes left on the table).' 'Sweets are sweet', and steamed puddings sometimes dry, but chocolate cream, and coffee and banana sponge, are praised. 'Cheddar and Stilton came with crisp oat biscuits.' There are friandises with coffee. The Sunday lunches (in two sittings) are popular. Girls serve in a natural manner, and Mr Kingsley 'in a piratical beard' expounds his English wines, from Genesis – a Suffolk example – onwards. Expect few revelations, and if you want red, you will have to drink Australian (or redcurrant, of course). Morning coffee (10–12). There is a secluded courtyard for summer eating.

*App: J. D. Muir, D. J. Penny, A. B. Stenhouse,
A.P.B.H., J.J., and others*

Prices quoted in entries now include VAT.

RIVER BISTRO   Map 13

15 Barnes High Street,
S.W.13
01-876 1471

It is close quarters at Mme Rivolta's welcoming red bistro and 'if there are tensions they spread,' but this can be said of much dearer London restaurants too. Mr Martel's cooking was good when tried: notably, fish soup, stuffed aubergine (95p), filet de boeuf au poivre (£3·65) with 'gorgeous juices', 'tender and succulent duck à l'orange' (£2·75), and a true flavour to mushrooms done in their own liquid, and potatoes in milk and onion. Expect profiteroles, chocolate mousse, or 'eggy crème caramel' for sweet, also good examples, and decent coffee. House wine (£2·85), 'an unexpected delight'. Recorded music.

Closed L; Sun D;
Apr 4 & 6; 3 weeks Aug;
Dec 24–26
Must book
D only, 7–11

Alc £6·20 (meal £9·45)

Service 12½%
Cover 40p

Seats 40 (parties 40)
 ♿ rest
Barclaycard

ROMEO & GIULIETTA   Map 15

11 Sutton Row, W.1
01-734 4914

At the northern (and cheaper) end of Soho Italian, this welcoming place has admirers for the first time in nearly ten years. An inspector disliked (true, on a Monday) the antipasto that others praise, but Luc Nankoo's osso buco was 'tender, with oomph', as was pollo Verona (£1·75). Daily specials ('wild duck with a nice sauce and fresh vegetables'), sole fillets in various ways, and beef fillet Petroniana (£3·50) are also worth trying. 'There seems to be an all-purpose tomato sauce.' 'Stereotyped' sweets tasted freshly made: profiteroles, Black Forest cake, and so on. Valpolicella or Soave £2·95; Brolio Chianti '74, £4·60 in 1979. Recorded music.

Closed Sun; Sat L;
public hols (exc May 5 &
26, Aug 25)
Must book
Meals 12.30–2.45,
6.15–11.45

Alc £5·95 (meal £8·95)

Cover 35p
Seats 48

No dogs
Access, Am Ex, Barclay,
Diners, Euro

Since each restaurant has a separate file in the Guide office, please use a separate form or sheet of paper for each report. Additional forms may be obtained free (no stamp required) from The Good Food Guide, Freepost, 14 Buckingham Street, London WC2N 6BR (unfortunately Freepost facilities are not available from the Channel Islands or the Republic of Ireland).

Please report to us on atmosphere, decor and – if you stayed – standard of accommodation, as well as on food, drink and prices (send bill if possible).

See p. 508 for the restaurant-goer's legal rights, and p. 510 for information on hygiene in restaurants.

LE ROUTIER   Map 12

Commercial Place,
Chalk Farm Road, N.W.1
01-485 0360

The barn-like room may need the sun on the canal and jazz on the bank to have a chance of charming. But the test meal that sank the kitchen without trace last time was forgiven in this year's well-fried Camembert with gooseberry jam (£1·10), fair soups, and trout stuffed with spinach and ricotta (£4·20, including unusually good roast potatoes and crunchy Kenya beans). 'Cloying' veal Maxime ('halve the port and double the lime') and 'disastrous' duck with armagnac revive doubts, but others report better luck with lamb, and duck with sage and honey. Perhaps blackcurrant fool 'the best of the mediocre sweets.' House wine £3·80 for a litre; Côtes du Rhône £3·75. You may eat outside in summer.

Closed Mon; public hols
(exc Apr 4 & 6, Jan 1)

Alc (min £2·50) £6·45
(meal £7·55)

Service inc

Seats 60
♿ rest; w.c.
Access, Am Ex

SABRAS   Map 12

263 High Road, N.W.10
01-459 0340

This Gujerati family take-away with a few clean plastic tables falls clearly into the 'if hungry in Willesden' category, yet the samosas, bhajias, and mung dhal balls heated on request, the 'fragrant bhel poori', and 'very hot' masala dosai with nuts and raisins in the filling as well as potato, make it worth knowing about. Unlicensed. Details approximate.

Closed Mon; 3 weeks
Nov/Dec
Open noon–8.45

Tdh about £2·50
Alc about £2·70
(meal £3·55)

Service 10%
Seats 16
Unlicensed

SALAMIS   Map 14

204 Fulham Road, S.W.10
01-352 9827

Greek overtones and Iberian tints give colour to the 'continental' menu at this welcoming long-settled restaurant. Ernest Victory, who was evacuated from Gibraltar in 1940, lauds his zarzuela and paella these days, but people also like squid, fried or en su tinta (£1·10) among familiar first courses; then kebab with hummus (£2·60), 'one of the best, carefully cooked', and a varied Greek salad. 'Golden Finale' pancake might well stop short at its filling of raisins and cheese, but the rich caramel sauce typifies house largesse. Soave is £2·60 a carafe. Loukoum with coffee.

Closed Sun; public hols
(exc May 5 & 26, Dec 26)
Must book
Meals 12.30–2.30, 6.30–12

Tdh £3 (meal £5·30)
Alc £6·30 (meal £9)

Cover 20p
Children's helpings

Seats 40
♿ rest (1 step)
No dogs
Access, Am Ex, Barclay,
Diners

SAN FREDIANO Map 14

62 Fulham Road, S.W.3
01-584 8375

Crowded tables and bare walls (relieved by a relief of old railway sleepers) make for noisy animation, but most customers like the sprightly Italian cooking and waiting. Even at a Monday lunch inspectors were surprised by freshly made paglia e fieno (£1·25) and the spinach and ricotta filling for crespolini. Mussels, pink wild duck, rare lamb steak with rosemary and buttery-lemony sauce for fish are also praised. Good salads. Strong coffee in enamel jugs. Sweets are more naive, but the wines are not: even the house Chianti '77 had 'a fine raspberry nose'.

Closed Sun; public hols
Must book
Meals 12.30–2.30,
7.15–11.30

Alc £6·45 (meal £9·60)

Cover 45p

Seats 85

⑤ rest (1 step)
Air-conditioning
No dogs
Access, Am Ex, Barclay,
Diners, Euro

SAN LORENZO FUORIPORTA Map 13

38 Worple Road Mews,
S.W.19
01-946 8463 *and* 8976

The notables or notorieties who frequent the in-town San Lorenzo have kept their counsel about it this year, which leaves the airy, leafy Wimbledon branch (with tables in the garden too) filling a more felt want. Service has been deft rather than doltish this year, and Elizio Giandomenici's tortino al spinacio, scaloppine di vitello San Lorenzo (with aubergine and Mozzarella, £4·50), chicken breast stuffed with butter and oregano, and the house sweet pancake are all creditable. Antipasti were generous. 'Drink the house white Sardinian,' advises an inspector. A proper pianist plays at night.

Closed Apr 6 & 7;
Dec 24–26; Jan 1
Meals 12.30–3, 7–11

Alc £9·80 (meal £13·65)

Service 10% (food)
Cover 50p

Seats 125 (parties 45)
⑤ rest
No dogs
Access, Am Ex, Barclay,
Diners, Euro

Prices of meals underlined are those which we consider represent unusual value for money. They are not necessarily the cheapest places in the Guide, or in the locality.

Inspections are carried out anonymously. Persons who pretend to be able to secure, arrange or prevent an entry in the Guide are impostors and their names or descriptions should be reported to us.

'Meal' indicates the cost of a meal for one, including food, coffee, a half-bottle of one of the cheapest wines listed, cover, service, and VAT (see 'How to use the Guide', p. 4).

The Guide accepts no advertising. Nor does it allow restaurateurs to use its name on brochures, menus, or in any form of advertisement. If you see any instances of this, please report them to us.

SATAY HOUSE   Map 12

13 Sale Place, W.2
01-723 6763

'Tatty Austrian cafe decor, plastic-wrapped with a hint of exoticism.' Nothing synthetic about the Malaysian food, however, nor the 'gentle and dignified service.' Praise for satay ('tender meat and a spicy sauce', £1·15), murtabak ('more a pancake than bread, with a generous meat stuffing', £1·35), sotong tumis ('chilli-hot and tender squid', £1·20), and rojak ('a good clean version of this salad', £1·10). Less enthusiasm for ayam percik ('blond and bland chicken') and tinned-pineapple curry (pajri nanas). Drink Tiger beer or jasmine tea, and skip the sweets. Recorded Malaysian music. The set meal (£4·50) allows you tastes of several different dishes. No dogs.

Closed Dec 25; Dec 26 L
Must book D
Meals 12–3, 6–11

Tdh (min 2 people) £4·50
 (meal £4·95)
Alc £2·85 (meal £3·60)

Service 10%

Seats 32
⌖ rest; w.c.
Air-conditioning
Access, Am Ex, Barclay

LA SCALA   Map 15

35 Southampton Street, W.C.2
01-240 1030

The scale is small, upstairs and down, but the waiters are expansive. Strand or Covent Garden theatre-goers – and performers – like the early evening opening and service 'which adjusts to one's needs'. Kind words for whitebait, minestrone, 'firm' spaghetti with tomato sauce, pollo alla Scala (in butter, mushroom and cream sauce), trout with almonds, fried courgettes and salad. Rognoncini trifolati con riso (£2·30) is a speciality. 'Coffee not worth a cantata.' Drink the Trebbiano and Sangiovese. 'Restrained' music.

Closed Sun; Sat L;
Aug 1–21; public hols
Must book
Meals 12–2.30, 6–11

Alc (min £1·20) £6·60
 (meal £9·30)

Service 12%
Cover 35p

Seats 60 (parties 25)
⌖ rest (2 steps)
No dogs
Access, Am Ex, Barclay, Diners, Euro

SEA SHELL FISH BAR   Map 12

33–35 Lisson Grove, N.W.1
01-723 8703

Diners who think nothing of shelling out £5 for limp fritto misto or goujons can ill afford to look down their noses at this over-popular fish and chip shop which simply fries perfectly. Huge servings of red-hot halibut, plaice (£2·50, with good chips), haddock, 'selected' skate, Dover sole, rock salmon or whatever the market provides. Take-away too. Dining area expanded, licence applied for, and other signs of up-grading in the offing. Recorded music.

Closed Sun; Mon;
Dec 24–26
Meals 12–2, 5.30–10.30

Alc £2·90

Seats 77

No dogs
Unlicensed

97

SHALIMAR Map 12

299 Finchley Road,
N.W.8
01-794 8344

Pale hands put pen to paper about this traditionally gloomy Indian place (related to the Maharani in Westbourne Grove), whose onion bhajia, lamb bhuna or masala with pilau rice (£1·80), mild lamb pasanda with cream and nuts, nargisi kofta, chicken moghlai, tandoori chicken and channa (chick peas) masaladar (£1) are among dishes praised by normally cautious members. 'Rice, nan, poppadums and stuffed parathas were freshly and well done too.' Lager.

Closed Dec 25
Meals 12–3, 6–12
(1 Sat & Sun)

Alc (min £2·35)
meal £4·75

Service 10%

Seats 70
No dogs
Access, Am Ex, Barclay,
Diners, Euro

SIENA Map 12

17–19 Highbury Corner,
N.5
01-607 3976

Highbury Corner would make a good course for the Palio, and pasta and veal here may reconcile you to juggernauts instead of horses. Seated without fuss on a busy night, a member liked her fried courgettes and zabaglione (hot 75p, cold 55p) though 'fagiolini might have been fresher.' Mr Bertoncini, who has cooked at this cafe-restaurant for 14 years, suggests saltimbocca, pollo parmigiana (£3·10) and scampi al funghetto (£4·60). Service is quick and likeable. Italian house wines, £3·15 a bottle. 'Soft' recorded music.

Closed Sun; public hols
(exc May 26)
Must book
Open noon–10 p.m.

Alc L £6·35 (meal £8·95),
D (min £3·50) £6·55
(meal £9·80)

Cover 50p D

Seats 68
Air-conditioning
No dogs
Barclaycard

SIMPSON'S Map 13

162 Lower Richmond
Road, S.W.15
01-788 3844

Closed L; Sun; Mon;
last 2 weeks Aug;
Dec 31; public hols
Must book
D only, 7.30–11

Alc £7·95 (meal £12·15)

Service 12½%
Cover 50p
Children's helpings
(under 12)
Seats 35

Cheek, some may say, but members and inspectors will reply that there is better English (with some French) cooking to be found in Ianthe Johns' and Alastair Little's chic but clattery restaurant near Putney police station than is to be had from their famous namesake in the Strand. Mr Little's menu is wisely short, and some of the details in a test meal showed that there is still room for improvement – 'no spoon for the mussel broth, rack of lamb poorly trimmed, and the vermouth sauce (for an enticing fricassee of John Dory, langoustine, monk-fish and scallops, £5·50) too cloying and sweet.' Still, both at this and other meals much has been admirably done: 'a really fresh and delicate vegetable terrine', 'delicate and creamy mousseline of smoked haddock', fish soup with a 'magnificent, garlic-laden rouille', 'superb feuilleté with great chunks of lobster', 'nicely cooked

rest (1 step)
No dogs
Am Ex, Barclay, Diners

duck with blackcurrants, the pink slices of breast wrapped round a leg', 'unusually separate and flavourful risotto', and pear mille-feuille 'very homely in appearance but tasting much better than I expected.' There are a few cheeses, often including goat ones, native or foreign. Service is courteous. The wines (from Corney & Barrow) make a sensible start while the owners await the chance to accumulate more: house claret or Blanc de Blancs, £3·75; Ch. Moulin-Pey-Labrie '73, £6. 'We do not sell cigars or cigarettes and would take action if smoking annoyed other customers.' They are planning to start serving lunches in the summer, perhaps on the new patio.

App: Alan Bruce, Pat & Jeremy Temple, Richard Orgill, Abigail Fawcett, Ellis Blackmore, and others

SKY CHINESE RESTAURANT   Map 12

17–18 New College Parade, Finchley Road, N.W.3
01-722 9605

Tdh from £3·75
Alc £5·65 (meal £6·45)

Seats 60

Regional Chinese cooking has lately invaded the Finchley Road in force, and some of the Szechuan dishes in this large restaurant are 'very hot, especially two minutes after you've swallowed and think you've survived.' This applied at a test meal to the Szechuan noodles and the shredded pork in hot and garlic sauce (£1·50), though gentler Pekinese classics such as crispy aromatic lamb with an aniseed dip, fried chicken with cucumber in garlic sauce (£1·50), and fried beef in oyster sauce have been good too. The trouble, as with most such places, is carelessness with food temperature, rice cookery, set meals, and presentation: 'for crab with black bean and garlic they brought one finger-bowl among five and no extra napkins – at the price, an insult.' More reports, please, in case they decide to take it easy in this well-trawled vicinity.

STANDARD INDIAN   Map 12

21–23 Westbourne Grove, W.2
01-727 4818 *and* 229 0600

Closed Dec 25
Must book D & weekends
Meals 12–3, 6–12

Tdh £4 (meal £4·80)
Alc (min £3) £3·70
(meal £4·40)

Service 10%
Seats 160 (parties 30)
rest

Apart from a member's 'diffident objection' back in March that he was seated for dinner in a construction site, with pieces of floor covering being hurled down the spiral stair as he ate, most people still like this large two-floor restaurant, with Ramlal Bedhan and M. Ishaque 'evidently running a very efficient kitchen, for my party of nine in a crowded restaurant was served accurately and with despatch.' The best things in that meal were the mild shahi korma made with good-quality lamb (£1·80), the juicy, cardamom-flavoured chicken tikka (£2), the dark-coated channa masaladar (spicy with black mustard seed, £1·15), and the pilau rice (75p), since they had forgotten to salt the plain. But the nan and other tandoori dishes are generally praised, along with butter chicken with its rich russet sauce (£4·60 for a whole one), lamb pasanda (£1·75)

No dogs
Access, Am Ex, Barclay,
Diners, Euro

and shaksu kar (a northern dish with minced meat, eggs and fresh coriander). Paratha was less good when tried. There are no reports this year of the kulfi, ras malai and other sweets. Drink Carlsberg (70p) or salt or sweet yoghourty lassi at 55p.

App: M. Milne-Day, L.B., C.P.D., B. C. Tillyard, and others

LE SUQUET Map 14

104 Draycott Avenue,
S.W.3
01-581 1785

Closed Mon; Tue L;
Dec 25, 26 & 31; Jan 1
Must book
Meals 12.30–2.30,
7.30–11.30

Alc £9 (meal £14·05)

Service 15%
Cover 70p
Seats 30
No dogs
Am Ex card

The chief problem at this very French fish restaurant (a sister of La Croisette, q.v.) is taming the service, which can be amiable as well as skilful but on other occasions could with advantage take lessons from London Frenchmen better used to Anglo-Saxon tastes: 'Unconcealed shrugs and impatient sighs accompanied our request to keep the bowl of aïoli on the table, and our next-door neighbours did not seem to fare much better.' However, it is also possible to sit up at the bar to eat their 'delicious whole crab and crevettes provençale, followed by fine escalope of poached salmon with beurre blanc and the renowned loup grillé' (£5·40). The equally renowned plateau de fruits de mer (£6·50) may require more elbow room, and of course the risk of a smoker at the next bar stool is serious unless you are prepared to be firm. The tarte aux pommes – or aux poires chaudes – makes a 'delicious' sweet. The house Estandon Blanc at £4·80 or Muscadet (Métaireau) at £5·50 are all most people need to drink, 'though their Sancerre is good too.'

App: P. & J. Temple, Robert Whitehouse, and others

SWEETINGS Map 12

39 Queen Victoria Street,
E.C.4
01-248 3062

The City hordes who relax at this Victorian 'ordinary' stay sleek by lunching on the day's Billingsgate catch. Others join them for fresh oysters (£2·50 for six in 1979), smoked salmon, good-sized Dover sole, turbot, mackerel and smoked haddock with a poached egg on top. All good meals, at counter or table, with Muscadet (£4) or a pint of Guinness, and joggers may make room for jam roll or bread-and-butter pudding. 'Chips are real', but 'avoid the sauces'. No coffee.

Closed D; Sat; Sun; Dec 24; public hols (exc Jan 1) L only, 12–2.30	Alc £5·80 (meal £8·25) Service 10%	Seats 30 ♿ rest (3 steps) Air-conditioning

Wine prices shown are for a 'standard' bottle of the wine concerned, unless another measure is stated (e.g. litre, 50 cl., or pint).

SWISS CENTRE RESTAURANT   Map 15

2 New Coventry Street,
W.1
01-734 1291

As well as a patisserie selling fine croissants and other things, there are five restaurants in this Swiss cantonment. The **Imbiss** (entrance in Wardour Street) is a snack place with good coffee; the **Rendez-Vous**, **Locanda** and **Taverne** are differently themed but broadly similar drop-in restaurants on the main floor, and the **Chesa** is the bookable room, comfortable when half-full. The system is semi-industrial (with close to a million meals a year served) and awfully Swiss. The British general manager must have an uphill task explaining to his fifteen Swiss co-directors what anarchic Londoners think of the till method and the service, but complaints about the limp, lukewarm rösti potatoes and shoddy gateaux (even in the Chesa) need no interpreter. Prices are stiff for what you get. But whether it is Gala toast (£1·75) in the Rendez-Vous, cheese fondue (£3·50) in the Taverne, or consommé à la moelle and Nuora dil Fuorn (lamb en croûte, £10·75 for two) in the Chesa, most people report at least something nice to eat, with good (if again, overpriced) Swiss and other wines. (When they say '7/10 bottle', they mean – being Swiss – a bottle.) There are non-smoking sections in the Rendez-Vous and the Locanda. When reporting, please mention which restaurant you have eaten in.

Closed Dec 25
Open 11.30 a.m.–
midnight

Tdh £4·75 (meal £8·85)

Alc £6·65 (meal £8·90),
(Chesa) £8·70
(meal £11·80)

Service inc
Seats 364

Air-conditioning
Car park
No dogs
Access, Am Ex, Barclay,
Diners

♥ TANTE CLAIRE   Map 14

68 Royal Hospital Road,
S.W.3
01-352 6045

Closed Sat; Sun;
3 weeks Aug; public hols
Must book
Meals 12.30–2, 7–11

Tdh L £9 (meal £13·30)
Alc (min D £10) £14·65
(meal £19)

Service inc (alc)
Cover 85p
Seats 36
⟨ rest
No dogs
Am Ex card

The fortune of London's tables has propelled Pierre Koffmann's Gavroche-born restaurant to an early prominence that in Paris would have come more slowly. But it would have come in the end, if only for the owner's virtuosity with fish, exemplified by his andouillette de mer au vinaigre de Cassis (£3·20), and his bar à la salade: the first (a 'sausage' of turbot surrounded by a delicately tangy sauce) 'a complex of subtle flavours'; the second 'one of the most distinguished dishes I have eaten in Britain, firm-fleshed yet melting sea bass whose exquisite wine sauce was combined with just crunchy courgettes and carrots.' The setting for these sensations is more relaxed than it was initially. The narrow room with its Klimt prints 'lacks *Stimmung*', someone says, 'but you are received with a benevolent gravity, as though to the confessional.' Anchovy *amuse-gueules* accompany an aperitif, and the *carte* is naturally short. A few disappointments are noted: indifferent bread,

101

and poorish pommes savoyarde, a 'collapsed and undistinguished' gâteau de foie de volaille, and 'lumpish, dry-fleshed volaille au Roquefort with surprisingly little taste in the sauce.' But even these criticisms are in the context of meals that included 'superb feuilleté d'asperges' (£3), 'tomato soup and sauces whose basil content announced itself from the next table', 'sweet scallops with an unctuous sauce that had a hint of bitterness from shredded endive', and 'quite splendid' poularde aux morilles. Foie de veau au citron vert (£6·30) and caneton aux épices (£6·70) are other specialities. Terrine de légumes 'pleased the palate as much as it ravished the eye', and in 1979 the set lunch was one of the best bargains in London, if you resisted the temptation to bump the bill up by drinking their stiffly marked-up wines. Saffron-rich mussel soup, filet de bar mouginoise, and hazelnut mousse 'the texture of quenelles floating in a pool of blood-red raspberry sauce' was one such meal; another, even better, included a poached egg in a cream sauce with mussels and artichoke hearts, a plump rare teal imported from France with an orangey sauce and a puree of celeriac, and a Munster cheese in prime condition. Puddings as a whole do not quite reach the standard of earlier courses (though great trouble is taken with the feuilleté aux poires, marquise au chocolat and other examples). It is also easy to choose three separate courses 'with liquid surrounds on over-large plates'. Coffee is excellent. Wine prices have not been notified, but a member reports 'very little under £10' (try the Muscat d'Alsace or the Gigondas) and over 200 per cent mark-up on the Listel Blanc that had a retail price of under £1·50 in 1979.

App: by too many members to list

A TASTE OF HONEY   Map 13

---

2 Kensington Park Road, W.11
01-229 6731 *and* 727 4146

People like the flowers and the homeliness but have doubts about the dim candlelight and some of the cooking, for Barbara Deane and Jonathon Hayes have served on occasion 'tinned ham wrapped round gritty leek' and carelessly prepared 'cheese parcel' as well as fair chicken liver pâté, lamb stew, and 'rather dry but well-flavoured' wild duck with 'crunchy broccoli'. Blackberries, either Romanoff or in a tart, sound good sweets. There are wines now (prices not notified) and Chimay bottled beer.

Closed L (exc Sat & Sun); public hols (exc Jan 1) Must book D Meals 12.30–3.30 (Sat & Sun), 6–11.30	Alc (min £3) £6·75 (meal £10·30) Service 10% Cover 40p	Children's helpings Seats 45 (parties 8) No dogs Am Ex, Diners

🍷 TATE GALLERY RESTAURANT   Map 16

Millbank, S.W.1
01-834 6754

Closed D; Sun (exc
Apr 6); Apr 4; May 5;
Dec 24–26; Jan 1
Must book
L only, 12–3

Alc (min £1·15) £9·55
(meal £13)

Children's helpings
(under 11)
Seats 130
🔽 rest (side entrance);
w.c.
Air-conditioning
No dogs

Recipe in *Second Dinner
Party Book:* buttered crab

'England should be proud' and 'the best exhibition in the gallery' are comments that will scarcely soothe the ruffled feelings of painters and curators, who would like to fill the Rex Whistler room with something more abstract than well-fed lunchers analysing their sensual response to Ch. Haut-Bailly '66: 'deep bricky colour, browning at the edges; a soft insinuating smell; and the taste round and mature with a fine backbone.' Visitors like this would not trade Tom Machen, his easily priced fine wines, and his alert, considerate waitresses for Sir Norman Reid and all his works. Their discontents have been minor this year. 'Perhaps the painful spectacle of people swilling Lafite as though it were Perrier and smoking their way through Taylor '55 port is the worst of it.' Michael Driver is at the helm in the kitchen, and most people have learnt that the enterprising English dishes, researched from original sources, often do little for great claret and burgundy. So drink the (very adequate) house wines at £3·28, perhaps, if you are eating spiced Welsh lamb with anchovy sauce or veal kidneys florentine, in which more than one person has detected 'an amazing back-taste of soap from one of the herbs used.' Still, the cooking has been better this year, by numerous accounts, and if you begin with the buttered crab (£1·80) or divide a portion of poached salmon trout sauce mousseline (£4·60) to match your white burgundy, and look on the short menu for a plain steak or 'lovely pink slices of roast Scotch beef and Yorkshire pudding', or steak and kidney pie, your Ch. Haut-Brion '66, c.b. (£17·25) or Grands Echézeaux, Domaine de la Romanée-Conti, '72 (£10·23) need not tremble. Salads are good too. At the sweet stage, English history can be allowed a freer rein, for the Victorian trifle recipe explains why the Italians called it zuppa inglese, and the soft fruit mousses or 11th-century 'pye with fruyt ryfshews' may be tried too – not forgetting that Ch. Suduiraut '72, c.b., to drink with it is a mere £5·65. The setting encourages animated conversation rather than hushed pretensions – 'I noticed a large party of women whose bags were labelled "Friends of the Koala Bear".' Remember that when you book you may request a table in the non-smoking section (other London restaurants, please imitate) and may ask for wine to be decanted or chilled as appropriate.

App: by too many members to list

When a restaurant says 'must book', the context of the entry usually indicates how much or how little it matters, but a preliminary telephone call averts a wasted journey to a closed door. *Always* telephone if a booking has to be cancelled; a small place (and its other customers) may suffer severely if this is not done.

THROGMORTON RESTAURANT
OAK ROOM   Map 12

27 Throgmorton Street,
E.C.2
01-588 1495 *and* 5165

As o.d as the century and wearing somewhat better, this oaken Lyons basement coddles waves of lunchers from the Bank and Stock Exchange with motherly service, modest prices and an undemanding menu. 'The place for a one-course meal of substance', perhaps roast sirloin (£2·65) or lamb, or grilled lemon sole (£3·20). Salad 'better than one would expect', and they leave the cream jug (16p) on the table with hot fruit pie (55p). 'Coffee as good as always.' House wine was £3·05 a bottle in 1979. Snacks and pressurised beers in the Buffet Bar and Bar Sinister.

Closed D; Sat; Sun;
public hols
L only (Mon–Fri), 11.45–3

Alc £4·55 (meal £7·45)

Service 12½%
Cover 27p
Seats 270
Air-conditioning

No dogs
Access, Am Ex, Barclay,
Diners, Euro

LA TOQUE BLANCHE   Map 13

21 Abingdon Road, W.8
01-937 5832

Closed Sat; Sun; Aug;
Dec 24 & 31; public hols
Must book D
Meals 12.30–1.45, 7–10.45

Alc £7·95 (meal £12·30)

Cover 60p
Seats 42
♿ rest
No dogs
Am Ex, Diners

'To avoid the crush and the smoke the only solution seems to be lunch or an early dinner,' say members about M Giovagnoli's long-running restaurant, which needs air-conditioning more than most. 'But the meals and service are an example to many. The fish soup, the veal normande, and the truite aux herbes flambé (£4·30) have all been excellent, and the cheeseboard is probably still London's largest.' Other critical eaters agree for the most part, mentioning other specialities – crêpes aux fruits de mer (£4·25), and ballotine de volaille bressane (£3·95) 'which had a most convincing Bresse taste and succulence, though I think that on its home ground the sauce would have been thinner and creamier. Green salad was satisfactorily dressed, though a fruity olive oil would have transformed it.' Langoustines à ma façon are ever popular (£5·60). Chicken Kiev and veau normande may be more routine, but on the whole if you concentrate on main courses and shun the bar drinks the final price need not be over-high. 'Some of the cheeses were in their second childhood, but I had an excellent Coutançais and a good Valençay Cendré.' Glace praliné with langues de chat made a very adequate finish. Wine prices again need care and a critical eye to shippers: the setting suggests Cendré de Novembre or Beaujolais rather than anything more complex.

App: V. Westerman, D. M. Gaythwaite, K. W. Daley, Eric Cline, and others

For the explanation of ♿, denoting accessibility for the disabled, see 'How to use the Guide', p. 4.

UPPER CRUST   Map 14

9 William Street, S.W.1
01-235 8444

The upper crust of Knightsbridge is impenetrable but the fillings under 'two inches of flaky pastry' persuade one to go native at this pine-and-tile pie shop. Steak and kidney or giblet and pickled walnut are popular at £2·65, with fresh bread, herb butter and the day's vegetables included in the cover charge. Besides pies (fisherman's, ham, chicken and raisin, or turkey, celery and cranberry), try roasts ('good rack of lamb'), and boiled meats (ham and – 'for fat-lovers' – brisket). 'Kedgeree, and Yorkshire pudding with chicken livers, were less good.' More pies for sweet, or plum pudding. 'The builders seemed to be in during lunch.' The house red wine has few friends.

Closed L Dec 25 & 25
Must book
Meals 11.30–3, 6–11.30

Alc (min £1·95) £4·75
(meal £8·05)

Cover 70p
Seats 155 (parties 40)

♿ rest (1 step)
Air-conditioning
No dogs
Access, Am Ex, Barclay, Diners

VALCHERA'S   Map 13

30 The Quadrant,
Richmond, Surrey
01-940 0648

The aspidistra, patterned crocks and Edwardiana, with crowded tables, almost lead you to expect Charlie Chaplin as a waiter, and indeed some call the service 'over-familiar'. Tough beef and 'crumbly' snails are among 1979 mishaps reported, but a test meal yielded 'excellent' grilled sardines (£1·25) and osso buco (£3·25), chicken Kiev 'with noticeable garlic and herbs', and fresh spinach. Parma ham with melon, inkfish salad, grilled sea bass and 'very dark' jugged hare are also mentioned. It is then best to ask for espresso coffee. House wines are £1·85 for 50 cl.

Closed Sun; public hols
Must book
Meals 12.15–2.30,
6.30–10.30

Tdh L about £2·85
(meal £5·45)
Alc £6·85 (meal £9·55)

Cover 45p

Children's helpings
Seats 75 (parties 35)
♿ rest
Access, Barclay, Diners

♥ VASCO AND PIERO'S PAVILION   Map 15

Poland Street/Oxford
Street, W.1
01-437 8774

Closed Sun; Sat L;
Apr 4 & 7; Dec 24 D;
Dec 25, 26 & 31; Jan 1
Must book
Meals 12–3, 6–11

Alc £8·35 (meal £12·50)

Even the *Guide*'s posted letters have not always found the midnight blue staircase to these two north Italians' gold 'pavilion' in the interstices of the Academy Cinema – and even when they got upstairs one couple found they were expected to prove at the door that they were not Scottish football fans in a predictable condition. The more pleasure to find such cordial hospitality – 'with the classical guitarist and the cat each adding his individual note to the atmosphere' – and fastidious cooking. Claudio Laponte's favourite dishes should be noted, for they have been admired

Children's helpings
Seats 45
No dogs
Access, Am Ex, Barclay, Diners

here for years: tenerelli pancakes stuffed with spinach and ricotta (£1·85), rich but 'judiciously helped' taglierini crema e funghi (£2), bean soup, and seafood lasagne among first courses; and then perhaps lambs' kidneys piccanti, calf's liver alla salvia, lamb cutlets Saporiti (£4·20) and breast of chicken with lemon and sage (£3·30). 'These strips of chicken showed simplicity and distinction of flavour, and my first taste of the grilled lamb, with the lemon and rosemary separately evident but not overpowering. took me straight back to a Tuscan holiday two years ago.' Salads are well dressed. The zuppa inglese is 'a sweet in its own right, not a parody of cafe trifle', and in the peach season try one with zabaglione sauce and Amaretti. Vasco understands Italian wine well, and the Trebbiano white or Montepulciano red at £2·50 for 50 cl are worth the small premium on other place's carafes. 'Ghemme '61 at £8 had profited from its bottle age and was impeccably handled' (it is '69 now, at £7·50) and other uncommon bottles include white Masianco '77 and red Carema in the £7 range. Coffee is 'hot and strong'. 'But I shall drink my grappa at home in future after paying £1·50 for a glass here.' No children under eight.

Recipe in *Second Dinner Party Book:* tenerelli

App: Celia Rushforth, C.H.C., Christopher Bolton, L.O'B., and others

---

VILLA BIANCA   Map 12

---

1 Perrins Court, N.W.3
01-435 3131

Ferrari and Costa's skittish restaurant with its upstairs bar is the place Hampstead loves to hate, but this time it is an out-of-towner who scolds 'tasteless' zuppa pavese, minestrone and veal escalopes, while Londoners admire tagliatelle Alfredo (or green ones with cottage cheese and tomato), 'plump and luscious' pollo sorpresa or alla Rino, 'garlicky sautéed mushrooms and fresh, crisply fried zucchini', escalopes with butter and lemon, 'fine salads', and strawberries 'with lemon not cream at my own request'. House Chianti or Straccali are £2·90, and Spanna or Chianti Classico £4·80. Tables outside.

Closed 1st 3 weeks Aug; public hols
Must book
Meals 12.30–2.30, 6.30–11.30

Alc (min £5) £8·55 (meal £12·45)

Service 12½%
Cover 60p

Children's helpings
Seats 65 (parties 14)
♿ rest
No dogs
Access, Am Ex, Barclay, Diners, Euro

Since each restaurant has a separate file in the Guide office, please use a separate form or sheet of paper for each report. Additional forms may be obtained free (no stamp required) from The Good Food Guide, Freepost, 14 Buckingham Street, London WC2N 6BR (unfortunately Freepost facilities are not available from the Channel Islands or the Republic of Ireland).

VILLAGE BISTRO   Map 12

38 Highgate High Street,
N.6
01-340 5165

'Highgate neuroses are shared or soothed' in this
Austrian-run room with an oriental chef who has a
deft hand with mushrooms provençale (£1·45) and
sauté potatoes. A modest range of other unpredictables
such as fondue bouillon 'with an interesting blue-
cheese sauce', and jarret de porc à la choucroute (red
cabbage, actually). Puddings unimportant; coffee good.
French red wine is £3·65. Some half-bottles are listed
for solitary lunchers.

Alc £6·55 (meal £9·60)   Service 10%   Seats 22
                             Cover 30p

WALTONS   Map 14

121 Walton Street, S.W.3
01-584 0204

Closed Sun D;
Dec 24 & 31;
public hols
Must book D
Meals 12.30–2.30,
7.30–11.30

Tdh L from £8
(meal from £11), D from
£15 (meal from £18)

Service inc
Seats 60 (parties 10)
Air-conditioning
No dogs
Access, Am Ex, Barclay,
Diners, Euro

As padded cells go, nothing but the prettiest in
primrose and grey is good enough for Walton's
('consultant designer, Lawrence of Arabia,' suggested
one visitor, feeling the give in the walls, but this does
enable you to bang your head with impunity when
the sheikhly bill arrives). The place's personality is
elusive. It is owned by a company, managed by Rolf
Amberge, and Murdo MacSween is still in the
kitchen, with a few of Michael Smith's dishes
surviving in the repertoire. On the whole, *Guide*
inspectors tend to think that anyone who chooses to
eat here when the same money or less would buy a
distinguished meal at other London addresses needs
his taste-buds examined. Yet some good things are
reported by critical people: 'Quenelles de turbot in
the set lunch were light and had an excellent sauce';
'hazelnut omelette in another such meal was an
interesting idea, professionally executed'; 'mousseline
of sea trout with saffron sauce was subtle and the
Stilton soup with walnuts and apple original'; 'collops
in the pan with pickled walnuts must have been a
miraculous accident, like penicillin'; 'my guest
consumed with apparent relish a concoction of
banana, raspberries, mint ice-cream and chocolate
sauce, but I think my conservative choice of a
savoury – prunes and bacon with water-chestnuts – was
more prudent.' So far, so dandy, and dinner may be
better groomed than lunch. But two separate
inspectors report boring menu composition, slipshod
cooking (of vegetables, especially) and 'cafe-level'
garnishing. The service also calls for firmer guidance;
one visitor who dropped in after hearing Mahler's
Third decided that the percussion section must have
followed him there. Little but Beaujolais and a couple
of clarets are still in single figures on the imposing list
of Bordeaux and burgundy, but the expense of the
wines derives partly from their eminence: Ch. Pétrus
'47, £130; Ch. Lafite-Rothschild '45, £200. But Ch.
La Mission-Haut-Brion '72 and Ch. Montrose

107

'71, both c.b., are a more accessible £12 or
so. 'Excellent Cafetière coffee and plenty of it.'
'Warre's '60 port is decanted every morning.'

*App: A. E. Hey, Ellis Blackmore, H. D. Rose,
J. R. Tyrie, H.W., P.G., P. G. Hollins, and others*

WARUNG JAVA TIMUR Map 12

45 Praed Street, W.2
01-402 6492

Mrs Chaudhry's homely Javanese snack bar closed
for a while in 1979 but is back in business, if you are
stranded at Paddington, for nasi rames ('a bed of
warm, moist rice with turmeric chicken, lamb,
sweetly barbecued liver, garlic and chilli, £1·32), pecel
(a chilli and peanut sauce for 'rather dull' vegetables),
kare ayam (chicken with coconut), and 'a layered
pink and white rice pudding'. Take-away service.
Unlicensed, and don't take your own: they disapprove.

Closed Wed; some	Open noon–7 p.m.	Seats 30
Moslem hols		No dogs
No bookings	Alc meal £3·55	Unlicensed

WEI HAI WEI Map 13

7 The Broadway, White
Hart Lane, S.W.13
01-876 1165

'If Mr Miao's chef Mr Miu can cook perfect Pekinese
prawns, lightly battered in a garlic and butter sauce,
why can't toffee bananas be less sodden and other
sauces more refined?' Barnes this may be, where
Chinese vegetables seem English enough, but decor
could be made more inviting and cooking less variable
with little effort. Grilled dumplings (75p), shrimp
toast (£2·40) and special fried rice (94p) hint at better
talents. Hirondelle £3·50 for 70 cl. Service 'cheerful
but detached'. Recorded music, but no caterwauling.

Closed L (Mon–Thur);	Tdh £3·80 (meal £4·50)	Seats 40
Dec 24–26	Alc £4·75 (meal £5·55)	♿ rest
Must book weekends		Air-conditioning
Meals 12–2.30, 6–11.30	Service 10%	No dogs

WIND IN THE WILLOWS Map 13

4 Elliott Road, W.4
01-995 2406

Closed L; Sun; Mon;
Dec 25, 26 & 31; Jan 1
Must book
D only, 7.30–11

Alc £6·95 (meal £9)

*Moles we have always with us, it seems, and the very
'English, unofficial' restaurant that Geoffrey Oldfield
and Dorothy Taylor have opened is certainly on Mole's
scale rather than Mr Toad's: hence the short (but
often changed) menu, since their gas stove has only
four rings. Both partners cook – one of them with a
leaning towards West Indian dishes – and people report,
for instance, 'large roasted marrow bones', 'super
curried aduki beans with chunks of apple', 'calvados-
flavoured pâté with whole hazelnuts contrasting with
the pink meat', and 'pigeon in wine, herbs and black
treacle, with admirably cooked fresh vegetables.'*

Children's helpings
Seats 16
No dogs

*However, though a test meal was mostly successful –
notably the breast of chicken coated with mustard and
breadcrumbs and finished with lemon juice, and the
chicken livers with apple, and malmsey sauce – there
are other hazards to be negotiated: 'By the time I had
penetrated a broken-down answering-machine and the
slow, gauche service on the spot I felt I had been to
Ballydehob or Samarkand and back, not Chiswick.'
'Coffee is apt to sit and sit, like the customers.'
However, good aperitifs (including madeiras and white
port), and interesting wines, honestly annotated and
priced (white Marqués de Cáceres from Rioja, £3·25;
Ghemme '61 from Piedmont, £6·95) suggest that
promise may be confirmed if the place is gently treated.
Recorded (intermittent) music. More reports, please.*

WOLFE'S   Map 15

34 Park Lane, W.1
01-499 6897

The thoughts of Ruskin share the menu with burgers
and sesame buns in this 'ritzy diner', which may suit
the staid patrons of Mayfair cinemas and hotels.
'Compares well with Kansas City' if you stick to
simple burgers (6 oz or 8 oz, £1·80 or £2·15), 'good
beef, rare and tasting of charcoal.' Mexican,
Provencal and German complications. Chips and plain
salad are *de rigueur* but grated potato pancakes (£1·70)
served with apple sauce or, on occasion, sour cream
are 'intriguing and delicious'. Ice-cream parlour
desserts. 'Pert service.' Drink beer, orange juice (£1
for 8 oz) or iced water rather than the house wine,
perhaps. 'Clean but cramped.'

Closed Dec 25 & 26
Open 11.30 a.m.–midnight

Alc £5·05 (meal £7·35)

Seats 60
♿ rest (1 step)
Air-conditioning

No dogs
Access, Am Ex, Barclay,
Diners

LONDON PUBS AND WINE BARS

THE ARCHDUKE   Map 16

Concert Hall Approach,
South Bank,
S.E.1
01-928 9370
11–3, 5.30–11
Closed Sat L; Sun

What with this scherzoid new wine bar's name,
Hoffnung drawings on the wine list, and such items as
Beethoven Bereich Nierstein '78 ('a mere bagatelle,
alas', £3·20), no one can forget its location under
Hungerford Bridge arches, handy for the Festival Hall
and Waterloo. 'Rather Conran' in its wood-and-
stripped brick decor ('gorgeous arched ceiling'),
'charmingly amiable in service.' The snacks offer
'higher prices, higher quality, and larger helpings':
'thick and tasty' rare roast beef (£1·75), ham or pork,
all carved from joints; quiche (£1·30); various terrines
and cold pies; inventive salads (25p a helping), all
with good rolls and decent dressings and pickles. The
house wine is £2·85 the bottle, 60p a glass; try
Sauvignon du Haut Poitou '78 at £5·35. 'Après-theatre'
suppers are being considered. Gallery restaurant
(bookable) does more extensive meals at lunch and
until 7.45 p.m. 'Bach's Fizz' is £1·25 (£2·50 made with
real Champagne) but Extrisimo Bach for pudding
ought to claim a niche too.

BALLS BROTHERS   Map 12

142 Strand, W.C.2
01-836 0156
11–3, 5.30–7.30
Closed weekends;
public hols

Comfortable, rather Citified wine bar (part of a chain)'
with friendly service. Bar food: smoked mackerel
(£1·15, with 'rather commercial' salads), quiche
Lorraine, various cold meats ('roast beef so rare it
was dripping on the counter', £1·75), cold pies,
sandwiches ('hearty not dainty', from 55p), cheese
and French bread (70p). Daily hot dish might be
cottage pie, mash and peas ('genuine mash', £1·45).
(Separate restaurant, L only: roast beef every
Wednesday, £2·70.) Good range of wines, from house
wine at £2·55 (53p the glass); Muscadet de
Sèvre-et-Maine '78, £3·35 (69p the glass); Corton Les
Maréchaudes '71 (estate-bottled) £8·90; Sauvignon
Clos Madelaine £2·90 (£1·70 the half). No dogs,
despite the decorative Victorian lamp-post outside.

Wine bars are represented by a wine glass on the maps, pubs by a tankard.

Inspections are carried out anonymously. Persons who pretend to be able to secure,
arrange or prevent an entry in the Guide are impostors and their names or
descriptions should be reported to us.

We rewrite every entry each year, and depend on fresh, detailed reports to confirm
the old, as well as to include the new. The further from London you are, the more
important this is.

BOOS Map 12

1 Glentworth Street,
N.W.1
01-935 3827
11–3, 5.30–8
Closed weekends; last
week Aug, 1st week Sept

'A warm welcome for all' at the Roses' clubby wine bar near Marylebone and Baker Street stations. They offer about a dozen 'generously filled' sandwiches on brown bread ('delicious freshly cut home-cured ham' 54p, 'coarse garlic pâté' 65p, smoked salmon £1·20) as well as home-made soup, quiches, pies, taramosalata ('why those depressing French toasts?') and cheeses. Maple cheesecake (50p) is 'superb' and 'even the coffee is good.' Seven house wines by the glass (from 55p for Muscadet) and many other interesting ones in carafe or bottle: Cumbrero Rioja £3·15 the bottle (£2·70 the carafe); Pernand-Vergelesses '72 (Verry Père et Fils) £6·85; Ch. Smith-Haut-Lafitte '73, c.b., £5·90; and a still Coteaux Champenois £4·95. Distinguished aperitifs include Chambéry (Gaudin) at 42p the glass and Palo Cortado sherry at 60p. A few tables outside in summer. No dogs.

BOOT AND FLOGGER Map 16

See Davy's Wine Bars

BOTTLESCRUE Map 12

See Davy's Wine Bars

BRAHMS AND LISZT Map 15

19 Russell Street, W.C.2
01-240 3661
11.30–3, 5.30–11
Closed Sun; public hols
Table service 10%

The pop cacophony will remind you that the respective followers of B and L spent their time in battle royal, and 'much the best meal here of 1979' was Saturday lunch in September, with hardly any customers and an eggy light tomato flan. Chunks of beef done up with bamboo shoots, ginger and soy also made a good light course at £1 (£2 as a main one), and lamb and aubergine casserole (£2·50) was 'worthy of a Turkish bistro.' But 'cheesecake now tastes synthetic and feels bouncy.' By the glass, nine table wines of little interest from 55p; better madeiras and ports from £1·05. By the bottle, California Zinfandel or Pinot Chardonnay, and Beaujolais Villages '78, under £5; Ch. Brane-Cantenac '73, c.b., £10·60.

BRAYS PLACE Map 14

198 Fulham Road, S.W.10
01-352 0251
11–3, 5.30–11
(Sun 7–10.30)

'A good place for a reasonably priced evening snack,' says an inspector after sampling a 'well-chosen and laid-out' charcuterie platter with salad (£1·65). The blackboard menu also offers home-made soups (85p), pâtés, quiche, pasties, oysters, 'as much as you like' from the cold table (£2·20), and a daily hot dish (from £2·20). About ten wines by the glass (house red Italian is 55p, £2·65 the bottle), and there is a 'special selection' of bottles from £4·40. 'Taped pop – but not deafening.'

COATES Map 12

(1) 109 Old Broad Street,
E.C.2
01-628 2411
11.30–3, 5–7.30
Closed weekends;
public hols

(2) 45 London Wall, E.C.2
01-628 5861
11.30–3, 5–7.30
Closed weekends;
public hols

This pair of places is marginal on food grounds,
though adequate if you expect no more of a wine bar
than 'meaty coarse-cut venison pâté (70p) and quiche
with a good eggy-cheesy filling but with warmed-over
pastry' (London Wall), and more than adequate if
your vice is the 'soft and crumbly fruit cake in the
Old Broad Street branch, a happy partner for a glass
of Bual Madeira (54p).' But it is for the Corney &
Barrow wines that City pin-stripes prop up the
mahogany panelling: 'ten by the glass, including
bicentenary wines in 1980', and beyond these, open
access to the main list at about a 50 per cent mark-up.
Note their exclusive '70s run of Ch. Trotanoy
(£6·25–£15), and other fine clarets. London Wall also
boasts about its Bloody Marys, perhaps because until
recently women were barred.

CORK AND BOTTLE Map 15

44–46 Cranbourn Street,
W.C.2
01-734 7807
11–3, 5.30–11
Closed Sun

Don and Jean Hewitson's cellar has to be visited very
early or very late in sessions, for if there were a dozen
such places round Leicester Square with the same
high standard of variety and value, all would be full.
(Happily, a younger relative, Shampers (q.v.), also
thrives near Carnaby Street.) 'Cloying' crab salad or
'leathery' quiche are noted now and then, but curried
chicken mayonnaise (£1·95) and meat loaf with spicy
tomato sauce (£1·85) are main dishes they are never
allowed to drop, and salads are colourful and better
seasoned than is usual (caraway is a favourite flavour).
The breads and terrines all make good company for
most wines. Afterwards there will be good Stilton,
gateau, or a fruit mousse in season, and Rombouts
coffee. 'The lavatories are rather continental.' About
twenty wines by the glass, including two South
Australians at 85p, and Quinta de Vargellas '69 port
at £1. Bottles are also strong in Alsace and Spanish
wines, and there is Provencal l'Estandon at £3·45 and,
for conservatives, Ch. Gruaud-Larose '73 at £6·95.
Classical guitarist.

CROWN Map 12

Aberdeen Place, N.W.8
01-289 1102
11–3, 5.30–11
Closed Dec 25 evening

'An architecturally interesting Victorian pub,
patronised by a good mixture of the young executive,
the student and the building worker.' Bar food (until
8.30): 'out of the ordinary' salads 30p–35p, pies and
pasties 35p–45p, sausages 30p–45p; 'very good range'
of pâtés and cold meats; hot daily dish such as chili
con carne or beef curry 75p–£1; cold food only in
the evening. Fuller's London Pride and ESB, Bass,
Ruddle's County, Young's Special and Samuel Smith's
bitter (pump). Wine. Juke-box; darts; fruit machine;
live music every evening. Tables outside.

DAVY'S WINE BARS

Boot and Flogger
(Map 16)
10–20 Redcross Way,
S.E.1
01-407 1184
11–3, 5.30–8.30
Closed weekends;
public hols

Many have wistfully said goodbye now to the great days of drinking fine wine at modest prices in the atmospheric, wood-and-candle rooms run by Davy's in the City and elsewhere. But it is not their fault that decent claret now costs a fiver upwards, and in fact £8 or so is not bad for Ch. Cantemerle or Ch. Malescot-St-Exupéry of the '71 vintage, and the 'vintage character port' at 85p the large glass is to be recommended. Rarer table and fortified wines are listed separately. The food is stereotyped: prawns, cold roasts, raised pies, and a few cheeses, but it is 'perfectly edible when the branch manager is efficient enough to see that bread is fresh, salad well dressed, and so on.' The odd place out in the attached list is the Croydon Wine Vaults, more distantly related to the parent body, which is now offering steaks as well: reports welcome. And even further out is the Davy's-owned pub, the White Hart in Exeter (*q.v.*).

Bottlescrue (Map 12)
Bath House,
Holborn Viaduct, E.C.1
01-248 2157
11.30–3, 5.30–8.30
Closed weekends;
public hols

Grapeshots (Map 12)
2/3 Artillery Passage, E.1
01-247 8215
11–2.30, 5.30–11
Closed weekends;
public hols

Gyngleboy (Map 12)
27 Spring Street, W.2
01-723 3351
11–3, 5.30–10.30
Closed weekends;
public hols

Wine Vaults (Map 3)
North End,
Croydon, Surrey
01-680 2419
11–2.30, 5.30–10.30
(Fri 11; Sat 7–11)
Closed Sun; public hols

DRAYCOTT'S   Map 14

114 Draycott Avenue,
S.W.3
01-584 5359
11–3, 5.30–11
Closed Sun; public hols;
3–4 days Chr

'Rather like a Paris cafe with bushes in tubs and a few tables on the pavement.' This wine bar (the newest venture of the Ebury wine bar, *q.v.*) is so popular with the smart set that it is difficult to get in – 'but fun when you do.' Cold food (sandwiches from £1·10, pâté, cheese, salads) is served at the far end of the long, thin bar. The upstairs restaurant, with waitress service, does lunches and dinners (except on Saturday evenings): watercress soup (75p), mackerel mousse, pastrami on rye (£1), with grilled steaks and chops and daily dishes (braised oxtail £3·65, with vegetables). Twenty Ebury wines: house wine £3·25 the bottle (55p the glass); Bordeaux Sauvignon Blanc £3·80 the bottle (65p the glass); Mercurey Domaine Pigneret '73, £6. And for those to the manor born, champagne by the glass, or a half-pint tankard of Buck's Fizz (£2·20), or even mulled wine in winter.

DUKE OF YORK   Map 12

2 St Ann's Terrace, N.W.8
01-722 4252
11–3, 5.30–11

A 'nice, spruce pub' with the menu chalked on a blackboard outside (Mon–Sat until 9 p.m., 40p–£1·50): minced beef chow mein, moussaka, cottage pie ('try with our chips'), gammon, plaice, bangers and mash, scampi, salads, sandwiches; menu changes daily. Watney's London bitter (air pressure). Wine. Fruit machine; Spoof. Tables outside.

113

EBURY WINE BAR Map 14

139 Ebury Street, S.W.1
01-730 5447
11–3, 5.30–11
(Sun 12–2.30, 7–10.30)
Closed 4 days Chr

The bow-fronted, bentwood-furnished Ebury looks,
and sometimes feels, like a very gentlemanly wine bar
that takes its trade from British Airways rather than
Victoria coach station, both nearby. (And its new
venture, Draycott's, *q.v.*, is positively Sloane Ranger.)
Perhaps this makes people unforgiving of tired-tasting
steak and kidney pie or blackberry and apple crumble.
'But the same meal did also include orange juice
freshly squeezed from four halves.' Daily dishes –
casseroles of beef, pork or veal – begin at £2·75. 'Hot
beetroot – lovely.' Also cold meats and salads from
£2·20. Meals, unless you sit up at the bar, should be
booked. Children are allowed in the restaurant area at
evenings and weekends. About 45 wines, from £3·25
(55p a glass). House claret is £3·95 ('*down* in price');
Ch. Malescot-St-Exupéry '73, £7·40, and Pilton
Manor '77, £5·30. Live music except on Sunday.

GOLDEN FLEECE Map 12

8 Queen Street, E.C.4
01-236 1433
11–3, 5–8.30
Closed weekends;
public hols

'An unusually agreeable place' though 'a bit tatty
inside and out.' Bar food (L only) includes sandwiches
from 33p, mussels, prawns, smoked mackerel,
'well-seasoned and tasty' shepherd's pie 45p, beef
curry, 'very good' breast of lamb, boiled bacon,
'genuine' chicken and ham pie 55p. Separate
restaurant (L only; 11.30–2). Fuller's London Pride,
Charrington IPA, Young's bitter (pump). Wine.
Darts; fruit machine.

GRAPESHOTS Map 12

See Davy's Wine Bars

GYNGLEBOY Map 12

See Davy's Wine Bars

LAMB AND FLAG Map 15

33 Rose Street, W.C.2
(off Garrick Street)
01-836 4108
11–3, 5.30–11

'Barely standing room and lots of people spilling out
into the street', but the bar food makes a visit
worthwhile: hot daily dishes (chili con carne, quiche),
'fresh, juicy' home-made game pie, cheeses, pâté,
plain and toasted sandwiches, salads. Courage
Directors (pump). Wine. Darts.

LONDON APPRENTICE Map 13

62 Church Street,
Isleworth, Middx
01-560 1915
11–3, 6–10.30
(11 Fri, Sat)

An attractive old pub on the water's edge. Bar food
(£1–£3) includes home-made chicken and ham pie, 'a
splendid array of cold meats', salads, smoked mackerel,
cheese. Separate restaurant. Watney's London and
Stag bitters (air pressure). Wine. Darts; fruit machine;
bar billiards. Patio. Car park.

LONDON PUBS AND WINE BARS

LOOSE BOX   Map 14

7 Cheval Place, S.W.7
01-584 8852
11–3, 5.30–11
Closed Sun; public hols

'Friendly personal service' at this 'smart, comfortable and honest' Searcy's wine bar on two floors ('the lower level is more informal'). Better at lunch-time than in the evening, apparently, for a varied range of salads, cold meats and cheeses, which supplement the daily home-cooked hot dishes. But by the end of the week the buffet may 'lack imagination'. 'Cheesecake is as good as ever.' Over a dozen wines by the glass (from 40p) and many bottles and half-bottles: Morgon '77, £4; Ch. La Tour Védrines '76, c.b., £3·25; Muscat d'Alsace '76, £4·75. Roof garden.

ORANGE TREE   Map 13

45 Kew Road,
Richmond, Surrey
01-940 0944
10.30–2.30, 5.30–10.30
(11 Fri, Sat)
Closed Dec 25 evening

Friendly service in a large Victorian pub, done out in Edwardian style. Self-service, home-cooked food in the cellar bar (not Sun) includes 'delicious' marinated beef, 'properly cooked pink' hamburger, sweet-and-sour fish £1·60, chicken in wine £1·90, kofte meatballs £1·70, three-course daily meal £1·90; menu varies daily. Young's bitter, special bitter, mild and Winter Warmer (pump). Wine. Darts. Tables on forecourt.

ORMES   Map 16

67 Abbeville Road, S.W.4
01-673 2568
12–3, 6.30–11
Closed Sun; public hols

An attractive wine bar, opened a year ago, 'rather Victorian modern', with an open hearth (gas 'log' fire), various levels, and curtained nooks for diners. The ambitious snacks include 'fresh-tasting' broccoli soup (60p), deep-fried mushrooms with garlic mayonnaise (90p), 'fishy and lemony' taramosalata with pitta, 'rather sludgy' port and Stilton mousse, various pies and casseroles, a vegetarian dish (stuffed aubergines with white wine, £1·40), and 'careful' puddings. 'Perfectly palatable French house wine' is £2·75 the bottle (50p the glass); others include Sardinian Monica (£2·65; 45p the glass); Ch. Margaux '72 at £10·95; Touraine Sauvignon at £3·50. Two pavement tables. Taped music: 'classical jazz and good pop.'

Prices quoted in entries now include VAT.

If you think you are suffering from food-poisoning after eating in a restaurant, report this immediately to the local Public Health Authority (and write to us).

Do not risk using an out-of-date Guide. A new edition will appear early in 1981.

See p. 443 for 'How to use the pub section.'

Wine bars are represented by a wine glass on the maps, pubs by a tankard.

Hours given are opening times. Food may not be served over the whole period.

PEACHEY'S   Map 12

205 Haverstock Hill,
N.W.3
01-435 6744
11–3, 5.30–12
(Sun 12–3)
Closed Sun D;
2 weeks Aug

'Fine in every way' is one verdict on this 'relaxed but
efficiently served' place, and 'prices are low for what
is offered' is another. According to the owners, 'the
food is more important than the wine.' The
multi-national menu includes 'delicious' garlic-stuffed
mushrooms (95p), taramosalata with pitta (£1·05),
Hungarian goulash, and wiener Schnitzel (£3·45), as
well as daily specials such as 'poussin in an excellent
sauce', roast guinea-fowl with port, or Armenian beef
pilaff. 'Tolerable' house claret is £3·50 a carafe (55p
the glass), while 'the more expensive bottles offer the
best value': Viña Real '66, £5·95; Coulée de Serrant
'75 (Mme Joly) £8·75; Ch. Palmer '73, £10·95. Soft
classical music 'sometimes'.

PRINCESS LOUISE   Map 12

208 High Holborn, W.C.1
01-405 8816
11–3, 5.30–11
(Sat 6.30)
Closed Dec 25 & 26

'Heaps of bar staff running around but serving
efficiently' in this large old pub, which stages live
music every evening. 'Well above average' lunchtime
bar food (Mon–Fri; 20p–95p): pizza, sausages, pâté,
cheese, 'very good' quiche, salads; hot daily specials
(cottage pie, steak and kidney pie). Range of beers,
including Godson's bitter, Archer's bitter and Samuel
Smith's bitter (pump). Wine. Fruit machine. The
Apples and Pears wine bar upstairs has a wider
choice of food.

RUSSKIES WINE CELLAR   Map 13

6 Wellington Terrace,
Bayswater Road, W.2
01-229 9128
11.30–3, 5.30–11
(Sun 7–10.30)
Closed Sun L;
Dec 25 & 26

'Congenial and delightful' basement opposite
'Millionaires' Row', with pleasing Edwardian clutter
and sometimes 'displeasing smoke'. Adequate bar
food: chili con carne, moussaka, veal parmigiana,
jacket potato with cheese (from 90p), some of them
microwaved before your eyes. Interesting wines,
especially strong on Australian: house wine is Spanish
Torres £3·25 the bottle (60p the glass); Yalumba
Riesling (Smith) £5·40; Heitz Zinfandel £4·50; English
Chilford Hundred £4. 'Strong coffee; gentle jazz.'

SHAMPERS   Map 15

4 Kingly Street, W.1
01-437 1692
11–3, 5.30–11
Closed Sun; Sat D;
public hols

'We stopped for a light lunch and it was so good we
came back for dinner,' say two Californian visitors to
'the Liberty's and Carnaby Street branch' of the
Hewitsons' Cork and Bottle (q.v.). The 'deli' style with
salads ('especially mushroom and green beans'), meat
loaf with tomato sauce, and other cold dishes is
augmented here at lunch-time by hot dishes such as
pork chops with peaches (£2·95, with potatoes and
salad) served by waitresses in the basement. Sweets
now seem fruitier and better. For wines (from £2·55)
see the parent place's entry, but expect too a
'champagne of the week' at £6·95 and interesting
choices elsewhere. Classical guitarist some nights.

WHITE SWAN   Map 13

Riverside,
Twickenham, Middx
01-892 2166
10.30–2.30, 5.30–10.30
(11 Fri, Sat)

A 'gem' by the riverside – 'not a trendy pub.' Bar lunches (12.30–2; 60p–£2·50): 'generous portions' of home-made soup, fresh meats and fish, steak and kidney pudding, haggis, stuffed vine leaves – menu changes daily. Self-service cold buffet on Sun (12.30–1.45) £2·50. Sandwiches and rolls in the evening. Watney's Stag and London bitters (air pressure). Wine. Children (accompanied). Darts; fruit machine; shove ha'penny; cards; dominoes. Garden. Outside gents'.

WINE VAULTS   Map 3

See Davy's Wine Bars

Restaurants, pubs and wine bars open on Sunday

Anarkali, W6
Ark, W8 (D)
Arlecchino, W8
Aziz, W6
Bagatelle, SW10
Bloomers Brasserie, SW13
Bloom's, E1
Brays Place, SW10 (D)
Bunny's, NW3
Il Camino, New Malden (L)
Capital Hotel Restaurant, SW3
Carlton Tower Chelsea Room, SW1
Carroll's Restaurant, W1
Chaglayan Kebab House, NW4 (D)
Chanterelle, SW7
Chuen-Cheng-Ku, W1
Connaught, W1 (Restaurant)
La Croisette, SW10
Crown, NW8
Curry House, NW11
Daphne's, SW3
Diwana Bhel Poori House, NW1 & W2
Down by the Riverside, Kingston (D)
Dragon Gate, W1
Drury Lane Hotel, Maudie's, WC2
Duke of York, NW8
Ebury Wine Bar, SW1
Fingals, SW6 (L winter)
Geeta, NW6
Gino's, Richmond
La Giralda, Pinner
Il Girasole, SW3
Gourmet Rendezvous, NW3
Green Jade, W2
Gurkhas Tandoori, W1
Hard Rock Cafe, W1
Holy Cow, W8
Joe Allen, WC2
Joy King Lau, WC2
Kew Rendezvous, Richmond
Kowloon, W1
Lamb & Flag, WC2

Lebanese, W2
Lee Ho Fook, NW3
Leith's, W11 (D)
Lemon Tree, SW19
Lichfield's, Richmond (L)
Lok Ho Fook, W1
London Apprentice, Isleworth
Loon Fung, W1
Mandarin, NW3 (D)
Mandarin, W2
Manzi's, WC2 (D)
Mata Hari, NW1
Maxim, W13
Monte Grappa, WC1
Munbhave, Croydon (D)
New Friends, E14
Nick's Restaurant, SW10
Orange Tree, Richmond
Le Palme, NW11
Peachey's Wine Bar, NW3 (L)
Pizza Express, W1
Prince of India, SW19
Princess Louise, WC1
Provans, SW10
The Refectory, Richmond (L)
Red Lion Chinese, Richmond
Le Routier, NW1
Russkies Wine Cellar, W2 (D)
Sabras, NW10
San Lorenzo Fuoriporta, SW19
Satay House, W2
Shalimar, NW8
Standard Indian, W2
Swiss Centre Restaurant, W1
Taste of Honey, W11
Upper Crust, SW1
Villa Bianca, NW3
Waltons, SW3 (L)
Warung Java Timur, W2
Wei Hai Wei, SW13
White Swan, Twickenham
Wolfe's, W1

Numbers are given for private parties only if they can be accommodated in a room separate from the main dining-room; when there are several such rooms, the capacity of the largest is given. Some restaurants will take party bookings at times when they are normally closed.

PLEASE keep sending in reports, as soon as possible after each meal. The cut-off date for the 1981 Guide is September 30, 1980, but reports are even more useful earlier in the year, especially for the remoter areas and new places. Late autumn reports can also affect corrections at proof stage.

Restaurants classified by the predominant nationality or style of their cuisine

American/hamburgers

Hard Rock Cafe, W1
Joe Allen, WC2
Wolfe's, W1

Austrian & Swiss

Kerzenstüberl, W1
Swiss Centre, W1

British (*see also Franco-British*)

The Grange, WC2
Lockets, SW1
Refectory, Richmond
Sweetings, EC4
Tate Gallery, SW1
Throgmorton Restaurant, EC2
Upper Crust, SW1

Chinese

Cantonese
Chuen-Cheng-Ku, W1
Green Jade, W2
Joy King Lau, WC2
Kowloon, W1
Lee Ho Fook, NW3
Lok Ho Fook, W1
Loon Fung, W1
New Friends, E14
Poon's & Co, WC2

Pekinese & Szechuan
Dragon Gate, W1
Gourmet Rendezvous, NW3
Green Jade, W2
Hung Foo, SW18
Kew Rendezvous, Richmond
Mandarin, W2
Mandarin, NW3
Maxim, W13
Red Lion, Richmond
Sky, NW3
Wei Hai Wei, SW13

Fish

La Croisette, SW10
Fogareiro, N3
Grahame's Sea Fare, W1
Manzi's, WC2
Poissonnerie de l'Avenue, SW3
Sea Shell Fish Bar, NW1
Le Suquet, SW3
Sweetings, EC4

Franco-British

Brinkley's, SW10
Carrier's, N1
Charing Cross Hotel, WC2
Connaught Hotel, W1
Leith's, W11
Mr Bunbury's, SW16
Provans, SW10
Simpsons, SW15

Franco-Italian

Lemon Tree, SW19

French (*see also Franco-British*)

Les Amoureux, SW19
Bagatelle, W10
Balzac Bistro, W12
Bloomers Brasserie, SW13
La Bourse Plate, EC3
Le Bressan, W8
Bubb's, EC1
Bunny's, NW3
Capital Hotel, SW3
Carlton Tower Chelsea Room, SW1
Chateaubriand, NW3
Le Chef, W2
Chez Moi, W11
La Croisette, SW10
Daphne's, SW3
L'Epicure, W1
L'Etoile, W1
Le Gavroche, SW1
Les Halles, WC1
Jonathan's, W14
Langan's Brasserie, W1
Lichfield's, Richmond
Ma Cuisine, SW3
M'sieur Frog, N1
Oven d'Or, Orpington
Poissonnerie de l'Avenue, SW3
La Poule au Pot, SW1
Au Provençal, SE24
River Bistro, SW13
Le Routier, NW1
Le Suquet, SW3
Tante Claire, SW3
La Toque Blanche, W8

Hungarian

Gay Hussar, W1

Indo-Pakistani

Anarkali, W6
Aziz, W6
Curry House, NW11
Diwana Bhel Poori House, NW1 & W2
Ganpath, WC1
Geeta, NW6
Gurkhas Tandoori, W1
Holy Cow, W8
Mandeer, W1
Munbhave, Croydon
Prince of India, SW19
Rama Sita, W11
Sabras, NW10
Shalimar, NW8
Standard Indian, W2

Italian (see also Franco-Italian)

L'Amico, SW1
Arlecchino, W8
Il Camino, New Malden
Canaletto, W2
Colombina, SW1
Gatamelata, W8
Gino's, Richmond
Il Girasole, SW3
Monte Grappa, WC1
Montpeliano, SW7
Osteria Lariana, W1
Le Palme, NW11
Pizza Express, W1
Pizza House, W1
Romeo & Giulietta, W1
San Frediano, SW3
San Lorenzo Fuoriporta, SW19
La Scala, WC2
Siena, N5
Valchera's, Richmond
Vasco & Piero's Pavilion, W1
Villa Bianca, NW3

Japanese

Ajimura, WC2

Jewish

Bloom's, El (Kosher)
Carroll's, W1
Grahame's Sea Fare, W1 (Kosher)

Middle Eastern

Averof, W1
Beotys, WC2
Chaglayan Kebab House, NW4
Cypriana Kebab House, W1
Efes Kebab House, W1
Jason's, SW11
Kolossi Grill, EC1
Lebanese, W2
Little Akropolis, W1
Nontas, NW1
Salamis, SW10

Portuguese & Spanish

Fogareiro, N3
La Giralda, Pinner

Scandinavian

Anna's Place, N1

South-East Asian

Arirang, W1
Bangkok, SW7
Chaopraya, W1
Mata Hari, NW1
Melati, W1
Satay House, W2
Warung Java Timur, W2

Vegetarian/Wholefood

Diwana Bhel Poori House, NW1 & W2
Food for Thought, WC2
Mandeer, W1
Sabras, NW10

Towns shown in black on our maps contain at least one recommended restaurant or pub (see map key). The dot denotes the location of the town or village, not the restaurant. Where necessary, we give directions to the restaurant in the entry. If you can, help us to improve them.

When a restaurant says 'must book', the context of the entry usually indicates how much or how little it matters, but a preliminary telephone call averts a wasted journey to a closed door. *Always* telephone if a booking has to be cancelled; a small place (and its other customers) may suffer severely if this is not done.

Restaurants open after midnight (*time of last orders in brackets*)

Cervantes, Coulsdon (12 weekends)

Chaglayan Kebab House, NW4 (12)

Chanterelle, SW7 (12)

Chateaubriand, NW3 (12)

Curry House, NW11 (12)

Daphne's, SW3 (12)

Le Gavroche, SW1 (12)

Gino's, Richmond (12 Fri & Sat)

Gourmet Rendezvous, NW3 (12)

Green Jade, W2 (12)

Hard Rock Cafe, W1 (12.30, 1 Fri & Sat)

Hung Foo, SW18 (12)

Jason's, SW11 (12)

Joe Allen, WC2 (1, 12 Sun)

Kolossi Grill, EC1 (12 Fri & Sat)

Kowloon, W1 (12)

Langan's Brasserie, W1 (12.45 Sat)

Leith's, W11 (12)

Lok Ho Fook, W1 (12)

Mandarin, W2 (12)

Mata Hari, NW1 (12 Fri & Sat)

Maxim, W13 (12 Fri & Sat)

Monte Grappa, WC1 (12)

Montpeliano, SW7 (12)

Pizza Express, W1 (12)

Provans, SW10 (12)

Salamis, SW10 (12)

Shalimar, NW8 (12, 1 Sat & Sun)

Standard Indian, W2 (12)

Swiss Centre Restaurant, W1 (12)

Wolfe's, W1 (12)

Since each restaurant has a separate file in the Guide office, please use a separate form or sheet of paper for each report. Additional forms may be obtained free (no stamp required) from The Good Food Guide, Freepost, 14 Buckingham Street, London WC2N 6BR (unfortunately Freepost facilities are not available from the Channel Islands or the Republic of Ireland).

Most places will accept cheques only when they are accompanied by a cheque card or adequate identification. Information about which credit cards are accepted is correct when printed, but restaurants may add to or subtract from the list without notice.

GLOSSARY

A rough-and-ready description of some of the dishes frequently encountered on restaurant menus and in the pages of the *Guide*.

Amer	American	*Fr*	French	*Mid East*	Middle Eastern
Arab	Arabian	*Ger*	German	*Pek*	Pekinese
Aust	Austrian	*Gk*	Greek	*Rus*	Russian
Austral	Australian	*Indo*	Indo-Pakistani	*Scot*	Scottish
Canton	Cantonese	*Ital*	Italian	*Span*	Spanish
Eng	English	*Jap*	Japanese	*Swed*	Swedish
Flem	Flemish	*Mex*	Mexican	*Sw*	Swiss

agrodolce (*Ital*) sweet-sour sauce, usually accompanying game or duck, which may contain pine nuts, sultanas, bitter chocolate and redcurrant jelly as well as the obligatory wine (or vinegar) and sugar (or honey)

aïoli (*Fr*) garlic mayonnaise

amandine (*Fr*) almonds as garnish (e.g. pommes amandine)

aranci caramelizzati (Ital) oranges, cooked whole in syrup, garnished with caramelised peel

Argenteuil (*Fr*) with an asparagus sauce or garnish (often served with eggs or chicken)

armoricaine (*Fr*) (américaine) ingredients include tomato, herbs, white wine, brandy and the coral (if the dish includes lobster)

Atholl brose (*Scot*) originally a thick drink made from oatmeal, water, honey and whisky. Modern versions are normally a syllabub-like sweet containing cream

avgolemono (*Gk*) chicken or fish broth with rice, eggs and lemon

baklava (*Gk*) thin pastry (filo) layered with nuts and spices, with a honey-and-lemon syrup poured over

béarnaise, sauce (*Fr*) an egg and butter sauce flavoured with vinegar and tarragon

béchamel, sauce (*Fr*) white sauce

beef Wellington see boeuf en croûte

biriani (*Indo*) elaborate dish of spiced saffron rice cooked with pieces of meat, chicken or prawns (dry)

blanquette (*Fr*) a 'white' stew, usually of veal, the sauce thickened with cream and egg yolks

boeuf en croûte (*Fr*) beef fillet cooked whole, seasoned with duxelles (*q.v.*), baked in puff pastry, served with a rich sauce, e.g. Madeira

boeuf Stroganoff (*Fr*) thin strips of fillet or sirloin steak, sour cream and onions (mushrooms and tomato puree may be added)

boeuf tartare (*Fr*) finely minced steak, served raw, garnished with a raw egg yolk, onion and capers

bordelaise (*Fr*) cooked in or served with a red wine sauce, often with beef marrow

borshch (*Rus*) beetroot soup (often garnished with sour cream)

boulangère (*Fr*) garnish of onions and potatoes cooked at the same time as a joint

boulangère, pommes (*Fr*) potatoes cooked in the oven with onions, dripping and stock

bourguignonne, à la (*Fr*) cooked with burgundy, onions and mushrooms

brandade de morue (*Fr*) cream of salt cod with milk, olive oil, garlic, served hot with croûtes (*q.v.*) or cold as an hors d'oeuvre

bretonne, à la (*Fr*) (of meat) served with haricot beans, sometimes as a puree; (of scallops) served in the shell with cream sauce and breadcrumbs

cacciatore (*Ital*) sauce includes tomatoes, herbs, onion and garlic

Café de Paris (*Fr*) garnish of truffles, asparagus, mushrooms, prawns, oysters, and lobster sauce

carbonara, alla (*Ital*) beaten eggs and chopped ham or bacon, used as a sauce for pasta

carbonnade flamande (*Flem*) beef cooked in beer, often with bread on top to form a crust

carbonnade nîmoise (*Fr*) mutton or lamb cooked slowly in a casserole with vegetables

ceviche (*Mex*) fillets of white fish – often scallops or sole – 'cooked' by marinating in lime juice with onions and seasonings

chasseur (*Fr*) sauce or dish which contains white wine, shallots, mushrooms and tomatoes

chateaubriand (*Fr*) thick centre cut of beef fillet (usually cooked for two)

chocolat turinois (*Fr*) sweet made from chestnuts, butter and chocolate

Choron (*Fr*) garnish (for tournedos) of artichoke bottoms filled with peas and pommes noisette (*q.v.*)

Choron, sauce (*Fr*) tomato-flavour sauce béarnaise (*q.v.*)

coq au vin (*Fr*) casseroled fowl in a rich, wine-based sauce

coquilles St Jacques (*Fr*) scallops

coulibiac (*Rus*) (koulibiak) a type of fish cake in pastry (usually salmon)

couscous (*Arab*) ground wheat (semolina) with vegetables and spices, usually served with mutton

crème pâtissière (*Fr*) confectioner's custard made of flour, eggs and milk, used as a filling for eclairs, profiteroles and fruit tarts (crème St Honoré has beaten egg whites added – see gâteau St Honoré)

créole (*Fr Carib*) ingredients include rice, peppers, tomatoes

crèpes Suzette (*Fr*) thin pancakes, flamed at table, in a sauce of butter, orange, lemon, curaçao and brandy

crespolini (*Ital*) spinach-filled pancakes and cheese in a béchamel sauce

croûte, croûton (*Fr*) bread, fried or toasted, used as base or garnish (see brandade de morue, tournedos Rossini, gazpacho)

croûte. en cooked in pastry case (see boeuf en croûte)

Cullen skink (*Scot*) fish soup made from smoked haddock, milk, onion and potato (named after a Morayshire village)

Dacquoise (*Fr*) layered meringues, often made with ground almonds, with cream, butter cream and/or fruit between the layers

darne (*Fr*) thick slice of a large fish

daube (*Fr*) slowly braised meat in an enriched wine stock with herbs
   à l'avignonnaise: made with mutton
    provençale: with tomatoes, garlic and olives

dauphine, pommes (*Fr*) duchesse potato mixture combined with unsweetened choux paste, formed into cork-like shapes, crumbed and deep fried

dauphinoise, gratin (*Fr*) sliced potatoes cooked in the oven with milk or cream, and garlic or cheese

dhal (*Indo*) lentils

dhansak (*Indo*) a Parsee curry of lamb or chicken cooked in dhal (*q.v.*)

dijonnaise (*Fr*) (sauce) containing Dijon mustard (sometimes mayonnaise-like)

dim-sum (*Canton*) light snacks, mostly savoury, and mostly served in the bamboo baskets in which they are steamed

dolmades (*Gk*) vine leaves stuffed with meat and/or rice and herbs

dopiaza (*Indo*) onion-based korma (*q.v.*) (wet)

duxelles (*Fr*) minced mushrooms, shallots, herbs, cooked in butter, used for seasoning (see boeuf en croûte)

Dug éré (*Fr*) (fish) poached in white wine, with cream and tomatoes added to the sauce

émincés (*Fr*) sliced or chopped left-over roast or braised meat, reheated in a sauce or gravy

émincés de veau zurichoise (*Fr*) sliced veal in a wine and cream sauce

escalope (*Fr*) thin slice of meat (usually veal, sometimes pork) cut from the leg or fillet (see saltimbocca, veal Cordon Bleu, and wiener Schnitzel)

estouffade (*Fr*) similar to daube (*q.v.*), though the meat is marinated and fried before braising

fish plaki (*Gk*) baked in a mixture of tomatoes, onions, garlic, parsley, wine and lemon juice

florentine (*Fr*) ingredients or garnish include spinach

fondue (*Sw*) melted cheese, wine and kirsch, served in a communal pot into which are dipped chunks of crusty bread on long forks

fondue bourguignonne (*Sw*) cubes of fillet steak are cooked by each diner in oil at the table and eaten with a selection of sauces

fritto misto (*Ital*) batter-fried morsels, either of vegetables and delicate meats, or of fish (di mare or di pesce)

gâteau St Honoré (*Fr*) choux paste balls, filled with a light crème pâtissière (*q.v.*) and caramel coated, piled on a pastry base

gazpacho (*Span*) cold soup, made from raw tomatoes, onions, garlic, cucumber, olive oil, garnished with croûtons and chopped vegetables

golubcy (*Rus*) stuffed cabbage

gougère (*Fr*) choux paste enriched with eggs and diced Gruyère cheese, eaten hot or cold as an hors d'oeuvre

gratin, au (*Fr*) (with) a browned topping of crumbs and butter or cheese

gratinée lyonnaise (*Fr*) consommé, enriched with egg and port, topped with bread and grated cheese, and browned in the oven

gravlax (*Swed*) (gravadlax) marinated or pickled salmon, dill flavoured, and usually served with a sweetish mustard sauce

grecque, à la (*Fr*) garnish of (hot) savoury rice and tomato sauce; method of marinating and cooking vegetables (artichokes, mushrooms) in white wine, water, oil, spices and herbs (served cold)

guacamole (*Mex*) a puree of avocado, oil, garlic and hot peppers, served as a dip for raw vegetables or savoury biscuits

hollandaise sauce (*Fr*) an egg, butter and lemon juice sauce

huevos a la flamenca (*Span*) eggs baked on a bed of onions, tomatoes and other vegetables, garnished with chorizo (garlic sausage), ham and pimento

hummus (*Mid East*) (homous) a paste of chick peas, lemon juice, mint, garlic, sesame and olive oil, used as a dip for bread or vegetables

jambalaya (*Amer*) a pilaff (*q.v.*) with ham, shrimps, peppers and spices

Kiev, chicken suprême (*q.v.*) stuffed with garlic butter, crumbed and fried

Kir (*Fr*) (vin blanc cassis) chilled white wine flavoured with blackcurrant liqueur

kofta (*Indo*) meat or vegetable balls, plain or stuffed, served dry or in a curry sauce

korma (*Indo*) mild meat curry, braised in yoghourt or cream (wet)

kromeski (*Rus*) (cromesquis) cutlets made from finely minced meat, deep fried in batter or egg and breadcrumbs

kulfi (*Indo*) ice-cream, often flavoured with pistachios or almonds

lamb Shrewsbury (*Eng*) lamb cutlets with mushrooms and a brown sauce flavoured with Worcestershire sauce and redcurrant jelly

lassi (*Indo*) yoghourt-based drink, either sweet or salt

lobster thermidor (*Fr*) served chopped in a shell, with a béchamel (*q.v.*) and wine sauce, with cheese and crumbs on top

macédoine (*Fr*) mixture of diced fruit or vegetables, the latter often bound with mayonnaise (*q.v.*) or white sauce

madrilène (*Fr*) (consommé or other dish) flavoured with tomato juice

marchand de vin (*Fr*) in a wine sauce

Marengo, poulet (*Fr*) chicken sauté with tomatoes, mushrooms, garlic, eggs and crawfish, finished with brandy

meunière (*Fr*) method of cooking fish, lightly floured, in butter (which is used as a sauce with lemon juice and parsley)

mille-feuille (*Fr*) layers of puff pastry and cream, crème pâtissière (*q.v.*), and/or fruit or jam

monosodium glutamate (MSG) white crystalline food additive, supposedly (but not really) tasteless, which accentuates the flavour of a dish

Montmorency (*Fr*) ingredients or garnish include cherries

Mornay (*Fr*) cheese sauce

moules marinière (*Fr*) mussels cooked in white wine with shallots

moussaka (*Mid East*) layered aubergines or potatoes and minced beef or lamb, with tomato sauce, and béchamel sauce (*q.v.*) or an egg custard on top

nan (*Indo*) bread cooked in a clay oven (see tandoori)

Nantua (*Fr*) sauce made from béchamel (*q.v.*), crawfish puree, cayenne and cream

noisettes (*Fr*) lamb: cutlets from the best end, boned and tied
              veal: miniature escalopes (*q.v.*) (sometimes called médaillons)
              pork: cut from the chump end of the loin, boned

noisette, pommes (*Fr*) garnish of small potato balls, browned in butter

normande (*Fr*) in a fish dish the ingredients include shrimps, mussels, mushrooms; with meat, cider and calvados; with puddings, apples

osso buco (*Ital*) shin of veal, with its marrow, cooked in white wine, tomatoes, garlic, parsley and lemon rind. The Milanese version is served with saffron-flavoured risotto

paella (*Span*) a mixture of fish, shellfish, onions, tomatoes, saffron, garlic, rice, usually chicken or chicken livers, pimento, peas (named after the dish in which it is cooked)

paloise sauce (*Fr*) similar to béarnaise (*q.v.*) with mint instead of tarragon

papillote, en (*Fr*) cooked in a packet of greaseproof paper or foil

Parmentier (*Fr*) ingredients include potatoes

Parmentier, pommes (*Fr*) $\frac{1}{2}''$ cubes of potato, cooked in clarified butter

pavé (*Fr*) (literally paving-stone) cold dish, either savoury (mousse with jelly coating) or sweet (sponge layered and coated with butter cream) made in a square or rectangular mould

Pavlova (*Austral*) a soft meringue case filled with fruit and cream

périgourdine (*Fr*) ingredients include truffles and sometimes pâté

pesto (*Ital*) a sauce for pasta (or other things) made from fresh basil, garlic, Parmesan cheese, pine nuts and olive oil

pilaff (*Fr*) (pilaf, pilau) rice cooked in stock, often flavoured and coloured with saffron, with meat, vegetables or fish added (pulao: Indo)

p'pérade (*Basque*) a mixture of eggs, onions, green peppers and tomatoes, with the texture of scrambled eggs

pistou, soupe au (*Fr*) soup with vegetables and thick vermicelli, flavoured with a liaison of pounded garlic, basil, tomatoes and oil

pitta (*Mid East*) round or oval bread, only slightly leavened, with a pocket in the centre. Served in strips with hummus and taramosalata (*q.v.*) or halved and filled with kebabs and salad

pizzaiola (*Ital*) highly seasoned sauce, with tomatoes and garlic

poivre vert (*Fr*) unripe green peppercorns, softer and with a milder flavour than ripe black or white ones

po.enta (*Ital*) yellow maize flour, boiled, or cooked in other ways

pollo sorpresa (*Ital*) Italian version of chicken Kiev (*q.v.*) (pollo: chicken)

pommes soufflées (*Fr*) thin, square slices of potato, fried in deep fat till partly cooked, removed and plunged into hotter fat so that they puff up

portugaise (*Fr*) ingredients include tomato

profiteroles (*Fr*) little balls of choux paste, usually filled with cream or ice-cream and often served with chocolate sauce, hot or cold

provençale (*Fr*) ingredients include oil, tomatoes and garlic

quenelles (*Fr*) light ovaı dumplings of fish (e.g. 'brochet' – pike), veal or chicken forcemeat, bound with eggs or bread. poached, served with a cream sauce (often sauce Nantua, *q.v.*)

quiche Lorraine (*Fr*) a savoury tart of bacon, cream and eggs

rasgulla (*Indo*) curd cheese balls in rose-water syrup

ratatouille (*Fr*) a stew of aubergines, courgettes, tomatoes, green and red peppers and onions, served hot or cold

rémoulade (*Fr*) mayonnaise sauce with mustard, chopped capers, parsley, herbs, and sometimes gherkins and anchovy essence

rillettes (*Fr*) potted pork, seasoned with herbs or spices

risi e bisi (*Ita·*) green peas and rice, cooked with ham and Parmesan cheese – Venetian dish

rogan gosht (*Indo*) Kashmiri lamb curry, aromatic rather than fiery

rösti (*Sw*) grated potato, mixed with onions and seasoning, and fried as a cake

rouille (*Fr*) creamy sauce, flavoured strongly with garlic and chillies, traditionally served with (or in) fish soups

sabayon (*Fr*) French version of zabaglione (*q.v.*) substitutes white wine for the Marsala, and uses whites as well as yolks of the eggs

salmis (*Fr*) duck or game, roasted, jointed and served in a strongly flavoured sauce made with stock from the carcase. Usually garnished with croûtons

salpicon (*Fr*) (savoury): cubed meats and/or vegetables, bound with a brown or white sauce, used to fill pastry cases, canapés, etc., or to make rissoles or stuffings; (sweet): fresh or candied fruits soaked in liqueur

saltimbocca (*Ital*) 'jump into the mouth', veal escalopes (*q.v.*) cooked with ham, sage and Marsala

sashimi (*Jap*) sliced raw fish (tunny, mackerel, bream, salmon, etc.), served with soy sauce, grated horseradish and sliced ginger

saupiquet (*Fr*) piquant cream sauce served with ham or game

scalopine, scaloppine (*Ital*) escalopes (*q.v.*)

shashlik (*Mid East*) lamb, mushrooms and onions, marinated and grilled on skewers (similar to kebabs)

shrikhand (*Indo*) curd cheese or yoghourt sweet, spiked with lemon and cardamom

smitane (*Fr*) (smetana, Rus) in a sour-cream and onion sauce

smokies (*Scot*) Scottish oak-smoked haddock, traditionally from Arbroath

sorpotel (*Goan*) spicy red curry of pork and other meats

soubise (*Fr*) a puree of onions and either béchamel (*q.v.*) or rice, used as a sauce for mutton or a stuffing for meat

steak Diane (*Fr*) fillet steak often cooked at table, usually with mushrooms, onions, Worcestershire sauce, flamed in brandy

stracciatella (*Ital*) chicken broth into which egg and grated Parmesan have been beaten

suédoise (*Fr*) (sweet): jellied fruit (apricot, plum) puree, usually served with cream or custard; (savoury): mayonnaise with apple puree and scraped horseradish

sugo (di carne) (*Ital*) standard Italian meat and tomato sauce to serve with pasta

sukiyaki (*Jap*) thinly sliced steak cooked at table with soy sauce, green onions, bean curd, transparent noodles, bamboo shoots. Served with a raw egg for dipping

suprême (*Fr*) the breast and wing of chicken (or other bird) removed raw in one piece from the carcase

sushi (*Jap*) morsels of vinegared rice with raw fish, dried kelp or egg, flavoured with ginger and horseradish

syllabub (*Eng*) traditionally made by milking a cow into a pan of white wine, this cold sweet is now usually cream with sugar, lemon, and white wine or sherry added

tandoori chicken (*Indo*) marinated in yoghourt, lemon juice, garlic and spices, cooked in a tandoor (clay oven) or over a charcoal grill

taramosalata (*Gk*) grey mullet roe or smoked cod's roe, pounded to a paste with garlic, lemon juice and olive oil, served with hot toast, or bread (pitta, *q.v.*). It is often 'lightened' with mashed potato, breadcrumbs, cream, or cream cheese

tempura (*Jap*) batter-fried morsels of fish and vegetables

toffee apples (*Pek*) apple segments, cooked in batter, coated with a caramel glaze, plunged into iced water to crisp the glaze

tournedos Rossini (*Fr*) a thick slice of beef fillet, sautéed in butter, topped with pâté, set on a croûte (*q.v.*), and covered with Madeira sauce

Turbigo (*Fr*) (usually fried kidneys) served with mushrooms and chipolatas and a tomato-and-wine sauce

vacherin (*Fr*) rounds of meringue layered with cream, fruit, and sometimes liqueur and ice-cream

vallée d'Auge (*Fr*) ingredients include calvados, apples and cream

veal Cordon Bleu (*Fr*) veal escalopes (*q.v.*), sandwiched with ham and Gruyère cheese, crumbed and fried

Véronique (*Fr*) garnish of white grapes (commonly served with sole or chicken)

vichyssoise (*Amer*) a cream soup made from leeks, potatoes and chicken stock, served hot or cold

vigneronne (*Fr*) ingredients or garnish include grapes

Walewska (*Fr*) garnish of Mornay sauce (*q.v.*), lobster and truffles (for poached fish)

wiener Schnitzel (*Aust*) veal or pork escalopes (*q.v.*), crumbed and fried, served with lemon and (sometimes) anchovies or capers (Schnitzel Holstein has a fried egg on top)

wun-tun (*Canton*) (won ton) thin wrappers of dough ('Chinese ravioli'), filled with minced pork, shrimp, vegetables or dates; served either as dumplings (dim-sum, *q.v.*), in soup, or deep fried

zabaglione (*Ital*) (zabaione) a frothy sweet made from egg yolks, sugar and Marsala, usually served warm

zarzuela (*Span*) mixed fish stew cooked with wine, onions, garlic and tomatoes, served with rice or boiled potatoes

zingara (*Fr*) garnish (usually for escalopes) of ham, tongue, mushrooms and truffles in a demi-glace sauce flavoured with tomato and tarragon

THE GOOD FOOD GUIDE
SECOND DINNER PARTY BOOK

Consumers' Association and
Hodder & Stoughton £5·95

This new hard-back successor to the immensely
popular first *Dinner Party Book* and the *Good
Cook's Guide* (both still available) is again
edited by Hilary Fawcett. It contains 200 recipes
from the chefs of many of the best restaurants
in the *Good Food Guide*, arranged in balanced
seasonal menus with lively introductions
covering different kinds of home entertaining,
useful suggestions for preparing and serving
dishes, and choosing appropriate wines.
Any reader of the *Guide* can expect to find
both dishes and whole meals that suit his or
her taste, technique, pocket, and company.

You can order your copy (or have one sent
direct to your friends) from Consumers'
Association at £5·95 post free. Simply send
your payment to:
The Good Food Club,
Caxton Hill,
Hertford SG13 8BR.

ENGLAND

AISLABY North Yorkshire   Map 8

Blacksmith's Arms
2 m NW of Pickering
on A170
Pickering (0751) 72182

Closed Tue; Dec 25 D
Must book D
Meals 12–2, 7.30–9.30

Alc £4·85 (meal £7·50)

Children's helpings
Seats 50 (parties 15)
 [&] rest
Car park
No dogs

William Murray's first entry (a short one) last year has brought admirers for what he attempts, often with success, and critics of faults he cannot yet control. The Tudor inn and quondam *blacksmith's forge have been ingeniously converted, even if the privies are still a stride away, and Mr Murray cooks well in both English and French regional styles. He commends his own smoked sausage with horseradish cream, local trout with juniper, and tranche d'agneau à la poitevine; an inspector and others add coquilles St Jacques en brioche (60p – 'a modest price indeed for a crisp and light shell and a creamy Mornay sauce'), rabbit pie, 'a giant of a lemon sole, fresh and delicious', and enterprising vegetables including 'excellent batter-fried cauliflower'. Praise is due for the vegetarian main dishes too. 'Sweets have a strong bias towards pancakes.' But ris de veau aux champignons (£3·60) at a test meal was only so-so, and ratatouille very poor. Several other reports stress 'inept service' which left cream and 'gruesome cheese packets' sitting in a hot sun by the window. (Rooms may, in fact, be too cold or too hot according to season.) A modest wine list (from £2·40) offers Côtes de Provence red at £3·40 and sweet white Monbazillac at £3·35. Recorded music. More reports, please.*

ALDERLEY EDGE Cheshire   Map 5

Le Rabelais
75 London Road
Alderley Edge (0625)
584848

Closed Sun; Sat L;
Aug 18–Sept 14; Dec 24
& 25; L public hols
Must book D
Meals 12–1.45, 7–11

Alc £6·50 (meal £10·15)

Service inc
Seats 45
No dogs
Access, Diners

A good many people have visited Patrick and Sally Guilbaud's 'unusually kind and welcoming' restaurant since last year's provisional entry, and this is just as well, for experience of it has been markedly uneven, sometimes within the same meal. An August inspector, for instance, reports good mussel soup, creamed turnips, and superb cheeses in fine condition (a cheese buyer adds he had to look some of them up when he got home); but indifferent meat, chipple-like chips, and some over-zealous scorching under the grill. Most – not all – visitors have done much better than this, reporting excellent seafood pancakes, coquilles St Jacques, 'steaks with fine sauces', veal en croûte with well-cooked spinach, and good fruit tarts on the sweets trolley. From time to time – perhaps during December – they may decide to offer a set lunch, and it proved good value when an inspector met it. Coffee is good. Provencal wines are under £5, and there are some fine ones too: Ch. Boyd-Cantenac '73, £9·45 in 1979, well served. 'Rather relentless' recorded music.

App: David Brickhill, Mrs P. M. Waldron, Shelagh Coleman, S. & A.G.

129

Johnnie Gurkhas Nepalese Cuisine
54 Station Road
Aldershot (0252) 27736

In a development Kipling never envisaged, 'Nepalese atmosphere and Nepalese cuisine' are delivered all the way to Aldershot by an ex-Gurkha engineer, Hari Karki, despite a menu and wine list ranging from avocado prawns and chicken Maryland to ouzo and Bulls Blood. Bypass this for the subtly spiced Nepalese dishes: lamb or chicken curry (£1·15), Gurkhali chicken chilli (£1·45), aloo tama (potato and bamboo shoots, £1·15), aloo til ko achar (pickled potatoes, 50p), tori ko gundruk ('typical Sherpa dried vegetable dish', £1·15) with Himalayan roti or samosas. Tandoori dishes too, and hotter ones if you wish (Madras, vindaloo). Helpful service, but as dishes are cooked to order, expect a wait. Drink lager or Notre Dame house wine at £3·15 for 'slightly less than a litre'. Recorded Nepalese music. More reports, please.

Closed L Dec 24 & 25
Must book D & weekends
Meals 12–2.45, 5.30–11.45

Alc (min £2) £3·55
(meal £4·75)

Seats 36 (parties 10)

♿ rest (1 step)
No dogs
Access, Am Ex, Barclay, Diners, Euro

Plough Inn
off A1079
Pocklington (075 92) 2349

New owners of this 'typical country pub' are reaping good-will after dinners of 'delicate salmon mousse', tasty lasagne, 'prime' steaks (£4·80 for fillet), sole in puff pastry with a mushroom and wine sauce, and carefully cooked vegetables. Sweets are less exciting. The young chef, from the Ilkley Box Tree (q.v.) offers simple Yorkshire puddings in onion gravy (70p) as well as gratin of smoked haddock in parsley and Pernod sauce (£1·30) and grilled liver with bacon and orange (£3·60). Lunchtime bar snacks include soups, pâté, lasagne and oxtail, sandwiches and sweets. Theakston's, Scottish & Newcastle, Younger's and Tetley's ales (pump). Various wines, from £3. 'Unobtrusive service.' Children under ten are charged half-price. Some tables on the front lawn. More reports, please.

Closed Mon (exc public hols & Apr 7 L);
Sun D (exc Apr 6)
Must book D & weekends
Meals 11.30–2, 7.15–10

Alc £6·30 (meal £8·85)

Children's helpings (under 10)

Seats 30
♿ rest
Car park
No dogs

The Guide News Supplement will be sent out as usual, in June, to everyone who buys the book directly from Consumers' Association and to all bookshop purchasers who return the card interleaved with their copy. Let us know of any changes that affect entries in the book, or of any new places you think should be looked at.

Wine prices shown are for a 'standard' bottle of the wine concerned, unless another measure is stated (e.g. litre, 50 cl., or pint).

ALRESFORD Hampshire   Map 2

O'Rorkes

34 Pound Hill
on A31
W of New Alresford
Square
Alresford (096 273) 2293

Closed Sun; last week
July; 1st week Aug;
Dec 25 & 26
Must book D
Meals 12–2, 7–9.30

Tdh D £9·50 (meal £12·05)

Alc L £5 (meal £7·35)

Seats 72
Car park
Access, Barclay

After 15 years' successive *Guide* entries, Brian
O'Rorke's civilised little restaurant, still with Michael
Harvey in the kitchen, has outlasted every other
serious place in its catchment area. 'Long life to them,'
somebody says. Habit or customers do not allow
them to depart very far from the favourite crespolini,
pike quenelles in shellfish sauce, guinea-fowl, pommes
dauphine and ratatouille or red cabbage. But
weatherbeaten members and inspectors who tasted
these things in 1979 report 'expert technique and a
sensitive balance of flavours, indeed, a well-balanced
set meal as a whole.' Smoked haddock mousse with a
dash of Pernod is another good first course, and the
guinea-fowl comes in at least two ways, with apple
and cream, or 'with salt pork, not bacon, and a real
red wine sauce.' Some of the more straightforward
meat dishes may disappoint on occasion. 'Rich but
light' chocolate mousse, and 'a French apple tart with
crisp pastry and a nice orange taste to the glaze'
make good sweets; 'coffee was freshly ground and
properly made.' Sometimes people feel starved by the
waitresses of the house's own sourdough bread. The
Berry Bros wines are well chosen and fairly priced –
'even the house ones', not listed to us this time, 'have
real character'. 'Chianti Classico '74 was in tip-top
condition' and 'it was a great treat to find two half-
bottles of good burgundy, Montagny '75 and Santenay
les Gravières '70, for under £6 the pair in 1979.' 'A
black mark for drawing the cork before presentation.'
Light lunches can be had à la carte, outside in fine
weather, and a fuller *carte* is planned when they open
a new extension in the spring – reports welcome.

*App: Stephen Coverly, G. B. Jackson, D. J. Ely,
R. F. Maddock, C.P.D., K. B. Bushen, and others*

ALSTON Cumbria   Map 8

High Fell
on A686
1½ m S of Alston
Alston (049 83) 597

Bet-hedging last year brings fair support for this snugly
converted 17th-century farmhouse. The French cuisine
the Chipmans desire sometimes falters, but from the
short à la carte menu people like duckling with plum
sauce (£5·60, including vegetables) and boeuf
Stroganoff. Home-grown vegetables, perhaps
courgettes with almonds, or carrots with fennel, win
praise all round. Peaches in brandy and grenadine or a
proper sherry trifle afterwards. Small, frequently
changing wine list. 'An agreeable overnight stay.'
'Light' music. No dogs.

Closed Jan
Must book
Meals 12.30–2, 7.30–9.30

Alc £7·05 (meal £11·55)

Children's helpings
Seats 20

Car park
7 rooms (2 with bath,
1 with shower)
B&B from £6·90

Apple Pie Eating House
Rydal Road
Ambleside (096 63) 3679

'Pub-section food really, with the scrum but without the licence.' Still, the summer queue forms because few pubs bake so well or charge so little for 'egg-custardy' quiche, 'apple pie with light pastry and real fruit', cheesecake, Chorley cake, various breads, biscuits and sandwiches, eaten on the spot or taken away up a fell. Coffee and tea, also both real.

Closed Nov–Easter
No bookings
Open 9–5.30

Alc L £2·05 (meal £2·30)

Service inc

Seats 60 (parties 30)
Unlicensed

Harvest
Compston Road
Ambleside (096 63) 3151

Strictly for vegetarians and non-smokers, perhaps, not to mention non-drinkers, but within these limitations tourists and inspectors have been pleased to find 'colourful salads' and 'beige but well-flavoured soups', and casseroles (chick pea, onion and aubergine, with brown rice, £1·35, including salad) in a mirrored, comfortable room. Fruit snow, damson crumble and other sweets 50p. Juices and coffee. Details approximate.

Open 10.30–8

Alc £2·70 (meal £3·25)

Seats 50
Unlicensed

Rothay Manor

Rothay Bridge
Ambleside (096 63) 3605

Closed Jan; Feb
Must book D & Sun L
Meals 12.30–2,
HT 3–5.30, 7.30–9

Tdh L £3·50 (meal £5·75),
D £10 (meal £12·90)

Children's helpings
Seats 45
♻ rest; w.c.
Air-conditioning
Car park
No dogs in public rooms
Am Ex, Diners
12 rooms (all with bath)
B&B £17·50–£25
D, B&B £27·50–£35
Fire cert

There is often a faint touch of forbearance in members' accounts of Bronwen Nixon's secluded (though traffic-girt) Georgian house and garden, as though affection outruns expectation and performance. Well, there are better tables in the Lakes, but they are not found in Ambleside or Langdale, and the subdued elegance of the dining-room here, along with the substantial breakfasts, the buffet lunches (which can be eaten in the garden) and the considerate if prentice staff, make the Manor a pleasant place to stay. Though they won a national competition for afternoon teas in 1979, they sometimes underbake their own bread and croissants. Soups are made with good ingredients; creamy pâtés and salady first courses are also praised. For main course, roasts and their gravies are less successful than meat that has been braised or casseroled in the first place, but note the mention of venison in red wine and herbs, duck strasbourgeoise, and guinea-fowl. Mushroom brioche and rolled brisket of beef with dumplings are other specialities. Char as well as trout are served on occasion. Mrs Nixon and her helper Jane Binns put effort into the sweets, and 'this place has become my standard for Sachertorte.' Butterscotch custard and Norwegian pudding are other good examples, but one guest calls grape brûlée 'watery'. Wines begin with Sidi Larbi at £1·75 for 50 cl, and they allow you to drink half a bottle of most things at ⅗ of the bottle price.

The list is strong in most departments, especially hock and claret if the items on the remnants list are included. Ch. Giscours '66, c.b., at £12·85 and Erbacher Michelmark Riesling Spätlese '71 at £6·90 are fair examples. Pressurised beer. No smoking in the restaurant. No children under five. (GHG)

Recipe in *Second Dinner Party Book:* Old English brisket with dumplings

App: Elizabeth Lever, Pamela Votier, C.G., Roy Mathias, R. J. & N. E. Stone, M. E. Cohen, F.K., C.L.C., and others

---

Sheila's Cottage
The Slack
Ambleside (096 63) 3079

Stewart Greaves and his cook Miss Wainwright close in the evening now to perfect their useful, simple English lunches; try the Scotch broth, quiche, cheeses and their oven-to-table Swiss raclette dish with mushroom cream sauce on a rye bread base (£2). Pastry, salads, sticky toffee pudding (60p), local nut and raisin tart, and less local engadiner Nusstorte are also popular. Tea or coffee (not served without food over the lunch period). You pay £1 a bottle corkage to bring your own wine or have it sent out for. Two non-smoking tables. Recorded classical music.

Closed D; Sun; Dec 25 & 26; Jan 1 Open 10–6 (L 12–2.30)	Alc L £3·15 (meal £3·80) Children's helpings (under 10)	Seats 40 No dogs Unlicensed

---

AMPNEY CRUCIS Gloucestershire Map 2

Crown of Crucis
on A417
3 m N of Cirencester
Poulton (028 585) 403

The Bamfords now run Nicholas Cripps's revived and smartened 15th-century inn. Over-thick sauces and a 'lurid, granular nursery trifle' marred a test meal, but Mrs Bamford's other instincts are more promising, to judge by good coarse pâté, crab mayonnaise, steak with Stilton, Cotswold beef (£4·45), salads, vegetables, oranges in Grand Marnier, and coffee. Sunday lunch is a traditional roast. There are bar snacks on the (also smart) pub side, and Courage or Arkell's bitters in cask. Saccone & Speed wines from £3 or so. No children under five. 'A minstrels' gallery but electronic minstrels, alas.' More reports, please.

Closed L (exc Sun); Wed; Apr 6 L; Dec 25 Must book D & weekends Meals 1 (Sun), 7.30–9	Tdh Sun L £4 (meal £6·65) Alc £7 (meal £9·95) Service 10%	Seats 60 (parties 30) ♿ rest; w.c. Car park No dogs in d/r

---

See p. 508 for the restaurant-goer's legal rights, and p. 510 for information on hygiene in restaurants.

Most places will accept cheques only when they are accompanied by a cheque card or adequate identification. Information about which credit cards are accepted is correct when printed, but restaurants may add to or subtract from the list without notice.

The Cottage
Bakewell (062 981) 2488

Closed Tue; Dec 25
Must book
Meals 1, 8

Tdh L £4 (meal £7),
D £5·50 (meal £8·70)

Seats 16
♿ rest (1 step); w.c.

'Why isn't there a whole Cottage industry', wonders one visitor, 'now that Mrs Rhodes has shown how the limitations of space and staff can be turned to advantage by a civilised woman who concentrates on doing a few dishes really well?' This sums up what the place is about, and the space problem explains, perhaps, why prams as well as dogs are turned away. The sample menus Mrs Rhodes sends are simple: for lunch, 'freshly juiced oranges', moussaka, and mince tart; for dinner, lentil roast with tomato sauce, soup, quail stuffed with minced steak accompanied by wine sauce, cabbage with herb butter, and garlic potatoes. But there is variety within this formula – 'we had excellent blinis with mackerel mousse, artichoke soup, and stuffed boned chicken.' You may choose to drink from a glass rather than from the pewter wine goblets. Wines are few, but Portuguese Dão Reserva was £4·05 in 1979. 'The lighting is rather dim.'

App: P. M. Reeve, T. J. David, C. E. Wilkinson

The Lornies
on A24
10 m N of Worthing
Ashington (0903) 892575

Closed L (exc by
arrangement); Sun; Mon;
public hols (exc Apr 4)
Must book
D only, 7.15–9.15

Alc £6·25 (meal £9·60)

Seats 20
♿ rest (1 step)
Am Ex card
1 suite (with bath)
D, B&B £45 (for 2 people)

The old brick, wood and stone of the Lornies' 16th-century farmhouse is allowed to speak for itself. It is an extension of home for many regulars when they decide that they do not fancy cooking that night, for they can depend on Gillies Lornie's seafood Saratoga (sole, scampi, scallops, prawns, onions and mushrooms in cream sauce, £4·80, including generally admirable fresh vegetables), or breaded lamb cutlets, or fillet of beef with madeira sauce. The short à la carte menu has changed little these ten years, and sweets, like first courses, are conventional enough (though the soup is home-made, even if the sorbet is not). Coffee might be stronger. A short Berry Bros wine list begins at £4. 'A light on the cobbled forecourt would encourage elderly visitors.' Smaller helpings for children. No dogs. Car park.

App: Angus Wells, A.F., R. & J.H.

Entries for places with distinctions carry symbols (pestle, tureen, bottle, glass). Credits are fully written entries, with approvers' names below the text. Passes are telegraphic entries (useful in the area) with details under the text. Provisional entries are in italics (see 'How to use the Guide', p. 4).

Since each restaurant has a separate file in the Guide office, please use a separate form or sheet of paper for each report. Additional forms may be obtained free (no stamp required) from The Good Food Guide, Freepost, 14 Buckingham Street, London WC2N 6BR (unfortunately Freepost facilities are not available outside the United Kingdom).

AUSTWICK North Yorkshire Map 8

Game Cock Inn
½ m off A65
17 m E of Lancaster
Clapham (046 85) 226

Members know what to expect from this tiny inn lying on the Craven Fault ('well known to geologists'). Nothing earth-shattering, but ramblers and potholers have found few fissures in steak, chicken, trout, and crispy duck in orange sauce ('a revelation'). Soups, though, suggest opened tins rather than opened heavens. Generous breakfasts; packed lunches only fair. Good simple bar food (not on Sundays). Yates & Jackson beer (electric pump) and basic wines. Service friendly but rushed (note the two sittings in summer and at weekends).

Closed Dec 24–26 & 31; Jan 1	Tdh L from £3·20 (meal £5·20), D from £5·75 (meal £8)	Car park
Must book		No dogs in d/r
Meals 12.30–1.30,		Barclaycard
7 & 8.30 (Fri, Sat & summer), 7–7.30 (Sun & winter)	Children's helpings	3 rooms
	Seats 24 (parties 10)	B&B £8·50–£9·50
	⅙ rest	D, B&B £14·50–£15·50
		Fire cert

BANBURY Oxfordshire Map 2

Peppermill
11 South Bar
Banbury (0295) 3610

Closed Sun; Sat L;
Dec 25 & 26; Jan 1
Must book
Meals 12–2, 6.30–10.30

Tdh L from £2 (meal £4·65)
Alc £5·45 (meal £8)

Children's helpings
Seats 32
⅙ rest; w.c.

It seems churlish to grumble when last year's entry should have had a lunchtime value underlining, and when the dinners in Peter and Denise Smith's unaffected restaurant by Banbury Cross also remain modest in price. But in March two midday visitors thought that at so low a figure the choice given was the enemy of quality, when 'better tasting and timing would have made a cheap meal into a good one.' Happily, later visitors found much to praise: at both meals, carefully made Melba toast; at lunch, improved soup, good chips, and sound roast beef, if 'rather stodgy' Yorkshire pudding; at dinner, the pâté, or smoked mackerel with shallots and cream (£1·05), scampi with avocado and mushrooms, garlicky chicken Kiev, and courgettes in batter. Mr Smith's own favourites include salmi of duck with grapes (£4·10, with vegetables), daube of lamb, and sometimes fresh salmon trout or roast pheasant in port and cream. Planter's ice-box cake, raspberry fool cake, and orange chocolate mousse are perhaps the best sweets. French table wine is £2·85 and there are about thirty others, rising to '70 clarets or Vosne-Romanée '70 at £8 or so. Smoke tends to drift through the trellis from the bar into the restaurant. Recorded music, but 'not at disco volume.'

App: J. Hardwick, L.A., M.P.D.

BANBURY see also pub section

Chez Maurice
on A30
5½ m W of Salisbury
Wilton (072 274) 2240

Closed L (exc Dec 25);
Apr 5 & 7; Dec 24 & 25;
Jan 1
Must book
D only, 7–9.30

Tdh from £6·50 (meal
£9·60)
Alc (min £3·60) £6·60
(meal £9·45)

Service 10%
Seats 40 (parties 16)
⟨ᕱ⟩ rest; w.c.
Car park
No dogs
Barclay, Diners

Gastronomically speaking, there is less temptation now
to linger over meals in Salisbury, and better cause to
try the Ricauds' conscientious, modern-style family
restaurant, which is poised on the first dog-leg turn
you meet after Wilton as you drive west on the A30.
Whether eating table d'hôte or à la carte, visitors
express great pleasure in Maurice Ricaud's crab soup,
potage, quenelles, caneton braisé au miel, and
accurately cooked entrecôte, either marchand de vin
or Mirabeau. There are August reports of boring hors
d'oeuvre and flabby duck, but both ratatouille and
raspberry ice-cream, others say, are far above the
West Country norm, and the bread rolls are made on
the premises. 'Chocolate mousse was the dense, dark
kind with some brandy in it.' Maurice's English wife
and their children do most of the service. The
house wines are Granvillons at £3·60 a litre; Edelzwicker
'76 is £4·80, and Ch. Doisy-Daëne Sec '77, a dry
version of the better-known Barsac, is £5·50. No
children under eight.

*App: J. R. Michaelis, R. T. Davies, N.R.H., C.P.D.,
Arden Winch, and others*

Blagraves House
The Bank
Teesdale (0833) 37668

Closed L; Sun;
Dec 24–26; Jan 1
Must book
D only, 7.30–9.15

Tdh from £6·90
(meal £9·65)

Seats 35 (parties 12)
No dogs
Barclaycard

The Davidsons' remarkable bow-windowed
Elizabethan house spent much of 1979 under the
restorers' scaffolding, but Josephine Davidson and
Paul Brodie have been working hard too. The dinner
menu is 'short but rich'; however, one Londoner was
much taken with his terrine of chicken with
Cumberland sauce, and very fresh baked trout with
cucumber sauce. Others report equally gratifying
smoked salmon mousse, 'light and delicate', and ham
and asparagus quiche. Carbonnade of beef with green
peppercorn sauce, accompanied by 'crunchy' mange-
tout peas and broccoli, or 'succulent' loin of lamb
with rosemary, served with aubergines, maintain this
promise, and sweets may include a period 'walnut
pye' to match the house. Wines begin at £3·75 for
Litre Vin, and are quite stiffly marked up, with red
Rioja '73 over £5, and Gewürztraminer '77 nearly £7
in 1979. Dessert Tokay may be had by the glass.

App: C. Lorenz, M. D. Watson, D. G. Foot

**Prices of meals underlined are those which we consider represent unusual value for
money. They are not necessarily the cheapest places in the Guide, or in the locality.**

Inspections are carried out anonymously. Persons who pretend to be able to secure,
arrange or prevent an entry in the Guide are impostors and their names or
descriptions should be reported to us.

BARNSTAPLE Devon   Map 1

Lynwood House
on A377
Barnstaple (0271) 3695

Closed Sun; Sat L; middle
2 weeks Nov; Dec 31 L;
1st week Jan; public hols
(exc Dec 26)
Must book
Meals 12–1.45, 7–9.30

Alc £7·40 (meal £10·90)

Children's helpings
Seats 50 (parties 20)
⟨&⟩ rest; w.c.
Car park
No dogs
Access, Am Ex, Barclay,
Diners

John and Ruth Roberts specialise – though not
exclusively – in fish at these invitingly set green and
gold rooms. Though more reports from the latter end
of the season would have been a help, early summer
visitors sound well content with their platters of cold
fish, the four pâtés ('the two best were of smoked fish,
and blue cheese') and pot of scallops, scampi, prawns,
crab, sole and so on, in wine sauce, at £5·25
(vegetables included). 'Between courses we were
given, unasked, a wisp of lemon sorbet "to cleanse
your palates".' Meat-eaters are equally pleased with
duckling in brandy and orange sauce, pork tenderloin
with mushrooms, jacket or garlic potatoes, 'delicious
stuffed tomatoes', and 'an unusual swede soufflé which
was superb.' Profiteroles, hazelnut mousse, grapefruit
in grenadine and other sweets are praised. French
table wine is £4·80 a litre and Ch. Malartic-Lagravière
'73, c.b., was £7·95 in 1979. Recorded music.

App: H. Machin, S.A., A. M. Carey

BASLOW Derbyshire   Map 5

Cavendish Hotel
on A619
3 m NE of Bakewell
Baslow (024 688) 2311

Must book D
Meals 12.30–2, 7–10

Tdh £5·20 (meal £7·90)
Alc £8·05 (meal £11·60)

Children's helpings
Seats 50 (parties 10)
⟨&⟩ rest
Car park
No dogs
Am Ex, Barclay
13 rooms (all with bath
& shower)
Room only, from £14·50
Breakfast from £2·50
Fire cert

One worries slightly about Eric Marsh, a hotelier
whose PR material devotes more lines to his own
pedigree than to his inn's. But lineage matters on the
Chatsworth estate, which has put money – and good
taste – into the refurbishment of an old stone building.
The service is normally smooth, and Nicholas
Buckingham's meals begin well with home-made bread
rolls. (They end equally well with plunger coffee pots
for each table.) In between, there are good ideas,
mostly well executed, from seafood Lido di Roma
(£2·55) to English oxtail with dumplings (£3·15). Fish
soup was watery when tried, but a trout stuffed with
seafood 'tasted delicious itself and included enough
prawns and mussels for a separate course.'
'Decapitation is preferred so that the diner is not
stared at reproachfully between mouthfuls': true
fish-lovers cope with this by attacking the head first.
Lamb's kidney vol-au-vent, and chicken Marie Louise
are also praised, but vegetables are less reliable and
sweets, say some, 'commonplace': 'a thick, bland,
tasteless, chocolate mousse' at a test meal. There are
useful bar snacks at lunch-time with Stones' bitter
on hand-pump. Carafino is £1·45 for 25 cl, but there
are also serious red wines, such as Savigny-les-Beaune
aux Guettes '76 at £10·75 (probably with many years
still ahead of it), and Ch. Cos d'Estournel '70 at
£14·40. Dress neatly. (GHG)

*App: Denis Tate, A. M. & H. Fessler, Nicholas Howell,
F. Joan Heyman, N. V. Crookdake, and others*

The Laden Table
7 Edgar Buildings,
George Street
Bath (0225) 64356

Closed Sun; Mon; Sat L;
public hols
Must book
Meals 12.30–1.30, 7.30–9

Tdh D from £7·50
(meal £10·85)
Alc (min £4·20) £7·50
(meal £10·85)

Seats 20
Access, Barclay

Tony Gulliford has gone rather silent lately in these Georgian rooms, and he has never had the flamboyance of George Perry-Smith, who taught him much of his craft. The result is 'a peaceful evening, with limited choice', but 'the menu had been compiled with obvious care and regard to food in season. The saucing and seasoning of our veal with white wine and tomatoes, noisettes of pork with red wine and cheese, and jugged hare, were of "pestle" quality, and the vegetables were admirably cooked too.' Sardines followed by guinea-fowl is another popular order, and for a finish, almond tart or strawberry pot de crème. Coffee is praised, but the Averys wines are – considering the source – unremarkable. No children under 14. No jeans; no pipes; no dogs. More reports, please, since the Bath scene sounded distinctly unstable at the time of writing. Details are for 1979.

Popjoy's
Beau Nash House,
Sawclose
Bath (0225) 60494

Closed L (Oct–Mar);
Sun; Mon L; public hols
(exc Apr 4, May 5,
D May 26 & Aug 25);
3 weeks Chr
Must book D
Meals 12–2, 6.45–10.30

Alc £12 (meal £14·80)

Service inc
Seats 30 (parties 30)
[&] rest
No dogs
Access, Am Ex, Euro

Recipe in *Second Dinner Party Book:* Provencal fish soup

The first-floor salon where Beau Nash used to hold court is confined to private functions now, so you assemble in the faintly clinical basement and eat at ground level in an elegant, 'sometimes dilatory' atmosphere. Stephen Ross, like his co-owner Kenneth Bell (of Thornbury Castle, *q.v.*), does his own cooking, and inventive successes include avocado mousse in glazed puff pastry (£2·10), and terrine of sole and salmon with a herb mayonnaise, £3. 'How can anyone refuse a second helping of the fish soup?' But the autumn brought two separate grumbles of heavy and over-buttered oeuf bénédictine (£1·75) and in one of Mr Ross's doubtless infrequent absences 'anyone fit to be left in charge of a £6·50 main course ought to make a better mint and onion puree for lamb, and know how to take the bitterness out of courgettes.' Poulet vallée d'Auge is a reliable main course speciality, though you may find it on the sweet side, as though local cider rather than alien calvados had gone to its making. Chicken in Pernod is another possibility. Gratin dauphinoise potatoes are routinely offered, and even at their best should be received warily if you contemplate one of the house's ice-creams ('try the Beaumes de Venise one') or the walnut tart with lemon cream, a recent idea (£1·50). The wines are first-rate, including the five house ones, four of them under £5, while well into double figures there are Chablis Fourchaume '76, fine '71 Germans, or 'really classy' Ch. Léoville-Lascases or Ch. Cantenac-Brown, both '70. But by popular request 'the glass symbol should vanish while parties are allowed to smoke cigars and cigarettes both on entering and between courses.'

App: R. P. B. Browne, John Wilkes, Walter Voyle, B. Marder, J.R.

Priory Hotel
Weston Road
Bath (0225) 331922

Closed Dec 24–26 & 31;
Jan 1
Must book D & Sun L
Meals 12.30–1.30,
7.30–9.30

Tdh L from £3·45
(meal £6), D from £9·80
(meal £12·35)

Service inc
Seats 40 (parties 25)
⌷ rest
Car park
No dogs
15 rooms (14 with bath,
1 with shower)
B&B from £21
Fire cert

It is good to see a long-admired hotel, dropped as is our custom when the owners changed, re-emerge with the esteem one expects with an experienced London manager (John Donnithorne), and a chef who has learnt some of his craft from the Roux brothers. The Georgian house and cedared garden on the outskirts of Bath are still, as a Wagnerian visitor puts it, a *Gesamtkunstwerk*, 'a total decorative experience, rounded off by dauntingly rich cooking for, well, the dauntingly rich.' That self-indulgent phrase is propped up by another man whom circumstances obliged to stay three weeks, and who was 'reduced to visiting simpler places like Popjoys (*q.v.*) for the sake of my waistline.' This said, a test meal included 'magically light and piquant spinach roulade, a masterly sole soufflé, gratin dauphinoise potatoes for once made both correctly and freshly', and – for those who enjoy the *frisson* – 'erotic négresse en chemise.' Little room was left for improvement, unless it were in the coffee. Robert Harrison's other specialities include terrine of scallops with beurre blanc sauce, and filet mignon of veal with chicken soufflé and madeira sauce. Lunch is a merciful buffet. The wines, from £4·15, are moderately priced for a place of this kind: Winkeler Hasensprung Riesling Auslese '76, £8·85; Ch. Gruaud-Larose '71, £11·95. No children under ten. No pipes or cigars in the dining-room. A credit entry is earned, but reports of the régime's maturing will be very welcome. (GHG)

App: Anthony Miller, A. E. Key, B.M., I.C.F., and others

Sweeney Todds
15 Milsom Street
Bath (0225) 62368

'Demotic rather than demonic' is one comment on this 'gutted hangar populated by the Armies of the Night.' Others find it a straightforward pizza bar, with ten ways of topping the crisp but not tough bases: praise for the Flame-Thrower (chillies, peperoni and pimento), the Vegetarian (green pepper, mushroom, onion and olives) – both pizzas are £1·75 in Neapolitan and £2·15 in Sicilian styles. Al Capone ('the works') is £2·90. Burgers, salads, stuffed potatoes and sweets are listed too (including a banana 'splint' should you need propping up, £1·25). Cocktails vie with the house French wine (£2·65 for 70 cl). 'Various' recorded music. More reports, please, on this and other bullets in the clip (see also under Oxford).

Closed Dec 24–26 & 31;
Jan 1
Open noon–midnight

Service 10%
(parties of 8 or more)
Seats 100

⌷ rest
Access, Barclay

Alc (min 90p) £3·85
(meal £6)

Unless otherwise stated, a restaurant is open all week and all year and is licensed.

Woods
9–13 Alfred Street
Bath (0225) 314812

Closed Sun; Mon
Must book D
Meals 12–2, 7–10

Tdh from £3·20
(meal from £6·10)
Alc (min L 85p, D £2)
£4·20 (meal £7·20)

Children's helpings
Seats 80 (parties 25)
⑤ rest (2 steps)
No dogs
Access, Am Ex, Barclay

All roads lead to Bath, it seems, for Cotswold and western caterers: Hugh Corbett from Broadway has now moved out of this elegant Georgian shop-window opposite the Assembly Rooms, and David Price from Rafters in Stow-on-the-Wold (q.v.) has moved in. It is very early days, and the first inspector found the food 'inventive but without an idiom of its own.' However, he was grateful for 'sweet and firm noisettes of lamb in thin gravy, not goo,' and 'innocently voluptuous chocolate fudge cake – a Pretty Baby pudding.' Others have already noticed tempting crudités 'as if from a kitchen garden' and 'pink, succulent' roast lamb. There are three set menus at different prices, and interchange with the competitively priced carte is possible. Main courses come with potatoes and salad. Note the low lunchtime minimum charge, and also the dishes Sharon Robinson, the cook, likes: smokies, sauté of chicken with cheese and onion, vegetarian dishes (£2) and bread-and-butter pudding. Snacks too, with pressurised beers. Basic French wines are £4·20 a litre and there are twenty others, some by the glass. Recorded music. 'No babies.' More reports, please.

BATH see also pub and wine bar sections

Pickwick's
The Square
Beaminster (0308) 862094

Closed L; Sun; Mon;
Dec 24 & 25
Must book
D only, 7.30–9.30

Tdh £8·25 (meal £10·85)

Service inc
Children's helpings
Seats 36
⑤ rest
Air-conditioning
No dogs
Access, Barclay

What with his penchant for game-shooting and the incandescent curries in which he indulges from time to time, Bill Mulligan seems to be reliving *Plain Tales from the Raj* down in this quiet corner of Dorset. Well, *Pickwick* itself was printed and published in Calcutta in serial form within a year of its appearance in England, and no doubt there are old India hands among the admirers of this mullioned restaurant with its skimpy bar – 'skimpy Dubonnets too,' says one visitor – but leisurely sittings at table over an enterprising short menu. Mildly curried prawns or kidneys make good first courses, 'pheasant was superb', and quails stuffed with grapes and served with harvest sauce, whatever that may be, are also popular. There is a choice of aïoli or mint and onion sauce to have with noisettes of lamb, and main courses come with salad or vegetables (now more lightly cooked). They keep a good Brie, and Jill Mulligan's strawberry shortcake and other cold sweets are also admired. Wine prices are mildly eccentric, with named clarets and sound red or white Hermitage little dearer than Lambrusco, which is more of a wink than a wine, but will cost you £5·10 here. They discourage smoking, mildly.

App: Lucia Ransom, Norman Hand, Charles Shepherd

BEESTON Cheshire   Map 5

Wild Boar Motor Lodge
L'Apéritif Restaurant
on A49
S of Beeston station
Bunbury (0829) 260309

Closed Sun D
Must book D & Sun L
Meals till 2.30, 7–9.30

Tdh L £5·65 (meal £10·05)
Alc (min £9) £9·35
(meal £13·70)

Service inc
Cover 60p
Seats 100 (parties 50)
Car park
Access, Am Ex, Barclay,
Diners
30 rooms (all with bath)
Room only, about £13
Breakfast from £1·50

As most readers know by now, this Tudor fastness under its aging king, Mr R. I. Roberts, has been at odds with the *Guide* and from time to time with otherwise inoffensive customers since – it sometimes feels – the Wars of the Roses. It survives here because if you can pay the price and avoid the huff and puff – and this year's inspectors were treated with unfailing politeness by both owner and staff – the food is as good as any in the county: 'a smooth but not bland pâté based on chicken livers, with Melba toast and unsalted Normandy butter; superlative bass (£3·10 as a first course, £6 or so as a main), delicate but firm, with a tarragon-flavoured Mornay sauce; true red wine sauce for entrecôte; and good suprême de volaille Marengo, if you like this dish that – *pace* Napoleon's chef – lacks a co-ordinating principle.' There are oddities like 'curry in the French dressing' and the service of potatoes with a dish that already has rice, but grapes or radishes on ice, and good coffee in plentiful quantities, reveal a better sense of detail. The Cheshire cheese and cream are also very fine: the former makes the set meal worth while. 'Crème brûlée had been properly made with egg yolks, not whole eggs.' The house white Alsace at £5·80 is sound, and the list is formidable in both length and price, though bargains can be found here and there: one visitor reports a half-bottle of Chambolle-Musigny '62 'mellow but still alive' at £4·80. Recorded music. Wear a tie. The attached Huntsman Grill is useful for quicker meals or when the restaurant is shut, since it also uses good materials.

App: A.G.S., Henry Bosworth, Richard Field

BELPER Derbyshire   Map 5

Rémy's
84 Bridge Street
Belper (077 382) 2246

Closed Sun; Sat L;
public hols (exc Apr 4)
Must book
Meals 12.30–2, 7.30–10

Alc £8·30 (meal £11·50)

Service 10%
Seats 45
Air-conditioning
No dogs
Am Ex, Euro

Lord George-Brown failed to ignite Francophile passions in Belper when he sat for the town, but Rémy Bopp has lately galloped into the old Chevin House with three French chefs ominously described as 'changed every eleven months'. The table settings and the little touches – like writing the customer's name on the pastry enclosing slices of lamb – are more remarkable than the lamb itself, an inspector thinks, and besides, rillettes were dry, and onion soup insipid. Still, Bopp's bonshommes have also produced promising boeuf Stroganoff, and good sauces for venison, tongue, and suprême de volaille. Apart from the trolley sweets, 'Grand Marnier soufflé (for two) had a true taste, though a rather wet texture.' French-bottled table wines are £3·30 and Juliénas '76 £6·95. Averys supply some wines, it seems, but you will do well to inspect the bottles: the list does not help. Recorded music. Dress smartly. More reports, please.

Christl's
118a High Street
Berkhamsted (044 27)
73707

An owl fetish ('should be sardines') in the cramped bar leads to more elegant dining-rooms, one red, one green, occupied by 'beefy steak-eaters with yes-dear wives.' But pâté is rich and good (£1), prawn cocktail served only on Saturday with the local market's prawns, and trout is also fresh and local. Praise too for smoked haddock in a herbed cheese sauce (£1·35), chicken Yassa (West African dish with lemon and chilli, £3·80) and whisky-based 'Highland Fling'. 'Gebäckene champignon' (£1·50) and sweet-and-sour chicken were more ordinary when tried, and gypsy goulash (£3·50) had better meat and sauce than pepper steak and Moroccan lamb. Like much else, the sweets are less Austrian than you might expect of the name. Good coffee 'in demi-semi-*tasses* – with refills.' More or less helpful service. French and Austrian house wines, £3·30 the bottle.

Closed Sun L; Apr 4 & 6;
Apr 7 L; Dec 24–26;
Jan 1
Must book D
Meals 12–2, 7–9.30
(10.30 Fri & Sat, 9 Sun)

Alc £8·85 (meal £12·20)

Service 10%
Seats 65 (parties 30)

Car park
No dogs
Barclaycard

La Fiorentina
21–23 Lower Kings Road
Berkhamsted (044 27)
3003

This British-owned shop conversion had a tentative entry last time, and Vincenzo Iannone has since cooked 'consistently and well'. 'I had the day's specials, paglia e fieno in a rich, creamy sauce, and calamari amalfitana. The squid tasted fresh and the sauce well spiced.' Minestrone, 'excellent tuna salad', just-baked lasagne, and traditional bistecca Fiorentina are also praised. Try, too, osso buco (£4, including vegetables), pollo Valdostana, and saltimbocca (both £3·65). Less has been heard of the sweets. Sangiovese is £3·65. Recorded light music. 'No babes in arms.'

Closed Sun; Mon;
Apr 4 L; 2 weeks summer;
Dec 25 & 26
Must book D
Meals 12–2, 7–9.30

Alc £5·80 (meal £8·70)

Service 10%
Seats 60

♿ rest
No dogs
Access, Am Ex, Barclay, Diners

Michelmersh Grange
1½ m off A30
5 m E of Shaftesbury
Donhead (074 788) 591

Closed L
Must book
D only, 7 for 7.30

The village is famously picturesque, but this guest-house on the Shaftesbury side, purpose-built for Vera and Richard Stevenson a few years back, already fits in. They have room for no more than eight eaters and half a dozen sleepers, and you take your own wine (no corkage charged). Inspectors who have tasted Mrs Stevenson's cordial hospitality and conscientious four-course dinners sound very pleased with both. One

Tdh £5·25 (meal £5·75)

Seats 8
Unlicensed
3 rooms (all with bath)
B&B £8–£12

should perhaps expect a carrot soup, smoked fish mousse, fried chicken breasts with duxelles, or veal with cheese and ham, and ice-creams or Pavlovas. Root vegetables may be better cooked than greens.
'Chocolate and chestnut turinois was served too cold, and coffee too weak.' They discourage smoking.
Car park. More reports, please.

BIDDENDEN Kent Map 3

Ye Maydes
High Street
Biddenden (0580) 291306

Closed Sun; Mon;
Dec 25 & 26; Jan 1 L
Must book D
Meals 12.15–1.45,
7.30–9.30

Tdh L £2·70 (meal £5·45)

Alc £7·25 (meal £10·45)

Seats 54 (parties 24)
♿ rest; w.c.
No dogs
Access card

This antique house and village are usefully near Sissinghurst, and the cooking coupled with sharp eyes and willingness in the service remain very promising. 'Our set lunch was good value.' 'My companion demolished her roast duckling with cherries and gooseberry sauce with gusto.' 'Ballotine de volaille indienne was a great success as a first course' (£1·40). In a test meal too, though rabbit soup was thin and the kitchen-made sweets enterprising rather than outstanding, main dishes showed real skill: 'côte de porc normande (£4·75) had a deliciously enhanced apple flavour, and paupiette de sole façon du chef, though I had my doubts about the breadcrumb coating and the tartare sauce, tasted well. Lyonnaise potatoes – the onion added at the last moment – were also properly done.' The Goustomé French table wines are £1·80 for 50 cl, but 'if you want to drink more than one glass, take the red.' Chianti or Gewürztraminer are in the £5 range. Pressurised beers, and Bob Luck's cider. As we went to press, David Daniels took on a chef, so report, please.

App: A. G. Thompson, Anthony Verney, H.L.F., A.J.H.

BIDDENDEN see also pub section

BILDESTON Suffolk Map 3

Bow Window
116 High Street
8 m SW of Stowmarket
Bildeston (0449) 740748

'A 16th-century oak-framed house and they still bake their own bread,' say people who find it 'a happiness' to eat Mary Cox's three-course dinners, competently and gently served. 'Goubiac – seafood with bechmele sauce in puff pastry' may sound like gobbledegook but is a good order, as is stuffed sirloin steak, and paella. 'We started with excellent soup and smoked fish mousse.' One or two simple but interesting puddings. French table wine £3·40; Ch. Malescot-St-Exupéry '73, £7·20. Recorded classical music.

Closed L (exc Dec 25);
Sun; Mon; Dec 25 D;
Dec 26
Must book

D only, 7.30–9.30

Tdh £6·05 (meal £9·05)

Seats 48
♿ rest (1 step)
No dogs
Access, Barclay

Jennie Wren
Groomsland House,
Pulborough Road,
Parbrook
Billingshurst (040 381)
2571

Closed Sun; Mon; Sat L;
Dec 25 & 26; Jan 1
Must book
Meals 12–2, 7–9.45
(10.15 Fri & Sat)

Tdh L £4 (meal £7·30)
Alc £7·70 (meal £11·35)

Cover 25p
Children's helpings
Seats 50 (parties 35)
♻ rest (1 step)
Car park
No dogs
Access, Am Ex, Barclay,
Diners, Euro

Jennie, who cooks, is actually Tilbury, and she and her husband start with the advantage of a 15th-century farmhouse complete with fossil floor, ingle-nook and bread oven in the bar. With a boy and girl to help serve, they make an efficient, enthusiastic team – 'as a host for a sizeable party, I was surprised to get through an entire meal without having to ask for anything except the bill.' The menu 'seems longer than it really is', but inspectors who have looked for dishes that must have taken trouble express pleasure in the chicken liver and pork terrine, mushrooms provençale, poulet Janine, and roast rack of lamb (£4·25); other suggestions include prawns maison (with sour cream, herbs and Parmesan, £1·65), crab mousse, scallops, entrecôte with red wine sauce, and duckling with peaches and brandy. A lethal meringue with chocolate, chestnut and rum is also reported, though orange sorbet was 'brick hard'. Hallgarten French-bottled table wine is £3·75, and wine-lovers might enjoy comparing Clair Däu's Pinot de Marsannay '72 with California Almaden Cabernet Sauvignon '73 at the same price (£5). Clarets, dessert whites, and vintage ports in bottle are also well above the usual Sussex run, and guests are not allowed to smoke cigars until everyone has finished eating. Wear a tie for dinner. Recorded classical music. More reports, please.

BILLINGSHURST see also wine bar section

BINHAM Norfolk   Map 6

Abbey House
4 m SW of Blakeney
Binham (032 875) 467

The Pryors' 17th-century country house, 'forbidding outside but welcoming within', overlooks Binham Abbey ruins, and in recent months various people have praised the owner's set meals ('excellent soup, casseroled chicken, vegetables and sweets') and also suggest exploring oeufs Jacqueline (£1), truite bretonne (£3·40) and escalope of pork with ginger wine (£2·95) à la carte. Croix St Pierre ordinaires; Ch. Gros-Caillou '71, £5·70. Recorded 'light orchestral' music. No dogs.

Closed L (exc Sun);
D Sun & Thur;
Dec 25 & 26; Jan; Feb
Must book
Meals 12.30–2, 7–9.30

Tdh Sun L £4·75
(meal £7·10), D £5·25
(meal £7·65)
Alc £6·25 (meal £8·75)

Service 10%
Children's helpings

Seats 40
♻ rest
Car park
Am Ex card
9 rooms (3 with bath,
1 with shower)
B&B from £10

We rewrite every entry each year, and depend on fresh, detailed reports to confirm the old, as well as to include the new. The further from London you are, the more important this is.

BIRMINGHAM West Midlands   Map 5

Blue Lamp
2 Robin Hood Lane,
Hall Green
on A34
at Robin Hood
roundabout
021-745 5445

Spelling on the eclectic menu ('choux croûte' led one visitor to expect something with pastry) and unanswered letters are not the only curiosities about this German-run place in a well-converted police station, and both service and cooking have been erratic. But for some, fair lobster bisque, pastrami, poulet chasseur or porc forestière, fresh vegetables and 'sound cheese or plentiful strawberries and cream' have added up to 'the best meal in a Birmingham week.' Wines from £3 or so. Witnesses please report at the *Guide*'s blue lamp sign in 1980.

Closed Sat L; Sun D;
May 26; Dec 25 D;
Dec 26 & 31; Jan 1
Must book weekends
Meals 12.30–2,
7.30–10.30 (10.45 Sat &
Sun)

Tdh L from £2·10
(meal £4·40), D (Mon–
Thur) £2·60 (meal £4·95)
Alc £7·80 (meal £10·70)

Service 12½%
Children's helpings
(under 10 Sun L)

Seats 38 (parties 25)
& rest; w.c.
Car park
Access, Am Ex,
Barclay, Diners, Euro

Dionysos
220 Broad Street
021-643 1500

Beware of flying sherds at night when resident Greeks and 'dozens of plates' take to the dance-floor. The cost of the knees-up (with live bouzouki music) is cheerfully borne by Midlands members unused to meze ('plenty of it': perhaps hummus, kalamarakia and stuffed aubergine, £2·80), tender grilled chicken Salonika, and kleftiko (£5·25) 'proudly served' amidst Cypriot linen and amphorae. Cretan house wine and a dozen other Greek brands. Summer eating in the courtyard. 'Jacket and tie preferred' – no satyrs or maenads.

Closed Sun; Sat L; Dec 25
Must book weekends
Meals 12–2, 7.30–12.30

Tdh L £3·75 (meal £6·30)

Alc £7·85 (meal £12·05)

Cover 50p D
Seats 200
& rest

Air-conditioning
No dogs
Access, Am Ex, Barclay,
Diners

Jonathans'
16 Wolverhampton Road,
Oldbury, Warley
1 m E of M5
junctions 2 & 3
021-429 3757

Closed Sun; Mon; Sat L;
1 week Easter; 3 weeks
Aug; 2 weeks New Year
Must book
Meals 12–2, 7–9.30

Town-planners have had so much stick in recent years that it is good to know from Jonathan Baker that there is a future for them in the restaurant business. (His partner, Jonathan Bedford, who cooks, used to be a publisher's rep.) Last year's tentative entry for their intimately Victorian room and imaginative English food is amply confirmed by members, from one whose 'alcoholic haze after supping their "pudding wine" prevented a fuller report' to a stalwart Wenceslas who ventured through snowdrifts that delayed the staff and made others cancel, called for flesh and wine, and was rewarded with jugged steak. Soups are good, whether cucumber and almond or ham and pea; turkey liver and sherry pâté is distinctive, and there

Tdh D (Sat & Thur)
£9·10 (meal £11·90)
Alc £6·75 (meal £9·80)

Seats 40 (parties 20)
Car park (4)
No dogs
Barclay, Diners

may follow poached salmon with anchovy butter, roast veal, or almond chicken ('they seem to go in a lot for nuts'). They are fertile inventors of new dishes (hot Stilton crab or Oldbury salmon packet are examples). Every other Thursday there is a set 'gourmet evening', and on Saturdays a 'country house' table d'hôte. Vegetables are left on a night-light warmer: perhaps beetroot and mushrooms, parsnip puree, Welsh onion cake, and others. Whim-wham (£1·25) or prune and brandy sorbet are sweets worth trying, though there is one grumble that helpings of them are small, with seconds charged at full price. The wines change almost as fast as the menus, but the flat-rate mark-up means that it pays one, in a sense, to venture beyond Loire Sauvignon at £3·20 or Côtes du Ventoux at £3·70 to Ch. Meyney '67 at £6·20 or even, for a grand occasion, Ch. Latour '67 at £21·70, since it might be hard to replace in Bordeaux itself at the price. Recorded music, 'baroque to Strauss'. You may eat outside in their new 'Victorian wine yard'.

App: Frank Cummins, G.H., W.N.

BIRMINGHAM see also wine bar section

BIRTLE Greater Manchester   Map 5

Normandie Hotel
top of Elbut Lane
off B6222
2½ m NE of Bury
061-764 3869

Closed Sun; Sat L;
3 weeks July; Dec 25 D;
Dec 26
Must book
Meals 12.30–2, 7–9.30

Alc £9·75 (meal £13·30)

Children's helpings
Seats 70 (parties 25)
🔄 rest (1 step)
Car park
No dogs
Access, Am Ex, Barclay,
Diners, Euro
21 rooms (17 with bath)
B&B £17·25
Fire cert

*The reign of Champeau frères in this functional but lavish hotel up Elbut Lane was so long that many members' horses or motors could find it blindfold – but others will need the advice to take exit 2 (Bury) from the M62, then Wash Lane and Willow Street to Bury Old Road (B6222). They will find the emotional atmosphere and the famous wine list somewhat lightened, but (it seems) fewer changes in the cooking, for M Marlot is still managing for the inn's Lancastrian owners, and M Dãho in the kitchen is the fastest garlic-chopper in the north-west, to judge by accounts of his snails, grilled sardines, and grenouilles à l'ail (£2·55) among first courses, and pommes bordelaise with the main course. Dishes to note at this point include julienne de canard maison (£5·30), côte de veau à la façon du chef (£5·75), and chevreuil sauce marrons (£5·65), but there are also contented accounts of the complex flavours in lobster and suckling pig.
Ratatouille and salads are mentioned, and sweets may include 'a rich but still tart lemon mousse', 'unusually fine crème caramel', and 'a pyramid of tiny profiteroles'. A menu glossary, it is suggested, might help to lead the businessmen beyond steaks. Bar prices are high, and they lightheartedly list Bonnes-Mares '34 at £350 (pre-VAT), perhaps for its own protection. But Birtle-bottled red and white French wines from good communes are accessible at £5·75 or so, and should suit both the culinary style and the smoke-beset room. Pressurised beers. More reports, please.*

BISHOP'S CLEEVE Gloucestershire Map 2

Cleeveway House
Evesham Road
on A435
3 m N of Cheltenham
Bishop's Cleeve (024 267)
2585

Closed Sun; Mon
(exc May 5); public hols;
Dec 24 D; 3 weeks
Aug–Sept; 1 week Chr
Must book
Meals 12–1.45, 7.15–9.45

Alc £6·30 (meal £9)

Children's helpings
Seats 38 (parties 14)
♻ rest (1 step); w.c.
No dogs
Access, Am Ex, Diners
3 rooms (all with bath)
B&B £11

Recipe in *Second Dinner
Party Book:* pheasant
with pâté, port,
mushrooms and cream

The Marfells have had ten years' exposure to fire in their Georgian house and garden just outside Cheltenham, and earn their medal even if (like us all) 'they are not at their best at breakfast'. John Marfell could fairly be described as a pestle-and-mortar chef working in an environment that may distract him too much or extend him too little. The cold table is famous, from the fresh salmon and pink roast beef or tender ox-tongue to the smoked fish and meat and cleverly varied salads (though there is one grumble of under-seasoning). More improvisatory hot dishes can be superb, from a chicken soup which satisfied even a member with a Jewish momma, to 'a dish self-deprecatingly described as a "fish gratin", which contained red mullet, haddock, salmon, crab, scallops, crayfish tails, shrimps and prawns, all in a creamy-cheesy sauce.' Crayfish tails in Stilton butter (£5·45), bream poached in white wine, chicken breasts in Pernod cream and Armenian lamb are good too, and woodcock, snipe, teal and pheasant may appear in season. Vegetables are 'well-timed'. Among Mrs Marfell's 'excellent' sweets, cherry and strawberry meringue, Cointreau cream with fresh pineapple, and 'outstanding summer pudding' are mentioned, though there is a school of thought that dislikes pippy grapes in fruit salad. The Averys wines seem less stiffly marked-up than they used to be, with St Maroc or white Bordeaux a bargain at £2·80, Ch. Truffet Pressac '75, £3·95, and Ch. Palmer '67, £12. White Montagny '76 (Louis Latour) is £7·20.

App: K. S. Mingle, D. C. Alcock, J. A. Taylor, Leonard Saffron, and others

BISHOP'S LYDEARD Somerset Map 2

Rose Cottage
on A358
1 m E of village
4¾ m NW of Taunton
Bishop's Lydeard
(0823) 432394

The Dale-Thomases are old hands, and their inn at the edge of the Quantocks is seldom short of customers for home-made bar lunches and more formally served dinners, with about half a dozen choices in each course: stuffed aubergine (£1·10), chicken livers with herbs and garlic; duck with orange, sweetbreads in a 'slightly floury' madeira sauce; pigeon braised in port with raisins (£5·10); lemon syllabub (95p) and other sweets. Wines – a personal collection formed over time – range from £3·50 to £26·40 (for Ch. Latour '60). Dorset IPA bitter in cask. Recorded music. You may eat outside.

Closed Sun; Mon;
Dec 23–Jan 10; public hols
Must book D
Meals 12–1.45 (bar),
7.45–9.30

Alc £5·75 (meal £8·60)

Seats 16 (30 Sat)
parties 20

♻ rest
Car park
No dogs in d/r

Angela's Chophouse
9 Northgate End
Bishop's Stortford (0279)
57316

'Expect beams and exposed bricks in an unhurried, sometimes jocular atmosphere', and while many praise the aviator-chef's tomato soup, smoked salmon mousse, beef or shoulder of lamb done as you like it, fresh carrots and spinach, and 'light' Black Forest gateau, an inspector and others wonder who is supervising whom, and late reports suggest strongly that lunch is better than dinner, and first courses better than main dishes. Wines from £2·90. More reports, please.

Closed Mon; 3 weeks Jan
Must book
Meals 12.30–2, 7–10.30

Tdh Sun L £5·50 (meal £8)

Alc £8·80 (meal £12·10)

Children's helpings
Seats 50

♿ rest (1 step)
Car park (6)
Access, Am Ex, Barclay, Diners, Euro

Mallory Court
Harbury Lane,
Tachbrook Mallory
off A452
2 m S of Leamington Spa
Leamington Spa (0926)
30214

Closed L (exc Dec 25);
Sun D (exc res); Dec 26;
Jan 1; last 2 weeks Feb
Must book
D only, 7.30–9.45

Tdh from £12·75
(meal £15·30)

Service inc
Seats 45 (parties 30)
Car park
No dogs
Access, Am Ex, Barclay,
Diners, Euro
6 rooms (4 with bath)
B&B from £17·80

An Edwardian mansion in ten acres near Warwick and Leamington does not have to fish far for guests, and since last year's provisional entry, Allan Holland (who cooks) and his co-owner Jeremy Mort have drawn a wide spectrum of praise and criticism. 'A splendid meal in the panelled dining-room' (which could do with a few good pictures), writes one member after 'featherlight' salmon soufflé wrapped in fillet of sole with asparagus sauce, and breast of chicken and hazelnut cream sauce, garnished with a tartlet laden with 'marbles' of apple. Other diners report equally good crêpes Alfredo (with spinach, ham and cheese sauce), tournedos Rossini 'with a smidgen of sauce madère', Dover sole stuffed with lobster, imaginatively cooked vegetables, 'delicious' orange bavarois, and a 'nicely tart' green fruit salad. Service on this occasion was prompt and friendly, but it is obvious that *longueurs* also occur, and that when they do, the precise placement of garnishing in the kitchen is an irritant, as though both the temperatures of food and the feelings of eaters were taking second place. 'I thought the Duke of Plaza Toro was about to inspect the Army Catering Corps.' Loin of lamb in pastry, with a spinach and calf's liver stuffing, is a speciality. Muscadet or Chinon are around £5 and Ch. Meyney '67, c.b., just under £12, from Seligmans. Dress smartly. Children under 14 are not accepted in either restaurant or hotel, which tells its own story perhaps (see Preface). Note that a cooked breakfast is £3 extra to the basic overnight charges. (GHG)

App: H. A. G. Durbridge, Mr & Mrs R. A. Hardwick, M.R., Capt. & Mrs J. S. Stewart, and others

BLACKPOOL Lancashire   Map 5

Danish Kitchen
95 Church Street
Blackpool (0253) 24291

Industrial democracy ('shared profits, free speech among staff but not to customers') is taking hold at the back of the Vernon Humpage shoe shop. Political scientists in autumn exile will note the servers' friendliness and the cleaners' zeal; others enjoy the 'variety of delicious snacks at fair prices': open sandwiches (from 55p), pizza, gateaux. Cream is piped, but not music. Chanson house wine £2·10 for 50 cl. 'Air-conditioning can cope with smoke,' they say.

Closed D; Sun;
Dec 25 & 26; Jan 1
Open 9.15–5.15

Tdh L £1·40 (meal £3·10)
Alc £1·70 (meal £3·40)

Service inc

Children's helpings
Seats 104
♿ rest
Air-conditioning

BLOCKLEY Gloucestershire   Map 2

As we went to press, the restaurant recommended here changed hands.

BONCHURCH see ISLE OF WIGHT

Please report to us on atmosphere, decor and – if you stayed – standard of accommodation, as well as on food, drink and prices (send bill if possible).

Most places will accept cheques only when they are accompanied by a cheque card or adequate identification. Information about which credit cards are accepted is correct when printed, but restaurants may add to or subtract from the list without notice.

The Guide News Supplement will be sent out as usual, in June, to everyone who buys the book directly from Consumers' Association and to all bookshop purchasers who return the card interleaved with their copy. Let us know of any changes that affect entries in the book, or of any new places you think should be looked at.

The Guide accepts no advertising. Nor does it allow restaurateurs to use its name on brochures, menus, or in any form of advertisement. If you see any instances of this, please report them to us.

Fountain House
St James Square
Boroughbridge (090 12)
2241

Closed L; Sun; Mon;
Dec 25 & 26; Jan 1
Must book
D only, 7.30–10

Tdh £10 (meal £12·90)

Seats 45 (parties 20)
♿ rest (2 steps)
No dogs

Peter Carwardine and two presumably eligible
spinsters (after all, if they can make Stilton and pear
pâté and Grand Marnier cheesecake . . .) occupy the
kitchen of this rambling house, whose entrance eludes
the passer-by. Rooms are well furnished, 'the loo
resplendent', and there are crudités and mayonnaise
on the lounge tables. An inspector found the salmon
centrepiece easily the tastiest part of his five-course
dinner, but other visitors are more complimentary
about smoked salmon pancake, devilled kidneys, and
orange and tomato soup. 'Main courses vary: the
sauce masked the flavour of the fish in fish pie, but
sole Mornay was admirable, and chicken breast
stuffed with chestnut puree in a sherry sauce even
better. Vegetables, too, kept their own flavours.' The
cheeses are Stilton and Wensleydale, and zabaglione,
bananas in rum, or pineapple in kirsch seem the
wisest sweets. The service is willing rather than expert,
and the French table wine at £3·50 a speculative
choice. Ch. Gloria '71, c.b., is £10·90, and they will
decant a vintage port (Dow '55, £32·20). The music
in the bar fortunately does not penetrate the
dining-room, and a regular visitor remarks: 'I would
be insulted if a guest in my house smoked – between
courses – while others were eating, but this is
permitted here.'

App: B.B., Stephen Adams, N.K., M.C., S.S.

---

*As we went to press, the restaurant recommended
here changed hands.*

When a restaurant says 'must book', the context of the entry usually indicates how
much or how little it matters, but a preliminary telephone call averts a wasted
journey to a closed door. *Always* telephone if a booking has to be cancelled: a small
place (and its other customers) may suffer severely if this is not done.

BOTALLACK Cornwall   Map 1

Count House
off B3306
1 m N of St Just
Penzance (0736) 788588

Closed L (exc Sun &
Dec 26); Mon (exc
May 26 & Aug 25);
Tue; Sun D; Dec 25;
Dec 26 D; Jan 1
Must book
Meals 12.30–1.45, 7.30–10

Tdh Sun L £3·50

(meal £5·90)
Alc £6·35 (meal £9·20)

Children's helpings
Seats 35
Car park
No dogs
Access, Am Ex, Barclay,
Diners, Euro

The old Botallack tin mine (formerly listed here under St Just in Penwith), whose converted workshop on the cliffs commands a superb view of sunsets over the Scillies, has held its place under the Longs for four years now. (From St Just, take the coast road from Land's End to St Ives [B3306], the second left past the Queen's Arms, and then follow the track.) In a wet south-westerly, the warmth and cordiality, with 'table settings so shiny that they squeaked', are as welcome as Mrs Long's carrot and coriander soup, 'very moist' marinated salmon, crab with marinated mushrooms, or terrine of fish sandwiched with garlicky chopped mushrooms. Main course specialities are meat rather than fish: marinated fillet steak with a sherry cream sauce (£4·25), and 'very succulent' escalopes of lamb, crumbed and fried and served with Cumberland sauce (£3). 'There was a very fresh lemon sole too.' Vegetables are lightly cooked, and for sweets 'it was difficult to choose but we settled on a light sponge roll with fresh raspberries and a shiny chocolate coating.' Another Cornish restaurateur praises the value given at Sunday lunch. The house wine is now French Gouttelette at a modest £3·30 a litre, and (depending on the year, which has not been vouchsafed) Ch. Lynch-Bages at £7·45 looks a bargain. 'Great care was taken with a finicky 12-year-old who ended up by consuming the largest meal of his life.' Local artists' pictures on the walls are for sale.

App: Jenny Fox, J. F. Sayers, Philippa Marnham, I. D. Nussey, J. Jewell, and others

BOURNEMOUTH Dorset   Map 2

Crust
1 Bus Station Arcade,
Exeter Road,
The Square
Bournemouth (0202) 21430

Closed Sun (Chr–Easter);
Dec 25 & 26; Jan 1;
Jan 6–20
Must book D
Meals 12–2.30, 6.30–11
(11.30 Sat)

Alc £6 (meal £9·45)

Service 10%
Cover 25p
Children's helpings
Seats 60

Bournemouth does not have the air of being down to its last crust, even round the bus station over which Paul Harper's croissant-shaped restaurant presides; and in spite of close tables and some casualness over drink orders at a test meal, it is a serious place, sensibly furnished, with a conscientious *chef-patron*. 'Perhaps the best feature is the vegetables: a large variety, all fresh, cooked to firm perfection, and buttered' – this from a most exacting inspector, who also warmly admired the crab and fish soup with saffron: 'exactly what it said, in a bowl that set off the soup handsomely.' Crust salad, with smoked chicken, gammon and Gruyère cheese, or with mushrooms and bacon, are other tasty first courses. Spare ribs, though well cooked and served, had too vinegary a sauce. Among main dishes are 'saddle of lamb with courgettes admirably prepared', 'grilled halibut very rich with cream and juices', 'properly cooked sweetbreads, perhaps in too thick a sauce',

♿ rest
Car park
No dogs
Access, Am Ex, Barclay,
Diners, Euro

and venison pie. Sweets and coffee fall off somewhat:
the ices and meringues are fine, but apple tart was
'the only flavourless dish' in a test meal. The house
wine is Italian Merlot or Riesling at £3·80 a litre, and
there is adequate choice thereafter: Rhônes and
Loires from Yapp, and Ch. Cantemerle or Ch. Cos
d'Estournel '66, both c.b., under £15. Recorded music.

App: A. E. Key, Mrs D. Hinton, John Haygarth,
M.J.M., G. J. Dykes, and others

BOURNEMOUTH Dorset   Map 2

La Rosticceria
107 Poole Road,
Westbourne
Bournemouth (0202)
767264

Essentially a pizzeria, offshoot of La Cappa nearby.
Either eat here 'with delightful service' or take
away the nine varieties of pizza (Rosticceria comes
with red peppers, mushrooms and Mozzarella cheese,
£1·45) or the same number of pasta dishes (rigatoni
al pescatore, £1·45). If you sit down, there are first
courses, salads and sweets, as well as a few
specialities. 'Ideal place for families.' Italian house
wine, £3·90 the litre. 'Basically Italian' recorded
music.

Closed Sun; public hol
Mons; Dec 25 & 26;
Jan 1
Must book
Meals 12–2, 6.30–11

Alc (min £1 D) £3·05
(meal £5·75)

Children's helpings

Seats 60
No dogs
Access, Barclay

BOURTON-ON-THE-WATER Gloucestershire
Map 2

Rose Tree

Riverside
Bourton-on-the-Water
(0451) 20635

Closed L (exc Sat & Sun);
Mon; Sun D; D Dec 25 &
26; 5 weeks from mid-Jan
Must book
Meals 12.30–2, 7.30–10

Tdh Sun L £4·95
(meal £6·65)
Alc £7·25 (meal £10·15)

Service 10%
Children's helpings (Sun L)
Seats 30
♿ rest (1 step); w.c.
2 rooms
B&B £7·50

Jane Mann and Iain Gaynor's Queen Anne house by
the Windrush sounds as if it is fulfilling its early
promise, in spite (or because) of an attached steak
bar to distract the kind of tourists in this much-harried
village who might not care for terrine de truite
Curnonsky (£1·75) and tranche d'agneau à la
poitevine (£4·10), two of Jane Mann's specialities.
Crab and lobster bisque (95p) and crêpes aux fruits de
mer créole (£3·95 as a main course) are other fishy
possibilities on the short menus, which change every
two months or so. Otherwise, a party of four who
began with quail pâté, garlic mushrooms en cocotte
and tomates farcies were equally pleased with their
choices, and indeed with the crudités and mayonnaise
on the table. 'Mignons de porc tasted duller than
their description', and 'second helpings of the accompanying new potatoes and spinach would have been
welcome.' 'Duck in cherry sauce was well-cooked and
not at all fatty.' Sweets are rich and creamy,
'especially the strawberry meringues', but a fine
Stilton served with a fresh apple provides an
alternative. French table wines are £3·75, burgundies
from Lionel Brück £3·95, and you are then invited

to browse among Mr Gaynor's 200 clarets, some of
them only bin-ends, but including (in 1979) a dozen
'61s, a few under £10. No smoking in the restaurant,
please. Lunchtime bar snacks in the garden in July
and August; Wadworth's 6X from the cask.
Sit-down lunches or late meals can be arranged with
notice. The bedrooms are an innovation. Recorded
music. No dogs.

App: Albert Ross, J. & J.W., L.O.B.

BOWNESS-ON-WINDERMERE Cumbria   Map 7

Porthole Eating House
3 Ash Street
Windermere (096 62) 2793

Gianni Berton's family régime has brought 'various
national styles of cooking' to this ancient tavern,
but most people seem to enjoy not too *outré* mushrooms in garlic sauce, prosciutto with fruit, pasta,
veal, lobster Newburg, Sicilian trifle and so on, in
cheery, cheek-by-jowl surroundings. Stroganoff
Porthole (£4·75) may be tried. You could mix a
powerful or blasphemous cocktail from the list of
eighty clarets (Ch. Smith-Haut-Lafitte '50, £15),
thirty English wines, twenty eaux-de-vie and countless
liqueurs that Gianni has assembled, but consult the
list in advance, perhaps. Prices are fair for what the
grands crus are.

Closed L; Tue; Dec; Jan;	Alc (min £4·50) £8·30	Seats 40
1st 2 weeks Feb	(meal £11·80)	No dogs
Must book		Am Ex card
D only, 7–10.30	Children's helpings	

BRADFORD West Yorkshire   Map 5

The Cottage
869 Thornton Road
Bradford (0274) 832752

'Though he is halfway to Halifax, Nikos Kkais
provides Bradford's nearest civilised eating,' says a
regular eater of 'thick soup, shellfish or sea bass to
start, then pink noisettes d'agneau and pigeon
moistly done ' Try also pâté de foie (95p), crêpe de
gibier, gigot d'agneau au vermouth, and canard
sauvage farci au citron. Vegetables and exotic fruit
are well varied. Trolley sweets are more routine, but
they keep a good Stilton, and serve strong coffee.
House wines are £5·50. White burgundies are oldish,
and 'if you drink '72 red, let it be burgundy, not
claret.' Wear a jacket and tie.

Closed Tue; Sat L;	Meals 12.15–2, 7.30–10	Seats 80 (parties 25)
Dec 25 D; Jan 1 L		Car park
Must book	Tdh D £9·75 (meal £14·75)	No dogs
	Alc L £7·45 (meal £12·25)	Access, Am Ex, Barclay

Numbers are given for private parties only if they can be accommodated in a room
separate from the main dining-room; when there are several such rooms, the
capacity of the largest is given. Some restaurants will take party bookings at times
when they are normally closed.

Last Pizza Show
48–50 Great Horton Road
Bradford (0274) 28173

Though movies ain't what they used to be, pizzas are bigger and better than ever. Mario Benericetti's Little Italy may not be the last word (entrecôte lumberjack, £3·20, a curious special) but a member found snails (£1·50) and pollo sorpresa ('beautifully cooked and presented', £3·10) a welcome change from central Bradford's choice between High Street English rubbish and backstreet Pakistani exotica. Specials include scaloppina al vino bianco and, among a dozen pizzas (£1·25–£1·50), quattro stagioni. An open kitchen is a recent innovation. A dozen wines 'imported direct from Italy.' Lambrusco (£3 for 80 cl) and Webster's Green label beer (pump). 'Italian music.'

Closed Sun L; L public
hols (exc Apr 4); Dec 25
Must book weekends
Meals 12–2, 6–11.30
(midnight Fri & Sat)

Tdh L £1·45 (meal £3·40)
Alc £3·05 (meal £5·35)

Service 10% (parties of 8
or more)

Children's helpings
Seats 120 (parties 50)
 ♿ rest (1 step)
No dogs

Farlam Hall
on A689
2½ m SE of Brampton
Hallbankgate (069 76) 234

Closed L (exc Sun,
Dec 25, Jan 1);
D Dec 25 & 26; Feb
Must book
Meals 12.30–1 (Sun),
7.30–7.45

Tdh Sun L £5·50
(meal £8·15), D £6·95
(meal £9·75)

Seats 50
♿ rest
Car park
No dogs in d/r (exc by
arrangement)
Access, Euro
11 rooms (4 with bath,
2 with shower)
B&B £10·50–£12
Fire cert

As a jumping on or off point for Hadrian's Wall – and as a peaceful historic house and garden in its own right – there is much to be said for the Quinions' hotel. As Lake District evening-out places go, it offers a fairly simple set meal, and dinner-time is inflexible, but the family of Home Counties vegetable growers who 'thought a *GFG* hotel would be good for the children's education' were delighted on all counts: 'besides, there were local pleasures such as gosling and sea bass, and good Stilton and blue Cheshire were served at the right point in the meal for proper appreciation.' Others praise the vegetables – 'roast parsnips, white cabbage with diced bacon, and buttered carrot matchsticks,' observes an inspector – though the effect can be slightly 'dry' unless there is a copious sauce elsewhere. Gnocchi, avocado mousse, grenadine of veal, saltimbocca, duck and other dishes have admirers, though 'two lamb cutlets was one too few.' Hot apple and blackberry or cold pear and walnut pies are praised. A conventional Christopher's wine list begins at £2·95: Beaune Teurons (Chanson Père et Fils) '71 is £9 50. The hotel is comfortable, and the family service 'overworks the word "gorgeous" but can be reproached with little else.' 'TV is in a separate room from the main lounge.' 'Toast-eating ducks parade in the gardens.' (GHG)

App: *Philip & Penelope Plumb, L. Lavender,
A. T. G. Wood, Mary E Lawrence, J. &. K.L.,
and others*

BRANSTON Staffordshire   Map 5

Riverside Inn
Warren Lane
Burton-on-Trent (0283)
63117

The Pumphreys' decently set-up hotel does lie by the Trent, and an inspector who hoped for little but beer in Burton reports well of the roast beef, steaks and foil-baked salmon, but wishes the home-made soups had more seasonal flair, and that the apple pie were served at least warm. There is a rudimentary wine list from £3·75 for various Yugoslav varietals; pressurised beers. Recorded music, and live on Wednesdays and Fridays to accompany the dancing. More reports, please.

Closed Sun D; Sat L
Must book
Meals 12–2.30, 7–10.30

Tdh L £4 (meal £6·50),
D £5 (meal £7·60)

Alc £6·50 (meal £9·20)

Service inc
Children's helpings
(under 5)
Seats 150
♿ rest; w.c.

Car park
No dogs
Access, Barclay, Euro
22 rooms (21 with bath,
1 with shower)
B&B from £9·50
Fire cert

BRAY Berkshire   Map 3

Waterside Inn

Ferry Road
Maidenhead (0628) 20691
and 22941

Closed Mon; Sun D (3rd
week Oct–Apr 13); from
Dec 26 D for 1 month
Must book
Meals 12.30–2, 7.30–10

Tdh L £12·75 (meal £17·05)
Alc £19·15 (meal £24·75)

Service inc
Children's helpings
Seats 80
♿ rest; w.c.
Car park
No dogs
Access, Barclay

'Perm any two *Guide* credit restaurants for one Waterside,' says one admirer of the Roux brothers' decorative, salmon-and-spinach restaurant, which pulls in millionaires and mashers alike by rowboat or Rolls. (Eyeing the lunchtime mix, one member suggests that this would be an ideal venue for the signing of a peace treaty between Israel and Saudi Arabia – with the Vicar of Bray in the chair, presumably.) For Albert and Michel Roux, notoriously, descriptions of a restaurant's clientele are the reddest of rags or herrings, but all the same, they have taken notice of the problems created for their very professional kitchen. Guests are now greeted more sympathetically, and at table they are advised more patiently. For a wonder (in a restaurant lying beyond the pale of the French culture that makes its existence possible) they get what they pay for: food of the highest class, both classical and contemporary. It takes a more than ordinarily confident Frenchman to offer an English-speaking audience oeufs brouillés à la rhubarbe (£3·30) or tourte chaude aux carottes (£3·75). But that tart filling was 'infinitely delicate and sweet: I thought only Gujeratis understood carrots so well.' (Eggs too: they have lately been doing here an 'oeuf aux oeufs' hors d'oeuvre to which hen, quail and sturgeon have all contributed their mite.) If none of these appeals, try the fish pâtés or crabe des îles or the 'creamy, eggy' mousseline de volaille with its reactor core of Roquefort and chopped walnuts, with a julienne of apple in the rich sauce. Clearly, with first courses like some of these, it is vital to build a meal carefully. Côte d'agneau Germaine would have delighted Paul Valéry (who once told a table neighbour, 'J'adore le mint-sauce') but many may look instead for the caneton sauvage aux myrtilles or faisan au porto (£9·65), 'dressed with a floral arrangement of pea and mushroom purees.' The treatments of bass and salmon should not be overlooked. Dish prices include 'légume ou garniture'. Just occasionally a dish errs on the salty side, or arrives tepid. Cheeses are a commanding range in fine condition, and as one expects of these owners, the patisserie is masterly: 'mille-feuille aux kiwis (on the Sunday set lunch): three layers of crisp pastry evenly sandwiched with perfect, sliced kiwi-fruit and a tangy cream, iced on top and feathered.' For sablé aux poires and tarte au citron, see previous entries. The wines are covetously priced from about £8·55 for Beaujolais Villages '78 or Lirac Rosé; Ch. Pape-Clément '70 was well forward in 1979 (£18·70). It is not at all difficult to pay three figures for La Tâche '59 or Taylor '27 port if your oil well has turned up trumps. Coffee (£1·35) is excellent, Malvern water free.

App: John Stevenson, T. Russell, G. A. Rose, A.J.H., Abigail Fawcett, Bruce Wright, and others

---

BRENTWOOD Essex   Map 3

Moat House
London Road
Brentwood (0277) 225252

The retreat to Suffolk is eased by this staging-post on the old coaching road. No surprises in the baronial dining-room, other than its very existence on the eastern flats. People single out avocado with fresh crab (£1·85) and meaty goulash soup (95p) to start, then noisettes d'agneau, lightly battered goujons of sole, 'moist' Dover sole (£5·60) and lamb cutlets from the busy grill. Profiteroles please and fruits astonish: mango, passion-fruit, and kiwi-fruit atop a trifle. French house wines are £3·90. 'Agreeably diverse staff.' 'Lovely garden.' 'Piped music with a minstrel on Friday nights.'

Must book **D**	Children's helpings	Access, Am Ex, Barclay,
Meals 12.30–2, 7–10	Seats 70 (parties 55)	Diners, Euro
	🅖 rest	26 rooms (21 with bath)
Tdh Sun L £4·90	Car park	Room only, from £15·50
(meal £9·20)	No dogs in public rooms	Breakfast from £1·90
Alc £9·40 (meal £13·15)		Fire cert

Wine prices shown are for a 'standard' bottle of the wine concerned, unless another measure is stated (e.g. litre, 50 cl., or pint).

Meal times refer to first and last orders.

The Guide accepts no advertising. Nor does it allow restaurateurs to use its name on brochures, menus, or in any form of advertisement. If you see any instances of this, please report them to us.

BRIDGNORTH Salop   Map 5

Bambers
65 St Mary's Street
Bridgnorth (074 62) 3139

'Comfortable, not down-at-heel,' says a rebuker of last year's comment, 'but not uppity either.' A warming fire in winter and 'seasonal menus' (though midsummer brought beef casserole provençale and baked gammon with cheese and onion sauce). 'Plenty of elbow-room', which diners may need to assemble their own hors d'oeuvre (popular at £1·05, as are lamb and salmon en croûte). Meringues, apple pie and other sweets seem to leave little impression. 'Pleasant service.' Litre Vin house wine is £3 for 83 cl. Quiet taped music.

Closed L (exc Dec 25);
Sun; Mon; Sept
Must book
D only, 7–9.30 (10 Sat)

Alc (min £2·25) £6·05
(meal £8·65)

Seats 40

♿ rest (2 steps)
Air-conditioning
No dogs

BRIDLINGTON Humberside   Map 8

Old Cooperage
High Street
Bridlington (0262) 75190

Closed Mon; Sun D;
Tue L; Dec 26
Must book D & weekends
Meals 12–2, 7.30–10.30
(11 summer)

Tdh L £4 (meal £6·05),
D £8·30 (meal £10·45)
Alc (min L £2, D £5) £8
(meal £10·05)

Service inc
Children's helpings
Seats 45 (parties 20)
♿ rest
Car park (6)
No dogs
Access, Barclay

' "You must be joking," my wife said when I suggested eating out in Bridlington. "After all, we live here." ' A glimpse of the amusement arcades prepared to receive coach parties from the smoky north Midlands explains the reaction, but there is an old town too, and Mr Henderson, with his manager Ace Nikuseuski and a husband-and-wife team in the kitchen, has made an inviting cane-furnished restaurant with real linen and 'a menu that actually changes every few weeks.' 'Faults tend to arise from excess zeal with the spirit bottle or the serving-spoon' – there are after all four courses at dinner – but there is no complaint of the quality of 'egg florentine made with delicious fresh spinach', or seafood pancakes 'with lots of fresh mussels and prawns in cream and cheese sauce.' Crab flan is another possible first course, and main dishes include lamb en croûte with duxelles, 'tender, delicate and creamy' veal hongroise, 'moist salmon in a sauce far removed from artificial aids', and a copiously sauced but crisp duck in peaches and brandy. 'The pause before sweets was welcome', but 'a legendary strawberry syllabub', 'raspberry mille-feuille of startling lightness' and even ungrudging praise of sherry trifle raise hopes further. Chocolate cream pie is another nomination from the Glovers in the kitchen. French Les Chevaliers table wine is £4·10, and they have yet to attach vintages to their wine list. Recorded music. More reports, please.

Do not risk using an out-of-date Guide. A new edition will appear early in 1981.

PLEASE keep sending in reports, as soon as possible after each meal. The cut-off date for the 1981 Guide is September 30, 1980, but reports are even more useful earlier in the year, especially for the remoter areas and new places. Late autumn reports can also affect corrections at proof stage.

157

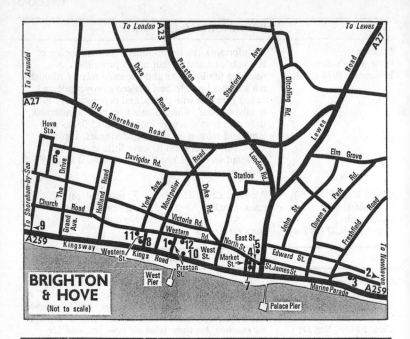

BRIGHTON & HOVE East Sussex   Map 3

(1) **Athenian Restaurant**
12 Preston Street
Brighton (0273) 28662

Consistent praise for this busy little family-run place near the West Pier. Greek specialities are still the favourites: hummus (80p), taramosalata (95p) and garithakia (cold fresh prawns in shell with mayonnaise, 85p). Generous helpings of main courses, perhaps charcoal-grilled lamb. Nor do they fall down on details like pitta, saffron rice, and salad. Good, small wine list; Greek house wine £4 the litre, 50p the glass. Recorded music.

Must book weekends
Meals 12–2.30, 6–12.30

Tdh L £2·80 (meal £4·80),
D £3·80 (meal £6)

Alc £3·90 (meal £7·35)

Service inc
Cover 20p D
Seats 50

🛆 rest
No dogs
Access, Am Ex, Barclay, Diners

(2) **Bannister's**
77 St George's Road,
Kemp Town
Brighton (0273) 687382

Closed L (exc Dec 25 &
26); Sun; Mon; Aug 25;
Dec 25 D
Must book weekends
D only, 7–11

The Roes have had their ups and downs here, and Mrs Roe (who serves) apparently had to cope with the stairs single-footed one evening. But it did not cramp her conversation, nor for that matter handicap her husband's production of 'delicately exuberant' scallops, crab cheese pancake, or salmon mousse; followed by venison with raisins and cashew nuts in a dark gravy ('the best restaurant main course I have had in years'), sweetbreads in cream sauce, or pigeon. Carré d'agneau aux herbes de Provence is a speciality (£5·75, including vegetables). The level of the best

Alc £7·50 (meal £11·90)

Seats 24
Air-conditioning
No dogs
Am Ex card

things is hard to maintain, however, and people who have returned for second or third meals in the same week – itself a high compliment – have noticed wide variations. Among sweets, ices, strawberry mousse, and chocolate pots with either armagnac and orange flower water, or dates, Tia Maria and apricot sauce, find admirers. Wines begin with Bordemer at £1·65 for half a litre, and Minervois, Corvo Bianco, or various fringe '75 clarets can be had for under £4. A Rhine Gewürztraminer – Guntersblumer Eiserne Hand Spätlese '75 – is £7·20. James Galway, Julian Bream and other gilded discs are played.

App: H. P. S. Forster, Capt. & Mrs J. S. Stewart, P. E. Birkett, J. N. Clogstoun-Willmott

---

(3) **Chez Moi**
113 St George's Road
Kemp Town
Brighton (0273) 680317

Closed L (exc Dec 25);
Apr 6; Dec 26;
annual hols
Must book
D only, 7.30–10.45

Tdh £7 (meal £10)

Children's helpings
(under 7)
Seats 32 (parties 22)
🔓 rest (1 step)
Air-conditioning
No dogs
Access, Am Ex, Barclay

At their little restaurant the Wilsons and their chef Keith Murray score by keeping prices at a reasonable level (for flash Brighton) and by not attempting more than they can perform; besides, they treat their customers warmly and civilly. Hence the praise received in recent months for their watercress soup, deep-fried mushrooms, goujons of smoked haddock, and grilled avocado with cream cheese and prawns, all first courses; and crisply roast duck with various garnishes or sweetbreads à la crème as main courses with unexpectedly good vegetables: 'lemony and buttery parsnip fingers', and deep-fried cauliflower florets. Raspberry cheesecake or a sorbet may close the set meal, 'and soft roes on toast were carefully done too.' The ordinaire at £3·35 is Arc de Triomphe, and there are few wines of any moment beyond. Recorded music. More reports, please.

---

(4) **D'Arcy's**
49 Market Street
Brighton (0273) 25560

Closed Sun; Mon;
Apr 4 D; Dec 25 & 26;
Jan 1
Must book
Meals 12.15–2, 6.30–9
(9.30 Sat)

Alc £7·70 (meal £10·70)

Seats 22
No dogs
Access, Barclay

Michael and Marie Veness have taken over this tiny place in the Lanes 'opposite the betting shop', and turned it into a bright and spotless preserve of 'the best seafood locally available'. Norwegian prawns in un-Scandinavian garlic butter are one example but the flat-fish gather the most praise. 'Sole is equally good grilled or fried', turbot 'couldn't be faulted' and an inspector's grilled plaice (£2·60) was 'absolutely fresh, very juicy and enlivened by half a lemon and crisp French fries.' Crab pancake (£1·70) is a filling start, but 'very good. If it must show its authenticity with bits of bone and shell, so be it.' Number two Whitstables are £3·10 for six. Salmon, lobster and mussels are offered when possible, and the eel revival is helped along by a stew with parsley sauce (£1·65). Green vegetables at 60p each are deemed expensive for what you get but sweets ('tasty gooseberry fool topped with whipped cream and hazelnuts', 75p) are

inviting. Seating is close enough for you to get
involved in a neighbour's choice of wine – ' "Have
the Sancerre," we chanted', but at £5·90 it may be
less good value than the house Blanc de Blancs at
£3·30 a bottle. Smoking does not suit the space. 'No
prams or pushchairs.'

App: G.C., G. H. Denton, S.S.

BRIGHTON & HOVE East Sussex   Map 3

(5) **Al Duomo**
7 Pavilion Buildings
Brighton (0273) 26741

Closed Sun; Apr 7;
3 weeks summer;
Dec 24–26 & 31; Jan 1
Must book weekends
Meals 12.30–2.30,
6.30–10.45

Tdh D £7 (meal £10·25)
Alc £5·80 (meal £8·90)

Service 10%
Cover 40p
Seats 60
🛆 rest
Access, Am Ex, Barclay

*Dino Azzarone of Al Forno (q.v.) has spread his wings
a good deal more widely in this new place on two floors
near the Pavilion. His table of cold antipasto has
ravished the eye and heart of many members and even
the odd inspector, with its 'stuffed tomatoes, aubergines
and peppers, veal polpette, and herby quiches'. The
variety of pasta dishes, from tagliolini with smoked
salmon to tortellini with walnut sauce, along with
calamari, prawns and fritto misto among the fish, is
also very promising, and in the evening there is a
formidable set meal with plenty of choice in all four
courses. A test meal also yielded good coffee.
Sangiovese or Trebbiano are a reasonable £3, and other
Italian wines are not overpriced. The house aperitif,
featuring red vermouth and cinnamon, is 'doubtless
good for conference hangovers of Regency proportions.'
More reports, please.*

---

(6) **Eaton Restaurant**
Eaton Gardens,
Hove
Brighton (0273) 738921

Forfars the Bakers maintain a conventional slap-up
restaurant with gardens and terraces, near Hove
Station. The style of menu promises and sometimes
achieves mediocrity, and an inspector was relieved to
eat well-made asparagus mousse ('spoilt by dried-up
smoked salmon with it'), tender and crisp duck wing,
and innocuous orange Boodle. Coq aux morilles (£6),
steak au poivre, and triple lamb cutlets are other
ideas, but a family Sunday lunch may be the best
choice Wines from £3·25 a litre for Baton, and poor
claret years too well represented thereafter. No pipes
in the dining-room. Recorded music.

Closed Sun D; Apr 4;	Tdh L £5·50 (meal £8·50),	Seats 90 (parties 100)
Dec 25	Sun L £5·75 (meal £8·80),	Car park
Must book	D £6·50 (meal £9·60),	No dogs
Meals 12.30–2, 6.30–10	Sat D £7·50 (meal £10·90)	Access, Am Ex, Barclay,
	Alc £8·85 (meal £12·05)	Diners, Euro

**'Meal' indicates the cost of a meal for one, including food, coffee, a half-bottle of
one of the cheapest wines listed, cover, service, and VAT (see 'How to use the
Guide', p. 4).**

1980 prices are as estimated by restaurateurs in the autumn of 1979 (including VAT).

(7) Al Forno
36 East Street
Brighton (0273) 24905

Though a long way down-market from the owner's new Al Duomo (*q.v.*), this cramped little trattoria (with a few tables outside in summer) is still pleasing students, pensioners and in-betweens with its pizzas, 'bubbling lasagne' with plenty of meat and a good cheese sauce (£1·20), salads and coffee. Some sweets may be shared with the other restaurant. Sangiovese and Trebbiano are £2·80 here. Recorded music.

Closed Mon (exc May 5 & 26, & Aug 25); Sun L; Apr 6 D; 3 weeks summer; Dec 24–26 & 31; Jan 1	Meals 12.30–2.30, 6.30–11.30	Service 10% Seats 55 Access, Am Ex
	Alc £3·30 (meal £5·50)	

(8) Le Grandgousier
15 Western Street
Brighton (0273) 772005

Last year's 'rather like dining in a train' prompts this year's 'more like school, with no hope of intimate talk.' You help yourself in succession to crudités with aïoli, salami, then a duck terrine; all before a limited choice of variable main courses, with limp vegetables sometimes; followed by a fine Brie; and sorbets (perhaps apricot) and sweets. Good bread and coffee. They shop rather than cook here, perhaps, and the service charge seems stiff when so much is your own work. They import French wines, and the £5·75 set price includes a half-bottle. Note that the 'mystery house aperitif' and the persuasively suggested armagnac are extra. 'Zealous young French waiters'. Recorded French music.

Closed Sun; Sat L; last 2 weeks Aug; Dec 24–26 & 31; Jan 1 Must book weekends	Meals 12.30–1.30, 7.30–9 (10.45 Fri & Sat)	Service 12% Seats 40 No dogs
	Tdh £5·75 (meal £6·90)	Access, Am Ex, Barclay, Euro

(9) Hove Manor Restaurant
Hove Street, Hove
Brighton (0273) 730850

The Anglo-Spanish owners of this polite, rather cramped restaurant at the foot of a block of flats duly list gazpacho, pollo catalana (£4) and other Spanish dishes. But we hear more about 'bargain' set lunches (£4, and £4·65 on Sundays): inviting hors d'oeuvre; well-cooked fish and roasts from the trolley (turkey, or 'the rarest of rare beef' with trimmings); good fresh fruit salad (trifle, though, would have been better for some sherry). 'Unlimited' coffee. No carafes, and better reckon on £4·50 or so for one of their recently added Spanish bottles. Light music. Dress neatly.

Closed Mon (exc May 5 & Aug 25); Sun D; Jan 1 Must book Meals 12.15–2, 7–10	Alc (min £3) £7·70 (meal £10·80)	Seats 40 ♿ rest Air-conditioning No dogs
Tdh L £4 (meal £6·75), Sun L £4·65 (meal £7·45), D £5·50 (meal £8·40)	Children's helpings (under 8)	Access, Am Ex, Barclay, Diners, Euro

(10) Oats
124 King's Road
Brighton (0273) 28221

'Oats – French Cuisine' sounds less than compatible, but in a basement between the Metropole and the West Pier Rita Forsey and Michael Moore have lately convinced critical locals and inspectors that their pâté, prawns gratinée, entrecôte Mirabeau, chicken en chemise and 'carefully bought and cooked vegetables' are the real thing. 'Good bread, service and coffee too.' Wines from £2·75 for Arc de Triomphe. Recorded music. Details approximate. More reports, please, with a view to later upgrading.

Closed L; Sun; Mon
Must book

D only, 7–10.30

Seats 40

Alc £5·10 (meal £7·55)

(11) Peking
9 Weston Road
Brighton (0273) 722090

Closed Dec 25 & 26
Must book
Meals 12–2.30, 5.30–11.30

Alc (min £2) £3·90
(meal £5·05)

Cover 15p
Seats 45
♿ rest
No dogs
Access, Am Ex, Barclay

Visitors to this smart Pekinese place 'on one of Brighton's main drags' have stopped saying, 'Never mind the food, feel the decor', and take the immaculate linen and glasses, the silver menu and the fresh roses in their stride. With Ying-Lam Man now in the kitchen, and John Man out front, reports of the food are less unanimous. Dried prawns and seaweed (90p) makes a better appetiser than sesame prawns nowadays. Soups, however, whether wun-tun, hot-and-sour ('better renamed furnace-and-sour'), or Shanghai-style fish 'with masses of fresh-tasting flaked fish', are generally liked. Sweet-and-sour pork varies from 'gristly with a bland sauce' to 'tender and golden in a syrupy yellow-bean sauce.' Aromatic crispy duck, listed as a speciality, served with pancakes and bean sauce (£7 a whole duck, £1·85 a quarter), is variously described as 'too fatty' and 'rather cold and lacking in flavour', but sliced duck with pineapple is 'generous and good' (£1·45). The tea is 'delicious', and 'toffee bananas looked beautiful and kept the children at the next table amused.' In Brighton many people like forks and knives with Chinese food – to say nothing of red wine, and coffee with demerara sugar – but ask for a bowl and chopsticks if you wish. More reports, please.

Towns shown in black on our maps contain at least one recommended restaurant, pub or wine bar (see map key). The dot denotes the location of the town or village, not the establishment. Where necessary, we give directions to it in the entry. If you can, help us to improve them.

For the explanation of ♿, denoting accessibility for the disabled, see 'How to use the Guide', p. 4.

If you think you are suffering from food-poisoning after eating in a restaurant, report this immediately to the local Public Health Authority (and write to us).

Prices quoted in entries now include VAT.

(12) **La Pergola**
41 Castle Street
Brighton (0273) 28653

'Patchy' was a member's verdict when Vito Vallone, all charm, was apparently factotum both out front and behind the scenes. Overcooked pasta and 'boring sauces with good steaks' fortunately seem to be exceptions to the rule of 'individual cooking' of spaghetti alle vongole, and 'delicious' scallops dry Martini. 'Fettuccine home-made, but I could not be sure of the mayonnaise.' No news of regional meals this year. 'Quiet, yes, but not always relaxed.' Valpolicella £3·30 for a litre.

Closed Sun; Apr 7; May 26; Aug 25; Dec 25 & 26 Must book D Meals 12.30–2, 7–9.30	Tdh D £6·50 (meal £9·25) Alc £5·95 (meal £8·65) Service 10% Children's helpings (under 8)	Seats 30 ♿ rest (2 steps) No dogs Access, Am Ex, Barclay

---

BRIGHTON see also pub section

BRISTOL Avon   Map 2

Gorny
13 Cotham Road South
Bristol (0272) 426444

German-born Michael Gorny hopes his chef's Swiss and French cooking provides good value for money; most members think it does. Roast duck with cream and cranberries and 'succulent' pork fillet with apples and calvados (firm vegetables included) win praise – or try venison in cream and madeira. First courses show zest (prawn and sweetcorn soup), but sweets 'from the blackboard' are little remarked. Friendly service, sometimes preoccupied. William Morris papers and recorded Scarlatti surpass bistro norm. Averys wines. No children under school age. No dogs.

Closed L; Sun; Mon; Aug; one week Chr; public hols	Must book weekends D only, 7–10.30 Seats 30	Tdh £5·25 (meal £7·95)

Michael's
129 Hotwell Road
Bristol (0272) 26190

Closed L (exc Sun
[Sept–May] & Dec 25);
Sun D; Mon; Aug;
Dec 25 D
Must book weekends
Meals 1.30–4.30 (Sun),
6.30–12

Tdh £8 (meal £11·65)

Service 10%
Seats 55 (parties 40)
♿ rest (1 step)

Michael McGowan has become a quayside fixture now in his ornate Victorian dining-room, where the cageful of stuffed birds is relieved by plenty of flowers. Indeed, local fruit and vegetable traders in 1978 conferred on him a 'freshest restaurant' award that was also earned in 1979, visitors say, by his 'leeks in cheesy sauce, nutty cabbage, aubergines au gratin and potatoes in cream with onions'. Others report crab pancakes, mussels in a curry cream sauce and 'exceptional' saumon en papillote among fish dishes. Pork loin in white wine, pork in cider with damsons, poussin with Restoration stuffing, and venison, in particular, are also praised. Mr McGowan himself advocates his aubergine caviare, duck breast with green peppercorns, and fillet steak in black coffee – but courage seems to have failed members at this point, for we lack reports. 'Peach Pavlova came with what tasted like a fresh raspberry sauce', and 'there was a first-rate choice of cheeses in good condition.' But another guest says, 'The waitresses were distracted by a raucous party, and my ice was served as a slush.' Averys Clochemerle red or white was £3·95 a litre in 1979, and there are a few finer bottles from the same source: Ch. de Sales '71, £6·55. 'It was particularly nice to have smoking confined to the bar.' Music, mostly classical, is similarly confined.

App: G. M. Wilson, E. Jenkins, K. I. Plum, F.I., J. Oxley, and others

---

BRISTOL Avon Map 2

Parks
51 Park Street
Bristol (0272) 28016

Mirrors, arches and exuberant ivy, with long opening hours and a sensible drinks policy, swell the youthful queues to eat at this lively place in a much-frequented Clifton street. Geoffrey Hale (ex-Dorchester) clearly cannot cook every dish served and quality control errs, says a local inspector, but turkey and potato broth, cheese and nutmeggy spinach in a crêpe (£1·55), robust cassoulet (£2·15) and wicked ice-creams (dark chocolate with fudge, or damson, 65p) excuse slips. Local Kingston Black cider, or wine from £2·50; two Californias under £4. Eclectic music.

Closed Dec 24–26 & 31; Jan 1	No bookings	Children's helpings
Open 11 a.m.–11 p.m.	Alc £3·15 (meal £5)	Seats 80

Rajdoot
83 Park Street
Bristol (0272) 28033

Punjabi cooking that once 'tickled the palates of the diplomatic corps' now evokes memos from Paul Scott adjutants. Even they linger on the stylish setting and hot crunchies before praising the tandoori fish (£2·35), chicken korma and 'ritual, infallible' rogan gosht (£1·95). Kidneys, in either a kebab or a masala ('cooked in cream') are listed. Dhal and 'meagre' rice. Indian music with a marked resemblance to jazz at times. Wine from £3·40; 'metallic' lager; 'warm' beer.

Closed L Sun & public hols; Dec 26; Dec 31 D	Tdh L £2·70 (meal £3·90), D from £5 (meal £6·15)	Cover 25p D Children's helpings
Must book D	Alc (min £3·50) £5·15 (meal £6·85)	Seats 58 ♿ rest (2 steps)
Meals 12–2.15, 6.30–11.30	Service 10%	No dogs Access, Am Ex, Barclay, Diners, Euro

---

BRISTOL see also wine bar section

Most places will accept cheques only when they are accompanied by a cheque card or adequate identification. Information about which credit cards are accepted is correct when printed, but restaurants may add to or subtract from the list without notice.

BRIXHAM Devon   Map 1

Flynn's Inn
39 Fore Street
Brixham (080 45) 4468

Closed Sun; D Mon &
Tue (Sept–May);
L public hols;
Dec 25 & 26; Jan 1
Must book D & weekends
Meals 11.30–2, 7.30–11

Tdh L £1·20
(meal £3·20),
D from £4 (meal £6·60)

Children's helpings
Seats 60
⑤ rest (2 steps)
Access, Am Ex, Barclay

*Robin Flynn was in and out of the kitchen during 1979,
but now spends his mornings on the casual self-service
lunches, perhaps with salad and quiche and blackcurrant
crumble to follow; and evenings turning out set meals
with plenty of choice: for main course, steaks various
ways (Bercy, poivre vert, marchand de vin), croustillon
montagnard, or poisson à la provençale (£5·25).
Visitors during the year do not think the changes have
affected much though ' "aïolli" was flavoured as
vaguely as it was spelt' and 'my wife's chicken Kiev
had lost its butter.' Sweets sound better than before.
Les Frères ordinaires at £4·05 a litre; Provencal
VDQS wines £3·25 a bottle in 1979. Recorded music,
and a cheerful atmosphere (dogs accepted at lunch-time).
More reports, please, since many of last year's refer to
the period when another chef was in charge.*

BROADSTAIRS Kent   Map 3

Marchesi Restaurant
18 Albion Street
Thanet (0843) 62481

Closed Dec 25 D;
Dec 26 L
Must book weekends
Meals 12–2, 6.30–10

Tdh L £3·95 (meal £6·55),
D £5·50 (meal £8·25)
Alc £7·50 (meal £10·45)

Service 10%
Cover 30p
Children's helpings
Seats 85 (parties 20)
⑤ rest (3 steps)
Car park
Access, Am Ex, Barclay,
Diners, Euro

*The Rogers family, girding themselves for their
centenary here (in 1984) have now taken on a French
chef (Jean-Pierre Raguenel) to operate the table
d'hôte and à la carte menus in these busy dining-rooms
and terrace overlooking Viking Bay. The challenge
seems to have stimulated everybody, for in a set meal
the hors d'oeuvre offered thirty items – including
various meaty dishes as well as French staples like
céleri rémoulade – and were followed by sweetbreads
grand'mère 'that would hold their own anywhere.' A la
carte, too, chicken Kiev (£3·45) was crisply coated
outside, and stuffed with a fragrant garlic and herb
butter; pommes lyonnaise 'must have been unsurpassed
in Kent that night.' Others report similarly good
whitebait and lemon sole, and M Raguenel suggests his
own chicken Pernod and tournedos du gourmet. Sweets
– even sherry trifle on occasion – have been found
adequate. Italian Settesoli ordinaires are £2·80, and the
cellar of French, German and Italian wines is
substantial; they also sell sweet Muscat de Beaumes
de Venise by the glass at a price (65p) that more
pretentious places could well copy. Please continue to
report progress.*

BROADWAY Hereford & Worcester   Map 2

Collin House Hotel
off A44
1 m W of Broadway
Broadway (038 681) 8354

*Jacobean stone and secluded gardens, and within, old
beams set off by Sanderson papers, give the Macleods
every advantage in their modernised farmhouse, and in
1979 various people have found their hospitality and
Philip Eveson's cooking equally commendable. The*

165

Closed Dec 24 to end Jan
Must book D
Meals 12–1.45, 7.30–9

Tdh D £7 (meal £9·95)
Alc £7·05 (meal £10)

Seats 22
Car park
No dogs in d/r
Access, Am Ex
6 rooms (5 with bath,
1 with shower)
B&B £12·50–£16·50
Fire cert

*kitchen garden, and the 'fennel, rosemary, tarragon,
mint and numerous others' in the cartwheel-shaped herb
garden, obviously contribute to the set dinners. A couple
who stayed two nights were able to try fresh sardines
in lime; salmon trout pickled in dill; cucumbers filled
with mayonnaise, horseradish and prawns; and crab
soufflé as first courses; then chicken in tarragon cream,
noisettes of lamb with apple and mint, strips of beef
with green peppercorns, and beef Wellington. The set
menus are altered every six weeks or so. Sweets are
often fruity as well as calorific, with strawberry
Pavlova and pineapple and lime cheesecake mentioned;
'Stilton was in unusually fine condition.' A few wines
were under £4 in 1979, on a short list; Ch. Malescot-
St-Exupéry '73, £8. No cigars or pipes in the
dining-room. No children under ten as residents. You
may eat outside. More reports, please.*

BROADWAY Hereford & Worcester   Map 2

Hunter's Lodge
High Street
Broadway (038 681) 3247

A fine old house at the north end of the High Street,
with a Swiss *chef-patron* offering simple grills and
salads at lunch-time (which you may eat outside):
also smoked fish, stuffed peppers, kidney and
mushroom risotto (£1·75), and 'the bear's paw'
(£1·90 – what is it?). Fancier dinner dishes,
gracefully served, include home-smoked beef with
spiced pear (£1·95), crème de poireaux au gratin
(£1·10), chicken Kiev with hot beetroot (£4·85) and
venison grand veneur (£5·40). Wines, from £3·45 for
Loire white; Barsac is 70p the glass – tell us which
sweets to drink it with.

Closed Mon; Sun D
Must book
Meals 12.30–1.45,
7.30–10

Alc L £4·65 (meal £7·40),
D £10·10 (meal £13·90)

Children's helpings
(under 8)
Seats 60 (parties 50)

🔲 rest (2 steps); w.c.
Car park
No dogs
Access, Am Ex, Barclay,
Diners

BUNGAY Suffolk   Map 6

Brownes
20 Earsham Street
Bungay (0986) 2545

Closed L; Sun; Mon;
Dec 25 & 26
Must book
D only, from 7.30

Alc £7·65 (meal £10·75)

Children's helpings
(under 8)
Seats 25

Timothy Brown (without an 'e', just to confuse you)
cooks and John Adams serves in this 'cosy Georgian
house' whose decor they change, they say, almost as
often as the menu. This must qualify them for a
paperhanger's medal, since their pleasure in seasonal
produce and culinary invention left one visitor
noticing on a second visit that 'every main course bar
one had been changed since the previous occasion.'
Both times, anyway, the meal was admirable, the
second time with fresh Norfolk samphire preceding
venison en croûte (from Woburn) with a sauce of red
wine, cranberries and juniper, and well-cooked fresh
vegetables. Others report comparable mushroom
soup, Stilton pâté, lamb with thyme and tarragon,

♿ rest; w.c.
No dogs
Access, Barclay

lobster in champagne sauce with black and white grapes, and a generously fruit-soaked summer pudding. Mr Brown himself notifies his blinis, lemon fish pie, chocolate and walnut cheesecake and other dishes. There are regular gourmet evenings at a set price (from £6·85). These tend to get booked up, but reports would be welcome. Châtelet ordinaires are £3·45, and there are about forty other wines. No under-fives. Recorded music 'was too heavy and soulful for me.'

App: Ian Beaumont, D. R. Raven, M.V.H.

BURFORD Oxfordshire   Map 2

Bay Tree
Burford (099 382) 3137

A handsome 400-year-old house, under the same owner for the last forty, but out of the *Guide* since 1974. Better reports now of the set meals (with the sensible alternative of a fourth course à la carte). Smoked fish, pâtés and prawn cocktail are expected, with conventional roasts, casseroles and steaks to follow, and 'rather nursery' sweets. Trainee girls serving under the mistress's eye 'recall St Agatha's.' Various reasonably priced wines, with Charbonnier at £1·65 for 50 cl. For the sake of the Russell Flints, if not you, 'no pipes in the dining-room'. (If you enjoy the pâtés and pastries, they are on sale in the owners' shop, Huffkins, in the High Street.) (GHG)

Must book D & weekends
Meals 1–1.45, 7.30–8.45

Tdh L £2·60 (meal £5),
D & Sun L £4·45 (meal
£7·05)

Children's helpings
(by arrangement)
Seats 50
♿ rest (1 step)
Car park
No dogs in public rooms

24 rooms (17 with bath)
B&B £9·60–£14
Full board (3 days or
more) £14 p.d.
Fire cert

BURGESS HILL West Sussex   Map 3

La Padella
2 Keymer Road
Burgess Hill (044 46) 3521

The Renzullis' local customers have kept their pleasure in meals here to themselves this year, so it falls to an outsider to hold the brief for this alpine trattoria opposite the station: 'Enjoyed plump grilled trout with almonds, rolling in butter, and fresh round beans.' Minestrone was an *omnium gatherum* but tasted fresher than the cannelloni. Daily specials have included Ogen melon with brandy or prawns (£1·45), Dover sole and roast duckling. Caramel orange to finish. 'Dignified' service. 'Barolo '73 good value.' 'Expect *arie amorose*.'

Closed Sun
Must book D

Alc £6·15 (meal £9·60)

Seats 40
Access, Am Ex, Barclay

See p. 508 for the restaurant-goer's legal rights, and p. 510 for information on hygiene in restaurants.

Toastmaster's Inn

Church Street
4½ m N of Maidstone
Medway (0634) 61299

Closed Sun; Mon;
2 weeks Aug; 1 week Chr;
Jan 1
Must book
Meals 12–2, 7–10

Alc £7·55 (meal £12·30)

Service 10%
Children's helpings
Seats 34
♿ rest (1 step); w.c.
Car park
No dogs in d/r
Barclaycard
No rooms

Gregory Ward's inn has now had ten *Guide* years to
mature, and most of the early tannic harshness has
softened. He has lately expanded into the terrace
cottage next door, which should enable him to offer
bar as well as restaurant meals in the evening, as at
lunch. He has also kept the same chefs (Tim Dalglish
and Paul Duvall), although they have always had to
play the second fiddles' steadying role to the
well-tuned wine cellar that created the inn's national
and international reputation. Both bar and restaurant
menus are thoughtful, and the cooking has lately
been simplified to advantage: it is easier than it used
to be to find a muted dish for a complex wine, or a
robust wine for an assertive dish. More plain roasting
of good birds, and more cooking with cream cheese
and herbs, may have helped. They are proud of their
home-smoked fish and meat (duck 'ham' with ripe
figs, £1·85 as an hors d'oeuvre, is much liked),
terrine de légumes frais, poulet de Bresse 'truffé' au
persil (£12·10 for two), and coussinet de saumon aux
algues champenoise. Inspectors and others this year
have also liked ragoût de fruits de mer with a (fairly
mild) aïoli, lamb with paloise or port and orange
sauce, sea bass with a lemony hollandaise,
'delicious nutmeggy creamed spinach, and crisp
courgette fritters', and the cheeses from Patrick Rance
of Streatley. But 'the sauce for duck bigarade was too
caramelised and marmalady'. The soft-fruit sweets
may be the best. In the cellar, both German and
California bins have lately been augmented, and, if
you choose, you may spend £16 or so on a '75 Pinot
Noir from Monterey, or on Scharlachberg
Steinkautweg Riesling Auslese '49 from Rheinhessen,
or for that matter on Château du Rayas '67 from
Châteauneuf-du-Pape or Ch. Gazin '52, c.b., from
Pomerol, or sweet white Ch. Rabaud '43, c.b., from
Bommes; or indeed you may spend very much more
or very much less, whether on Ch. d'Angludet '61,
c.b., £28 or 'a strapping young Roussillon' which,
with other house wines, often changed, may be
offered at £4·15 (70p the glass). Other interesting
wines by the glass, with at least four real ales in the
bar, make a brief stop for cannelloni or a dish of
scallops tempting if you are passing through this
gloomy part of Kent. No pipes or cigars in the
restaurant.

*App: John Field, Dennis McDonnell, J. & M.B.,
Dr R. J. von Witt*

**Inspections are carried out anonymously. Persons who pretend to be able to secure,
arrange or prevent an entry in the Guide are impostors and their names or
descriptions should be reported to us.**

BURNHAM MARKET Norfolk   Map 6

Fishes'

Market Place
on B1155
Burnham Market
(032 873) 588

Closed Mon (mid-Sept to
mid-July); Sun D (Oct–
June); Dec 24 D;
Dec 25 & 26
Must book
Meals 12–1.45, 7–9.30
(9 Nov–Easter)

Tdh weekday L £3·40
(meal £6·10),
Sun L £4·50 (meal £7·30)
Alc £6·35 (meal £9·40)

Children's helpings
(under 12)
Seats 48 (parties 20)
&. rest (1 step)
Air-conditioning
Am Ex card

Fishes' vicissitudes (try saying that after a good
dinner as well as before) are not confined to frayed
lino, but everyone this year has thought Gillian Cape's
informal restaurant well suited to this pretty coastal
village. 'Dover soles grilled to perfection,' says one
visitor, and a test set lunch proved good value,
including, as it did, avocado and tomato salad, a
vegetable soup rather less than hot, generous fresh
salmon with a slightly sweet mayonnaise, 'absolutely
delicious' apple, almond and raisin salad and good
cheesecake with fresh peach. 'Noticeably, tomatoes
and apples tasted better than Home Counties
equivalents, and the bread was good too.' Scallop
soup, whitebait, fishcakes with crab sauce, 'superb
mussels in cider with apple and celery, hot crab-meat
with peppers and almonds', and various home-made
ice-creams and mousses are also praised. The judicious
wine list, from £2 for 50 cl of Italian, has fewer gaps
now, and with good bottlings of Vouvray, Sancerre,
Pinot Blanc d'Alsace and others in the £6 range, as
well as a few cheaper wines, good sherry, and Abbot
ale from the cask, you could visit many more famous
fish restaurants and do far worse. No dogs.

*App: Rosemary Royle, Michael Sharpin, Geoffrey
Finsberg, R. Howgego, L. & J.H., and others*

BURNHAM-ON-CROUCH Essex   Map 3

Contented Sole
80 High Street
Maldon (0621) 782139

Closed Sun; Mon;
1 month Chr; 2 weeks July
Must book
Meals 12.15–1.45,
7–9.30

Tdh L £3·45 (meal £5·55)
Alc £9 (meal £11·05)

Service inc
Children's helpings
Seats 70 (parties 30)
&. rest (1 step)
No dogs

Yachtsmen, however contented, are slow to tell us
enough about Mr R. T. Walton's smartly served
restaurant, but inspectors report that it loses little of
its *élan* as the years pass. 'It is not a place to eat
curried veal in,' suggests one man who tried and was
disappointed, but in his Sunday lunch the 'puffy'
sardine and tomato quiche, braised duckling in cherry
sauce with Manzanilla, and cream caramel reached a
higher standard. So, on another occasion, did roulade
de crabe frite, leek and potato soup, steak and kidney
pudding with surprising but well-buttered swede, and
filet de sole royale in a prawn sauce. Crêpe de fruits
de mer (£4·50) is a house speciality. Crème brûlée was
'good and rich', and apple pie, though the pastry was
open to criticism, was amply filled with apples and zest
of orange. The wine list offers sensible bottles to drink
with fish at sensible prices (from £3·30; Brauneberger
Mandelgraben Kabinett '77, £5·20).

App: E.S., P.A., Ron Salmon, and others

See p. 441 for the pub section, and p. 491 for the wine bars.

CADNAM Hampshire   Map 2

Le Chanteclerc
Romsey Road
on A31
Cadnam (042 127) 3271

Closed Sun; Mon; Sat L;
Dec 25 & 26; Jan 1
Must book
Meals 12–1.30, 7–9.45

Alc £9·25 (meal £12·25)

Children's helpings
(under 12)
Seats 50 (parties 18)
 rest (2 steps)
Car park
No dogs
Access, Barclay

*Take exit 1 from the M27 – or play safe by staying on
the A31 – to find the Denats' suave, set-back
restaurant by a BP garage just east of Cadnam
roundabout. It is time we heard from more customers,
for it is a busy place, courteously served in various
people's experience, with an ambitious repertoire. The
virtues of a test meal were the plump orange mussels in
natural juices, chicken with a real taste, home-made
game chips with moist partridge (at a modest seasonal
price), and runny Brie. Faults included 'unripe, tasteless
tomatoes at a season when better ones could be found
for tomates à l'antiboise, noticeably anglicised
mayonnaise, sauces and seasoning, and unimpressive
sweets.' M Denat's own suggestions are caneton
à la cévenole, côte de veau vallée d'Auge, and sole
dieppoise (all £5·85), perhaps with buckwheat pancakes
au rhum to follow. French ordinaire is £3·65 a litre and
relatively, the dearer wines are better value here, with
Ch. Lynch-Moussas '73 at £8·05, and Ch. Smith-Haut-
Lafitte, '61, c.b., at £12·35. More reports, please.*

CALDBECK Cumbria   Map 7

Parkend
1½ m W of Caldbeck
on B5299
Caldbeck (069 98) 442

Closed Mon; D Dec 25 &
26; Jan; Feb
Must book
Meals 12–1.45, 7–8.45

Tdh D from £7·20
(meal £8·75)

Alc L £4·25 (meal £6·05),
D £6·05 (meal £7·90)

Service inc
Children's helpings
Seats 32
 rest
Car park
No dogs
Access card

Joyce Woodcock, and her parents the Arnesens, are
remote from both tourist and commercial populations
in their calm 17th-century farmhouse, and last year's
petrol anxieties make them doubtful about their lunch
trade, so telephone before a midday visit. But their
primary concern is to keep faith with the regulars
who know what value they are given. A test meal
yielded simple hors d'oeuvre, a good tomato and
orange soup laced with sherry, chicken casseroled in a
slightly over-thick mushroom sauce with crisp sauté
potatoes and deftly cooked green vegetables, and
profiterole-like orange salambô, with orange cream
inside the choux buns, and a brittle caramel crown.
English cheeses in good condition were also offered.
A la carte, the dishes sound less exciting but are
cooked with equal care. Other possibilities mentioned
either by Mrs Woodcock or by other visitors include
bean soup with almonds, 'excellent salmon trout',
mixed grill (£4·85 à la carte), medallions of pork in
cream, lemon and chives, and roast duck with orange
salad. 'Strawberry flan had a real home-made pastry
crust.' Bar snacks are served at lunch-time only –
there is no pub licence, only a restaurant one, and
'you do not let your hair down at Parkend, but you
do get good food nicely presented at a fair price.'
Argentine table wines are £3·10 for 75 cl and
Marqués de Riscal '73 (Rioja) is about £5. Pressurised
beers. No children under eight at dinner. There is a
small terrace for outside eating.

App: S. W. H. Perry, R. J. Bocock, K.L.J.

CAMBRIDGE Cambridgeshire   Map 3

Peking
21 Burleigh Street
Cambridge (0223) 354755

Closed Mon; last 2 weeks
Sept; Dec 25–31
Must book D & weekends
Meals 12–2, 6–10.30

Tdh D £6·50 (meal £7·55)
Alc £5·60 (meal £6·65)

Service 10%
Seats 64 (parties 30)
Air-conditioning
No dogs

For reasons obscure even to an Oxford man,
Cambridge has never been especially well-fed, and
one or two who have made the long march to Mr
Mao's 'dull façade in a seedy street in the Kite' have
wondered, after excess salt or sugar, whether the place
has the qualifications expected of a solitary
standard-bearer. But others, an inspector included,
remain impressed with the fried mixed vegetables (no
bad test): 'striking crispness combined with great
succulence.' At a test meal, prawns with green peppers
(£3.30) were 'the very biggest and curliest animals' –
and the sauces for chicken with almonds and fillet
of pork in sweet-sour sauce (£2·10) were both
carefully differentiated; prawns with sesame seeds,
'roast duck with sundries', and sliced beef with garlic
are also praised. Mr Mao and his five chefs further
recommend grilled chicken Peking-style (£2·30),
sliced pork with leeks and garlic, bean curd with
mince meat in hot pepper sauce, and deep-fried
shredded beef with chilli ('very hot, £3'). It is probably
best to eat à la carte. Hirondelle is £3.

App: John Wilkes, E. Rigbey, E.S., D.J.W.

CAMBRIDGE see also pub section

CANTERBURY Kent   Map 3

The Longport
Monastery Street
Canterbury (0227) 51204

Closed Dec 24–26 & 31;
Jan 1
Must book weekends
Meals 12–2.30, 6–11

Tdh £3·80 (meal £6)

Seats 45 (parties 18)

*'From the outside it looks more likely to appeal to a
tosspot from the Canterbury Tales', and indeed the
real ales on hand-pump have something of this
character too. But people who care more for cooking
than for chic and chicanery take pleasure in Mrs
Golding's simple fare, amply served in a plain setting.
Hot dishes are brought to the table; the rest is up to
you. An early nominator mentions the bread, salads,
pâté, vegetable curry (£1), Mexican hot-pot (£1·50)
and chicken pie. 'They also make a good coffee and
walnut cake and don't call it gateau.' Others commend
the savoury rice with kidneys, but wish the quiches were
not made heavy by wholemeal flour. A test meal
confirmed these impressions, and both the fresh tomato
soup (60p) and red cabbage salad would have been
hailed with delight in more pretentious restaurants.
Drink beer or Taunton cider, or the house red wine
(£2·80), rather than anything dearer. Mostly classical
records at lunch, 'modern' ones at dinner, whatever that
may say about the clientele. More reports, please.*

We rewrite every entry each year, and depend on fresh, detailed reports to confirm
the old, as well as to include the new. The further from London you are, the more
important this is.

171

Aynsome Manor Hotel
off A590 (M6 exit 36)
2 m NW of
Grange-over-Sands
Cartmel (044 854) 276

Closed L (exc Sun);
Sun D (exc res)
Must book
Meals 1–1.30 (Sun),
7–8.30

Tdh Sun L £5·50
(meal £8·70), D £8
(meal £11·45)

Children's helpings
(under 12)
Seats 40 (parties 10)
 ⌖ rest
Car park
No dogs in public rooms
Access card
16 rooms (13 with bath)
D, B&B from £12
Fire cert

Eight centuries have gone since Cartmel Priory was founded by an earl whose descendants later lived in this tranquil manor, now run (with a converted stable annexe) by the Williams family to the power of four (Alan, Sue, Jill and Evelyn). 'We cook to please our guests and not ourselves,' writes Alan, explaining meat past pinkness and vegetables past crunchiness; fair enough, but some people wish that he would not recite what they are about to eat with quite such repetitive gusto. Meals begin well with praise of pâté, strips of plaice in almonds, and mousses of salmon or tongue. There is also high praise of the roast lamb with redcurrant and orange sauce. 'Sweets are not put out on the trolley so early that they droop', 'apricot Dacquoise still lingers on the tongue', and 'fresh raspberry ganache was delightful.' Cheeses could well be fewer, and so better. The table settings sparkle and the service is efficient as well as friendly. The dining-room light level is perhaps too low for those who like to see as well as taste. Nicolas ordinaires are £4 a litre and a bottle of Loire red or white costs about the same: in 1979, Ch. la Rose Figeac '71 and Louis Latour's Clos de la Vigne au Saint '70 hovered round £7, which sounds reasonable. Breakfasts are good. There are bar lunches with pressurised beers for residents (except on Sundays). No children under five at dinner (but they may take supper in their rooms). Smokers are asked to drink coffee in the lounge. Recorded music mostly string or baroque. (GHG)

App: Mr & Mrs J. D. Cranston, Dr R. Filer Cooper, R. Sykes, David Murdoch, A. T. Langton, M. S. Kirk, and others

CAULDON LOWE Staffordshire   Map 5

Jean-Pierre

on A52
7 m W of Ashbourne
Waterhouses (053 86) 338

Closed Sun; Sat L;
Dec 25; Jan 1
Must book
Meals 12–1.30, 7.30–9.30

Alc £6·85 (meal £10·85)

Service inc
Cover £1 (Sat)
Seats 25
 ⌖ rest (2 steps)

Jean-Pierre Champeau took in good part the last edition's mischievous reproduction of the accent all Englishmen love, since it has led so many to discover that he cooks as Norman as he is and sounds: that is, with the lightest of touches in rich-sounding dishes. 'To think,' writes one member from what another calls 'the effete end of the Pennines' – 'to think that I of all people actually devoured four courses in this little place, and cleaned the plate every time, including mousseline sauce with asparagus, lots and lots of garlic butter with snails, gooseberry sauce with wild duck (the meat slashed across to tenderise and flavour it), and a quietly lethal coupe glacée au Grand Marnier at the end.' Not everyone exhibits stamina of this order, but it is evident that this meal was no flash in the *sauteuse*. The jambon cru and the venison pâté; the saumon au Champagne and the langoustines or scallops au

Car park
No dogs

gratin (£2·20 as an intermediate, £4·40 as a main course); the navarin au cidre and the cuisses de grenouilles – all are lovingly described. So is a fascinating dish called 'sot-l'y-laisse au cidre' (£3·65): if you have ever wondered what to do with the two nuggets of tender dark meat found low down a chicken's back, buy a dozen birds and ask here. There is even a Jean-Pierre fan club – 'a family who knew him from his days at Birtle had made the journey just to eat.' A more critical admirer, not quite ready to buy his scarf and rattle, points out that bar nibbles are poor, Kirs not always chilled and délices d'Argenteuil an indifferent version; moreover, that the spirits kept are more interesting than the wines (which begin at £2 for 50 cl of French Gamay, Pinot, or Cabernet). But the cheeses, the willingness to buy cèpes or inkcaps people bring in to sell, the bread, the sorbets, the *trou normand*, the coffee, and the memory that gives a returned guest his vegetables after the meat because that is how he liked them last time: all this has made the white stone house with chequered bistro table-cloths 'Staffordshire's best discovery since Primitive Methodism'. Please do not smoke. Leave under-14s at home, and expect a few long waits – perhaps cold feet on the tiled floor too.

App: Christopher Forman, Katherine Muir, Geoffrey Hands, M.A.S., Cynthia McDowall, Ruth Johnson, and many others

---

CHAGFORD Devon Map 1

Gidleigh Park

2 m W of Chagford
Chagford (064 73) 2367
and 2225

Must book
Meals 12–2.30 (bar),
7.30–9.30

Tdh D £12 (meal £14·30)
Alc bar L about £4,
D £12·35 (meal £15·35)

Service inc
Cover 50p L (non-res)
Seats 30 (parties 12)
rest
No dogs
Access, Am Ex, Barclays,
Diners
11 rooms (all with bath)
B&B from £22

You will reach Paul and Kay Henderson's 'mercantile Tudor' house if you start from Chagford and persevere; only foxes make it from Gidleigh. 'A rising star', one Scandinavian visitor calls it after last year's provisional entry for this ambitious but charming American couple with developed tastes in food and wine. They are calling it a restaurant with rooms rather than a hotel this year, and this is all one or two of the attics deserve – though the public rooms are a pleasure to sit in. Mrs Henderson's cooking is serious: there is limited choice, and it is bad luck if you find an unpeeled tomato. 'After quenelles of Tamar salmon with a sauce of prawns and cream, we had veal fillet with white wine sauce and lemon, then a choice of at least a dozen cheeses sent up by Patrick Rance or Paxton and Whitfield or both, and finally a delicious walnut gateau.' 'Crêpes stuffed with cream cheese and spinach were light and piquant.' 'Mange-tout peas were about 3 cm long: a triumph to buy as well as to cook.' The best things in a test meal were fully up to these raptures: the fragile vegetable tartlets passed round in the bar, and the pink slivers of magret de canard, arranged fanwise with chopped red pepper and green peppercorns, in

173

the duck's own juices. But neither the vegetable soup nor the vegetables on this occasion matched the rest, and neither savoury nor sweet pastry shells were as fragile as the tartlets. Another visitor reports tough veal too. Cranberry sorbet, chocolate meringue gateau, and other sweets are praised. Service is informal, 'perhaps more pert than its skills justify.' The wines are understood, fairly priced, and served in the right glasses, with champagne as an aperitif 'cheaper than gin and tonic', and pipes and cigars are forbidden in the dining-room. It is worth asking the host's advice (noting also his enthusiasm for California Cabernets and Chardonnays) but there is plenty of fine claret to play with: Ch. Troplong-Mondot '64, Ch. Talbot '67, Clos Fourtet '70, Clos René '71 and Ch. Palmer '73 were all under £12 in 1979; and Salon le Mesnil '71 champagne £15. House wines, brandies and eaux-de-vie are also good. Pressurised beers. Children are 'treated and charged as adults'. The bar lunches look promising (or they will pack up one for you), and there are thirty acres of land before you get to Dartmoor. (GHG)

App: Jens Ulltveit Moe, B. J. Whittaker, A.J.B., Henry Clarendon, W. L. Sleigh, and others

---

CHAGFORD see also **DREWSTEIGNTON** and **FRENCHBEER**

CHELTENHAM Gloucestershire   Map 2

Aubergine
Belgrave House,
Imperial Square
Cheltenham (0242) 31402

Closed Sun; Mon L;
public hols (exc May 5,
Dec 31, & Jan 1)
Must book D
Meals 12–1.45, 7–9.30

Alc £6·75 (meal £9·85)

Service 10%
Children's helpings
(under 12)
Seats 40 (parties 20)
⟨⟩ rest (3 steps); w.c.
Am Ex, Diners

Inaki and Sue Beguiristain's downstairs restaurant, decorated with old cameras and portrait photographs, has appeared here for nine years now – though want of charm has often erased impressions of skilful cooking. A nadir was reached when a policeman was summoned to persuade a reputable local tradesman to pay in full for a party's meals that the staff were unable to serve hot, and unwilling to heat up. Later visitors, including an inspector, report happily of the gazpacho (65p), the superb lunchtime stuffed omelettes (£1·55 for a 'light, creamy, perfectly rolled one with chicken livers') and main dishes such as 'steak au poivre with correctly cooked vegetables' or veal escalope and tongue with madeira sauce (£4·30). But these people too make it clear that the service problem arises from the 'Cheltenham lady' waitresses, too few in number and perhaps too uninformed about their job. Wines (from £3·65 for Rioja) are mediocre for the price. There is a small garden for summer eating. More reports, please.

The Guide accepts no advertising. Nor does it allow restaurateurs to use its name on brochures, menus, or in any form of advertisement. If you see any instances of this, please report them to us.

Food for Thought

10 Grosvenor Street
Cheltenham (0242) 29836

Closed L; Sun; Mon;
2 weeks Sept; Dec 25,
26 & 31; Jan 1;
Cheltenham Gold Cup
Week
Must book
D only, 7.30–9

Tdh £8·95 (meal £10·80)

Service inc
Seats 20
♿ rest
Air-conditioning
No dogs

Recipe in *Second Dinner
Party Book:* grapefruit
cheesecake

'Summa cum laude' was the verdict on a deceptively simple test meal this time, and though it comes in a year when 'bouncy' Christopher Wickens and Joanna Jane Mahon have changed places with each other in kitchen and bar, as piano duettists might change ends of the keyboard, it is only fair to say that their first pestle consummates a period of steady development in a partnership first formed in a neighbouring county. Early in the year, another inspector's difficulty in booking suggested that Cheltenham punters know a winner when they see one – and at a modest stake too, considering how few tables there are. The street is unfashionable and the exterior shabby – as one member says, 'I can remember it as the Hurry Curry.' But with the shelves of cookery books, the hospitable welcome, and a correctly mixed Kir leading to well-balanced chicken liver pâté and delicate slivers of smoked haddock in cream with cheese and celery, the local favourite was already beginning to pull clear of the field, in spite of 'wet chicken, wet courgettes and wet salad' one evening. For the *Guide's* hardened Scouts and O'Sullivans, the issue was decided by the main courses on two different occasions, a beef in beer casserole, with vegetable flavours distinct and a crunchy breadcrumb and Parmesan topping, and 'splendidly juicy, rose-pink roast lamb with a delicate béarnaise on the side, chastely steamed broccoli, and an equally restrained salad of lettuce hearts and diced cucumber.' Sirloin of beef and pork chop with port and orange have proved as good, and that is without counting the owners' own preferences for stuffed trout in garlic butter and devilled roast duckling. Final fences are jumped with ease: the strawberry and mulberry ice-creams, the crème brûlée and the grapefruit cheesecake, the Stilton (with good bread) and the generous bowl of fresh fruit. But for reluctance to stock half-bottles (though they will break into the cheaper full ones for lone diners) the wine policy is also beyond reproach, with smokers politely deterred, and affectionate service from a good list (mostly by Robin Yapp and Christopher Tatham). It begins with Beaudet table wines at £3.75, includes sound Riojas and is predictably strong on Rhônes and Loires, with Ch. Rausan-Ségla '73 in magnum at £16 a fair example of restraint in (inclusive) pricing. Recorded classical music.

App: Mr & Mrs D. M. Bowdell, K. S. Mingle, R.A.C. Hellier, A.J.B., J. & J.W., H.L.W., and others

---

CHELTENHAM see also wine bar section

Prices of meals underlined are those which we consider represent unusual value for money. They are not necessarily the cheapest places in the Guide, or in the locality.

Jean's Kitchen
1 Newtown Close,
St Anne Street
Chester (0244) 24239

Tony Lacey has a local fast-food outlet too now, but says he still helps his wife Jean in her red-checked kitchen near Northgate Arena. 'Perhaps the best in Chester,' suggests one man, and sausage meats with garlic roll, mushrooms in white wine, veal cutlet with tomato and cheese, or the Laceys' preferred estofat albigeoise, chicken hongroise and gigot provençale (all £3·55) bear this out. But 'too much rice lurked under seafood in salad, and sweets were over-rich.' The £2·85 set lunch is also available in the evening till 7 p.m. Spanish Talamanca at £1·50 for 33 cl, which is plenty. Recorded music. No dogs.

Closed Sun; L public hols; Dec 25
Must book
Meals 12–2, 5.30–9.30

Tdh L £2·85 (meal £4·95), D £5 (meal £7·30)
Alc (min Sat D £6)
£5·45 (meal £8·70)

Service 10%
Children's helpings
Seats 32
Access card

Kinchs

on A4095
3 m SW of Bicester
Bicester (086 92) 41444

Closed L (exc Sun & Dec 25); Mon; Sun D; 1st week Jan; public hols (exc Apr 4)
Must book
Meals 12–1.30 (Sun), 7–9.30

Tdh Sun L £6·75 (meal £10·15), D £8 (meal £11·55)

Service 10%
Children's helpings (under 8)
Seats 40
rest (3 steps)
Car park
No dogs

'An enchanting place both inside and out,' says one visitor to Christopher Greatorex's candle-lit refectory. There is a slight question-mark over its place this year, for since a serious illness early in 1979 he has been looking round for a partner. But with one or two exceptions people found standards of food and service well maintained by his womenfolk during this difficult period, and he is now back in the kitchen, so doubts may stop short of italic type (though progress reports will be welcome). There is plenty of choice in the set dinners, and the owner's favourite dishes are worth noting: turbot and vegetable mousse with herb mayonnaise, salmon trout baked in sorrel leaves, poussin cooked with garlic and fines herbes, and fillet of lamb baked with basil in pastry. This list hints at the well-stocked vegetable and herb garden which has been his pride and consolation. A guest reports 'a meal to remember' that began with a drink that one of the wine suppliers (Yapp of Mere) calls a Myr (white wine with a dash of Crème de Myrtilles). 'I began with prawns in a skilful sauce, with lettuce and fennel, then very tender Grecian spiced beef, with white cabbage and slender beans, and a bottle of Château de Vannières '72 (an excellent Bandol from Reynier). Note that garlic bread is 30p extra.' Another visitor praises the coriander mushrooms, the prune and cream sauce for noisettes of pork, and 'the excellent red and white French house wines' in the £4 range. Sweets have been extended lately. A current list of likely ones is not to hand, but the soft fruit ices are good. Beyond the wines already mentioned, there is formidable claret and burgundy, most of it in double figures. Ch. Rausan-Ségla '73, '67, and '70, all c.b., are priced in ascending order from £9·50 to

Recipe in *Second Dinner Party Book:* chicken cocotte with garlic and fines herbes

£14. Sometimes they hold wine evenings, and (though there is otherwise no music) Elizabethan banquets with minstrels in the gallery. Restraint is expected of smokers.

App: Stanley John, R. J. Haerdi, Paul Fletcher, S.P.B.M., J. Tovar-Graü, and others

---

CHICHESTER West Sussex   Map 3

Christophers
149 St Pancras
Chichester (0243) 788724

Closed Sun; Mon;
public hols (exc Apr 4,
Jan 1)
Must book D & weekends
Meals 12–2, 7–10 (later
for theatre parties)

Tdh L £4 (meal £6.30),
D £8·40 (meal £11·15)

Service 10%
Cover £1 (after 9.30)
Seats 35
⌖ rest (2 steps); w.c. (m)
Air-conditioning
No dogs
Access, Am Ex, Barclay,
Diners

Christophers has been out of the *Guide* since the original Christopher moved out years ago, but members now seem at last to feel more confident about the present owner Philip Mitchell's cooking, and even indignant at not finding the place in the last edition. A test meal in 1979 suggested that we were indeed missing something: that is, a well-judged meal served with courtesy but without airs. The room is small but the tables are well spaced and napkins are linen in the evening. Kipper pâté or seafood crêpes or garlic-buttered prawns make good first courses, and a lunchtime inspector was very taken by the cold lemon soup. Among main courses, steamed chicken breasts with crab stuffing are at least a brave shot at the *cuisine minceur* style, poulet vallée d'Auge is another favourite chicken dish, duck 'could have been carved with a saucer' (if that is how you like duck) and sweetbreads with cream and mushrooms had 'that rich buttery taste you only get at home or in France.' Saddle of lamb with gooseberry sauce is a speciality. Among sweets, look out for apricot Dacquoise and the 'flavoury, un-smooth blackcurrant ice-cream'. Wines (from Arthur Purchase) begin with red burgundy or Tarn white at £2·65 for 65 cl (under a bottle) and Ch. Brane-Cantenac '73, c.b., was £8·95 late in 1979. Recorded music.

App: Imogen Nichols, A. W Hakim, J.O.H., H.F.

Little London Restaurant
38 Little London
off East Street
Chichester (0243) 884899

Closed Sun; Mon;
Dec 25–27; Jan 1
Must book
Meals 12–2, 7–10 (later
after theatre)

Tdh L from £3·90
(meal from £7·05)
Alc £8·40 (meal £12·80)
Alc meal (Savourie)
about £5

To judge by the number of reports this year, Philip Stroud must be more dependent on Good Food Club members than he cares to admit; besides, most of them sound pleased, even when they have also had 'the faint sense of having gate-crashed a county cocktail party.' Two restaurants are contrived out of the house, bijou though it is in estate-agentese. Downstairs, where you now eat surrounded by two tones of pink, the cost (which guests are not allowed to see) would quickly provoke criticism if the 'creamy and thrilling' curried apple soup, fried langoustines, and filled avocados failed to get meals off to a good start, and if double-figure lobster and grouse dishes were carelessly cooked. But mistakes are rare, and there is praise too for duck with gooseberry sauce, mignons de porc sautés, and chicken breasts stuffed with crab and served with apple and orange sauce.

Cover L 20p, D 50p
(75p after theatre)
Seats 40 (parties 14)
⟨&⟩ rest; w.c.
No dogs

Bread and butter are both good, and 'I did not need
to be apprehensive about the menu's apparent offer
to overcook vegetables on request.' 'Lamb fricassee –
and supposedly spicy dishes generally – may need
more zest.' Sweets keep up the standard: 'excellent
summer pudding, and hazelnut meringue with Melba
sauce'; 'memorable meringues with bitter chocolate.'
'We found the service friendly without being familiar.'
The set lunch is also called good value. Upstairs in
the Savourie, the system is self-service, and control is
less tight, to judge by occasional notes of unskimmed
soups, 'unfortunate' sardine and tomato pâté, dryish
gateaux, and 'warm Beaujolais'. But, again, regulars
find the salads, individual fish or chicken pies, and
home-made puddings 'consistently good, and the
service welcoming. I am lucky to work so near – and
on fine days you can eat on the terrace.' The house
wines from Arthur Purchase are sound at about £4,
and perhaps relatively better value than some of the
dearer ones. No pipes, or over-casual dress in the
restaurant. No young children. Recorded classical
music in the Savourie. Details are approximate:
telephone about after-theatre suppers and charges.

*App: Robert Ellis, Ron Salmon, B. G. Laker, J. N.
Cooper, J. Fox, Mrs T. Cavanna, and many others*

CHIPPING CAMPDEN Gloucestershire   Map 2

Kings Arms
Evesham (0386) 840256

Closed Mon, Sun D,
Tue L (Nov–Mar)
Must book D
Meals 12.15–2 (bar),
7.30–9.30

Tdh D £6·75 (meal £9·25),
Sun L £6·25 (meal £8·70)

Service 10%
Seats 35 (parties 18)
⟨&⟩ rest (1 step)
Car park
No dogs in public rooms
Access, Am Ex, Barclay,
Diners
14 rooms (2 with bath)
B&B £6–£12
Fire cert

*Hugh Corbett's traditional inn had the rare distinction,
two years ago, of being dropped from the* Guide *by
mistake, or at least by misapprehension, though the
inspector who ran the gauntlet of the 'débutante' service
the following year amended this to 'by mistake on
purpose.' Mr Corbett himself is a volatile figure in
Cotswold catering, and has put the Willmotts in charge
here, with Rosemary Willmott in the kitchen, and, it
seems, more efficient service now. Summer visitors have
especially enjoyed the 'mildly curried fish-cakes with
hollandaise', hot tagliatelle, cold chicken with curry
mayonnaise, crudités, rack of lamb cooked pink with
fresh mint and yoghourt, and other dishes on a sensibly
varied set dinner or Sunday lunch menu. Sweets by and
large are mercifully simple, and 'the Stilton is super.'
There are weekday bar lunches, perhaps outside in
summer. Les Frères ordinaire is £2·40 a bottle and other
wines have been listed to us without vintages. The bitter
in cask is Hook Norton. More reports, please.*

CHITTLEHAMHOLT Devon Map 1

Highbullen Hotel

off B3226
5 m SW of South Molton
Chittlehamholt (076 94)
248

Closed L (exc Sun & res);
Apr 6 L
Must book
Meals 1–2 (Sun), 7.30–9

Tdh L £6, D £7 (meal
£8·90)

Service inc
Seats 60
 ♿ rest
Car park
No dogs
26 rooms (all with bath)
D, B&B £17·50–£25
Fire cert

The number of reports on file takes one back to the earlier days of the Neils' régime at this under-served but very involving hotel on a peaceful plateau. No wonder that so many visitors' book entries cite the *Guide* as their introduction to it, and as one of them says: 'It is the only hotel I can think of where the guests on a snow-bound New Year's Eve would toast the proprietors, and consider it an honour to be asked to help wash up.' It is naturally not like that in summer, and there are, as always, accounts of casualness over bookings, long waits at meal-times and poorly cooked main courses at dinner to set against the warm praise of serious people who return year by year and have noticed, this time, not just the gradual improvement of sporting and other facilities but also rather more innovation on the menu than usual. 'We had three different soups and as many different pâtés in our short stay, underdone sirloin in port sauce was generous and excellent, and côte de veau in a creamy, garlicky brandy sauce was also delicious.' Mushrooms arménienne is a familiar first course; fresh sardines with spinach, or avocado cream with smoked salmon and prawns, are novelties here; at the pudding stage too 'one or two duds seem to have gone, but we particularly enjoyed hazelnut meringue with nicely tart dried apricots, frosted almond cream with a dash of Grand Marnier, and several rich variations on the chocolate theme; we always seem to want just a nibble of cheese after puddings like these, but were too shy to ask until we noticed a neighbour demanding and getting a cut at a whole Stilton.' Breakfasts are mainly self-service 'with Olympic sprints for the toast placed on a central table', but they will cook you anything at a small extra charge. The wines remain, in some cases, well under what they would now cost to replace. It would be unsporting to specify the bargains too closely, but not many of us will be drinking again Ch. Giscours '66, c.b., at £10·70, or Bonnes-Mares '72 (Amance) at £12, or half-bottles of Ch. Coutet '73 at £3·50. A couple who left some wine in their bottle for the next day and had it drunk up by Mr Neil in error were amiably presented with a full bottle in atonement. Smoking in the dining-room is discouraged. Residents may eat their lunchtime bar snacks in the courtyard; pressurised beer. Children under 13 are not accepted in either restaurant or hotel, and in season meals are for residents only. (GHG)

App: by too many members to list

Wine prices shown are for a 'standard' bottle of the wine concerned, unless another
measure is stated (e.g. litre, 50 cl., or pint).

Splinters

🍷

12 Church Street
Christchurch (0202)
483454

Closed L; Sun
Must book
D only, 6.30–10.30

Alc £6·45 (meal £10·05)

Seats 36
No dogs

As often, more people find this wine-distinguished
little restaurant, run by a harmonious quartet, than
ever report to the *Guide*: please make the detour to
this coastal town and tell us more about Peter
Hornsby and Juanita Franke's cooking, for in 1979 it
noticeably surpassed the restaurant of the same name
and ownership in Winchester (now dropped). 'The
smoking can be a menace, though a lighted candle on
the table helps to dispel the clouds', but 'we have had
some of the best and hottest French onion soup we
have tasted, admirable turbot and beef Stroganoff,
and raspberry sorbet and fresh blueberries were
equally good.' Champignons provençale, artichoke
soup, Dover soles, or filet de sole Barfleur (£4·85),
and chicken Célestine (£3·20) are other favourite dishes.
So is filet de porc basquaise, but 'tournedos were
tepid, small, and mediocre.' The Carters' wines may
direct drinkers to cheese rather than a sweet, though
most clarets are in double figures now: compare
perhaps Klüsserather Bruderschaft and Bernkasteler
Bratenhöfchen, both '71 Auslese Mosels, at £7·30; or
Châteauneuf-du-Pape La Bernardine and Côte-Rôtie,
both '73 or '76, with half-bottles available.
London-bottled Chapoutier wines are £6·10.
'Occasionally there is music from an antique polyphon.'

App: G. J. Dykes, C.L.J., Robin Woolf, and others

The Plough
Clanfield (036 781) 222

Must book weekends
Meals 12–1.45, 7–9.30

Tdh L £5·85 (meal £8·65)
Alc £7·90 (meal £11·70)

Children's helpings
(Sun L)
Seats 60 (parties 10)
🔥 rest
Car park
No dogs
Am Ex card
6 rooms (1 with bath)
B&B £13·50–£20
Fire cert

*Tony Barnes and his German wife Hedy (who cooks)
sound as if they had a rough tractor ride when they
embarked on this much-cultivated manorial hotel in the
furrows of the former owners. Though it is now shorn
of the neighbouring pub, there is much work for a
woman used only to private entertaining, and the
service has yet to settle down. 'Splendid' cream of
prawn soup, interesting crudités with sweet-and-sour
sauce, and good goulash or Elizabethan pork (£4·50),
followed by various gateaux and petits fours, earn the
place a tentative entry. But the wary may prefer to
give it a first trial at lunch prices, and drink the
Wadworth's 6X bitter on hand pump, or the French
house wines (at £4 for 80 cl) from Giddings of Devizes,
rather than plunge blind in the double-figure grands
crus that Harry Norton must have left behind him
when he moved to Rookery Hall (Worleston, Cheshire,
if you contemplate a visit, but reports are still mixed).
Note that there is no minimum charge for people who
want a light dinner. No children under five in the
restaurant, or under ten in the hotel. Dress neatly. You
may eat outside in the rose garden. More reports,
please.* (GHG)

CLAUGHTON Lancashire   Map 8

As we went to press the restaurant recommended here changed hands.

CLEEVE HILL Gloucestershire   Map 2

Malvern View Hotel

🍷

on A46
4½ m NE of Cheltenham
Bishops Cleeve (024 267)
2017

Closed L; Sun (exc res);
Dec 24–26 & 31;
Jan 1
Must book
D only, 7.30–9.30
(Sun at 7.30)

Tdh £7·50 (meal £10·20)

Service inc
Seats 42 (parties 20)
Car park
No dogs
7 rooms (5 with bath,
2 with shower)
B&B £12·50–£15
Fire cert

The competition for gastronomic primacy in the Cheltenham district is severe, but the Sparks's hotel is at least a contender. The view of the Malvern hills is a further bonus (till the dining-room windows steam up) and though there are one or two murmurs about hyper-organisation, some fairly sensitive residents warmly praise comfort, housekeeping and courtesy alike. Apart from a poor taramosalata and – at a test meal – merely dull mushrooms à la grecque, Mr Sparks's set dinner accumulates many admirers of avocado filled with crab and celery, and other hors d'oeuvre, among them fresh grilled sardines, and escargots Malvern View; followed perhaps by lamb en croûte that an inspector dares to call triumphal, with light and crisp pastry and hints of rosemary and Marsala, or 'expertly defatted' duckling bigarade, or 'moist and delicious' trout in cider, or guinea-fowl with calvados and cream. Salads are well dressed, vegetables apt to be over-buttered. Sweets may include a good syllabub or water-ice, but the touch is less certain here: 'Chocolate and brandy mousse and oranges in caramel are easily surpassed elsewhere.' (So is the Stilton.) It is a slight surprise to find coffee separately (and stiffly) priced in a meal of this kind, nor is it always strong enough. A farmer who enjoyed his breakfast 'was tempted to ask what bacon was served but did not in case what he liked was Danish.' The wines begin with the *patron*'s red or white burgundy (Bouchard Aîné) at £4·40 (£2·45 a half, 70p a glass) and beyond that, the clarets command attention, from magnums of Ch. Haut-Marbuzet '71 at £17·10 to bottles of Ch. Cantemerle '66 at the same

181

price. Morey St Denis '70 (Louis Latour) is £10·70 and Hermitage Blanc '73, £5·35: it is a fairly conservative list, but there are enough half-bottles. 'What a pity they use wine cradles instead of decanting.' Wear a jacket and tie for preference, and leave young children at home. Lunchtime snacks (with bottled beers) and afternoon tea for residents. (GHG)

App: B. P. Levitt, Ian Wilson, R. Boyer, M. R. Judd, Margaret Major, Ivor Hall, and many others

---

COATHAM MUNDEVILLE Co Durham   Map 8

Hall Garth Hotel
½ m off A1(M)
at junction with A167
4 m N of Darlington
Aycliffe (0325) 313333

Closed Sun D (exc res);
public hols (exc Apr 4 &
6; D Apr 7, May 5 & 26,
Aug 25)
Must book
Meals 12–1.30, 7.15–9.15

Tdh L £5·95 (meal £8·95),
D £7·50 (meal £10·70)

Children's helpings
Seats 55
[symbol] rest
Car park
No dogs in public rooms
11 rooms (8 with bath,
1 with shower)
B&B from £12·65
D, B&B (2 nights) from
£34 (off-season)

Ernest Williamson, 'wandering around in his butcher' apron with a pencil tucked into his massive beard', is a much more enthusiastic hotelier than anyone expects, and his partner Janice Crocker's cooking also graces a district where fresh food itself is atypical. The old house rambles but is comfortable, with well-furnished lounges. There are still some (though fewer than in 1978) who conclude that the pair were overstretched by their move from a restaurant to a hotel: 'a complete let-down'; 'the food was extremely ordinary and one vegetable which looked like mashed turnip proved to be butter beans when disturbed.' Service is erratic. But other well-travelled guests have been delighted with their rooms, set dinners, and English breakfasts (£1·75 extra – 'my boiled egg might have been just snatched from under the hen'). 'Prawns in Alabama sauce, avocado with fish pâté, lobster in wine with herbs and diced vegetables, and turbot in a light, creamy cheese sauce were all delicious fish courses, and we liked the simple fresh vegetables, left on the table for seconds.' 'Leg of pork in gooseberry sauce looked and tasted marvellous.' Soup stemmed from a glut of tomatoes in the garden. 'Cabbage at lunch was cooked better than I remember in a restaurant, still crunchy, and with sultanas.' Blackberry sorbet, treacle lick, and rhubarb fool are among sweets praised, but bland flavours or heavy textures are not unknown. Wines begin with Valgardello red or white at £1·75 for 50 cl, and there is a good list of Yapp's Rhônes and Loires: Gigondas '74 (Roger Meffre) £5·70, Sancerre Rosé '77 (Jean Vatan), £5·70, Viognier Condrieu '77, £9·50. They prefer no smoking, but 'a man who ignored this request blatantly from the outset turned out to be one of the local hospital consultants.' (GHG)

App: P. H. Tattersall, Pat & Jeremy Temple, G. P. Knowles, Helen Gane, Roger & Judy Thompson, and others

---

Unless otherwise stated, a restaurant is open all week and all year and is licensed.

COLCHESTER Essex   Map 3

The Barn
Williams Walk
off East Stockwell Street
Colchester (0206) 67867

Locally loved, very trim and clean conversion tucked away in the 'old Dutch quarter' behind the George Hotel ('chilly in winter, though'). It shares owners with Bistro Nine (*q.v.*), but Maggie Symonds here just does 'lovely healthy lunches': counter-service of home-made soups, quiches, hot smokies 'with nice dry brown rice', cold chicken with interesting sauces and salads (large 70p, small 35p; cucumber with honey dressing, or cauliflower, green pepper and peanut). Home-made puddings, cakes and biscuits all day. Charbonnier carafes; cider or fresh fruit juices by the glass too; bottled beers. No dogs. You may eat on the forecourt in summer.

Closed D; Sun; Mon;
1 week Chr; public hols
(exc Apr 4, May 5
& Jan 1); Dec 24

Open 9.30–5.30 (L 11.45–3)
(May–Sept), 10–4.30
(Oct–Apr)

Alc L £2·65 (meal £4·35)

Seats 80 (parties 30)
♿ rest

Bistro Nine
9 North Hill
Colchester (0206) 76466

Some think these 'fairly poky rooms' have fallen off somewhat in value and quality, but the 'traditional English and other' food, eaten at wooden stalls, still fills a niche between the Bistro's competitor and its stable companion (*q.v.*). In season you may find some 'wholesome and unusual' dishes: fair tagliatelle with haddock, peppers and tomatoes (£3·55) and good but skimpy compote of cherries in red wine (£1·05). Home-made bread and ice-creams. 'They may put more effort in at dinner than at lunch.' Poorish coffee. Obliging but sometimes weary service. Charbonnier house wines, £3·45 the litre. Bottled beers and cider.

Closed Sun; Mon (exc
May 5); Dec 25 & 26
Must book weekends
Meals 12–1.45, 7–10.45

Alc £4·65 (meal £8·10)

Children's helpings
Seats 70 (parties 35)

♿ rest (3 steps)
No dogs
Access, Barclay

Most places will accept cheques only when they are accompanied by a cheque card or adequate identification. Information about which credit cards are accepted is correct when printed, but restaurants may add to or subtract from the list without notice.

Inspections are carried out anonymously. Persons who pretend to be able to secure, arrange or prevent an entry in the Guide are impostors and their names or descriptions should be reported to us.

We rewrite every entry each year, and depend on fresh, detailed reports to confirm the old, as well as to include the new. The further from London you are, the more important this is.

Numbers are given for private parties only if they can be accommodated in a room separate from the main dining-room: when there are several such rooms, the capacity of the largest is given. Some restaurants will take party bookings at times when they are normally closed.

The third restaurant recommended here changed hands as we went to press.

COLYTON Devon   Map 2

Old Bakehouse

Colyton (0297) 52518

Closed L; Sun D
(exc res); Nov–Feb
Must book
D only, 7–9

Alc £8·65 (meal £12·55)

Service 10%
Children's helpings
Seats 28
 🔾 rest (1 step)
Car park
No dogs
7 rooms (1 with bath)
B&B from £11·50
D, B&B from
£109·25 p.w.
Fire cert

Susan Keen's cooking for this 17th-century restaurant with rooms shows exceptional devotion to French cuisine bourgeoise, and apart from one or two obvious off-days, or problems with main-dish timing or temperature, very few people's expectations have been disappointed. (That includes one person who cooks for a living and stayed longer than a week.) Indeed, there have clearly been evenings that most of the guests spent discussing the *Guide* entry with each other, as at a club or seminar. Both the quantities and the very pains taken make it food for an occasion rather than a holiday, some think, and not everyone gets as far as the rich sweets that others admire. But 'we paced ourselves better the second night and had an outstanding meal: chilled lettuce soup (£1·10), and scallops bretonne (£2·75); grey mullet madrilène (cooked in Muscat de Beaumes de Venise with tomatoes, onion and tarragon, £5·05, including vegetables) and ham jurassienne (baked with Gruyère and cream, and served with a tomato and port sauce); good vegetables (crisp cauliflower with almonds); then green salad; and two marvellous sweets, Dacquoise and gateau Diane (£1·30 each). We ended with a glass of vintage port (they decant one every few days – once it was Sandeman's '17).' Friands provençale (£1·95) or rissolettes de fromage are first-course favourites of the cook, and other dishes worth looking for include duck albigeoise, daube de Périgord, and chicken Célestine (though 'not much more than the sum of its parts,' says one critic). 'Sea bream should at least have been scaled, and morello cherries are vital to Black Forest gateau.' Floating island (usually the lightest sweet), raspberry hazelnut meringue, and other sweets are praised. There are usually a French and an English cheese. Breakfasts are excellent, the rooms adequate, the lounge 'TV-free'. Small children may be offered high tea. Stephen Keen – 'more astringent than his wife', and that is an understatement for one example of his correspondence shown to us – has bought good wine for some time, and it shows, with Volnay les Santenots '64 at £13·20, Ch. Cos d'Estournel '66, £9·90, good half-bottles and sweet whites, and everyday Sémillon white or Cabernet Sauvignon at a relatively stiffer £4·25. 'All were carefully served and the claret decanted, with smoking in the dining-room barred.' Enquire about occasional regional dinners. The village is charming and – except when the September carnival sent the Bakehouse staff on a French kick – quiet. (GHG)

App: Adrian & Catharine Edwards, Roger Chance, S.A.B.P., Robert & Gilly Jamieson, Mayer Resnick, and many others

---

COMBEINTEIGNHEAD Devon   Map 1

Netherton House
Shaldon (062 687) 3251

The Godfreys match their ambitions to their resources at this isolated house in twenty wooded acres. 'The dinner menus with modest choice are sensibly varied, composed and cooked, and the service is quiet and efficient.' White onion soup, poached Teign salmon, baked gammon with apricots, roast topside, steak, kidney and mushroom pie, and the country-house sweets are worth noting; so is 'creamy scrambled egg for breakfast.' Lunchtime bar snacks (with pressurised beers) are for residents only. Wines in bottle begin at £3·65 or so for Bereich Nierstein. No children under ten. Wear a jacket and tie at dinner.

Closed L; Sun; Dec 31; Jan 1	Seats 30	11 rooms (5 with bath, 2 with shower)
Must book	🔊 rest	B&B £12–£17·50
D only, 7.15–8.30	Car park	D, B&B £14·50–£21
	No dogs in public rooms	Fire cert
Tdh £6·50 (meal £9·15)		

Do not risk using an out-of-date Guide. A new edition will appear early in 1981.

For the explanation of 🔊, denoting accessibility for the disabled, see 'How to use the Guide', p. 4.

'Meal' indicates the cost of a meal for one, including food, coffee, a half-bottle of one of the cheapest wines listed, cover, service, and VAT (see 'How to use the Guide', p. 4).

Numbers are given for private parties only if they can be accommodated in a room separate from the main dining-room; when there are several such rooms, the capacity of the largest is given. Some restaurants will take party bookings at times when they are normally closed.

185

Withies Inn
off B3000
1 m S of junction with A3
Godalming (048 68) 21158

Closed Sun D; 3 weeks
Aug (poss)
Must book
Meals 12.30–2, 7.30–9.30

Alc (min £3) £7·05
(meal £10·70)

Service 10%
Cover 30p
Seats 32
Access, Am Ex, Barclay,
Diners

More than one visitor has noticed – before, during or after his meal – the touch of complacency that mars Gaston Magnin's popular and over-crowded inn. Negligent order-taking, cramped tables (in spite of two sittings sometimes), limp whitebait and inaccurate grilling are reported along with major merits, such as 'superb' house pâté, 'escalope viennoise as good as anywhere', fine halibut and formidable – if sometimes fatty – duck with peach sauce. 'Coffee is better, but sweets are still mostly variations on ice-cream.' Service as a whole is good. French ordinaires are £4·35 a litre and there are about sixty other wines, not listed to us this year. Bar snacks with pressurised beers. No children under five. No rooms. Car park. No dogs. You may eat outside at tables under the pergola.

App: R. Franklin, D.H.B., A.F., and others

Le Radier
19–21 Station Hill Parade
Bourne End (062 85)
25775

Closed L; Sun; public hols
(exc Apr 4, May 5)
Must book
D only, 7–9.30

Alc £6·10 (meal £9·55)

Service inc
Seats 30
Car park
No dogs

There are more restaurants than there are good dinners in the Thames Valley, and Lucien Voisin's little timber-and-brown cottage must be the least assertive of them all. Madame Voisin serves it single-handed, but bookings are usually phased to make this feasible, and anyway even the first courses are worth waiting for: potage Léontine 'a real French vegetable cream soup made with spinach, lettuce, potatoes and mint' (70p), and scrambled eggs with creamed salt cod 'a delicious combination'. A severe critic prefers the ratatouille to the pipérade and the courgettes 'filled with a sort of pease pudding'. Main courses such as mignons de veau with sage and tarragon, gigot d'agneau, and a delicately cooked pintade normande with cream, calvados and apple come with well-judged vegetables. 'The thick spicy sauce for salmon trout seemed inappropriate.' The sweets are conventional enough for a French place but normally well made: Mont Blanc, apple pancake, and St Emilion au chocolat. There are grumbles of persistent over-salting (another French trait), and of a grossly sweet melon sorbet. The red wines begin at £3·80 with Bergerac and one member speaks well of Ch. Guibeau '75 at £6·90. But 'Frenchmen ought to be able to find better wines for less.' Recorded music.

*App: Mr & Mrs F. Williams, Douglas Brooks,
J. B. MacGill, R. E. Collins, Joan Taylor, P. Flatter,
and others*

1980 prices are as estimated by restaurateurs in the autumn of 1979 (including VAT).

CORBRIDGE Northumberland   Map 8

Ramblers of Corbridge
18 Front Street
Corbridge (043 471) 2424

Closed L; Sun; Mon;
public hols (exc Apr 4)
Must book
D only, 7–10

Alc £6·15 (meal £9·80)

Children's helpings
Seats 55
♿ rest (2 steps)
No dogs
Access, Barclay

'We seem to have to book earlier every time we go,' says one member (to be fair, it is probably something to do with Heini Herrmann's local TV appearance as well as with six years of *Guide* entries). Worthy competition in the region for this roughstone house in a quiet street would help customers and perhaps the restaurant too: they ought to know by now not to serve cheeses and parfaits straight from fridge or freezer. But on the whole the couple and their staff take good care of their guests, who also enjoy rolling their tongues round the German dish titles (explained in English): gebackene Käsestangen (£1·30) or dicke Muschelsuppe, perhaps, followed by Regenbogen Forelle (which Schubert-lovers at least ought to recognise), eingelegtes Sattelstück (marinated and roasted lamb) or helgoländisches Kalbsschnitzel (£5·10, including vegetables) which is veal escalope stuffed with sardine and lemon. Fischermann's Tasche too had 'delicate pastry and expensive shellfish in its sauce'. For sweet, 'fresh fruit brûlée was an unqualified success', and more conventional blackcurrant flan, coffee gateau or black cherry cheesecake are also admired. Spanish Don Cortez carafes are £2·90; Gau-Odernheimer Petersberg Spätlese '76 is £5·20. Recorded music. It is time to go home when you can no longer say gepfeffertes Zwischenrippenstück (pepper steak).

App: J. D. Cranston, A.G.H., R. & M. Graham

CORNHILL-ON-TWEED Northumberland   Map 8

Collingwood Arms
Coldstream (0890) 2424

One Swallow hotel does not make a Borders summer, but James Mair's cooking for this creeper-clad house graced an inspector's short stay – 'a real tomato concassé in sauces for scampi and pork chops.' Roast chicken, too, had an original oatmeal stuffing, and try game pie, dressed crab, and braised wood-pigeon. Sweets are more routine. Others report well of the rooms (at least, the back ones), the bar snacks (not served on Sundays) with pressurised beers, and the kitchen garden. Wines, from £2·20 for 'just under a bottle' of La Navette, are 'humdrum'.

Must book weekends	Service inc	No dogs in d/r
Meals 12.30–2, HT 5–6, 7–8.30	Children's helpings (under 12)	Access, Am Ex, Barclay, Diners, Euro
	Seats 60 (parties 30)	16 rooms (8 with bath)
Tdh L £3·75 (meal £4·85), D £5·50 (meal £6·60)	♿ rest (2 steps); w.c. Car park	B&B £10·50–£13·50 Fire cert

Prices quoted in entries now include VAT.

Corse Lawn House
on B4211
5 m SW of Tewkesbury
Tirley (045 278) 479

Closed Mon; Sun D
Must book D
Meals 12.30–2, 7–10

Alc £7·30 (meal £10·85)

Service inc
Children's helpings
Seats 40 (parties 30)
♿ rest
Car park
No dogs
Access, Am Ex, Barclay,
Diners

The first thing you notice on approaching this Queen Anne house is the enormous lily pond, and if the first thing you taste is Mrs Hine's hot shrimps en croustade or pâté cognac the distinctive impression left by a meal here may well be reinforced. The Hines had mixed notices in their early months, despite their previous reputation elsewhere, but with one or two residual doubts about tough mallard, seafood pancake 'overweighted with whelks', and desultory reception, everyone sounds happier now. 'Filets mignons in a tasty sauce of onion and herbs were exquisite and not too heavy for a hot evening'; 'escalope de veau à la crème, a severe test for a chef because of its simplicity, was memorably delicate'; 'I particularly recommend the steak tartare that has to be pre-ordered.' Noisettes of venison with roebuck sauce (£5·45) is another speciality. The sweets 'look like a dieter's mirage' but are often agreeably light in spite of that, especially the brandy cheesecake and the chocolate pancake filled with crème de menthe cream (£1·30). 'As an unashamed coffee snob I was delighted to see it properly made and served with respect rather than with longlife cream.' Wines (from Tanners of Shrewsbury) begin with red or white vin de table at £3·85 and include Bonnes-Mares (domaine Clair Däu) '72 at £19·15; the sweet white Coteaux du Layon at £4·60 may be useful later (but please not with the chocolate pancake). Mr Hine has failed to list his brandies to us but they are predictably formidable. They provide bar lunches with pressurised beers. You may eat in the garden in summer.

App: A. D. Johnson, P. de B. Turtle, A. & N.R.,
G. Adams, Charlotte Brady, P.P., and others

Fox and Hounds
Sparsholt (096 272) 285

As for ten years past, locals and travellers are pleased to find Janet Marsden's bar lunches, with home-made soups, Sparsholt smokies, and salads; or in the little dining-room 'excellent poached salmon with lightly cooked green beans', seasonal game, and sound joints or steaks from John Robinson of Stockbridge. 'An evident symbiosis between this cosy brick pub and the IBA at Crawley Manor.' Sweets and coffee not mentioned this time. Pompey Royal bitter (hand pump); Berry Bros red ordinaire £4·25 a litre. Other wines seem mostly Stowells.

Closed Mon; Sun D;
Dec 25 & 26
Must book
Meals 12.30–2, 7.30–10

Tdh Sun L £5 (meal £7·15)
Alc £7·10 (meal £9·25)

Service inc

Seats 30
♿ rest; w.c.
Car park
No dogs in d/r

CROSBY-ON-EDEN Cumbria   Map 7

Crosby Lodge Hotel
S of B2624
Crosby-on-Eden
(022 873) 618

Closed Sun D; Apr 7;
Aug 25; Dec 24–Jan 23
Must book
Meals 12.30–1.30 (Sun 1),
7.30–8.45

Tdh L £5·50 (meal £8·15),
D £7·75 (meal £11·05)
Alc £11·20 (meal £13·50)

Service inc
Seats 50
♿ rest (2 steps)
Am Ex, Diners
7 rooms (3 with bath,
2 with shower)
B&B £15–£18·50
Fire cert

Once again the Lake District seems to be offering battlemented comfort in the Sedgwicks' decently furnished house, halfway between Carlise and Brampton. 'Home-made scones with morning coffee made a good start to the day,' says a visitor who had a business rendezvous there. The set meals are carefully cooked by the proprietor: 'ham and pea soup with cheese snippets', 'browned shrimps on hot garlic bread,' 'moist and tasty' smoked capon and jambon cru, 'good beef in a winey gravy,' and 'excellent duckling'. A 'junior and less flamboyant version of Sharrow Bay's sweets trolley' yielded walnut fudge flan with good pastry, and a light coffee meringue. The wines (from £3·50 for Valpolicella or Soave) come from a Workington firm and the list is properly guarded about the enterprising Rhine and Rumanian reds at £5 that humbler mortals will need to substitute for Ch. Cos d'Estournel '61 at £35·50. There is red Chassagne-Montrachet '72 (Drouhin) at £10·75 too. Bar lunches (except on Sundays) and pressurised beers. Car park. No dogs. Wear a jacket and tie at night. More reports, please.

CUCKFIELD West Sussex   Map 3

Elvira's
45 High Street
Haywards Heath (0444)
59000

A tiny, rather trendy place, more earthy in its catering: 'They stress wholesome nourishment rather than artful style.' Expect, then, generous helpings, strong (sometimes too strong) flavours – and occasional flops. Successes include fresh prawns with garlic mayonnaise (£1·10), salade niçoise, 'very fresh' Dover sole (with prawns and mushrooms in a wine sauce, £3·40), steak au poivre 'more peppery than creamy', and a rich chocolate gateau. Main dish prices include vegetables, and there are lighter dishes and salads at lunch-time ('good for children: there's so much to look at that they behave'). Italian house wine, £3·40 the litre. Recorded music. More reports, please.

Closed Sun; Mon;
Dec 25; Jan 1
Must book D

Meals 12.30–2.15,
7.30–10.30

Seats 25
No dogs

Alc £4·85 (meal £7·30)

DARTINGTON Devon Map 1

Cranks
Shinners Bridge
Totnes (0803) 862388

'High standards, in their cranky way. Besides there are few places where you can eat for so little with drinkable table wine, and admire the design of the arts complex too.' Celery soup, tomato and cheese quiche, date and apple crumble, salads and juices from the wholefood menu, 'eaten at a non-smoking table,' underline this verdict for a passing inspector. Recorded classical music. You may eat outside overlooking the river.

Closed D; Sun; Apr 7;
Dec 25 & 26
Open 10–5 (L from 11.30)

Alc L £2·55 (meal £4·90)

Service inc

Seats 80
Car park
No dogs

DARTMOUTH Devon Map 1

Carved Angel

2 South Embankment
Dartmouth (080 43) 2465

Closed Mon; Sun D;
Dec 24–26
Must book D
Meals 12.30–1.45,
6.30–10.30

Alc £10·10 (meal £12·85)

Service inc
Children's helpings
Seats 50 (parties 20)
🛇 rest (3 steps)
No dogs

Carved in marble or some even less perishable material, one hopes, for this graceful restaurant, transparent behind its picture window to the quayside passer-by, has become the 'bench-mark' by which other talented West Country restaurateurs assess their own achievements. As for mere customers, 'I dine here two or three times a year and consider it one of the dozen best in the land, London not excepted. The food is superb and changes with the seasons just as it should; the people who run it are as charming and helpful as it is possible to be.' The régime rests upon a secure tripod: Tom Jaine as owner-manager, Joyce Molyneux as cook, and Sally Agnew as diplomatist. Between meals, as it were, Mr Jaine collects books and wine, and writes papers on fish or the history of Dartmouth; Miss Molyneux extends her already capacious repertoire, or composes Christmas puddings and English conserves for sale in the annual fair at Caen. (Miss Agnew's extra-curricular activities have yet to be revealed.) People of conservative temperament would think a Dartmouth meal incomplete if it did not begin with the porridge-textured fish soup, to which one gentleman helped himself three times without even regretting it when he came to the salmon in pastry with currants and ginger, followed by ice-cream which 'albeit home-made and delicious, took some swallowing at £1·50.' But a tart of scallops with saffron cream (£1·95 as a first course); 'unusual and delightful' leg of chicken stuffed with crab, served with lemon sauce; and home-made fettuccine with pesto, give a further idea of the style. So do chicken canaille, and the superbly unpredictable fish from the harbour. 'I was not so sure about the aubergine stuffed with under-spiced lamb, and I think the Italian ham-veal-and-cheese trick is better done with thinner veal.' Sweet things may rise to the consummate standard of the rest chiefly in the soft-fruit season, but this may be grossly unfair to the Russian paskha ('exceedingly rich, like Eliza Acton's prescription for a publisher's pudding'), frangipane tart, and St Emilion au chocolat which a Devonian Eliza Doolittle calls 'bloody gorgeous'. Sources of wine have been diversified. You crash the double-figure barrier all too early now: that is, at Montagny '76 (Louis Latour), Ch. Fourcas-Hosten '66, c.b., and sweet white Bonnezeaux Château les Gauliers '59. But you can idle with the house wines at £5 if you prefer, or go to afterburners with Ch. Haut-Brion '67 at £26; note too that tips above the inclusive prices will be politely declined.

App: *Stephen Parish, Melvyn Jones, W.W., P.H., R.L., and others*

DEDDINGTON Oxfordshire   Map 2

Holcombe Hotel
High Street
Deddington (0869) 38274

Closed Sun D;
Dec 25 & 26
Must book
Meals 12–2, 7.30–9.30

Tdh L £3 (meal £5·70)

Alc £5·80 (meal £8·85)

Children's helpings
Seats 60 (parties 20)
♿ rest
Car park
No dogs in d/r
Access, Am Ex, Barclay,
Diners. Euro
12 rooms (1 with bath,
1 with shower)
B&B £12

A Cotswold stone family hotel, built 300 years or so ago, offering enterprising food and year-round inclusive weekend prices, sounds a little too good to be true – and is, according to one member who found the housekeeping patchy, the front rooms noisy, and dinner and breakfast poorly cooked. However, despite minor quarrels some have had with vegetables or breakfast coffee during otherwise enjoyable meals and stays, other experienced diners report very happily of tomato salad or coupe Caprice to start with, then the favourite zrazy Nelson (with kümmel sauce, £4·15: 'we daren't take it off the menu,' says Ishbel Daniel), porc Modigliani (which is not as slimming as admirers of the painter might suppose) and tournedos Lilli (with artichoke hearts and madeira). The feminine team in the kitchen take trouble with the sweets, by accounts of Jamaican banana ('remind the waitress that the rum sinks to the bottom'), crème caramel, and pineapple ginger cake. Dolamore's Italian carafe wine is £1·85 for 50 cl but the same merchant's College range at £3·65 a bottle may be preferable. Not all the wines are from this source. A good evening bar snack of 'juicy cold roast beef and a respectable savoury flan' is reported. Hook Norton on hand pump. 'Recorded music seems to have been soft-pedalled lately, thank goodness.' No children under ten at dinner, unless sharp at 7.30.

App: *D. Westoby, Michael Latham, E.F.T., G.H. & P.K.W., David Head*

Prices quoted in entries now include VAT.

When a restaurant says 'must book', the context of the entry usually indicates how much or how little it matters, but a preliminary telephone call averts a wasted journey to a closed door. *Always* telephone if a booking has to be cancelled: a small place (and its other customers) may suffer severely if this is not done.

Le Talbooth

Gun Hill
off A12
7 m NE of Colchester
at Stratford St Mary
Colchester (0206) 323150
(Maison Talbooth–
322367)

Closed 1 week Chr
Must book
Meals 12.30–2, 7.30–9

Alc £9·25 (meal £13·05)

Service 10%
Children's helpings
Seats 80 (parties 50)
⅃ rest
Car park
No dogs
Access, Barclay
10 rooms (9 with bath,
1 with shower)
B&B £21–£35
Fire cert

Gerald Milsom has successfully exported his ideas on restaurant management to Harwich (*q.v.*) but the home market at this resplendent 16th-century house and garden remains buoyant. (Its residential lodge, Maison Talbooth, half a mile away is modern, quiet, and luxurious for a short stay.) You are unlikely to forget that you are in the richest, most-visited corner of Essex, but Samuel Chalmers' cooking – if not the younger end of the local service – is equal to most demands made, and there are few complaints of moment. First courses are particularly noticed: 'a delicious artichoke soup'; 'a well-browned smoked haddock soufflé, delicate, with good chunks of fish and a cheesy crust'; 'a wonderful concoction of Stilton, port and celery'; 'Brie cooked in a very light pastry case'; and 'julienne of herring with beetroot in mayonnaise – a good combination.' Colchester oysters at £8 a dozen are a seasonal alternative if the price slides down as easily as the oyster. They are proud of their steak and kidney pie (£5) and Dover sole belle Gabrielle (£8·50), and an inspector is no less pleased with the duck, stuffed with almonds and apricots. Other main dishes praised include lamb cutlets in puff pastry, spring chicken with mustard sauce, pork Holstein 'as delicate as calf's liver', and the roast beef for Sunday lunch. Creamed carrots made an interesting vegetable. Cheeses are sound, and the sweets, criticised last year, seem improved, by accounts of plum pie, 'burn't cream' to remind us it doesn't belong to the French, and ginger ice-cream. There is one cross note about the coffee, and if you have eaten three courses you may be inclined to skip the fudge (which otherwise makes a substitute for a sweet). The house red and white wines at £3·75 are good choices and the main Lay & Wheeler list is fine if dear, with Ch. Meyney '73, £8·40 and Ch. Pétrus '67, £31. On the useful subsidiary list of wines under £6 the previously remarked shortage of half-bottles has been remedied. (GHG)

App: T. S. Green, H.W., R.E., S.R., and others

DEDHAM see also pub section

Entries for places with distinctions carry symbols (pestle, tureen, bottle, glass). Credits are fully written entries, with approvers' names below the text. Passes are telegraphic entries (useful in the area) with details under the text. Provisional entries are in italics (see 'How to use the Guide', p. 4).

Most places will accept cheques only when they are accompanied by a cheque card or adequate identification. Information about which credit cards are accepted is correct when printed, but restaurants may add to or subtract from the list without notice.

DENT Cumbria   Map 8

Country Kitchen
10 m E of junction 37
on M6
Dent (058 75) 376

A remote and delightful village, with cobbled streets and 17th-century stone cottages, houses a 'warm and friendly' mother-and-daughter team offering simple Sunday lunches and set dinners four nights a week. People praise leek and potato soup, avocado pâté with warm wholemeal rolls, chicken with tarragon and grapes, game pie (venison, hare and guinea-fowl on one occasion) with well-cooked vegetables, apple pie, and home-made rum-and-raisin ice-cream. Other choices might include roasts, Yorkshire rabbit, venison, tipsy cake and almond tart, with good Wensleydale among the cheeses. Recorded classical music. There may be a licence shortly; no corkage as yet.

Closed L (exc Sun &
Dec 25); Mon; Tue;
Sun D; Dec 24 & 26;
Dec 25 D; Jan 1
Must book
Meals 12.30–1.30, 7–8.30

Tdh L £4 (meal £4·40),
D £5·75 (meal £6·60)

Children's helpings
(under 12)

Seats 30
♻ rest (1 step)
No dogs
Unlicensed

DERBY Derbyshire   Map 5

Ben Bowers
13–15 Chapel Street
Derby (0332) 367688 *and*
365988

Gastronomic thrill it is not, but Glancz and Suthers' restaurant and Blessington Carriage pub, 'in a fine converted house by a multi-storey par cark', serves its turn in Derby. From the Phineas Foggish menu, they propose chicken Kiev (£3·25), landbayrischer Röstbraten (£3·95) and seafood platter (£4); an inspector found the mayonnaise, other sauces, and cheesecake perfunctory or heavy but the vegetables were good, 'and so are the Blessington bar snacks with real ales on pump' (unavailable in the restaurant). French or Italian table wines are about £4·50 a litre. Live music on occasion, otherwise recorded.

Closed Sun D; Sat L;
Dec 25 & 26; L public
hols
Must book D
Meals 12–2, 7–11

Tdh L £3·65 (meal £6·40)
Alc £6·30 (meal £9·30)

Children's helpings
Seats 65 (parties 30)

Air-conditioning
No dogs
Access, Am Ex, Barclay,
Diners, Euro

Ristorante Sanremo
5 Sadler Gate
Derby (0332) 41752

Closed Sun; Mon D;
public hols (exc Apr 4);
3 weeks July/Aug
Must book
Meals 12–2, 7–10

Luigi Negro's tenth *Guide* entry for his popular place in the pedestrian precinct finds him, his chef Giovanni Fappiano, and his customers in good order: 'Not many provincial cities have a better Italian restaurant,' with 'friendly, talkative staff and little niceties like showing meat before they cook it.' It is better not to be talked into asparagus out of season, but lasagne – 'a one-dish meal', 'delicious tomato-flavoured risotto alla marinara', eggs fiorentina, and 'snails with an ideal amount of garlic juice' are good first courses.

Tdh L £2·55 (meal £4·45)
Alc (min £2) £5·60
(meal £9·25)

Cover 30p D
Children's helpings
Seats 45
No dogs
Diners card

Italian classic veal dishes (alla crema, Cordon Bleu,
or Marsala with oregano) are also praised, but
'kidneys siciliano were not as good as I remembered
them.' They do not spare the liquor for the flambé
sweets. The set lunches look good value still, but we
lack reports. Torrenova table wines are £2·65, and
Barolo was £4·35 in 1979. Recorded music.

*App: Bruce King, W.F., R. G. Hopkinson,
B. M. Hopewell, and others*

DEREHAM (EAST) Norfolk   Map 6

Phoenix Hotel
Church Street
Dereham (0362) 2276

After 22 visits in 14 years to this 'excellent hideaway'
near Cowper's death-place, a member calls the table
d'hôte the best bet (perhaps 'thick' celery soup, a
small breast of duck stuffed with bacon, plain
vegetables and fancier trolley sweets, for £5). Forays
à la carte may consume time to little purpose but
note two pâtés (£1·15), lentil and smoked ham soup,
and escalope of pork with prawns and green peppers
(£3·90). Attentive and mostly efficient staff, and a
clean, modern THF hotel. Arc de Triomphe table
wine £3·10. Weekday lunchtime bar snacks; Adnams'
and Abbot on pump. Dancing on Saturdays in winter.
Dress smartly. Enquire about bargain weekends.

Must book	Alc £7·40 (meal £9·40)	Car park
Meals 12.30–2.15, 7.30–10		No dogs in d/r
(Sun 9.30, Fri & Sat 10.30)	Service inc	Access, Am Ex, Barclay,
	Children's helpings	Diners, Euro
Tdh L from £4 (meal	Seats 80 (parties 150)	28 rooms (17 with bath)
£5·55), D from £4·25	🔾 rest (2 steps)	B&B £12–£14
(meal £5·80)		Fire cert

DREWSTEIGNTON Devon   Map 1

Castle Drogo
3½ m S of A30
between Exeter and
Okehampton
Chagford (064 73) 3306

Lutyens built his farewell to the Middle Ages for the
Drewe family here. You don't eat in his dining-room,
but Rosemary Collins runs the spruce restaurant for
the National Trust, with a warm welcome for walking
breeches and rompers alike. A simple all-day menu
begins with 'real coffee and leaf tea' and rises to
home-made soups, local pasties, good bread and
shortbread, and 'light, very lemony mousse'. Good
local service and cider; some would like a drier white
wine by the glass (60p). 'Excellent value.' No
smoking; no dogs: *tout comme il faut.*

Closed D; Nov–Mar	Alc £2·95 (meal £5·50)	Seats 90 (parties 45)
Open 12–5.30 (L 12–1.45)		🔾 rest; w.c.
	Children's helpings	Car park

DULVERTON Somerset   Map 1

Rendez-Vous
High Street
Dulverton (0398) 23613

Closed Nov; mid-Jan to
Mar
Must book D
Meals 12–2, 7–9.30

Tdh L £4·45 (meal £6·60),
D £5·90 (meal £8·20),
L & D £7·30 (meal £9·70)

Seats 35
 rest (1 step)

Since autumn 1978 several visitors from neighbouring counties have nominated François Prudon's simple restaurant, saying that his turkey and pork pâté, crêpes aux fruits de mer, 'fine, tangy mayonnaise' and sauces for everything from tripe and brains to lobster and veal live up to his long experience abroad. However, he is closing till Easter 1980 to allow his English wife time to cope with a new baby, so be sure to telephone before a visit ('and don't miss the village of Selworthy nearby,' advises an inspector). Wines begin at £3·05 for Yugoslav Riesling and £3·50 for Côtes du Rhône or Entre-Deux-Mers. Recorded classical music. Young children are not encouraged in the evening, but are given smaller helpings at lunch-time. No dogs. More reports, please.

DURHAM Durham   Map 8

Undercroft
The College
Cathedral Cloisters
Durham (0385) 63721

From coffee after terce to scones before vespers, there is 'good home baking' self-served at almost every (weekday) canonical hour 'in the 13th-century crypt opposite the jewel house.' A change of cooks has not affected members' joy in 'wholesome' rice with nuts, 'uplifting' mushroom salad and quiches 'more spiritual than temporal' (50p). Frankfurter soup, and apple crumble with 'plentiful cream' are among Milburn Bakers' earthier pleasures. Wine 50p a glass. 'Excellent coffee, cheaper black.' 'Clean, attractive place, a model of its kind.' On Sundays and public holidays they serve afternoon teas only. No music – and no sleeping it off in the dormitory upstairs, even if you are a monk.

Closed D; L Sun &
public hols
Open 10–5 (L 12–2);
2.30–5 (Sun & public hols)

Alc L £2·50 (meal £3·25)

Service inc

Children's helpings
Seats 85
 rest; w.c.

PLEASE keep sending in reports, as soon as possible after each meal. The cut-off date for the 1981 Guide is September 30, 1980, but reports are even more useful earlier in the year, especially for the remoter areas and new places. Late autumn reports can also affect corrections at proof stage.

Towns shown in black on our maps contain at least one recommended restaurant, pub or wine bar (see map key). The dot denotes the location of the town or village, not the establishment. Where necessary, we give directions to it in the entry. If you can, help us to improve them.

The Guide News Supplement will be sent out as usual, in June, to everyone who buys the book directly from Consumers' Association and to all bookshop purchasers who return the card interleaved with their copy. Let us know of any changes that affect entries in the book, or of any new places you think should be looked at.

EARLS COLNE Essex   Map 3

Draper's House
53 High Street
Earls Colne (078 75) 2484

'Warm welcome, pleasantly subdued lighting, relaxed atmosphere' made a good beginning to a dinner of mushrooms à la crème (£1), 'perfect' lobster pâté ('could have done with a bigger portion, but lobster-anything is like that'), rich and carefully spit-roasted pheasant with stuffing (£6·30), amply served steak and kidney pudding (winter only), with 'too little gravy' (£4), but deftly cooked fresh vegetables (haricot beans in parsley and garlic sauce). Good old-fashioned puddings: 'real' trifle, 'light and delicious' steamed syrup pudding. Over a hundred wines, from Spanish at £3·70 the litre; '63 port 'still £1·40 a glass'. Adnams' ale from the cask. Recorded 'instrumental music'. No dogs.

Closed Sun; Mon; Sat L; Apr 4; Dec 25 & 26; Jan 1 Must book	Tdh L £3·20 (meal £5·90) Alc £8·35 (meal £11·60)	Seats 50 (parties 36) ♿ rest (3 steps) Car park
Meals 12–1.45, 7.15–9 (9.45 Fri & Sat)	Service 10% Children's helpings	Access, Am Ex, Barclay, Diners, Euro

EASTBOURNE East Sussex   Map 3

Bistro Byron
6 Crown Street,
Old Town
Eastbourne (0323) 20171

Closed L; Sun;
Dec 25 & 26
Must book
D only, 7.30–10.30

Alc £6·70 (meal £9·90)

Cover 30p
Children's helpings
Seats 24 (parties 10)
No dogs
Barclaycard

'Steer between St Mary's and the Lamb' to find Simon and Marian Scrutton's little restaurant, says a bipartisan supporter. The spectrum of opinion set the *Guide* a problem in 1979, for it ran all the way from an experienced and critical inspectorial couple suggesting a pestle-and-mortar to 'you must be joking' from separate visitors complaining of scruffy appointments and inferior meat or fish. (Another complaint was so regretfully and thoughtfully – if firmly – answered by Mrs Scrutton that it makes ambivalent evidence.) It is best to conclude, with the concurrence of regular visitors, that these are two talented people working to narrow margins of human and financial resource, capable of 'taramasalata which, like the olives served with aperitifs, easily surpasses most Greek examples', 'pâté de canard with hazelnuts that would have been a pleasant surprise in the Périgord', 'fresh prawns with a reeking aïoli', 'gorgeous lamb cooked pink', 'classic' suprême de volaille sauce madère and escalope de veau savoyarde, good aubergines and haricots verts in a Provencal manner, and 'mange-tout peas that had me lining up for a third helping.' Chocolate and brandy dessert is good; 'intensely flavoured greengage sorbet even better.' The VDQS or AOC house wines are £3·45 and there are a few other wines, chosen with some care. Cigars and pipes are discouraged until after 10 p.m.: it is a tiny place. 'Recorded music may infiltrate from the kitchen.' Please report fully.

App: E. Jenkins, J. & M.B., A.M.W., and others

Porthole
8 Cornfield Terrace
Eastbourne (0323) 20767

Peter Puplett is altering and enlarging his restaurant early in 1980, so please report. However, in 1979 most people found it unspectacular but sound for vegetable soup, fresh grilled plaice on the bone, game pie, and 'sweetbreads in a delicious sauce' (£2·95). 'Mushy courgettes and tinned figs were a let-down.' Home-made steak and kidney pies or puddings are a set lunch speciality of the chef, Filipe Fernandes, and bar lunches are also provided. The owner's wine suppliers offer table wine from Angers at £2·95, and about sixty other bins, including nine English from £3·80. Smokers are directed to the first floor. Children are not encouraged at dinner. Recorded music.

Closed Mon; Sun D;	Tdh L from £2·95	Seats 38 (parties 22)
D Dec 25 & 26	(meal £5·30)	♿ rest
Must book	Alc (min £5) £6·35	Air-conditioning
Meals 12–2, 6.30–10	(meal £9)	No dogs
		Access, Barclay, Diners
	Service 10%	

EAST BUCKLAND Devon   Map 1

Lower Pitt
5 m NW of
South Molton
off A361
Filleigh (059 86) 243

For a simpler (and cheaper) place than many of the Guide's West Country entries, Suzanne Lyons' old farmhouse sounds worth a try. Near and distant visitors describe with pleasure her terrine of pork fillet (85p), lamb à la grecque (£4·40, including vegetables), pork Stroganoff, roast duckling, coffee soufflé and other dishes. Wines from £4 a litre for Choix du Roy; Ch. Gassiot '71, is £5·20. Recorded music. More reports, please.

Closed L; Sun; Mon	Alc (min £4) £6·35	Car park
(exc D public hols);	(meal £9·30)	No dogs
Dec 25; Jan		2 rooms
Must book	Children's helpings	B&B from £6
D only, 7.30–9.30	Seats 32 (parties 14)	

EAST GRINSTEAD West Sussex   Map 3

Gravetye Manor

5 m SW of East Grinstead
off B2110
at sign West Hoathly
Sharpthorne (0342) 810567

Must book
Meals 12.30–1.45,
7.30–8.45

Alc £11 (meal £18·55)

Service 12½%

Unlucky the man who (like the Editor) visits Peter Herbert's creeper-clad Elizabethan manor on a day too wet to perambulate the 200-acre estate and William Robinson's famous gardens. Lucky those who stay the night, enjoying unusually polished service and most of the creature comforts known to country-house-goers. And lucky, with few exceptions, those who know how to eat and drink. Mr Herbert took amiss last year's scepticism – justified at the time – about the first months under Michael Quinn, who inherited Karl Löderer's *toque* in 1978. This year, numerous members write in well-observed detail about the ambitious repertoire (there are even three savouries listed with the sweets). Few Easter Sunday lunchers can have sat down to four such first courses

Cover 30p
Seats 40 (parties 16)
♿ rest (bar entrance)
Car park
No dogs in d/r or
bedrooms
14 rooms (12 with bath,
2 with shower)
Room only, from £14
Breakfast from £2
Fire cert

as langoustines à la nage sauce aïoli (complete with pincers, prongs, and finger-bowls), 'hot and delicate' salmon mousse in puff pastry with two contrasting sauces, the well-tried mushroom and Gruyère sandwich, deep fried, and oeuf en cocotte à la truffe (for a well-disciplined nine-year-old who gave the slice of truffle to his mother). The fish pâté (£2·50) at a test meal, encasing a core of French beans set lengthways, was also notable, and a main dish on this occasion, suprême de poulet au crabe (£5·70), overcame the eater's prejudices against this kind of miscegenation by the very freshness of the crab. 'Venison tends to be underhung and carp poached soft', but aiguillettes de caneton au poivre vert, or poussin Quinn (in a rich madeira sauce), are well worth considering. 'Oddly,' says a weekend visitor, 'wild duck was superb one night, steak the next day tough.' But roast lamb with rosemary, creamed potatoes with silverskin onions, and mange-tout peas were 'beyond criticism'. So was the red-wine sorbet and almond pastry tulip with Cointreau cream and fresh peach that followed, and 'crêpe kirscher (£1·70) was one of the cheaper sweets, but a masterpiece if you had the room: a freshly made pancake with generous slices of a fine mango inside, in a hot, very sweet syrup tasting strongly of Cointreau and kirsch. It would have been a blasphemy to add cream.' Cheeses, coffee – and breakfasts – are all admirable. The wines are very fine, though the list itself does not always reflect the contents of the cellar, nor has it been furnished to the *Guide* this year, so the 'bottle' distinction must remain suspended. A request for a glass of white with the fish brought a fine Pouilly Fumé '76 at £1, and the party who paid about £40 for Eitelsbacher Karthäuserhofberg Kronenberg Auslese '71, Meursault-Charmes '73 (Louis Jadot), Ch. Beychevelle '66, c.b., and a half-bottle of Iphofener Silvaner Beerenauslese '67 will not soon forget a series of tastes that seemed to sum up all seasons in the gardens, winter perhaps excepted. Ports and cognacs are comparable, and everything can be savoured because pipe or cigar smoking is not permitted – 'indeed, even motorists are asked not to park with their exhaust pipes near the flowers.' (GHG)

App: Pat & Jeremy Temple, F. Kuhlmann, A. E. Key,
W. E. Cowl, C.P.D., M. C. Whiting,
C. D. L. Menzies, and many others

We rewrite every entry each year, and depend on fresh, detailed reports to confirm the old, as well as to include the new. The further from London you are, the more important this is.

Inspections are carried out anonymously. Persons who pretend to be able to secure, arrange or prevent an entry in the Guide are impostors and their names or descriptions should be reported to us.

EAST HORSLEY Surrey   Map 3

Tudor Rose
15 Bishopsmead Parade
East Horsley (048 65)
4484

Closed L (exc Sat & Sun);
Mon; Sun D; public hols
(exc L Apr 6, Dec 25 &
26)
Must book
Meals 12–2.30, 7–9.30

Tdh L £3·15 (meal £5·45)
Alc £4·55 (meal £7·30)

Seats 28
Access, Am Ex, Barclay,
Diners

The three leading features of this improbable suburban restaurant have always been honest and good cooking, the remarkable value given, and disputes or embarrassment arising from the lack of anywhere to wait for a booked table to be ready. Since Mr Chapman's death in 1979, his widow has kept the first two features and is now tackling the third by having a bar constructed. She has also now discontinued weekday lunches. So expect Stilton soup (65p), 'hors d'oeuvre with so much smoked salmon that it must have been a bargain', always excellent' roast duck with orange and Grand Marnier (£2·95), veal with Marsala and cream (£4), and 'good vegetables, especially the sauté potatoes.' Sweets are adequate. The carafe wine is Caldorino and an inspector thinks the house burgundy is not what it was – 'but at least it is under £4·50.' Go early if you are sensitive to smoke in a confined space. Car park. No dogs. More reports, please.

EAST LOOE Cornwall   Map 1

Runnelstone Restaurant
Buller Street
Looe (050 36) 2240

'A delightful surprise among the wimpys and whelks' is this quaint old place 'with double stable-doors and nautical decoration'. Take a pew – literally – and enjoy scallops simply fried in butter (£1·50), 'fresh and plump' butter-grilled lemon sole with crisp chips (£3·10), a seafood platter 'like a fritto misto' (£2·90) or a Cornish improvement on 'turf 'n'surf': 'a large tender sirloin with about 12 oz of fresh crab claw-meat and less interesting frozen prawns.' Non-fishy starters – and sweets – are only moderate, but the coffee came 'hot, fresh and strong'. Pleasant and competent service. St Austell Brewery wines, with Argentine Estancia at 60p the glass. 'Light' music on tape. Cream teas and snacks available from 2.30 to 6 p.m.

Closed Oct–Easter
Open noon–10 p.m.

Tdh L £1·95
(meal £3·90)
Alc £6·20 (meal £8·15)

Children's helpings
(under 6)
Seats 34
Air-conditioning

EAST MOLESEY Surrey   Map 3

The Lantern
20 Bridge Road
01-979 1531

Closed L; Sun;
public hols (exc Apr 4)
Must book
D only, 7–11

Alc £7·90 (meal £11·55)

Lunchtime closure helps Peter Morphew avoid the overspill from Hampton Court so that the evening's welcome appears genuine and the cooking sincere. Yet visitors to the palace of *le roi gourmand* would find this discreet restaurant trying very hard to be French: 'The *patron* is said to read Guérard in bed', and regional dinners were 'the best complete meals I had in 1979.' 'Crab soup, oeufs basquaise (two baked eggs with ham and aubergine), an over-sized main course, grapes in Grand Marnier, and a bottle of

Service 10%
Cover 40p
Children's helpings
(under 8)
Seats 48 (parties 20)
No dogs
Access, Am Ex, Barclay,
Diners

sparkling Saumur are an example.' If portions suit *les forts des Halles,* seasoning is over-fine. An inspector's terrine de porc en sanglier 'began better than it continued.' Rabbit in mustard sauce was 'too tame' and vegetables 'indistinct'. But the kitchen works hard and a February visitor could not fault home-made sausages with sauerkraut (sometimes with oysters, £1·75), rare médaillons de boeuf Bercy (£4·25) and a 'delectable gateau, flavoured with orange and piled high with strawberries and cream', almost as summery as another member's pudding of berries and currants bound with pureed plums. Service is usually exemplary, but 'I would have expected the wine list before the pâté.' 'Choice is limited and information lacking'; however, there are a number of halves, and French table wine is £3·50 for 73 cl. 'General' music, though one member found operatic arias specifically indigestible.

App: J M. Brushfield, M.R., E.L.F.

EASTRY Kent   Map 3

Coach and Horses
Lower Street
Sandwich (0304) 611692

Closed Tue; Sat L;
Dec 25 & 26
Must book
Meals 12.30–1.30, 7.30–10

Alc £6·90 (meal £10·60)

Service 10%
Seats 18
♿ rest
Car park
No dogs

The Longs are not the first people to realise that the risk and the frazzle of restaurant operation are reduced if you can persuade customers to order in advance from a menu circulated by post. They work this system tactfully, and people all seem to enjoy their dinner parties by a log fire, with sparkling glass and silver on the tables. Mrs Long cooks everything 'from crusty bread to exquisite ices', and in between a severe critic has found very little fault with her scallops in garlicky tomato sauce, 'the crispest puff pastry for sea supreme (£4·80 for two), filled with prawns, sole and other fish', equally crisp canard calvados (£4·30 – 'the apple sauce, though, was rather sweet and bland'), and accurate steaks. Halibut florentine and chicken Pappagallo are other good dishes. Sauces are generally delicate, and vegetables (included in the dish price) 'brought at no extra charge the first asparagus of the season.' 'Wild strawberry ices and lemon sorbet flavoured with Pernod completed a really good meal.' 'Rum chocolate truffles were good, but mediocre coffee was poor value.' The house claret is £4·70 and Muscadet '76 or Fleurie '78 expensive at nearly £7. They offer white wine by the glass, and do not sell cigars or cigarettes.

App: David Stanley, R.J.B., H.W.

Please report to us on atmosphere, decor and – if you stayed – standard of accommodation, as well as on food, drink and prices (send bill if possible).

See p. 508 for the restaurant-goer's legal rights, and p. 510 for information on hygiene in restaurants.

ELLAND West Yorkshire   Map 5

Bertie's Bistro
9 Town Hall
Elland (0422) 78533

Nothing Woosterish (or Worcesterish) about 'Bertie' Woodward's saucy and sumptuous Edwardian-style bistro in the heavy woollen district. Hubbub by design, but careful cooking all the same of chicken liver vol-au-vent, carrot and orange soup, moussaka (£2·50), glazed loin of lamb (£3·30), banana and Marsala syllabub. The kitchen's 'young men and women' advocate mushrooms in garlic (80p), crab and Stilton croquettes, and poussin (£3·15). No bookings, so prepare to gulp French house wine (£3·15 a litre) at the bar. 'Fifties music.'

Closed L; Mon;
Dec 24–26
No bookings
D only, 7–11 (11.30
Fri & Sat, 5–10 Sun)

Alc £4·85 (meal £7·40)

Children's helpings
Seats 100

♻ rest
Air-conditioning
No dogs

ELY Cambridgeshire   Map 6

Old Fire Engine House
25 St Mary's Street
Ely (0353) 2582

Closed Sun;
Dec 24 for 2 weeks;
public hols
Must book
Meals 12.30–2, 7.30–9

Alc L £4·05 (£6·60),
D £5·25 (meal £7·95)

Children's helpings
Seats 34 (parties 22)
Car park
No dogs in d/r

'Simple and unprofessional' is Ann Ford and Michael Jarman's own description of their slightly scatty Fenland fire-station just beyond the shadow of the Cathedral's splendid octagon. 'Ample, noisy and enjoyable' is the terse summary of one member after 'abundant helpings of well-rounded dishes by buxom waitresses.' A party of sixteen was seduced by an offer of seconds, but simplicity here means more than bulk. 'An honest use of local produce, enhanced by the cooking' is the kitchen's creed, borne out by experience of beef in ale, pigeon in red wine, steak and kidney pie, and turkey breast in cream sauce. But 'home-made broth was rather watery and fatty.' The specialities of the kitchen team include chicken in herb and cream sauce (£3·60) and, in season, wild duck casserole (£4·30) and stewed eel (the city's namesake, according to Bede). Vegetables are fresh and sweets 'gooey' (including 'very good meringue'). Advance warning is necessary for most fine wines (Ch. Phélan-Ségur '71, £8·50) but Adnams' bitter needs just a pull on the pump. Otherwise, Pedrotti red is now £3·60 a litre and Aspall House supplies cider and apple juice. People are fascinated by the paintings. Bar snacks 'when we're able'; and afternoon teas (3.30–5.30 p.m.), perhaps in the garden.

App: J. M. Hodgson, R.R., and others

If you think you are suffering from food-poisoning after eating in a restaurant, report this immediately to the local Public Health Authority (and write to us).

Prices of meals underlined are those which we consider represent unusual value for money. They are not necessarily the cheapest places in the Guide, or in the locality.

Phantasy
19 The Strand
Exmouth (039 52) 5147

Closed Mon D (exc
May 26); Apr 7; May 5;
Aug 25; Dec 25 & 26;
Jan 1; D Nov–May
(exc Fri & Sat)
Must book
Meals 12–2, 7–10

Alc L £4·05 (meal £6·25),
D £5·50 (meal £7·85)

Service 10%
Children's helpings
Seats 34
No dogs
Access, Barclay, Euro

An element of phantasy is not unwelcome in Exmouth, and it was a happy day for everybody, it seems, when Shirley and Michael Wilkes sold their house in the Midlands to open here a grocery and gift shop with a restaurant above, where they could cook for money what they had always cooked for friends. Dependably, they offer something for fish-lovers and vegetarians as well as more predictable grills. Mrs Wilkes's omelettes or crab-stuffed pancakes, local plaice, sole and halibut in 'good sauces, not over-rich' (£3·50, including vegetables) and 'cuddly chicken' are popular. So are her vegetables – 'a choice between lemon-buttered carrots, crisp white cabbage cooked with onion and wine, cauliflower, and celery with nuts.' Sweets are called 'outstanding for a place of this type' by a visitor who counted ten home-made confections (75p) from chestnut and coffee cake to black cherry and almond flan. 'Fresh peach and raspberries with ice-cream and Grand Marnier ended our meal superbly.' Coffee may be weak. Service is 'informal, friendly and honest'. French Solitaire red or Yugoslav Riesling are £2·60 a litre, and Muscadet Château la Noë '77 was £4·75 in 1979 on the short list. Recorded music. 'There is no room for push-chairs.' More reports, please.

Plough Inn
off A170
2½ m N of
Kirkbymoorside
Kirkbymoorside (0751)
31515

Closed L (exc bar Sun &
public hols [exc Apr 4]);
Sun (exc bar L); Mon;
1 week May, Oct & Feb;
Dec 24–26 & 31; Jan 1
Must book D
Meals 12–1.30 (bar),
7.30–8.30

Tdh from £4·70 (meal
£6·65)

Service inc (food only)
Seats 28 (parties 14)
Car park
No dogs in d/r
No rooms

Kath Brown has gone back to part-time help and 'support from husband' in the kitchen after a less than happy experience with full-time staff. But the summer's problems have not stopped people reporting 'happy evenings spent eating the delicious food and enjoying Mr Brown's welcome' in this simple whitewashed pub on the village green. It is a pub but more than a pub, not just because dinners begin at £4·70 and rise beyond, but because specialities such as smoked salmon mousseline with sorrel sauce, chicken and sweetbread pie, prawns provençale, mushrooms en cocotte, and parsnip fritters are unlikely to be general in British pubs until the millenium dawns. 'Nor are you hurried to eat.' 'The vegetables are as excellent as always.' Crème au fromage, redcurrant sorbet, and rum-baked bananas are among the sweets confected. The curries, quiches and other snacks in the bar (with Cameron's Strongarm bitter on pump) are now confined to lunch on Sundays and public holidays 'when we do not have to prepare an evening meal.' Wines (from £3·10) are accessibly priced, and that includes serious clarets such as Ch. Fonbadet '70 at £7·15 or Ch. Rauzan-Gassies '67 at £9·80, both c.b. Children must be over eight and able to eat a full meal.

App: G. R. McKee, Anita Schubert, B.H.F.G., C. N. Hobson, D. & M. Worrall, and others

FALMOUTH Cornwall   Map 1

Continental
29 High Street
Falmouth (0326) 313003

Closed L; Sun;
Dec 25 & 26; Jan 1
Must book
D only, 7–10

Alc £5·50 (meal £8·40)

Children's helpings
Seats 32
No dogs
Diners card

Not much has been heard about the Pozos' 'well-polished' cellar restaurant since last year's entry, but a test meal suggested that Jeremy Adkins' cooking was well up to 'credit' standard, with a muted but distinct Spanish accent. Savoury pancakes, stuffed with mushrooms, chicken and peppers, had a good dark wine sauce, as did tournedos courtbois (£3·45); salteado de carne, with an onion and tomato cream sauce, and good pilaf rice, made a well-balanced dish; good veal had been found for escalopes viscayenne, and home-made meringues and profiteroles with dark chocolate sauce preceded strong coffee. The local Spanish wine firm, Laymont and Shaw, provide suitable wines modestly marked up (Viña Ardanza '73, £4·40 in 1979). Recorded music. More reports, please.

FALMOUTH see also pub section

FARNHAM Surrey   Map 3

Castle Coffee House
68 Castle Street
Farnham (0252) 714 721

Next to the Latour (*q.v.*) in Farnham's conservation area, but an independent enterprise. The Gibbonses provide a simple set meal (£1·95) and self-service salad bar at lunch-time, with soup and baked potatoes too in winter. More ambitious dinners have included 'an enormous plateful of crisply cooked whitebait' (70p), daube avignonnaise, peppered fillet steak (£4·25, including fresh vegetables), tournedos Rossini (£5·25), and game in season. No news of the sweets, but coffee is 'freshly made and good.' Everything is cooked to order, so expect a wait or two. Friendly and willing service. Various wines from £2·75 the bottle. 'Subdued background music' at dinner.

Closed Sun; Mon;
Dec 24 to mid-Jan
Must book weekends
Meals 12–2, 7–10.30

Tdh L £1·95
(meal £3·90)
Alc £6 (meal £8·40)

Children's helpings

Seats 70 (parties 24)
No dogs
Access, Barclay

Latour
69 Castle Street
Farnham (0252) 721133

Closed Sun; Mon; Sat L;
Aug; Dec 24–26
Dec 31 L; Jan 1
Must book weekends
Meals 12.30–2.30,
7.30–10.30

The Strasbergs' mews restaurant (once a 16th-century granary, and more recently the Castle Theatre) is 'very French', from the staff (including chef Patrick Gramaglia) to the live accordion music, with dancing at weekends. The accent of the food is harder to identify, though there are two set dinner menus, with the 'gastronomique' offering frogs' legs, brains, snails, poussin à l'estragon, filet au poivre vert, and, at a £1·50 supplement, filet mignon Prunier (with oysters, brandy and cream). The regular menu (changed monthly, £6·75) might list velouté de cresson, salade frisée aux croûtons, or feuilleté de jambon ('rather

Tdh L £4·95 (meal £7·65),
D £6·75 & £9·75
(meal £8·75 & £11·75)

Service 10%
Seats 40 (parties 60)
🔥 rest (1 step)
No dogs
Access, Am Ex, Barclay,
Euro

*soggy pastry') as first courses; then, perhaps, veal
('tender') with peaches ('tinned'), well-balanced
médaillons de porc à la moutarde, lapin aux pruneaux,
or cabillaud aux câpres. Vegetables are plainly cooked
and generally well judged; sweets, apart from chocolate
or coffee mousse, are less successful. M Strasberg
imports his own wine and has an interesting range of
regional ones from France (Provencal Mas de Lune,
£3·50) as well as more distinguished bottles (Volnay
Clos des Chênes '70, £12·50). There are a few tables
on the terrace in summer. More reports, please.*

FARNHAM see also wine bar section

FARRINGTON GURNEY Avon   Map 2

Old Parsonage
on A37
7½ m N of
Shepton Mallet
Temple Cloud (0761)
52211

Closed (exc res) Mon
(exc May 5); Sun D;
Apr 4 & 6; Dec 25 & 26
Must book
Meals 12.30–1.30, 7–10

Alc £8·85 (meal £11·40)

Service 10%
Seats 14 (parties 14)
🔥 rest (1 step); w.c.
Car park
No dogs
3 rooms (2 with bath)
B&B £11·50
Fire cert

'Difficult place to break into' is one (law-abider's)
comment on this Queen Anne parsonage. However,
once you have found a door ('think ours was the
wrong one'), rung to gain admission, and cracked a
smile out of Mr Gofton-Watson, all is sweetness and
light. Amid handsome mahogany furniture and
effusively patterned walls and floors, 'he will keep you
in line as punctiliously as he keeps the cruet', but 'I
warmed to the owner's dry sense of humour,' and *he*
warms to guests who care what they eat and drink.
His wife does most of the cooking now, with Ann
Oakes as her relief, and the proprietor himself as
universal understudy. It makes a strong, consistent
team, and apart from a liverish inspector's complaint
that there seemed to be cream with everything and
another visitor's 'shame they have a mushroom
fetish', members delight in hot wholemeal rolls and
'the crispest Melba toast I've ever eaten', with
excellent butter; 'a superb ripe half-Charentais melon
with black grapes, fresh mint and a good vinaigrette'
(£1·90); 'buttery' gratin of prawns and mushrooms in
wine and cream (£2); pork fillet in a 'succulent' black
cherry sauce (£5·75); and fillet steak ('perfect: thick,
tender and bloody') either with a Stilton sauce or
with port and cream (£6). Vegetables (included in main
dish prices) are an object lesson: 'tiny, earthy-tasting
new potatoes', Kenya beans 'with a squeak to them',
crisp courgettes and broccoli. Sweets are more
variable, with plum brûlée judged less successful than
'a boozy chocolate thing with cream', and the coffee
could be improved, by several accounts. The wines,
from various sources, include a fine half-bottle of
Aloxe-Corton '71 (Averys) at £5·50, and the French
house wines are £3·25 a litre. (The current list is not
to hand.) 'Large breakfasts – the mushrooms were
welcome here.' 'It can be unnervingly quiet – but this
is nowadays a virtue.' Babes in arms are barred.

*App: Nova Whyte, J.B.W., David Head, R. Goldstein,
Henry Fawcett, and others*

FIDDLEFORD Dorset   Map 2

Fiddleford Inn
Sturminster Newton
(0258) 72489

Closed L (exc bar); Sun;
Tue; Dec 25, 26 & 31
Must book D
Meals 12–2 (bar), 7–10

Tdh £7 (meal £9·85)

Service 10%
Children's helpings
(under 12)
Seats 30
▣ rest
Car park
No dogs
6 rooms (1 with bath)
B&B from £7–£8

The Fishes – well remembered by Dorset weekenders from their long spell at Piddletrenthide – are back in calm water at this creeper-covered inn on the Blandford road from Sturminster. They have kept the pattern of bar service that in different hands earned a place in our pub section, but they have also found Julian Harrison – a keen, hitherto amateur chef – for their appealing chocolate-brown restaurant. Either way, early results sound good. An inspector's party in the bar had tasty if small smoked mackerel pâté (85p), stuffed pancakes (they do blinis at night too), and fair chicken curry, with hazelnut gateau and chocolate roulade – in the landlord's words – 'a frightfully refined Swiss roll' – to follow. In the dining-room, an autumn visitor used to eating well all over Europe was bowled over by Mr Harrison's fresh prawns in garlic sauce, and found the wild duck 'crisp but juicy, with firm fresh vegetables.' Cailles au façon du chef and carré d'agneau persillé are also worth trying. Litre Vin carafes are £2·90 a litre. Other wines come from Yapp and Cleeve House, with Gamay de l'Ardèche £4 and Ch. Giscours '71, £14·50. Wadworth's 6X and Old Timer beers are on pump. You may eat outside in the garden. Simple rooms: no children under 14 to stay. More reports, please.

FINDON West Sussex   Map 3

Darlings Bistro
The Square
off A24
Findon (090 671) 3817

Closed Sun; Mon;
L Tue & Sat; 3 weeks
Aug; public hols (exc
Apr 4; May 5; Aug 25)
Must book
Meals 12–1.45, 7.30–9.30

Alc £7 (meal £9·80)

Seats 16
No dogs
Access, Am Ex, Barclay

Brian Lavers often has to be both chef and captain in his shop conversion opposite the Gun pub, and this does much to excuse longish waits and unadorned vegetables, as well as making for an individual, helpful atmosphere (even when a vegetarian turns up). Devilled kidneys and Indonesian pork satay are approved among first courses, and if the stuffed mushrooms are one cap too few, the main dishes are copious: 'The scallops would have defeated a hungry schoolboy (but not my brother).' Venison – 'more tender than the sirloin steaks' – came with 'a delicious sauce of port and black cherries.' Pork fillets with onions, mushrooms and white wine (£4·35) are a speciality. We have heard little of the puddings. Mr Lavers, though capable of saying that Anjou Rosé 'goes with anything', is justly pleased with the value he gives the wine drinker, from Italian Caldorino at £2·75 to less basic '72 burgundy and '78 Beaujolais, or Ch. de By '73 at £5·75. No pipes. There is 'mixed' recorded music, and dancing every now and then.

App: P. A. Burden, J.R.T., R. & J.H.

Wine prices shown are for a 'standard' bottle of the wine concerned, unless another measure is stated (e.g. litre, 50 cl., or pint).

Findon Manor
Findon (090 671) 2269

Closed L; Sun; Mon;
public hols (exc Apr 4)
Must book
D only, from 7.30

Alc £8·45 (meal £13·55)

Cover 50p
Seats 35 (parties 20)
&. rest
Car park
No dogs
5 rooms (4 with bath,
1 with shower)
B&B £14·15

'Five periods of architecture are represented' in the Bannisters' rambling mansion, and almost as many contradictory features evidently appear in the way they run their hotel and restaurant. Accounts of stays range all the way from fascinated horror – 'we were left to drift through the weekend, cold and unattended, like passengers on the Marie Céleste' – to delighted appreciation: 'I was warmly welcomed and treated with the greatest kindness and hospitality throughout my stay.' It is impossible to adjudicate, for both genres of account have the ring of truth about the different dates to which they relate. If you can take all this and the overnight prices in your stride, tell us your own experience – but this entry appears in Roman type because there are fewer doubts about Adrian Bannister's cooking – 'a haven after a bizarre afternoon in Chichester theatre.' People admire the two-stage wild duck dish, the breast cooked with fresh limes, the legs in a mustard coating, 'all done without any hint of dryness or grease, served with an artist's intensity, and accompanied by simple vegetables or salad.' Crab bisque, asparagus, quails and 'properly high' venison are also approved, and Mr Bannister and his assistant Jonas Tester also recommend their brioches aux poissons fumés ('the brioche itself is not light enough yet'), quenelles de brochet au coulis de homard, and perdreau au chou rouge. 'The selection of English cheeses was fabulous', and 'we finished with soufflé glacé Grand Marnier.' French Gamay or Blanc de Blancs table wines are £4, and at a different level 'Beaujolais Blanc (Duboeuf) '77 at £6·35, Château Corton-Grancey '73 at £13·80, and a fine marc de Corton-Grancey at the end sent us floating home.' Bar lunches can now be had with Stones' bitter, perhaps on the terrace. Occasional recorded music. In the dining-room, both smoking and young children are discouraged.

App: M. C. & V. H. Whiting, L.W., J.N.C.,
J. Dobbing, S.P.B., Adrian Underwood, R. D. Carswell,
and others

When a restaurant says 'must book', the context of the entry usually indicates how much or how little it matters, but a preliminary telephone call averts a wasted journey to a closed door. *Always* telephone if a booking has to be cancelled: a small place (and its other customers) may suffer severely if this is not done.

Numbers are given for private parties only if they can be accommodated in a room separate from the main dining-room; when there are several such rooms, the capacity of the largest is given. Some restaurants will take party bookings at times when they are normally closed.

Unless otherwise stated, a restaurant is open all week and all year and is licensed.

FINGEST Buckinghamshire   Map 3

Chequers Inn
7 m NW of Marlow
Turville Heath
(049 163) 335

A chequered year for this busy pub in a sleepy village rather too near Henley and Marlow. Between a pleasant bar lunch of tender steak and kidney pie, with a good pint of Brakspear's, and a painful evening of 'ham-handed cooking and high-handed service' falls an inspector's 'patchy' meal: 'decent mild pâté, convincing minestrone, crunchy cauliflower and courgettes, and thick chocolate mousse; but harsh gravy and half-cooked pastry in meat pie.' Changes in the kitchen may or may not explain all. The beer seems a better choice than French ordinaire at £4 a litre. You may eat outside in the garden.

Closed Mon (exc public hols); Sun D (exc Apr 6); Dec 26; Jan 1
Must book
Meals 12.45–2, 7.30–10

Tdh L £4·95 (meal £8·20)
Alc £7·40 (meal £10·85)

Service 10%
Cover 30p

Seats 35
♿ rest (2 steps)
Car park
No dogs
Am Ex, Barclay

FLITTON Bedfordshire   Map 3

White Hart
off A507
2½ m SE of Ampthill
Silsoe (0525) 60403

Closed Sun; public hols; Dec 24 D
Must book
Meals 12–2, 7.30–10

Tdh £4·55 (meal £7·85)
Alc £8·30 (meal £12·05)

Cover 40p
Seats 50 (parties 16)
Car park
No dogs

Sarah Austin, late of Horton (*q.v.*), is now helping Somerset Moore at this individual inn, which may allow the proprietor more time for his garden, vineyard, *pétanque,* sign collection and other diversions. A French Partridge pupil might be expected to refine the style somewhat – though there is as yet no sign of reduction in often over-generous helpings here. Still, critical visitors have found much to enjoy this year. Mr Moore has a leaning towards fish, and steers plenty of it to Flitton: his best dishes, he thinks, might well include his mousse of scallops, 'superior plate of fresh shellfish', and fresh hake with salsa verde. Oysters, *nephrops norvegicus* with garlic mayonnaise, and 'a mountain of hot crab' are also liked. Quail, venison sausages, and smoked chicken (with the horseradish sauce that Mr Moore's French wife makes) are other good ideas. They bake their own bread, make a 'chocolate and rum stockade' that is guaranteed to keep hunger at bay for a week, and compose a fine bowl of fresh fruit – 'would that equal care were given to the condition of the cheeses, which should never have left the kitchen the night we were there.' The staff, though, are both well-conditioned and well-favoured. Wells bitter and Fargo for the bar snacks are in cask, and they keep a sensible small collection of wines in simplified price ranges: Côtes du Rhône, Sauvignon, and red or white Rioja at £3·60, better Loires (over-chilled) and moselles at £5·45, and Ch. Brane-Cantenac '73, c.b., at £5·90. Two tables for non-smokers.

App: E. David, J. R. Tyrie, M. & R.H., John Foster, and others

Emilio's Restaurant Portofino
124a Sandgate Road
Folkestone (0303) 55866
and 55162

Closed Mon; public hols
(exc Apr 4)
Must book
Meals 12–2.15, 6–10.30

Tdh L £3·50 (meal £6·55)
Alc £6·20 (meal £9·50)

Cover 40p
Children's helpings
(under 12)
Seats 55
♿ rest; w.c.
Air-conditioning
No dogs
Access, Am Ex, Barclay,
Diners

After twelve consecutive *Guide* entries, it is hard to find anything new to say in praise of Emilio Bevilacqua and his chef Eric Randall. The menu and other details were forwarded this year by their accountants, but judging by the value given at set lunches these gentlemen are kept more firmly in their place than is common. 'There was a typical Italianate menu, with minestrone and excellent hors d'oeuvre followed by turbot mugnaia, veal in Marsala, and liver Veneziana; we have had all these at one time or another. From a choice of three sweets, we had a fine gateau, and neither the linen nor the service could be faulted.' Newcomers posted to the south coast on business, somewhat against their inclination, were reconciled by the light textures and clean tastes of their dinners here, with cannelloni, crab salad, fritto misto and 'unsurpassed roast partridge' the most vivid memories. 'By mistake, my companion was served with bread sauce thinking it was tartare, but he found it so nice that he ate it with his fish.' 'Lovely, lemony grilled sardines' and scallops in a delicate Mornay sauce are also much liked. It is worth asking about sweetbreads alla Sassi (£3·50) if they are not on the printed menu. 'Waiters removed empty plates before all of us had finished, in spite of being asked not to.' Pedrotti carafe wines are £3·30 for 82 cl, and other Italian bottles begin at £4·80. No music – a further unusual virtue in an Italian place.

App: David Kibble, H.L.F., W.F., A.A.B.C., and others

FOLKESTONE see also wine bar section

FOWEY Cornwall   Map 1

Cordon Bleu
3 Esplanade
Fowey (072 683) 2359

The local reputation of Rolf Keilbart's well-set and 'maternally served' restaurant is undimmed after fifteen years. At different times, when tried, crab au gratin, minestrone, 'chateaubriand with well-assorted vegetables' and 'venison steaks with some taste in a cream and brandy sauce, unthickened' (£4·20) all showed well. Fish is quayside luck: Mr Keilbart limits himself to familiar species. Sweets mostly iced or flambé. Short sensible wine list from £3·95, with good '71 and '76 Germans.

Closed L; Sun (exc Apr 6);
Dec 24–26 & 31; Jan 1
Must book

D only, 6.45–11

Alc £7 (meal £10·30)

Seats 48 (parties 30)
♿ rest
No dogs

Do not risk using an out-of-date Guide. A new edition will appear early in 1981.

Food for Thought
Town Quay
Fowey (072 683) 2221

Closed L (exc Sun);
Dec 24–26 & 31; Jan 1
Must book
Meals 12–2, 7–10.30

Alc £7·05 (meal £9·95)

Seats 35
No dogs
Access, Barclay

Exposed beams, original stonework, a flagstoned floor, as well as the newly imported candles, checked cloths and (everlasting) flowers, contribute to the relaxed bistro atmosphere of Martin and Caroline Billingsley's recently opened place. Service is genial if under-informed (especially about wines – you may get the wrong bottle and be undercharged). The menu changes monthly: start, perhaps, with mushroom soup ('almost creamed mushrooms', 75p) or avocado with 'interesting fillings' or a moist livery pâté; continue with tender lambs' kidneys in a rich sauce, local fresh fish (scallops provençale, £3·75, or Dover sole) or steaks (filet mignon parisienne, £3·95) with carefully cooked vegetables; and finish – if you survive the generous helpings – with pears in burgundy or cheese-cake. Though the rolls are good, the bread with pâté is packeted pre-sliced, and noisettes of lamb have been tough – 'it may be the butcher's fault,' says a member, explaining his soft heart away by saying that for fresh food, imaginatively cooked and nicely presented, he will forgive a great deal. About thirty wines (mostly lacking vintages on the list) with Hallgarten French house wine at £3·25 for 70 cl. 'Gentle classical guitar' on record in the bar area. More reports, please.

FOWEY see also pub section

FRAMFIELD East Sussex   Map 3

Coach House
off B2102
2 m SE of Uckfield
Framfield (082 582) 636

The original tiny coach house remnants are buried in a comfortable modern extension, with swimming-pool. Praise for the generous set lunch (prawn and Stilton quiche, grilled plaice or roast topside, apple tart or strawberry sundae) and more ambitious dinners: smoked salmon and caviare blinis (£1·80), avocado Venus ('good avocado, rather bland filling', £1·60), Cretan shrimp soup (95p), grilled trout or scallops on a skewer, carpetbagger steak (stuffed with oysters, £5·85). 'Portmanteau sweets trolley, the Granthams' pride': at least ten, including profiteroles, Bakewell tart, green fig flan and a fine lemon meringue pie. Various fairly priced wines with French carafes £4 the litre. 'Light classical' music on tape. No children under five at dinner. Cold meals can be eaten in the garden. Pipes and cigars 'confined to the bar, please.'

Closed Mon; Sun D;
Apr 26–May 3; last 2
weeks Oct; Dec 24–26;
Jan 1
Must book
Meals 12.15–1.45, 7–9
(9.30 Sat)

Tdh L £3·50 (meal £6·20),
Sun L £3·75 (meal £6·45)
Alc £7·45 (meal £10·70)

Service 10%
Children's helpings
(exc Sun L)

Seats 36 (parties 10)
&. rest
Air-conditioning
Car park
No dogs

Teignworthy Hotel
3 m SW of Chagford
Chagford (064 73) 3355

Closed L (exc Sun & bar)
Must book
Meals 12.45–2 (Sun &
bar), 7.30–9

Tdh Sun L £6 (meal £8·70),
D £10 (meal £13·10)

Seats 20
 rest (2 steps)
Car park
No dogs
7 rooms (6 with bath,
1 with shower)
B&B £13·50–£18·50
D, B&B £20–£25
Fire cert

With one fairly vigorous exception, people sound very pleased with themselves to have found the Newells, at the head of a south-facing Dartmoor horseshoe. (Once there, the firm-footed hardly need a car.) The house, built for comfort by the craftsmen Lutyens gathered for Castle Drogo, is 'my idea of a perfect hotel,' says one member of early Postgate vintage. When more non-residents start booking dinners, the atmosphere will surely be too convivial to recall 'an Agatha Christie house party'. The cooking, which Mr Newell shares with his daughters, is careful, and the set dinner menus necessarily short. (Sunday lunch is normally a cold buffet, and very good value. On weekdays residents are offered snacks in the bar.) Soups of watercress or onion, guacamole, mushrooms in wine, taramosalata, mackerel pâté, shoulder of lamb stuffed with asparagus, local red mullet, and chicken Michel Guérard crop up in reports, and the kitchen is not afraid of a touch of pinkness at the bone. 'Too much, though, is lukewarm.' It must be an atypical visitor who found the sweets 'all things I do at home and fill the freezer with', for others are content. Cheeses turn over too slowly, and Brie may be a mistake in this context. Breakfasts 'remain superb'. The wine list is thoughtfully compiled, with Trento red or Riesling £3·75 a litre or pro rata for less, Maître d'Estournel '76 (bottled at Ch. Cos d'Estournel) £4, and Gigondas '74, £5·90, if you are eating venison, perhaps. Pressurised beers. Smoking in the dining-room is discouraged, children under 14 ruled out, and service is 'neither charged nor expected.' Note that they offer a special rate for two or more nights' stay in winter. From Chagford, follow signs to Kestor and Thornworthy. Turn left at Yeo before you get to Thornworthy to find the house. (GHG)

App: D. R. Whittle, E. J. Pointon, Helen Gane, D.F., T.J.S., R. Slaney, W. S. Tillyard, H.D. & A.L.R., and others

Fox and Goose
❦

Fressingfield (037 986) 247

Closed Tue; Dec 21–28
Must book
Meals 12–1.15, 7–9

Alc £10·25 (meal £14)

Service 10%

'There is a strange feeling that you have pulled up at a slightly forbidding old inn in Normandy,' says an expert traveller about this place, built in the time of Henry VIII. The Clarkes had got so used to their ten-year sojourn in the *Guide* that they took it amiss when a clear majority vote went against them last year. Transfer between kitchen generations and a general want of self-criticism in pricing and presentation were the main problems. But they are homely people when you know them, members say, and a test meal with Adrian Clarke cooking yielded 'splendid bread and mayonnaise' for a generously

Seats 26
⌖ rest (3 steps)
Car park
No dogs

assembled seafood platter, and 'a delicate, non-floury and well-seasoned cream sauce for guinea-fowl.' Pommes Anna, courgettes provençale, and cauliflower were well cooked too. Others (ordering from the printed but unpriced menu despatched when you book) report equally fine scallops en croûte ('the pastry light and crisp'), buttery home-grown asparagus, good beef, and 'lamb en croûte cooked past pink (but we forgot to ask) in superb gravy.' Helpings are of East Anglian *grosseur*. The admiration of regulars for the special liquor-soaked sponge and chocolate sweet is not shared by inspectors, but 'raspberry sorbet, chocolate mousse, and coffee were good.' There are about 300 wines, from £3·65 for Granvillons and a little more for Alsace and Gard wines shipped by Jean Passot. The fine wines are Mr Clarke's pride, and perhaps solace, for the prices of £150 for Ch. Margaux '45 and £40 for half-bottles of Ch. Haut-Brion '61 protect them from marauders.

App: Michael Mowbray Silver, D.C.A.C., J. N. Murphy, S.L., C.W., and others

---

GITTISHAM Devon   Map 2

Combe House

off A30
2 m SW of Honiton
Honiton (0404) 2756

Must book Sun
Meals 12–2, 7.30–9.30

Tdh Sun L £6·40 (meal £9·75)
Alc £9·60 (meal £12·95)

Service inc
Children's helpings (Sun L)
Seats 60 (parties 40)
⌖ rest
Car park
No dogs in d/r
Access, Am Ex, Barclay, Diners
13 rooms (8 with bath, 3 with shower)
B&B £16·50
Fire cert

John and Thérèse Boswell have owned Combe for ten years, and though this does not compare with the 232 years that the peppery Putts held this serene wooded estate and Elizabethan mansion, their régime has matured in a way that might surprise visitors from their more ragged early years. The service this year has been smoother 'though still loud and showy', and 'the lofty, elegant rooms were enhanced in a chilly August by roaring log fires.' People describe it as a superb place to stay even though the style (rather than the sheer expense) of the à la carte dinners makes it advisable to eat elsewhere at least every other night. This, and the lack of weekly terms, seem to put Combe *hors-concours* as a 'tureen' hotel. Mrs Boswell cooks, and her food is rich, as the first courses (which may double as bar snacks) suggest: 'first-rate crab gratinée (£2) and beignets soufflés au fromage with sauce provençale', 'delicious garlic bread, champignons en cocotte, and hors d'oeuvre de poisson.' Main course specialities include filets de sole homardin with cream and hollandaise sauces (£7·30), salmon quenelles sauce Nantua (£5·25) and médaillons de filet de boeuf aux champignons; plainer (if that is the word) tournedos Rossini with spinach and chopped, lightly cooked cabbage also delighted a previous critic. 'We were further indulged at the sweet stage with a choice of six, including caramel profiteroles, chocolate and orange mousse and various fruit tartlets.' Packed lunches and breakfasts ('albeit without kippers') are good. The wine list is not long

211

by the standards of a house of this kind, but it is chosen (mostly from Corney & Barrow) by a wine-lover, from the house claret and white burgundy at £4·95, to Ch. La Venelle '73 or Beaujolais-Villages '78 in the £7 range, and Auxey-Duresses '72 (Leroy) and Ch. Coutet '71 if you consider that such rich fish and puddings demand white wines of double-figure stature. Pressurised beers with bar lunches (which can be eaten in the garden). Pipe and cigar smokers are 'encouraged' into the lounges. No children under ten for dinner. (GHG)

App: T. M. Wilson, Joseph M. Thomson, P.H.L., Jill Mulligan, M. J. Kelly, Kay Desmonde, and others

---

GLASTONBURY Somerset   Map 2

No 3 Dining Rooms

Magdalene Street
Glastonbury (0458) 32129

Closed L (exc Sun &
Dec 25); Mon (exc
May 26); Sun D; May;
Nov; Dec 25 D
Must book
Meals 12.30–1.30 (Sun),
7.30–9.30

Tdh from £9·80
(meal £12·70)

Seats 24 (parties 12)
&. rest (2 steps)
Car park
No dogs

'Noel Coward held that the only difference between amateur and professional is practice,' say Charles Foden and George Atkinson, refugees from non-culinary vocations. Their Georgian house, furnished with contemporary Lombard lightness, 'would make a suitable stage set for Bernard Levin to bound through the French windows crying "Anyone for lobster?".' The owners are sincere in their devotion to excellence in materials, and Mr Atkinson's cooking proves it. They are also friendly people, though a hint of self-congratulation is not missed by visitors – 'We half expected to see previous *Guide* entries reproduced as table mats.' A test meal this year did not, in fact, bear out all hopes, mainly because of 'a misguided experiment called a pork eclair', and a residual doubt about the freshness of a sauce base. Happily, so much in this and in other people's meals during the year has been finely – though often too richly – achieved that genuine merit is not in doubt. Choice of main dish reveals (alas, to host only) the price of meals. First courses have yielded, for instance, superb bourride, and celery soup with walnuts, or turbot salad. They permit you to eat scampi and steak of high quality if you insist, but would sooner you tried, perhaps, saumon en papillote with hollandaise and buttered cucumber, or 'amazing sweetbreads', or 'calf's liver in an orange and port sauce', or 'tender, highish, and succulent' quails Véronique with (surprisingly) black grapes. Vegetables, though mistimed for one visitor, are generally good, and salads well dressed. In spite of the richness, 'this is the only place where I have eaten three puddings in a row,' confesses a West Countryman (naturally): if one of the three was the chocolate truffle or 'die echte Sachertorte' one hopes the brandy sorbet figured too. Cheddar and apple flan is also worth a note. Cheeses on their own are less remarkable, but the coffee is good. The French red and Hungarian white wines are sound for £4·20 a litre. Other Averys clarets and burgundies command attention, though the owners are not experts. Ch. Croizet-Bages '71 and Ch. Guiraud '67 for the fruitier puddings were both around £10 in 1979. No pipes, though the owners have the curious notion that cigar smoke and women's perfume go well together – and with food. No guests below the age of consent (as it stands at the time of writing). Dress up to the occasion.

App: J. A. Croxford, John Rowlands, W. C. Voyle, D. & M.W., J. D. Acland, Cdr G. F. Barnett, Mrs P. Holbrook, and others

---

GRASMERE Cumbria   Map 7

Michael's Nook
Grasmere (096 65) 496

Must book
Meals 12.30 for 1, 7.30
for 8 (Sat in season 7 for
7.15, 9 for 9.15)

Tdh L £6·55 (meal £10),
D £9·95 (meal £14)

Service 10%
Seats 30
♿ rest; w.c.
Car park
No dogs in public rooms
10 rooms (6 with bath,
2 with shower)
D, B&B £22·50–£34·40

By the end of the poem, Wordsworth's Michael 'never lifted up a single stone', but Mr Gifford will have turned over plenty (not personally, perhaps) by the time he has finished the grandiose new Wordsworth Hotel planned for this village in 1981 (turn off the A591 at the Swan, north of the village). In Michael's Nook itself (a century-old mansion furnished with more and better Victorian antiques than any other in this book, with a live parrot to complete the effect) his worries have been diminished this year by the stability of Nigel Marriage in the kitchen, whose cooking some people admire above other distinguished places in the district. The style is rich (and the house itself warmed to transatlantic taste), but at a test meal the smoked trout quiche, milky onion soup, plainly and pinkly roast lamb with garlic and rosemary, and sultana meringue pie made a balanced programme for a robust appetite. Vegetables – 'including nutmeggy creamed swede' – were admirably cooked and presented. In a longer stay, another visitor praises among first courses Stilton and port quiche, sweetbreads soubise, and grilled sardines with mustard mousseline; and among main dishes roast quail, escalope de veau Holstein, and braised ox tongue with black cherry sauce. 'Superbly roasted' beef and duck are mentioned in other accounts. There are fresh orange juice and Cumberland sausage at breakfast (which is served with less despatch than dinner). The Costa Rican coffee is consistently good. 'Mr Gifford wants charm if anything is found amiss' but 'will talk wine if he knows you.' The Youdell list gives plenty to discuss, with fifteen clarets and as many burgundies (beginning at just under £6) and one or two £50 treasures. 'If you click with the place you may think it "tureen" standard, but the owner is caviare to the general.'

App: E. Radcliffe, Michael A. Shiffman, J.K.L., Mrs F. Millward, Christopher Rae, G.B., and others

White Moss House

Rydal Water
on A591
1 m S of Grasmere
Grasmere (096 65) 295

Closed L; Wed; end-Oct
to mid-Mar
Must book
D only, 7 for 7.30

Tdh £9 (meal £11·60)

Seats 18
⚹ rest (1 step)
Car park
No dogs
7 rooms (5 with bath)
D, B&B from £23
Fire cert

Recipe in *Second Dinner
Party Book:* Sussex pond
pudding

It was a positive relief to hear that one Tuesday in
May 1979 Mrs Butterworth cooked an unambiguously
second-rate meal – and a relief too to know that the
eater of it stayed long enough in this sedate granite
house to see his hostess 'back on form as only very
few cooks can be.' 'English food cooked in a way
that shows up so many other kitchens' is another
typical remark about a place that also shows, more
positively, how much can be achieved by thoughtful,
civilised people who give their minds and hearts to
getting things right. 'Mr Butterworth forgot nothing
though he alone waited on 18 people at dinner and
saw to the wine expertly too.' It is difficult to select
individual dishes from meals so lovingly listed;
indeed, the internal balance of menus is part of the
point, so that you proceed, say, from scallop and
artichoke soup to terrine of pigeon with Cumberland
sauce and garlic bread, then pork chop baked with
fresh pineapple, various accurately cooked garden
vegetables, and only reach a choice at the sweet
stage, with cheese strudel or almond and chocolate
meringue gateau with Tia Maria cream. But other
particular favourites include tipsy shrimps, fresh herb
pâté with kiwi-fruit salad and home-made date and
walnut bread, 'wonderful roast lamb with redcurrant,
orange and mint jelly and cheesy potatoes', 'chicken
livers in cream and Chambéry – a classic of their
kind', 'chicken breast with parsley and almond
stuffing and a lovely sorrel sauce', 'the marriage of
suet crust and lemons in Sussex pond pudding',
'English cheeses with home-made oatmeal biscuits',
pickled damsons, and so on, ad infinitum. A few
minor lapses are reported, and one or two vigorous
walkers mention the restraint (otherwise welcome)
over helpings. 'Anyone on honeymoon could hardly
do better than the annexe, Brockstone, up the hill,
especially as it rains so much and one needn't bother
to go out.' The wines, from just over £3 for a Rioja
Montecillo '71, are well chosen and served –
'Meursault Charmes '67 was the best white wine I
have ever tasted, Le Montrachet included', and
though that has gone now, other Chanson or Latour
burgundies are compelling. The half-bottles provided
encourage discussion and experiment. Comforts
abound – books included – and breakfasts match the
rest. Snack or packed lunches are made for residents.
No smoking in the dining-room. Recorded classical
music. No children under 15. Jacket and tie are
preferred at dinner. (GHG)

*App: M. E. Cohen, M. J. Young, R. J. & N. E. Stone,
Roy Mathias, Mrs F. Millward, N. V. Crookdake,
A.C.S., and others*

GREAT BARRINGTON Gloucestershire   Map 2

Inn for All Seasons
on A40
3 m W of Burford
Windrush (045 14) 324

Closed Dec 25, 26 & 31
Meals (Buttery) 12–2,
6–9.45 (Sun 7–9.45);
(d/r) 7.30–8.45

Tdh D (res only) £4·75
(meal £6·85)
Alc (Buttery – min £2)
£4·55 (meal £7·05)

Seats (Buttery) 20, (d/r) 26
[symbol] rest
8 rooms (6 with bath)
B&B £10–£14·30
Fire cert

Kenneth West's stone-built Georgian house and garden appeared in last year's pub section on the strength of the carefully cooked soup, lasagne 'up to Italian standard', steak and kidney pie and other dishes served in the cosy Buttery Bar (no bookings). He relies on word-of-mouth recommendation to bring resident guests, and the dining-room is reserved for them. A member speaks very well of all this, from the double-glazed rooms and breakfast eggs 'exactly to my taste' to 'unbelievable crackling with the roast pork and a genuine sherry trifle.' (The cooking is done by Cordon Bleu girls who may vary from season to season.) Wadworth's 6X is probably the best drink, since the brewer also supplies the wine. Recorded music in the buttery. No children under ten. No dogs. Between November and April they offer a special dinner, bed and breakfast rate of £25 for two nights. More reports, please, on all operations.

GREAT WITLEY Hereford & Worcester   Map 2

Hundred House
on A443
11 m NW of Worcester
Great Witley (029 921)
215 *and* 565

Closed D Sun & Mon
(exc May 5); L Dec 25;
D Dec 26
Must book weekends
Meals 12–2, 8–9

Tdh buffet L £3·50 (meal
£5·95), D £8·55 (meal
£12·05)

Service 10%
Children's helpings L
(under 7)
Seats L 150, D 80
(parties 20)
Car park
No dogs
Access, Am Ex, Barclay

The Italianate parish church is recommended without reservation but reports on the Tansleys' simply dressed restaurant are fewer and less fulsome this year. The lunchtime cold table (which is mostly independent of the dinner), while still good value, is called 'not what it was'. Helpings (including soup, cheese, fruit and good coffee) are unlimited, but choice narrows: 'Gone are the pâtés and quiches, only Edam and mousetrap for cheese,' mourns a regular. Salads are 'tasty' and carnivores make do with cold beef, ham, pork and chicken legs. Good materials mark 'restful' dinners: 'Vegetables were so good I asked about their garden.' Others wonder whether they also own an ocean, for fresh turbot (£5·25), squid (£1·95), scallops (in saffron sauce, also used with fish mousseline), salmon and halibut 'recur with agreeable frequency.' Langoustine kebab (£5·25) and lambs' sweetbreads are praised; baked trout in yoghourt (£2·25) and calf's liver with sage and avocado (£4·75) sound worthwhile. White wines are surprisingly limited (Frascati Superiore is cheapest at £3·80), but there is plenty of red meat to match the clarets.

App: R. O. Marshall, G. A. Wright, P.B.W.

PLEASE keep sending in reports, as soon as possible after each meal. The cut-off date for the 1981 Guide is September 30, 1980, but reports are even more useful earlier in the year, especially for the remoter areas and new places. Late autumn reports can also affect corrections at proof stage.

The Haven
Hornby (0468) 21274

Closed L; Sun; Mon; Fri
Must book
D only, 8 p.m.

Tdh about £5·50

Seats 25
Car park
Unlicensed

Mrs Hogg's cottage with its 'cordial host and inviting smells' is one of those places that belong in any guide to well-cooked dinners but do not actually need or even enjoy the book's advocacy. After several years' gap, one couple was pleased to find so little changed: 'Creamy and flavourful salmon soup – a decided success – with hot wholemeal rolls was followed by the usual sole in a cheesy but well-balanced sauce, and then by judiciously stuffed and crisply cooked duck with roast and duchesse potatoes, leeks in a fine creamy sauce, and a Lancastrian ratatouille.' Apricot pie and hazelnut meringue with apricot sauce were both made with fresh fruit – 'delicious: believe it or not we were also offered, and accepted, lemon meringue pie after the coffee, for quantities were generous without being overfacing.' You must take you own wine, which naturally makes the evening even better value. Prices given are those current in 1979.

App: Mr & Mrs R. J. Stone, Abigail Fawcett, L.O'B.

Black Horse Inn
on A151
4 m NW of Bourne
Edenham (077 832) 247

In three years, Mr and Mrs Fisher have moved from advertising their entry in the *Guide* to regretting it, but there has been little other change: gross helpings of rich food that sounds more English and more flavourful than it tastes (apart from 'pleasantly butyric butter'), in a welcoming stone house noisily sited on a bend. Spinach soup, Fenland omelette, local sausages, devilled kidneys, Mrs Beeton's steak pie, syllabub, breakfasts, and Italian Cabernet (£3·45 in 1979) are variously praised. Pressurised beers. No children under five in the restaurant. Wear a tie at night. Details are approximate.

Closed Sun; Apr 6;
Dec 25
Must book
Meals 12–1.30, 7–9.30

Alc £6·20 (meal £11·40)

Service 10%
Children's helpings
Seats 50

♿ rest
Car park
No dogs in d/r
5 rooms
B&B from £10

Since each restaurant has a separate file in the Guide office, please use a separate form or sheet of paper for each report. Additional forms may be obtained free (no stamp required) from The Good Food Guide, Freepost, 14 Buckingham Street, London WC2N 6BR (unfortunately Freepost facilities are not available from the Channel Islands or the Republic of Ireland).

For the explanation of ♿, denoting accessibility for the disabled, see 'How to use the Guide', p. 4.

Prices quoted in entries now include VAT.

GUILDFORD Surrey Map 3

Cranks
35 Castle Street
Guildford (0483) 68258

'High-priced wholefood but high quality too' in the self-service vegetarian restaurant attached to a health-food shop in the centre of town. Pottery, pine and wicker chime with 'vegetarian' pizza (60p), cheese and onion pie (95p), curried vegetables, salads and sweets (figs, date and apple torte, pears and nuts in yoghourt). 'Special, unsprayed' cider and elderflower wine as well as the grape sort. 'Crowded and cramped at lunch', when smoking is banned.

Closed D; Sun;
public hols
No bookings
Open 10–5

Alc L £3·25 (meal £3·90)

Service inc

Seats 21
♿ rest (1 step)
No dogs

GUILDFORD see also wine bar section

GUIST Norfolk Map 6

Tollbridge Restaurant
on B1110
10 m SW of Holt
Foulsham (036 284) 359

Closed Mon; Sun D;
Sat L; 1st week Oct;
Dec 25 & 26; Jan 1;
Jan 7–31
Must book
Meals 12–1.30, 7–9.30

Tdh L £3·40 (meal £5·65)

Sun L £4·30 (meal £6·95)

Alc £4·75 (meal £7·95)

Children's helpings
Seats 35
♿ rest
Car park
No dogs

William Stark's family restaurant on the banks of the Wensum, half-way between Norwich and the Wash, was evidently one of the last edition's most pleasing finds, for quality and value alike. The set lunch, with adequate choice, could hardly be more accessibly priced, and for quality 'several times during the winter we have had Mr Stark's partridge Véronique (£4·55, including vegetables), cooked rare as we have never found it outside France.' Mousseline of pike and local clams in garlic butter are first-course specialities, not to mention langoustine aïoli, soupe de poisson, and other more homely soups. Sweetbreads are tender, crab and turbot are safe orders, and vegetables carefully cooked. Sweets include 'delicious creamy gateaux, fresh fruit, brandy and mincemeat flan, and enormous meringues.' Moreover, 'the children, both in their early teens, were offered a two-thirds menu more than lived up to its proportion.' 'Service is a good balance of friendliness, information, and unobtrusiveness.' There are one or two suggestions for further improvement: better control or segregation of smokers; more Rhônes or Riojas on the wine list for the game; real ale in the bar, and better coffee. You may eat on the riverside lawns if you wish.

App: Kate Harwood and Tony Marks, John Bruce, J. P. G. Rogerson, R. Whitehead, and others

Entries for places with distinctions carry symbols (pestle, tureen, bottle, glass). Credits are fully written entries, with approvers' names below the text. Passes are telegraphic entries (useful in the area) with details under the text. Provisional entries are in italics (see 'How to use the Guide', p. 4).

Horn of Plenty

✌ ❢

3 m W of Tavistock
off A390
Gunnislake (0822) 832528

Closed Thur; Fri L
Must book D & Sun L
Meals 12.15–2, 7.15–9

Tdh D (inc wine) £15·70
(meal £18·10)
Alc £8·45 (meal £12·60)

Cover 65p
Children's helpings L
Seats 60
♿ rest (3 steps); w.c.
Car park
No dogs

Recipe in *Second Dinner
Party Book*: potato
pancakes

As with other performing arts, one test of cookery in
its upper flights is the length of time a taste remains
in the memory. More so, for Kreisler or Caruso are
recorded, and Edith Evans filmed, but who is to bottle
Bocuse? So the precision with which a member
describes in October a dinner he ate in April, and
another 'a meal I shall remember as clearly as one at
the Hole in the Wall over seven years ago', is relevant
to this family house above the Tamar valley, now in
its twelfth *Guide* year under Patrick and Sonia
Stevenson (who cooks). In that time, plenty of dishes
have miscarried or voices been raised: it is not for
belt-and-braces predictability that one treasures this
restaurant. Again, some might hold that an Easter
menu that included both 'egg and shellfish in pastry
topped with hollandaise' and îles flottantes was
literally over-egging the theological pudding. But 'the
first dish was a miracle' and it remained one after six
months. More agnostic (and recent) inspectors have
commited to memory the hot mousse of crab with a
freshly made hollandaise sauce (£1·75), a duck-shaped
but subtle galantine of duck, the 'peppery and
delicious' hare soup, the 'exquisitely flavoured chicken
in a cream sauce with Pinot d'Alsace' (£4·45), and the
'divinely rich' speciality, langouste et fruits de mer en
croustade (£6·85, or £3·60 as a first course). Other
masterpieces have included the Inca duck, with fresh
coriander leaves and 'perfectly greaseless' meat and
rice, or 'the *tour de force* of calf's sweetbreads en
brioche, combining an outrageous visual pun with
harmonious flavours and textures.' Vegetables – apart
from the favourite potato pancakes – and salads are
adequate rather than distinguished, and some would
say the same of the cheeses and the puddings, but
here again, if a delivery has just arrived from Patrick
Rance, or blackberries are in season for a fruit pie
with clotted cream, judgment may have to be revised.
The set meal is a regional dinner, appropriate wine
included. Wines are researched by David Wolfe: you
never quite know what you will find, except that the
proprietor will have tried and liked it, from
Yugoslav Prokupac and Poitou Chardonnay under £5
in 1979, to a Californian echo of Sancerre, or major
bottles such as Ch. Cheval Blanc '73 under £20. The
waitresses charm even when they hurry their patients.
No children under ten to dine. You may eat outside
under the vine-covered terrace. 'Mr Stevenson
approached – twice – to ask us whether everything
was all right but looking rather as though he wanted
to borrow the condiments.'

*App: R. G. W. Caldicott, V. H. Vanstone, A.J.B.,
J. Birmingham, J. & P.S., Andrew Tozer,
John Sherlock, M. I. Bradbury, and others*

HADLEIGH Suffolk   Map 3

Tavitons
103 High Street
Hadleigh (0473) 822820

Closed from 22nd to end
of every month (exc Dec);
Sat L; Dec 25 D; Dec 26
Must book
Meals 12.30–2, 7.30–9.45

Tdh D £8·25 (meal £9·40)
Alc L £4·90 (meal £6·40)

Service inc
Seats 22
Car park (res only)
No dogs
Access, Barclay
2 rooms (1 with bath)
B&B £9

The cooks now named in this Georgian house – 'Ian and Sue Weeks with help from Sue's mum as pastry-cook' – sound a refreshing change from the former owner, now gone sailabout. Ex-teachers, 'they may be amateur,' says an inspector, 'but they understand food and are charming and considerate.' Indeed, a test meal that included their spiced pâté, beetroot and orange salad, fennel and almond fish soup, and beef with prunes suggested that the Weeks had been in business months or years rather than weeks, and even fish quenelles, though not quite classic, were light and delicate in a well-made shrimp sauce. Prawn pâté with lime and coriander, tomato and tarragon soup, steak and pigeon pie, and raspberry bombe are other favourite dishes on the monthly menus; chestnut parfait and chocolate apricot slice are 'wickedly rich'; and blue Cheshire cheese was 'nicely presented with slices of apple and home-made wheatmeal biscuits.' An overnight stayer was not surprised to find breakfast equally conscientious, with squeezed oranges and good toast. Châtelet table wines are £3·50 and on a very promising list Ch. Gazin '71 is a modest £4·75. No smoking in the dining-room; no children under 12. Recorded music. The adjoining bistro/wine bar is now separately owned. More reports, please.

HALESWORTH Suffolk   Map 6

Bassett's

London Road
Halesworth (098 67) 3154

Closed L; Sun;
Dec 24–26; Jan 1
Must book
D only, 7.30–10

Tdh £7 (meal £9·25)

Seats 40 (parties 18)
♿ rest (2 steps)
Car park
No dogs

Restaurants, like other performers, must either develop or recede: they cannot stand still. Stewart Bassett has been one of East Anglia's most interesting *chef-patrons* and wine-lovers, and was not lightly awarded his *Guide* pestle. Nor it is lightly withdrawn, for serious and regular eaters at his unsmart, rush-and-wood house near the church continue to find the food outstanding: 'notably pheasants' eggs in tarragon sauce, the chicken liver and soft herring roe pâtés, the forcemeat stuffings and wine, cream and mustard sauces for joints, the cheesecake, and inventive ice-creams such as gooseberry and rosemary.' But even if the strains of single-handed work are taken into account, too many correspondents in 1979 echoed the conclusions drawn from a winter test meal: that 'the simple things were best, in tune with the country-blacksmith decor, and the terrines and vegetables were excellent; but parsnip and curry soup was too bland, the sauces for braised veal and walnut-stuffed pigeon flawed, and chocolate brandy cake (to an admirer of the original recipe) unrecognisable.' Other critics have mentioned the ill-advised use of pork for stuffing duck, with *'écoeurant'* results, and dry cakes; admirers take pleasure in the hot crab, fish and game, meringues and crème brûlée. The wines, and the value generally, are still unstintedly admired. Corbières red or Loire white are £2·85, there are good '75 moselles under £7, and a lost world of clarets from Ch. Cissac '71 at £6 to two '61s and three '45s at prices that are at any rate understandable (Ch. Cheval Blanc '49 is £94) – 'though you'd think they could afford more than one wine list to pass round the bar.' No cigars before 9 p.m.

App: Stanley John, J. M., J. B. Wilkin, and others

HALSETOWN Cornwall   Map 1

Chef's Kitchen
off B3311
2 m S of St Ives
St Ives (073 670) 6218

Closed L; Sun; Apr 4;
Dec 25 & 26
Must book
D only, 7–10

Alc £6·65 (meal £8·60)

Service inc
Seats 32
&. rest (3 steps)
Air-conditioning
Car park
No dogs

Recipe in *Second Dinner Party Book:* crab fritters

From the B3311, branch east at the Halsetown Arms to find the Tetleys' restaurant, which has now broken into the cottage next door, 'though our bank manager has not yet taken in that we now seat fewer people than before but have more lounge space.' Mr Tetley's ambitions – or rather his own past – are metropolitan; and he knows enough to know that 'there is a best and a worst day for every item on the menu.' One visitor in a crowded August hit the worst for the crab fritters that others praise, and found the sauce for boned duck too sweet. But in general there is little but pleasure taken in the hazelnut bread, 'light and crisp' seafood vol-au-vents, and other good sauces for brill, or sole stuffed with John Dory. Spinach and other vegetables are also carefully cooked. Hazelnut meringue is 'apt to rebound' but 'I had a delicious iced soufflé with Tia Maria.' Coffee appears to be chicoried, and they like you to drink it in the lounge. 'The waitresses are out of *Poldark* but they coped politely with a lady who said she was on a fat-free diet and promptly ordered avocado vinaigrette and duckling.' Wines, from £3 in 1979 from Merchant Vintners, include '78 Beaujolais under £4. Recorded music.

App: Gwenda Shaw, Diana Chapman, R. W. Simpson, I. D. Nussey, and others

---

HAMPOLE South Yorkshire   Map 5

Hampole Priory
off A638
1 m W of A1(M)
Doncaster (0302) 723740
and 724602

Steady praise continues for this small, calm, candlelit restaurant, once a vicarage. The approach to both cooking and service is tidy and earnest; after a fishy beginning (seafood pancakes £1·45), or a rough pâté, there is always one choice each of pork, veal, chicken, lamb and steak, in varying guises. Vegetables are treated plainly but well. Pineapple Martinique is a favourite sweet. Plentiful coffee. Small wine list; French carafe £3 for 70 cl. Recorded music.

Closed L; Sun; Mon;
public hols (exc Apr 4;
Dec 26; Jan 1)
Must book
D only, 7–9.30

Alc £7·45 (meal £9·45)

Service inc
Children's helpings
(under 10)

Seats 26
Car park
No dogs
Access, Euro

HARROGATE North Yorkshire   Map 5

Au Charbon de Bois
Studley Hotel
Swan Road
Harrogate (0423) 60425

A busy, spick-and-span hotel dining-room dressed in spartan Greek Revival. Grills, kebabs and brochettes carry the day: kidneys, sardines or 'cheese-topped' avocado to start, then coquilles au lard, judi kebab ('tasty well-timed chicken and aubergines, dull sauce,' £4·35) and brochette burger with concassé tomatoes (£3·75). 'Imaginative salad' and other careful details. But 'dry caneton aux pêches with a single peach and sticky sauce' (£4·60). 'Good custard in limp mille-feuille from a trolley too full to move.' Service 'friendly but stretched'. Les Celliers carafes £3·20 for 75 cl. Recorded music. No children under seven in the hotel. Car park. (GHG)

Closed Dec 25 D (exc res)	Service 10% (Sat D, Sun L & parties of 6 or more)	No dogs in public rooms
Must book		Access, Am Ex, Barclay, Diners
Meals 12.30–2, 7.30–10.30	Children's helpings (under 7)	25 rooms (23 with bath, 1 with shower)
Tdh L £3 (meal £5·50)	Seats 55	B&B £15–£16
Alc £7·70 (meal £10·70)	🔲 rest	Fire cert

Number Six
6 Ripon Road
Harrogate (0423) 502908

Closed L; Mon (exc
May 5 D); last week July,
1st 2 weeks Aug;
Dec 25 & 26; Jan 1
Must book
D only, 7.30–10

Tdh from £7·95
(meal £10·50)

Seats 58 (parties 24)
Car park
No dogs

If the art of restaurant operation is disguise, the di Silvestros have done well, for they lost their chef after the last *Guide* entry was written, and soldiered on themselves until John Beardsley took over at Easter 1979 without visitors noticing anything altered or amiss. True, there are faults, but only the usual ones (do not necessarily expect the waiter to rescue you from ordering too many creamy dishes in your set meal). Otherwise, a summer visitor's late dinner after a concert began well with fresh crab salad, followed by a substantial and well-flavoured mushroom soup. Loin of lamb coated with a crust of breadcrumbs and mint showed pink when cut, vegetables were carefully cooked, and though the sweets trolley betrayed the lateness of the evening, lemon soufflé and oranges in caramel were both pleasing. Other contented notes include the crudités on the tables, 'enormous Dublin Bay prawns with good mayonnaise', 'lovely' pork fillet in cream and mushroom sauce, and roast poussin. Wines that need it are now decanted, but members say that the level of smoking permitted (including cigars between courses) must forbid any distinction for the excellent wine list, which is unusually strong in Rhine, Mosel (Wehlener Sonnenuhr '71, £9·75) and Alsace wines as well as in claret and burgundy. But if you contemplate spending £20 on Musigny '70 (Louis Jadot) or Ch. Grand-Puy-Lacoste '59, c.b., better be in your place early before the atmosphere thickens.

App: B. A. Boucher, I. & K. Oswald, A.V.,
K. S. Mingle, J.S.S., and others

221

Oliver Restaurant
24 Kings Road
Harrogate (0423) 68600

Closed L; Sun; public hols
(exc Apr 4)
Must book
D only, 7–10.30

Tdh from £7·50
(meal £10·60)

Seats 80
&. rest
Air-conditioning
No dogs
Access, Am Ex

It takes all sorts to make a restaurant's customers, from a member who daringly calls Harrogate the Surbiton of Yorkshire and delighted in chicken with prawn and lobster sauce, to an elderly trio who 'brought their indigestion pills and could be heard saying (after tasting Peter Jones's delicate cauliflower Mornay, new potatoes and courgettes), that they preferred tinned carrots.' However, apart from one grumble of mediocre smoked trout, sweetened savoury dishes and bland sweets, and another of desultory greeting and wine waiting, everyone thinks they have been treated very well in this purple and lilac dining-room. First courses are often unusual and generous – 'at successive dinners, high quality asparagus with butter sauce, and delicious lamb's liver on toast'; 'rather filling salmagundy'; 'superb trout baked with cheese and egg.' The soup that follows – perhaps French onion, or cream of broccoli – is also good. Main courses are professionally cooked – for example, beef Wellington, chicken breast with juniper and gin sauce, and roast duckling with pineapple and liqueur. They are also proud of their salmon and grouse. But steak pieces en brochette came 'overdone and dry'. 'Vegetables were particularly well treated.' Apricot and almond trifle is called 'inconsequential', but strawberries with a sauce of raspberries and kirsch were 'prime'. The wines, from £3·45, are serious, and effort has been made to find beguiling bottles from unfashionable regions under £6. Montagny '77 (Ponnelle) and minor '73 clarets are in the £8 range. Half-bottles of sweet white Bordeaux are kept. Recorded music, and, as at Oliver's chief local rival, no restraint on smoking.

App: A. Taylor, J.S.S., Gerald C. Longhurst, K. S. Mingle, P. & P.P., F.K.

The Pier at Harwich
The Quay
Harwich (025 55) 3363

Closed Dec 24–26
Must book
Meals 12.30–2, 6.30–10
(Sun 7–10)

Alc £5·65 (meal £8·30)

Children's helpings
Seats 130 (parties 100)
&. rest

If obliged – like one hapless member – to pass two whole days waiting for a fair wind in this busy but oddly underdeveloped port, you may find yourself enjoying a view of the yachts in the bay and spending most of your ship ha'pennies at this nautically converted pub opposite the ferry landing-stage. Gerald Milsom of Le Talbooth at Dedham (*q.v.*) and his wine merchant Richard Wheeler are co-owners. The (mainly fishy) menu is adapted to different levels of the market: à la carte dishes may come from either the 'captain's table' or the 'wardroom table' but there is no lower deck. One à la carte meal included 'superb bread' and 'hot, cheesy crab pastries', then baked haddock topped with horseradish and

Car park
No dogs
Access, Barclay

breadcrumbs. The cost seemed reasonable. Cullen skink and clam chowder are both admired soups, baked mussels are worth trying, and goujons of sole Maharajah (£4·10) were 'very handsomely presented considering how few maharajahs now enter Britain through Harwich.' (Paella, though, was 'only as Spanish as Benidorm', and some may prefer an oil-and-vinegar alternative to the house salad dressing.) Sweets are mostly iced and one visitor fell foul of a fermenting summer pudding, but otherwise contentment is general. The bitter is Adnams', and the wines sensibly chosen, with quite a few half-bottles. It is worth paying the extra for the dearer house wine, Moutier Blanc, at £3·95. Alsace and white burgundy are mostly over £8. Recorded pier music.

App: Paul Palmer, P. I. Robbins, C.P.D., Lt. Col. C. A. Brooks, and others

---

HEALD GREEN Greater Manchester   Map 5

La Bonne Auberge

🍷

224 Finney Lane
061-437 5701

Closed Sun; Mon D;
public hols (exc Dec 25 L)
Must book
Meals 12–2, 7–9.30

Tdh L £2·90 (meal £5·50)
Alc (min £7) £7·35
(meal £10·55)

Service 10%
Children's helpings
(under 7 L)
Seats 70 (parties 35)
🔥 rest
Car park
No dogs
Am Ex, Diners

The awning breaks the shopping parade, and the new green-and-white check theme to the decor has vastly lightened the feel of Roger and Cecilia Boutinot's long-loved restaurant on the rim of Stockport; their son Paul, too, has now brought new zest and knowledge of wine to the enterprise. It is a shame that a grumble about far-from-*bleu* tournedos brought the service out in flounces for one party, but this apart, both the set lunches and the à la carte dinners are as reliable as ever. 'Vegetables were a little soft for my taste,' an inspector says, but the coquilles St Jacques 'with prawns and mushrooms, under a cheesy crust' (£1·75), chicken suprême and tournedos Rossini – accurately cooked this time – were good. So were the sweets, including apricot pie with a very rich shortcrust, and a raspberry meringue gateau. Quiche Lorraine (£1·60), scampi biarotte (£3·70) and crêpes normande with calvados (£3 for two) are other ideas. White Côtes du Luberon at £3·35 or red Minervois at £3·70 may be the best cheap wine choices, but the carefully described Dopff & Irion Alsace wines, Pernand-Vergelesses '72 (Chanson) and '70 clarets in higher reaches inspire confidence. Recorded music in the evening. To find the place from the M56 (junction 5), steer between the airport and the Excelsior hotel, turning left at Styal road and right at traffic lights.

App: R. E. Carter, R.H., Henry Fawcett

1980 prices are as estimated by restaurateurs in the autumn of 1979 (including VAT).

Towns shown in black on our maps contain at least one recommended restaurant, pub or wine bar (see map key). The dot denotes the location of the town or village, not the establishment. Where necessary, we give directions to it in the entry. If you can, help us to improve them.

Andwells
on A33
8 m S of Reading
Heckfield (073 583) 202

Must book weekends
Meals 12.15–1.45,
7.15–9.45

Alc £10·70 (meal £16·55)

Service 12½%
Cover 75p
Children's helpings
Seats 40 (parties 15)
🔽 rest (1 step); w.c.
Air-conditioning
Car park
No dogs
Access, Am Ex, Barclay,
Diners, Euro

It is possible to dine well at the Strattons' brocaded restaurant for a little under £20 a head. Whether you will want to depends on a personal reaction to what some describe as scrupulous devotion to classical cuisine, and others call in their politer moments 'ghastly good taste, coupled with elements of extortion.' Arbitration is difficult. Not all dishes have been as generous or well served as they should be, and some dishes on customers' July and August bills exceeded prices shown on the menu supplied to the *Guide* in October. But if price as well as cooking matters to you, consider soup or egg dishes, followed by kidneys or sweetbreads with a single vegetable perhaps, rather than lobster and asparagus, however admirable. Wines under £10 include Gewürztraminer '76 (Hugel) and Vieux-Château Tropchaud '71. There are also half-bottles of some fine wines (Ch. Haut-Brion '66, £22·90). As always here, please report experiences in detail.

App: D. L. Shead, W. R. Fletcher, R.J.M., and others

Riverside

off B3293
Manaccan (032 623) 443

Closed L (exc Sun);
D Sun & Mon (exc res);
public hols (exc Apr 4 D)
Must book
Meals 12.45–2.15, 7.30–10

Tdh Sun L £8·50 (meal
£10·70),
D £10·50 (meal £12·75)

Service inc
Seats 40
Car park (res)
No dogs
4 rooms (all with bath)
B&B £10·50

For George Perry-Smith, there is always one more river to cross, even after Helford's (take the Lizard road out of Helston), and during 1979 admirers' hearts were in their mouths while he threatened to cross the same river twice. As in previous periods of restlessness, everything slipped slightly except the actual cooking, where *noblesse* obliges – though even here, it is well to remember that if the maestro is going to err, it will be in the direction of the raw and the raucous, not the limp and the bland. Still, when the omens are favourable, 'this is what the *Guide* is all about, and we spent two days in our delightful room savouring the exquisite aromas wafting from the kitchen from mid-afternoon till we could wait no longer.' 'I had the parsley, artichoke and fennel soup and the pink lamb, both superb. The little touches made the visit: crisp cheese straws in the bar, individual coffee pots at breakfast, the smell of the hot rolls and croissants, the daffodils in my bedroom, and the grace with which they mended my boot in the kitchen without a cobbling charge.' 'My wife had a very good avocado and turbot concoction followed by sea bass, and I had the fish stew, which would have fed three people comfortably.' Rissoles parisienne, in fragile pastry, guinea-fowl terrine with salsify, breast of lamb Ste Ménéhould, osso buco with home-made noodles and gremolata, and the *patron*'s very own great dish – salmon in pastry with currants and ginger, at extra charge – are other ideas. St Emilion au chocolat may be the favourite but is not necessarily the best sweet: try quince ice-cream, perhaps, or walnut treacle tart. The wines (and ports and whiskies and everything else) are well chosen, but often lackadaisically served. You may expect to drink Ronsac red or Clochemerle white under £5, sound Loires and Rhônes under £7, and acceptable Averys burgundies under £9; after that the sky or at any rate £65 is the limit, though the choice of '66 clarets under £20 or so ought to satisfy anyone. There are a few tables outside.

App: Helen Gane, E. A. Lawson, B. S. Bourne, N.R.H., Mrs J. C. Broughton, J. P. Read, and others

---

HELFORD see also pub section

HEMEL HEMPSTEAD Hertfordshire   Map 3

Casanova
75 Waterhouse Street
opposite water gardens
Hemel Hempstead (0442)
47482

Closed Sun; Sat L;
public hols (exc
L Dec 25 & 31)
Must book
Meals 12–3, 6.30–11.30

Alc £6·90 (meal £10·25)

Service 12½%
Cover 35p
Seats 60
♿ rest
Air-conditioning
Car park
Access, Barclay, Diners,
Euro

A team of 'young, brisk and highly articulate cooks and waiters' sounds all too like the amorous diarist who gave this restaurant its name, and indeed Alberto (who cooks) and Carlo make few bones about their conviction that women are there to be admired, men to pay the bill. At the same time, says a shrewd eater, 'the food has a touch of personal artistry about it, and the tomato, wine and herb sauces for pasta call to mind an Italian minceur *style. Fish is particularly good: a superbly creamy crab mousse, a very aromatic stew of scampi with garlic and chilli, served in terrines with "soldiers" of real bread, tender calamari in a spicy Sicilian sauce, and sole with mushrooms in a very light pancake, served with béchamel on a bed of spinach.' Others who have followed a different route through the menu and eaten minestrone, lasagne, piccatine di vitello with cream and port (£3·25), 'glistening pink and brown entrecôte', and 'heavenly zabaglione beaten for twenty minutes by the owners' muscular English colleague' sound equally content. Montevino red or white wine is £3·15 and there are several other Italian wines. Recorded music. No dogs. More reports, please.*

Lautrec
95 High Street
Hemel Hempstead
(0442) 55146

Closed Sun; Sat L;
3 weeks July;
public hols; Dec 31 L
Must book D & weekends
Meals 12–2, 7.30–10.30

Tdh L £4·55 (meal £7·05)

Alc £5·65 (meal £8·80)

What with the cramped quarters, dim lighting, 'pre-war French' loo and reports early in the year of 'very perfunctory' mushrooms à la grecque and entrecôte berrichonne, inspectors approached Pierre Briançon's restaurant in Hemel's agreeable old town with a certain scepticism. Still, for the price the 'bush' of whitebait (90p), truite meunière (£2·45) with small potatoes in their skins, and poulet bergerette with 'a fresh-tasting wine and cream sauce of good consistency and colour' did the kitchen credit. M Briançon himself suggests poached salmon (£4) and rognons flambés (£2·55). Others too report tasty watercress soup and garlic bread, entrecôte au poivre done as ordered, rather too much tomato here and there in the

225

Service 10%
(parties of 6 or more)
Cover 25p
Children's helpings
Seats 40
No dogs
Access, Am Ex, Barclay,
Diners, Euro

vegetables, and sensible desserts: cherries in brandy, strawberry granita, and 'subtle and delicious' bavarois à la vanille. Valpolicella or Soave are £3·20 a litre, Roussillon red or white Corbières £4 a bottle, and Ch. La Fontaine '71, c.b. (Fronsac), £5·45. Recorded French music.

App: N. H. Fletcher, C.I.S., J.T., C.H.C., and others

HENLEY-IN-ARDEN Warwickshire   Map 2

Le Filbert Cottage

64 High Street
Henley-in-Arden
(056 42) 2700

Closed L; Sun; Sat;
3 weeks July/Aug;
3 weeks Chr; public hols
Must book
D only, 7.30–9.15

Alc £10·90 (meal £14·95)

Seats 22
No dogs

'It is going to be difficult not to make a habit of it,' says one member after two meals within the month at Jean-Yves Guerrot's Tudor nook in Arden. M Guerrot has made restraint easier by ceasing to serve lunch – a pity on other grounds, though in fact a poorly cooked lunch after a public holiday was the only serious count against the restaurant in 1979. The bar is uninviting, but 'any place that greets me with a Mozart piano concerto starts well,' says a diner whose meal, too, started well with feuilleté de fruits de mer (£2·80) with a light and flaky crust, and cuisses de grenouille à la julienne de concombre. An inspector started a test meal with a snail version of that feuilleté and called it 'a really distinguished dish'. This was also true of the petit poussin en cocotte au citron vert (£3·75) that followed, notable for its tangy thin sauce of lime peel and mushroom slivers. Sole braisée à l'oseille, and filet de boeuf poêlé au poivre vert are also worth considering if they appear on the short à la carte menu, and simple rack of lamb with mint (though cooked past pink for one customer who requested otherwise) is good too. 'Vegetables were much better than on the previous visit even though Mme Guerrot had had a baby the previous week.' Perhaps, though, this happy event had prevented the ice-cream from being made at home. Other sweets are simple: profiteroles, admirable orange curaçao pancakes, and so on. French girls serve very competently. Litre Vin ordinaires are £2 for 50 cl. Clarets, conscientiously divided into communes, are better (though not cheaper) than one has come to expect from Frenchmen's restaurants in Britain: Ch. Meyney '70, £8·95; Ch. Pavie '62, £14·20.

App: Frank Cummins, P.B.W., T.M.F., P.S.A.W., A.H., and others

---

Most places will accept cheques only when they are accompanied by a cheque card or adequate identification. Information about which credit cards are accepted is correct when printed, but restaurants may add to or subtract from the list without notice.

Inspections are carried out anonymously. Persons who pretend to be able to secure, arrange or prevent an entry in the Guide are impostors and their names or descriptions should be reported to us.

226

HERSTMONCEUX East Sussex   Map 3

The Sundial
Herstmonceux (032 181)
2217

Closed Mon; Sun D;
last 3 weeks Aug;
1 week Chr; Jan
Must book D & Sun L
Meals 12.30–2, 7.30–9.30

Tdh L £4·95 (meal £9·20)
Alc £7·95 (meal £13)

Children's helpings
(under 10)
Seats 45 (parties 20)
⅙ rest (1 step); w.c.
Car park
No dogs
Barclay, Diners

Give or take a few vicissitudes, Guiseppe Bertoli and
his French wife Laurette are entering their second
Guide decade now in their elaborately restored cottage.
Understandably, reports concentrate upon lunch, for
the set meal (not offered at night) has nothing
perfunctory about it. A member who 'dropped in for
a casual, unintended lunch on a wet Sunday' was
delighted with 'a real mini-bouillabaisse with cheesy
croûtons served separately'; an inspector was much
taken with moules farcies, 'really delicious' lambs'
kidneys in red wine sauce, and light, crisp, courgette
fritters. 'No complaint this time about the amount of
rum in the babas either.' The choice is wide, and
there an even wider *carte*, with specialities such as
selle d'agneau aux trois épices (£9 for two), suprême de
saumon gentillesse, and magret de caneton aux pêches
(£5·15). Chocolate mousse 'had a rather blancmangy
consistency' but it is worth noting the menu advice
that four people may order at the outset of their
meal a soufflé Grand Marnier (£8·05) as a finale.
Italian Merlot or French Sauvignon wine is £4·30 and
beyond this lies a formidable collection of double-figure
clarets and burgundies bottled at source: Echézeaux
(Veuve A. Clerget) '71, £14·90; Ch. Léoville-Poyferré
'66, and so on. But if you choose to drink them, start
before the (human) chimneys smoke. Recorded music.
You can eat outside in summer.

*App: A. G. Thompson, M. du M., J. & M.B.,
V. Westerman*

HERTFORD Hertfordshire   Map 3

Dimsdale's
Beadle House,
Bull Plain
Hertford (0992) 52193

Closed Sat L; Sun D
(exc Apr 6); Mon D;
public hols (exc Apr 6;
L Dec 25)
Must book
Meals 12.30–2.15, 7–10

Tdh L £3·75 (meal £6·10),
Sun L £4·90 (meal £7·20)
Alc £7·45 (meal £9·80)

Service inc
Children's helpings
(under 10 Sun L)
Seats 55 (parties 12)
Am Ex, Barclay

*David Ricketts – whose Maison Carton appeared in the
last* Guide *– moved to this Queen Anne house,
discreetly decorated in oatmeal and green, just in time
for members to commend, and an inspector to confirm,
the smoothness of the transition, though with an
ambitious menu and three chefs in the kitchen praise of
the garlic bread, soup 'stiff with chopped mushroom',
'pink and tender calf's liver with avocado', and 'golden
brown cockerel with a piquant herb stuffing' must
remain tentative. Moules marinière (£1·90) and lamb
en croûte (£4·25) are specialities. The cooking of
potatoes and greens is a further sign of promise
(though mushrooms à la grecque and salads were
'oily'), and lime flan, lemon posset, and black cherry
gateau taste lighter than they sound or look. Provencal
table wines are £3·40, and there are others, at stiffish
prices: Ch. Lascombes '73, £9·50; and ominously
numerous champagnes for Home Counties binges.
Recorded music, said to be classical. Pipes are
discouraged. No dogs. More reports, please.*

HIGH EASTER Essex   Map 3

Punch Bowl
off A414/A1060
6 m NW of Chelmsford
Good Easter (024 531) 222
and 264

After two *Guide* entries people look at the Clarks' crowded menu and restaurant more critically. Roquefort quiche, casserolettes of crab, scallops and mussels, quail and guinea-fowl, steak, kidney and smoked oyster pie (£3·95), and generous Sunday lunches are liked. But the dried herbs and 'floury, cube-flavoured' sauce for neck of lamb suggest that 'they would do a lot better with a simpler menu.' Trolley sweets are more cheering. Castel Frères ordinaires are £4·60 a litre and the Marcel Amance house wines £4·90 a bottle; Ch. Boyd-Cantenac '73, c.b., £9·50. Pressurised beers. Recorded music.

Closed L (exc Sun); Mon; Sun D; Dec 25 & 26; 1st 2 weeks Jan Must book Meals 12.30–2.30 (Sun), 7.30–10.30	Tdh Sun L £4·90 (meal £7·35) Alc £8·45 (meal £14·30) Cover 50p D Children's helpings	Seats 60 ☐ rest (1 step) Car park No dogs Access, Am Ex, Barclay, Diners, Euro

HINDHEAD Surrey   Map 3

La Masia d'Avinyo
15 London Road
Hindhead (042 873) 5171

Closed Mon; L Tue &
Sat; Dec 25 D; Dec 26;
L Dec 31 & Jan 1
Must book D
Meals 12–2.30, 7–12

Tdh Sun L £6·25
(meal £8·75)
Alc £6·90 (meal £11·90)

Children's helpings
(under 5)
Seats 42
☐ rest (1 step); w.c.
Car park
No dogs
Access, Am Ex, Barclay,
Diners, Euro

Maxine Houlden may be a chip off the old 'I've always wanted to run a restaurant' brigade but she has had the good sense to retain the services of the Spaniards – Sabino and Genara Soto – who worked for the previous owner. After an initial stumble or two – and a very poor meal in May – people are prepared to call this the best fish restaurant for miles around, unexpected in a nondescript Surrey high street. 'Grilled sardines put me in mind of Portugal, and their new dish, parrillada de mariscos, contained clams, scallops, mussels, crayfish, Dublin Bay prawns and crab claws all amazingly fresh, with a hot and piquant sauce that brought out the flavour of the fish.' Paella is praised too. Veal La Masia (£4·50, with ratatouille and Parmesan cheese) was 'vast but well garnished'. Crème caramel reminded one veteran observer of 'Peterhouse, Cambridge, fifty years ago'. Bavarian lemon gateau is another possibility. The Torres wines begin at £4 but we have not seen the full list. A singer/guitarist performs on Friday and Saturday nights, but at other times you must expect a canned version. Please tell us more about the Sunday lunch.

App: G. A. Wright, R. T. Davies, P. M. Walker

If you think you are suffering from food-poisoning after eating in a restaurant, report this immediately to the local Public Health Authority (and write to us).

HINTLESHAM Suffolk   Map 3

Hintlesham Hall

on A1071
5 m W of Ipswich
Hintlesham (047 387) 227
and 268

Closed Jan 1
Must book
Meals 12.30–2.30,
7.30–10.30

Tdh L from £10·05
(meal £13·55), D from
£11·80 (meal £15·50)

Service 12½%
Children's helpings
Seats 100 (parties 110)
[] rest (1 step)
Car park
No dogs
Am Ex card

On a fine summer evening, few settings for superior gluttony outrun this house and park, which in four centuries of remodelling has passed through the manicured hands of nobles, Treasury men and judges before finding a New World grandee, Robert Carrier. Perhaps 'gluttony' is unfair, for the *grosseur* if not the price of the set meals here (still cooked by Nigel Rolfe and Stig Henriksen under Paul Lewis's management) has slimmed in obedience to the prevailing wind of contemporary taste. Kids bleat at tether outside, less in terror of the spit than in the promise that the house has its own goat cheese; the herb garden may make you wish that you were, in Catullus's phrase, *totum nasum*; and the creation of a swans' walk is a recent instruction to the gardener. This all raises expectation, but there are patches of dissatisfaction; inspectors early in 1979 lunched superbly but found the service slow and the housekeeping slack. A later (dinner) visitor, equally exacting, found the napery impeccable and the year's intake of young men and women from the Continent more smoothly groomed, but at table he became acutely conscious of saltiness as the dominant taste in a pâté made of vitello tonnato, in cold consommé, and even (because of the grilled Parmesan topping) in the gratin dauphinoise potatoes. But technically, it is easy to admire the cooking and presentation of cromesquis de ris de veau or diplomate aux grenouilles, and of main dishes such as gigot de volaille nouvelle cuisine (stuffed with a sweetbread mixture and accompanied by watercress sauce) or lamb done in the manner of game. Filet de turbot aux poireaux and aiguillettes de canard aux herbes are other new dishes. Salsify in cream sauce and crunchy beans or mange-tout peas tossed in a 'herb of the evening' revive the flagging palate; so do the three sorbets, garnished with kiwi fruit, melon and raspberry, perhaps, or the tulipe d'été, 'a lovely mélange of seasonal fruits and good ice-cream, crowned by a mint leaf and exquisite candied orange peel coated in chocolate.' Richer puddings are equally good. The wholemeal rolls are apt to be heavy. Coffee is good but not outstanding. The wines are outstanding if you have £45 for Ch. Pétrus '66 or £11 for Ch. Fourcas-Hosten '66, both c.b. of course, and the dearer wines are modestly marked up. There is also now a new leaning towards lesser known wines at lesser cost: Rully Rouge, Domaine de la Renarde, '76, £6·45. Babies, but not toddlers under five, are allowed. 'An agreeably relaxed atmosphere in spite of the very conscious food and period decor.'

App: Paul Palmer, N. O. R. Hall, J. & M.B., C.P.D., E.R., and others

Knights
Black Lion Court,
High Street
Honiton (0404) 3777

'Encourage the German bias of Peter Oswald's simple, panelled restaurant (and covered courtyard) in a well-designed shopping precinct,' says an inspector. Herrings, pickles and prawns in sour cream (£1·35) and Rohkostsalat ('raw vegetables in water melon with banana and mango dressing', £1·25) are first course examples. Main courses include Schnitzel, Pfeffersteak (with green peppercorns), and game in season and, at a special German evening, Sauerbraten followed by Zwetschgendatschi (plum cake with almonds). 'Wine-bar style' lunches: perhaps cold cuts and a jacket potato or a Bratwurst with Sauerkraut (£1·25). A dozen German wines from £3. 'James Last and zither music.'

Closed Sun; Mon (Nov–Mar); Mon D (Apr–Oct); Tue D; public hols Must book D	Meals 12–2.15, 7.30–9.30 Alc L £3·25 (meal £5·50) D £6 (meal £8·70)	Children's helpings Seats 30 ⅃ rest Car park D No dogs

Low Hall
Calverley Lane
off A6120
Horsforth (0532) 588221

'Mixed feelings' says a member paying his own bill at Kenneth Monkman's modernised Elizabethan house and garden. 'A typical business meal of pâté, prawn cocktail, beef Stroganoff, but the summery sweets were the best of it. Service looked quicker than it was, but they opened the wine before bringing it to table.' Others, though, are sure an entry is deserved after a four-course set meal in which kidneys in brandy and cream and blackcurrant cheesecake stood out. Recorded music is intermittent, it seems, and the silences are praised.

Closed Sun; Sat L; 10 days Aug/Sept; most public hols Must book Meals 12.30–2, 7.30–10 Tdh £9·10 (meal £11)	Alc L (min £3·35) £6·05 (meal £8·25) Service inc Children's helpings (prior notice)	Seats 70 (parties 112) ⅃ rest Car park No dogs Access, Barclay

French Partridge

on B526
6 m SE of Northampton
M1 exit 15
Northampton (0604)
870033

There are not so many restaurants where a diner who complains that his claret has not been decanted in advance as requested is told in extenuation that the defendant (Mrs Partridge) has been in court all day, decanting justice for this quiet part of Northants. She is very much in control here, too, of evenings which for fifteen years have been adjudged the most civilised and, for the quality, the most fairly priced that can be found anywhere in the London–

Closed L; Sun; Mon;
3 weeks summer;
2 weeks Chr
Must book
D only, 7.30–9.30

Tdh £7·90 (meal £9·20)

Service inc
Cover 50p (Sat)
Seats 60
♿ rest
Car park
No dogs

Manchester corridor. The key to this is David
Partridge, whose portrait hangs in the dowdy little
bar but who is otherwise invisible, bent over pâté de
poisson Traktir sauce verte, pintadeau farci au porc,
and chevreuil rôti à l'allemande (which are some of
the dishes he thinks best on his set dinners). As these
suggest, his strength is savoury rather than sweet (nor
is he a man to sweeten his savoury dishes, in the
hateful modern mode). An inspector reports happily
of the fish pâté, 'looking for all the world like a slice
of cassata', and the 'very light' feuilleté filled with
hot, creamy shellfish. A pepper steak and suprêmes
de pigeonneaux à la Marigny followed, both very well
done, though the accompanying rösti potatoes were a
little greasy. Smoked fish salad, chicken liver pâté,
chicken breast stuffed with walnuts, a good fresh
savarin aux fruits and 'rather leathery profiteroles'
are among other dishes described in reports. 'The
Cona coffee had sat too long, and they seem to have
trouble keeping plates and dishes hot.' The times are
against the claret-lovers who have been coming here
for so long but foresight and storage still yielded in
1979 Ch. Chasse-Spleen '70 at £6, Ch. Guillotin '61
at £9·50 and half-bottles of Ch. La Lagune '70 at
£3·70, with comparable white burgundies and hocks:
Auxey-Duresses '72, £5·90; three Hattenheimers of '75
and '76 vintages under £6. Vins du patron from £2·60
include various French regional wines and (at £7·50)
a Bouché Fils champagne. It all makes a complex
restaurant to serve, but the waitresses try hard. They
endeavour to keep non-smokers and cigar-puffers
apart by discreet observation in the bar beforehand,
but do not always succeed.

*App: R. C. Godber, E.L.F., S. Laundon,
R. J. Haerdi, D.G., T.M., and others*

HOVINGHAM North Yorkshire   Map 8

Worsley Arms
on B1257 between Malton
and Helmsley
Hovingham (065 382) 234

A charming village and a comfortable, courteously
served Georgian inn make people kind about the
traditional – sometimes all too traditional – cooking.
Good steaks, roast beef, lambs' kidneys in wine, and
mince tart are reported, but 'their mousse would have
been called shape in my childhood.' Other faults
appear. (Mr Rowe says he does not change his way of
serving Stilton: fair enough, but a May visitor wonders
when he last changed the cheese.) Robust lunchtime
bar snacks. Wines, and Theakston's beers. (GHG)

Closed Dec 25
Must book
Meals 12.30–1.45, 7–9

Tdh L £3·85 (meal £6·55),
D £6·50 (meal £9·50)

Service inc
Children's helpings
Seats 60 (parties 12)
♿ rest (2 steps)
Car park

No dogs in d/r
Access, Barclay
14 rooms (all with bath)
B&B from £13·20
Fire cert

Shabab
37–39 New Street
Huddersfield (0484) 49514

Justice and – in Huddersfield – desperation demand a mention for this branch of the Leeds Shabab (q.v.), with the same attentive service bells on the chairs, menu and style. 'Onion pakoras were hard going but murgh tikka, gosht dhansak (£1·80), gosht korma and chapatis were good.' Karahi gosht (lamb with garlic, ginger and tomatoes, £2·90) is one of Mehmood Ahmad's specialities, as are birianis and chicken tandoori. 'Good kulfi.' Wines from £3·30 if you must. More reports, please.

Closed Sun L
Must book D & weekends
Meals 11.30–2.30, 6–11.45

Tdh L £1·95 (meal £2·90)
Alc £4·35 (meal £6·30)

Service 10%
Seats 62 (parties 30)

Air-conditioning
No dogs
Access Am Ex, Barclay,
Diners, Euro

Hunstrete House
on A368
8 m SW of Bath
Compton Dando
(076 18) 570 *and* 578

Closed Sun D;
Dec 24–Jan 3
Must book
Meals 12.30–1.45,
7.30–9.15

Tdh L £5·20 (meal £7·30),
D £9·20 (meal £11·30)

Service inc
Seats 40 (parties 28)
[&] rest
Car park
No dogs
Am Ex card
19 rooms (all with bath)
B&B £18·40–£28·75

John and Thea Dupays, late of the Priory in Bath (q.v.) opened this elaborately converted Georgian house and extensive grounds in May 1978, with an explicit eye to the guides (not this one) which lock up their editions six months before the year that appears on the cover. They had their reward – along with a Good Food Club member's complaint of being 'fed and accommodated on a building site', and much later, a deplorable test meal that clinched exclusion as far as our own 1979 edition was concerned. Reports since then, while still slightly guarded about 'prompt, smiling, but uninformed' service and 'a taste of mediocrity here and there', generally approve Alain Dubois' cooking: 'cucumber soup, lobster Newburg, noisettes d'agneau – all excellent'; 'spinach roulade tasty and fresh, as from their own kitchen garden'; 'guinea-fowl, so often dry and tasteless, was moist and appetising, with vegetables lightly done'; 'chicken with Gruyère and walnuts an interesting and effective conception'; 'dreamy Scotch mist for pudding.' Ices need more work – 'sorbets reminiscent of melted lollipop.' Still, says yet another visitor, 'they served us with fine dinners five days running, and the Sunday evening cold buffet was irreproachable.' And 'if you can afford to pay 35p on the bill for the Daily Telegraph, *all human life is there.' The wines, from £3·25 for Anjou rosé, are carefully chosen, and more modestly marked up. No under-nines. You may eat outside. More reports, please.* (GHG)

Please report to us on atmosphere, decor and – if you stayed – standard of accommodation, as well as on food, drink and prices (send bill if possible).

Prices of meals underlined are those which we consider represent unusual value for money. They are not necessarily the cheapest places in the Guide, or in the locality.

HUNTINGDON Cambridgeshire   Map 6

Old Bridge Hotel
1 High Street
Huntingdon (0480) 52681

Closed Dec 24 D; Dec 25
Must book
Meals 12.30–2.30,
7.30–10.30

Alc (bar) £3·15
(meal £6·15), £6·35
(meal £10·20)

Service inc
Cover 25p
Seats 50 (parties 25)
No dogs in d/r
Access, Am Ex, Barclay,
Diners
25 rooms (13 with bath)
B&B from £11·75
Fire cert

'If you don't mind eating and sleeping on an overgrown traffic island' – but the situation is not the fault of Poste Hotels, and food, rooms and youthful, sometimes rather desultory, service leave most people content. The all-day meals available in the bar are a particular virtue, and two tired January guests were mightily relieved to find well-cooked and generous whitebait (95p) and goujons of sole with chips (£1·65), followed by a helping of Stilton with hot bread that sufficed for two. In the dining-room, the 'rare and tender' roast beef may well be the best, because most conservative, order, but James Bate's kidneys, guinea-fowl, and breast of chicken with crab-meat in a cream sauce are also worth considering. 'Vegetables were dire and the beef tough,' counters a November visitor. Puddings are for the most part creamily conventional. The carafe wine is Lilliano red or white, but the wine list (standard for the group, and sensible) is not yet to hand. Pressurised beers. You can eat outside on the terrace. Car park. (GHG)

App: Pam & Keith Holmes, L.S.H., Geoffrey Sealey

HUSBANDS BOSWORTH Leicestershire   Map 5

Fernie Lodge
Berridges Lane
on A50
6 m SW of Market
Harborough
Market Harborough
(0858) 880551

Closed Sun; Mon; Sat L;
2 weeks July;
Dec 24–26 & 31; Jan 1
Must book
Meals 12.15–1.15, 7–9.30

Tdh L from £3·65
(meal £5·70), D £7·50
(meal £9·90)

Seats 90
♿ rest (1 step)
Car park
No dogs

The East Midlands are looking a little less thin on the *Guide*'s map than they used to, but locals and M1 travellers will not be quickly seduced away from the Speight's meals and prices in this comfortable Victorian house. 'They are served competently, quickly and informally, with plenty of choice at the modest set prices without necessity to ponder culinary French, varying prices, or hidden extras.' Where so much is done for so little, mistakes do occur: at a test meal, ordered potatoes failed to arrive, and the crab flan – a speciality – was over-seasoned and onion-dominated. But the pastry for this and for the contrasted patties that made another visitor's first course was light and crisp, and the hors d'oeuvre, though served on the plate, inventively composed. The cooking is not naive: they decline to grill rump steak beyond medium-rare, and chicken and mushroom pancake in cheese sauce may be set off by cashew nuts, and breast of chicken may be stuffed with prawns and Pernod butter. Finally, at the sweet stage, 'a syllabub resting on whole raspberries was exactly the smooth and astringent close the palate required.' The cheeses are Stilton and red Leicester. There are about eighty wines, from £3 for Minervois or Italian white, with too many '72 clarets, but nice sweet white Rhine or Bordeaux for £6 or so. A pianist plays at night. Wear a tie.

App: A. B. X. Fenwick, D. Carr, A.M.

233

Duke of York
on B3217
3½ m NE of Hatherleigh
Hatherleigh (083 781) 253

Closed Sun L; Mon D
Must book D
Meals 12.30–2, 8–9

Tdh L £3·45 (meal £4·60),
D £6·90 (meal £8)

Service inc
Children's helpings
(under 10)
Seats 26
🚹 rest (1 step); w.c.
No dogs in d/r
8 rooms (3 with bath,
3 with shower)
B&B £6·30–£8·60

The Balls' atmospheric old pub, deeply buried in
Devon lanes, is one of those *Guide* places that needs
to select its clientele carefully. But most people are
prepared to put up with the odd chill, churl, or
cobweb for the sake of mostly skilful home cooking
('Mrs Ball had a disaster with the cheesecake one
night but did not try to hide it') and a relaxed
weekend with plenty of Inch's cider or Whitbread
best flowing from the casks (for the lunchtime bar
snacks). One visitor even sympathises with Tony
Ball's firmness with customers: 'We had three
bachelors in the room above who spent their days
golfing, their evenings drinking, and what was left of
the nights falling out of bed.' All the same, it is a
place you can take children to enjoy the breakfasts,
lunches, and if old enough, set dinners. These may
begin with soup, or tomato mousse, or both; there
are now two alternative main courses such as baked
ham in wine, crisply roast duck, 'super stuffed lamb',
pork fillet fried in breadcrumbs, and boeuf
bourguignonne. You are also expected to try two
sweets: 'On the second evening we had a
power-packed slice of chocolate brandy cake and a
light strawberry meringue, followed by Stilton.'
French Cabernet or Sauvignon are only £1·75 and
there is a fair range of other wines at £4 or so. No
smoking till the meal ends. You may eat outside.

*App: Ray & Beverley Williams, Nial Brannigan, D.C.,
P. L. Leonard, and others*

Box Tree
Church Street (A65)
Ilkley (0943) 608484

Closed L; Sun; Mon;
Dec 25 & 26; Jan 1
Must book
D only, from 7.30

Tdh £14·95 (meal £20·75)

Seats 50 (parties 25)
🚹 rest
No dogs
Access, Am Ex, Barclay,
Diners

'A gingerbread house' is fair comment on the
glorified Hansel and Gretel decor of Malcolm Reid
and Colin Long's nest of rooms. Inevitably, coupled
with the high expense of the four-course dinners here,
the decor and the assiduous description of dishes
bring out the culture-snob in visitors: 'The service
was thoughtful and good but the total effect
overpowering; somehow the vowel sounds of both
staff and clientele made one more conscious of
alienation.' Serious eaters take all this in their stride
if the food is good, which it often is, but not
rigorously so. The displeasing sweetness of many
sauces, and saltiness of others, suggests that dishes
are tasted, if at all, by someone whose own palate
is coarse. Moreover, a knowledgeable admirer of the
fish soup and terrine, the salade grande ferme, the
sablé aux fraises and other items received the
impression that he was also expected to admire
willy-nilly chicken terrine – 'edible marquetry, but
stodgy and dry' – leaden feuilleté d'artichauts, the
cloying sauces and other miscarriages. Still, only an

accomplished technician could turn out the dariole de champignons truffés, mousseline de sole, tarte de fromage and other dishes described (they are best followed, some think, by more plainly cooked fish, flesh, or fowl. 'Melon sorbet was divinity itself.' The Yorkshire Fine Wines list is long and dear as well as fine, though the cheaper wines subsidise the more expensive, and, for instance, 'the silky elegance of Bonnes-Mares '59, domaine-bottled (Pierre Ponnelle), as it developed over the evening fully justified the £20 or so paid for it.' A '76 Beaujolais and a few other bottles remain around £7. Low ceilings and cigar-happy customers, will guide members' choices.

App: C. J. Richardson, David Wooff, M.M., C.J.D., W.F., M. Freegrove, and others

---

Sabera
9 Wells Road
Ilkley (0943) 607104

From box-tree to bo-tree is a leap of faith for Ilkley visitors. The novice is helped by the garrulous menu (waiters are 'friendly and quick but not fluent'); others, however, query the chicken dhansak (£2·10) with a 'runny' sauce of pineapple, oil, milk and (little) garlic which 'barely succeeded'. 'Hot, crisp bhajia' (75p) and 'tasty' fried vegetables (75p). Pine panelling and wagon wheels from a previous incarnation. Italian Cavitello £1·85 for 50 cl. Recorded Indian music. More reports, please.

Closed Dec 25
Meals 12–2.30, 6–12

Tdh weekday L £1·85
(meal £2·45)
Alc £4·05 (meal £5·20)

Seats 44
♿ rest; w.c.
No dogs

IPSWICH Suffolk   Map 3

Rosie's Place
200 St Helen's Street
Ipswich (0473) 55236

Closed L; from 23rd to
end of every month
(exc Dec 24)
Must book
D only, 7–10.30

Tdh (Sat) £6·90 (meal
£8·60)
Alc (min £3·50) £6·20
(meal £8·70)

Service inc
Seats 32
♿ rest
Car park (3)
No dogs
Am Ex card

Rosie Farrell is on her own in the kitchen now, for Bud Woolsey has cut loose from the business, and though this does not imply a slide, the change is substantial enough to make more reports a good idea. 'Merrie-English' cooking, the Observer called it, and on the whole accounts are cheerful enough, right down to the outdoor privies ('the only primitive feature'). 'The salmon mousse was solid salmon and there was horseradish in the dumplings for beef stew.' Soup, buttered parsnips, and other homely things are praised, and it is worth trying steak and kidney pie (£4·60, including vegetables), vegetable pie, baked bread pudding (72p) and candied wardens (85p). 'Chocolate Marie was as delicious as ever, and rhubarb fool also good.' Saturday dinner is a four-course set meal 'but only one of us made it to the end.' Look for bargains and bin-ends (sometimes under £3) if you wish to advance from the Peatling and Cawdron Spanish table wines, but Hattenheimer Engelmannsberg Riesling Spätlese '71 also seems fair at £5·90. Under-eights must be serious eaters to be admitted. Recorded music. They prefer you not to smoke.

Peacock Vane

🍷

Bonchurch
Ventnor (0983) 852019

Closed Mon D; Sat L;
May 5; Dec 25; Jan 2–
Feb 16
Must book
Meals 1–1.45, 8–9.30

Tdh L £5 (meal £6·40),
D £10 (meal £11·40)

Service inc
Seats 40
⟨ᕱ⟩ rest
Car park
No dogs in d/r
Access, Am Ex, Barclay
Diners
6 rooms (4 with bath)
D, B&B £20–£28
Fire cert

'Battered elegance' is one visitor's phrase for this long-admired survivor from the days of the Old Queen. It is now in its second generation of Wolfendens, with 'a hungry third generation competing for the *chef-patronne*'s attention', and most such families have problems with upkeep and heating bills these days. Most people are still very happy with their stays, set lunches and dinners, and a regular visitor praises the care taken to devise interesting soups, and bring the Sunday beef 'cooked exactly as requested rather than something vaguely short of medium.' Fish dishes have been consistently good, notably sea bass stuffed with fennel, and poached brill. 'Guinea-fowl with watercress stuffing and the Sunday evening cold buffet – with generous helpings of an overwhelming variety of meats – were alike memorable.' Helpings in the set meals are also well judged on the whole, and 'they will always respond to Oliver Twists.' Grilled soles, scallops with bacon, 'moist roast goose with apple, celery and walnut stuffing' and various other dishes are mentioned. Vegetables are 'not exceptional'. The sweets trolley 'bulges with creamy delights' from raspberry gateau to Bavarian cream, and good cheeses are kept, though 'kept too long sometimes, and they scoop their Stilton.' Breakfasts and service faded late in the season. The wines are intelligently chosen and fairly priced, with Chanson's red and white at £2·80, and a remarkable range of more serious Beaunes in the £7·50 to £15 range. Rhônes and Loires are also good, over a wide range of types and prices; two '73 clarets, Chx. d'Issan and Haut-Batailley, c.b., are £8. Half-bottles of dessert wine will be decanted at 60 per cent of the bottle price. Service is good, and 'for residents everything goes on the bill, including the aperitifs housed on the grand piano.' (GHG)

*App: P. B. Scott, B.E., D. Robson, K.W.D.,
B. R. Mackness, Christopher Rae, H.I., and others*

The Cottage
8 Eastcliff Road,
Shanklin
Shanklin (098 386) 2504

'Tiny cottage in a side street', with pink decor, lace cloths and cat-suited waiters. Set lunches and à la carte dinners offer rather a wide choice, but members praise mushrooms portugaise, lobster bisque (£1), generous helpings of venison grand veneur (£4·20), and fruit tarts or vacherins. Local produce is used as far as possible: try sole Newburg, tournedos Rossini (£4·60, including vegetables) or veal Cordon Bleu. A few wines (Chianti Classico '71, £3·95); house wine 50p the glass. Recorded music. More reports, please.

Closed Wed; Sun D;
Dec 26; Dec 31 D
Must book

Meals 12–2, 7.30–9.45

Tdh L £3 (meal £5·45)
Alc £5·85 (meal £8·65)

Service 10%
Seats 24
No dogs

ISLE OF WIGHT see also pub section

IVINGHOE Buckinghamshire   Map 3

Kings Head
Cheddington (0296)
668388 *and* 668264

Trusthouse Forte sensibly leave Georges de Maison
to run his own show at this well-groomed pub, and
one member, after Nigel Flood's devilled whitebait,
braised oxtail (£3·75), and caramel oranges with cream
– and three wines – 'stayed submerged for 24 hours.'
Crisp duck is liked too. But a cook found the cream
sauce for guinea-fowl 'odd-tasting', and there are
two accounts of the magic vegetable trick: 'a choice',
then individually charged. At current prices, complain
if a helping of potatoes and 'seasonal vegetables'
costs more than £1·40 a head. (Stuffed cabbage, a
speciality, is a modest £1·75, but you pay £5·25 to
drink even Don Cortez with it.) Wear a tie.

Must book D & Sun L	Service 12½%	Car park
Meals 12.30–2 7.30–9.30	Cover 45p alc	No dogs
	Seats 65 (parties 100)	Access, Am Ex, Barclay,
Tdh £6·75 (meal £10·55)	♿ rest (1 step)	Diners, Euro
Alc £8·15 (meal £13·25)	Air-conditioning	

JEVINGTON East Sussex   Map 3

Hungry Monk
on B2105
4 m NW of Eastbourne
Polegate (032 12) 2178

Closed L (exc Sun);
Dec 24 & 25
Must book
Meals 12.15–2 7–10

Tdh Sun L £6·30
(meal £9·40), D £7·45
(meal £10·65)

Seats 28
Car park
No dogs in d/r

As the Mackenzies are the first to concede, monks
are not the only people these days who go hungry
rather than pay restaurant prices – but theirs are by
no means the most penitential in the district, and
minor service sins noticed last time appear to have
been blotted out. True, there is a slight tendency to
overblow everything from the Yorkshire pudding to
the 'garden-freshness' of the vegetables (true of some
but not all). However, Ian Dowding and Kent Austin
have been labouring here for years, as though they had
taken vows, and a test Sunday lunch of prawn and
egg mayonnaise, roast duck with apple sauce, and
treacle tart was 'really very creditable, especially the
last – and essential details such as the mayonnaise and
the bird's stuffing were not scamped.' Fresh crab
roulade with prawn and smoked salmon filling 'brings
tears of joy to the eyes,' Mr Mackenzie says: the ink
has not run on anyone's reports of this, nor of the
roast rack of lamb with Shrewsbury sauce, fillet of
beef Wellington, and hot madeira cake with butterscotch sauce, but try them all the same. The wines
are accessible, from Corbières red or white at £3·80
to nine other French regional house wines around
£5, and serious claret beyond. No cigars in the
dining-room. Better coffee might be more welcome
than the complimentary port. No children under five.
Recorded classical music.

App: E.J., H. Joyce, S.S., and others

Restaurant Bosquet

97a Warwick Road
Kenilworth (0926) 52463

Closed L; Sun; Mon;
Apr 4; Dec 25, 26 & 31;
Jan 1
Must book
D only, 7–10

Alc £8·20 (meal £11·50)

Seats 24
♿ rest (2 steps)
No dogs

'This little restaurant welcomed us like friends after the smell had enticed us in,' says a newcomer to David Groves' cooking – now in its fourth year of *Guide* distinction. Gradually this and the other fine restaurants nearby have created their own clientele in a formerly undiscriminating district. True, one or two visitors in early summer wonder whether Mr Groves' remark about his own dishes – 'all of the same quality' – could be sustained, for terrine de chevreuil aux noix palled too easily, sauces are apt to be over-thickened, and guinea-fowl in cream, white wine and mushrooms 'is not the kitchen's best version of this bird: it seems to need the sting of calvados.' However, vol-au-vents 'deliciously stuffed with prawns, tomatoes and herbs', courgettes with hollandaise, stuffed mushrooms, tournedos chasseur, and boeuf Philomène proved a more than adequate reassurance. Another guest, delighted by prawns with mayonnaise followed by oxtail with excellent vegetables and a *chambré* Santenay adds for good measure: 'Yippee, still no music.' Vegetables, like sweets, may vary comparatively little here, but it is difficult to improve upon pommes Chamonix and crêpes aux fraises, for originality and technique together. Remember, too, that the words 'soufflé' or 'beignet' are here an invitation worth accepting. One visitor wishes the table settings were more dignified, but the service is cordial and competent. The wines and their service are open to criticism – 'the second bottle not cooled, the Beaujolais all '77' – and if you can bypass the Litre Vin carafes (£3·80) for white Hermitage of Ch. Fombrauge '71, c.b., at £10·10, or, if you have just sold the Rolls, Richebourg '71 (Charles Viénot) at £26·50.

App: Katharine Goodwin, Joe Philp, P.R.M., Robert B. Fairweather, R. A. Wartnaby, and others

---

Romano's
60 Waverly Road
Kenilworth (0926) 57473

Romano has been to Rome and back and his restaurant has moved round the corner since the last edition: a migration often makes a difference, so please report further. But 'good smells, soups, rare steaks, and vitello Romano' go far to commend the place, as does 'honesty about the bought-in ice-creams'. (Anna Goldoni makes her own cannelloni and lasagne, £1·10, instead.) The Soave or red Capricci Ticino is £4 a litre. The Sardinian house red Cannonau or sweetish Girò at £4·60 and £4·95 may be worth trying. Recorded music. Wear a tie. No dogs.

Closed Sun; Sat L;
Aug 17–31; Dec 25 D;
Dec 26
Must book D & weekends

Meals 12.30–2, 7.30–10.30

Tdh L £3·45 (meal £5·35)
Alc £7·15 (meal £9·10)

Service inc
Seats 26
Car park
Am Ex card

KERSEY Suffolk   Map 3

Quills
The Street
off B1070
1½ m NW of Hadleigh
Hadleigh (0473) 827161

As in Hadleigh nearby (*q.v.*) there is 'charm, enthusiasm and invention' in this tiny cottage with a bar reached by a spiral stair. Large helpings, too, 'but fallible taste' says a benignly fierce inspector after admiring fried stuffed mushrooms, 'parts of the hors d'oeuvre', steaks with Stilton butter, crisp sprouts, and brandy praline cream, but rejecting ill-judged kebab en croûte, tough kidneys, and 'wrong' sauces. Gravadlax and stuffed pork chops are among Frankie Cooper's favourites; also potato pie ('*trompe-l'oeil* for gratin dauphinoise', in one comment). Argentine Franchette wines a modest £3 a litre; Barolo '73, £4·50.

Closed L; Sun; Mon; 2 weeks May; 2 weeks Oct; Dec 25 & 26 Must book

D only, 7.30–9

Tdh £8 (meal £9·50)

Service inc
Seats 30
No dogs

KESWICK Cumbria   Map 7

Yan . . . Tyan . . . Tethera
70 Main Street
Keswick (0596) 72033

Learn how to count sheep in Borrowdale while tasting England in these tidy 16th-century cottages. 'Munchies', 'Goodies' and 'raspberry mmmm' (that is, sorbet £1) may not, as words, rise often to the lips of Alvar Lidell, but others relax over lunchtime scrambled eggs (55p), game pie, baked trout (£1·30), and filled potatoes, and tea-time rum butter. The shorter dinner menu starts with pâté and stock-pot soup ('meaty game with a nutty cobber roll'), then 'giant shrimps' with mayonnaise and tomato sauce or a hearty venison casserole (£4·80). Small wine list includes Berry Bros Good Ordinary Claret, £3·75, and five English whites at the same price. 'Relaxed and amiable.' Classical music.

Closed Mon D; D Sun, Tue & Wed (Nov–Apr); Dec 25 Must book D

Meals 11–2.30, 6.30–10 (later after theatre)

Alc L £2·25 (meal £3·70), D £5·45 (meal £6·90)

Service inc
Children's helpings
Seats 46
♿ rest
Air-conditioning

KINGS LANGLEY Hertfordshire   Map 3

Old Cottage
18 High Street
Kings Langley (092 77) 63823

Closed Sun; Mon; Dec 25 & 26; Jan 1 Must book

In a diverting, if basically forbearing, account of Ron Titley and Annie Maudsley's ancient cottage on the main road, an inspector says the 'bucolic' evening reminded him of the New York caterer's advertisement: 'courteous and efficient self-service.' However, the cooking is much more dexterous than this implies, with brave (sometimes oriental) ideas cheek by jowl with conventional kidneys Turbigo or chicken paprika on the short à la carte menus.

239

Meals 12.30–2, 7.30–9.30
(10.30 Fri & Sat)

Alc £7·50 (meal £10·85)

Children's helpings
Seats 65 (parties 35)
♿ rest (3 steps); w.c.
No dogs
Access, Am Ex, Barclay,
Diners, Euro

Monthly 'gourmet' dinners occur on the last Friday in the month. Szechuan prawns (£2) and Mexican enchiladas (95p) began one meal, oeufs à la tripe another, and spinach and ham roulade (£1·50) is another favourite. If Ron is cooking, look for his stuffed sea trout; if Annie, try crêpe langoustine (both dishes are £5 or so); lamb rémoulade and steaks stuffed with asparagus and Stilton are also well spoken of. Puddings may be bought in or otherwise mediocre ('queen of puddings had been exiled to the fridge for too long') but soft fruit fools and sorbets may be better. Coffee is skippable and the wines (from £3·35) unremarkable, but they seem generous about corkage if you bring your own.

App: H. J. Swain, Tricia Cavendish, C.F.M., M.S.

KINTBURY Berkshire   Map 2

Dundas Arms
off A4
5½ m W of Newbury
Kintbury (048 85) 263

Closed L (exc bar); Sun;
Mon; Royal Ascot Week;
Dec 24–26 & 31; Jan 1
Must book
D only, 7.30–9.15

Tdh from £9·80
(meal £13·60)

Seats 40
♿ rest (2 steps); w.c.
Car park
No dogs
Access, Am Ex, Barclay,
Diners
6 rooms (with bath)
B&B from £18·40
Fire cert

'Still the same old place,' writes David Dalzell-Piper of his weekenders' haunt between Kennet and Avon, with the M. C. Escher ducks-into-fish drawing on the billheads. Disconcertingly, many members this year have wondered whether this confidence is entirely justified. Extensions have been notified, and also changes in the kitchen which were preceded or succeeded by very patchy reports in the spring, including transparent failures with normally reliable (and expensive) meat dishes. Nor is the wine list quite what it was: that is, the library of clarets accumulated over time is still there, but marked up to and beyond current Bordeaux repurchase levels, so that people have to root around among less impressive Rhônes and Loires (or unnamed carafe wine at £4) for drink they can afford. Happily, summer and autumn accounts of the cooking improved, with mushrooms and mussels in garlic butter, crab au gratin (also served as a bar snack), and duck liver pâté perhaps the best first courses; then roast duckling with mint and lemon, noisettes d'agneau, and steak and kidney pie praised among main dishes. 'Chicory in Stilton sauce was excellent.' 'Apricot – earlier in the season raspberry – mille-feuille was just right.' 'They do a good breakfast with fresh toast and home-made marmalade.' Morland's, Arkell's and John Smith's beers (pump). Note that they close in Ascot week. More reports, please. (GHG)

We rewrite every entry each year, and depend on fresh, detailed reports to confirm the old, as well as to include the new. The further from London you are, the more important this is.

The Guide News Supplement will be sent out as usual, in June, to everyone who buys the book directly from Consumers' Association and to all bookshop purchasers who return the card interleaved with their copy. Let us know of any changes that affect entries in the book, or of any new places you think should be looked at.

KNUTSFORD Cheshire Map 5

La Belle Epoque
60 King Street
Knutsford (0565) 3060

Closed L; Sun;
public hols; Dec 24
Must book
D only, 7.30–10

Alc £8 (meal £12·95)

Service 10%
Seats 80 (parties 70)
Car park (8)
Access, Am Ex, Barclay,
Diners, Euro
5 rooms (2 with bath,
1 with shower)
B&B £8·25–£14
Fire cert

These are the dreaming towers of Knutsford, and
Richard Watt, the Edwardian merchant who
conceived them, has dowered the present owners
(Keith and Nerys Mooney) with every decorative
theme from *Jugendstijl* to Tuscan pantile. The
Mooneys market it all with verve, but if the recorded
music obtrudes in the restaurant, 'our room at the
back was very quiet and comfortable.' Moreover,
Yvonne Shelmerdine's French-accented food pleases
almost everybody this year, including a private party
who praise their hot rolls with parsley butter, melon
salad, filet de sole farci, and boeuf mâconnaise.
Another dinner yielded 'lobster pancake with very
little lobster' but a good steak au poivre and
well-judged French beans. Beignets aux foies de
volaille (£1·75), grenouilles au calvados, and snails
with hazelnuts are among the less predictable first
courses; rognons dijonnaise with an onion puree
sound worth trying, and the trolley sweets are liked,
though one unrepentant m.c.p. finds the waitresses
'even more delectable'. French table wines are £4,
and red Saumur-Champigny or Bandol, or Dopff &
Irion Alsace Riesling and Gewürztraminer, all in the
£6–£7 range, sound sensible choices. No children
under 12 either to stay or to eat.

*App: C. Lorenz, S. J. Monkcom, R. W. Lowe,
C. T. Edge, Stella Martin, and others*

David's Place
10 Princess Street
Knutsford (0565) 3356

Closed Sun; Mon L;
last 2 weeks Aug;
Dec 25 & 26; Dec 31 L;
Jan 1
Must book
Meals 12.30–2.30,
7.15–10 (10.30 Sat)

Tdh L £4·95 (meal £7·85)
Alc £8·80 (meal £12·10)

Children's helpings
Seats 60 (parties 40)
🔲 rest
No dogs
Access, Am Ex, Diners

'Less spacious, more homely' is one visitor's brief
comparison of David Molloy's restaurant (for which
he and Colin Williams cook) with Knutsford's
other entry. Their best efforts, it seems, go into main
courses, which is as it should be. Helpings are
generous, and two specialities, duck with green
peppercorn sauce (£6·25) and fillet steak Maurice
(cooked with pâté and horseradish), are also
mentioned in reports, along with 'very good if
expensive vegetables': sautéed parsnips, broccoli,
and gratin dauphinoise potatoes. Baked ham with
mushroom puree (£4·25) and calf's liver in Marsala
are also suggested. First courses, mostly over £1·50
now, may include samosas, mousses of ham or
haddock, petits fondus and other ideas. The sweets
have provoked little comment. French or Argentine
table wines are £3·20, and, given the prices for all but
the youngest and obscurest clarets, Rioja or Valdepeñas
wines or Alsace Gewürztraminer may be the soundest
choice thereafter. Stones' bitter on pump with soup
or pâté at lunch-time. Recorded music. Please confine
pipes and large cigars to the bar.

App: W. N. Greenwood, Stuart Monkcom, L.O'B.

At the Sign of the Angel
3 m S of Chippenham
M4 exit 17
Lacock (024 973) 230

Closed Sat L; Sun D;
L Apr 4 & 7, May 26,
Aug 25; Dec 23–Jan 1
Must book
Meals 1–1.15, 7.30–8

Tdh L £8·50 (meal £12·10),
D £9 (meal £12·65)

Seats 35
No dogs in public rooms
6 rooms (all with bath)
B&B from £15
Fire cert

The pipes rumble in 14th-century ways, and until current fiscal potions shrink British children back to medieval stature, you may find the walls and ceilings rather near. But this, with genuine English food and capable Wiltshire service, is part of the charm, says a letter written from the Tokyo Sheraton. Charm is not the word for the chow, to judge by the dog warnings issued, and some of the Levis family's cooking, though not gruff, is plain – 'vegetables could have done with either butter or a sauce.' Fish pâtés or mousses are bettered elsewhere, but turkey and vegetable broth and other soups are good. There is no choice of main course, but 'superbly roast' duckling, or pork with 'the crispest crackling imaginable' and virtuous stuffing, and good lamb or beef, also testify to a good butcher. Potatoes are well cooked. Plum tart with good pastry and 'lovely sharp whole fruit', Danish chocolate gateau, or treacle lick, are the style of sweets: there is a choice of first and last courses. Cheeses are limited but well chosen, and breakfasts are decently English too. Labastide-de-Lévis (a coincidence of names, and a sensible choice from Bordeaux Direct) is £3·80, and there are sound Riojas under £5; also halves of Ch. Coutet '72 for pudding. 'A careful list for a place of this kind.' No children under 12: this age limit seems to be rising, for whatever reason. Note that there is no food at all on Sunday evenings, and no pub licence. (GHG)

App: Geoffrey Auckland, F.K., and others

Dockie's Bistro
20 Westgate Street
Launceston (0566) 3873

A relaxed bistro, offering fine soups (leek, lettuce or cream of celery), Caribbean pepperpot, spaghetti with 'special meat sauce', slivers of beefsteak in a red wine sauce with mussels, boned chicken stuffed with spinach and cheese, or crêpes with local crab-meat, all with mostly fresh vegetables. Sweets include fresh pineapple and orange in liqueur, and 'chocolate pud'. 'Charming service.' The wine policy keeps all bottles below the cost of a dinner (£6·25; lunches are à la carte), but most people drink Bonatello at £3·40 the litre; or try Fell Down Head cider from Tavistock. 'Unruly children are not welcome.' Recorded music.

Closed Sun; public hols
(exc D public hol Mons);
Dec 31–Mar
Must book Aug & Sept

Meals 12–2.15, 7–10

Tdh D £6·25 (meal £8·75)
Alc L £3·40 (meal £6·05)

Children's helpings
Seats 45 (parties 12)
No dogs

See p. 508 for the restaurant-goer's legal rights, and p. 510 for information on hygiene in restaurants.

LEEDS West Yorkshire   Map 5

Shabab
2 Eastgate
Leeds (0532) 468988

'Food justifies pretensions,' writes one member after a stimulating set lunch of mulligatawny, murgh massalam with vegetables and pilau, and sweet sevian ('chilled Indian spaghetti'). Even ascetics, shying away from the glitter, must face silver leaf on the rice pudding. Lamb korma 'justified our move from London.' Specialities include tandoori chicken and karahi (Indian wok) cooking. 'Thoughtful' service. Chatty menu and wine primer. Bottled beers. Recorded Indian music but no dancing now, it seems. There is a new branch in Huddersfield (*q.v.*).

Closed Sun L; Dec 25	Tdh weekday L £2·30	Seats 72 (parties 80)
Must book D & weekends	(meal £2·90)	Air-conditioning
Meals 11.30–2.30,	Alc £3·80 (meal £5)	No dogs
6–11.45		Access, Am Ex, Barclay,
(Sat 11.30 a.m.–11.45 p.m.)	Service 10%	Diners, Euro

LEEDS see also HORSFORTH

LEICESTER Leicestershire   Map 5

Acropolis
270 Loughborough Road
(A6)
Leicester (0533) 63106

No sign of last year's promised face-lift to the outside of this Greek-Cypriot place, but inside all is 'cool and severe, with efficient service – also cool sometimes.' Roles have been switched within the Menicou family but the authentic flavours are unchanged in taramosalata, avgolemono (60p), moussaka (with rice and salad, £3), and afel'a. The Acropolis special brings tastes of kebab, sheftalia and dolmades for £3·50. Limited choice of honeyed pastries. They seem to have dropped the set meals now. Greek-Cypriot wines are fiercely priced, from Cypriot Troodos at £2·75 for 50 cl. Recorded Greek music.

Closed Sun; Sat L;	Alc £5·05 (meal £7·50)	♿ rest
1st 2 weeks July;		No dogs
Dec 25 D	Service 10%	Am Ex card
Must book	Seats 45 (parties 35)	
Meals 12.30–2.30,		
6.30–10.30		

Prices quoted in entries now include VAT.

Unless otherwise stated, a restaurant is open all week and all year and is licensed.

STD telephone codes are given in brackets. Remember that in some cases, different local codes may apply within the district.

For the explanation of ♿, denoting accessibility for the disabled, see 'How to use the Guide', p. 4.

Bull House
92 High Street
Lewes (079 16) 3936

Postgate would have been pleased to admit here a house where Tom Paine lived. Nothing revolutionary about Eric Cook's cooking, but unusually honest vegetable soup, entrecôte bordelaise, chips and coffee, in one inspector's experience, and cod's roe pâté, salmon and crabmeat pancakes (£4·50, including vegetables), escalope forestière, and chicken livers with mushrooms sauce madère, should be tried too. Charbonnier £4·25 a litre; well-chosen Loires and half-bottles on the short Christopher's wine list. Recorded music. No pipes. No children under eight.

Closed Mon; D Sun &
Tue; D Wed & Thur
(Nov–Easter); Dec 24–
26 & 31; Jan 1
Must book D & Sun L
Meals 12–1.45, 6.30–9.15

Tdh L £3·50 (meal £6·60),
Sun L £4·75 (meal £8)
Alc £6·90 (meal £10·75)

Cover 35p

Children's helpings
Seats 30 (parties 15)
No dogs
Access, Am Ex, Barclay,
Diners

La Cucina
13 Station Street
Lewes (079 16) 6707

Closed Sun; public hols;
Dec 23–Jan 1
Must book D
Meals 12–2, 6.30–11

Alc £5·40 (meal £7·85)

Service 10%
(parties over 6)
Seats 50 (parties 20)
No dogs
Access, Barclay

Glyndebourne on the one hand and Newhaven on the other bring the Lincolns and the Cuthbertsons a polyglot as well as an Anglo-Saxon clientele, and more regular customers also praise Ray Lincoln's energetic marketing and inventive cooking. 'There was plenty of garlic in the air and in my stuffed peppers,' says one, but another finds well balanced sauces as well as forthright ratatouille. Helpings are generous – 'the next table had a size 15 Dover sole' – and 'though the feuilletage of fresh salmon and prawns (a speciality at £3·50) was a little thick, and scorched on top, it was otherwise skilfully done, and the filling was excellent. So were the vegetables.' Veal chop with rosemary, red wine and mushrooms (£3·25) is also worth trying, and sweets such as Banoffi pie, orange and Bacardi cheesecake (95p) and lemon soufflé live up to the rest. Perhaps at this level there ought not to be a separate charge for roll and butter. Italian Ticino red or Trebbiano white are £2·80 and the better wines are also mostly Italian. Recorded music – though usually enough noise in the crowded room to drown it.

App: R. C. Ellis, Jane Pitcairn, M. C. Mitchell, Joanna McQueen, and others

---

Meal times refer to first and last orders.

Do not risk using an out-of-date Guide. A new edition will appear early in 1981.

When a restaurant says 'must book', the context of the entry usually indicates how much or how little it matters, but a preliminary telephone call averts a wasted journey to a closed door. *Always* telephone if a booking has to be cancelled: a small place (and its other customers) may suffer severely if this is not done.

Pelham Arms
Sussex Kitchen
High Street
Lewes (079 16) 6149

A lost silencer in a thriving high street led one motorist to soothing homely fare at this Olde Worlde pub. 'Proper fish pie' with hard-boiled eggs and chicken curry 'worth the detour', if not the breakdown. Other food, including hand-drawn Harvey's bitter, is 'above average' (oxtail soup, boiled beef; sandwiches and Scotch eggs on Sunday). Crab cocktail (95p) and steak and kidney pie (£2·50) à la carte give pleasure in the 'comfy dining-room with roaring gas log fires.' French and Italian house wine, £3·15 a bottle.

Closed Sun; Mon; Apr 4; last week Aug; 1st week Sept; Dec 25 & 26; Jan 1 Must book Meals 12.15–1.30, 7–9.30	Tdh L £2·75 (meal £5·10) Alc (min £2·60) £4·30 (meal £7) Service 10% (parties of 5 or more)	Cover 18p (alc) Seats 38 ♿ rest (1 step) Air-conditioning Car park No rooms

---

Trumps
19–20 Station Street
Lewes (079 16) 3906

Closed L; Sun; Mon;
1st 2 weeks Oct;
2 weeks from Dec 24;
1 week Mar (1981)
Must book
D only, 6.45–10

Alc (min £5·50) £8·35
(meal £11·45)

Service 10%
Seats 30
No dogs

Christopher Goff's cooking for this restaurant that his partner Bryan Chaffer manages is in the style that demands prospective and retrospective abstinence. *Guide* inspectors, not unnaturally, tend to react against this, but if you have the constitution for Mr Goff's smoked haddock cream, brill or sole in creamy white wine sauce, or his personal version of beef Wellington ('though cooked well over medium'), reaction may well be warmer. Hot avocado sunburst (£1·80) or Provencal fish soup with aïoli (£1·50) are other first courses, and main dish specialities include fillet of pork with sage, bacon and apple, or veal steak pizzaiola au gratin (£5·60, including vegetables). 'French-fried potatoes were good, but cauliflower au gratin a misjudgment,' says the eater of a test meal. French table wines are £3·10 and there are eighty others. Recorded music. Because the food is fresh, late arrivals may have limited choice.

App: A.W., E. Moonman, S.S., and others

LEYBURN North Yorkshire   Map 8

Bolton Arms
Wensleydale (0969) 23327

Closed D Sun & Mon
Must book D & Sun L
Meals 12–2, 7.45–9

Alc £4·90 (meal £7·50)

Children's helpings
(under 10)
Seats 80 (parties 25)
♿ rest (by arrangement)
Car park
No dogs in d/r

The Stevens' modest Dales pub stands four-square at the head of the busy market-place, 'looming lugubriously, just like Armley Gaol', according to a West Riding or recidivist inspector. Sandwiches casually served in the smoky bar (not on Sundays) seemed punitive to one member, though 'straightforward' hot dishes brought a critical visitor back for more. All is peace and tranquillity upstairs in the expansive dining-room, however, where a weary family of three generations was revived by 'garlicky' pâté ('a novelty in the Dales'), 'juicy' prawn cocktail, rare roast beef, salmon steak in prawn sauce, and a rich venison stew in port and cream. Cream added to 'egregious quail stuffed with pâté' seemed excessive when 'apricots with Tia Maria and cream roofed with meringue' were still to come. For the liverish, there is always Yorkshire's version of *minceur* style: 'genuine' vegetable soup, roast ham, and a fresh fruit salad of pineapple, peaches and strawberries (in July). Bread has been pre-sliced and coffee thin, but cheerful ladies meet complaints quickly and generously. Yorkshire Fine Wines list; house claret £3·75. Pressurised beers. Recorded pop.

App: Rev. and Mrs. J. Beech, C.L.C., and others

LIMPLEY STOKE Wiltshire   Map 2

Danielle
The Bridge
5 m S of Bath
on B3108
Limpley Stoke (022 122)
3150

Closed L (exc Sun
Sept–July, Dec 25 &
Jan 1); Mon (exc D
public hols); Sun D;
Dec 25 D; Dec 26
Must book
Meals 1–2.30 (Sun),
7.30–10

Tdh Sun L £8 (meal £9·65),
D meal £11
Alc £8·25 (meal from
£10·45)

Service inc (tdh)
Service 12%
(parties of 6 or more)
Children's helpings
(L under 10)
Seats 34
[&] rest
Car park
No dogs
Access, Am Ex, Barclay,
Diners

Since the Tearles left this 'square, small building 30 feet below and 75 feet to the side of the main line to Paddington', Ned Carlton Smith (who cooks) and his wife Danielle (who keeps a charming but firm eye on the front of house) have had to earn their own fare back to these pages. They have not suffered by the high esteem in which the previous owners were held. Their own style is more middle-of-the-road French, perhaps, but 'clams in a peppery, garlicky butter with plenty of crushed parsley were light, piquant and appetising', and onion soup 'markedly rich and thick with a beefy base.' 'Seafood crêpe is another first course worth trying, and may be followed by lamb in mustard sauce, 'tasty and filling cassoulet', 'chicken in cheese sauce tasting unusually of itself', or seasonal pheasant with apples and a delicate sauce. Mousse of chicken livers (£1·35), boeuf à la mode du chef and chocolate torte are other house suggestions. 'Madame had got up early to buy the broccoli and it was worth it. She also noticed that I had not wanted the waitress to sugar my strawberries, and changed them.' Chocolate mousse and Belgian damson pie impressed an inspector. At Sunday lunch (well cooked and fair value, by two accounts), children can be served separately and packed off upstairs under supervision while parents eat. There is no pressure to drink – 'indeed, I was steered to the cheaper of two clarets' – but if you want to advance beyond the Hérault or Tarn table wines at £3·30, Ch. Gruaud-Larose '73, c.b., is £10·50. Recorded classical music, agreeable pictures, and 'dancing on Danielle's birthday as well as at Christmas and New Year.' The set dinner price – it is not clear whether or not it is always offered – includes half a bottle of wine. They plan to do garden lunches.

App: D.W.D., F.I., Jane Tosh, N.L.F. & S.R.M., and others

The Guide accepts no advertising. Nor does it allow restaurateurs to use its name on brochures, menus, or in any form of advertisement. If you see any instances of this, please report them to us.

LINCOLN Lincolnshire   Map 6

White's
The Jew's House,
15 The Strait
Lincoln (0522) 24851

Closed Sun; Mon L;
public hols (exc Apr 4 &
Dec 26); 2 weeks Aug;
2 weeks Jan
Must book
Meals 12.30–1.30, 7.30–10

Alc £5·55 (meal £9·85)

Children's helpings
Seats 30
♿ rest
No dogs

'Potentially a major restaurant,' says an early visitor. *Nothing less befits the Jew's House (which is about eight centuries too old to get a mortgage on), nor indeed this cathedral city, which has seldom had much luck even with minor restaurants. Colin White settled here with his wife Gwen after earning* Guide *entries for his work at Newport, Dyfed, and more recently Wickham, Hampshire. His dining-room is small, decorously furnished, and as yet nervously served: 'We had to put them at their ease,' runs one report, which is understandable on a day that produced the line, 'James is so difficult to feed: I mean, he won't even eat avocados.' 'Helpings are too big, for substantial lamb cutlets en croûte provençale and the accompanying pile of gently cooked vegetables came after delicious jambon persillé done in a sharp white wine jelly.' Chilled fresh tomato soup, and hot crab bisque with croûtons, with the tureens left on the table, also at once tempt and turn the appetite. 'Both pork terrine and cream cheese quiche were delicately herbed.' Main courses already warmly admired on the weekly-changing menu include salmon in white wine and butter, oxtail, honey-roasted duck with pineapple, and 'a boned stuffed chicken in a crust with a splendid mushroom and madeira sauce.' There is a long list of home-made ice-creams, with reports too of 'a fine orange curaçao trifle.' The best value on the wine list (from £3·50 for Coteaux d'Aix-en-Provence) may be the Riojas from Laymont & Shaw, but Brauneberger Juffer Riesling Auslese and Quarts de Chaume '75 at under £7 may be noted when something honeyed or actually sweet is needed. Note that pre-booked after-theatre dinners are also offered. More reports, please.*

LINCOLN see also pub section

LIVERPOOL Merseyside   Map 5

Everyman Bistro
Everyman Theatre
Hope Street
051-708 0338

Closed Sun; Sat L;
Mon D; public hols
(poss exc May 5)
Open from 10 a.m.
(meals 12–2, 6–11.30)

Alc £2·40 (meal £3·85)

Don't shy off the 'grossly informal' atmosphere (their description) or the term-time queues to eat at this restaurant and cafe-bar under the theatre, for the Everyman is all things to all men and the co-operative quintet who run it care much more than most bistroperators about the sources of the food they serve and cook. 'Home-made soups vary daily in composition but seldom in quality.' 'Pâté is generous, butter less so.' Vegetable pies, lamb casserole, dried fruit salad, yoghourt, flapjacks, cheeses and much else are liked. 'Always a good pint of Higson's if you're inured to that brew.' Several wines are still under £3, and a little more will buy a thumping Rioja or half a litre of Tokay '71 (4 putts.) 'reputed to be a

Seats 140 (parties 50)
No dogs

powerful aphrodisiac' (as if this were locally necessary). Better ventilation than of yore. Go early, though, especially if you have children with you. Later, dishes will be off, pop highly audible (on Thursdays), and drinks 10 per cent dearer (on Fridays and Saturdays).

App: Mr & Mrs Samuel H. Finnerman, T.M.H., Alan Kevin Grice, and others

---

LIVERPOOL Merseyside   Map 5

Oriel
Oriel Chambers
Water Street near pierhead
051-236 4664

Closed Sun; Sat L;
public hols
Must book
Meals 12–2.15, 7–10.15

Alc £11·90 (meal £15·30)

Service inc
Seats 100 (parties 40)
Air-conditioning
No dogs
Access, Am Ex, Barclay,
Diners, Euro

The country's first iron-clad building (they say) towers above, but you feel safe enough – give or take understandable anxiety about the bill – in the padded technicolour womb that Andrea Coticelli manages for R. I. Roberts's Groveland Inns (see also Beeston, Wild Boar). 'Slap-up' is a phrase that occurs, on glancing at the decor and the jacketed and tied company, but the staff are surprisingly polite in their halting English to eccentrics who bring their own wine and order cheese before pudding, or to women who arrive without a male escort. Early in the year, some were hesitant or worse about James Swain's cooking but he seemed to have settled down by the time one or two *bonnes fourchettes* paid return visits for the fish that is the kitchen's forte: 'excellently fresh seafood pancake' with a touch of lemon in the batter itself, delicate brill in cream and wine, 'outstanding' sea trout in a tangy cucumber and butter sauce. Meat dishes such as noisettes d'agneau Brouilly or steak au poivre tend to be over-produced, but the vegetables are buttered rather than drenched, and the sweets are light considering their richness (which is heightened by the house's heavy Jersey cream). Profiteroles, apricot tart, or strawberry gateau are a wiser choice than trifle, though. The blue Cheshire cheese, the Cafetière coffee, and most of the petits fours are further luxuries. The inclusive wine prices may drive some to the (unusually wide) choice of half-bottles, but there is much dead wood on the list. If you have £10, try Alsace for fish or Ch. Chasse-Spleen '71, c.b., for meat, perhaps; even Ruffino Chianti or La Flora Blanche is £6·50. There is a trickle of recorded music. No children under five. The set meal seems to have vanished, alas.

App: Stuart J. Monkcom, Marcia Macleod, D. S. Cottrell, A. & J.L., and others

---

Numbers are given for private parties only if they can be accommodated in a room separate from the main dining-room; when there are several such rooms, the capacity of the largest is given. Some restaurants will take party bookings at times when they are normally closed.

Prices quoted in entries now include VAT.

Singapore
471 Smithdown Road,
Allerton
051-733 0723

Suburban Allerton is on the way up, with antique shops and restaurants displacing motor-cycles and launderettes, but the Pangs soldier on consistently in their simple little place. 'Thoughtful service' of mixed meat satay ('well-cooked if rather small for £1·60' – but that's how it comes), generous sweet-and-sour wun-tun, Singapore meatballs, duck and vegetables ('mostly duck'), nasigoreng and fried rice. The Pangs recommend their set meals, Singapore special ribs with sauce, and sliced beef with ginger and onions. Licensed. 'Dress tidily.' Recorded wallpaper music.

Closed L; Dec 25	Tdh from £4	Children's helpings
Must book weekends	(meal from £4·40)	(under 8)
D only, 6.30–12.45	Alc £4·80 (meal £5·70)	Seats 80 (parties 35)
(Fri & Sat 1.15)		No dogs
	Service 10%	
	(parties of 10 or more)	

Yuet Ben
1–3 Upper Duke Street
051-709 5772

Closed Mon; L Sat &
Sun; Dec 25 & 26; Jan 1
Must book D & weekends
Meals 12–2, 5.30–11

Tdh D £4 (meal £5)
Alc £3·65 (meal £4·60)

Seats 75 (parties 45)
No dogs
Access, Am Ex, Barclay,
Diners

This once-popular Pekinese place (last in the Guide *in 1977) has resurfaced at a new address, with discreet western decor, polite service and only occasional rumbles from the underground railway beneath. First impressions are good, and inspectors report happily on a meal which began with two soups: well-balanced and aromatic hot-and-sour, and delicate and unusual cucumber and meatball (75p). The 'special' sweet-and-sour pork (£1·95) was judged too sweet to be special, and beef in chilli also suffered from a sweet and glutinous sauce. Sesame prawn, however, was generously prawned and carefully fried (£3·20), and Peking chicken was 'at least half a chicken, crisp and juicy, with a thin, rather salty soy-based sauce' (£2·65); it put crispy duck ('no pancakes') in the shade. Chef Yuh Ho Yau also recommends his barbecued spare ribs (£1·95), lamb and leeks (£2·10), and Hung Shao fish fillet (£2·20). Finish with toffee mixed fruits (unusually, apple, banana and pineapple, £1). There are various wines (house wine, £2·80 the litre); Chinese tea is 20p. Banquets can be arranged, from £4 a head, but such an interesting à la carte menu deserves leisurely exploration, and helpings are large enough to share round. More reports, please.*

LOOE see under EAST LOOE

Since each restaurant has a separate file in the Guide office, please use a separate form or sheet of paper for each report. Additional forms may be obtained free (no stamp required) from The Good Food Guide, Freepost, 14 Buckingham Street, London WC2N 6BR (unfortunately Freepost facilities are not available from the Channel Islands or the Republic of Ireland).

'Meal' indicates the cost of a meal for one, including food, coffee, a half-bottle of one of the cheapest wines listed, cover, service, and VAT (see 'How to use the Guide', p. 4).

Old Farmhouse Hotel
on A436
1 m W of Stow
Stow-on-the-Wold
(0451) 30232

'Considerate to the old' can be a put-off, like 'popular with children', but the Gladstones do not practise ageism in either direction, and deserve the credit. Creaky floors, courteous service, good breakfasts, and inventive Sunday lunches are other features. Main dishes such as roast chicken, venison or braised pheasant with calvados may be better or more generous than avocado and anchovy, or 'jellified' chocolate cream, though 'smoked salmon roll with prawns and cheese was fine and huge.' Wines from £3·25 for Nicolas. Weekday 'knee lunches' (omelettes from 40p, seafood platter £1·75), perhaps in the garden. Pressurised beers. No smoking at table.

Closed L (exc Sun & bar); Sun D (exc res); Dec 24 to mid-Jan Must book D & Sun L Meals 12.15–2, 7.30–9	Tdh Sun L £4·95 (meal £6·60), D £7·50 (meal £9·15) Service inc Seats 25	No dogs Access, Euro 5 rooms (1 with bath, 1 with shower) B&B from £10·30 Fire cert

Penny Anthony
5 Church Street
Ludlow (0584) 3282

Closed Sun; Thur;
Apr 27–May 11;
Nov 23–Dec 7
Must book weekends &
D summer
Open 10–2.30 (L from 12),
7–10

Alc £5·60 (meal £7·75)

Children's helpings
Seats 48
&. rest (1 step)

Call it Salop or call it (in Anglo-Saxon) Scrobbesbyrigscir, the county would still be a gastronomic Arizona. This sets a dilemma to a conscientious restaurateur who then has to be all things at all prices to all men, but Mrs Penny Anthony has thought her way through it and she is well served by her local chef Colin Hingston. 'After a week of dreadful pub sandwiches and dinners the very smell of this place was welcome,' says one woman. The look, too, of the old shop-front and interior has been upgraded without detriment to the pleasing informality of reception and service. Good nibbles are provided with aperitifs, 'and from an interesting menu chose with success the carrot soup, seafood pancake (£2·50, or £1·25 as a first course), rum and chocolate mousse, and crème de menthe syllabub.' At a test meal, casseroled leg of lamb with apricots and raisins, and plaice in blue cheese sauce were both highly enjoyable; the vegetables included fried lettuce, and broad beans chopped and cooked in their jackets. Kidneys with madeira, gammon with cider and honey (£3·95, including vegetables), and baked trout in pastry are specialities. Vegetarians are also offered a 'very rich' bean pot. Choix du Roy ordinaires are £1·70 for 50 cl but Bergerac red at £5·25 and Rioja red at £5 or so may be a better choice. Pressurised beers. A classical guitar is played on Mondays and Wednesdays.

App: Mr & Mrs C. D. Wickenden, M. W. Wheeler, J.G., H.W. & T.S.

LUSTLEIGH Devon   Map 1

Moorwood Cottage
on A382
2½ m S of
Moretonhampstead
Lustleigh (064 77) 341

Closed L; Sun; Dec 25
Must book
D only, 7–9.30

Alc £6·10 (meal £10·75)

Seats 24 (parties 20)
🔴 rest (1 step)
Car park
No dogs

'I fear that after so long in the Guide, the only people who bother to send in reports are those who haven't been entirely pleased,' writes Claudia Harris. If anything, the opposite is true, but there are not enough of either: hence italics in the hope of a better seasonal spread next time. Game, fish, and shellfish are the Harrises' preferred resources (they both cook), and as well as their seafood bonnes bouches, scallops and mussels, and venison and quail, 'trout pâté, escalope of veal, and chocolate and brandy mousse remain as good as ever.' In the intervals of patiently explaining to customers that 'crème brûlée is not the same as crème caramel and is meant to be hard on top', and supplying the address of the local undertaker to any smoker who asks for it, Mrs Harris makes her own ice-creams and sorbets too. Wines begin at £2·30 for 50 cl of French dry white, sweeter German, and light red Italian, with a carefully chosen list beyond. They prefer their guests to have reached the age of puberty, but 'not to flaunt the fact in their dress or lack of it.' More reports, please.

LYME REGIS Dorset   Map 2

Toni
14–15 Monmouth Street
Lyme Regis (029 74) 2079

Peter Taylor is an architect, which shows in the building; his wife Ingrid is Austrian, but, as the name of the place implies, the culinary style is Italian, with pollo alla Valdostana and filetto di bue alla norcese (£5, with fresh vegetables included) among main dishes praised. Usefully, spaghetti alla carbonara or lasagne may be eaten either as first or main courses (£1·50 and £3·50). Please tell us more about the sweets and cheeses next time. Valpolicella or Soave are £2·10 for 50 cl and there are about 30 other wines. Recorded music; 'ad hoc' dancing.

Closed L; Sun;
Oct–Easter
Must book
D only 7–10.30

Alc £7·35 (meal £10·25)

Children's helpings

Seats 28
No dogs
Am Ex Barclay. Diners

LYTHAM ST ANNE'S Lancashire   Map 5

Lidun Cottage
5 Church Road
Lytham (0253)
736936

Closed Mon L; Dec 25 &
26; Jan 1
Must book
Meals 12–2, 7.30–9.30

Inexperience still shows behind the criss-cross panes of glass that front Paul Caddy's little restaurant and cramped bar, but 'food was all freshly cooked and hot, with attention to detail such as the olives in the bar and salt-mills on the tables.' Various lunchtime visitors further report, for instance, home-made tomato soup, 'peppery avocado mexicaine', correctly cooked omelettes, 'large and juicy fillets of plaice in a nice Mornay sauce', and interesting (not always successful) batter-fried cauliflower. At dinner, the monthly menus have also produced mango with

251

Tdh Sun L £3·65
(meal £5·95)
Alc L £3·85 (meal £6·25),
D £6·40 (meal £9·10)

Children's helpings
Seats 34
♿ rest (1 step)
Air-conditioning
No dogs
Am Ex, Barclay

grilled Stilton – a success – and blackberry and Pernod fool 'in which the two flavours fought each other, with casualties on both sides.' Main courses and their vegetables are more debatable, for they include 'cremated' noisettes of lamb and 'medium stewed' (supposedly rare) steak as well as enterprising, if mild, beef curry Madras and breast of chicken orientale. 'Vinaigrette without oil' and 'cold hard-boiled eggs in Mornay sauce' are other eccentricities met with. The fruity sweets, or port and lemon syllabub, sound the best finishers, and the coffee is 'strong and good'. The (unnamed) house wines are £2·95, and Ch. Haut-Batailley '73, c.b., was a reasonable £8·50 in 1979. Recorded music – 'easy listening', they say, which is what some people find hardest.

App: Geoff & Elizabeth Key, W.J. & R. Webster, M.A.P., H. Wilson, L.K.J., and others

---

MAIDENHEAD Berkshire   Map 3

Chef Peking
74 King Street
Maidenhead (0628) 32591
and 32851

Closed Dec 25 & 26
Must book weekends
Meals 12–2.30, 6–11.30

Alc £5·70 (meal £7·15)

Service 10%
Seats 80
No dogs
Access, Am Ex, Barclay,
Diners

The *Guide* is the wall newspaper for the Maidenhead Pekinese struggle, and though loyalties and ratings are volatile in this context, as they are in the political one, Mr Yi and Mr Ching do seem to be creaming off the cadres to their 'sprightly, restful, not visually Chinese' place. (Ask for bowls rather than a plate or you will find chopsticks difficult.) An inspector and others have found the cooking 'well up to the best London Rendezvous', though 'rice was overcooked and sweet-and-sour pork inferior.' 'What a gorge' is one verdict on a meal with everything from spare ribs and crispy seaweed to Peking duck and chicken with almonds. At a test meal, the seaweed was 'bland and sweet, without that lovely salty fishy taste', and nine seasons prawn (£2·75) was also over-sugared. But sesame prawn toasts (£2·30), mutton with spring onion (£2·10), and 'colourful, flavourful, very lightly cooked mixed vegetables' (£1) and toffee fruits were all excellent of their kind. Try, too, deep-fried beef with spicy vegetables (£2·15). Wines if you must, mostly over £4, and rapid tea refills. Allow time for the town's parking problem.

App: V. Westerman, S.L., Abigail Fawcett

PLEASE keep sending in reports, as soon as possible after each meal. The cut-off date for the 1981 Guide is September 30, 1980, but reports are even more useful earlier in the year, especially for the remoter areas and new places. Late autumn reports can also affect corrections at proof stage.

Most places will accept cheques only when they are accompanied by a cheque card or adequate identification. Information about which credit cards are accepted is correct when printed, but restaurants may add to or subtract from the list without notice.

Maidenhead Chinese Restaurant
45/47 Queen Street
Maidenhead (0628) 24545

'Pekinese' rather than just 'Chinese', and a test meal (with other pleased accounts) showed that Mr Ng the noodle-knitter may cook with a more vigorous north Chinese accent than his local rival ('big prawns in crisp batter with a devilish hot chilli sauce sent us running for the teapot'). Fried seaweed was 'salt-sweet and fishy' as it should be, and fried three meats (£2·90) delicate. But dishes go awry sometimes, and both duck with pancakes and toffee apple had lost their crunch when tried. 'Some portions seem small for the price and tea too is dear.' Attentive service. Wines. Recorded music.

Closed Sun; Dec 25 & 26
Must book D
Meals 12–2, 6–11.30

Tdh D from £5·60
(meal from £6·20)
Alc £4·80 (meal £5·40)

Service inc
Seats 80

♿ rest (1 step); w.c.
Air-conditioning
No dogs
Am Ex, Diners

La Riva
Ray Mead Road
Maidenhead (0628) 33522

Oddly uneven cooking and attentive if sombre service in Mr Trapani's swish *ristorante* by the bridge. Robert Owen Gabbar's best dishes seem to be avocado or prawn cocktail, turtle soup, fegato di vitello alla veneziana (£3·20), chicken Kiev, and roast duck with apple, cherry or orange sauce (£3·40). Veal may be dry or too highly seasoned, and the tournedos with madeira, though tender, is small. Cauliflower in cream sauce and ratatouille are vegetables of the year rather than the day, but well cooked. Routine sweets, with oranges in caramel perhaps the best choice. Hedges & Butler wines: Orvieto cost £3·80 in 1979. Recorded music.

Closed Sun; Apr 4;
Dec 26
Must book
Meals 12.30–2.30, 7–10.30

Alc (min £5) £7
(meal £10·70)

Cover 40p
Seats 40

♿ rest (3 steps)
Car park
No dogs
Access, Am Ex, Barclay, Diners, Euro

MALVERN WELLS Hereford & Worcester   Map 2

Croque-en-Bouche

🍷 🍴

221 Wells Road
on A449
2 m S of Malvern
Malvern (068 45) 656 12

Closed L (exc Sun);
Sun D; Mon; Tue;
Dec 25 & 26
Must book
Meals 12.45–2 (Sun),
from 8

Apart from one or two diffident suggestions that the customer is not always wrong (and a man whose wife cooks and looks like Marion Jones may be forgiven a touch of *hauteur*) almost everyone has fallen in love with this cosy house opposite a filling station (with a much better view from the bar). Their success, with timed arrivals and unaided control of a five-course set dinner with some choice (Sunday lunch is simpler), goes beyond their previous, more peccable, staff-dependent place in London. An old friend from Lavender Hill days reports 'hors d'oeuvre better than anything we had in a fortnight's Loire Valley eating, a Bresse chicken which tasted like it, a dreamy raspberry Pavlova, and the usual fine French cheeses.' A new

253

Tdh Sun L £5·75
(meal £9·05), D £8·50
(meal £12·05)
Tdh D for two
(inc wine) £18·50
(meal £21)

Service 10%
Children's helpings
Seats 22 (parties 10)
 🔲 rest (1 step)
Car park
No dogs
Access, Am Ex, Barclay,
Diners

friend from Pershore is no less impressed by vegetable soup, turbot in sorrel sauce, 'lately live' crab in cheese sauce, 'delectable entrecôte, singed outside, perfectly pink within', creamy pommes dauphinoise, a green salad with garden herbs and a French-tasting dressing, three different goat cheeses, and a comfortably small pot à la crème d'orange. (The tart with crème pâtissière and calvados was 'slightly disappointing'.) An exacting inspector confirmed most of this, especially the hors d'oeuvre – 'outstanding gravadlax, soft, succulent and well dilled; in general nice contrasts of crunch, colour, flavour, and viscosity.' Main dishes such as pork bigarade and poulet Pépitoria with their vegetables were comparable, though 'Mrs Jones mustn't let the thyme and rosemary in her garden go to her head.' There was good chocolate in the mousse, and good coffee in the Cafetière. Aperitifs offer a wide French range as well as chilled Manzanilla. It is a pity about the wine glasses, but what goes into them is well chosen (and informally served): 'a lovely range of Loires with helpful notes – "¼ dry" was just right for Vouvray '73 (Marc Brédif) at £5·10'. The list has lately diversified into Alsace and white burgundy, and the claret too is good. The house wines are Fitou red and dry Bordeaux white at £3·65. No pipes in the dining-room 'and we do not sell tobacco.' Note the closure between Sunday lunch and Wednesday dinner. If the Malverns are knickerbocker country, this for the moment is their knickerbocker glory. The 'dinner for two' price shown is for a five-course meal chosen by the restaurant.

App: J. T. C. Wilson, Eileen O'Keefe, Ken Vaus, B. W. Jack, D. & F.N., J. N. Bennitt, John and Lesley Wilson, and others

---

MANCHESTER Map 5

**(1) Armenia Hotel
Shish Kebab House**
125 Palatine Road,
Didsbury
061-434 1122

Closed Sun; Sat L;
Apr 4 & 7; Dec 25 & 26;
Jan 1
Must book weekends
Meals 12–2.30, 7.30–10.45

Alc £4·85 (meal £8·05)

Service 10%
Children's helpings
Seats 70 & 50 (parties 50)

History, as George Mardirossian's menu points out at learned length, has dealt the Armenians an unkind cup, and some people, looking at the last line of their accounts at this cosseted caravanserai in south Manchester, wonder whether they are paying not just for their dinner but for the sins of Huns, Khazars, Seljuks, Mongols, and Mamelukes, to name but a few. But others who have been faithful to George and his family's cooking in the fifteen years since the old Shish Kebab House days, say that he only gives his prices a full turn of the screw every other year; and that Britain still boasts few Middle Eastern matches for 'Tale of Three Cities' kebabs, rice, and perhaps a nibble of lahma bi ajeen (Persian pizza) or a sip of borshch to start with, and equally distinctive baklava or gatnabour (rice pudding, in a sense) at the end. Aznieve Boursalian's couscous, and (with notice)

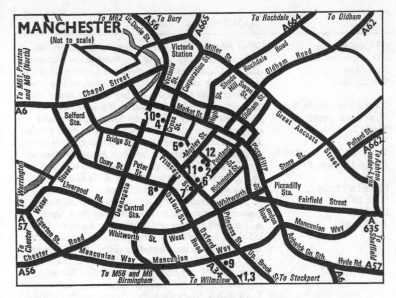

Air-conditioning
Car park
No dogs
Am Ex, Barclay, Diners
23 rooms (5 with bath, 18 with shower)
B&B £11·75–£17·20
Fire cert

levtzvarz varyag (a chicken dish 'with liver, snobar, walnuts and brandy' for two, £7·10) are also specialities. You might as well drink the Lebanese ordinaires at under £4 unless the various Tokays at about £5 for 50 cl appeal. Recorded music – Armenian, of course.

App: S. P. E. Tucker, B.M., and others

---

(2) **Ashiana**
34 Charlotte Street
061-236 1085

'Delicate helpings and delicate spicing' are the keynotes of this South Indian vegetarian place (in former Kwok Man premises, 'still vaguely oriental'). Various set meals allow you a taste of several dishes: thali de luxe (£3·40) offers 'light and puffy' puris, pilau rice, lentils and other spiced vegetables, poppadums, raita and tea. A la carte, try bhel puri (55p), dahi vada (black-pea fritters with yoghourt, 50p), dosai de luxe (crisp potato-stuffed pancake, 80p), katchori (deep-fried lentil balls in pastry, 65p); and for sweet, kulfi (ice-cream), shrikhand or barfi. Drink sweet or salt lassi, and end, if you dare, by chewing a pan ('toothpaste-flavoured birdseed'). 'Competently unfussy' service. Licensed. More reports, please.

Closed Mon; L Sat & Sun
Must book weekends
Meals 12–2.30, 6–11.30
(Sat & Sun 4–11.30)

Tdh L from £1
(meal £1·80), D from £3
(meal £3·85)
Alc £2·40 (meal £3·30)

Service inc
Children's helpings

Seats 100 (parties 50)
No dogs
Access, Am Ex, Barclay, Diners

255

(3) Casa España
100 Wilmslow Road,
Rusholme
061-224 6826

Closed Sun; public hols
Must book weekends
Meals 12–2.30, 6.30–10.45

Tdh L £2·25 (meal £4·65)
Alc £6·35 (meal £9·15)

Children's helpings
Seats 60
No dogs
Am Ex card

After fourteen years, the partnership here is broken, with Manuel Puro opening the Andalucia in Didsbury. But Mr Galdeano and his chef Juan Lopez seem just as busy in their 'decorative' basement – indeed, overbooking and long waits forced one of their earliest customers to find dinner elsewhere. Seasoning is guarded even by the standards of today's Costa del Sol, but pickers and choosers are rewarded. A frequent visitor from Scotland took supreme pleasure in the wines, detecting 'a taste of Russian birch juice' in his Gran Reserva Paternina, which 'perfectly suited gambas pimpinela with pine nuts in a spicy tomato sauce' (£1·60). A '64 red from the same estate in Castille (£6·85) was a 'revelation', naturally overshadowing a good paella of 'chickens, prawns, mussels, red peppers, etc.' For once, Ogen melon (with shrimps and Marie Rose sauce, £1·55) is admired; note also mejillones (mussels) a la marinera, calamares fritos and chipirones (baby squid) in their own ink (£1·25) and, among main courses, riñones al Jerez (£2·70) and albondigas madrileña ('five spicy meatballs in a sherry and almond sauce'), both also set lunch dishes. 'But even if they cannot get the right fish for zarzuela they don't have to use powdered garlic and dried herbs.' Sweets are rather dim, and 'is queso worth the quest?' Sangria is now £3·70 a jug. Recorded Spanish music. More reports, please, on the Manchester Spanish reshuffle.

---

(4) Danish Food Centre
Royal Exchange Buildings,
Cross Street
061-832 9924

Popularity has extended all three sections: the shop, the self-service Danmark Inn where (between 9 a.m. and 11.15 p.m.) you may eat open sandwiches and pastries, and the Copenhagen Room, which offers a short *carte* of simple dishes (chicken in horseradish, £3·75) or the help-yourself cold table (waitresses serve the soup). 'Every type of fish you can think of – and a few more besides', but more limited and less enticing cold meats and cheeses, and competent sweets. Drink akvavit, lager, or Granvillons carafe wine at £2·25 for 50 cl. 'Mass market music on the quadrophonic system, and a live pianist on Saturdays.' No dogs.

Closed Sun; public hols
Must book
Open 9–11.15,
(Copenhagen) 12–2.30,
6–11.15

Tdh L £3·45 (meal £6·15),
L (cold table) £5·25
(meal £7·95),
D (cold table) £6·90
(meal £9·60)
Alc £7·85 (meal £10·55)

Service inc
Children's helpings
(under 12)
Seats 200 (parties 80)
Air-conditioning
Access, Am Ex, Barclay,
Diners

1980 prices are as estimated by restaurateurs in the autumn of 1979 (including VAT).

Meal times refer to first and last orders.

(5) Isola Bella
6 Booth Street
061-236 6417

Closed Sun; public hols
Must book
Meals 12.30–2.15, 7–11

Alc £7·45 (meal £10·45)

Service inc
Seats 70
Air-conditioning
No dogs
Am Ex, Barclay, Diners

Manchester's experience of Italian restaurants has been patchy, to say the least, but one customer of Evandro Barbieri's spacious basement praises Tino Giacometti's 'genius for dealing with food, especially hors d'oeuvre and vegetables.' Mixed salad keeps up this leguminous record, and more substantially, bean and rice soup, spare ribs, grilled chops, lasagne verdi, osso buco, pollo sorpresa, and escalope mafiosa (with pepper and spices) have pleased customers, all the way from media men and model girls to 'a Jewish gourmet from yesterday's Ancoats.' Trota alla mandorla (£3·80) is a speciality. Black Forest cake and other puddings are praised. Chianti or Tuscan white wine is £2·50 for 50 cl, and you can pay £15 for Barolo '61. Recorded music. More reports, please.

---

(6) Kai's
16 Nicholas Street
061-236 2041

The Chans' tardiness in returning the *Guide*'s form is an encouragement if anything, for the modest place is *echt* Chinese. 'Like Dr Fu Manchu, I shall return', an inspector says, for one-dish meals of duck on rice or chicken with congee, 'wall dishes' in Chinese characters, such as frogs' legs (£2·50) or Cantonese cockles and oysters at £2, and more conventional fish-head and bean curd soup with vegetables, wun-tun soup, and 'best of all, fillet steak Chinese-style (£3), sweet but well balanced.' Wines, and recorded music.

Open noon–2 a.m.

Tdh L £1·10, D from
£3·50

Alc meal £4·35

Service 10%
Seats 90

Air-conditioning
No dogs
Am Ex, Diners

---

(7) Kwok Man
28–32 Princess Street
061-228 2620

Open noon–4.45 a.m.

Tdh L £1·30, D £4·50

Alc £4·95 (meal £6·05)

Service 10%
Seats 200
Air-conditioning
No dogs
Am Ex, Diners

Tony Lai's transmogrified Kwok Man (if you are a wedding couple you may dine framed in a 'dragon and phoenix' arch) has stood up very well to a year's scrutiny. The service (raided from other Chinese places in the city) has an edge that has surprised old customers. Dim-sum are not necessarily a strong point, but prearranged banquets (as opposed to the set meals ordered on the spot) are well worth trying, and meals that include wun-tun soup, Chinese mushroom with prawn meat stuffing, baked spare ribs with salted pepper, Hong Kong roast duck, beef steak with mixed vegetables, lemon chicken ('a superlative version') and Peking crunch duck should not go far wrong. And that is leaving out the specialities listed this year: sea bass, crab with ginger and spring onion, prawn and fresh fruit salad (£1·55) and green pepper stuffed with prawn (£3). Note the one-dish rice meals and items such as beef brisket and crispy pork which may appear in Chinese only, but can always be enquired for. There are wines in bottle from £3·65. Recorded music, and a tableside conjuror.

App: N. J., William Ward, and others

257

(8) Midland Hotel
French Restaurant

Peter Street
061-236 3333

Closed Sun; Sat L;
Apr 4 & 7; Dec 25 & 26;
Jan 1
Must book D
Meals 12.30–2.30, 7–11

Alc £11·65 (meal £14·05)

Service inc
Seats 70
Air-conditioning
No dogs in public rooms
Access, Am Ex, Barclay,
Diners, Euro
304 rooms (252 with bath,
2 with shower)
B&B from £20·50
Fire cert

Gilbert Lefèvre, doyen of British Transport Hotels'
French chefs, might be able to explain why talent
and tomfoolery vie with each other in this dignified
dining-room, with 'the largest frogs' legs I have seen,
in a deliciously garlicky mustard sauce' (£5·45), and
an admirable veal steak with apple and chicken liver
(£6·30) offset by 'fillet of sole that actually contrived
to be tough' and – at a test meal – 'soft and leaden
pastry poorly filled' doing duty for mille-feuille. (The
inspector warmed more to the breakfast coffee, croissant
and runny poached egg in the hotel's Narrow Boat
coffee shop.) It is good to know that, along with
other high-sounding successes or failures, peasant
rillettes and tripes à la mode also emerge from this
kitchen, and the latter may better withstand lamp
reheating and often inept service. The BTH wines
(from £3·45) are a much needed consolation: though
the list has been pruned somewhat, it has also been
diversified, with good Rhônes, from Gamay de
l'Ardèche at £4·70 to Gigondas '67 (Jaboulet) at
£9·05. For comparison, Ch. Bel-Orme Tronquoy de
Lalande '66, c.b., is £9·15. Expect a pianist at night;
and wear a jacket and tie.

App: Dr T. J. David, Helen Macintosh, M.H.N.

---

(9) On the Eighth Day
111 Oxford Road,
All Saints
061-273 4878

This wholefood vegetarian co-op is about to expand
into two adjoining shops – and enjoy a spring clean,
one hopes. They plan to be open by Easter for
dinner and all-day snacks. Eavesdrops come free ('a
Maharishi man expounding on his levitation
experiences'). Generous bowls of grains and vegetables
or salads for about £1 please lunchers, as do the
goat's milk yoghourt, fruit juices, wholemeal bread,
and variety of teas. Children may take half-portions.
No smoking. Recorded music 'from rock to classics.'
Take home from their thriving shop a jar of bluebell
honey and hedgehog ointment – for Scottish
love-bites, perhaps.

Closed D; Sun;
public hols; 1 week Chr
L only, 12–3

Alc meal about £2·05

Service inc

Children's helpings
Seats 32
No dogs
Unlicensed

Entries for places with distinctions carry symbols (pestle, tureen, bottle, glass).
Credits are fully written entries, with approvers' names below the text. Passes are
telegraphic entries (useful in the area) with details under the text. Provisional
entries are in italics (see 'How to use the Guide', 4p.).

Inspections are carried out anonymously. Persons who pretend to be able to secure,
arrange or prevent an entry in the Guide are impostors and their names or
descriptions should be reported to us.

(10) **The Royal Exchange**
St Ann's Square
061-833 9682

Closed Sun; Sat L; Apr 7;
last 3 weeks Aug; Dec 25;
L Dec 26 & Jan 1
Meals 12–2.15, 6–11

Tdh D £5·50 (meal £7·85)
Alc £7·25 (meal £10·25)

Service 10%
Seats 54 (parties 12)
♿ rest
Access, Barclay, Diners

Roy Pegram has left this restaurant, tucked away in the marble halls of the old Cotton Exchange, since his own theatrical talents in the kitchen ceased to fit with the operation of an actual theatre in the same building. Stuart Maxwell is still a probationer, by members' accounts, but 'worth encouraging' in the light of a test meal that produced 'pink and tender' kidneys Benedict (£1) and crisp duck, but too copious sauces, variable vegetables, and fairly ordinary sweets. Others note good pea and ham soup, escalope à la crème, and cabbage with onion and tomato. Chevreuil d'Uzès is a speciality. The red Cuvée du Patron (£3·30) has displeased two critics lately, and it may be better to pay a little more for Provence, Loire, or Bergerac. Service 'willing but naive'. Smaller helpings for children. Air-conditioning. No dogs. More reports, please.

(11) **Woo Sang**
19–21 George Street
061-236 3697 *and* 4107

Closed Dec 25 & 26
Open noon–midnight

Tdh L £1·40 (meal £1·80),
D £1·85 (meal £2·30)
Alc £5·45 (meal £6·30)

Service 10%
(with bookings)
Seats 200 (parties 100)
Air-conditioning
No dogs
Access, Am Ex, Barclay,
Diners, Euro

Cantonese cooking has lately been added to the longish list of things that Manchester does either earlier or better than London, and 'it was a happy day when Mr Woo gave up cleaning windows.' His popular restaurant (with Yek Yan Tsim in the kitchen) is the local market leader in the sense that, of the authentic places, it is the most adapted to European demands for service, intelligibility, and meal-shaping. It also has good dim-sum, which enabled a member with small children in his party to entertain them with salt and pepper ribs, prawn dumplings, and mushroom with prawn meat stuffing before proceeding to beef with chilli and black bean, steamed lemon sole, chicken in lemon sauce, cold pork 'with a lovely soy and anise char siu marinade', 'moist crunch duck with excellent prawn stuffing', and an egg tart for the youngest at the end. Roast duck is also good cold here (£3·45), and king prawns with salted pepper (£3) is a speciality. Other visitors – one of them on his way to a conference on organ studies – report no less happily of oysters in batter, wun-tun soup, char siu po (a meat-stuffed bun), stuffed bean curd ('more like a soup') and stewed beef brisket with vegetables and rice (£1·85), not to mention – for students of obscure organs – duck and chicken webs, or stewed assorted meat in spiced seeds. Wines are from £3·65, and tea is automatic. They make a service charge if you book, one member advises, which is certainly necessary after 8 p.m. Recorded music.

App: Michael M. Silver, R. Hutson, D. Sefton-Jenkins, N.J., and others

---

If you think you are suffering from food-poisoning after eating in a restaurant, report this immediately to the local Public Health Authority (and write to us).

See p. 508 for the restaurant-goer's legal rights, and p. 510 for information on hygiene in restaurants.

(12) Yang Sing
17 George Street
061-236 2200

Closed Dec 25 & 26
Must book
Meals noon–11.45

Alc £4·40 (meal £5·35)

Seats 70
Air-conditioning
No dogs
Am Ex, Barclay

It is a good sign when a pair of adjoining restaurants each has devoted advocates (and a few detached arbiters) as though they were Early Christian heresies. The Yeung family's awkwardly laid-out basement, with their marginally more Europeanised neighbour (overleaf), helps to explain why 'there is no need to eat a poor or boring Chinese meal in Manchester'. The Yeungs themselves offer over two hundred dishes, and if this is sometimes at the expense of the rice cookery or other basics, their ambitions are confirmed by one inspector's experience with fish lips, duck's web and ox tripe, or in more conventional company, steamed prawns with soya and chilli, chicken in honey and lemon, and steak in onion and ginger; and by another man's endorsement of salt and pepper ribs, char siu cheung fun, bat col siu mai, and Chinese mushroom with mixed meat stuffing among the all-day dim-sum snacks. Other successes among substantial dishes are 'superb' stewed chicken and liver, three roasts on rice, and braised brisket in barbecue sauce. 'Waitresses get aggravated easily if things fail to run smoothly', says one critic, but others praise the service. German table wine was a modest £2·70 in 1979; Chinese white £4·50. Anglo-oriental music.

App: W. B. O'Neill, N.F.J., C.P.D., Braham Murray, and others

MANCHESTER see also HEALD GREEN

MARSTON TRUSSELL Northamptonshire   Map 5

Sun Inn
off A427
3 m SW of Market
Harborough
Market Harborough
(0858) 65531

Young chefs joining the Farmers' small hotel will not lack for company (six in the kitchen at the last count), but may be more daunted than challenged by the three-page, closely printed menu. Visitors often confine themselves to steaks at night and the cooked breakfasts in the morning, but note also roast quail (£4·15) and rainbow trout in red wine (£1·95 as an appetiser), 'above-average' fresh vegetables (other kinds also listed), and packeted butter that seems incongruous beside Dover sole 'fresh from Grimsby'. Wines from £2·75. Pressurised beers for the weekday lunchtime bar snacks. Efficient service, 'excellent warm, quiet rooms.' 'Executive dress preferred.'

Closed Dec 25 & 26
Must book D & weekends
Meals 12.30–1.45, 7–9.30

Tdh Sun L £3·50
(meal £5·35)

Alc £6·40 (meal £8·95)

Service inc
Children's helpings
Seats 40 (parties 12)
♿ rest (1 step)

Car park
No dogs
Am Ex, Diners
10 rooms (all with bath)
B&B from £9·75
Fire cert

MASHAM North Yorkshire Map 8

Danby's
Silver Street
Masham (076 582) 310

No relation to the Danby family entombed across the huge market square, this elegant, 'vaguely Victorian' bistro earns a niche. Special dinners (on Hallowe'en or '*minceur*' themes), and various grape juices hint at the zeal of the chef, Rev. A. J. Sandys, who is devoted to lamb Marinetti with dates and pistachios (£4·50) from *La Cucina Futurista*, 'rich' game pâté (80p) and soup, 'peppery' potatoes baked in tomato juice, and bilberry ice-cream. 'Friendly service.' House Mosel £3 for 70 cl. 'No pop music.' They also serve morning coffee and afternoon tea.

Closed L (exc Dec 25);
Sun; Mon (exc D
public hols); Thur;
Dec 24 & 26; Dec 25 D;
Jan 1

Must book
D only, 7.30–9.30

Alc £7·45 (meal £10·30)

Children's helpings
Seats 32
No dogs

MAYFIELD East Sussex Map 3

Rose and Crown
Fletching Street
Mayfield (043 55) 2200

Closed L (exc bar); Sun;
D Mon & Tue; Dec 24–
26 & 31; Jan 1
Must book D
Meals 12.15–2 (bar),
7.45–9.30

Tdh £7·20 (meal £10·25)

Seats 22 (parties 24)
Air-conditioning
Car park
No dogs in d/r
No rooms

Promotion from the pub section was suggested in 1979 by people who had eaten Mrs Leet's set dinners and remarked her husband's knowledgeable and friendly service. 'We had very good crab vol-au-vents and guinea-fowl in wine sauce, fine Stilton, and well-made cold sweets, but the supply of sea salt and a pepper-mill, and good coffee, was even more of a surprise.' There is not much room in the low-beamed coaching-house except for the bars, but inspection confirmed these judgments on the whole: pork tenderloin in ginger and lemon sauce, and poussin stuffed with spinach and bacon, were both unusual dishes, well-cooked, and the same could be said of the brandy, walnut and date trifle; cold chicken soufflé as a first course had not worked so well, and simpler vegetables might have been a better idea. The menu changes every four weeks, as does the enterprising lunchtime bar menu. La Borie ordinaire is £4·20, and there are about sixty other wines from various sources, with four real ales on hand pump, including Everards Old Original.

App: D. G. Crawley, M.L.H., R.K., A.J.B.

The Guide News Supplement will be sent out as usual, in June, to everyone who buys the book directly from Consumers' Association and to all bookshop purchasers who return the card interleaved with their copy. Let us know of any changes that affect entries in the book, or of any new places you think should be looked at.

Unless otherwise stated, a restaurant is open all week and all year and is licensed.

Please report to us on atmosphere, decor and – if you stayed – standard of accommodation, as well as on food, drink and prices (send bill if possible).

MELBOURN Cambridgeshire Map 3

Pink Geranium
on A10
11 m S of Cambridge
Royston (0763) 60215

Ellen Shepperson, a *Guide* indestructible, does not attempt too much in her flowery, pink-and-white, beamed cottage, and sauces may make you wish for even plainer ways with the steaks and well-roast duck (£3·75). Salad may be better than vegetables. But leek and potato soup (70p) or prawn cocktail, and lemon soufflé, flanked the main dishes adequately at a test meal, thoughtfully served. Wines from £2·95 include Ch. Gazin '71, c.b., at £7·95.

Closed L; Sun; Mon;
last 2 weeks Aug;
public hols
Must book

D only, 7–10

Alc £6·90 (meal £9·75)

Seats 32 (parties 18)
Car park
No dogs

MENTMORE Buckinghamshire Map 3

The Stag
off B488
4 m S of Leighton Buzzard
Cheddington (0296)
668423

'Consistency and continuity' recommend this snug country inn, once part of the Towers estate, and still handy for neighbouring grandees or a stroll on the Ridgeway Path. The best things are predictable: Sunday roast beef (£4·55, including vegetables), entrecôte bordelaise or roast duckling. Vegetables come from a nearby garden.'The usual fruity and creamy sweets.' Service is smooth. No vintages named, so stick to the house wines from Hérault or Loire at £3·20. Bar snacks and Charles Wells beers.

Closed Mon
Must book
Meals 12.30–2.15, 7.30–10

Tdh L £4 (meal £7)

Alc £6·75 (meal £10·05)

Service 10%
Cover 20p
Children's helpings
Seats 65 (parties 30)

🔥 rest
Car park
No dogs in rest
Access, Am Ex, Barclay,
Diners
No rooms

MEVAGISSEY Cornwall Map 1

Mr Bistro
East Quay
Mevagissey (072 684) 2432

An informal, family-run quayside place, with 'candle-lit pine booths and cork walls which enclose both smoke and talk.' Local fish is favoured, much of it inventively cooked: 'We change the lobster and crawfish recipes to save chef's boredom.' Try red mullet 'rubbed with fresh fennel' (£4) or John Dory with orange and sherry sauce (£4·50). Meat-eaters have enjoyed lamb in lemon and walnut sauce, and beef hot-pot. Well-cooked fresh vegetables. 'We take pride in our sweets trolley.' Light meals and a children's midday menu. Bacchante is £3·50 the litre, on a short list, with 'some better wines if required.' No dogs.

Closed Nov–Mar
(exc weekends)
Must book D
Meals 12–2, 7–10

Alc L £2·40 (meal £4·50),
D £6·40 (meal £9·35)

Children's helpings

Seats 30
🔥 rest (1 step)
Access, Am Ex, Barclay,
Euro

MIDDLEWICH Cheshire   Map 5

Franco's
51 Wheelock Street
Middlewich (060 684) 3204

'For an Italian, Franco is almost taciturn', but his cooking invites discerning visitors to this friendly little place by the canal. The menu changes every month, and uses fresh materials for such dishes as rigatoni con Emmental (£1·40), fagiolini con acciughe, crêpes de fruits de mer à l'indienne (£2·30), stuffed green peppers with spaghetti (£4·90) and veal escalopes in various ways (Franco recommends the foie gras version with a truffled sauce, £6·85). Humdrum sweets and good coffee. There are light lunches on weekdays. Mainly Italian wines (Nebbiolo d'Alba, £3·85); wine by the glass, 55p. Light recorded music.

Closed Sun; L Mon & Sat; 1st 2 weeks May; Dec 25 & 26; Jan 1 Must book D

Meals 12–1.45, 7–9.45

Alc £8·10 (meal £11·25)

Children's helpings
Seats 40
  rest (1 step)
No dogs

MILFORD-ON-SEA Hampshire   Map 2

Westover Hall
Park Lane
Milford-on-Sea (059 069) 3044

Closed Mon; Sat L;
L Tue–Fri (winter);
May 5–12; Nov 3–10;
Jan 1
Must book D & Sun L
Meals 12–1.45, 6.30–9.30

Tdh L £5 (meal £7·10)
Alc £7·15 (meal £10·65)

Children's helpings
(under 10)
Seats 40 (parties 40)
  rest (3 steps)
Car park
No dogs
Access, Am Ex, Barclay,
Diners, Euro
3 rooms
B&B £9·50–£12·50

'The elegance of the building dictates our style,' says James Perkins of his 'restaurant with rooms', 'and Mark Hewitt our chef has never heard of fast food.' For that matter, the magnate who built this Victorian Tudor mansion overlooking the Needles and the Solent had never heard of the labour and energy crises, or envisaged dancing in his entrance-hall (on Fridays and Saturdays) to 'an electronic organ touched by one of the proprietors.' Several members have been very happy with their dinners: perhaps baked avocado with walnut and butter sauce, wrapped in bacon, or duck pâté or crab cocktail; followed by venison and burgundy pie or other game dishes, 'richly sauced' halibut, steak stuffed with mushrooms, or Mr Hewitt's own suggested noisettes d'agneau maréchal. 'Mixed vegetables included fennel in a delightful sauce.' Salads look interesting too. Syllabub, Stilton, and the croûte Windsor savoury are variously praised, as are the brandy-snaps served with coffee. The wine list is both long and well-chosen: house burgundy (Chanson) is £4·50 a litre, and Mr Perkins is proud of his German Müller-Thurgau at only £3·80 for the same amount. Claret-lovers might help drink up Ch. Canon-le-Gaffelière '67, c.b. at £16·50, or experiment with the Napa Valley Cabernet Sauvignon '74 at £8·95. Bar snacks; Courage Directors is on pump. Wear a tie. More reports, please.

1980 prices are as estimated by restaurateurs in the autumn of 1979 (including VAT).

Towns shown in black on our maps contain at least one recommended restaurant, pub or wine bar (see map key). The dot denotes the location of the town or village, not the establishment. Where necessary, we give directions to it in the entry. If you can, help us to improve them.

Milton Ernest Hall
on A6
4 m N of Bedford
Oakley (023 02) 4111

Closed Mon; Sun D;
public hols (exc Apr 4);
1st week Sept;
1st 2 weeks Jan
Must book D
Meals 12.30–1.30, 8–9.30

Alc £8 (meal £11·05)

Service 10%
Seats 58 (parties 35)
☻ rest; w.c.
Car park
No dogs in d/r
Access, Barclay, Euro
6 rooms (5 with bath)
B&B £13·20–£23
Fire cert

William Butterfield, architect of this 'splendid' if impractical pile between the Grand Union Canal and the Ouse, had never come across the energy problem. That belongs to Francis Harmar-Brown instead, who has survived as a hotelier these eight years because, as he remarked in a *New Society* notice of Mark Girouard's *The Victorian Country House*, most people respond well to the air of dotty grandeur, though one customer vanished with the line: 'I should be *afraid* to ask for a drink in a place like this.' Mr Harmar-Brown 'sometimes goes overboard in the attempt to cheer the place up', and one victim of an all-night party was later advised to insist on rooms 5 or 7. But even he conceded that Robert Andrews' dinner had been admirable, and others report 'creamy and scalding artichoke soup with wholemeal bread', crisp and succulent roast duck with oranges and a tart apple sauce, set off by a warming casserole of root vegetables, and, at the end, a pile of Atholl brose, a sharp lemon mousse with almonds, and strong Cafetière coffee. Steaks – and a speciality banana pudding (85p) – are also of Victorian amplitude. The wine list has the owner's personal attention too , with £3·15 the basic price for Côtes du Rhône. Thereafter, prices rise quickly: Muscadet Château de la Galissonnière '78, is £4·80, Ch. Pichon-Lalande '67, c.b., £17·25. Charles Wells's Fargo bitter is in cask. During dining hours, the recorded music played is classical. (GHG)

App: M. M. Silver, E.L.F., T.J., and others

Beaconside
2½ m S of Bideford
on A388
Bideford (023 72) 77205

Closed D Sun & Mon
(exc res); L Wed & Sat;
Dec–Feb
Must book D & weekends
Meals 12.30–1.30, 8–9

Tdh D £7·50 (meal £8·90)
Alc snack L about £2·50

Service inc
Seats 28
☻ rest
8 rooms (6 with bath,
2 with shower)
B&B £13·80–£17·25
Fire cert

Andrew and Thea Brand have opened a relaxed well-furnished Victorian house near Bideford. From panoramic views and a heated swimming-pool to a one-hole golf course and a £2 high tea for resident children in school holidays, the owners work hard at making their guests content, and reports of Mrs Brand's set dinners suggest early success. Orange and tomato soup, sea-trout béarnaise, and strawberries in wine is one example, and 'we had only one glutinous sauce and one tepid dish in the whole holiday.' Soups, such as sorrel, or curried marrow, are a pride and joy, as is sea-bass vendangeuse ('a peasant version of Véronique') and blackberry frangipane. They make their own cider from Beaconside apples 'if you are brave enough to try it', and keep various fairly priced wines, with Balls Bros' Plonque Rouge at £3 the litre. Snack lunches (beef salad £2), perhaps on the terrace. Recorded classical music 'sometimes'. No dogs (because they have their own) but advice is offered on K.C.-approved kennels nearby. More reports, please.

MONTACUTE Somerset   Map 2

Milk House

17 The Borough
4 m W of Yeovil
Martock (093 582) 3823

Closed L (exc Dec 25);
Sun; Dec 25 D
Must book
D only, 7–9.30

Alc £7·25 (meal £9·10)

Service inc
Children's helpings
Seats 50 (parties 20)
⅃ rest
No dogs
Access, Am Ex, Barclay

The Donovans' 15th-century Ham stone house in
Montacute's quadrangle has been a local favourite
for six years now, and remains so, though Mr
Donovan's adjustment to a partner in the kitchen
(Graham Bayley) cannot have been entirely smooth,
to judge by a summer grumble of 'tasteless, lumpy and
lukewarm' crab au gratin, overcooked paupiettes de
boeuf and veal paprika, and perfunctory sweets.
However, this must have been an aberration, for
others at the same season found the kitchen on form,
and 'would especially recommend the aubergine first
course.' The owner himself suggests haddock à la
crème (£1·50), duck Grand Marnier (£4·25), lamb
Shrewsbury (£3·95) and chocolate and Cointreau
roulade (£1) as among their best dishes – though with
sweets 'someone is addicted to unbrowned supermarket
almonds.' Notre Dame carafe wines are £2·80, but
under £4 one would do much better with Yugoslav
Traminer or Averys dry white Bordeaux and
burgundy, or David Baillie's Prince Pirate claret;
more seriously, Ch. Fombrauge '71, c.b., at £8·45, or
halves of Ch. Coutet '72 Barsac at £4·30 appear on a
substantial list, and are well served, with cigars and
pipes banned. No children under three.

App: S.P., N. P. Bray, Leo & Betty Clynes, and others

MORETON-IN-MARSH Gloucestershire   Map 2

Lamb's
High Street
Moreton-in-Marsh
(0608) 50251

Closed Sun L (Mar–Oct);
weekday L (Nov–Mar);
Mon; Tue L (Mar–Oct);
Dec 25 D
Must book weekends
Meals 12–2, 7–11

Tdh Sun L £6·25
(meal £9·30)
Alc weekday L £4·50
(meal £7·35), D £8·95
(meal £12·30)

Service 10%
Children's helpings
(under 8, Sun)
Seats 65 (parties 24)
⅃ rest
No dogs in d/r
Access, Barclay, Euro

'An oasis in a desert of oolitic limestone,' says a
geologist of Ian Mackenzie's spacious restaurant – 'so
spacious that several people wandered in and out
with their shopping at midday.' Whether at the
wine-bar-style lunches, or at a busy Saturday
dinner, Paul Barnard's cooking seems consistent.
One member, whose party included 'a Frenchwoman
and one of the best home cooks I know', reports
general pleasure in melon salad, lambs' kidneys in
madeira sauce with grapes, and boned poussin
stuffed with rice; another's large group tried most
of the different dishes in a Sunday set lunch, and
'highlights were the seafood crêpe, bacon and fennel
Mornay, and calf's liver and veal terrine with
Cumberland sauce among first courses; and then
quail with cream, apple and calvados, and paupiettes
of veal with ham and Stilton stuffing.' Again 'steak
and scallop pie had light flaky pastry covering
succulent beef and tender scallops, all very hot.'
What is evidently a versatile kitchen further suggests
terrine of eel with tomato and sherry sauce (£1·95),
'Jack Daniel's mushrooms', roast teal with
horseradish ('one bird £3·50, two £6·50'), and roast
boned best end of lamb with kidney and marjoram
stuffing. 'Wild duck done in Guinness (would Ibsen

265

approve?) was very tasty.' Vegetables, if good, are dearish. 'I wondered whether the impressive fruit bowl had a false bottom, and what I was supposed to do with the lemons, but with a generous helping of Brie this made a good alternative to creamy meringues and profiteroles.' 'Redcurrant soufflé was bland and tasteless.' Service is usually prompt. Baronette wine is £3·20, and the short list is sensibly composed, though there is little under £5, and stock-keeping is called erratic. Ch. Cissac '71 (£9) is also to be had in halves and magnums. Perhaps Mr Mackenzie could subsidise the serious drinker by exacting, as he has hinted he might, special deposits from diners during Cheltenham Gold Cup week, when he had 37 defaulters.

App: Michael Latham, Susan Miles, Clive Kerridge, T.M.F., D. C. Alcock, G.H., Eileen Davies, and others

---

MORPETH Northumberland   Map 8

Gourmet
59 Bridge Street
Morpeth (0670) 56200

The table-sized menu at Pierre Paesano's outpost is more gourmand than gourmet, perhaps, but an inspector was hard pressed to recall better tomato soup (65p), chateaubriand au porto (£10·25 for two) and 'alcoholic' zabaglione. 'Too thick' fettuccine al burro and over-cooked vegetables fell short, but venison in 'rich and spicy orange sauce' and roast quail with chestnuts were both 'first class'. Vegetarian dishes and economical and varied bar lunches are useful. Service is 'good when supervised'. Ordinary ordinaire (Donnini Italian £3·75 a litre) and over a hundred other bottles. Pressurised beers. Music, like the menu, polyglot.

Closed Sun; Mon; public hols	Alc (min £2·75) £7·20 (meal £10·35)	Seats 50 (parties 50) Car park
Must book Sat		No dogs
Meals 12–2.30, 7–11.30	Children's helpings (under 10)	Access, Am Ex, Barclay, Diners, Euro
Tdh L £4·25 (meal £7·20)		

MOULTON North Yorkshire   Map 8

Black Bull
off A1
1½ m SE of Scotch Corner
Barton (032 577) 289

Closed Sun; Apr 13 L;
Dec 24–31
Must book D
(exc fish bar)
Meals 12–2, 7–10.30

'An accurate and helpful description in the 1979 edition' is a member's verdict, not George Pagendam's, it seems, though it is not easy to summarise the four ways of eating at this vastly enlarged, very popular pub near Scotch Corner. Hasty motorway travellers choose 'delicious cream of asparagus soup (90p) and smoked salmon sandwiches' (£1) in the bar. With more time, there is a choice between the fish bar and the conservatory-like main dining-room. Accounts of the fish bar describe 'very genuine' smoked salmon pâté (indeed, says another visitor, the seafood pâtés are 'strong enough to take some getting used to'),

Alc (fish bar) £7·55 (meal
£11·85); (main rest) from
£8·55 (meal £12·30);
(Hazel) £8·90 (meal
£13·15)

Seats 30, 20 & 20
(parties 20 & 10)
&. rest & fish bar
Car park
No dogs

good lobster, and sole florentine (£5·25), finishing with
'knickerbocker glory reminiscent of childhood summer
holidays.' In the conservatory, the new à la carte
service of steaks, poached salmon hollandaise, brandy
snaps, pancakes in Grand Marnier and the like, has
not seemed an improvement on the previous set meals.
The fourth, and for couples the most agreeable choice
(with its two-seater tables), is dinner in Hazel, a 1932
Pullman coach from the Brighton Belle, restored to
its original glory. 'After a longish wait in the bar we
had light and delicious spinach and salmon pancake
and meaty scallops in an excellent Mornay sauce,
then two immense Dover soles, with well-cooked
vegetables, and ended with profiteroles and "Brontë"
ice-cream. Like his chef Charles Somerville,
Mr Pagendam has simple tastes for good materials,
whether it is offal for supper or a Rolls on the road.
As agent for Duboeuf and Métaireau, he has access
to good wine – 'a fine Rully '78 for £5,' and sensible
Spanish bottles too. Clarets and half-bottles alike
do the place credit, and a vintage port is kept
decanted. They have failed to supply a list this year.
Theakston's bitter. Details are approximate.

*App: D. G. Foot, C. G. Ferguson, J. P. Elliott, W.F.,
Jean Dundas, W. A. Rinaldi-Butcher, and others*

NANTWICH Cheshire   Map 5

Churche's Mansion
150 Hospital Street
Nantwich (0270) 65933

Closed Sun D; Dec 24 D;
Dec 25–27; Jan 1
Must book
Meals 12–2, 7–8.30

Tdh L from £3·50
(meal £5·70), D from
£6·50 (meal £8·70)

Service inc
Cover £1
Seats 60 (parties 20)
&. rest (1 step)
Car park
No dogs

The Myott family's superbly preserved and restored
Elizabethan house counts years the way insomniacs
count sheep ('400, 401, 402') and the count of *Guide*
years for the restaurant is already up to 24. (An
expatriate correspondent from Canada remembers
being taken by his mother to eat there when the
Myotts first opened.) It has never been a place for a
soigné dinner (besides, if you arrive at a fashionably
late hour half the dishes may be off). Popularity, and
comparative cheapness, at once cause and excuse
plenty of slips between pan and palate. But most
people are readily consoled by the generous drink
measures and the honest attempt to cook and serve
real English food in keeping with the surroundings:
not mock-Tudor or mock-French but kipper pâté
perhaps (take the rolls, not the toast) or a mousse of
cream cheese and peppers, then 'four or five large,
plump and juicy scallops, with a gorgeous flavour and
never mind a grain of grit, served with a rasher of
back bacon', and damson mousse or bilberries and
cream among the puddings. 'Really fresh, crisply
fried plaice', roast suckling pig, braised pigeon, veal
Marengo, and carbonnade of beef are other main
dishes mentioned. Vegetables are at least 'adequate'.
The cheeses are worthy of the county, which is saying
much. The Averys wines are clustered in five price
groups, rather as motor cars are for insurance purposes.

Half a litre of St Maroc is £2·40 and after that you may pay £4·75 to choose between Ch. Truffet (Pressac) '75 or Italian Vernaccia, or £8·50 if your eye is on Santenay Gravières '72 or Ockfener Bockstein Auslese '75. Dessert wines are notable too, and Hyde's bitter is in cask. Sherry may be served 'warm, just before the soup arrives.' No pipes.

App: R. T. Davies, M.A.S.,J. & K.L., Dr C. K. Knapper

NAYLAND Suffolk   Map 3

The Bear
Bear Street
Nayland (0206) 262204

Closed L (exc Sun); Mon;
Tue; Sun D; 1 week
Easter; 3 weeks late
summer; Dec 25 & 26;
Jan 1; 1 week Jan
Must book
Meals 12.30–2, 7.30–9.30

Tdh L £6·30 (meal £9·10),
D £6·95 (meal £10·25)

Children's helpings
Seats 75 (parties 24 & 55)
⟨&⟩ rest (2 steps)
Car park

Gerard and Jane Ford run a very natural restaurant, in a rambling house and grounds that look older than they really are, and while the bar may be too small for the numbers, people find the atmosphere benign in the panelled, well-spaced dining-room. The cooking 'has its moments of silliness, like boiled carrots with cannelloni', but choices are restricted to about half a dozen in each course, and 'fresh salmon, and wild duck with red cabbage, were finely cooked when we tried them.' Pâté, boeuf en croûte (£5·55, including vegetables), and cold chocolate soufflé or Eton mess (strawberries and cream) are also praised, and the owners (who both cook) suggest their garlic-stuffed mussels and mushrooms (£1·25), boned game, boned and stuffed chickens, and for pudding brown bread ice-cream, fruit mousses, or crème brûlée (£1·05). 'Mr Ford correctly advised us that we would enjoy Ch. Gloria '66 and a half-bottle of sweet Loupiac with the pudding.' House wines are good too: red Ch. Peconnet and white Poitou Sauvignon '78, both £3·90. Pressurised beers. You may eat outside on the terrace.

App: Derek Butterfield, B. L. Underwood, L.O'B, Henry Fawcett

---

NEWBURY Berkshire   Map 2

Tandoorium
21–22 Park Way
Newbury (0635) 44699
and 47420

'Most agreeable – I plan to become a regular,' says a local resident happily of this tandoori house nearby. The menu sounds familiar, with kebabs and tikkas in various ways (from £2·30), but tandoori chicken (£2·05 for half) was 'striking in colour and delicate in flavour.' So was prawn butterfly (£1·10), though 'rather marred by the crumb coating.' Praise too for creamy murgh massalam (£1·95) and seekh kebab (95p). Sweets are tinned fruits or syrupy balls and twists (jelabi, 70p). Smooth service. Various wines; Carlsberg. 'Soft' Indian music on tape. No dogs. More reports, please.

Closed Dec 25
Meals 12–3, 6–12

Tdh L from £2·50
(meal £3·40), D £5·50
(meal £6·70)
Alc £3·95 (meal £4·75)

Children's helpings
(under 12)
Seats 50 (parties 20)
Access, Barclay, Diners

Black Gate Restaurant
The Side
Newcastle upon Tyne
(0632) 26661

Closed Sun; Mon D;
Sat L; public hols
Must book
Meals 12–2, 7–10.30

Tdh L £3·50 (meal £6·25),
D £9·75 (meal £13·70)
Alc £9 (meal £12·85)

Children's helpings
Seats 70
 ♿ rest
No dogs
Access, Barclay, Diners

'The best restaurant in Newcastle' has not been an extravagant compliment these thirty years past, and the chief peril for Bryan Lant and his chef Douglas Jordan is that they should come to think it is. They try hard to please, but most correspondents find a few thorns among the roses: 'disastrous vegetables', 'grotesquely large' helpings (though 'very civilised doggy bags, which enabled us to feed two teenage boys more than adequately when we got home'), undressed salads, a danger of overcooked steak and 'cheesecake with too much gelatine'. But menus are enterprising, and much is made on the premises, from bread downwards. The door by the Cathedral is modest, music and the decor 'inter-war eclectic, with everything from suspended violins to a stuffed Baltistani goat.' A lunch of celery and walnut soup, estouffade of beef, and a sweet, with coffee included, seemed good value, and 'the cabbage was *al dente* on this occasion.' Coquilles St Jacques, grilled halibut, and salmon stuffed with mackerel suggest interest in fish; sweetbreads with apple rings, and rack of lamb with tarragon also sound hopeful. The kitchen's repertoire is large (too large perhaps, for they claim not to have repeated a lunch menu in two years). Valgardello carafes are £4·40 a litre and though the wine list has not been forwarded, it too sounds from customers' comments to be open to criticism. But cherish the place, in hope of further improvement.

App: Dr I. J. Runcie, C. K. Grant, M.C.K., J.E.F., and others

Forge Restaurant
Parkgate Road
5 m S of Dorking
off A24
Newdigate (030 677) 582

Closed Sun; Mon; Sat L;
Dec 26; Jan 1
Must book
Meals 12–2, 7–10

Alc £10·65 (meal £13·55)

Service inc
Seats 36
 ♿ rest
Access, Am Ex, Barclay,
Diners, Euro

There is nothing here, perhaps, to write an Oxford prize poem about, but the Essls are rhyming and scanning with Austrian craft in their quietly furnished restaurant opposite the Surrey Oaks pub, on the northern edge of the village. Various people report unusually tender and crisp duck, and the schnitzel, veal zurichoise, and lunchtime oxtail may be worth trying. Game is another speciality. Vegetable prices are stiff (salads are cheaper). An inspector reports genuine lobster bisque, and for pudding 'light sponge with apricot jam and icing of good chocolate, then proper coffee, served with home-made crystallised fruits.' Austrian Gumpoldskirchner '76 is £5·70 and the next wine list step brings Fleurie '78 (Duboeuf) at £7·10; double figures are soon reached thereafter. Recorded Viennese music. Wear a collar and tie. No children under eight. No dogs. Car park. More reports, please.

See p. 441 for the pub section, and p. 491 for the wine bars.

Bridge End House
on A3052
Colaton Raleigh (0395)
68411

Closed L (exc Sun);
Mon; Sun D;
Sept 22–Oct 7;
Dec 25 & 26
Must book
Meals 12.15–1.15 (Sun),
7–10

Tdh Sun L £3·35 (meal
£6·15)
Alc £6·65 (meal £9·85)

Service 10%
Children's helpings
Seats 45
Car park
No dogs
3 rooms
B&B £5·50

As before, drive carefully and sleep soundly if you contemplate a night at the Coxes' hospitable house on a main-road corner, but these are not the only two caveats this time. Various reports in the late summer and autumn of 1979, after an apparently minor change in the owning partnership, mention flaws that range from 'dust and dog hairs' in the bedroom to 'cloying sauces', and 'slivers of ice in a pheasant's leg joint'. Some differences of opinion are cultural rather than technical: 'I like to be able to see my food clearly ... vegetables did not go with the main dishes ... chicken legs stuffed with prawns not worth the trouble, given tasteless primary ingredients ... unnecessary clotted cream with already luscious sweets.' The same report, though, pays tribute to the civility, the table settings, and the generosity of the place: others concur, with high praise of 'fresh and flavourful fish', ballotine of duck, breast of chicken with ham in béchamel, beef Wellington, steak Marseilles (£3·70), and 'potatoes three ways: sauté with bacon, sliced with cheese and cream, and crisply fried in allumettes.' Quail normande (£4·20) is a speciality; so is nabob's delight (80p) among the puddings. Home-made ices are 'much recommended'. Table wines from France and Italy are £3·75 a litre; Ch. Lyonnat '67, c.b., from David Baillie Vintners is £7·20. Pressurised beers. 'We enjoy having good children in our restaurant.' More reports, please, since temporary illness may have caused the troubles reported.

Romanby Court
High Street
Northallerton (0609) 4918

Closed L (exc 2 weeks
before Chr); Sun; Mon;
Dec 25 & 26; 3 weeks Aug;
1 week Feb
Must book
D only, 7.30–10

Tdh from £7·05 (meal £10)

Seats 30 (parties 15)
&. rest (1 step)
No dogs

The Collu-Pala partnership is Sardinia's gift to North Yorkshire, according to a rigorous critic who adduces 'edifying standards of materials and preparation despite dismally undemanding clientele.' (Others, though, lately report 'easy and mundane steaks'.) Two women diners, vulnerable as usual, were gratified to be welcomed warmly and taken seriously: 'When we needed a rest between the four courses, we got it.' The menu changes every few months, and autumn may bring roast grouse or duck, accompanied by 'outstanding vegetables'. A magisterial member, made wary by the chilly lounge, an awkwardly placed table and a poor Barolo (£7·50), marched without effort through prawn pancake, vegetable soup, 'a brace of teal, small but full of flavour' (£6·75), dessert ('crème OK, more brûlée s.v.p.') and 'expert cappuccino complete with chocolate sprinkling.' Carafe wines vary with the market; house claret is £4·15. Recorded Italian music 'operatic and romantic'. You may eat outside in summer.

App: P.O'R.S., H.J.W., H.M.D.

NORTHAMPTON Northamptonshire   Map 3

St Matthews Cellar
23 St Matthews Parade,
Kettering Road
Northampton (0604)
713821

'A useful alternative to motorway catering' – and a much warmer welcome in this small restaurant below a hotel, according to grateful travellers. The Colleys offer a sensibly limited menu (sole, scampi, steaks and a roast for main courses, say) with additional *plats du jour*: mussels provençale (£1·30), half a roast duck with apricot stuffing (£4·80) or salmon with hollandaise (main dish prices include salad or vegetables). Duc Henri house wine £3 a litre; Ch. Fombrauge '73, £5·30. 'Light jazz' on tape.

Closed Sun; Mon; Sat L;
Dec 25 & 26
Meals 12.15–2, 7–10

Tdh L £2·20 (meal £4·30),
D £6·70 (meal £9·50)

Service 10%
Children's helpings
Seats 50
No dogs

NORTHLEACH Gloucestershire   Map 2

Country Friends
Market Place
Northleach (045 16) 421

Closed Mon; Sun D;
D Dec 25 & 26; Feb
Must book D & weekends
Meals 12–2, 7–9.30

Tdh L £4 (meal £6·65),
Sun L £4·75 (meal £7·50)
Alc £7·10 (meal £10·10)

Seats 18
Barclaycard

Northleach may be surprised to find itself a centre of good eating, but Pauline Whittaker's seasonally conscious cooking in this 17th-century house has drawn cordial admirers over the past twelve months for onion and Stilton soup, pigeon pâté, sole and scallop brochette, noisettes of lamb with orange sauce, stuffed chicken, game pie (£3·75) and other conceptions. Charles Whittaker, who serves, says his wife tries to make everything from cheese biscuits to tiffin cake for afternoon tea, and (a relief, this) that her style is 'definitely not Cordon Bleu'. Opening times may be flexible, according to bookings. Batisque ordinaire is £3·25 and there are a few other wines. Recorded music. Smaller helpings for children under ten. No dogs. More reports, please.

Old Woolhouse

The Square
Northleach (045 16) 366

Closed L; Sun; 5 weeks
May/June; 1 week Chr
Must book
D only, from 8.15

Tdh about £10·50
(meal about £13)

Service inc
Seats 14
♿ rest (1 step)

'It is easier to become a Mason than to book a table for two at Jacques Astic's house', partly because of the demand on a tiny place where serious cooking is done, partly because he is understandably distrustful of defaulters (and also of restaurant guides). But 'there is nothing to touch M Astic and the value he gives round here: why more restaurants cannot see that you do not need dozens of dishes to be successful, if you concentrate on the few you can do really well, amazes me.' True, if the quality of the dishes solemnly recited falls even slightly below expectation, irritation burgeons: 'I found several dishes – the crab tartlets, the marzipan-stuffed prunes – no more than the sum of their parts, as is often true of home-cooking: flavours and textures never quite coalesced. Veal kidneys and the accompanying potatoes were not intrinsically good enough to stand without further support.' An inspector differs, recollecting in tranquillity hot chicken liver mousse

271

and 'marvellously warm-tasting' rib of beef in mustard sauce. 'Chicken actually tasted of chicken, not some macabre supermarket fish-bird. Contrary to the last *Guide*'s account, dauphinois potatoes and the salad dressing made a well-judged contrast to the suave sauces.' Sweets are the least French offering, in their profusion ('We were urged by Madame to try five') and also in other senses ('salty butter cream in chocolate cake, unpeeled grapes in over-sweet Pavlova'). However, 'almond tart was slightly severe, but excellent.' 'When a couple at the next table refused cheese, M Astic looked as though he might cry' (which is explained by his insistence on direct imports from his native Lyonnais, served *à point*, or not at all). 'There was good, plentiful coffee, and good, plentiful (if unnecessary) petits fours: I admit we finished them.' The wine list is short, well balanced and practically priced, with Ch. Lyonnat '67, £8·50 and Volnay Santenots '69, £9 in 1979. Details are approximate.

App: Tom Hamilton, A. & J.L., C.J.M., and others

NORTHREPPS Norfolk   Map 6

Church Barn
off A149
3 m SE of Cromer
Overstrand (026 378) 588

This converted flint barn by the church has expanded (gracefully) into the Granary Bar. The Foxalls plan to serve light meals (soups, flans and pies with Adnams' BB from the cask) at weekday lunch-times and on Sunday and Monday evenings. The main restaurant still stresses set meals with fresh fish and shellfish ('my Cromer lobster tasted like that day's catch') and traditional roasts. Soused herring or seafood cocktail are good openers and chef-made cassis sorbet is popular. Sauces – mayonnaise included – may be 'drab'. French house wines are £4·25 for 70 cl. 'Infrequent' recorded music. A few tables outside.

Closed L (exc weekday bar & Sun); D Sun & Mon (exc bar & public hols); Dec 25 D; Dec 26; Jan 15–Mar 1 Must book Meals 12.15–2, 7.15–10	Tdh Sun L £5 (meal £8·35), D £6·50 (meal £10) Children's helpings (exc Sat D)	Seats 50 (parties 30) ⅙ rest Car park No dogs Access, Barclay

---

NORWICH Norfolk   Map 6

Marco's
17 Pottergate
Norwich (0603) 24044

Closed Sun; Mon; Apr 4; Aug; Dec 25 & 26; Jan 1
Must book
Meals 12.30–2, 7.30–10

'The kind of restaurant that I should like to visit every week,' says one valued correspondent. Perhaps Marco Vessalio's formula – and after nine *Guide* years, he knows his own worth to Norwich – might pall with that frequency, to say nothing of the crowded tables in the bright, sprucely set room. But the cooking is sound, and within limits varied. 'Cozze alla marinara were outstandingly fresh (£2·30 as a first course) and

Tdh L £5·75 (meal £8·85)

Alc £9·80 (meal £13·70)

Seats 40
& rest
No dogs
Access, Am Ex, Barclay,
Diners

though the cheese, cream and mushroom filling for cannelloni was too rich and white for my taste, the dish was sizzling and indisputably good.' Burrida alla genovese is another fishy speciality (sometimes shown on the bargain set lunch) and Marco also suggests pollo alla diavola, saltimbocca, and scampi allo spumante. Main courses à la carte start at £4·15. Braised fennel on the vegetable list sounds promising, but aubergine fritters (80p) were unimpressive at a test meal which, however, ended well with 'lovely honey ice-cream, and espresso coffee just as it should be.' Barbera or Frascati are £3 for 50 cl, and there are about 65 other Italian wines to try, with Chianti Classico about £5·75. Recorded 'Italian' music.

App: D. G. Poole, L.W., M.A.B., P.G.U., and others

Parson Woodforde
1 Old Post Office Yard,
19/21 Bedford Street
Norwich (0603) 24280

Closed Sun D; Apr 6
Must book D & weekends
Meals 12–2.30, 7–10.30

Alc £8·75 (meal £12·15)

Seats 48
Car park (D)
No dogs
Access, Barclay, Diners,
Euro

The mid-18th-century volume of the *Oxford History of English Literature* omits to mention that Parson Woodforde was not only a verbose diarist but an exceptionally greedy man; the owners of this agreeable timbered hall supply the reminder with Paddy Heyland's (and others') anchovy whets, wild duck with port and orange, and the pie called 'the Charter' (chicken, cream and leeks). The parson would have eaten the lot, 'since the whets were a modest portion for the price' (£1·25), and his successor 'should be demoted to the curacy' for charred sprouts and excess rosemary with lamb. But others like the hot mushrooms in mint and anchovy sauce, sweetbreads in mushroom sauce ('somewhat over-garnished', £4·50), rib of beef, good fresh vegetables, and 'worthy bread-and-butter pudding, though more nutmeg and a less aerated texture would have improved it.' Chocolate mousse with walnuts is an alternative. The bread, and cheese dip at the beginning, are praised: we have heard little of the cheeses. French Monceny table wines are £3·40 and the ales are in bottle, alas, but someone takes an educated interest in the clarets and dessert wines: Ch. Troplong-Mondot '71, £10·70; Neusiedler Altenberg Beerenauslese '75, £14·50 – though the latter would be better kept a while. Good ports and eaux-de-vie too. Recorded Handel and Mozart. *Please report also on the same owners' Winkles Sea Food Bar in the 14th-century crypt, where the music is 'alas coeval with the staff', not the stones', but where good fish and chips and smoked fish salads have been noted at £1·70 or so.*

App: M. Sanderson Walker, P.G.U., M.H., and others

Wine prices shown are for a 'standard' bottle of the wine concerned, unless another measure is stated (e.g. litre, 50 cl., or pint).

Meal times refer to first and last orders.

273

Tatlers
21 Tombland
Norwich (0603) 21822

Closed Dec 25 & 26;
Jan 1
Must book D
Meals 12–2.30, 6.30–11.30

Alc £5·45 (meal £7·95)

Seats 70 (parties 25)
♿ rest (2 steps); w.c.
No dogs

' 'Tis substantial happiness to eat' at this youthful town house in Tombland near the Cathedral. The rough and not-yet-ready atmosphere can be irksome, but most members are prepared to accept 'inordinate waits', uncomfortable benches and 'eclectic' music as the *sine qua non* of gifted amateur cooking. ('Yet unquiet meals make ill digestions,' they quote on the menu.) One inspector thought the gamey fare 'more carefully assembled now'; another concurred after moist pigeon in red wine sauce 'though the stuffing was unadventurous' (£2·55). The 'rough and satisfying game pâté' may be a by-product of the main courses: pigeon, wild rabbit in 'strong, well-judged rosemary and mustard sauce', and perhaps mallard in elderberry wine (£3·75) or partridge stuffed with plums (£4·95). Cashew nut stew (£1·40) has been added this year, but not all dishes are so provocative: smoked cod in cheese sauce (£1·90), fresh prawn salad, 'perfect ratatouille and excessively, delightfully rich trifle' (65p). A dissenter found the bar a dingy place to wait for 'mackerel with too much garlic in its butter and offhand jugged hare', but could not withhold praise from the extensive wine list (Ch. Phélan-Ségur '71, £6·85). Abbot IPA from the cask. 'Be-jeaned waitresses charm but need prodding.' Better not try, perhaps, even in this liberated atmosphere.

App: L.W., Peter Andrews, Stuart Manger

NORWICH see also wine bar section

Ben Bowers
128 Derby Road
Nottingham (0602) 43288
and 47488

'An international restaurant must expect to be judged by the same standards', bemoans a rigorous and veteran diner from the West Indies after 'dry prawns with garlic, grey cauliflower and uninspired ratatouille' before praising a 'fresh, light gateau'. Low stocks of beer and wine irked another man but the less severe rest content with venison in 'a delightful plum sauce' (£4·25) or with chestnuts. Green figs in ouzo still please. 'Cramped' seating; cigar-smokers are dispatched to the coffee lounge. Lunch in Betty's Buffet (£1·12) and snacks and a bar supper in the wine bar (Mon–Sat: 12–2.30, 5.30–10.30). House wines from £3·80 a litre. Recorded music.

Closed Sun; Sat L;
L public hols (exc Apr 4);
Dec 25 & 26
Must book
Meals 12–2, 7–11

Alc £6·10 (meal £8·90)

Children's helpings
Seats 50

Air-conditioning
No dogs
Access, Am Ex, Barclay,
Diners, Euro

La Grenouille
32 Lenton Boulevard
Nottingham (0602) 411088

'Not good enough for a credit entry,' say various visitors and an inspector about Yves Bouanchaud's 'cheerfully shabby' and cramped bistro. Support is stronger for his soup, jambon à la crème, navarin, mushroom omelette (£1·10), pot au feu, casseroled vegetables and bananes flambées. Saumon à la crème (£3·75) is a speciality. Helpings are 'navvy-sized'. But it is best to choose meat dishes that allow the butcher and the saucier a margin of error. Chocolate cake and ices are praised. Chaumière ordinaires are £2·20 for 50 cl. Recorded 'popular' music. Please keep us posted.

Closed Sun; Sat L; Dec 23–Jan 1; public hols (exc Apr 4 D) Must book Meals 12.30–1.30, 7.30–9.30	Tdh £4 (meal £5·55) Alc £5·90 (meal £8·75) Service 10%	Children's helpings (under 8) Seats 24 No dogs

Laguna Tandoori
43 Mount Street
Nottingham (0602) 49110

Even detractors call D. B. Mali's Punjabi cooking 'above local average'. Regulars club together for tandoori specialities: cardamom-flavoured chicken shashlik, 'generous' chicken tikka and 'acutely spiced' seekh kebab (£1·45) – all as first courses. Praise also for 'subtle' Begum Behar (£1·55) and 'positive additions to pilau', but scented towels do not make up for mild dhal, 'empty' raita and smallish portions. Drink lager or tap water. 'Relaxed' service. Recorded Indian music.

Closed Dec 25 & 26 Must book D Meals 12.30–2.30, 6.30–11.30	Tdh from £3 (meal £4·30) Alc £4·60 (meal £6·10) Service 12½%	Seats 75 No dogs Access, Am Ex. Barclay, Diners

OBORNE Dorset   Map 2

The Grange
Sherborne (093 581) 3463

Mauro (who cooks) and Lucio (who greets guests macaronically) preside over this small manor in a quiet village just north of the A30. 'Not quite gracious living, and smoky late at night, but cheerful.' At a test meal, eggs Valentine (£1·10) and a ham-and-herb version of chicken Kiev, with crisp courgettes and French-fried potatoes, were skilfully done, but sauce for saltimbocca was mediocre. Main dishes are about £4. 'Lovely roast beef for Sunday lunch.' 'Devilish rich' chocolate gateau. Expect little of the house Chianti at £3·50 a litre, but other Italian bottles are dear. 'Try Aurum with your coffee.' Recorded music.

Closed L (exc Sun); D Sun & Mon; Apr 6; Dec 25 D; Dec 26; Jan 1 Must book Meals 12–1.30, 7–11	Tdh (Sun) L £4·50 (meal £6·90) Alc £7·30 (meal £10·40) Service 10%	Seats 45 ⓹ rest Car park No dogs

Butley-Orford Oysterage
Market Hill
on B1084
12 m E of Woodbridge
Orford (039 45) 277

Closed Dec 25 & 26;
D Jan & Feb
Must book
Meals 12–2, 6.15–8.15

Alc £2·55 (meal £4·65)

Seats 50 (parties 20)
 ♿ rest

The Pinney family's note on their simple cafe virtually suffices: 'We smoke salmon, trout, eels, cod's roe, mackerel and so on, and grow our own oysters in the local estuary. We also keep our own fishing-boats and serve sole, skate and cod when they are to be had, notifying these items on blackboards.' Since Mrs Pinney runs the kitchen it is our place rather than theirs to advocate the raw rather than the cooked, for pork and clam stew at a test meal was 'calamitous', though 'angels on horseback (85p) saved the situation.' The 'gorgeous' Butley oysters (£2·60 a dozen) and 'unsurpassed' smoked salmon would grace any table in the land. Only bread and butter are served with the fish. Both coffee and wines are better than the surroundings promise: try the local Finn Valley Müller-Thurgau (£3·10), a member advises, though the '76 has now become the '77. Skip sweets, and nip round the corner to their take-away shop for all your lucky friends.

App: J. B. Wilkin, Ron Salmon, T. M. S. Tosswill, Rodney & Pamela Giesler, J. & P.S., and others

The Lodge
17 Silver Street
Ottery St Mary
(040 481) 2356

Closed Mon; Sun D;
public hols (exc Apr 6,
& Jan 1)
Must book
Meals 12.30–1.30,
7.30–9.30

Alc £6·65 (meal £9·30)

Seats 24 (parties 20)
No dogs

'The customer is always right,' say John and Anne Freeman-Cowen – and that extends to the one who said, 'Why don't you knock down this wall and give yourselves a larger ante-room?' The *Guide*'s customers are at least sure they were right to visit this little town – delightfully self-contained in the matter of produce – and its church too. Many begin their meals with mushrooms Cockaigne (stuffed with almonds, £1·35), but frogs' legs in tomato and crab mayonnaise are among the alternatives. Seafood casserole (£4·50) and 'gratifyingly original' chicken Zuleika (marinated in spices and served on the bone with ginger and pineapple) are very popular, and an interesting range of vegetables, such as ratatouille, dauphinois potatoes, cabbage with green peppers and spinach with nutmeg 'showed no sign of overcooking'. If you happen not to fancy one of the creamy sweets, both the Stilton and the strong mature Cheddar from Newton St Cyres are worth eating. Gresham Bordeaux ordinaires are £2·75 and fine claret (Ch. Latour '71, c.b., £20) is fairly marked up. Pipes are 'not encouraged'. 'Men's shirts should be buttoned above the navel' – perhaps in Ottery the female navel is seldom or never exhibited?

App: B.A., J. B. Ainscough, Brenda Shewring

Do not risk using an out-of-date Guide. A new edition will appear early in 1981.

Wheel House
25 Silver Street
Ottery St Mary (040 481)
2262

Closed Mon; Tue; Sun D;
2 weeks Oct/Nov;
Dec 24–26; 2 weeks
Jan/Feb
Must book
Meals 12.30–1.30, 7.30–9

Alc L £2·65 (meal £4·85),
D £5·25 (meal £7·75)

Children's helpings
(under 7)
Seats 20
♿ rest (1 step)
No dogs
2 rooms
B&B £7

*Vaunda Corinaldesi (who cooks) and her sister
Eleanor Wragg succeeded a short-lived régime in this
Georgian cottage by the church late in 1978, and have
attracted notice for the obvious affection with which
they are serving a judiciously modest range of food and
wine. A member who reckons on eating well was very
pleased with the fine furniture and 'domestic' atmosphere,
as well as with 'good vegetable soup, delicious
tagliatelle with herbs and cream, breast of chicken with
tarragon and lightly cooked vegetables, and apricot
tart.' Others have enjoyed the carbonnade of beef,
Atholl brose and chocolate roulade. The owners – who
like their guests not to feel constrained to eat three-
course meals – also commend their own pâtés (from
75p), tenderloin of pork normande (£3·85, including
vegetables) and ginger syllabub (80p). On their days
closed they will happily take bookings for parties, for
they are their own mistresses and employ no staff.
There are about a dozen wines, with bottles of Prince
Pirate Bordeaux from Baillie Vintners under £4 in
1979. Smoking is discouraged. They accept children 'at
discretion if under seven'. The walled cottage garden is
agreeable to eat in on a fine day. More reports, please.*

OUNDLE Northamptonshire   Map 6

Tyrrells
6–8 New Street
Oundle (083 22) 2347

Closed Mon; Sun D;
Dec 26; Jan 1
Must book D & weekends
Meals 12–2, 7–10.30

Tdh L £3·25 (meal £6·20)
Alc £6·05 (meal £9·60)

Cover 25p (alc)
Seats 46
No dogs
Access, Barclay

Mike and Hilary Tyrrell's little restaurant opposite
the school gates, with its pretty walled courtyard
complete with vine and peach-tree, succeeded quickly
– and deservedly, according to a visitor from a distance
who called in for a business lunch of melon cocktail,
beef bourguignonne and sorbet; and an inspector who
was 'knocked out, but nicely' by mushrooms filled
with Stilton, crumbed and fried, pepper steak in
cream and brandy (£5·20), and crunchy almond
soufflé. Richard Pool in the kitchen does a proper
carpetbagger steak, too, as well as mussels en
brochette and Basque lamb with an anchovy topping
and port and redcurrant sauce (£3·75). Third-course
ideas include Brie with black grapes, and 'Aunt No's
brandy cream'. Recorded music; 'ad hoc' dancing.

App: Elizabeth Brigg, R.V.M., L.O'B. and others

We rewrite every entry each year, and depend on fresh, detailed reports to confirm
the old, as well as to include the new. The further from London you are, the more
important this is.

Since each restaurant has a separate file in the Guide office, please use a separate
form or sheet of paper for each report. Additional forms may be obtained free (no
stamp required) from The Good Food Guide, Freepost, 14 Buckingham Street,
London WC2N 6BR (unfortunately Freepost facilities are not available from the
Channel Islands or the Republic of Ireland).

Meal times refer to first and last orders.

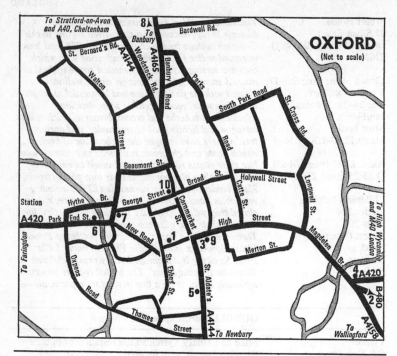

OXFORD Oxfordshire Map 2

(1) La Cantina di Capri
34 Queen Street
Oxford (0865) 47760

Closed Mon (exc Apr 7,
May 5, Aug 25); Dec 24–
26 & 31; Jan 1
Must book
Meals 12–2.30, 6–11.30

Alc £5·05 (meal £7·65)

Cover 30p
Children's helpings
(under 8)
Seats 60
No dogs
Access, Am Ex, Barclay,
Diners

'Zeal, all zeal, Mr Easy' explains both the faults and
the virtues of Reno Pizi's modestly lit cellar. From
the 'bonhomous welcome to the quixotic refusal
to serve a dish they thought I would not like' and the
'brandy-fuelled pyrotechnics with snails, clearly as
frightening to the waiter as they were entertaining to
the customer', everyone seems to have enjoyed this
example of the restaurant as *commedia dell'arte*. The
food is pretty good too, if approached with
commonsense: onion soup may be 'weirdly sweet',
vegetables various but erratic, and profiteroles
'drowning in cocoa'; but cannelloni is 'excellent',
coquille de fruits de mer an inviting version, veal and
chicken breast dishes 'delicious', courgettes crisply
fried, and the sweets very suitable for sweet-toothed
Oxford. (Stray bachelor dons more interested in the
cheese and the coffee may be disappointed.) The
house wines are Merlot or Tocai at a frugal £2·60
and there is a judicious Italian choice between £4 and
£5: white Verduzzo '77 and red Rubesco Torgiano
'75, for example. Recorded music. Not a place for a
hot night, perhaps, and if the customers cannot set a
better example over smoking, at least the staff should.

*App: Benedict Coldstream, Geoffrey & Jenifer Rowntree,
Doug Miles, Frank Cummins, T.S., and others*

278

(2) La Capannina
247 Cowley Road
Oxford (0865) 48200

Busy, family-run Italian place, redecorated since last year, but still providing generous helpings of good minestrone (30p), pasta (sometimes overcooked), and veal or chicken ('excellent' saltimbocca £2, chicken cacciatore £1·90). A salad may be a better choice than vegetables. Usual sweets. Service can be slapdash when they are rushed. Italian carafe £3 the litre, 50p the glass. Muted music.

Closed Sun; Apr 6;
Dec 25 & 26; Jan 1
Must book D
Meals 12–1.45, 6.15–10.45

Alc £5·10 (meal £7·85)

Service 10%
(5 or more)

Children's helpings
Seats 60
♿ rest (2 steps)
No dogs

---

(3) Casse-Croûte
130a High Street
Oxford (0865) 41320

With the same chef as its relation upstairs, the Sorbonne (q.v.), this small cafe provides relatively cheap and speedy lunches for students, traders and shoppers. 'Not much money spent on the decor.' Worth minor discomfort, some think, to enjoy rather thin vichyssoise (60p), coarse and peppery pâté de canard, truite belle meunière ('large and tasty', £2·10) and tender and high – though bony – civet de lièvre (£1·80), with competent vegetables included. The blackboard menu also offers several soups, tarts, omelettes, steaks and salads. Sweets are hardly worth it. House wine is £2·40 for 50 cl.

Closed D; Sun; last week
Aug; 1st week Sept;
public hols
L only, 12–2.30

Alc (min £1·95) £3·30
(meal £6·65)

Seats 18
No dogs
Am Ex, Diners

---

(4) Clements
37 St Clements
Oxford (0865) 41431

Closed Wed; 1st 2 weeks
Sept; Dec 25 & 26; Jan 1
Must book D
Meals 12.15–2.15, 7.30–11

Tdh Sun L £4·80
(meal £7·50)
Alc £6·55 (meal £9·40)

Children's helpings
Seats 35 (parties 40)
♿ rest
No dogs

Michel Sadones' restaurant, with Richard Sarney as chef, is quieter than it looks, and more French than you fear, in this dreary street beyond Magdalen Bridge. The à la carte menu is wisely short, and 1979 visitors report good crudités and ratatouille or artichoke vinaigrette among first courses; then 'a handsome salmon trout', or 'chicken Véronique with black grapes (a pity, I thought) and firm potatoes in buttery brown skins', or 'good John Dory portugaise, and spicy kidneys.' Dacquoise, 'tangy, not over-sweetened loganberry mousse', and summer pudding sound superior to the usual French formula. Specialities, though, are savoury: quenelles de saumon sauce Nantua (£3·80), and côte de boeuf aux trois sauces (béarnaise, poivre, et provençale) £12 for two, including vegetables. Wines (from £3·20) are being extended beyond the standard Grierson-Blumenthal French examples, and just as well. Recorded music. More reports, please, Sunday lunch included.

The Guide accepts no advertising. Nor does it allow restaurateurs to use its name on brochures, menus, or in any form of advertisement. If you see any instances of this, please report them to us.

(5) Restaurant Elizabeth

84 St Aldates
Oxford (0865) 42230

Closed L (exc Sun); Mon;
3 weeks Aug; public hols
Must book
Meals 12.30–2.30 (Sun),
6.30–11 (7–10.30 Sun)

Alc (min £6·25) £9·50
(meal £13·35)

Service inc
Cover 95p
Seats 55
No dogs
Access, Barclay, Euro

There are some academics – and for that matter undergraduates – who find contemporary Oxford so rich in restaurants that they wish one could be spared for Cambridge. But it had better not be Antonio Lopez's upstairs room, now better lit and spaced than it used to be. For a dozen years or more, he has kept the loyalties of many whose lean and hungry youth has yielded to mid-career *embonpoint*. This habit-forming process continues: 'At Sunday lunch, the mean age must have been about 25 – where do they get the money from?' The service, though often kind and competent, languishes sadly when Mr Lopez's mild and magnificent eye is off it. The cooking, too, seldom quite fulfils its potential. 'Ttoro and pipérade were both competent rather than inspired, the soup neither the fishiest nor the best, though perhaps the most original, I have tasted. Suprême de volaille au vin blanc was an excellent piece of meat in a good sauce, subtly flavoured – with nasty croquette potatoes.' A test meal that included avgolemono soup, carbonnade de boeuf flamande (£6·30) and truite Alhambra (stuffed with a shellfish mousse) confirmed this judgement in essentials: the soup and the main dishes were admirably cooked, though their accompaniments (green salad apart) were ill-conceived: what is one to think of a major restaurant that allows its customers to yawn over the same rice and potatoes for a dozen years? Charcoaled prawns with aïoli – 'lovely little things,' says a heartless sentimentalist, poulet au porto, entrecôte au poivre vert, and carré d'agneau are other sound orders. Crème brûlée, when tested, was burnt beyond the recipe's intention, but this, with syllabub, chocolate mousse, and praline ice-cream, is all most people seem to desire of sweets here. The cellar is very fine: 'all bottles are racehorses, no hacks,' says an inspector generously, resolutely settling for Alsace Gewürztraminer and vigorous red Hermitage rather than Chx. Branaire-Ducru or Boyd-Cantenac, both '67, at £18·55, or one of the dozen '61s ('the four *premiers crus* are impartially priced at £101·20 each'), or the 'delightful' Wachenheimer Mandelgarten Trockenbeerenauslese '70 (Bürklin-Wolf) at £36·80. 'If you order a German wine, give the number, because the waiters can't pronounce them' – who can? 'Janneau armagnac '37 is a reasonable £1·45 a glass.'

App: Christopher Forman, J. M. Thomson, A.A.B.C., J.C.M., Mr & Mrs F. Williams, J.T., and others

---

'Meal' indicates the cost of a meal for one, including food, coffee, a half-bottle of one of the cheapest wines listed, cover, service, and VAT (see 'How to use the Guide', p. 4).

(6) Munchy Munchy
6 Park End Street
Oxford (0865) 45710

'Oo' and 'Mmm' is Oxford's response to Mrs Ow's pine-built Indonesian food bar, 'which any poor student (or don) can afford.' Inspectors familiar with the genre are thankful for the short daily menu and the skill shown in fried beef with coconut and chilli (£1·40) and gosht ka rai (beef braised with cardamom and other spices), pork with tamarind and ginger, itek panggang tyen (roast duck with ginger and wine), ayam limau (chicken with lime), sodi ('pineapple and leek in turmeric and coconut sauce – fascinating'), other vegetarian dishes, and treatments of fish, squid and prawns. Cheesecake if you want a sweet. Drink fruit juices and exotic teas, or take your own and pay a 10 per cent service charge. Book, or expect a queue.

Closed Sun; Mon L;
2 weeks Sept;
2 weeks Dec; public hols
Must book D & weekends
Meals 12–2.15, 5.30–9.15

Alc (min £2) £2·30
(meal £3)

Seats 26

♿ rest
No dogs
Unlicensed

---

(7) Opium Den
79 George Street
Oxford (0865) 48080

Closed Dec 25 & 26
Must book D & weekends
Meals 12–2.20, 6–12

Tdh L £1·60 (meal £2·15),
D £4 (meal £4·75)
Alc £5·35 (meal £6·25)

Seats 140 (parties 30)
♿ rest
Air-conditioning
No dogs
Access, Am Ex, Barclay,
Diners, Euro

'Hectic but lovely' is one phrase for Shu Man Tse's 'womb-dark' restaurant on a corner near bus and railway stations, and toll car park. An inspector's late lunch-hour visit was equally hectic, for staff with itchy feet gave him 'the fastest service ever seen in a Chinese restaurant.' But unless it were 'cold and sparse pancakes for crispy duck', there was nothing slack about the cooking of dishes from the 100-dish menu, and 'tastes that linger in the mind include the salty deep-fried squid in pepper and garlic dressing (£2·10) and the baked vegetable in coconut sauce' (£1·75). Roasted pork spare ribs (£1) and 'sizzling' beef Cantonese-style (£2·50) were also good examples. 'Another time, I shall try oyster with spring onions and ginger, stir-fried beef with salt cabbage, and (out of curiosity) "jor jou (hot)" .' Even the cheap set lunch of soup, beef with Chinese greens, peaches in syrup, and percolated coffee has been found acceptable.

App: R. Whitehouse, C.P.D., E.E., S.M.T.

---

(8) Les Quat' Saisons
👍

272 Banbury Road
Oxford (0865) 53540

Closed Sun; Mon;
public hols (exc May 5 &
26, & Aug 25); Apr 8;
July 14–Aug 14;
Dec 24 & 31
Must book D

'Just locate Oxfam and you're not far away' is one man's advice on finding Raymond and Jenny Blanc's restaurant in the Summertown shopping area. This does not seem to have spoilt many people's meals, and indeed, 'we made a detour to eat here on the way to a wedding and nearly missed the ceremony, as neither of us could bear to pass up a pudding and we hate a bustle.' Prices rose sharply in 1979, and not only with the dropping of the gentle set lunch. But this apart, M Blanc has been the man for all seasons, far beyond the confines of Oxford. Spring, summer, autumn and winter meals have all treated critical eaters to the

281

Meals 12.15–2, 7.15–10

Alc (min £5) £12·50
(meal £15)

Service inc
Cover 50p
Children's helpings
Seats 55
&. rest; w.c.
Air-conditioning
No dogs
Barclaycard

impressive spectacle of a Frenchman in his stride.
'Apart from pappy bread rolls and cool plates, everything was quietly but decisively professional,' says a
good cook renewing his acquaintance with the pancake-
wrapped turbot pâté sauce beurre blanc (£2·85), and
introducing himself to the 'intensely rich and savoury
experience' of poularde aux morilles (£5·15) with its
sauce of Jura wine and marc de Bourgogne. Inspectors'
petit pain truffé sauce porto (a mousse of duck's
liver, beef and veal) and 'gâteau' of Jerusalem
artichokes with an asparagus-flavoured sauce verte,
showed mastery in the marriage of fragility and
unctuousness; ris de veau cressonière (£6·90) confirmed
the *joie de vivre*, and autumnal râble de lièvre sauce
poivrade (£14·95 for two, done rare on request), had
a tangy sauce based on good demi-glace, cranberry
sauce tartlets and other garnishes, and 'sweet and
tender salsify in cream among the vegetables' –
though the gratin dauphinoise potatoes were mediocre.
The repertoire is enlarging all the time, and keep an
eye open for the seasonal or fishy specialities, and less
expensive *plats du jour*. 'For once, eye and palate are
courted together.' But do not expect copiousness,
either of sauce or vegetables: 'It is possible to eat here
often and keep a waistline.' Willingness to cook hot
puddings (order these at the start) yielded 'puffy
soufflés Grand Marnier' (£5·30 for two), 'a lovely
clafouti of cherries marinated in kirsch', and feuilleté
de pommes flambé au calvados. They will not mind
you sharing a mousse glacée pralinée (£1·70) instead.
Service is French, and competent. Coffee is adequate,
no more. House burgundies, red and white, are
£3·85 (the Bordeaux district table wines are £2·35 for
50 cl). Other wines from Edward Sheldon match the
quality and price of the food, with Morey-St-Denis,
Clos des Lambrays '69, domaine-bottled, £14·25.
Château Chalon '59, is £23·30 – they do not actually
say that this is the 'Jura wine' they use for the chicken
dish, but it would make a delightful (sweetish) aperitif
for a large party.

*App: Curzon Couper, Ronald Jones, J. C. Crawford,
Evelyn Rose, A.H., Neil Fairlamb, S. C. Coverly, E.H.,
and many others*

OXFORD Oxfordshire   Map 2

(9) **La Sorbonne**
130a High Street
Oxford (0865) 41320

Closed Sun; public hols;
last week Aug;
1st week Sept
Must book
Meals 12–2.30, 7–10.30

Drake-like, André Chavagnon may insist on finishing
his game of *pétanque* (in which he plays for England)
before joining Mr Benadel in the gallery or cockpit of
this medievally-timbered restaurant near Carfax. But
apart from one spring visitor whose salade niçoise
was a disgrace and médaillons de veau orangina not
much better, scrupulous inspectors award him at least
an alpha-beta for unusual and professional dishes:
gâteau châpon fin (£2·50) or soup (£1·50) or a 'poetic'

Alc £10·30 (meal £14·65)

Seats 60 (parties 30)
No dogs
Am Ex, Diners

artichoke as first courses, followed by veal kidneys in 'a delicious cream and brandy sauce', or cailles aux raisins, or quenelles de brochet lyonnaise, or the longstanding favourite râble de lièvre sauce poivrade (no wonder the Casse-Croûte downstairs, *q.v.*, offers civet). Scampis flambés au Ricard is another speciality. So is crème brûlée, though Cambridge here has something to teach both France and Oxford: even when the Sorbonne's is good it gives the impression of depending on more than just cream, egg yolks, and vanilla sugar, and a Dutch visitor was slightly surprised to be offered the dish with a carapace still bubbling from the grill. Apple sorbet 'awash with calvados' is an alternative. A few grumbles over the coffee. Wines are very dear – ludicrously so in some instances – and the air often smoky, so there is no need to grit your teeth before ordering the house wine (Carafino at £2·40 for 50 cl) or Loires at £6 or so, rather than Ch. Montrose '48, c.b., at £115.

App: Mr & Mrs F. Williams, C.H.C.,
Susan Kellerman, M.M., and others

---

(10) **Sweeney Todds**
6–12 George Street
Oxford (0865) 723421 *and*
45024

'A crust almost French in delicacy'; 'stodgy and greasy pizzas'; 'cheap, adequate toppings, but dry and hard based.' The search for the ideal pizza may be yet another lost cause but a narrow majority prefer Sweeney's bland baking to his demonic barbering. There are 19 pizzas to debate (Sicilian or Neapolitan – £1 to £2·90). 'Friendly service,' and a 50p fee secures you a table-side conjuror. House wine £2·65 a bottle. The tapes 'to our own requirements' (not yours?), the juke-box, the piano and welcomed dogs turn dinner into din-din. More reports, please, of this and the Bath branch (q.v.).

Closed Dec 25 & 26
No bookings
Meals noon–midnight

Alc (min 90p) £3·85
(meal £6)

Service 10%
(parties over 8)

Seats 140
♿ rest
Air-conditioning
Access, Barclay

OXFORD see also wine bar section

When a restaurant says 'must book', the context of the entry usually indicates how much or how little it matters, but a preliminary telephone call averts a wasted journey to a closed door. *Always* telephone if a booking has to be cancelled: a small place (and its other customers) may suffer severely if this is not done.

Numbers are given for private parties only if they can be accommodated in a room separate from the main dining-room; when there are several such rooms, the capacity of the largest is given. Some restaurants will take party bookings at times when they are normally closed.

Country Elephant
New Street
Painswick (0452) 813564

Closed L (exc Sun,
Dec 31 & Jan 1);
Mon; Sun D (exc Apr 6);
mid-Oct to mid-Nov;
Dec 24–26
Must book
Meals 12.30–2, 7.15–10

Tdh Sun L £4·30 (meal
£6·90)
Alc (min £5) £6·55 (meal
£9·30)

Service 10%
Children's helpings
(L under 12)
Seats 38
♿ rest (1 step)
No dogs
Am Ex, Barclay, Diners

Elephantalia (painted, moulded, carved, snapped and alcoholic) and 'original English dishes' on a pink menu comprise the Medforths' version of *la vie en rose*. Painswick is pure Cotswold and the cooking in the elegant dining-room of this stone house follows suit in its blend of rustic and urbane. An inspector charmed by sea salt, fresh butter and sweet peas on the table was further beguiled by crunchy, stuffed cabbage, a feathery pancake of mushroom, onion and bacon (£1·15), Arbroath haddock pie ('not a bone in sight') and a large serving of steak and mushroom pie in 'beautiful' flaky pastry: 'couldn't taste wine but lovely gravy anyway.' Cheese and cream sauces are over-worked. Most vegetables lack the precision and imagination of a member's 'garlicky' gratin dauphinoise. After chicken liver and brandy pâté (£1·10) and a fatty pork chop stuffed with apricots, raisins and almonds in a 'slightly sharp' cider sauce (£4·55), a meringue conch filled with cream and thin butterscotch sauce seemed decadent – and delicious – to one diner. Brown bread ice-cream is at least Victorian. California wines head the thorough list; Napa Valley Pinot Noir '75 (Mondavi) is £4·60; Ch. de Pez '67 is £6·10, and the house burgundy (£3·40) pleases. 'Vegetarians are welcome' at a day's notice.

App: A.J.B., J. H. F. Taylor

Foxdown Manor
near Bideford
off A39
5 m SW of Bideford
Horns Cross (023 75) 325

Closed L; Nov–Mar
(exc Chr)
Must book
D only, 8–9

Tdh £7·50 (meal £9·70)

Service 10%
Seats 38
♿ rest; special cottage
No dogs in hotel
Access card
7 rooms (4 with bath,
2 with shower)
B&B £38–£68 p.w.
D, B&B £80–£110 p.w.
Fire cert

It seems to have been a fast run on good snow in 1979 for these two ex-ski instructors. The Luxmoore-Rosses recently married and set up hotel, with her catering and his eating experience, in a large Victorian manor. There are outlying, self-contained residential cottages where 'the hot water flow is sometimes erratic.' True, the owners are evidently well aware that one customer who fills in a *Guide* form is worth three who don't, but there is nothing perfunctory about the pleasure people express in the woods, lawns and pool, nor in the attempts of a sociable couple to see that their guests meet each other and enjoy themselves. The price of the set dinners has been kept down by eliminating choice, and perhaps also by presenting main courses on large platters complete with (lightly cooked) vegetables. Meals seem well balanced, and Belinda Luxmoore-Ross's soups, 'very crabby quiche', 'admirably served duck à l'abricot or beef in madeira', and 'professional' crème brûlée or coffee brandy meringue are among dishes individually admired. Criticisms include some under-salting, the tendency of the breakfast hot-plates to 'steam' fried foods, and the absence of half-bottles on what is, however, an accessibly priced wine list, drawn from various sources. Hayward's (Provencal?) Sur le Pont ordinaires are £2·60; Ch. Lyonnat '73, c.b., is £5·50. Smoking in the dining-room is discouraged. A pianist plays 'mainly classical' music two nights a week after dinner. Small patio for outside eating. Children and dogs – cats too – are welcome in the cottages, but not in the hotel. (GHG)

App: N. C. Heavisides, Anne Murray, Brian Martin, L. C. Elliott, Gordon Hands, David van de Poll, and others

---

PENZANCE Cornwall   Map 1

Bistro One
46 New Street
Penzance (0736) 4408

Closed L; Apr 6; May 5;
Dec 25 & 26; Jan 1
Must book
D only, 7–10

Alc £7 (meal £10·95)

Service 10%
Cover 25p
Seats 30
Am Ex, Barclay

'The prices are firm, by local standards' but perhaps that judgement of the Harrises' Victorian rooms owes something to the 'bistro' title, for returned visitors 'had no complaints of service, food quality, and general neatness.' 'Avocado and crab were delicately flavoured, garlic bread was superb, duck in port and orange, and John Dory with cheese sauce, just right, vegetables well cooked, chocolate gateau very light, and pot au chocolat luscious.' 'Helpings are if anything too generous.' There are one or two doubters, especially of the wine prices, with French carafes £4·20 a litre, and Ch. Rausan-Ségla '73, c.b., £9. No dogs.

App: Philippa Marnham, M. Dunne

PEWSEY Wiltshire   Map 2

The Close Restaurant
Pewsey (067 26) 3226

Closed Mon (exc Apr 7);
Sun L; Oct 22–29;
Dec 25 D; Dec 31
Must book
Meals 12.30–1.30,
7.30–9.30

Tdh L £4·75 (meal £6·75),
Sun L £5·75 (meal £7·50),
D from £7·35 (meal
from £9·50)

Children's helpings
Seats 35 (parties 16)
♿ rest (1 step)
Car park
No dogs
Am Ex, Diners

It is a far cry from Tighnabruaich, Argyll (where the Aitkens' regime will be remembered by several members from the early '70s) to the chestnut avenue by the Council offices that leads to their handsomely furnished house here. 'Mr Aitken, a slightly Jeevesian figure who also gives off tea-planting vibrations, kept a creditably stiff upper lip when our small daughter addressed him with: "This orange juice is very nice, man." ' Rhona Aitken cooks, as before. Guests fill in appreciative comment cards for the set dinners, perhaps with Elizabethan pork or oxtail braised in burgundy, with lightly cooked vegetables and redcurrant sorbet afterwards; and especially for the Sunday 'tiffin' lunches, with curries and similarly spicy dishes from various lands, at prices the owners hope are within the range of retired people. An inspector's perhaps franker comment card to the Guide *also reported 'virtuous but slightly dull soup and fish mousse, some miscalculations over salt, and unfortunate gooseberry cheesecake, but these are early days, and besides, the coffee was good.' The wines, from £2·75, include a few economical Yugoslav, Spanish and even South African bottles. More reports, please.*

Stilton Dish
on A30
8 m E of Basingstoke
Hartley Wintney (025 126)
2107

An epic-length menu and a Homeric love of epithet (sauces labelled Washington, Carmencita, Mozart and White Horse) disturb some of the Schweimlers' partisans. 'Stick to specialities,' advises one wary man, leading the way with tournedos stuffed with Stilton in port sauce (£4·80). Whitebait has also pleased, but soft vegetables and poor Stilton are complaints. Sweets are passable, and they make their own ices. Wines (Hungarian 50p a glass) 'not styled for big spenders.' 'Many kinds' of recorded music.

Closed L (exc by arrangement); Sun; public hols (exc Apr 4) Must book D only, 7–9.30	Alc £6·65 (meal £9·65) Service 10% (6 or more) Cover 25p Seats 35	🔥 rest (2 steps) Car park No dogs Access, Am Ex

The Kitchen
Fish Na Bridge
on A387
Polperro (0503) 72780

At thirty-one, David Porter 'retired from the world of paper to the world of weight', in this bright, 'open-plan' cottage, and is still learning, he says. Praise for Mrs Porter's cooking and 'unprompted counsel and unfussy efficiency' out front: 'subtle turnip soup, good fisherman's pie (too lavish with potato), ratatouille (50p) and fudgy chocolate cake (75p).' Nicolas white £2·20 for 50 cl. Babies discouraged. Recorded music. No dogs.

Closed L; Mon; Nov–Mar (poss) Must book	D only, 6.30–9.30 Alc £5·55 (meal £7·85)	Seats 12 Access, Am Ex, Barclay. Diners, Euro

Dolphin Hotel
Towngate Restaurant
Poole (020 13) 3612

The Dolphin – a modern building – rolled to the surface in 1979, it seems, because of its carvery, breakfasts, and wine bar: 'Roast beef, Yorkshire pudding, Stilton and kippers are revealing tests for English food, passed easily.' 'Yesterday a ragout of lamb came with fresh rosemary: what a difference.' The Musgraves' chef, M Berthet, also suggests prawns sicilienne (£1·85). Bar snacks too. Wines eagerly chosen and described: Ch. Clerc-Milon '71, £7·95; Baton carafes £2·05 for 50 cl. Well-kept Bass from the cask. Recorded music 'may drown talk, alas.' More reports, please.

Must book Meals 12–1.45, 7–9.45 Tdh (carvery) £3·45 (meal £5·90) Alc (min £3·45) £5·80 (meal £8·90)	Children's helpings (under 12) Seats 60 (parties 60) 🔥 rest Car park No dogs in public rooms	Access, Am Ex, Barclay, Diners, Euro 74 rooms (37 with bath, 13 with shower) B&B from £14 Fire cert

The Warehouse
The Quay
Poole (020 13) 77238

Closed Sun; Sat L;
L public hols;
Dec 24–26 & 31; Jan 1
Must book
Meals 12–2, 7–10
(Fri & Sat 11)

Alc £7·20 (meal £11·25)

Service 10%
Seats 85 (parties 40)
No dogs
Access, Am Ex, Barclay,
Diners

*Military men and others may wonder how Rachel
Greig's Marc Bertrand – named as chef both this year
and last – fitted in (according to her) his year's
French national service between Guide editions.
Visitors reporting inferior meals and slow or confused
service in May and June may be privy to the secret,
and in spite of last year's italics the case must be called
not proven again, particularly as M Bertrand is said to
have returned from France full of cuisine minceur
longings. But, happily, others like the place and its
outlook on the quay, and praise especially the
scallops en brochette ('at £3·25, the best dish any of us
had'), 'accurately cooked whole plaice on the bone, a
difficult thing to do', 'tender and delicious venison
grand veneur with a rather sweet, rich, peppery sauce',
and 'pink lamb cutlets done to a turn.' Potatoes and
salad may be a better choice than vegetables, and 'a
whole Stilton in a Victorian cheese dish' preferable to
humdrum sweets. 'But Polish crystallised plums in
chocolate made a welcome change from After Eights.'
Rhône or Loire house wines are £3·85; Ch. Gruaud-
Larose '67, c.b., £10·20; sweet Ch. Brouset '71, c.b.,
£8·25. More reports, please.*

POOL-IN-WHARFEDALE West Yorkshire   Map 5

Pool Court

Pool Bank
4 m E of Otley
Arthington (0532) 842288

Closed L; Sun; Mon;
Dec 25, 26 & 31;
July 27–Aug 11;
1st 2 weeks Jan
Must book
D only, 6.30–9.30

Tdh £10·75 (meal £14·75)

Seats 65 (parties 24)
♿ rest (1 step, Regency)
Air-conditioning
Car park
No dogs
Barclay, Diners

Michael Gill's well-padded (though to the eye less
inviting) Dales restaurant counts as many *Guide* years
as the Editor does, most of them with food and wine
distinctions. In its attentive but unservile way, its
appeal is catholic: 'There are not many places that
embrace an executive squeezing a contract out of a
Frenchman, a young couple in search of the meal of a
lifetime, a bunch of substantial Yorkshire farmers,
and a brace of London media trendies, but there
they all were, munching away.' Roger Grime cooks,
with Melvin Jordan, and they need to be on their
mettle, given the quality of criticism they receive: 'My
meal no match for Brussels, but prices going that
way. The menu too flowery, the vegetables too
numerous.' 'The trouble with their four-course dinner
was that nearly everything arrived in little gratin
dishes, as at 30,000 feet. The kitchen is over-fond of
nuts and the main sauce for duck was too sweet, but
the vegetables were excellent (including little tarts
filled with creamed parsnips) and the lemon and
chicken terrine I began with was very good indeed.'
Sweetness is criticised by others too, but most people
are more than happy with their evenings, and even
when mistakes are made, they are remedied with
despatch and aplomb. 'The diffident might lose a little
bit of heaven if unaware that the kitchen is very
happy to serve extra sauce with the main dish if
asked.' In detail, note the chefs' own favourites:
carrot and chervil gateau, cream of Stilton and
Guinness soup, flétan la Napoule, and médaillons des

trois filets. Reports also mention gravadlax, 'an architectural mélange of Ogen and other melons enclosing a sorbet of lemon and mint', lamb, salmon, apricot mousse 'with a Persian dome of spun sugar', ices (try lemon and rose petal) and many other things from the cheese pastries in the bar to the petits fours at the end. They have abandoned a brief experiment with cheaper meals in the Cellar, but again people ask, 'with different rooms to play with, surely smoking could be banned in one of them?' The wines and the advice given about them are excellent but 'service is rote-like: they tremble for a diner keen enough to lift a bottle but are reluctant to bring or leave water. They also try to edge you to the lounge for coffee even if you are sitting over wine.' They have picked a dozen wines from £3·25 to £4·70 (Ch. Senailhac '76, c.b.) for everyday drinking; or you may browse among Yorkshire Fine Wines' Montrachets or Romanée-St-Vivants at ten times as much. Those who remember Raymond Postgate's tastes will be interested to see the long run of Ch. Cissac – alas, mostly in double figures. 'There is usually a Gill about to see you off.'

App: D. M. Gaythwaite, J.S.S., G. M. F. Boucher, W.F., Anne Hardy, D. E. W. Bennett, and others

---

PORLOCK WEIR Somerset   Map 1

Ship Inn
on B3225
1½ m NW of Porlock
Porlock (0643) 862753

Closed L (exc bar & winter); Dec 25 D
Must book D
Meals 12.30–1.45, 7.30–8.45

Tdh L from £3·50
(meal £6·15), D from £5
(meal £8)

Seats 24
⑤ rest (2 steps)
Car park
No dogs in public rooms
5 rooms (all with bath)
B&B £9
D, B&B (3 nights) £35

Pandy Sechiari confesses to slight surprise at receiving the *Guide*'s questionnaire after a year of upheavals and alterations – 'at times I have been truly ashamed of the standard of food.' One or two visitors share the surprise – 'awash in poor sauces . . . no clear-cut tastes' – but most people are grateful for an on-the-spot proprietor who actually notices 'everything down to a missing butter-knife', and is not above helping his wife and chef in the kitchen in spite of owning, now, two hotels. (He has bought the Anchor next door, and people mostly report well of their stays and breakfasts there, but prefer on balance to eat their midday bar snacks and evening dinners at the antique Ship.) 'I stayed for eight days and did not have a single dish twice, or a single frozen vegetable, even in May. Apart from an overcooked duck and plaster-of-Paris meringues, the cooking was excellent, especially a locally made boudin aux pommes, and a peach pie with superlative pastry.' Whitebait ('my American table neighbour was explaining to his friends that the eyes didn't bother you if you put each one in head first'), mackerel, steak and kidney pie and crème brûlée are also praised, and lobster sometimes arrives on the set meals (the price is governed by your main-course choice). Italian Primanova red or white wine is £2·70 a litre, Bass and Courage bitters are on hand-pump, and the

main wine list (not yet seen this year) is by David Baillie
Vintners. No pipes; 'collar and tie preferred'; and
children are discouraged in both hotel and restaurant.
Mr Sechiari was not Savoy-trained for nothing.

*App: R. C. Lang, H. F. H. Barclay, Peggy Moore,
John S. Gordon*

PORTHLEVEN Cornwall   Map 1

That Mott
Cliff Road
Helston (032 65) 62460

The keen young owners of this simple little place
bridle easily, even at admiring comments in the
Guide, but this reflects their own high standards. They
offer 'an extensive cold buffet at lunch-time in
summer', 'really fresh plaice', 'excellent' oxtail,
'lovely home-made soups', 'a lobster Newburg to
compare with Mme Prunier's', 'light and
well-composed puddings.' Set dinners with a
frequently changed menu (crab pâté, mushrooms à la
grecque, moussaka, kidneys in sherry sauce, banana
fool with rum); conventional Sunday roast lunch;
home-made cakes at tea-time. Service is friendly and
competent. Small, reasonably priced wine list, with
good 'house plonk' at under £3 the litre.

Must book

Tdh L £2·25 (meal £4),   Seats 28
D £5·85 (meal £8·20)

PORT ISAAC Cornwall   Map 1

Slipway Hotel
Port Isaac (020 888) 264

*The Slipway nearly slid out of sight this time but a sale
fell through and the Scotherns are here for another
season, to the relief of 1979 visitors who have enjoyed
the owners' cooking and comfortable housekeeping.
'They find and keep good local suppliers', and fish may
be best: 'very light salmon mousse'; 'clean-tasting
sole florentine.' But roast lamb, guinea-fowl, fresh
vegetables, home-made bread, and 'alluring' sweets
(apricot in madeira meringue and raspberry and
cherry brandy trifle) are also praised. 'Informal service,
sometimes harrassed, but friendly.' Please keep us
informed.*

Closed L; Dec 24–26
& 31; Jan 1
Must book
D only, 7.45–9.30

Tdh £5·85 (meal £8·25)

Alc £8·35 (meal £11·05)

Children's helpings
(under 12)
Seats 40

Car park (res)
No dogs
11 rooms (2 with shower)
D, B&B from £16
Fire cert

PLEASE keep sending in reports, as soon as possible after each meal. The cut-off
date for the 1981 Guide is September 30, 1980, but reports are even more useful
earlier in the year, especially for the remoter areas and new places. Late autumn
reports can also affect corrections at proof stage.

Potters Lodge
1 Barnet Road
Potters Bar (0707) 59976

On a glance at the international section of Costas Nichols' menu you may murmur the old *Guide* line *timeo Danaos et scampi ferentes* but kebabs, moussaka, kleftiko and stifado can be eaten here more comfortably and (at under £3) no more dearly than elsewhere. Take the Greek wines rather than the carafe or the dearer French ones. 'No jeans.' Music.

Closed Sun; Dec 25 & 26
Must book weekends
Meals 12–2.30, 6–11.30

Alc £5·20 (meal £6·60)

Service 10%
Cover 30p
Children's helpings
(under 12)
Seats 60

🚫 rest
Car park
No dogs
Access, Am Ex, Barclay, Diners

Well House
🍷

3½ m S of Taunton
Blagdon Hill (082 342) 566

Closed L (weekdays
mid-Sept to mid-May,
exc Dec 25); Mon;
Sun D; Tue L; Dec 25 D
Must book weekends
Meals 12.30–1.30, 7–9.30

Tdh Sun L £6·30 (meal
£9·20)
Alc £6·80 (meal £9·70)

Children's helpings
Seats 40
🚫 rest (1 step)
Car park
No dogs

In recent years, this Tudor 'Great Kitchen' in the rolling country between Taunton and the Blackdown hills has been one of the West Country's most scrutinised places, and it now shows signs of settling down under Ralph Vivian-Neal, with Laurie Boston taking an interest in the wine list from retirement nearby, and Graham and Margaret Cornish as chef and manager. They are kind to children, and one visitor calls the place 'triumphantly British' after three months in the US, and that was on the strength of chicken liver pâté and Armenian kebabs for dinner rather than the roast beef Sunday lunch. (A landscape historian was pleased to find 18th-century parish maps as table mats, though he had little time to stare at them since 'the meal was served promptly and efficiently.') Graham Cornish's specialities are themselves native rather than foreign, with rabbit brawn and pickled cherries (85p) as a first course, and Devonshire squab pie (£3·75) or pheasant on spiced lentil puree (£4·30) as main courses. 'Playce with garlick and mustard (c. 1680)' should also be noted, and spicy tomato soup, salmon and lamb are praised. But 'the Sunday beef was tough and hacked about in Mr Cornish's absence, and the squab pie showed an inch gap between the hard pastry and the contents below.' 'Crème velour is exceedingly rich with cream cheese and chocolate', so for lighter relief try, perhaps, the ginger ice-cream or peaches in vermouth with hazelnut biscuits (95p). 'Excellent coffee.' The new wine list continues Mr Boston's exploration of unfamiliar areas, beginning with 15 table wines in the £2–£4 range, chosen by six named wine merchants. Beyond this, Ch. Frontenac '75 is £7·45 and half-bottles of sweet Cérons £2·60. There are a few tables in the garden.

App: M. W. Beresford, Eileen Mitchell, S. J. A. Mort, R. G. W. Caldicott, H.W., and others

POYNINGS West Sussex   Map 3

Au Petit Normand
2 The Street
off A281
6 m NW of Brighton
Poynings (079 156) 346

Closed L (exc Sun);
Mon; 1st week Sept;
Dec 25 & 26; Jan 1; Feb
Must book
Meals 12.15–2 (Sun),
7–9 (9.30 Sat)

Tdh Sun L £3·25 & £4·50
(meal from £5·95)

Alc £7·45 (meal £10·85)

Cover L 15p, D 40p
Seats 22
⑤ rest (2 steps)
No dogs
Access, Am Ex, Barclay

'Take a torch if you eat late, for there's no street light for miles,' says one visitor to Christian and Wendy Debu's diminutive restaurant (itself if anything too well lit). The service is 'affable but sometimes shoestring', but there are no complaints of M Debu's cooking, including the Sunday set lunch – 'by far the best value we have found.' At dinner, 'ficelle normande (£1·10) was hot and creamy and cheesy as it should be, and even a vegetarian mother-in-law found the avocado moussed to perfection (with leeks). Poussin à la moutarde and saumon grillé were both excellent, and not many places would warn diners off the quail because "it came boned so it's a bit flat".' 'Flat or not,' says another man, 'quails in apple and calvados sauce were gorgeous.' Canard aux poires (£3) and médaillons de boeuf périgourdine (£4·70) are specialities. For sweet, expect tarte normande or crème brûlée, followed by good coffee. Red or white vin du patron is £3·25 and there are others in most categories under £5 on the short list, as well as Normandy cider sometimes. Recorded music. 'Children over five are welcome.'

App: Angus Wells, Alan Sayer, H.N.M., and others

PRIDDY Somerset   Map 2

Miners' Arms
4 m NW of Wells
at junction of B3134 &
B3135
Priddy (074 987) 217

Plain Elizabethan inn on the Mendip plateau, 'used by travellers, sheep drovers and freelance lead miners', and now handy for Cheddar Gorge or Chewton Mendip's cheese-making farm, the Priory. New owners (the Haslams) recommend the local snails (£1·15 for six), home-smoked loin of pork, and Priddy oggy with scrumpy sauce (£3·10). Their set lunch saddened an inspector ('tough meat, mushy vegetables'), but from the *carte* others like whitebait, scampi bisque (£1), steak Theodora (tender beef with brandy and herbs, but tinned peach and sweetcorn), and almond and mocha galette. French house wine £3·80 the litre; Eldridge Pope (IPA) from the cask or ale 'from the smallest brewery in the country' (O.G. 1047). 'Light' recorded music. No pipes. No children under five at dinner.

Closed Mon; Sun D
(exc Apr 6); Dec 25 & 26
Must book
Meals 12–2, 7–10

Tdh £3·80 (meal £6·55)
Alc £6·70 (meal £9·85)

Children's helpings
(under 10)
Seats 45

⑤ rest
Car park
No dogs
Barclay, Diners
3 rooms
B&B £6·90–£10·35

For the explanation of ⑤, denoting accessibility for the disabled, see 'How to use the Guide', p. 4.

PRIORS HARDWICK Warwickshire Map 2

Butchers Arms
5 m SE of Southam
Byfield (0327) 60504

Lino Pires is a surprising landlord to find in these parts. Soup, grilled sardines, langostinos, and mixed fried fish are worth ordering in this 600-year-old inn, along with the steaks and game Midlanders expect. But hors d'oeuvre may be preserved rather than invented, venison terrine and bread both 'rubbery', and vegetables and sweets 'uninspiring'. Drink the Portuguese wines in the £6 range rather than the double-figure clarets. 'Chaotic service sometimes.' You may eat outside in summer. Bar snacks (except on Sunday); pressurised beers.

Closed Sat L; Sun D;
D Dec 25 & 26; Jan 1
Must book D & Sun L
Meals 12.30–2, 7.30–11

Tdh Sun L £5 (meal £7·35)
Alc £7 (meal £9·35)

Service inc

Children's helpings
Seats 90 (parties 38)
 ♿ rest
Car park
No dogs

PULBOROUGH West Sussex Map 3

Stane Street Hollow
Codmore Hill
on A29
Pulborough (079 82) 2819

Closed Sun; Mon; Sat L;
last 2 weeks Apr;
3 weeks Oct; public
hols (exc Apr 4 & Jan 1)
Must book
Meals 12.30–1.15, 7.15–
9.15

Tdh L £2·50 (meal £5·40)

Alc £6·20 (meal £9·45)

Children's helpings
Seats 32 (parties 24)
♿ rest (2 steps)
Car park
No dogs

Fresh food, serious cooking – and the custom that both attract – are hard work, and one admiring visitor wondered how the Kaisers coped as he retreated from the crowded bar to his table for an aperitif. But give or take the kind of delay that is actually rather encouraging if you have ordered duck, this cottage remains the 'best value in the district'. First courses are especially imaginative: 'oeuf en cocotte royale (65p), in a ragoût fin of chicken livers and madeira sauce, was delicious'; 'the thin, deep-fried slices of ham filled with cream cheese, asparagus and garlic impressed me greatly.' Chicken variants, and tongue ('better than the ham', an inspector suggests) with a flavoury caper sauce, are popular main courses, and it is worth waiting for René Kaiser's crisply cooked half-ducks with interesting sauces based on vegetables or fruit, not flour. Trois filets mignons, with a mushroom cream sauce (£5·15, including vegetables, probably from the garden) is another speciality. Blackberry bombe (85p), hazelnut meringue with apricots, and other less seasonal sweets are up to the best Swiss standards, and the good coffee comes with 'home-made shortbread as a pleasant change from After Eights.' Nicolas ordinaires are £4 a litre, and in 1979 Ch. Meyney '67, c.b., was £8·95.

App: B. G. Laker, T.R.J., M.R., J. A. Seiffert

Prices quoted in entries now include VAT.

Most places will accept cheques only when they are accompanied by a cheque card or adequate identification. Information about which credit cards are accepted is correct when printed, but restaurants may add to or subtract from the list without notice.

RAMSBURY Wiltshire   Map 2

The Bell at Ramsbury
5 m NW of Hungerford
Ramsbury (067 22) 230

Closed Mon; Sun D;
public hols (exc Apr 6 D,
Jan 1)
Must book D
Meals 12.30–1.45,
7.30–9.45

Tdh L £5·50 (meal £7·85),
D £6·50 (meal £8·95)
Alc £10·45 (meal £13·30)

Service 10%
Children's helpings
Seats 60 (parties 40)
Air-conditioning
Car park
No dogs
Am Ex, Diners

'Brian and Rosemary O'Malley looking after
everything, as usual,' writes the *chef-patron* merrily
– optimistically, suggests one dissenter who arrived
early and was exiled to the crowded bar to await the
typing of menus. Others bear the wait with patience
and fortitude, knowing that these virtues are less
required at table; in fact, the odd vice might come in
handy, for the heartiness of the 'true English food'
invites gluttony and promotes sloth. The next 'cold,
cold evening' will tempt one ever-hungry inspector
back for a share of the electric log fire and another go
at 'creamy smoked mackerel pâté (£1·65), Dublin Bay
prawns deftly combined with dill mayonnaise, moist
grilled salmon (£5·75) and sharp apricot brandy
cream (more apricot than brandy, but very good all
the same).' Many first courses issue from the smokehouse – loin of pork with orange salad (£1·70),
'salty' cod's roe (£1) – and even smoked chicken
grilled with bacon (£4·50) among the main courses.
(Diners are 'discreetly discouraged' from smoking
their own nearest and dearest at table.) Boursin and
watercress mousse is a rare concession to delicacy,
roast beef and Yorkshire was 'too much but too good
to leave.' The 'ordinary' set menu offers an interesting
choice of humbler dishes such as steak and pigeon pie
and devilled kidneys, though the alluring puddings
cannot veil their richness: 'exotic rhubarb and ginger
mousse, splendid syrup and lemon tart' and 'a
powerful blackcurrant sorbet'. Bar lunches (which can
be eaten in the garden) are even better value, but
stale rolls and 'inappropriate' vegetables are hazards.
'Prompt and helpful staff (some *very* young) serve.'
Fair prices on wines from Berry Bros and others
include ordinary claret at £3·60, and many half-bottles
(Ch. Cos d'Estournel '67, £4·85, Ch. Montrose '67,
£4·90) among finer wines. Wadworth's 6X and IPA
are on hand pumps. No children under ten at night.
'Clean' dress requested.

App: M.A.P., C. A. Mitchell, C.A.W., A. T. Langton

RAMSGATE Kent   Map 3

Mallet's

58 Queen Street
Thanet (0843) 52854

Closed L; Sun; Mon;
Dec 25, 26 & 31; Jan
Must book
D only, 7.30–10.30

Perhaps the Liberal Assembly went to Margate in
1979 solely so that the more discerning delegates and
media men could drive round to Ramsgate to eat: at
any rate, Simon Mallet's converted shop is a band-
wagon that members have been jumping on as early
as they could. Mr Mallet's career includes the Wife of
Bath at Wye and the Riverside at Helford (both *q.v.*)
and a patisserie venture in London. Here, apart from
reservations about 'noise, smoke and heat, especially
late in the evening', experienced inspectors have few
hesitations, from the dish of plump olives on the

Alc £6·45 (meal £9·75)

Cover 35p
Children's helpings
Seats 40
♿ rest; w.c. (2 steps)
Access, Barclay

tables at the start to the fudge with coffee. 'There is a sense of caring for people and food even when the two conflict, as with the party at the next table who drank coffee before the meal and wanted a dish based on rare steak to be well-cooked.' 'Fresh gooseberry chutney with the lamb was not even on the menu but they offered me some to try.' 'When I asked for a spoon to finish the sauce of the tripe a second helping was suggested.' First course ideas include monkfish dusted with Parmesan and deep fried, 'very garlicky' mushrooms with bacon in red wine on a crisp croûton, and 'best of all, brandade of smoked mackerel, hot in little pastry turnovers, with a dill-seed cream as a perfect foil.' Main courses at a test meal, generously helped, were the pot-roast shoulder of lamb with butter, garlic and rosemary, and a crisp duck done with green olives and thyme. Both were excellent, though 'the salad with a good lemony dressing was a better accompaniment than the vegetables (normally excellent) actually served that night.' Fish naturally varies with local landings. Sweets have included fresh dates with a lemon-flavoured cream cheese, a pile of apricots and cherries in white wine, a tangy lemon sorbet, and blander vanilla ice-cream with blackberry puree. The Costières du Gard red or Bastide white ordinaires at £3·50 and £3·20 seem sound – just as well since most of the few clarets are in double figures. Recorded music does not make it any quieter.

App: D. R. Gildersleve, H. J. Hooper, W. I. Jenkins, J. & M.B., and others

---

REDLYNCH Wiltshire   Map 2

Langley Wood
off B3080
6 m SE of Salisbury
Earldoms (079 439) 348

Down in the woods, someone is stirring a pot at the Pearces' isolated house – but enquire for detailed directions when you book, as well as anything else you need to know, since they are silent this year. 'Not outstanding, but worth an entry round here for eagerly described pear suprême (80p), guinea-fowl in brandy and cream (£4·10) with fair vegetables, and strawberry Pavlova.' Other cooked first courses, along with a heavy programme of main dishes, do the owners' energy credit. Routine wines with few half-bottles, apart from white Graves at £2·35. Expect a certain formality, easy or uneasy.

Closed L; Sun; Dec 25 & 26; Jan 1
Must book
D only, 7.30–9.30

Alc £7·80 (meal £10·85)

Children's helpings
Seats 40

♿ rest (1 step); w.c. (M)
Car park
No dogs

See p. 441 for the pub section, and p. 491 for wine bars.

1980 prices are as estimated by restaurateurs in the autumn of 1979 (including VAT).

REETH North Yorkshire   Map 8

Burgoyne Hotel
9 m W of Richmond
Reeth (074 884) 292

Wild Swaledale, ramblers' breakfasts and unforced geniality make up, people say, for the Cordingleys' drab decoration and 'mixed cooking'. The care that marks beef in beer, boiled mutton in caper sauce, lamb chops, or even tandoori chicken, should also yield better vegetables and cheeses ('take the Wensleydale'). Smoked haddock quiche and aubergine casserole make fair first courses. 'Effort also goes into sweets': rhubarb tart, grape and blackcurrant brûlée. The Spanish carafe is £1·90 for 50 cl and Entre-Deux-Mers '78 is £3·70; or drink pressurised Webster's bitter (one rain-drenched visitor was offered a pint in the bath). 'It pays to be punctual.'

Closed L (exc Sun, Apr 7, May 5 & 26, Aug 25); Dec 24–26 & 31; Jan 1 Must book Meals 1–1.45 (Sun), 7.30–8	Tdh Sun L £3·15 (meal £5), D £5·90 (meal £8·05) Service 10% Children's helpings (under 10) Seats 35	♿ rest Car park No dogs in d/r 10 rooms B&B £8·35 Fire cert

RICHMOND North Yorkshire   Map 8

Serino's
Rosemary Lane
Richmond (0748) 3664

A simple and friendly little Italian place (due to expand onto two floors) with a relative in Yarm (q.v.). The menu – short enough to inspire trust – might offer prawns with garlic butter and a wine sauce (£1·70), cannelloni, or devilled chicken livers, followed by pork fillet with an orange and raisin stuffing and orange sauce ('tender and tangy', £3·60) or lamb either with a pepper sauce or pizzaiola (£3·30). Vegetables are admirably al dente (and included in main-dish prices). The star of the sweets is a rum-flavoured chocolate pot. Italian house wine, £3 the litre; Barolo '73, £4·20. More reports, please.

Closed Sun; Apr 4; Dec 25 D; Dec 26; Jan 1 Must book D Meals 12–2, 7.30–10.15	Alc £6·15 (meal £9·05) Children's helpings (under 12)	Seats 25 No dogs Diners card

---

Towns shown in black on our maps contain at least one recommended restaurant, pub or wine bar (see map key). The dot denotes the location of the town or village, not the establishment. Where necessary, we give directions to it in the entry. If you can, help us to improve them.

Inspections are carried out anonymously. Persons who pretend to be able to secure, arrange or prevent an entry in the Guide are impostors and their names or descriptions should be reported to us.

If you think you are suffering from food-poisoning after eating in a restaurant, report this immediately to the local Public Health Authority (and write to us).

RIPON North Yorkshire   Map 8

Hornblower
Duck Hill
Ripon (0765) 4841

'An elegant place', though service seems moribund at times. Set dinners, priced by choice of main course, may offer 'excellent' cheese poppets or cannelloni, white fish au gratin or Italian stuffed mushrooms; then devilled crab, 'delicious steak au poivre with a hot, rich sauce' (£6·75), or chicken breast in Marsala and cream (£6·20 – prices include fresh vegetables). Pineapple Romanoff and fruit pies may be wiser than brown bread ice-cream. 'Complaints well received.' Still some bargain Rhône wines: Gigondas Domaine de la Chapelle '76, £5·95. French house wine £3·30 the bottle; Muscat de Beaumes de Venise by the glass. Children must eat early.

Closed L; Sun; Mon; Dec 25 & 26 Must book D only, 7–9.30	Tdh from £6·95 (meal £9·80) Children's helpings	Seats 22 No dogs Barclaycard

RIPPONDEN West Yorkshire   Map 5

Over the Bridge
on A58
6 m SW of Halifax
M62 exit 22 or 24
Ripponden (042 289) 3722

Over the bridge (and hard to find) but not over the hill, members say. Set dinners with fair choice in each of four courses. Flowery setting, competent service. Dishes liked include gazpacho, cock-a-leekie 'with chicken enough for a main dish', spinach and shrimp crêpe, crab mousse, stuffed fillet of pork, 'moist and heavenly salmon', ballotine of duck with a nut stuffing and sauce, with good vegetables and sweets. First courses may be too heavy for rich main ones. No wine details from the owners, but halves of Chablis '77 or Kreuznacher Kahlenberg were under £3 in 1979. No under-tens. The related Old Bridge Inn on the other bank serves a weekday lunchtime buffet.

Closed L; Sun; public hols (exc Apr 4 & May 26) Must book D only, 7.30–9.30	Tdh £9·75 (meal £11·40) Service inc Seats 45	♿ rest Car park No dogs Am Ex card

---

The Guide News Supplement will be sent out as usual, in June, to everyone who buys the book directly from Consumers' Association and to all bookshop purchasers who return the card interleaved with their copy. Let us know of any changes that affect entries in the book, or of any new places you think should be looked at.

See p. 508 for the restaurant-goer's legal rights, and p. 510 for information on hygiene in restaurants.

Unless otherwise stated, a restaurant is open all week and all year and is licensed.

Please report to us on atmosphere, decor and – if you stayed – standard of accommodation, as well as on food, drink and prices (send bill if possible).

ROMILEY Greater Manchester   Map 5

Waterside
166 Stockport Road
3 m E of Stockport
between A560 & A626
061–430 4302

A Mancunian deserts his local 'dear and dismal dives' for the set lunch at Monty Small's 18th-century cottage by the canal. The warm welcome is sometimes only metaphorical, and someone's mother ate in her coat and gloves. The *carte* is overlong and many dishes clumsily presented, but people praise amply helped pâté, bisque de homard (£1·45), game pie (on the set lunch), jugged hare and 'tipsy hedgehog, heavy, boozy and delicious.' Vegetables, sometimes too soft, may include salsify. Gently priced wines (n.v. Veuve Clicquot or Moët & Chandon, £8·30 in 1979); Italian or French house wine, £3·30 the litre. Wear a tie.

Closed Mon; Sun D;
Sat L; Dec 25 & 26;
Jan 1
Must book
Meals 12–1.45, 7–9.30

Tdh L £3·60 (meal £6·05)
Alc £7·75 (meal £10·60)

Children's helpings
(under 12)

Seats 36
♿ rest
Car park
No dogs
Access card

ROWSLEY Derbyshire   Map 5

Peacock Hotel
on A6
3½ m S of Bakewell
Darley Dale (062 983) 3518

Hedgehogs in the garden, grayling in the Derwent, Haddon Hall down the road and a good breakfast in a comfortable stone house go far with many. Main meals are more pot-lucky: 'If they did less they might do it better.' Sweetbreads and roast duckling have been praised, but the wise may look for simple smoked trout, roast beef, steak and kidney pie and suchlike. Expect steaks and vegetables to be overdone; sweets seem to have fallen off in 1979; but be grateful for baked bread and raw but willing service. Weekday lunchtime bar snacks; Burton ale (pump); and routine big hotel wines (Fleur de Lys, £3·20). (GHG)

Must book
Meals 12.30–1.30, 7–9
(Sun 7–7.45)

Tdh L £4·50 (meal £6·60),
D £7·75 (meal £9·85)

Service inc
Children's helpings
Seats 50 (parties 30)
Car park
No dogs in public rooms

Access, Am Ex, Barclay,
Diners, Euro
20 rooms (11 with bath,
4 with shower)
B&B £13
Fire cert

RUGBY Warwickshire   Map 5

Andalucia

10 Henry Street
Rugby (0788) 76404

Closed Dec 25 D; Dec 26
Must book weekends
Meals 12–1.30, 7–10.30

Last year's entry, for the first time in fifteen years, had the tone of an awkward interview in Dr Arnold's study, but the Izquierdos and their loyal chef Carlos Garcia seem to have taken the hint. Habitués, too, have emerged to defend an old favourite against charges of slackness: 'The boisterousness and even the showing-off on the unvarying menu are well meant, the service is genial, and you can eat very well if you keep to the Spanish seafood dishes and flambés that they are good at.' Duck liver pâté, crab soup, whitebait, and fresh sardines are among the first

Tdh L £3·45 (meal £6·50)
Alc £6·70 (meal £11·65)

Cover 25p D
Children's helpings
(under 12)
Seats 60 (parties 50)
 ♿ rest
Air-conditioning
No dogs
Access, Am Ex, Barclay,
Diners

courses praised, and 'medallones of lobster and chicken lived up to their description.' So did paella marinera (£4·30), zarzuela de mariscos (£5·15) and banderilla Moruna (£3·75) for other visitors. Kidneys al Jerez (£2·30) is a more modestly priced speciality. Set lunches, whether with braised ham or a curtailed version of the paella, remain good value, and at slack times they will let you have a first course as a casual snack. Most of the sweets are mildly nonsensical but 'we always find crêpes Suzette hard to resist', and 'if they can be persuaded to do it, their cold zabaglione is splendid.' The Spanish wines are beguiling, from their own imported Rioja '74 red or Banda Dorada white '74 at £4·60 to comparative rarities such as Faustino Primero '70 at £7·75. Live and recorded flamenco music.

App: Katharine Goodwin, Robert Whitehouse, P.J.R.J., M. F. a'Brook, Gerald Froyd, A. Taylor, and others

---

RUSHLAKE GREEN East Sussex Map 3

The Priory
6 m SE of Heathfield
Rushlake Green (043 56)
553

Closed Dec 23–Jan 17
Must book
Meals 12.30–1.45, 7.30–9

Tdh L £5·75 (meal £9·10),
D £8·95 (meal £12·15)

Service 12½ % (res)
Seats 38 (parties 18)
Car park
No dogs in public rooms
Access, Barclay, Diners
10 rooms (all with bath)
B&B £16·45–£20·80
Fire cert

Augustinian monks from Hastings began to build on this site in 1412, and lived here until Henry VIII bestowed the house on his Attorney-General; somehow it has kept the thousand peaceful wooded acres in which it stands. So much initially rested on the Dunns' first manager and chef Karen Roozen (*q.v.* under West Stoughton) that last year's entry was suspended when she left, but the present team of cooks (unnamed) have been doing consistently well, it seems. One visitor reports 'an outstanding meal in which rather dry croquette potatoes and past-rare noisettes of venison were the only perceptible faults. Prawns with aïoli, and caramel mousse, were perhaps the high points.' A test lunch confirmed this good opinion, featuring chicken liver pâté with prunes, a terrine with herbs and chicken fragments, and chicken in red wine with onions and mushrooms. 'Roast beef was cooked rare, and though I have had better gravies than the thick one that smothered too much of it, the Yorkshire pudding was creditable and the roast potatoes and runner beans both delightful.' Devilled seafood pancakes, duck with elderberries, and rack of lamb with pepper sauce are other dishes to look out for, and among sweets, prune and port fool and chocolate and Cointreau ice-cream. The bread rolls are home-made and good. The wines (from £3·75 for French red or white) are of little moment and too reticently described: if you are spending £5–£6, though, take Spanish red rather than English white; beyond that, there are sound '73 clarets. No pipes or cigars in the dining-room. No children under nine as residents. (GHG)

App: Mr & Mrs F. L. Lees, E. Bickerstaff, J. & M.B.

RYE East Sussex   Map 3

The Monastery
6 High Street
Rye (079 73) 3272

Closed Tue; L Oct–Mar
(exc Sun)
Must book D
Meals 12.30–2, 7–9.30

Tdh L £4·50 (meal £7·65)
Alc £6·30 (meal £9·60)

Service 10%
Cover 25p
Seats 44
♿ rest
No dogs
8 rooms (7 with shower)
B&B £8–£11
Fire cert

This restaurant with rooms ('the nature of the building is against them on the hotel side, but at least the rooms are clean and reasonably priced') was taken over in 1979 by Messrs Culverhouse and Moore. Welcoming smiles are backed up by the aroma of freshly baked bread or simmering fish soup, and the menu might then offer creamed spinach tart with 'a good balance of cream sauce and spinach' (90p), prawn thermidor, pâté or salads, followed by Dover sole in cider and cream (£4·50), pigeon pie, Romney roast ('a full best end of lamb remarkably tender though not quite pink enough for me, seasoned with garlic and rosemary', £8·50 for two) or kidneys Cantator (with burgundy, mushrooms and peppers, £4·30). Vegetables are crisply cooked – 'though the duchess potatoes were slightly dry.' The trolley sweets may include 'a generous and magnificent raspberry and almond slice', and there are sorbets and ices, as well as 'good strong coffee'. The wine list is unambitious, but Givry '76 (Louis Latour) at £6·90 in 1979 was thought good value; Cuvée St Pierre house wine is £2 for 50 cl. Note that children under seven are accepted only by special arrangement, and that weekday lunches are served in summer only. Recorded classical music. More reports, please, of further changes and improvements, including the campaign to stop all Romney pré-salé lamb going to France, rather than to browbeat the French into letting it in.

RYE see also pub section

ST ALBANS Hertfordshire   Map 3

Aspelia
17 Heritage Close,
High Street
St Albans (0727) 66067

Seasoned travellers from Sir John Mandeville's ancient city whitewash their Hellenic memories at this busy place in a modern shopping precinct. Some lapses in taste or temperature, but taramosalata 'smooth and tangy' and psarosoupa (salmon, that day) 'beautiful'. Fillet steak in cream and brandy sauce (£3·75), and year-round strawberries (£1·50) mix happily with dolmades, kebabs, and moussaka (short on aubergines at times). Meze – tastes of many dishes – costs £5·75. Greek and Cypriot wines around £4. 'Attentive' waiters: 'I defy anyone to refill his own glass.' 'Hectic' eating in the wine bar or on the terrace. Recorded Greek music, 'ancient and modern'.

Closed Sun; public hols
Must book D
Meals 12–3, 6.30–11

Alc £6·25 (meal £9·55)

Cover 50p
Seats 70

♿ rest
Air-conditioning
No dogs
Access, Am Ex, Barclay,
Diners

Diomides Taverna
97 St Peter's Street
St Albans (0727) 33330
and 34155

Closed Sun; L Dec 25 &
26; L Jan 1
Must book
Meals 12–3, 6–11.30

Alc £6·50 (meal £9·50)

Service 10%
Cover 30p D
Seats 50 (parties 40)
No dogs
Access, Am Ex, Barclay,
Diners

Spelt after the extrovert Famagustan owner rather
than the lumpish Argive hero, this immaculate,
'wicker, rush and cane' restaurant on the old A6 has
hoovered up a local Clean Food Award as well as
praise for its cooking and 'Cypriot hospitality'. 'The
atmosphere is more refined than the usual taverna',
and the open grill consumes £5 worth of charcoal a
day. Sheftalia, 'home-made sausages stuffed with
chopped pork, onion, rice and fresh herbs', are
£3·40 and served with lemon, good rice and 'a very
mixed salad (including tasty mushrooms).' Olives,
peppers and hot pitta are gratis at lunch, so moussaka
at £3·30 is not such a bad deal: lamb, plenty of
aubergines, and 'eggy custard'. Tsatsiki is a 'stimulating'
first course; and note too the grilled haloumi goat's
cheese, 'excellent' taramosalata (95p) and grilled
loukanika and pastourma sausages. Grilled fish would
make a nice addition to the lamb and pork. A 'tangy'
sponge covered with orange and lemon cream is
reported; home-made yoghourt and baby walnut
preserve are other alternatives to bought-in sticky
sweets and there is loukoum with the coffee. Greek
house wine is £3·50 a bottle, or drink water from
'exquisite terracotta ewers'. 'Pop and bouzouki music
unquenched.'

App: H.C., S.S., J.T.

Cotehele House
off A390 and A388
2 m E of St Dominick
St Dominick (0579) 50434

They cook simply as 'a service to National Trust
members and paying visitors' in this medieval manor,
but the fresh food and cheerful staff ('kind to children
too') are alone worth the trip. One or two hot dishes
(apricot roast lamb, £1·90, 'excellent steak and kidney
pie', £2·10, with fresh vegetables), tasty soups (45p),
fruit gateaux, queen of puddings, crumbles, pâté,
ploughman's and cold buffet for snacks. Milton Abbot
Countryman cider. Routine wines, 60p the glass.
Cornish cream teas. Up to 50 per cent reduction for
children. No smoking, and 'fresh air a-plenty.'

Closed D; Nov–Mar
Open 12–5.30 (L 12–2.30)

Alc L £3·50 (meal £6·45)

Children's helpings
Seats 100

♿ rest; w.c.
Car park
No dogs

Wine prices shown are for a 'standard' bottle of the wine concerned, unless another
measure is stated (e.g. litre, 50 cl., or pint).

Meal times refer to first and last orders.

Do not risk using an out-of-date Guide. A new edition will appear early in 1981.

ST IVES Cambridgeshire   Map 6

Slepe Hall
Rugeley's Restaurant
Ramsey Road
St Ives (0480) 63122

Peter and Maggie Scott's restaurant (with James Edwards as chef) succeeds better than the public rooms and service in their hotel (a revamped Victorian mansion). 'Even on the food side, more goodwill should accompany the amateurism that had a waiter open a carving trolley with a flourish, only to find no beef there.' But 'Bell Inn smokies are far better than the present Bell Inn's', joints have good gravy, and 'sweets are good, notably a cream with raspberry liqueur.' Stilton croquettes with tomato dip (£1·20) and omelette normande (£7·45) are specialities. Ample bar snacks which you may eat outside at lunch-time; pressurised beers. Wines from £3·60, some fine.

Closed Dec 25
Must book D
Meals 12–2, 7–10

Tdh £6·05 (meal £9·25)
Alc £8·90 (meal £13·90)

Children's helpings
Seats 50 (parties 28)
Car park
No dogs in d/r
Access, Am Ex, Barclay, Diners

15 rooms (9 with bath)
B&B £12·50–£19
D, B&B £14–£25 (min 2 nights)
Fire cert

ST JUST Cornwal.   Map 1

Seabird
West Place
4 m N of Land's End
St Just (0736) 788 509

'Making an effort' runs an early report on this 'semi-formal place'. It fits the steak pattern to a T-bone, but cuts few corners: crab soup 'hot, home-made and served with fresh brown rolls'; 'properly trimmed and grilled' lemon sole. Steaks of various sizes, plain or sauced (sirloin £3·20, including vegetables). Frozen scampi and (with sweets) tinned cherry topping may be locally demanded. 'Cream with cheesecake is otiose except in Cornwall.' Stowells wines and beer. There is smoke on both sides of the bar. 'Light' music. 'Small, polite dogs only.'

Closed L; Sun (winter);
Mon (exc May 5 &
Aug 25); Dec 25 & 26
Must book

D only, 6.30–10.30

Alc £4·10 (meal £7·20)

Children's helpings
Seats 50
♾ rest; w.c.
Car park

ST JUST IN PENWITH see under BOTALLACK

ST MARTIN IN MENEAGE Cornwall   Map 1

Boskenna

off B3293
5 m SE of Helston
Manaccan (032 623) 230

Closed L; Dec 24–26
Must book

As Parsifal, Clarissa and others tend to show, it is hard to make virtue interesting, and what is one to do about a house whose every visitor makes it clear to the *Guide* that here, in the far west, is where the rainbow ends? John and Patricia Munro, no less unusually, are equally kind about the people the *Guide* has sent them, and with few bedrooms and so many repeat bookings it is tempting to let them all get on with it, but for the fact that providers and consumers

D only (res only), 7.30–8
(or by arrangement)

Tdh £5 (meal £5·50)

Service 10%
Seats 8
♿ rest
Car park
No dogs
Unlicensed
4 rooms (1 with bath)
B&B £8

elsewhere need to know what can be achieved by two hospitable and civilised people with a graceful house, tactful pets ('even the parrot only spoke when we were not listening') and a rare talent for cooking. A couple used to the best in restaurants do not expect to eat a better meal anywhere than Mr Munro's crab soup, made from that morning's deliveries, served with just the right seasoning and delicate croûtons, and his crisp, succulent roast duck with brandy and fresh orange sauce, and 'peas so delicious we ate them with our fingers'; followed by Mrs Munro's raspberry Pavlova, with a perfect contrast of fruit and meringue, tartness and sweetness. 'A casual remark about sweet things with coffee brought Mrs Munro back into the dining-room half an hour later with a dish of still-warm walnut fudge.' Some have wondered about the breadth of the repertoire, but many reputations have been built on less than the Munros' own (incomplete) list: borshch and consommé with cream and caviare for soups, fish pâté and devilled crab, avocado mousse and mushroom provençale, lasagne and fisherman's pie, roast beef with herby Yorkshire pudding or 'slices of sublime lamb with apple jelly', 'whisky pud,' and crème brûlée with fresh pear or white peach (there is no choice until the sweet stage) – never forgetting the breakfasts which evidently make parting guests reluctant to tear themselves away. Packed lunches can be provided. The place is not suitable for children under 14, dining-room smokers, or evening jeans-wearers, though there exists a TV as well as stereo, grand piano, and books. 'Now go and do likewise,' one is tempted to say to any hotelier who has read this far – but at these prices, something like sanctity must be accounted a necessary qualification. Remember to pack your own wines and spirits, which are served without corkage.

App: David & Ann Murdoch, Dr & Mrs D. Worrall, G. Wilson, F. & L. Gill, Steven Parsons, and many others

---

ST MAWES Cornwall Map 1

Green Lantern
Marine Parade
St Mawes (032 66) 502

Closed L (exc Sun);
mid-Dec to mid-Feb
Must book
Meals 12.30–2, 7–9.30

Tdh L £4 (meal £5·70),
D £7·50 (meal £9·20)

Service inc

'My only criticism is of cold plates.' The panorama of the busy harbour and bay from this comfortable, recently redecorated hotel would soften rebuke anyway, but the Browns allow the critic few openings. We could do with more in-season reports, but early visitors were impressed by Elizabeth Brown's deft treatment of a menu that would pall in lesser hands: scampi provençale and deep-fried mushrooms with garlic mayonnaise much liked, duckling blessed with crisp skin and 'balanced orange sauce'. 'Excellent seafood Mornay and entrecôte bordelaise.' Browns cook, greet, serve and draw beer so it is no surprise that the family boat doubles as a trawler, though the

Seats 50
No dogs
Am Ex, Barclay, Diners
11 rooms (4 with bath,
1 with shower)
B&B £9·80
D, B&B £15·50
Fire cert

table's share of the catch is conservative: plaice, sole, crab claws and lobster (thermidor or salad, £4·60 extra). One visitor reports 'ratatouille beyond words'; others an unvarying choice of vegetables for residents. 'Trolley sweets – chocolate roulade, lemon torte, black cherry cake – were creamy yet light.' Wine prices make other places look greedy, with plenty under £6 (Hérault, Domaine de la Caumette, £2·95; Ch. Bellevue '71, £4). Pressurised beers. No children under ten. Recorded music in the bar.

App: A. S. Mercer, V.L., and others

Rising Sun
St Mawes (032 66) 233

Closed Nov 20–Dec 29
Must book
Meals 1–1.45, 7.30–8.45

Alc (min £5) £6·85 (meal
£10·75)

Service 10%
Seats 50
♿ rest
Air-conditioning
Car park
No dogs in d/r
20 rooms (13 with bath,
2 with shower)
B&B £14·55–£18·70
Fire cert

Recipe in *Second Dinner
Party Book:* Ogen melon
with raspberry sherbet

The effluxion of time means that Mrs Campbell Marshall's flowery doll's-house hotel by the sea front 'has a period Noel Coward feel whose formality is disconcerting if you have just landed from a damp dinghy.' But this and other writers say that the staff are in fact very kind, and that Jeffry West's cooking gets better and better 'at prices tolerable for the age.' 'Lamorna fish soup was this time an excellent white soup with plenty of fish in it, and the terrine was good too. We shared a rack of lamb and enjoyed the salsify and the mint and orange sauce that went with it.' Another guest recalls 'an outstanding vol-au-vent filled with chicken, mushrooms and sweetbreads in a subtle cream and wine sauce, fennel very well cooked and served with butter and parsley, and crisp green beans dusted with nutmeg.' The home-made rolls – perhaps flavoured with garlic, or orange and parsley – are a pleasure, as was 'a fresh trout for breakfast, steamed with butter and oregano.' (Sometimes fried fish has had commercial crumbs.) Scallops au gratin, baked grey mullet stuffed with crab and avocado (£5·20, including vegetables) and melon with raspberry sherbet are other favourite dishes, and 'there were mountains of strawberries and cream.' Other helpings too are far from doll's-house. The ordinaires are Carcassonne red or Bordeaux white, and other wines include Wehlener Sonnenuhr Spätlese '75 (Bergweiler) and Vosne-Romanée Les Beaumonts '70 in the £8–£9 range. The lunchtime bar snacks are deservedly popular (you may eat them outside). Pressurised St Austell beers.

App: Mrs K. Warner, Sheila Griffiths, F.M.J., N.R.H., Ron Salmon

---

Entries for places with distinctions carry symbols (pestle, tureen, bottle, glass). Credits are fully written entries, with approvers' names below the text. Passes are telegraphic entries (useful in the area) with details under the text. Provisional entries are in italics (see 'How to use the Guide', p. 4).

Prices of meals underlined are those which we consider represent unusual value for money. They are not necessarily the cheapest places in the Guide, or in the locality.

Rivermede Country House Hotel
on A586
9 m NW of Preston
St Michaels (099 58) 267

Horse-and-groom has given way to bride-and-groom here, but the style of the Fielding family's hotel is set now: 'mannered but pleasing decor', 'really good glass and china', 'well-drilled unobtrusive service.' Grooming is less obvious in the kitchen, 'though they have got over the floral-platter stage of Cordon Bleu.' Hits in the four-course dinners include 'delicate but positive' chilled cucumber soup, garlicky chicken liver pâté, guinea-fowl with lovage sauce, 'ideal' beef Stroganoff, and 'very light' gooseberry and almond tart. But cream of lettuce soup may lack both cream and seasoning, roast pork has been tough, hollandaise for fresh salmon watery, and vegetables over-sauced and overcooked. 'Bloated rather than transported,' is an inspector's phrase. House wine, £3·99 the litre. 'Well-behaved and forewarned' children are welcome. (GHG)

Closed L; Tue; Dec 25–Jan 31
Must book
D only, 7–9

Tdh £8·95 (meal £11·90)

Children's helpings (under 10)
Seats 50 (parties 10)
♿ rest (3 steps); w.c.
Car park

No dogs
Access, Am Ex
3 rooms (with bath)
B&B £14

Wellington's
84 Fore Street
Salcombe (054 884) 3385

Closed L; Sun (Oct–Mar);
Dec 25 & 26;
mid-Jan to end Feb
Must book
D only, 7–11

Alc £7·15 (meal £10·70)

Service 10%
Children's helpings
Seats 72
♿ rest
No dogs
Access, Am Ex, Barclay, Diners

The Duke of Wellington's own boots form the menu logo, but the Hales and the Evanses accept the drenched sou'westers of yachtsmen into their sunnily furnished room as easily as they do the greatcoats of more sedate winter customers. Their chef, Terence Pates (with Penny Distin to do the puddings), has wandered Australasia and Indonesia before settling here, so along with a feeling for shellfish expressed in the plateau de fruits de mer and crab with garlic mayonnaise you may find Chinese spare ribs, Afghan skewered lamb, and Javanese chicken (ayam roedjak). The menu changes twice a year. A very satisfactory test meal included the crab bisque (85p) and venison cutlets in 'a rather sweet gooseberry and wine sauce which nevertheless matched the venison well.' 'Carrots and creamed leeks were overcooked.' Speciality steaks are also popular. 'A huge helping of bass béarnaise (£4·95) was taken back for filleting at once when the waiter saw that a guest's aged mother could not cope.' 'Understandably, they can never take raspberry and hazelnut meringue off the menu' (95p). Johnson-Marr vin de pays red or Blanc de Blancs is £2·75 for 50 cl on a short list – too short and conventional for a lover of fish and white wine together. Children under twelve may be fed at reduced rates in the early evening: enquire. Recorded music. More reports, please.

SALISBURY Wiltshire   Map 2

Le Provençal
14 Ox Row,
Market Place
Salisbury (0722) 28923

Closed Sun; Sat L;
Dec 24–26 & 31; Jan 1
Must book
Meals 12–1.30, 6–10.30

Tdh L £3·60 (meal £6·30)
Alc (min L £3·60, D £4)
£8·25 (meal £11·45)

Seats 34 (parties 20)
Air-conditioning (lower rest)
No dogs
Am Ex, Barclay, Diners

'Don't laugh, but we are doing lunches yet again,'
writes Edward Moss, disarming as usual, and possibly
not unaware that a change of regime at Crane's half a
mile away gave his own close-packed two floors a fresh
opportunity. By bad luck, it is too early to tell about
the lunches, whereas some of the early autumn's dinners
suggested that Mr Moss and his young assistant Peter
Barker had not yet mastered the new pressure or
devised dishes proof against lapses in timing or taste.
Few restaurants with similarly stretched resources stand
in greater need of the maxim faites simple. At its best,
the food is excellent: 'crab soup with chilli such a
change from dingy bisque; duck with cherries as crisp
and delicious as I can remember'; 'splendid crudités and
ragout of smoked fish'; and 'good crème brûlée even if a
pickaxe was needed for the top.' But hot avocado,
mushrooms à la grecque, and médaillons de porc have
all been examples of dishes that would be better with
fewer elements, and sauces have been floury sometimes.
Service is heavily worked, and though wines (from
£3·30 for the house Gamay or Sauvignon) are
enterprising, especially in the Rhône and Loire sections,
unrestrained smoking can still be a nuisance. Also,
'half-way through a first course is too late to be told
that the red wine one has ordered is "off".' No children
under seven. Please report further as reorganisation
proceeds.

SANDBACH Cheshire   Map 5

Wheatsheaf
1 Hightown
Sandbach (093 67) 2013

Closed Sun; Dec 25 D;
Jan 1
Must book D
Meals 12–2.30, 7.30–10

Alc buffet L about £2,
D (min £3·75) £6·25 (meal £9·10)

Cover D 20p
Seats 24 (parties 20)
♿ rest
Car park
No dogs in d/r
Access, Am Ex, Barclay, Diners

*For want of anything better to do with this pub on the
family estate, Colin Crewe (Quentin's brother) has
made a restaurant of it, with trompe l'oeil effects in
the dining-room, and two young people in charge:
Keith Read, who waits dapperly, and Caroline
Swatland, who cooks. The range is sensibly limited,
with a cold table and hot dish at lunch-time, and in the
evening à la carte dinners, with about half a dozen
choices in each course. Mushroom tartlets and Cheshire
cheese beignets with tomato sauce (£1·05) are first
course specialities. An inspector reports good crudités
with garlic bread along with first course pâté and
salmon mousse, competent rolled lamb cutlets and
bouchée aux fruits de mer, 'outstanding' pommes
dauphine, other good vegetables (including baby onions
in brown sugar and white wine), and agreeable home-
made ginger or brown bread ice-creams. 'Even the
biscuits in the bar seemed home-made.' The wines
(from £3·15) are modest. John Courage from the cask.
Recorded music. More reports, please.*

For the explanation of ♿, denoting accessibility for the disabled, see 'How to use the Guide', p. 4.

Lanterna Ristorante
33 Queen Street
Scarborough (0723) 63616

Closed Sun; Mon;
Dec 24–26 & 31; Jan 1
Must book D
Meals 12–1.30, 7–9.30

Alc £7·35 (meal £10·60)

Seats 36
♿ rest
No dogs
Barclaycard

For all its faults – an inspector who enjoyed the food counted ten 'on the periphery' – Gianluigi Arecco's bay-windowed restaurant is without peer in the area. In consequence, celebrities and carpet-baggers compete for attention with local lunchers. Yet serious (though never solemn) eaters have priority and are indulged with second and third helpings. The owner's forays to London may bring fennel or asparagus, and lobster or sole may adorn the table inside the door, but the *carte* is conventional enough. Daily specials keep the interest of diners (and perhaps the chef): at one meal, fresh crab (£1·70), 'tender carne (beef) tonnato in a fragrant bath of tuna mayonnaise and capers' (£1·15), polpette in tomato sauce, and osso buco – 'three veal knuckles with saffron rice, a sharp garlic and lemon peel garnish, a mild tomato sauce and a marrow spoon (£5·20).' Begin with lasagne or, better, 'paradigmatic' spaghetti carbonara (£1·15), rather than taking them as a main course (£4). The fruit gateaux are extravagant – 'layers of cream and raspberries stacked on a light sponge and crowned with peaches, almonds, and strawberries.' Brandy-snaps served with coffee are put in the shade. Bread, though home-made, is dry sometimes, and Neptune Cocktail 'should stay in the depths.' Signor Arecco imports his Barbera wines from Piedmont: 'serviceable' in carafe (£3·45 for 75 cl) and 'admirable' in bottle ('71 is £4·60). Italian halves are elusive. Smoke, close tables and chafing dishes make for discomfort and the 'spirited waitresses could be better informed.' No babies. Recorded music, 'sometimes loud'.

App: P.O'R.S., P.H., D.N.C.F., J.R.D.

Yew Tree
8 m SW of Keswick
Borrowdale (059 684) 634

'Why aren't there more places serving decent, casual food outside scheduled hours?' demands one grateful afternoon visitor to the Martins' fell-walkers' refuge at the foot of Honister Pass. Teas with home-made scones and jams are popular. Even more so are ham and vegetable broth, bacon and egg, Cumberland sausage with salad and mushrooms (£2), 'lovely omelettes', grilled sirloin (£3·75) and apple pie and cream. 'They are very nice to children', and allow them smaller helpings at two-thirds price. Pressurised beer; a few wines (from £3 for 75 cl).

Closed Mon; Sat L;
Nov 8–Mar 31
Must book D
Open noon–8 (6–9.30 Sat)

Alc £4·05 (meal 6·60)

Children's helpings
Seats 45

♿ rest
No dogs
Access card

SEAVINGTON ST MARY Somerset   Map 2

The Pheasant
off A303
at Seavington St Michael
South Petherton (0460)
40502

Tenth *Guide* year for this cheerful and 'reliable' thatched hotel and restaurant off the main road: 'good for an overnight stay.' Bar and buttery lunches (which can be eaten on the terrace) are 'useful and ample': meat platters, help-yourself salads, and a few hot dishes. The kitchen's evening favourites coincide with dining-room choices: haddock in crab and sherry sauce (£2·70), duck with liver, onion and wine sauce (£2.70). Ham and mushroom pancake before, and walnut gateau after, are also singled out from the long menu. Generous coffee. No carafes, but a long, tolerably priced list from £2·90; pressurised beer; good malt whiskies. Dress neatly for dinner. (GHG)

Closed Sun D (exc res);
last 2 weeks Sept & Feb;
Dec 25 & 26
Must book D
Meals 12–2, 7–9.30

Alc £5·60 (meal £8·20)

Seats 56
♿ rest
Car park

No dogs
11 rooms (8 with bath)
B&B from £9
Fire cert

SELLACK Hereford & Worcester   Map 2

Lovepool Inn
3½ m NW of Ross-on-Wye
Harewood End (098 987)
236

Closed L (exc bar); Sun;
Dec 25
Must book
Meals (bar) 12–2.30,
7–10.45; (rest) 7–9.30

Alc £5·90 (meal £7·85)

Service inc
Children's helpings
Seats 36
♿ rest
Air-conditioning
Car park
No dogs

Richard and Trish Stammers added this sensibly furnished restaurant, built of surplus elm, to their black-and-white 17th-century inn shortly after they took it over. Their other addition was two young cooks, Susan Price and Karen Haydon, who have already astonished two critical visitors by the provision of 'a dish, not a blob' of home-made mayonnaise with a simple pub lunch of smoked mackerel and salad, and by a dinner whose precisely cooked potatoes, cauliflower and courgettes commanded attention even before the pork olives, veal chasseur, veal with fennel and olives, fruity cheesecakes, and raspberry and loganberry meringue that others also mention. Fully inclusive dish prices for specialities include venison in red wine (£4·25), pork fillet with Marsala and mushrooms (£3·50), chicken Foy (with white wine and prawns, £3·20), and half a duckling with Grand Marnier sauce (£4·50). Choix du Roy carafes are £3 a litre, but it would be wiser to skip direct from the Wadworth and Penrhos bitters or Weston's rough cider on hand pump to Mr Stammers' enterprising list of wines from unfashionable regions. This provides plenty of drinking under £3, as well as striking if, alas, irreplaceable burgundies such as Morey-St-Denis '70 at £8·80. Cockburn's '67 port is 75p a glass. Monday night may be 'grill night'. You can eat outside. No rooms. More reports, please.

When a restaurant says 'must book', the context of the entry usually indicates how much or how little it matters, but a preliminary telephone call averts a wasted journey to a closed door. *Always* telephone if a booking has to be cancelled: a small place (and its other customers) may suffer severely if this is not done.

Corin's
Church Farm
off A27
7 m SE of Lewes
Ripe (032 183) 343

Closed L (exc Sun);
D Sun & Mon; Dec 24–
26 & 31; Jan 1
Must book
Meals 1 (Sun), 7–11

Tdh Sun L £3·50
(meal £5·75), D £6·50
(meal £9·05)

Seats 24
♿ rest
Car park
Access, Barclay

Lewis Carroll wrote *Alice Through the Looking Glass* in this village, and though the walrus moustaches of Sussex embrace prawn cocktail more often than oysters under the blanched beams of this 1602 farmhouse, Geoff Corin's cooking of four-course dinners has a refinement Dean Liddell's daughter would have approved, by inspectors' accounts of his lovage or lettuce and cucumber soups, seafood mousse with tomato sauce, fillet of plaice with prawns and spinach and 'excellent Sunday roast beef with a rare centre.' Potatoes, carrots and cabbage were alike well cooked. Beef Louisette is another speciality, and Mr Corin is making some very suave sweets now: 'very light' raspberry gateau, Elizabethan orange flan, and 'darkly oozing' French apple tart. French table wine is £3·45, and there is a sound list (not supplied) beyond, with good Vouvray, and Ch. Beychevelle '71, c.b., at £14·25. The family wait very competently.

App: E.L.F., S.S., Angela Frost

SELMESTON see also pub section

SHANKLIN see ISLE OF WIGHT

Just Cooking
16 Carver Street
Sheffield (0742) 27869

Cheerful and friendly self-service spot in the basement of the Shape Design Shop. Well-spaced, swiftly cleared tables, with flowers and jugs of water – and special touches like heart-shaped cakes for Valentine's day – win a loyal following. Praise for 'hearty or delicate soups' (barley broth or avgolemono), a light hand with pastry for quiches (65p) and steak and kidney pie (£1·20), the daily casserole (lamb comes with lemon, or prunes and almonds, £1·60), various salads and fruity puddings (chocolate cheese triangle 'less prosaic than its name', 65p). French house wine, £2·15 for 50 cl; fresh fruit juices. No-smoking area. Recorded classical music. They will also open in the evenings for sizeable parties.

Closed D; Sun; Mon;
Apr 4; Dec 25, 26 & 31;
Jan 1
No bookings

Open 10–5.15 (L 11.45–
2.45)

Alc L £2·80 (meal £5·15)

Service inc
Children's helpings
Seats 70
Air-conditioning
No dogs

We rewrite every entry each year, and depend on fresh, detailed reports to confirm the old, as well as to include the new. The further from London you are, the more important this is.

SHEPTON MALLET Somerset Map 2

Blostin's
29 Waterloo Road
Shepton Mallet (0749)
3648

Closed L; Sun; Dec 24–26;
Jan 1
Must book
D only, 7–10

Alc £5·80 (meal £9·75)

Children's helpings
Seats 28
♿ rest
No dogs

There is not much room for either chefs or guests here, and the recorded music (or behind-the-bar smoker) may make the place seem even smaller. But Bill Austin is a resourceful man ('the rabbits which ate three hundred broccoli plants in one night later found themselves cooking gently in white wine and mustard at £3·30 a helping'), and people praise his mushrooms with aïoli, salmon mayonnaise as a first course, chicken breast stuffed with Stilton, and roast suckling kid with rosemary and garlic in a sauce that leans on the scrumpy he gets from Worthy Farm. Mange-tout peas are a vegetable the rabbits missed. Zuccotto, chocolate turinois (85p) and other sweets are praised, but in view of much cream elsewhere there ought to be an escape route at this stage. Service and presentation are variable. Wine prices are fair, at £3·30 for Averys St Maroc or Bordeaux Blanc, and £18·35 for magnums of Ch. Gruaud-Larose, c.b., '71. The three Spanish bottles under £5·50 are also worth a glance.

App: M. G. & V. A. Hart, W. Voyle, M. J. Cox, L.D.R., G. S. James, and others

Bowlish House

Wells Road
off A371
Shepton Mallet (0749)
2022

Closed Sun L; Dec 25 &
26
Must book
Meals 12–1.30, 7–11

Alc £8·90 (meal £12·70)

Service 12½%
Children's helpings
Seats 30
♿ rest; w.c.
Car park
No dogs
5 rooms (1 with bath)
B&B from £10

Brian Jordan has always lifted a pretty fork, whether in his old mechanical handling days or now as a restaurateur. The regime in this solid, secluded, Georgian merchant's house is looking more stable than its predecessor's, with a heavy ballast of wine in the cellar and Martin Schwaller in the kitchen, assisted by Mrs Jordan (who will take over if Mr Schwaller moves on) and Barbara Swire. Rooms, too, are being upgraded, and a disabled guest reports generous treatment. Most people are well content with their meals now that the owners are getting over their terror that guests might leave hungry – though 'an ample lady appeared in the bar fanning herself and declaring that she was unused to meals of this magnitude and nothing but a large brandy would settle her.' The bread at the start is 'claggy and tempting' with the garlic and fresh herb butters supplied – 'the garlic one greatly improved the mushrooms Café de Paris first course.' Lotte à l'escargot (£2) and Ogen melon filled with a mixture of apple, orange, cucumber and mint in local scrumpy are other possible beginnings. Turbot with sorrel, kidneys with cream and mustard, and lightly cooked vegetables are also praised, though steaks are apt to be done a minute too long, and at a test meal 'capers and brown-fried onions destroyed all delicacy in porc dijonnaise.' Arabian lamb, red mullet with olive and avocado sauce, and boeuf en croûte cochonnaille are other ideas. Sweets usually repay the effort that goes into them, and 'a crisp flan with caramel-and-walnut filling and a chocolate topping was a sensation.' An inspector's Chewton Mendip Cheddar 'would have benefited from six more months in the cellar to mature.' Mr Jordan now runs his own wine firm, and offers more than 65 at under £4·50, including six house and six dessert wines by the glass, not to mention Michael Eavis's scrumpy. At higher levels, the eyes dazzle at the '67 clarets in the £12 range and the '66s in the £20 one, and dessert wines are most beguiling. No pipes or cigars in the dining-room. Enquire about the winter weekend rates.

App: John MacAuslan, Felicity Riddick,
R. J. Parish, H.F., D.J.M., and others

SHIPSTON ON STOUR Warwickshire Map 2

White Bear
High Street
Shipston on Stour (0608)
61558

Closed Sun; Mon D;
Sat L; Jan 3–Feb 4;
public hols (exc Apr 4 &
Jan 1)
Must book L & weekends
Meals 12–2, 7.15–9.15

Alc £5·55 (meal £8·30)

Service 10%
Seats 25
♿ rest; w.c.
Car park
No dogs in d/r
7 rooms
B&B £6–£7
Fire cert

Hugh and Suzanne Roberts' homely old pub was a tentative last-minute choice for the 1979 edition, but apart from a couple of dissentients who criticised both the food and the housekeeping in May, people are warmly grateful for the value given in an over-priced district. Mrs Roberts varies her weekly à la carte menus with zest, and they are better balanced than they used to be. Mushrooms à la crème and spare ribs with garlic and honey are 'especially good first courses', says a man who called in for a glass of beer and stayed for a month; smoked fish hors d'oeuvre and 'delicious parsley and lovage soup' began another couple's dinner that continued with fillet of pork in pastry, steak, and fresh vegetables, restoring faith in the provender of rural inns. Cassoulet (£3·20) or scallop kebab (£3·40) and 'an intriguing duck, sage and apple pancake' are other dishes to look out for. Sweets may include treacle tart (50p), pavé au chocolat, or home-made ice-creams. 'But I ought to have known better than to try zabaglione trifle.' Bar lunches (with hand-pumped Bass and M&B XI) are simpler but here too, much will be home-baked. Spanish Rocamar is £3·20 a litre, and there are a few better wines, mostly under £5. 'Children often eat high tea with our own.' 'No music and not much other noise, though the bar is the only public room, and the restaurant tightly packed.'

App: Julian Lloyd Webber, Michael Hordern, R.G.,
E. H. Webb, R. Brown, R. J. Knecht, J.S., and others

The Guide accepts no advertising. Nor does it allow restaurateurs to use its name on brochures, menus, or in any form of advertisement. If you see any instances of this, please report them to us.

'Meal' indicates the cost of a meal for one, including food, coffee, a half-bottle of one of the cheapest wines listed, cover, service, and VAT (see 'How to use the Guide', p. 4).

SHREWSBURY Salop   Map 5

Penny Farthing
23 Abbey Foregate
Shrewsbury (0743) 56119

Closed Sun; Mon; Apr 4;
Dec 25 & 26
Must book
Meals 12.30–1.45, 7–9.30

Tdh L £6·25 (meal £8·50)
Alc £7·60 (meal £10·50)

Service 10%
Children's helpings
(under 10)
Seats 32
 ♿ rest (1 step)
Car park
No dogs
Access, Diners

Twelve consecutive *Guide* entries is no bad record for anybody, even though Chris Greenhow's 'cluttered dark room, claustrophobic like granny's parlour', has always had its critics as well as its admirers. However, one of the former returned this year to praise his scallops au gratin – 'for once the dish was full of large pieces of fish' – and half a duckling in cider and honey sauce – 'an idea I can't wait to try at home.' Rack of lamb with rosemary provided the eater with five pink cutlets, a well-made madeira sauce and a fingerbowl on the side. A test meal found the mushroom and lovage soup, the pepper toulonnaise (£1·40) and the sweets superior to the main courses (fresh turbot with a rather runny hollandaise and entrecôte with an under-seasoned sauce au poivre vert). Wild duck Grand Marnier (£5·25, including vegetables) is a speciality, but 'partridge in October was so tough that it may be inadvisable.' Banana and honey ice-cream (85p) remains a favourite, and may even be less sweet than the chocolate roulade. The Tanners of Shrewsbury wine list is enterprising and fairly priced, with six house wines from France, Spain, Italy and Yugoslavia under £4, and much claret of good years under £10: Ch. Gruaud-Larose '73, c.b., £8·20. 'No smoking preferred.'

App: Stephen Adams, T.S. & H.J.W., John Tyrie

SKIPTON North Yorkshire   Map 5

Oats
Chapel Hill
Skipton (0756) 3604

Not everyone can expect the free litre of house wine that was bestowed on one visitor for demanding seconds of strawberry vacherin, but most agree that 'sweets are something special' (whisky and oatmeal syllabub, plum and port fool). Stilton and onion soup and deep-fried Camembert are imaginative and popular starters. 'Excellent kidneys in rich wine sauce' versus 'over-rich oeufs en cocotte and spaghetti alla carbonara.' Discrepant reports on the treatment of the scruffy in this 'preserve of the nattily-suited.' 'Boisterous' staff may need prompting. Italian Valgardello £3·75 for a litre. There is a terrace for outside eating. 'Subdued' music.

Closed Sun; Mon;	Tdh D £10·50 (meal	Seats 62 (parties 25)
Dec 25 & 26; Jan 1	£13·85)	♿ rest; w.c.
Must book D	Alc L £4·95 (meal £7·75)	Car park
Meals 12–1.30, 7.15–9.30		No dogs
	Children's helpings	Access, Barclay

If you think you are suffering from food-poisoning after eating in a restaurant, report this immediately to the local Public Health Authority (and write to us).

Stumbles
134 East Street
on A361
South Molton (076 95)
3683

Closed Sun; Dec 24–26;
Jan 1; 2 weeks Jan
Must book
Meals 12.30–2, 7.30–10

Alc £5·40 (meal £7·95)

Service 10%
Seats 36
Access, Am Ex, Barclay,
Diners
3 rooms (all with bath)
B&B £9–£10
Fire cert

Colette Neil has left her parents' home at Chittlehamholt (q.v.) to open up on her own in this little restaurant with rooms, an easy stumble from the square. Her home training – augmented by the Hole in the Wall in Perry-Smith days – appears to be standing her in good stead, according to early but warm reports of lunchtime stuffed pancakes and 'deliciously dressed fresh salad', and various hamburgers in the courtyard at the back. The carte is more elaborate, and Colette recommends her hot crab puffs (£1·15), calf's liver in red wine and herbs (£3·15), chicken Xérès (£2·95) and apricot and almond flan. Others mention the vegetable soup, 'delicious' seafood gratin, 'vast and rich' steak in port, chocolate and chestnut ice-cream, and the Stilton. 'Service started rather dour, but it thawed.' There are some interesting wines, at modest prices, and the French and German house wines are £3·25 for 70 cl. 'Soft background' music. Smaller helpings for children. Car park. No dogs. The building next door will become a 'small, high-class hotel' if the planners approve. More reports, please.

Oaklands

8 Palmer Street
South Petherton (0460)
40272

Closed (rest) L (exc Sun);
Sun D; Mon; 2–3 weeks
June & Oct; Dec 25 & 26
Closed (Pump Room)
Dec 25 & 26
Must book
Meals 12.30–1.45 (Sun),
7–9.30

Tdh Sun L £5 (meal
£7·05), D £7·70 (meal £10)

Service 10%
Children's helpings
Seats 40 (parties 16)
♿ rest; w.c.
Car park
No dogs
Am Ex, Diners
3 rooms (1 with bath)
B&B £8–£10·50

Six years have lodged the Chapmans' early Victorian house off the A303 very firmly in members' affections, and its quality is now singularly even, whether you are looking for a celebration dinner, a passing meal in the (sometimes wintry) Pump Room where 'smoked mackerel pâté and steaks are both models of their kind', or a short stay in a quietly served, well-furnished house with books on the shelves. (With so few rooms, a 'tureen' distinction would extend a promise hard to fulfil.) Hilary Chapman's set meals are cleverly composed and interesting to read – 'we always end up taking samples from each other's plates.' One such menu presented, among first courses, fresh crab and cucumber tarts, 'delicious fondant de volaille Père Bise with really hot toast', succulent baked prawns in garlic butter, and – for robust appetites, considering the rest of the meal – a Burmese fish curry with well-cooked rice. Salmon quenelles, too, are 'fluffy and light'. Poached salmon hollandaise, likewise, 'preserved the flavour and texture better than any other versions I have tasted', and piccata alla Marsala had 'a delicious, slightly sharp sauce'. Vegetables, mostly home-grown, are much better cooked than they used to be. An inspector's roast beef for Sunday lunch 'had its own gravy, and a good home-made horseradish sauce.' Among the owners' favourite dishes, note baked sea bass with Pernod, and Heidelberg gateau. Margaret Siddall makes the sweets now, and there are notes of 'unbelievably light apricot Pavlova' and 'dark, chocolaty mousse'. 'It is the best pudding trolley we have ever been offered twice.' Stilton and Cheddar may be taken before or after this indecorous orgy. Some think coffee might be improved, but breakfasts are praised. The wines, from various sources, are more than a match for the kitchen's best efforts, with half a dozen ordinaries from £3 upwards, well-chosen Spanish, English, Rhône and Loire wines in the £4–£7 range, including four vintages of Noël Sabon's Châteauneuf-du-Pape, and better clarets in half-bottle than are normally seen (among '70s under £6, Chx. Pontet-Canet, Cantenac-Brown, Lynch-Moussas and others). The '71 hocks are no less impressive. Recorded classical music. No pipes or cigars in the dining-room. They prefer you to dress formally. Enquire about special winter dinner, bed and breakfast rates.

App: by too many members to list

Old Bakehouse
20 St James Street
South Petherton (0460)
41117

Closed Sun; Dec 26 & 26;
L Jan 1
Must book D & weekends
Meals 12.30–2.30, 7.30–10

Alc L £2·10 (meal £4·30),
D £5·20 (meal £7·70)

Seats 30
⑤ rest (2 steps)
No dogs

Duncan Gordon, for many years chef at Charlton House, Shepton Mallet, has settled in a quietly converted shop in this now well-favoured village, and is cooking, by early accounts, virtuous, often inviting, food at bearable prices. Tenderloin of pork with calvados and apple (£3·40, including good vegetables) and a 'vast' salmon steak with fennel and cream seemed the best value on a trial visit. Cheese beignets (80p) had the fresh tomato sauce over, not around, cream of watercress soup was 'too white to be encouraging' (celeriac and Stilton soup, 60p, may be better) and raspberry slice 'had mostly crisp pastry, and was not too sweet.' Wines began modestly at £2·80 a litre for ordinaire in 1979, with a few others. Smaller helpings for children under eight. Recorded music is 'mainly Peter Skellern on the piano.' More reports, please.

SOUTHPORT Merseyside   Map 5

Peking Garden
52 King Street
Southport (0704) 30169

Warm towels may be the real reason, but members claim that the spirited cooking alone has revived their interest in this friendly place, out of the *Guide* since 1977. In this genre, set meals are worthwhile: the chef chooses, and apart from 'cornfloury' soup has done well with crispy duck pancakes, 'delicate prawn' or 'wafer-thin marinated beef' with crunchy peppers, and even 'good, lean sweet-and-sour pork'. Crispy seaweed and sesame prawn toast (£2·20) win approval à la carte; mutton and spring onion deserves investigation. Peking dry white wine is 68p a glass.

Closed L; Mon;
Dec 25 & 26
Must book
D only, 5.30–11
(Sat 11.30, Sun 10.30)

Tdh from £3·50 (meal
from £4·35)
Alc £3·70 (meal £4·55)

Seats 60
No dogs

Squires
78 King Street
Southport (0704) 30046

Closed L; Sun;
2 weeks midsummer;
2 weeks from Chr
Must book
D only, 7–10.30

Alc £7·70 (meal £11·15)

Service 10%
Seats 40
♿ rest (1 step)
Air-conditioning
No dogs
Access, Am Ex, Barclay,
Diners, Euro

Enrique and Susan Darias clearly hate standing or
sitting still. It does not seem long since they closed
their Spanish restaurant and opened this inviting
brass-knockered French one instead, yet they are
already converting the cottage next door for their
young assistant to run as a bistro (reports welcome).
For the moment, though, knowledge as opposed to
speculation is confined to Enrique Darias' very
professional cooking here of 'creamy potage,
generously served', crêpe ma façon (a beef and
spinach pancake brought in its cast-iron pan with a
cheesy sauce, £1·30), a delicately spiced mousseline
de mer (£1·35), and similarly rich but not cloying
suprême de volaille homardine (£5) and escalope de
veau savoyarde – both pieces of meat that 'cut like
butter'. Another visitor praises the 'salad with three
kinds of fish on top' and 'a huge steak with dried
cèpes in the sauce'. Scallops and various other
fish are also worth looking out for. Vegetables at a
test meal were as deftly treated as the rest, notably
pommes Anna and ratatouille, though 'green beans
were slightly dark and stringy.' Blackberry cheesecake
is fine if you have not eaten two rich courses already,
and 'the hot chocolate sauce with almond ice-cream
reminded me of Louis at the Ripon Old Deanery.'
Wines start at £4 and the owners have gathered
together a good list now, mostly under £10, and that
includes Ch. Figeac '70 and Ch. Cantemerle '66, both
c.b. One would like to know rather more about the
provenance of the estate-bottled burgundies before
contemplating a 'glass' symbol. Service is well
supervised. Recorded classical guitar music.

App: F. Kuhlmann, G.R., L.K.J., W.E.M.

SOUTHWOLD Suffolk   Map 6

*As we went to press, the restaurant
recommended here changed hands.*

STEEPLE ASTON Oxfordshire   Map 2

Red Lion
South Street
Steeple Aston (0869)
40225

Closed L (exc bar); Sun;
Mon D; 2 weeks Apr;
2 weeks Aug;
Dec 25 & 26
Must book
Meals 12–2 (bar),
7.30–9.45
D only, 7.30–9.45

Tdh D £6·80
(meal £9·40)

Children's helpings
Seats 20
Car park
No dogs in d/r
Access, Barclay

'This lovely old pub is a place where one will always be a friend, whether old or new' is a fine testimonial from a man who is even rash enough to go on: 'If only all wives cooked like Margaret Mead.' Others too this year have warmed to Colin Mead's Wadworth's bitter in cask and the weekday bar lunches as well as to the informally served dinners in the little dining-room. 'Freshly made toast was brought for the flavoury smoked mackerel pâté as we sat down. Chicken Kiev – two huge, indeed rather overwhelming, pieces – had a crisp coating and just the right hint of garlic.' Smoked haddock in cream sauce, 'duck bigarade with a crisply edible skin', 'salmon trout simply done', and well-chosen vegetables are also praised. Veal in Marsala and pork in calvados may be less dependable. Sweets are simple: one visitor likes the syllabub; another found chocolate mousse 'bland in flavour and lumpy in texture'. The wine list has not reached us this year. Smokers are asked to consider fellow-diners. You may also eat outside.

App: Michael Copp, M. J. Walker, B.J., D.S.C., Dr & Mrs S. W. Wells

STOKE GOLDINGTON Buckinghamshire   Map 3

Forest Retreat
Eakley Lanes
on B526
1 m NW of Stoke
Goldington
Stoke Goldington
(090 855) 305

The sense of roadside discovery, and the engaging resolve of Lucilla Randall (who cooks) and her sister Alicia to buy good materials at source, may add up to more than the menu really achieves; but vegetable soup, pâté, fillet steak with cheese and Guinness sauce, fresh vegetables, raspberry mousse, home-made coffee ice-cream and good coffee pleased most 1979 visitors. Portuguese wines are £3·90, with sufficient others. Recorded music.

Closed Mon; Sun D;
Sat L;
Dec 25 & 26
Must book

Meals 12–1.45, 7.30–9

Tdh £8·15 (meal £11·10)
Alc £8·05 (meal £11·60)

Seats 24
[] rest (2 steps); w.c.
Car park
No dogs

Inspections are carried out anonymously. Persons who pretend to be able to secure, arrange or prevent an entry in the Guide are impostors and their names or descriptions should be reported to us.

Since each restaurant has a separate file in the Guide office, please use a separate form or sheet of paper for each report. Additional forms may be obtained free (no stamp required) from The Good Food Guide, Freepost, 14 Buckingham Street, London WC2N 6BR (unfortunately Freepost facilities are not available from the Channel Islands or the Republic of Ireland).

Prices quoted in entries now include VAT.

Manleys
Manleys Hill
Storrington (090 66) 2331

Closed Mon; Sun D;
Dec 25 D for 2 weeks
Must book D & weekends
Meals 12.30–2.15,
7.15–9.30

Tdh Sun L £6·80 (meal
£10·50)
Alc £10·40 (meal £15·15),
L (one-course) about
£3·50

Service 12½%
Cover 50p (exc Sun L)
Children's helpings
Seats 40 (parties 10)
🔾 rest (3 steps)
Car park
No dogs
Access, Am Ex, Euro

Karl Löderer's Queen Anne house and garden on the Steyning road is an address that can be recommended to a veteran *conférencier* in search of the kind of food that assuages the chore of putting the world together again after one of its periodic eruptions. The service, it is true, is not what the Emperor Franz-Josef was accustomed to, and when the elaboration of the cooking comes to grief, it does so resoundingly: 'Blanc et noir – veal and steak – and the accompanying *bouquetière* of vegetables resembled a cloud of harmonies inaccurately rendered; fraisalia pancake was sloppy, with mushy strawberries and an overheated sauce of gum and kirsch.' Even this off-day, though, also produced 'delicious loin lamb chops cooked as ordered and accompanied by succulent haricots verts and carrots in a straw potato basket', and most visitors find the cooking 'divine': 'smoked haddock in a tangy cream sauce was followed by a large veal chop, split and stuffed with baby scallops, covered in a delicious lobster sauce, and served on a bed of vegetables, mange-tout peas included. For sweets we had elaborate fruity meringues and pancakes.' And this was merely the set Sunday lunch. (On other days you may opt for a light lunch.) A la carte specialities include the mushroom pousse d'automne (£1·10) and médaillons de chevreuil Baden-Baden (with black cherries, £5·20), not to mention züricher Geschnetzeltes with rösti potatoes (£5·60) and sweet salzburger Nockerln. 'On one occasion we were saved a long perusal of the menu by news from the kitchen that the lobsters had come in, and we were correctly advised that after a whole one (£8) with sumptuous mayonnaise we would not want anything else.' The wines, though no match for Gravetye Manor (*q.v.* under East Grinstead) where Mr Löderer formerly worked, are adequate; they begin at £4, with Alsace bottles £6·50, and Ch. Malartic-Lagravière '71, c.b., £11·50. Wear a tie in the evening.

*App: Helen Miedema, Charles E. Markus,
A. N. Attwell, J. C. Greenleaf, and others*

PLEASE keep sending in reports, as soon as possible after each meal. The cut-off date for the 1981 Guide is September 30, 1980, but reports are even more useful earlier in the year, especially for the remoter areas and new places. Late autumn reports can also affect corrections at proof stage.

1980 prices are as estimated by restaurateurs in the autumn of 1979 (including VAT).

Towns shown in black on our maps contain at least one recommended restaurant, pub or wine bar (see map key). The dot denotes the location of the town or village, not the establishment. Where necessary, we give directions to it in the entry. If you can, help us to improve them.

STOW-ON-THE-WOLD Gloucestershire   Map 2

Rafters
Park Street
Stow-on-the-Wold (0451)
30200

Closed Mon; Sun D;
2 weeks June;
Dec 24–26; Jan
Must book D
Meals 12.15–2 (2.30 Sun);
7.15–9.30 (10 Sat)

Tdh Sun L £6·25 (meal
£7·80)
Alc L £4·45 (meal £7·10),
D £6·55 (meal £8·60)

Service inc
Children's helpings
(under 10)
Seats 40
⚹ rest (2 steps)
No dogs
Access, Am Ex, Barclay,
Diners

One member's spelling of the new owner – 'Keith Maybe' – need not be copied, for Mr Maby is in fact not an uncertain quantity, after his sojourns at Corse Lawn (*q.v.*) and Cottage in the Wood (Malvern Wells). He has also had a full year at this well-spaced restaurant (a *Guide* entry under its previous owners) to attract reports: 'I liked this place before it changed hands and I like it better now, on the strength of the quenelles.' 'He even emerged from Mothering Sunday and Stow Horse Fair with flying colours.' An August Saturday dinner – hardly more auspicious – yielded terrine of écrevisses with tomato sauce and feuilleté de ris de veau (£1·55) which delighted a visitor fresh from great names across the Channel, and trout, lobster, pork fillet with apple and cider, and hasselback potatoes are also warmly praised. Mousseline of scallops with orange cream sauce (£1·95) is another first course speciality. The sweets divide opinion more often, and lemon and almond ice-cream (85p) may be safer than ones that depend on choux pastry and 'overblown' cream. The menu changes every five weeks. Italian Merlot or Gambellara are £3·10 and Ch. La Rose Figeac '71, c.b., £8·50. The Mabys are also enlightened enough to serve Hook Norton bitter from the cask.

App: T. J. Mallinson, Patricia Moore, E. V. Hibbert, William McFarland, Hugh Ross, P.M.S., and others

STRATFORD-UPON-AVON Warwickshire   Map 2

Ashburton House
27 Evesham Place
Stratford-upon-Avon
(0789) 292444

Closed L; Sun; Dec 22–
Jan 11
Must book
D only, 6–7.45

Tdh £5 & £7·50 (meal
£6·20 & £8·70)

Service inc
Seats 12
Car park (3)
No dogs
5 rooms
B&B £6·70
Fire cert

'It seemed a shame that *Twelfth Night* should be booked solid while there were empty places at Mrs Fraser's pre-theatre dinner,' says one August visitor to this unassuming guest-house near the Elfin nursery school. Sir Toby Belch himself could not have hoped for better than lettuce soup, fresh brown rolls, trout stuffed with prunes, and Swedish apple tart; 'besides, advance order brought an extra course, cheese soufflé, to two fellow-guests who were enraptured by it.' Careful cooking and unhurried but competent service make up for want of choice, and others have been equally content with, for instance, parsnip soup with cream and the lethally hot Jamaican pepper wine, Hungarian fillet of beef, and raspberry sorbet or lemon Cotswold. Wines – and cheeses – are elementary. Breakfasts are traditionally English, and rooms are small but adequate. No children under ten. No smoking in the dining-room. If you are non-resident, book at least twelve hours in advance. (No meals for anyone on Sundays after breakfast.)

App: J. B. & S. Barnes, E.C., D. R. & A. J. Linnell, Mr & Mrs S. J. Jones, J.E.H., and others

Marianne
3 Greenhill Street
Stratford-upon-Avon
(0789) 293563

Closed Sun; public hols;
Oct 12; Dec 24
Must book weekends
Meals 12.30–2, 7–11.30

Tdh £3 (meal £5·25)
Alc D £7·70 (meal £11·20)

Service 10%
Cover 20p D
Children's helpings
Seats 54 (parties 25)
♿ rest (1 step)
No dogs
Am Ex, Diners

Italics two years running is bad luck for any restaurant, let alone one that is enjoying its tenth consecutive entry here, but Pierre Denervaux has had a new chef (John Moore) since September. Early reports in favour of his handling of the restaurant's long-popular deep-fried mushrooms, onion soup, veal with tarragon and fruity sorbets need to be confirmed. Avocado with pounded walnuts and tomato (£1·15), entrecôte with garlic mayonnaise, 'crunchy carrots, juicy ratatouille, and chewy spinach' are also praised. 'We shared an excellent chocolate pudding.' 'Tables are rather close together if you are unlucky enough to draw a smoking neighbour.' 'The lady who serves us is invariably sprightly and sweet-tempered.' These verdicts tend to cancel out one or two contrary ones during the year, and with a few blackboard specials, Languedoc ordinaire at £3·80 a litre, and a modestly priced set meal, visitors to the town's theatre and hotel may well bless the day M Denervaux settled there, though we must still ask for more reports, please.

Plumber Manor
off A357
on road to Hazelbury
Bryan
2 m SW of Sturminster
Newton
Sturminster Newton
(0258) 72507

Closed L (exc Dec 25);
Sun (exc res Nov–Mar);
Mon (exc May 5);
1st 2 weeks Nov; Jan 1;
Feb
Must book
D only, 7.30–9.30

Tdh £8 (meal £10·80)

Seats 60 (parties 40)
♿ rest
Car park
No dogs
6 rooms (all with bath)
B&B £11–£15
Fire cert

Once upon a time the younger sprigs of the gentry were expected to become clergymen. But at this well-groomed Jacobean manor and garden, which the family have occupied since the 17th century, the name 'Brian Prideaux-Brune, Chef' signifies an altered orientation, and all visitors seem to agree that with brother Richard and his wife to lend suavity to the whole enterprise as owners and managers, the pleasures of a meal or a weekend here are atmospheric as well as simply physical. True, one visitor found the bed so wide that he mislaid his wife, and the range of services belongs to a 'restaurant with rooms' rather than to a full-dress hotel. At table, though occasional dishes miscarry and Stilton 'has shown signs of being a slow-mover', the cooking is rich in style and professional in technique. 'Pancake stuffed with ham and asparagus was excellent', but it may be best to take a simple first course such as smoked chicken, or prawns with garlic butter before embarking on 'absolutely delicious' scallops Newburg with a well-brandied sauce or beef Wellington, which has long been a speciality here. They ask you how you like your vegetables done. The sweets look and are formidable: 'no complaints about crème brûlée, done just right, coffee gateau soaked in Tia Maria, and Atholl brose.' Averys Ronsac red or Clochemerle white is £3·60; consult the proprietor about further choices. Wear a jacket and tie. No children under 12. (GHG)

App: Norman Siggers, Cynthia McDowall, Herbert Tint, B. E. Tustain, A. T. Langton

SUMMER BRIDGE North Yorkshire   Map 8

Knox Manor
(Brimham Room)
3 m SE of Pateley Bridge
Harrogate (0423) 780473

Closed L (exc Sun);
Sun D; Mon; Dec 25 &
26; Jan 1
Must book weekends
Meals 12–2 (Sun), 7.30–9

Tdh Sun L £4·95 (meal
£7·15), D £10 (meal
£12·70)

Children's helpings
Seats 50
♿ rest; w.c.
Car park
No dogs
Access, Barclay

Chris Cope, the owner of this reconstructed 18th-century flax mill, likes to trace the district's recorded history to the Brigantes, the tribe the Romans found here when they came looking for lead. But he and his chef Peter Ward are commendably anxious to cook and serve English rather than Roman or French food in their grand dining-room (complete with minstrels' gallery). Visitors in recent months have expressed pleasure in the obviously fresh preparation of their first courses and vegetables. 'Our four-course Sunday lunch began with a whole peach, stoned and filled with brown crab-meat in thin mayonnaise, topped with two prawns in shell. Another of us started with two Yorkshire puddings the size of saucers in a gravy that could have been served as onion soup; we went on to steak, kidney and mushroom pie and a whole boned poussin stuffed with a rather too strong liver and mushroom farce. Not surprisingly, we had to take half home to eat cold the next day.' Yorkshire appetites here are also directed to all kinds of game in season, Nidd Valley ducks, and local trout, fresh or smoked. Fortunately, perhaps, they are as generous with soft fruit at the sweet stage as they are with cream. The house red and white burgundy, shipped by Pierre Ponnelle, is £3·95, and the wine list is already considerable, with plenty of Alsace, Rhône, cru bourgeois clarets, and '76 Beaujolais to choose from in the £5–£10 range before domaine-bottled Clos de Tart '70 and other important burgundies at £15 or so. No children under ten. Recorded music, though they could surely confine it to their less formal Dalesman's bar and buttery, where snacks or full meals are served at lunch as well as in the evening (closed on Sundays). Pressurised beers. More reports, please, of both rooms.

SWAY Hampshire   Map 2

Pine Trees
Mead End Road
(NW of Station)
off B3055
4 m NW of Lymington
Lymington (0590) 682288

Closed L; Dec 25 & 26
Must book
D only, 7.45–9

Tdh £8 (meal £9·50)

Service inc
Children's helpings
Seats 18 (parties 6)
♿ rest

'Not luxury, but intelligence, comfort and consideration' is what weekenders have come to expect from the Davids' regime at their well-worn Victorian house, set in wooded, bird-haunted grounds. The owners make the most of what can be done at the price, and from their own resources, with attention to details such as flowers, iced water, and croissants for breakfast. The five-course dinners, though lacking choice until – refreshingly – the cheese stage, are simply cooked from good ingredients. True, one or two visitors have been surprised to find a dish based (in August) on tinned rather than fresh peaches, but 'first courses are very good, including light soufflés and a tasty fried lemon sole.' Fillet steak may be 'cut too thin and dried out' but roast lamb at a test meal, carbonnade of beef, and filet de veau ma façon sound much better, and the condition of the cheeses is as impressive as their number. Sweets are variably

Car park
No dogs
Am Ex, Barclay
7 rooms (1 with bath,
4 with shower)
B&B £10–£14·75
Fire cert

successful: 'Coupe française was fantastic' but chocolate mousse could well have been rummier, and ratafia pudding was served too cold (still, 'at least there was real raspberry sauce'). An inspector did not much care for the house's French red ordinaire at £3 but a '73 Côtes de Bourg at £4·60 or '76 Côtes du Rhône may prove better. Packed lunches can be provided but we have no note about them. No children under 12 as residents. 'Good value for a winter break.'

App: G. F. Fletcher, Clive Richards, Rita Masseron, T. E. Nunn, D. Carswell, M.A.P., and others

---

TALKIN Cumbria   Map 8

Tarn End Hotel
2 m S of Brampton
Brampton (069 77) 2340

Closed Oct; Dec 25
Must book
Meals 12.30–1.45, 7.30–9

Tdh L £4·60 (meal £6·70),
D £6·90 (meal £9)

Alc (min as tdh)
£9 (meal £11·75)

Service 10%
Seats 40
Car park
No dogs
6 rooms
D, B&B £15·50

'We have developed an interest in Hadrian's Wall in order to visit Tarn End,' says one Scot, and a Canadian was taken back to northern Ontario by a sunset glimpse of 'opalescent water, pine trees, and canoes'. True, the interior decor may also make sunglasses advisable, and the mien of the hotel is Germanic without being *gemütlich* – but they did dry out one soaked cyclist without complaint. Anyway, Martin Hoefkens' cooking – though he attempts too much on an overlong set menu – makes up for many faults. At a test meal, beignets de crabe and pommes dauphine were heavyish, and pommes Biarritz deplorable. Some main dishes and green vegetables may be cooked too long. But terrine of pheasant, 'succulent home-preserved confit d'oie with garlicky sauté potatoes', 'carefully boned' perch in herb sauce, fillet of pike in a pastry case with lemon and fennel, quail, guinea-fowl and other dishes are warmly praised. The cheeses vary, but add to the generous effect created by the puddings: 'good and fresh' raspberry shortcake, 'delectable hazelnut cake with a caramelly filling and nutty outside', 'light but spirituous apple cream calvados', and 'exquisite petits fours and fondants with coffee'. The wines (from £2·55 for a pint of Bonatello or Soave) are mediocre (cocktails are better), but regulars who take their own wines have been charged modest corkage. Breakfasts are good, and if the service wants grace, some customers want discretion – 'like the lady who inquired of the waitress, "Are you a Mary Queen of Scots person or an Elizabeth person? I do think that is *such* a good guide to a person's character".' Wear a jacket and tie to dinner rather than doublet and hose, and extinguish pipes. No under-eights in the restaurant or under-15s in the hotel.

App: J. Stephenson, David & Melanie Worrall, Anthea Rose, H. D. O'Reilly, H. & A. M. Fessler, and others

TEMPLE SOWERBY Cumbria   Map 7

Temple Sowerby House
on A66
6 m NW of Appleby
Kirkby Thore (093 06) 578

John Kennedy and Joseph Armstrong have moved to 'the queen of villages' from Ambleside, and their early Georgian house in a walled garden has handsome panelling and two four-posters. Praise for the four-course set dinners: perhaps 'plump prawns baked in sour cream', onion and Stilton flan or 'a good rough pâté'; cream of carrot or chicken and almond soup; then 'nicely underdone' roast beef, or wild duck with gooseberry sauce, with fresh vegetables, well cooked. Finish with a creamy pudding (crème brûlée, banana toffee pie or 'subtly sour' rum and raisin cheesecake). Thoughtful service. Youdell wines, from £2·75. No under-fives.

Closed L; Dec 24–26 & 31; Jan 1 Must book D only, 8	Tdh £8 (meal £10·30) Seats 36 🔥 rest; w.c. Car park	No dogs in public rooms Access, Barclay 12 rooms (10 with bath) B&B £10·95–£15 Fire cert

THORNBURY Avon   Map 2

Thornbury Castle

Thornbury (0454) 412647

Closed L (exc Sun); Mon; Sun D; Dec 25 & 26; Jan 1
Must book
Meals 12.30–2 (Sun), 7.30–9.30

Tdh D £10·75 (meal £13·20)
Alc £8·90 (meal £12)

Service 12½%
Cover 50p (Sat & Sun)
Seats 60 (parties 40)
🔥 rest
Car park
No dogs
Access, Am Ex, Barclay

If not to the manor born, Kenneth Bell can fairly think of himself as to the manor bred, after fourteen years as *châtelain* of this 16th-century keep, latterly surrounded by its own vines. He is acknowledged to be one of the land's more skilful *cuisiniers*, and if his kitchen here suffers occasional miasmic patches, the fault can probably be attributed to a deputy – 'but at £5·75 plus 27½% for a main course, I expect the vice-regent to be as good as the king.' Still, a customer who claims to have eaten chez Bell about twice a year for the past decade finds his latest meal well up in the rank order, with 'magnificently fiery, creamy and frothy gazpacho' followed by 'plump poulet au vin rouge et au vinaigre de vin, the sauce dark and winey without being too rich.' Note that the gratin dauphinoise potatoes – which *are* rich – come automatically, while much-needed salad does not, and it tends to be 'an apologetic version' even when it is requested. A clergyman 'found dariole de caneton so fine that I am experimenting with this creation myself', and the saumon en croûte and gooseberry sorbet that followed 'balanced the meal perfectly.' Salmon pickled in olive oil and orange juice, devilled crab, and mousseline of sole are other fishy successes. 'Alas, the madeira sauce with paupiette de veau was gluey in texture, muddy grey in colour, and floury in taste, and raspberry sorbet tasted overpoweringly of framboise, drowning rather than heightening the flavour of the fruit.' Service is also erratic: some customers find it too chilly or uninformative; others report 'a waiter willing to discuss a painting from the school of Caravaggio.' Wines in this house have always been dependably excellent, and fairly priced. 'The house Sauvignon is classically flavoury and fresh; claret half-bottles are abundant (Ch. Cissac '62, £3); but it seems a pity to offer three different Muscats de Beaumes de Venise but not one by the glass.' Details are approximate.

App: Robin Butterell, M. F. a'Brook, J.J.B., Mrs M. A. Hodgkiss, J.G., Christopher Forman

---

THORNTON-LE-DALE North Yorkshire   Map 8

Hall Hotel
3 m E of Pickering
Thornton Dale (075 14)
780

Handsome 16th-century house and park, with dawn screeches from the peacocks, and a watercress stream in the surrounding village. 'Obliging if not faultless' sums up the staff – and the cooking. Set meals may include smoked mackerel, 'hot and thick' ham and pea soup, 'very tasty' grilled plaice, 'large pork chops with sage and onion stuffing (good except for the gravy)', roast beef and 'fresh peach in a well-brandied caramel sauce.' Vegetables are 'palatable'. A la carte, the chef suggests chicken baked with Pernod and prawns (£3), trout with whisky butter, and sweetbreads braised with tomatoes and brandy (£3·25). Routine wines from £3·15 for Chianti. Tetley's and John Smith's beers on hand pump. Hearty breakfasts (try the 'full grill'), and bar lunches, on the lawn in good weather. A room away from the road avoids both noise and floodlights. More reports, please.

Must book weekends	Alc (min £4·50) £6·10	🪑 rest (1 step)
Meals 12.30–2, 7–9	(meal £8·80)	Car park
		No dogs in d/r
Tdh L £3·75 (meal £6·20),	Service 10%	Access, Am Ex, Diners
D from £4 (meal £6·45)	Children's helpings	26 rooms (23 with bath,
	Seats 60 (parties 100)	1 with shower)
		B&B from £10

TIMPERLEY Greater Manchester   Map 5

Le Bon Viveur
Hare and Hounds Hotel
Wood Lane
on A560
1 m from Altrincham
061-904 0266 *and* 980 8299

Closed Sun; Mon D;
Sat L; public hols (exc
Apr 4 & Dec 26 D)
Must book
Meals 12–2, 7.30–10

Tdh L £4 (meal £6·35)
Alc £6·70 (meal £10)

Frances and Jim Cunningham describe themselves as 'relatively new to catering' but they sound quick learners: running a busy restaurant with a French chef (Yannick Herin), annexed to a real-ale pub with a prosperous weekday lunch-time cold buffet trade, is no job for tyros. Anyway, local nominations of the restaurant are confirmed by more than one inspector, pleasantly surprised in the context by both food and presentation. Frogs' legs in a tomato, onion and garlic sauce followed by puff pastry bouchées 'packed full of fat langoustines, mussels and mushrooms in a light cream sauce' made a particularly inviting meal, for the vegetables were mostly well cooked (perhaps they all would be if there were fewer of them). Even prawn cocktail Alabama had a kick beyond normal Cheshire expectation, and entrecôte provençale and trout with

Children's helpings
(under 5)
Seats 40
♿ rest (1 step)
Air-conditioning
No dogs in d/r
Am Ex, Barclay, Diners

*almonds were both well cooked at a test meal.
Escalope de saumon au Champagne is another
speciality (£5·85, including vegetables), and 'dauphinois
potatoes were delicious' when tried. Cordier ordinaires
are £3·50 and other wine prices may steer some towards
the Marston's Pedigree bitter in cask. Recorded music.
You may eat outside. Car park. No rooms. More
reports, please.*

TIVERTON Devon   Map 1

Henderson's
18 Newport Street
Tiverton (088 42) 4256

Closed Sun; Mon
Must book weekends
Meals 12–2, 7.15–10

Alc L £6 (meal £9),
D £6·90 (meal £10·15)

Children's helpings
Seats 50
♿ rest (2 steps)
Air-conditioning
No dogs
Access card

*The italic type is or should be no more than a formality
here, for up to 1977 the Amblers ran one of the
Guide's better Devon places (Haldon Thatch), and
Elisabeth Ambler has spent the intervening period
cooking at two others (the Carved Angel, Dartmouth
and Combe House, Gittisham, both q.v.). But they are
themselves keen to be reassessed thoroughly in this
restaurant, whose name they inherited from former
owners. (They also say they are always happy to see
someone who wants to consult their food and wine
library.) So far, reactions are warm, and a glance at
the menu reveals several new-old ideas, notably for the
fish landed at Brixham: fritto misto del mare with
tomato coulis (85p); turbot sauce Messine (£3·90). For
one gourmandising traveller, green summer pâté and
vitello tonnato as first courses, followed by 'beautifully
tender, pink and garlicky' rack of lamb (£4·55,
including vegetables) puts the kitchen high up the
Devon league table. A simple but more than ample
lunch of spinach soup, 'real chili con carne', and home-
made vanilla ice convinced others. (Equally, you may
take just a dish of the day and coffee for lunch if you
prefer.) Nevill Ambler's wines bid fair to recapture the
distinction formerly awarded. His house wine policy
makes it easy to drink something different with each
course, and the 'no-nonsense' division of the list into
red and white of whatever region, coupled with careful
description, also makes it easy to lay out £20 on a
fistful of finer bottles: say, Tokay d'Alsace '75 (Preiss
Zimmer), Côte-Rôtie '72 (Emile Champet), and half a
bottle of Ch. Coutet '71. After-dinner smokers are
discreetly shunted towards the bar. Classical guitar
records sometimes. More reports, please.*

Numbers are given for private parties only if they can be accommodated in a room
separate from the main dining-room; when there are several such rooms, the
capacity of the largest is given. Some restaurants will take party bookings at times
when they are normally closed.

Most places will accept cheques only when they are accompanied by a cheque card or
adequate identification. Information about which credit cards are accepted is correct
when printed, but restaurants may add to or subtract from the list without notice.

1980 prices are as estimated by restaurateurs in the autumn of 1979 (including VAT).

The Lowman

♥

45 Gold Street
Tiverton (088 42) 57311

Closed Thur; Wed D;
Apr 4; June 5–19; 2 weeks
Nov; Dec 25 D; Dec 26;
Jan 1
Must book D
Meals 12.30–2, 7–9.45

Alc L £4·45 (meal £6·45),
L (quick service) £2·20
(meal £4), D & Sun L
£5·25 (meal £7·50)

Children's helpings
Seats 30
No dogs

'The middle ground of people paying their own bills' is Timothy and Susan Harvey's laudable target in their Queen Anne house, which offers quick-service casual weekday lunches along with other more formal meals and Sunday lunches. The setting, and some of the techniques employed, are a drawback: as one evening visitor says, 'How they equate plastic table-cloths and refreshed vegetables with £30 bottles of wine is beyond me.' But within the place's limitations, French onion soup, beef and cheese pie, jugged steak 'evidently marinated', 'curry of the day', apple Grasmere, and apple and almond pudding are worth trying. 'Lowman oggie', medallions of pork (£3·25) and beef Auckland are other dishes suggested. Mr Harvey, a Master of Wine, has collected one of the West Country's best cellars, from a dozen humble wines (mostly under £4 a litre) and inviting Spanish, Chilean, Hungarian and French regional bottles at almost equally low prices, to the great classics: Ch. Cantemerle '67, c.b., £8·50, Ch. Branaire-Ducru '55, c.b., £14·90, half-bottles of Ch. Doisy-Daëne (Barsac) '71, c.b., at £2·70 and so on.

App: J. B. Ainscough, T. A. Brocklebank, R. J. S. Marsh, and others

Toorak Hotel
Chestnut Avenue
Torquay (0803) 211866

A comfortable hotel in well-wooded grounds, 'splendidly run by the owners and their hard-working staff.' Families return year after year for the swimming-pool, dinner-dances and other pastimes, as well as the simple set meals: 'lovely game soup', melon with mushrooms and smoked salmon 'in a rich sauce', fried fish, roast lamb, beef or turkey, and 'a special word for the Dart salmon.' Vegetables sound inventive (cabbage with garlic, green peppers with celery) and sweets appealing (mincemeat slice, beignet soufflé). Routine wines; French carafes £3·10 the pint. Wear jacket and tie at dinner. 'Light' music on record.

Closed L Apr 6;
Dec 25, 26 & 31;
Jan 1–10
Must book
Meals 1–1.50, 7–8.15

Tdh L £4·10 (meal £5·65),
D £6·50 (meal £8·05)

Alc £9 (meal £11·90)

Service inc
Children's helpings
(under 8)
Seats 200 (parties 30)
♿ rest

Car park
No dogs in public rooms
80 rooms (49 with bath)
B&B from £13·50
D, B&B £16 (2 nights or
more; exc mid-June to
mid-Sept)
Full board from £142

See p. 508 for the restaurant-goer's legal rights, and p. 510 for information on hygiene in restaurants.

TOTNES Devon   Map 1

Elbow Room
6 North Street
Totnes (0803) 863480

The Sellicks' converted cider press is well hidden behind the congested High Street, and more easily spotted from the town wall car park. The menu's effusions disguise sound cooking of 'fluffy' semolina gnocchi (£1·60), delicate salmon mousse, soft roes, tournedos Opéra and roast duck (in burgundy sauce with mushrooms, or à l'anglaise with sage and onion, £5). Vegetables 'good and less usual' (carrots and sultanas, for example). 'Lashings of cream improve more ordinary sweets.' Argentine house wine, £3·10. 'Romantic music.' No blue jeans. No under-sixes.

Closed L; Sun; Mon (exc May 5 & 26); Apr 4; Dec 25 & 26
Must book

D only, 7.30–10

Alc (min £4·50) £8·85 (meal £12·05)

Children's helpings
Seats 30
No dogs
Am Ex, Barclay, Euro

TREGONY Cornwall   Map 1

Kea House
Tregony (087 253) 642

Closed L; Sun; Dec 25; Jan 1
Must book
D only, 7.30–9.45

Alc £5·35 (meal £8·15)

Children's helpings
Seats 32
♿ rest
No dogs
Access card

'Once past the unpromising raspberry façade' of Paul and Teresa Folkes's converted pub in a terrace, 'Madame Prunier herself would definitely have approved.' Or again, 'Jane Grigson's *Fish Cookery* seems to be the Bible.' The point, though, is not so much the recipes used, or even culinary skill (though it is seldom that Mrs Folkes miscalculates the texture or saltiness of a sauce). The surprise is that the spider-crabs, monk-fish, and John Dory that the instructed visitor to Cornwall looks for (mostly in vain) actually appear here. Moreover, says a local, 'if they know you and you are bringing a party you are not always tied to the menu. A few words in advance and you could sit down to a whole turbot or gilthead bream or a huge gurnard' (from £3·70 a head, including vegetables). Apart from the 'milky and succulent' spider-crab claws, you may find deep-fried scallops, crab agnolotti (£1·25) or fish soup with croûtons and rouille as first courses; vegetables are deftly cooked. A meat dish is always available for ichthyophobes. There are two or three home-made sweets; adequate cheeses. The Spanish wines from Laymont & Shaw of Falmouth are 'modestly priced: you feel a second bottle would not break you.' (The best buys are the red Riojas, perhaps, but the white Marqués de Murrieta was £3·55 in 1979, and Extrisimo Bach supplies a sweet counterpoint for dessert.) The *patron* is still occasionally rebarbative 'but the customers see less of this side than the cook', we are told. One customer was more than surprised to be served wine by an apparent chain-smoker. No toddlers, but cot-bound or otherwise dependable children welcome.

App: W. L. Sleigh, D. G. Shields, V. S. Abell, R.S., Grp Capt. A. C. P. Carver, K.M.B., and others

TRING Hertfordshire   Map 3

Waterfall
75 High Street
Tring (044 282) 5283

Closed Dec 23–26
Meals 12–2, 6–11

Tdh from £5 (meal £6·15)
Alc £4 (meal £5·10)

Service 10%
Seats 65
No dogs
Access, Am Ex, Barclay,
Diners

The waterfall is 'only a fountain with plants and fish', but everything else about this newish Pekinese place sounds genuine, from the flocked and mirrored decor to the noodle-spinning shows most weekends. The Chows are firmly helpful hosts, and if you venture beyond the 'leave it to us' feasts (from £5 a head) your solecisms may be pointed out. However, with or without advice, members have enjoyed crisp sesame prawn fingers (£1·50), 'hot and peanutty' bang-bang chicken shreds (£1·80), 'deliciously garlicky' cold Go Tar chicken (£1·50), 'robust' hot-and-sour soup, prawns either Ganshow (Szechuan-style) or with green ginger and spring onions (£2·20), crisp-fried shredded beef with carrots (£1·50), egg-fried fish (£2·20) and lettuce in smoked oyster sauce (80p). 'All the usual dishes' are apparently well done too, and the best sweets are toffee apples or bananas. Various wines; Hirondelle £3 for 70 cl. Some prefer jasmine tea; Chinese coffee on offer, made with Mei Kwei Lu (expect a whiff of dried roses). Or try fiery Mao Tai, 'known in China as Nixon's ruin.' Recorded Chinese music. More reports, please, of this and of the sister branch in Enfield.

TUNBRIDGE WELLS Kent   Map 3

L'Hermitage Hotel
A Marianne
30–33 London Road
Tunbridge Wells (0892)
24277

Closed Sun D;
D Dec 25 & 26; Jan
Must book
Meals 12.30, 8 p.m.

Tdh L £4 (meal £4·40)
Alc £6·85 (meal £9·85)

Service 10%
Seats 30
No dogs
Access, Am Ex, Barclay,
Diners
19 rooms (1 with bath)
B&B £8–£11
Fire cert

The Maillards opened their hotel on Bastille Day after moving from A la Bonne Franquette (see previous Guides), and some early visitors who entered via the public bar to an unsmiling reception felt that liberation, or at any rate light relief, was overdue. However, inspection after early troubles at least proved that M Maillard's cooking has not suffered in the transfer, for croustade de courgettes and 'extremely rich but gorgeous-tasting' crab soup (85p) made two admirable first courses, and cassoulet (£3·60) was a generous and well-cooked version. Quenelles de brochet sauce Nantua (£2·40), and confit de canard aux navets (£5) sound equally enticing. Pommes dauphine are popular, and salad is probably better than cooked vegetables. 'Chocolate mousse was light as well as creamy and had a faint flavour of both orange and mint; crêpes were stuffed with a syllabub-like mixture, with a hot, clear orange sauce poured over: contemplate neither unless you have room for more richness.' 'Déclassé' Mâcon or Loire wines are £3·20 for 50 cl. Quiches, gnocchi and other snacks may be had at lunch-time. They do not sell cigarettes or cigars. More reports, please.

Please report to us on atmosphere, decor and – if you stayed – standard of accommodation, as well as on food, drink and prices (send bill if possible).

Prices of meals underlined are those which we consider represent unusual value for money. They are not necessarily the cheapest places in the Guide, or in the locality.

Hoover Chinese Restaurant
Calverley Road
Tunbridge Wells
(0892) 33723

Pekinese cooking is hardly a household word in Kent, and this place may be becoming too domesticated as well as over-extended. At its best it pleases with 'Grand Hors d'Oeuvre' (tastes of prawn toasts, satay pork, marinated beef and tongue, fried fish, seaweed, pancake roll and batter baskets with bean sprouts), wun-tun soup, sliced pork with chilli, crisp vegetables and toffee fruit. Less good choices from the lengthy menu have been 'mouth-puckering' Peking soup, over-sweet and glutinous sweet-and-sour sauce (better with pork than fish), and a strange ratio of chicken to almonds with yellow-bean sauce. 'Rice was a case of one lump or two.' 'Company rather noisy – but so were we.' 'Quiet and efficient' service. Drink tea or lager. Recorded music sometimes. Details approximate.

Closed Dec 25 & 26
Meals 12–2.30, 5.30–12

Alc £5·50 (meal £6·05)

Service 10%

Seats 70
Access, Am Ex, Barclay, Diners

Mount Edgcumbe Hotel
The Common
Tunbridge Wells
(0892) 20197

The Higginses' 'over-heated and over-decorated' hotel on the Common offers rich food in a style learnt at Gravetye (q.v. under East Grinstead). Much of it works: artichauts à la diable (spiced, crumbed and fried, with garlic mayonnaise, £2·40), mushrooms done similarly, salmon mousse, wild duck with cherry sauce (£5·10), turbotin Renaissance (poached with lobster, wine and cream, £4·50). Other sauces have tended to overbear roast rack of lamb or poussin à l'estragon, and the vegetables, though well cooked, are too copiously served. 'Rather heavy hand' with sweet omelette and the sugar in syllabub. French house wine is £3·75 the bottle; a short, dull, dearish list beyond. 'No cigars or pipes in the restaurant.' Wear a tie. Recorded music.

Closed Sun; Mon
(exc May 5 & Aug 25)
Must book
Meals 12–2.30, 7–12

Alc £9·40 (meal £13·50)

Service 10%
Seats 34
Car park

No dogs
6 rooms (1 with bath)
B&B £9·50
D, B&B £12·50
Fire cert

TUNBRIDGE WELLS see also pub section

PLEASE keep sending in reports, as soon as possible after each meal. The cut-off date for the 1981 Guide is September 30, 1980, but reports are even more useful earlier in the year, especially for the remoter areas and new places. Late autumn reports can also affect corrections at proof stage.

Entries for places with distinctions carry symbols (pestle, tureen, bottle, glass). Credits are fully written entries, with approvers' names below the text. Passes are telegraphic entries (useful in the area) with details under the text. Provisional entries are in italics (see 'How to use the Guide', p. 4).

Sharrow Bay

2 m S of Pooley Bridge
M6 exit 40
Pooley Bridge (085 36)
301 *and* 483

Closed Dec–Feb
Must book
Meals 1–1.30, 7.45–8.30

Tdh L £10·35 (meal
£12·30), D £11·80 (meal
£13·75)

Service inc
Seats 60
  rest (1 step)
Car park
No dogs
28 rooms (19 with bath,
2 with shower)
D, B&B from £35

Not all correspondents are able to take Sharrow and
its owners quite as solemnly as the owners take themselves, 'down to the last half-strawberry on the fish.'
But Francis Coulson and Brian Sack's stone-built,
rococo-furnished house on the Howtown shore of the
lake has become an ancient monument in its own
lifetime, a witness to lost days of labour intensity in
the kitchen, over-stuffing in the dining-room, and –
throughout the hotel – 'solicitude with a human face.'
At its best, Mr Coulson's cooking touches poetry: at
least, this is deducible from the man whose first two
courses 'made me tingle all over', like A. E. Housman
reporting the physical effect of a fine line. But his art
knows no restraint whatsoever – 'my Eden salmon
stuffed with mousseline of sole in tarragon and cream
sauce I would have preferred as three separate
courses in reverse order'; and 'I am unused to having
my tastebuds assaulted by thirty different flavours in
one meal: it must surely bring the first coronary a
little closer.' Still, 'terrine of turbot and sole with
beurre blanc sauce and suissesses remains a triumph';
and to summarise a single meal, 'orange and sorrel
soup, paupiette of turbot, traditional roast lamb and
guinea-fowl, and lemon sorbet in the middle'
transported a critical Oxonian. But 'after a day on
Striding Edge we did so much justice to the home-
made brown and white rolls before the meal that we
could not accept more sweetmeats after rich ice-
cream and syllabub.' (Sharrow's guests must develop
a fellow-feeling for Strasbourg geese.) 'Breakfast was
also super, with delicious croissants, and a huge jug
of coffee for me alone.' They will supply a packed
lunch, too, which you would indeed be wise to walk
up a mountain with if you contemplate returning for
afternoon tea. One advantage of the hotel's longevity –
'and even our waiter was a nice, bald, elderly gentleman
who must have been on vacation from a Regius
Chair of Ancient History' – is the accumulation of fine
wines at now-historic prices in the cellar. 'We had
a château-bottled claret at £6·55 that tasted twice the
price, and reminded me of Ch. Brane-Cantenac which
I saw listed at £14·60.' The luscious hocks, too, are
tempting with food in this style. Leave under-13s at
home, and dress conventionally. They reserve one
dining-room for non-smokers. Details are approximate.
(GHG)

*App: R.A.S., A. G. Hodgkin, J. P. Brown,
L.F.L., T.H., J.J., and many others*

**Inspections are carried out anonymously. Persons who pretend to be able to secure,
arrange or prevent an entry in the Guide are impostors and their names or
descriptions should be reported to us.**

UNDERBARROW Cumbria   Map 7

Greenriggs Country House
3 m W of Kendal
M6 exit 36 or 37
Crosthwaite (044 88) 387

Closed L; Sun; Jan;
Mon–Thur (Nov–Mar)
Must book
D only, 8 p.m.

Tdh £7 (meal £9·75)

Seats 40 (parties 14)
Car park
No dogs in public rooms
12 rooms (8 with bath)
B&B £12–£14
D, B&B £16–£18
Fire cert

Frank and Christine Jackson and their 18th-century house in the tranquil Lyth valley seem to take firmer root in the *Guide* as the years pass, and though several visitors say that Mr Jackson's cooking is not in the same league as the best the Lakes can offer, they go on to write favourable notices. Well, the half-praise of people with high standards is worth more than the ecstasies of people with none. Rooms, garden, cordiality and fair value for money also count for much. Breakfasts seem to have got better, and at dinner there is adequate choice. Particular dishes mentioned include shrimp soup, hot spicy peaches, and Stilton and onion flan among first courses, then poussin with peaches, roast beef with savoury pancakes (or well-roast potatoes), and summer pudding or cherry brandy meringue. 'But there is still a tendency for flavours to be over-assertive – capers, for example – or over-elusive: flair is missing somewhere.' Santa Fé Spanish carafes are £2·90 and there is a sensible Youdell wine list: Pineau de la Loire '78, £3·60; Ch. Meyney '70, c.b., £7·80; pressurised beers. Smoking is discouraged, and children must be over ten to dine.

App: Kevin & Jane O'Mahoney, N. V. Crookdake, Regina Glick, M. E. Cohen, M. J. Young, H.R.

Tullythwaite House
4 m W of Kendal
M6 exit 36 or 37
Crosthwaite (044 88) 397

Closed L (exc Sun); Mon;
Fri; Sun D; public hols
(exc D Apr 4); Dec–
Easter
Must book
Meals 12.30 (Sun), HT
4–5 (Sun), 7

Tdh Sun L from £7·50
(meal £8·25), D £8 (meal
£8·80)

Children's helpings
(under 10 L)
Seats 20 (parties 8)
⑤ rest
Car park
No dogs
Unlicensed

'It was rather like meeting the composer at the end of a new string quartet when Mrs Johnson senior emerged at the end of the meal to acknowledge our decorous appreciation.' The analogy breaks down, of course, not because she is eighty in the shade and still composing – after all, no doubt Elizabeth Lutyens will manage that – but because the Lakeland farmhouse style of cooking is recognisably the same as it would have been in Hannah Glasse's time. This does not exclude new ideas, perhaps partially attributable to Mrs Johnson's daughter-in-law who is named as fellow cook, such as the avocado mousse, 'miraculously light prawn cheesecake' and 'parcels of tongue and chicken liver pâté, daringly served with cherry sauce.' But flavours are designed for combination, not contest, and the centre-piece of all dinners will be a traditional roast: crisp duckling with a proper orange sauce, or beef and Yorkshire with home-made horseradish sauce; followed by, 'to our delight, a whole strawberry shortcake and a lemon mousse left on our table, so different from a portion spooned from a trolley, and far above the standard of our own kitchen'; then Stilton in its pierced dish from the Gillow sideboard, with home-made wheaten biscuits; and fruit; 'and admirable coffee.' You take your own bottle, which will be carefully treated; and if you are wise, you will bring a civilised foreign friend who does not believe that there is such a thing as English food. (Even tea-time will do if you cannot manage dinner, and you can sit in the garden then.) Wear a jacket and tie at dinner. It would not be fair to pick out such a place for the symbol of distinction that attracts, inevitably, more geese than swans. But supply it silently if you like.

App: R. J. & N. E. Stone, David & Melanie Worrall, D.R.T., Mrs R. Slaney, and others

---

UPPINGHAM Leicestershire   Map 5

Lake Isle

♟

16 High Street East
Uppingham (057 282) 2951

Closed L; Sun; Mon;
public hols (exc Apr 4,
Dec 26, Jan 1)
Must book
D only, 7.30–9.30

Tdh £7·50 (meal £8·60)

Service inc
Seats 40
 🔲 rest
No dogs

'Makes the job worthwhile' is the encouraging comment from one inspector who arose and went very promptly to the Lake Isle, as soon as the *Guide*'s intelligence system told him that behind this double shop-front in a public-school village Roy Richards was applying lessons about food and wine he learnt at Thornbury Castle (*q.v.*) and elsewhere. There are no frills to the setting, 'we serve only one vegetable with the main course', and service is 'sketchy', so prices are a long way short of Thornbury's. But several experienced judges have already praised the high quality of what is actually attempted in the five-course, modestly varied set dinners. Mentions include gazpacho and carrot soups; fried squid, or pork and spinach terrine; poulet au citron and canard aux abricots; admirable ratatouille and green vegetables (no doubt from the 'nine bean rows') and fine cheeses (including blue Cheshire); chocolate and walnut pudding or a delicate fresh fruit salad; and coffee not only generous but good. Mr Richards has his own wine business and in the restaurant adopts the blessedly serious and fair policy of charging the wholesale price plus £1·50 plus service and VAT: many who frequent other Midlands restaurants will be surprised how little that leaves them paying for, say, magnums of Ch. Batailley '70 or Ch. Mouton-Rothschild '73 (£19 in each case) or bottles of Winkeler Jesuitengarten Spätlese (£7), or Taylor's '60 port (£11·50). Claret at all prices is the backbone of the list, but there are also fine Paternina Spanish reds, and Yugoslav Cabernet or Traminer for the nursery slopes at £2·75. Give notice for fine wines: they are kept in the cellar. No ban on smoking, though the *patron* dislikes it. Please report how they cope with greater pressure this year, but a full entry and 'glass' distinction seem well merited already.

App: Michael Latham, W. Frankland, A.M., R. J. Haerdi, R. Boyse, and others

---

Wine prices shown are for a 'standard' bottle of the wine concerned, unless another measure is stated (e.g. litre, 50 cl., or pint).

VERYAN Cornwall   Map 1

Treverbyn House
7 m SW of Mevagissey
Veryan (087 250) 201

The Gardners seem 'anxious to please' at their guest-house 'in one of Roseland's prettier villages'. 'Flowers everywhere', and a sensibly limited French provincial menu to which the kitchen is equal. An inspector 'could have made a meal of carefully cooked carrots and immaculate gooseberry pie' but also liked carbonnade and porc niçoise. Family service 'with an eye to detail'. Modest wine list, priced accordingly (Egri Bikavér, £2·80). 'Jacket and tie preferred.'

Closed L; Dec 24–26 &
31; Jan 1
Must book
D only, 7.30–8.45

Tdh £6 (meal £8·15)

Children's helpings
Seats 20

Car park
No dogs
4 rooms
D, B&B £14

WAREHAM Dorset   Map 2

Olivers
West Street
Wareham (092 95) 6164

A gruelling, semi-public inquest into the pedigree of the steaks sapped two members' desire to return, but the Twists still please with haddock mousse, entrecôte and pigeon aux cerises (which 'might have been more tender'); add to the list this year whitebait, peppery venison, beef Stroganoff and 'savoury cucumber' bound with bacon, mushrooms and rice. 'Refreshing sorbets, but crème brûlée topping tacky.' Soave is £3·50 for 75 cl. 'Efficient, never bustling.' No children under five. 'John Williams on record.'

Closed L; Sun & Mon
(Oct–Apr); public hols
(exc Apr 4 & 6, Jan 1)
Must book
D only, 7–10.30

Alc £6·45 (meal £8·65)

Service 10% (6 or more)
Children's helpings

Seats 30
♿ rest
No dogs
Barclaycard

Priory Hotel
Church Green
Wareham (092 95) 2772

Must book D
Meals 12.30–2, HT 6–7,
7.30–9.45

Tdh D (Mon–Fri) £6·60
(meal £8·90), Sat D £7.50
(meal £9·90)
Alc £6·40 (meal £9)

Seats 48 & 24
♿ rest; w.c.
Access, Am Ex, Barclay,
Diners
15 rooms (all with bath)
B&B from £10
Fire cert

Accountants are often coolly received when they branch out as catering entrepreneurs, and the Turner brothers are no exception. But after two years in this priory (whose grounds run down to the river), their hotel and 'crypt-like' restaurant are more warmly praised by an inspector who stayed a week and found Ian Price's set dinners imaginatively composed and sensitively cooked. 'First courses usually included a good soup and a salad of some kind. Beef was excellent every time we tried it, and duck or pheasant too. Fresh vegetables included fennel more than once. Cheeses were in good condition, and the seasonal fruit that went into the puddings was a further encouragement. Service seemed concerned and cheerful.' There are all-day bar snacks. Bordeaux table wines are £3, and a considerable cellar is kept: Ch. Lynch-Moussas (£8·95) among many distinguished '73s; Ockfener Bockstein Spätlese '76 (£6·90); and a dozen vintage ports (Graham '63, £12). Pressurised beers. A guitarist plays on Saturday evenings. You may eat outside. Car park. No dogs. More reports, please.

WATFORD Hertfordshire   Map 3

Flower Drum
16 Market Street
Watford (0923) 26711

The thorough Szechuan and Pekinese menu solicits fire-eaters with flames marked against spicy dishes, but spares the roof of the mouth when it comes to the point. Tubular cane chairs and 'familiar' service ease the transition but flavours could be more exotic in chicken 'salad', crispy duck and 'greasy beef with black beans' (£1·90). Soho standards are reached with prawn toasts and seaweed with grated scallop (£1·40), and set meals tempt with kungpo chilli prawns and 'Bang Bang' chicken (in sesame dressing with cucumber, £1·80). 'Crowding brings discomforts.' Recorded music.

Closed Dec 24–26
Must book D & weekends
Meals 12–2.30, 6–11.30

Tdh L £3 (meal £3·75),
D £6 (meal £7·05)
Alc £5·05 (meal £6)

Service 10%
Seats 54
  rest (1 step)
Access, Am Ex, Barclay, Diners, Euro

WELL Hampshire   Map 2

Chequers
3 m SE of Odiham
off A32
M3 exit 5
Long Sutton (025 681) 605

An ancient coaching-inn with a bistro grafted on – either too French by half, or not nearly French enough, some say. Bonuses are suave service (though 'cool to complaints'), 'really fat and juicy' frogs' legs provençale (£2·50), tender sweetbreads à la crème (£3·95) and braised duck Brillat-Savarin ('for those who find it too rich when roast'), with *croquant* vegetables, varied cheeses and fair sweets. Debits include French salting, English garnishing ('pâté and crêpe hiding in greenery'), Franglais smoking in the dining-room. Interesting French wines; house wine £3·75 for 70 cl. Snacks (onion soup, quiche Lorraine) and Badger bitter (pump) are served at lunch-time in a separate area.

Closed Sun; Mon;
Dec 25–30
Must book D
Meals 12.30–1.30, 7.30–9

Alc £7·65 (meal £10·85)

Service 10% (parties over 5)
Children's helpings

Seats 50
  rest
Car park
No dogs
Diners card

WESTERHAM Kent   Map 3

Alison Burt's
1 Market Square
Westerham (0959) 62245

Closed L; Sun; public hols
Must book
D only, 7.30–9.30

'We would stop if it weren't fun.' Alison Burt and her sister Kate Sutherland show no sign of letting up, and Kentish diners tempted by the painted façade and gentle prices enjoy themselves in spite of the informal furnishing (which at least implies expenditure where it matters). The monthly menu offers four or five choices for first and second courses, various enough to satisfy all tastes and appetites. September's had spare ribs, jugged hare, Alsace chicken, poached

Tdh £6·25 (meal £8·40)

Children's helpings
Seats 40
No dogs
Access, Barclay

lemon sole, and an ambitious stuffed ox tongue in tomato sauce. Their version for December was suitably escapist with 'unremarkable' Dutch pea soup, pheasant vallée d'Auge and Jamaican torte as well as carefully prepared cauliflower and walnut vinaigrette and lemon sorbet. A test meal of 'thin but fresh and delicious spicy tomato soup', robust Caribbean pork stew with skilfully cooked vegetables, and 'a very good version of Russian paskha which only one other diner had the sense to try' was most rewarding, though Alison Burt's recipe for pâté produced 'an odd taste and a wet texture.' Members like the full descriptions of food and wines. Caldorino is £2·75 a litre and Corney and Barrow's claret is £2·75 a bottle. 'Informal, as in France', and you can buy the owners' cookery books to read under Churchill's gaze from the statue across the road. 'Light, popular' music.

App: R. M. Ganderton, N. Hayter, C. R. Hart, A.J.B.

WEST RUNTON Norfolk Map 6

Mirabelle

West Runton (026 375) 396

Closed Mon; Sun D
(Nov–May); Dec 25
Must book
Meals 12.30–2, 7–9

Tdh L £3·45 (meal £5·85),
D £6·10 (meal £8·75)
Alc £7·05 (meal £9·80)

Children's helpings
Seats 48
♿ rest
Car park
No dogs
Am Ex card

'Six or seven visits during the year, every one confirming the consistent excellence of food and service' is a pretty good chit for Manfred Hollwöger's surprising Swiss restaurant near a suburban stretch of seaside. The more so when an inspector's party on a single Saturday lunchtime visit found the same evenness across all dishes in the set meal, along with 'a refreshing air of quiet, amiable efficiency over finding tables, taking orders, and delivering dishes. Good linen too.' In detail, 'frying was dazzlingly good, whether of the fresh, ungraded whitebait that teem offshore, or aubergines viennoise; the vegetable soup was a classic and subtle potage; sweetbreads à la crème had real taste and a russet sauce; and small whole lobsters, fresh in taste though a little flabby in texture, were a derisory 50p extra on the very modest lunch price. Salmon trout meunière, though, should not be served in the darkened frying butter, and vegetables do not match the standard of the rest.' Sweets have 'a typically Swiss' unctuousness, with fresh peach in the Melba, and chocolate gateau (as distinct from Sachertorte, also served) 'very light, with real butter-cream filling.' 'Cheeses are rather meagre.' The wines are much improved, with Côtes du Luberon (£3·50) a sensible step up from the Charbonnier carafes at £2·90, and desirable clarets and burgundies (though watch out for the off-years). White Hermitage '75 at £5·50 and Ch. Rauzan-Gassies '71, c.b., at £10·20 seem tempting when the food prices are so reasonable.

*App: M.S., C.P.D., M.E.D., R.N.A.S., J.C.B.,
Ron & Liz Fritz*

Eethuys
Cypress House
1½ m NW of Wedmore
Wedmore (0934) 712527

Closed L; Sun; Mon;
Dec 25; 3 weeks Jan/Feb
Must book
D only, 7.30–9

Tdh £7·25 (meal £10·10)

Seats 16
 ♿ rest
Car park
No dogs

Some faint-hearts may need reminding that it is under an hour from Bristol – take the Blackford road from Wedmore, then after a mile turn left towards Stoughton. Once you have arrived at the crossroads another mile further on, Karen Roozen (who cooks) and her partner Erie Ten-Oever create a soothing and civilised atmosphere (with no pipes or cigars in the dining-room) even before the food has been tasted. In one sense, the food is less soothing, for it was 'desperately unbalanced on the creamy side' when a surfeited inspector called. But robust appetites happy to begin with 'divine coarse brown bread', corn chowder or devilled prawn pancakes, and more delicate ones that can face only melon with Dubonnet, are alike rewarded. 'Duck was faultlessly roasted with a sharp cherry plum sauce.' Vegetables are imaginative – sometimes too imaginative for the dishes they accompany – and not overcooked. As befits a Dutchwoman, Mrs Roozen will do rijsttaffel for a party of a dozen or more, and 'if I weren't proud of it I wouldn't have it on the menu.' 'A delicate sonata of a lemon mousse finished the concert,' says one visitor, jutting his chin in George Steiner's direction; others have praised the apple sorbet with calvados, vanilla soufflé with Crème de Cassis, and cabinet pudding 'with more unannounced cream'. Coffee comes with good fudge. The wines (from £2·90 for Gamay or Frascati) are few, and fairly priced: Ch. Léoville-Poyferré '67, £12·50.

App: Susan Loppert, Mrs D. Collins, F.I., Nova Whyte, A.H.

Fantails
on B6263
5 m SE of Carlisle
M6 exit 42 or 43
Wetheral (0228) 60239

Fans' tales of this two-family affair in a converted barn on the village green suggest amiable service and careful cooking. Deep-fried mushrooms (95p) came with home-made tartare sauce and wholemeal buns, and fish is a popular main course (though 'the portion of good plaice in wine sauce would have been better as a fish course'). 'Crisp potatoes and onion rings.' 'Excellent eclairs and lemon mousse', but lunch sweets were survivors from dinner. Soup and trifle disappointed one member. Yugoslav Riesling and Pinot Noir, £3·25 for 70 cl.

Closed L Nov–Mar
Must book D
Meals 12–2, 6 (Sun 7)–9.30

Alc £6·05 (meal £9)

Children's helpings
Seats 48 (parties 25)

Car park
No dogs
Access, Am Ex, Barclay, Diners, Euro

See p. 441 for pubs and p. 491 for wine bars.

WEYBOURNE Norfolk   Map 6

Gasché's
on A149
3 m W of Sheringham
Weybourne (026 370) 220

Closed Mon; Sun D;
Dec 25
Must book
Meals 12.30–2, 7–9

Tdh L £3·85 (meal £6·40),
D £6·50 (meal £9·30),
& £7·50 (meal £10·40)
Alc £9·25 (meal £12·55)

Children's helpings
Seats 70 (parties 14)
⌖ rest; w.c.
Car park
Am Ex, Diners

'I'd give up a lot before I gave up Gasché's,' writes a Norfolk member who 'feels disloyal and is usually disappointed' if he deserts Mr Steiner-Gasché and his chef Nigel Massingham for places nearer home. The pebble and thatch 'Swiss cafe', now in its second generation, has remained here for nigh on thirty years, for the value given is remarkable, even when the cooking is in a mundane patch and the throughput of customers uncomfortably fast. 'We were told we could have fresh salmon – not on the menu – at no extra charge to the £3·85 set lunch.' Soup is a better start than hors d'oeuvre, perhaps; aubergine viennoise will be well fried, and trout well grilled. Dressings tend to be insipid or overpowering by turns, and vegetables casually cooked. Sweetbreads à la crème or wiener Schnitzel are good main course orders, fish risotto is a speciality for two at £9·90, and for sweet try Swiss apple tart or praline surprise. André Simon table wines are £2·40 for 50 cl, and it may be courting financial punishment to venture beyond.

App: R. Whitehead, P.W.C., Yorick Wilks, R.P., J.C.B.

WEYBRIDGE Surrey   Map 3

Casa Romana
2 Temple Hall,
Monument Hill
Weybridge (0932) 43470
and 54221

Closed Mon; Sat L;
Apr 6 D; Apr 7;
Aug 25; Dec 25 & 26
Must book
Meals 12.15–2.15, 7–10.45
(Sun 7–10)

Tdh L £3·45 (meal £6·90)
Alc (min L £3·45, D
£4·75) £9·35 (meal £14·40)

Cover 60p
Seats 75
⌖ rest (3 steps); w.c.
Air-conditioning
Car park
No dogs

Ballerini and di Michele run one of the most successful Italian restaurants outside London, and though one evening visitor goes so far as to suggest they might with advantage offer guests ear-plugs and a blindfold, not to mention more space between the tables, even he has little quarrel with the cooking. Anyway, at lunch it is quieter, and an equally sensitive member found the 'rams' heads swathed in fruit' less distressing than the sight of his fellow men opting for avocado vinaigrette or egg mayonnaise after being shown a trolley laden with 'mouth-watering king prawns, crab claws, smoked turkey and stuffed aubergines.' (It is advisable to ask the price, though.) The aubergines can also be had hot, lightly stuffed with tomato, onion and herbs, and another hot first course – clams gratinée (£2·50) – proved 'entirely successful'. Chicken dishes are good: with asparagus tips, almond sauce, or stuffed with cheese and Mortadella – 'a satisfying harmony.' Pork in cream sauce with noodles, and 'rich and delicate' fettina di bue alla Don Corleone also sound worth recording. The owners further recommend sogliola Corrado, faraona in crostata, and vitello Ostia Antica at prices (well over £5) which fortunately include vegetables. Italianate sweets may be better than plain apple pie. Wines begin with Frascati at £3·25 but most Italian wines are over £4·75. Recorded music.

App: Roy Mathias, Ellis Blackmore, J.R.T.

Dulcinea
73 Queen's Road
Weybridge (0932) 42895

Closed Sun; Mon L
(exc public hols);
Apr 4; Dec 25 & 26
Must book weekends
Meals 12–3, 6.30–11.30

Tdh L £3·75 (meal £5·95)
Alc £8·40 (meal £11·50)

Children's helpings
(under 10)
Seats 35
♿ rest; w.c.
No dogs
Access, Am Ex, Barclay,
Diners, Euro

Recipe in *Second Dinner
Party Book*: sopa de
pescadores

For most of the past decade, Longinos Benavides has been quietly expressing Spanishness on the Costa del Southern Railway, and is still finding new customers who have 'passed this little turquoise room many times thinking it worth a try one day.' One day, when it arrived, produced 'truly splendid' eggs in Rioja style (hot both ways), and a nicely presented zarzuela, 'not the usual sloshy, hyped-up fish stew.' It sounds better than the 'suspect, curry-flavoured paella' another member regretted. Guacamole, sopa de pescadores (£1·25), casseroled monk-fish sometimes, and pollo Sara-Lucia (with artichoke sauce, £3·75) are other suggestions; moreover, suckling pig ordered in advance, or breast of pigeon with duck liver in the winter season, argue enterprise. In a Spanish place, nougat or dulce de membrillo with coffee may be a good alternative to more conventional sweets. The wine list is dominated by over forty mostly distinguished Spanish wines; Gran Coronas Reserva '71, is £6·75; San Ignacio, n.v., a dry white Panades £3·50; Codorniu, n.v. (sparkling), £4·50. The house Rioja is £3·35. Please try the set lunch.

App: B.E., S.J.M., P. S. Chester

Sea Cow Bistro
7 Custom House Quay
Weymouth (0305) 783524

This popular little whitewashed bistro by the harbour changed hands early in 1979, but reports still favour good fresh fish (matelote of squid, crab bisque, baked brill or 'sole in a lovely sauce') and even gammon with banana and cheese (£2·85) and a fine chocolate mousse. The mid-day table (now £4·35) offers soup and sweet and various fish, meat and salads ('try bean sprout, nut and peach'), but flavours seem blander and the joints less juicy than before. French and Spanish house wines, £1·85 for 50 cl; Muscadet-sur-Lie, £4. Children (usually) half-price plus 50p. More reports, please.

Closed Sun; last 3 weeks
Oct; Dec 25 & 26; Jan 1
Must book D & weekends
Meals 12–2, 7.30–10.15

Tdh L £4·35 (meal £6·35),
D £5·95 (meal £8·55)

Children's helpings

Seats 54 (parties 35)
♿ rest
No dogs
Access, Barclay

Towns shown in black on our maps contain at least one recommended restaurant, pub or wine bar (see map key). The dot denotes the location of the town or village, not the establishment. Where necessary, we give directions to it in the entry. If you can, help us to improve them.

We rewrite every entry each year, and depend on fresh, detailed reports to confirm the old, as well as to include the new. The further from London you are, the more important this is.

WHITEWELL Lancashire   Map 5

The Inn at Whitewell
Dunsop Bridge (020 08)
222

Closed D Mon & Tue
(exc res & exc Apr 7,
May 5, May 26);
D Dec 25 & 26 (exc res)
Must book D
Meals 12–2 (1.30 Sun),
7–9

Alc £6·80 (meal £10)

Service 10%
Seats 50 (parties 25)
&. rest
Car park
No dogs
Am Ex, Barclay, Diners
10 rooms (6 with bath)
B&B from £8·50
Fire cert

Once you find it, this remote hotel on the River
Hodder with good views of the Trough of Bowland
proves ideal for fishin', shootin', paintin' and eatin'.
Robert and Lesley Orr, late of Whitbreads and
Leith's cookery school respectively, have prompted
many worthwhile detours by offering 'painstaking
cooking, happy and informed service and a dignified
but homely setting.' Log fires in the winter and
antiques galore comfort stragglers, and breakfasts are
unsparing, but dinners get most attention. An
inspector predicted success after fluffy crêpe farcie au
jambon (£1·20), an encyclopaedic vegetable soup 'in
good brown stock', courgette stuffed with prawns
(£1·50), trout Bélin ('a plump fish filled with spinach
and mushroom and nicely garnished with lime and
watercress', £4·20) and a fruit puree with banana and
brandy, topped with burnt sugar (90p). Others have
praised prawns and mushrooms in cheese sauce, veal
florentine, breast of chicken provençale (£4·50) and
'superior' bar lunches of pâté, quiche and crisp salads.
House burgundy is £4 a litre and Robert Orr 'shows
a sound working knowledge' of his thorough list.
Whitbread Trophy and mild on electric pump. You
may eat outside.

*App: Jean Wilding, P.K.D.H., J.G., J. & K.L.,
and others*

WHITSTABLE Kent   Map 3

Giovanni's
49–55 Canterbury Road
Whitstable (0227) 273034

'Very modern and extremely comfortable now,' says
an inspector about this *Guide* veteran, using fewer
superlatives on the cooking (still Italian, but with a
few French gestures). The set lunch is standard but
varied, and notable value for the hors d'oeuvre such
as mushroom and walnut salad and coppa. At a test
meal 'noisette' of chicken with orange and gherkins
'succeeded technically' but aubergines with 'bland'
seafood (£1·70) 'failed to gel', and trifle was 'more
Black Forest than inglese'. 'Crisp sauté potatoes, other
vegetables old or ordinary.' House Italian wines are
now £3·25. Brisk service. 'Quiet' Italian music.
Air-conditioning, 'with some effect.' 'Clean and tidy
dress', please.

Closed Mon; Dec 26
Must book D
Meals 12–2.30, 6.30–10.45

Tdh L £3·45 (meal £5·95),
Sun L £3·95 (meal £6·50)

Alc (min £3) £6·60
(meal £9·90)

Service 10%
Cover 35p
Children's helpings
Seats 65

&. rest (1 step)
Air-conditioning
Car park
No dogs
Access, Am Ex, Barclay,
Diners, Euro

White House Hotel
on A39
1½ m SE of Watchet
Williton (0984) 32306

Closed L; mid-Oct to
mid-May
Must book
D only, 7.30–8.15

Tdh £7 (meal £9·70)

Seats 30
⎣ rest (1 step)
Car park
No dogs in d/r
14 rooms (7 with bath)
B&B from £11·70
D, B&B from £16
Fire cert

Smith, Smith, Smith, Smith and Smith are
responsible for what's eaten at this shuttered house
(say that quickly to reproduce the sound of
Williton's vintage loco getting up steam). True, the
eight-year-old's repertoire is restricted to after-dinner
mints, and the limitations of family service make it
wise for you to skip like a young ram when you hear
the dinner gong. But the housekeeping is impeccable
and the cooking honest. A couple who began with
smoked mackerel quiche, then ate porc aux pruneaux
with 'three perfectly cooked vegetables', and finished
with coffee eclairs and strawberry crème brûlée
considered themselves fortunate and stayed eight days
to prove it. Rillettes de lapin, saupiquet nivernaise
and other enterprising dishes often owe much to
local herbs and thick cream. Piña colada ice-cream is
a speciality, and the Stilton and Cheddar are sound.
'Order apricot pancakes in advance.' Richard
Smith's interest in wine ensures that the house Gamay
de l'Ardèche and Sauvignon are fairly priced at £3,
and beyond this there is a long list of Yapp Rhônes,
from Vacqueyras '76 at £5·80 to runs of Jaboulet
Aîné's Hermitage and Noël Sabon's Châteauneuf-du-
Pape. (GHG)

*App: P. A. Bull, J.S., B.F.H., Juliet Richters,
R. Curzon, and others*

Banners
18 Little Minster Street
Winchester (0962) 67212

Manners makyth man, Banners a full man. Godsends
are to be hoped for in Winchester, and the sprightly
food dished up at this modest place pleases natives
and visitors alike. The Law Courts adjourn here for a
quick lunch of mushroom or Stilton quiche (£1·10),
filled potatoes and 'creamy' curried egg mayonnaise.
Dinners are more ambitious: perhaps cream cheese
and cucumber mousse (95p), hare braised in port
with juniper (£4), and greengage sorbet (85p).
Eldridge Pope wines. 'Decor gives asceticism a good
name.' 'Varied music', live and recorded.

Closed Sun; Mon D;
public hols
Meals 12–2.15, 7–10

Alc L £3·30 (meal £5·95),
D £7·20 (meal £10·45)

Cover 20p D

Children's helpings
Seats 46 (parties 20)
⎣ rest
No dogs

WINCHESTER see also wine bar section

**The Guide accepts no advertising. Nor does it allow restaurateurs to use its name on
brochures, menus, or in any form of advertisement. If you see any instances of this,
please report them to us.**

WINDERMERE Cumbria   Map 7

Miller Howe

Rayrigg Road
on A592
Windermere (096 62) 2536

Closed L; Dec 14–early
Mar
Must book
D only, 8 for 8.30
(two sittings Sat)

Tdh £11 (meal £14·35)

Service 12½%
Seats 70 (parties 30)
♿ rest
Air-conditioning
Car park
No dogs in public rooms
Am Ex, Diners
13 rooms (12 with bath,
1 with shower)
D, B&B from £26
Fire cert

There are at least two John Toveys not quite at peace on this promontory with its restful view of lake and Langdale: an obsessional craftsman of the kitchen with the lightest pastry hand in the business, and a Diaghilev of the dinner-table, whose evening production (now in its ninth year, still pulling in customers from Milan and Missouri along with a few diffident English) could be translated entire, dimmer lights and all, to a theatre as one of the *Eccentricities of Cardinal Pirelli*. Which Tovey you see may depend more on you than on him. ('We go to Miller Howe because we find 24 hours there is the equivalent of 36 hours anywhere else.') One inspector who admired the show more than some of the substance is doubtful, like many others, about the wisdom of the 'seven vegetables of the apocalypse' that are served with every main course. An equally shrewd critic compares the kitchen team (staff turnover in this house is almost nil) with too many *outré* effects in the same bar used by a master of orchestration who never allows oboe or trombones a tune unadorned. Others, though – including professional cooks who go there to recharge their imaginations by tasting, say, the chilled mutton broth with dry sherry and mint – pay less attention to the dining-room parade of a leg of lamb 'complete with the hay in which it was roasted' than they do to the 'tender, pink and juicy meat, perfectly set off by a puree of cauliflower with pine kernels.' They also know that for this pinnacle to be reached Mr Tovey has compared for taste roasted joints from carcasses of local lamb that have been hung for four, eleven, and eighteen days respectively (the last won). That joint, besides, was only the centre-piece of a dinner (choiceless, as always, till the sweet stage) that ran the gamut from a peach coated with savoury cream cheese and browned under the grill, chicken and water melon consommé ('a most subtle balance of flavours'), and turbot in a tangy lime butter, to original Cointreau and orange ice-box pudding (it might equally have been mango fool, or kiwi fruit and almond meringue gateau . . .) On the hotel side, the unforced courtesy of the staff, the Buck's Fizz for breakfast and (piling Ossa upon Pelion) the packed lunches and afternoon teas, readily excuse the prices. Wines (from £3·50) are now more enterprisingly chosen from numerous regions besides the classic ones. A Gewürztraminer and one of the Chanson Beaunes, perhaps, will together cost well under £20 and suit a genre of cooking which will smother a weak wine and sabotage a great one. No smoking in the dining-room, thanks be. No children under twelve. Amiable recorded music. (GHG)

App: by too many members to list

WINDERMERE Cumbria   Map 7

Postern Gate
Broad Street
Windermere (096 62) 3344

A plush, Victorian restaurant with waitresses in long black dresses, gingham pinafores and mob caps. The Buntings aim 'between cafe and gourmet' and succeed, to judge from an inspector's 'pretty' curried prawn risotto (£1·85), Chelsea meat pie (£3·80) 'with good gravy and flaky crust', and modestly named almond slice, 'layers of cherry preserve around almond filling on sweet short crust.' Guinea-fowl (£5·90) and Windermere char please; 'crunchy' sauté potatoes but 'runner beans also-ran'. Are blackboard lunches subsidised by dinners? French house wines, £3·50 for 70 cl. 'Air-conditioned', but smoke is rife. 'Unobtrusive' music.

Closed L (exc Sat); Sun D;
Dec 24–26 & 31; Jan 1
Must book
Meals 12.30–1.30, 7–9.30

Tdh Sat L from £2
(meal £4·60)
Alc D £7·80 (meal £11)

Children's helpings
Seats 32

♿ rest
Air-conditioning
No dogs
Access, Am Ex, Barclay, Diners

WOLVERHAMPTON West Midlands   Map 5

Tandoor
46 Queen Street
Wolverhampton
(0902) 20747

Some wonder whether the clay-oven cooking at the Hans brothers' restaurant needs or deserves such magnificence. But others are flattered by the attention 'which suits the first-rate food.' Tandoori chicken is 'thoughtfully spiced' but nan may be heavy. Sauced dishes have been less rewarding, and chutneys and pickles, when they appear, fail to compensate. Kebabs are good, though, and raita 'was more than yoghourt.' 'Superb kulfi and creamy, sweet lassi.' Hirondelle £3·50. Various beers. 'Expect delays – and hot towels between courses.' Recorded Indian music sometimes.

Closed Sun L; L Apr 7,
Aug 25 & Jan 1
Must book weekends
Meals 12–2.30, 6.30–12.30

Tdh L from £2 (meal
£2·60), D £4·50 (meal
£5·55)
Alc (min £1·75) £4·05
(meal £5·50)

Cover 25p D

Seats 90 (parties 40)
♿ rest (1 step)
Air-conditioning
No dogs
Access, Am Ex, Barclay, Diners

The Guide News Supplement will be sent out as usual, in June, to everyone who buys the book directly from Consumers' Association and to all bookshop purchasers who return the card interleaved with their copy. Let us know of any changes that affect entries in the book, or of any new places you think should be looked at.

When a restaurant says 'must book', the context of the entry usually indicates how much or how little it matters, but a preliminary telephone call averts a wasted journey to a closed door. *Always* telephone if a booking has to be cancelled: a small place (and its other customers) may suffer severely if this is not done.

WOODSTOCK Oxfordshire   Map 2

Luis
19 High Street
Woodstock (0993) 811017

Closed Mon L; Apr 7;
May 26; Aug 25; Dec 26;
Jan 1
Must book D
Meals 12–2.30, 6.30–11

Tdh L £3·95 (meal
£7·75), D £4·50
(meal £8·35)
Alc £8·45 (meal £12·75)

Service 10%
Cover 35p
Children's helpings
(under 6)
Seats 32
♿ rest
No dogs
Am Ex, Barclay, Diners

'The best place for miles around,' says one veteran eater, presumably excluding Oxford itself from this generous catchment. Another member whose set dinner included a 'violent' sauce for pork and 'a rather odd' crème brûlée dissents violently. But a test meal at Luis Castro's Pyrenean restaurant leant to the former judgement. Even the set meal, with duck and bacon terrine (served with Cumberland sauce), poached trout, fried aubergines, and 'hard-topped but acceptable' crème brûlée was satisfactory; and if you keep an eye on the Castros' specialities (they do their own cooking) you may do very well with shellfish soup (£1), fresh squid, scallops and langoustines in various ways, breast of chicken either stuffed with crab and served with hollandaise or done with a Pernod and garlic sauce, or crab soufflé. A customer who telephoned to notify a flight delay sat down to a warm welcome and an excellent dinner at or after the usual closing time. Carafe Merlot is now £4·40 a litre, but an inspector counsels instead 'a glass of chilled San Patricio, and a bottle of Marqués de Riscal red' (£5 in 1979). Please contain smoking to the bar upstairs. Recorded music.

App: Gerald Landau, S.C.J., M.A.P.

WOOTTON BASSETT Wiltshire   Map 2

Loaves and Fishes
The Old Lime Kiln House
on A420
M4 exit 16
Wootton Bassett (079 370)
3597

Closed Mon; Sat L;
Sun D; Dec 24 D;
Dec 25, 26 & 31; Jan 1
Must book
Meals 12.30–1.30,
7.30–8.30

Alc £7·50 (meal £10·95)

Children's helpings
(under 8)
Seats 20 (parties 6)
Car park
No dogs in d/r
Access card

Doubts centre not on the food but on the security of tenure, so be sure to give warning of approach. But, as before, 'there is no better place for an escape from the bedlam of the M4 for a Friday evening dinner' than Angela Rawson and Nikki Kedge's Elizabethan house and walled garden. They have the sense and strength of character to offer very little choice until the sweet stage. If something miscarries there are no excuses, but this is a rare event, and an inspector reports a deliciously seasonal Sunday lunch of 'very crabby' crab mousse with fennel garnishing, chilled cucumber soup as an alternative, roast poussin with herb sauce and plainly but accurately cooked vegetables, and to finish, an inspirational orange and Cointreau gateau decorated with daffodil heads. Trout pâté, avocado mousse, roast pork, raspberry sorbet and other items are also praised. Argentine red or white wine is £3·85, with English Adgestone '77, £6, Les Ormes-de-Pez '73, £9, and agreeable port and madeira by the glass. No smoking in the dining-room while others are eating. No children under eight for dinner. Recorded classical music. More reports, please.

For the explanation of ♿, denoting accessibility for the disabled, see 'How to use the Guide', p. 4.

King Charles II
29 New Street
Worcester (0905) 22449

Charles merely changed disguises at this half-timbered house. Decent dress is still preferred in the Pedrini regime but lingering is now worthwhile. A member who 'knows real lasagne when I see it', saw it, and stayed to enjoy orange poached in syrup with Grand Marnier (£1). 'A better menu than one expects', with fish salad (£1·80), fresh prawns and cannelloni alla piemontese possible first courses, and beef Wellington (£5·80), saltimbocca (£4) and salmon trout au vin blanc the owner-chef's favourite main courses. Muscadet was £4·60 in 1979. 'Very good coffee, pleasant service.' No children under ten at dinner.

Closed Sun; public hols
(exc Apr 4); last 3 weeks
July
Must book

Meals 12.30–1.45,
7.30–9.30

Tdh L £5 (meal £8)
Alc £8·30 (meal £11·60)

Seats 35
No dogs
Access, Am Ex, Barclay,
Euro

Poyers Farm
off A361
4 m NW of Barnstaple
Braunton (0271) 812149

Ring the doorbell long and loud to penetrate this roadside farmhouse, thatch without, cut glass and silver within. (Take the road to the west off the A361 opposite the Williams Arms.) The menu too aspires to grandeur, but ignore Rossini and Henry IV styles and take good roast saddle of venison (though when tried, the meat was fought down by the aromatic sauce), salmon Biaka at a day's notice and goose, perhaps, at Christmas. 'Veal was tough.' Ratatouille pleases among the five vegetables included in main dish prices. 'Juicy' grilled fish and soups 'the only cooked first courses.' Creamy sweets. Wines are dear (Rioja cheapest at £4·25). Lunches now Sunday only; they plan to provide accommodation from Easter. 'Modern' music: Bee Gees or Berg?

Closed L (exc Sun);
Sun D (exc summer);
Dec 25 & 26; Jan 1;
last week Feb
Must book
Meals 1–2 (Sun),
7.30–9.30 (10 Sat)

Tdh Sun L £4·85
(meal £7·30)
Alc £7·95 (meal £12·10)

Service inc
Seats 42 (parties 20)
♻ rest (1 step)

Car park
No dogs
Am Ex card
10 rooms (all with bath)
B&B from £15

Since each restaurant has a separate file in the Guide office, please use a separate form or sheet of paper for each report. Additional forms may be obtained free (no stamp required) from The Good Food Guide, Freepost, 14 Buckingham Street, London WC2N 6BR (unfortunately Freepost facilities are not available from the Channel Islands or the Republic of Ireland).

Unless otherwise stated, a restaurant is open all week and all year and is licensed.

WRELTON North Yorkshire   Map 8

Huntsman
off A170
2 m NW of Pickering
Pickering (0751) 72530

Closed Mon; Sun D;
Dec 25
Must book D & weekends
Meals 12–2, 7–9.30

Tdh L from £2·95
(meal £5·15), D from
£5·90 (meal £8·10)

Service inc
Children's helpings
Seats 40 (parties 15)
 rest
Car park
No dogs in public rooms
3 rooms
B&B £15
Fire cert

David and Annette Bell have done wonders with this stone-fronted pub in sporting country off the A170 since they left the Worsley Arms at Hovingham (*q.v.*) three years ago. Clear tastes and willing service are impressions that remain in visitors' minds – perhaps too willing on occasion, for 'we had to wait for our claret to cool.' The cooking offers something for most generations of food preferences. A Londoner praises the soups, shellfish barquette (95p extra as a first course on the set menu), 'very fresh local trout with mushroom sauce', lamb in tarragon sauce, and imaginative vegetables, including stuffed courgettes. More local and frequent visitors are no less pleased with a half-duck in celery sauce, and lamb cutlets, cooked pink to request, with a Pernod-tinged sauce. The puddings, too, are enterprising: blackberry or hazelnut meringue, a Black Forest gateau that stood south German comparisons, fruit pies, peaches in caramel, and ginger chocolate fudge. The short Yorkshire Fine Wines list begins at £3·60, and beers are pressurised. The bar snacks are good, but not served at weekends. Recorded music.

*App: Peter Hall, John Beech, D. A. Slade,
C.M.R., H.G., and others*

WYE Kent   Map 3

Wife of Bath
🍷
4 Upper Bridge Street
Wye (0233) 812540

Closed Sun; Mon (exc
May 5 & 26, & Aug 25);
Apr 4; Dec 24–26 & 31
Must book
Meals 12–2, 7–10

Alc £6·75 (meal £10·05)

Cover 45p
Children's helpings
Seats 65 (parties 18)
 rest
Car park
No dogs

It is always dispiriting for a restaurant to lose a long-held *Guide* distinction, but the year's reports of this 'oasis among the oast-houses' suggest that members were right in thinking that a certain *élan* had been lost. Michael Waterfield still has a half-time role, and Robert Johnson still cooks, with Brian Boots managing. The kitchen also still produces on occasion dishes of the highest class: an inspector's ham mousse, served with a dill, cucumber and cream sauce, was 'more than a nod in the direction of Eugénie-les-Bains.' Fritters of fennel 'which we have had before with tomato and basil sauce, this time came with walnut and anchovy, a delicious variation. How many places would think of serving gurnard as a first course, or include John Dory in an aromatic bourride? Turbot and roast guinea-fowl have been our best main courses; duck normande has been flabby' (a criticism lately repeated by others). Salmon and lobster en croûte apart, August and September seem to have been months when too little went right; nor do coffee and service sound reliably what they were. At the sweet stage, the creamy ices and intense sorbets or perhaps a tarte aux fruits may be the best. 'White-wine fanciers are well catered for, as you might expect where the owners have also been English

343

vignerons; red-wine lovers may have to look harder, though (if it is still there) an inspector puts in a word for Ch. de Fieuzal '72. Glasses of dessert Muscat or Quarts de Chaume are always pleasing.

App: Philip Young, Wilson Plant, Sir John Stow, Neil Fairlamb, C. P. Cretton, J. & P.S., and others

---

YARM Cleveland   Map 8

Santoro
47 High Street
Eaglescliffe (0642) 781305

The Serinos divide their time between Richmond (q.v.) and this 'intimate' restaurant on Yarm's broad High Street. 'Try filetto di maiale fiorentina (£4) in a cheesy sauce, and intoxicating rum and raisin trifle.' 'A huge sole filled with crab and prawns', and stuffed potatoes, are also praised. Tagliatelle carbonara (£1·50), calamari livornese and duckling alla pesca (£4·90) vie with potted prawns provençale and halibut portugese on the shortish menu. Weekday bar snacks (lasagne, crab salad, seafood pancake). 'Various Italian wines.' Pressurised beers. Guitar music, sometimes live, and dancing. No jeans. More reports, please.

Closed Sun; Sat L; public hols Must book D Meals 12–2, 7.30–10.15	Tdh L £3·75 (meal £6·25) Alc £7·05 (meal £10·35) Service 10% (food)	Children's helpings (under 12) Seats 48 No dogs Barclay, Diners

---

YORK North Yorkshire   Map 5

Lew's Place
King's Staith
York (0904) 28167

'Very busy, people have to wait, seats still hard!' writes Lewis Speight in triumph. Most members also accept loud music and 'breathless' (though 'cheerful') service in exchange for huge helpings at prices that belie the careful cooking and presentation. 'Yummy mushrooms, stuffed, pushed together, crumbed and deep fried (75p), daunting steak and kidney, large cheeseboard.' Automatic rice with curry and 'provençale' dishes, 'crisp' chips with grills and fish. Tables crowded with salads, self-helped. 'Sharp dressings, solid trifle.' Bass and Stones on hand-pump; wines listed by price (Ch. La Terrasse '74, £4·20, comes twelfth). 'No children in later evening' and little food.

Closed Sun; Apr 7; 1st 2 weeks Sept; Dec 25, 26 & 31 No bookings	Meals 12–2, 6.45–10 Alc £4·50 (meal £7·55)	Seats 45 ♿ rest (2 steps) No dogs

---

Numbers are given for private parties only if they can be accommodated in a room separate from the main dining-room; when there are several such rooms, the capacity of the largest is given. Some restaurants will take party bookings at times when they are normally closed.

St William's Restaurant
College Street
York (0904) 34830

Gluttony is next to godliness in this medieval (but often altered) house for chantry priests just east of the Minster. As at the Undercroft in Durham (*q.v.*), Milburns' daily bread extends to cheese and nut pudding, 'proper' shepherd's pie, and light but tasty quiche (50p) as well as daily soups, 'juicy' cold cuts and zestful salads (raw mushroom, cauliflower à la grecque, creamed beans, 20p), and tempting sweets (date and fig pie, 'real' trifle). 'Semi-self-service', though friendly young staff preside. They will provide set meals for parties (from £2·85) and afternoon teas (also on summer Sundays). Sansovino £3 a litre. Flexible seating indoors and out, 'ideal for families'. No-smoking area. Parties in medieval rooms by arrangement.

Closed D (exc by arrangement); Sun (exc 2–5.30 summer); Dec 25 & 26

Open 10–5 (5.30 summer), L 12–2

Alc L £2·15 (meal £3·90)

Service inc
Seats 80 (parties 150)
♿ rest (2 steps)
Car park (6)

WALES

Bronheulog Hotel
off A499
6 m SW of Pwllheli
Abersoch (075 881) 2177

Closed L; Sun; Mon
(exc summer); Apr 6;
Dec 24–26 & 31; Jan 1
Must book
D only, 7–9

Tdh £7·70 (meal £10·15)

Service inc
Seats 50
Car park
No dogs in public rooms
5 rooms
B&B £8–£9·50
Fire cert

For six years now the Welsh section has begun with this 'hotel on a hill in the sun' – 'a little gem of a place' (built by Clough Williams-Ellis). It is run by Stefano Zanier (who cooks) and his Welsh wife, with grandma's help, and their punctual, considerate service relaxes people easily. Besides, 'at dinner one picks up the menu with pleasurable anticipation, and the knowledge that they will go out of their way to please you.' Fresh mussel soup may arrive, says Mr Zanier, 'when tides permit', but local crab with lemon juice and cream, brill with white-wine sauce, and cannelloni are less subject to the phases of the moon. Avocado, artichoke and prawn salad was an enterprising first course, though the vinaigrette was too vinegary. At a test meal, the roast veal in armagnac and cream sauce and, above all, the medallions of beef in red wine sauce (£3·60) did credit alike to the butcher and the *saucier*. Puddings included a light lemon mousse 'full of flecks of rind' and a 'lightly cooked peach in a lovely brandy syrup'. 'Brandy-snaps to end all brandy-snaps are normal fare at Bronheulog.' It is a great pity, from a long-stayer's point of view, that the wines (from £4 a litre for Cavitello carafes) are so humdrum, and that there are only bottled beers. No children under 12 as residents, and younger children must be *bonnes fourchettes* to eat in the dining-room, though the Zaniers are kind to them.

App: E. F. Haylock, J.R., L.O'B., Helen Murray

Porth Tocyn Hotel
9½ m SW of Pwllheli
Abersoch (075 881) 2966

Closed Nov; Dec; mid-
week (Jan & Feb)
Must book
Meals 1–1.30, 7.30–9.30

Tdh L from £5·55 (meal
from £8·75), D from £8
(meal from £11·70)

Children's helpings
Seats 60
♿ rest (1 step) & hotel
Car park
No dogs

This prosperous-looking house above Cardigan Bay has been in the same family for thirty years, and Mrs Fletcher-Brewer and her son Nicholas seem to have brought its head back into the wind after uncertain veering a while ago. Much money has been spent on heating and general upgrading, and the reward is a lawyer's comment that, 'If you must go to Abersoch in mid-winter, this is obviously the place to stay or eat. The hospitality was outstanding, and I was surprised at that season to find so much choice at dinner, including rich onion soup, a good home-made pâté, grilled sole with fresh winter vegetables (sautéed swede, crisp cabbage and garlic potatoes), and home-made mint ice-cream followed by both fruit and cheese.' One summer inspector found the cooking more chequered, with 'expert and delicious' Zwiebelfleisch preceded by 'dry and tasteless trout and apple pâté' and followed by 'leaden' gâteau

Access, Am Ex, Diners
17 rooms (15 with bath)
B&B prices on application

Pithiviers. But another was delighted by the apricot and mint sauce for lamb, and the coffee crunch cheesecake, and even the basket of fruit 'including nectarines'. Miss Elliott's best dishes, she thinks, also include port and oxtail soup, asparagus and smoked chicken quiche, roast guinea-fowl with peach and ginger sauce, courgettes in soured cream, and orange and kirsch soufflé. Service is 'pretty and pleasant, and if they don't know they go and ask.' Wines begin with house red or white burgundy at a modest £3·70, and there is a ceiling on mark-ups so that Ch. Malescot-St-Exupéry '67, c.b., is relatively better value than the immature Ch. Grand Barrail '76 (£5·50). You may eat in the garden. Dancing 'in winter occasionally'. They prefer a jacket and tie at night. (GHG)

App: D. R. Saunders, G. G. Gee, R. Plastow, P.M., J.R., and others

---

ABERYSTWYTH Dyfed   Map 4

Julia's
17 Bridge Street
Aberystwyth (0970)
617090

Closed Sun; Mon;
Dec 25 & 26; Jan 1;
2 weeks Jan
Must book D
Meals 12.30–2, 7.30–10

Tdh D £6·25 (meal £8·90)
Alc L £3·15 (meal £5·50),
D £7·15 (meal £9·90)

Children's helpings
(under 12)
Seats 35
No dogs in d/r

Julia Hallinan is said to be a 23-year-old missionary from Cardiff to Ystwyth's coral coasts, armed with sackfuls of Tourist Board money for the creation of this green and pink interior in an early Victorian terrace. The arrival of Rosie's (q.v.) in the same wave suggests that hostesses, like Mormons, come in pairs, but local gossips and eaters have gracefully accepted this devotion to their welfare: 'We were delighted by the chilled cucumber soup, crab pâté, pigeon in white wine, nutty cabbage and orange syllabub in our set dinner.' Inspectors, who betray a Catholic or Calvinist impatience with upstart sects of this type, endorse instead another member's comment: 'Go with patience and a sense of humour.' For though soups have been uniformly successful, salmon moist, and tournedos poivre vert (£4·95 à la carte) competently cooked, quiche pastry was wet, vegetables erratic, cream sauces amateurish, sweets and cheeses 'good value only by good fortune', and the service neophyte – 'stunned by queries, and slow to mop up even their own spillages.' Table wines are £2·80, Fronsac £3·40, and there are a couple of dozen others. More reports, please.

Within parts of these old county boundaries, alcohol is not served on Sunday, except to hotel residents: Anglesey, Cardigan, Carmarthen, Merioneth.

'Meal' indicates the cost of a meal for one, including food, coffee, a half-bottle of one of the cheapest wines listed, cover, service, and VAT (see 'How to use the Guide', p. 4).

Meal times refer to first and last orders.

Do not risk using an out-of-date Guide. A new edition will appear early in 1981.

ABERYSTWYTH Dyfed   Map 4

Rosie's
The Gables,
Penglais Road
Aberystwyth (0970) 4397

Small – even cramped – restaurant run by a doctor's
wife in a Victorian house on the hill up to the new
university campus. Note the limited opening times.
'Charming' staff, flowers and an open fire support the
set dinner, changed every two weeks: perhaps rough
country pâté or tasty onion soup; pork cutlet or
ballotine of duck with mostly correctly cooked
vegetables; apricot and apple crunch or blackberry
and apple flan. (The small *carte* changes almost as
often.) Sauces are sometimes amateurish. Litre Vin
carafes £2 for 50 cl. Recorded classical music.

Closed L; Sun; Mon;	Tdh £6·90 (meal £9·70)	Seats 24
Tue; Thur	Alc £6·65 (meal £10·55)	🔥 rest
Must book		Car park
D only, 7.15–9.15	Cover 50p alc	

BEAUMARIS Anglesey, Gwynedd   Map 4

Hobson's Choice
13 Castle Street
Beaumaris (0248) 810323

Closed Sun; Mon L;
Dec 24–26
Must book D
Meals 12–2, 7–10

Alc L £2·65 (meal £4·85),
D £6·15 (meal £9·30)

Service 10%
Cover 15p D
Children's helpings
Seats 65 (parties 40)
🔥 rest (1 step)
No dogs
Access card

'A discovery that amply repaid the cost of my *Guide*,'
says a member kindly, approaching Anglesey with a
certain scepticism. Not everyone was as fortunate in
the early part of the year, and an autumn inspector
was relieved to find 'authentic' cream of watercress
soup with good wholemeal bread, equally tasty
chicken and duck liver pâté, and 'meltingly tender'
roast lamb with garlic and oregano, not overcooked.
Scallops in mushroom, cheese and white wine sauce,
and the vegetables, required a more delicate touch.
Ian Mirrlees's grilled king prawns with melted butter,
roast guinea-fowl, bass with sultanas, almonds and
tomatoes (£4·20), winter pheasant casserole with
chestnuts, and simpler lunch dishes are also worth
trying. 'Peaches in brandy made a more successful
sweet than the profiteroles, and it was good to see
fresh mangoes as well as raspberries on offer in
September.' The low-beamed bar and close quarters in
the dining-room make people regret Patricia Talbot's
reluctance to curb smoking. Litre Vin carafes are
£3·50 for 80 cl, and Ch. Talbot '73, c.b., was £8 in
1979. A young man sings to a guitar three nights
a week.

App: J. G. S. Scott, K.S.M., W.H., R.V.M., J.F.G.

BROAD HAVEN Dyfed   Map 4

Druidstone Hotel
Druidstone Haven
2 m N of Broad Haven
on coast road
Broad Haven (043 783)
221

'A beast, but a just beast' (a Rugby schoolboy's
famous description of his headmaster) roughly
represents Rod and Jane Bell's view of the *Guide*.
Over the years we have sent them, they say, families
who enjoy the scatty *Survivors* atmosphere on this
sublime cliff-top, along with unusually good (and

Closed Sun D; Nov;
Dec 24–26 (exc res)
Must book D & Sun L
Meals 12.30–2, 7.30–9.30

Tdh L £5·50 (meal £7·95),
D £7 (meal £9·60)

Children's helpings
(under 12)
Seats 36
♿ rest; w.c.
Car park
No dogs in d/r
8 rooms
B&B £9
D, B&B from £12
Fire cert

careful) food at modest prices. We have also deterred
more fastidious visitors who, in the words of one of
them, 'would only think the grazing safe when all
those atrocious children with bows and arrows were
safely in bed.' (Children are, in fact, expected to eat
high tea before dinner.) Inspectors, though, agree on
the merits of Mrs Bell's food: for instance, the
home-baked bread, local bass and mackerel inventively
treated, comforting soups ('hot peanut', one visitor
reports), salmon and halibut kebabs with
hollandaise, legs of chicken enlivened by soy, ginger
and garlic and served with a crisp salad at half the
price a self-service wine bar would charge, vegetables –
from mushrooms in sour cream to beetroot in onion
sauce – and good puddings (though fudge and nut
tart demands a dangerously sweet tooth). 'Rod's beef
casserole with beer, treacle and vinegar' comes first
on the kitchen's own list. At a test meal, even the
coffee was good. Notre Dame carafes are £2·50 for
50 cl and there is a good range of other wines:
Vieux-Château-Tropchaud '71, £8·05 or £4·25 a half;
Winkeler Hönigberg Spätlese '75, £5·75; an uncommon
Basque white at £5·05. There are bar snacks at
lunch-time in season (except Saturday) and Sunday
evening brings a fine cold buffet. There are some
tables outside. Music is confined to the cellar bar or
'grot' as a punning member calls it. Service is
relaxed, and telephone bookings may go astray.

App: R. Marsh, Joan Taylor, J.R., P.O'R.S.,
Paul Brown, and others

BULL BAY Anglesey, Gwynedd   Map 4

Pot Luck
Amlwch
Amlwch (0407) 830885

Closed L; Sun;
Mon (exc public hols);
Tue (exc July & Aug);
Oct–Easter
Must book
D only, 7.30–9

Alc (min £4) £4·45
(meal £6·65)

Seats 16
No dogs

'Less of a gamble than the name implies,' says a
crusted inspector who reacted against the repro
furniture and tangerine paper napery of Ann Peters's
dining-room (an experiment in expansion was
called off during the year), but he found the cooking
as good as anything he had lately tried on the North
Wales beat. The owner has 'two faithful helpers', and
her avocado mousse, stuffed spinach pancake with
béchamel, tomatoes stuffed with cream cheese,
walnuts and celery, and Stilton soup are reliably
good first courses. Liver italienne, fish flan (£2·50) or
carbonnade of beef may be the best main dishes,
but all the tastes are 'clean'. Charlotte russe at a test
meal was 'marvellously light considering its richness',
and Miss Peters is a dab hand at Pavlovas. The wines
(from £2·70) are elementary. Good coffee. Recorded
music.

App: C. Brian Davies, R.J., and others

1980 prices are as estimated by restaurateurs in the autumn of 1979 (including VAT).

Field's
99 Wyeverne Road,
Cathays
Cardiff (0222) 23554

Vegetarian wholefood restaurant in 'farmhouse kitchen style' (dowdy, say some), trying to produce food that even carnivores enjoy. Some success with stuffed savoury pancakes; pizzas; buckwheat, hazelnut and lentil sausages; and 'out of this world' banana fritters – related to the 'infinite avocado' listed? Try too walnut oatburgers with tamari sauce (£1·85), Russian vegetable pie (£1·90) and cauliflower and mushroom pudding (£1·90). Salads, juices and teas as well. Frequently changed menu; eat here or take away. Recorded music.

Closed Sun; Mon; Aug;
1 week Chr; Dec 31
Open noon–11 (L 12–2)

Alc L £3·50 (meal £3·70)

Service inc
Children's helpings

Seats 36
♿ rest
No dogs
Unlicensed

Gibson's
6–8 Romilly Crescent,
Canton
Cardiff (0222) 41264

Closed Sun; Mon;
1 week Chr; public hols
Must book
Meals 12.30–2.30, 7.30–10

Tdh D (Tue–Thur) £6·75
(meal £9·90)
Alc £6·30 (meal £9·85)

Service 10%
Cover 40p (Fri & Sat)
Children's helpings
Seats 36
Car park (4)
No dogs
Access, Am Ex, Barclay,
Diners

It is time we had a better spread of reports on Irene Canning's 'elusive' and to the casual eye uninviting restaurant, where cooking well above the Cardiff average has been observed these seven years past. For one thing, Matthew Canning has joined his mother and the others in the kitchen; for another, an early admirer, after a rather mixed dinner, recalls the days 'when they were still engagingly surprised that one thought their food good; now that it is less good, they are less surprised.' The best meals, almost certainly, are the mid-week five-course regional dinners at set prices, with adequate choice: Provence, Alsace, and so on, with the very dish names an evocation. A la carte, a test meal fell down on freshness of fish and judgement of seasoning; its best features, unusually, were the cooking of potatoes, green beans and other vegetables, the raspberries and nectarines in the gateau of the day, and the coffee. On the changing carte, note, perhaps, soups (85p), 'robust' pâté de campagne – 'a hefty slice, as it should be at £1·50', steak in overcoat (£4·60), and guinea-fowl with gin and juniper. The wines, from good sources, are fairly priced, with Vin Vivant £3·60 a litre in 1979, Saumur '76 or Burglayer Schloss Kapelle '77 just under £5, and Pernand-Vergelesses '72, £8·95. Mrs Canning makes it easy for her guests to smoke, but says she discourages it when it is a nuisance: a career in politics clearly lies open to her. More reports, please.

PLEASE keep sending in reports, as soon as possible after each meal. The cut-off date for the 1981 Guide is September 30, 1980, but reports are even more useful earlier in the year, especially for the remoter areas and new places. Late autumn reports can also affect corrections at proof stage.

Within parts of these old county boundaries, alcohol is not served on Sunday, except to hotel residents: Anglesey, Cardigan, Carmarthen, Merioneth.

Harvesters
5 Pontcanna Street
off Cathedral Road
Cardiff (0222) 32616

Giampero Fama is famous for filling you up with a flair, and though 1979 brought an untypical report of tasteless potted shrimps, tough beef and veal, and ill-cooked vegetables, his pea soup, kidneys in brandy sauce, kedgeree (£1·45), pasta Ty Mawr (£4·30) and jugged hare (£5·85) may reassure. Treacle tart has friends too. Wines from £3·75 for French or German; California Cabernet Sauvignon £5·75. No pipes.

Closed L; Sun; Mon; 3 weeks Aug; Dec 25 & 26; Jan 1
Must book

D only, 7–11

Alc (min £4·30) £7·85 (meal £10·05)

Children's helpings
Seats 38
Air-conditioning
No dogs

Riverside
44 Tudor Street
Cardiff (0222) 372163

Must book
Open noon–midnight

Tdh D from £4 (meal from £4·85)
Alc £5·30 (meal £6·25)

Service 10%
Seats 140
Air-conditioning
No dogs
Access, Am Ex, Barclay, Diners, Euro

Speaker George Thomas's taste in Cardiff Chinese restaurants (his opening of Mr Chan's place is commemorated in a plaque on the wall) has been confirmed by appreciative reports during the year. Although one diner was pursued into the street by irate waiters after she had withheld a service charge on the grounds of a two and a half hours' wait to be fed. But the service is on the whole civil and ungrasping, and the ayes have it that this is one of the best Cantonese places outside London, taking into account the egg-fried rice (60p, and usually a good test), spare ribs, deep-fried crispy king prawns, fried sliced beef Cantonese-style, crispy chicken, duck with ginger and spring onions, 'crunchy' mixed vegetables, and even the set dinners. As the owners point out, you could eat a different meal every day for two months, and the list of dim-sum (served from noon till 8 p.m. – reports welcome) argues the presence of a specialist chef. Other specialities include stuffed duck (£5), and baked crab and lobster. A French wine firm based in Cardiff (Luc Lacerre) provides a long list, fancily priced, but a local doctor perversely prescribes dry white Chefoo Shansi at £4·50. Decor and table settings are wearing already. Repetitive music.

App: J. R. Wardley, H. L. Young, D.J.G., J.I.J., J. S. & F. Waters, Patrick Bromley, and others

---

CASTLE MORRIS Dyfed   Map 4

Y Gwesty Bach
on B4331
3½ m W of Letterston
Letterston (034 84) 337

Closed L; Sun; Mon & Tue (mid-Nov to May 27); Wed (mid-Nov to Apr 2); mid-Oct to mid-Nov; Dec 25 & 26; Jan 1; Feb

Students of language go to this corner of England in Wales to study macaronic mixtures – 'I heard one long burst of Welsh ending with "appendix bust".' Whiz Collis, with Laura Ashley patterns in her dining-room and teeming hippopotami in her hall, is herself not above a few macaronic flights, what with her leek roulade and Welsh salt duck, her fiori di zucchini ripieni al pilaf (which few restaurants outside Italy do), her youvarlakia me avgolemono and her tandoori chicken. The implicit challenge to herself is bold, and usually met: 'indeed, she nudges

351

Must book
D only, 7.30–9.30

Tdh £7·50 (meal £10·75)

Service 10%
Children's helpings
Seats 30
♿ rest
Car park
No dogs

higher distinction.' An experienced inspector reckons on remembering for a long time the 'simple, delicate-tasting' hot scallop mousse that began his set dinner, and the 'irresistible' blackcurrant crème brûlée that ended it; another was equally admiring of 'huge mushrooms in a very light and crisp batter, served with hollandaise', a true bordelaise sauce for fillet steak, 'tender and gamey' pigeon, and profiteroles filled with a 'soft, light chocolate mixture, with hazelnut meringue as an alternative temptation.' Sometimes meals can be faulted for balance: the tandoori spiced, marinated chicken with 'superbly cooked vegetables and rice' at a test meal made the puddings afterwards look too sumptuous, and if you are unlucky, Stilton (normally praised) will be 'long past its best'. The dining-room and bar ('now dominated by a stuffed albatross'), are run by Tony Roberts 'in his half-moon specs', author of *A Guide to Walking the Pembrokeshire Coast Path*. The house wines are Vermorel red or Gaudet white at £3·40 a litre.

App: J. Meyrick Thomas, P.O'R.S., J.R., J.R.D., A.A.B.C., and others

---

COLWYN BAY Clwyd   Map 4

Holland Arms
on B5113
6 m S of Colwyn Bay
Tynygroes (049 267) 308

This 'Sanderson-curtained and cushioned' place 'must once have been a coaching-inn – it's in the middle of nowhere.' The handwritten menu follows the straight and narrow of fillet, escalope and suprême in sauce but first courses and sweets diverge a little. 'Tender' kidneys (either curried or in garlic sauce, 95p), mushrooms provençale and Dolcelatte mousse (better than a prawn and cream cheese version) may contrast with 'poor meat, floury sauces and boiled vegetables' later, but guinea-fowl and seafood provençale have impressed. 'Grainy' blackberry sorbet, brown sugar meringues and iced coffee gateau. House wine £3·45. Pressurised beers. Soft recorded music. You may eat outside.

Closed Sun & Mon
(exc L May 26–end Aug);
Tue D; Dec 24–26;
Jan 1 L
Must book D

Meals 12–2.30, 7.30–9.30

Alc £7·55 (meal £10·70)

Children's helpings

Seats 50 (parties 30)
♿ rest
Car park
No dogs
Access, Am Ex, Diners, Euro

Entries for places with distinctions carry symbols (pestle, tureen, bottle, glass). Credits are fully written entries, with approvers' names below the text. Passes are telegraphic entries (useful in the area) with details under the text. Provisional entries are in italics (see 'How to use the Guide', p. 4).

If you think you are suffering from food-poisoning after eating in a restaurant, report this immediately to the local Public Health Authority (and write to us).

CRICIETH Gwynedd Map 4

Moelwyn Restaurant
29 Mona Terrace
Cricieth (076 671) 2500

'Informal, but neither cafe nor bistro,' writes an inspector thankfully of the Booths' creeper-clad Victorian house above Cardigan Bay, whence the mackerel (£2·50 and 'tasty') arrive. The dinner menu is frenchified (and included asparagus in July) but pride is taken in local fish and lamb. 'Mushy' vegetables. Lunch includes a cold buffet with 'excellent dressed crab', or quiche and pâté in the bar. Argentine Franchette wines £2 for 50 cl. 'Light classics' on tape. 'Heavy smokers eased towards coffee lounge.'

Closed Mon & D Sun (exc mid-July to mid-Sept); mid-Oct to Easter (exc weekends & L Dec 25) Must book D	Meals 12.30–2, 7–9 Tdh L £2·90 (meal £5·40), D £4·35 (meal £7) Alc L £3·25 (meal £5·80), D £5·80 (meal £8·60)	Children's helpings Seats 30 ⑤ rest (1 step) Air-conditioning No dogs

CRICKHOWELL Powys Map 4

Gliffaes Country House
off A40
2½ m W of Crickhowell
Bwlch (0874) 730371

'Guard your handbag from the labrador' who escorts round the estate those who forgo Black Mountain walks and the Usk's salmon fishing. Several visitors are cool to 'amateurish' cooking and service, with some dinners strongly suggesting a cook's day off. But in the buffet lunches and set dinners (the order reversed on Sunday) others praise marinated kippers, quiche, roast lamb, duckling in black cherry sauce, beef stew in kidney sauce and bread-and-butter pudding or butterscotch gateau. Choice starts at the sweet and cheese stage. House wine, by the glass only, is 50p. John Smith's beer from the cask. Smoking discouraged. 'Jacket and tie at dinner.' A few tables outside. (GHG)

Closed Dec 31 to mid-Mar Must book Meals 1–2, 7.45–9 Tdh L £4·80 (meal £6·30), D £6·70 (meal £8·20)	Service inc Children's helpings Seats 40 (parties 40) ⑤ rest Car park No dogs	21 rooms (11 with bath) B&B £10·30–£15·30 Full board £16–£24·50 p.d. Fire cert

Towns shown in black on our maps contain at least one recommended restaurant, pub or wine bar (see map key). The dot denotes the location of the town or village, not the establishment. Where necessary, we give directions to it in the entry. If you can, help us to improve them.

Most places will accept cheques only when they are accompanied by a cheque card or adequate identification. Information about which credit cards are accepted is correct when printed, but restaurants may add to or subtract from the list without notice.

See p. 508 for the restaurant-goer's legal rights, and p. 510 for information on hygiene in restaurants.

Nantyffin Cider Mill
Talgarth Road
at junction of A40 &
A479
Crickhowell (0873) 810775

Thundering traffic pains the pleasure gardens at this pink-washed stone house by the Usk. Imbibers of pints and Radio One augment the hubbub. Yet the Ambroses' cooking brings quiet folk too to the bar for sandwiches and snacks ('perfect' cottage pie, rare roast beef but 'boring' lasagne). In another room mushrooms and onions in wine, sweetbreads, steak au poivre, fresh vegetables, and melon and ginger ice-cream made one dinner; soused mackerel in cider, mushroom and other mousses, and lime ice-cream also sound inviting, though 'fish pie had dull potato and too little salmon.' Short wine line, from £4·50 for a litre of white Clochemerle. Good beers on pump, and Weston's, Symonds' and Bulmers' ciders on tap. 'Shirts must be worn.' Tables in the garden.

Closed Dec 25	Alc (bar) £3·70 (meal	Seats 30
Must book D & weekends	£4·45), (rest) £7·05	🔧 rest (3 steps)
Meals 11.30–2.30, 6.30–10	(meal £10·50)	Car park
(Sun 12–1.40, 7–9.30)		No dogs in d/r

Rhos-yr-Hafod Inn
at junction of B4337 &
B4577
Nebo (097 46) 644

A rocking-horse would leave fewer saddle-sores than the rickety chairs in the Rileys' converted stable. January chills and tardy ostlers also cloud an inspector's praise of 'humble, wholesome food': 'succulent stuffed peppers', 'Welsh' guacamole, 'authentic, generous soups', spiced plum fool. Main courses are bistro-style, vegetables 'commonplace'. Bar meals, though mostly with chips, are ordered straight from the kitchen and have included 'delicious' lobster salad and the like on occasion. 'A friendly place.' Hancock's HB and Bass on hand pump more carefully kept than wine. Garden for bar food (also served at lunch-time).

Closed L (exc bar); Sun;	Meals 12–2.15 (bar), 7–9	Seats 26
Mon (exc public hols);		🔧 rest (2 steps)
Dec 25 & 26	Tdh £6 (meal £8·05)	Car park
Must book		No dogs in d/r
	Children's helpings	No rooms

The Guide News Supplement will be sent out as usual, in June, to everyone who buys the book directly from Consumers' Association and to all bookshop purchasers who return the card interleaved with their copy. Let us know of any changes that affect entries in the book, or of any new places you think should be looked at.

Please report to us on atmosphere, decor and – if you stayed – standard of accommodation, as well as on food, drink and prices (send bill if possible).

Within parts of these old county boundaries, alcohol is not served on Sunday, except to hotel residents: Anglesey, Cardigan, Carmarthen, Merioneth.

DENBIGH Clwyd   Map 4

Yr Hen Gartre
53 High Street
Denbigh (074 571) 2513

The winner of the *Liverpool Daily Post*'s 'Warmest welcome in Wales and the North-West' is helping to revive this 'forgotten market town' with simple meals served in a parlour full of bric-à-brac (the 1922 Eisteddfod chair draws admirers). People enjoy home-made soup (creamy vegetable, mushroom) with wholemeal bread at lunch, moussaka 'without finesse but clearly fresh', plum and apple tarts. Dinner runs to savoury pancakes (£1·40), beef Karoline ('ground sirloin topped with Gruyère', £5·20), trout from the fishmonger next door. Grapes, nuts and crackling at the bar. Wine is usually taken by the glass (45p). Children half-price. Recorded classical music.

Closed Sun; Mon D;
public hols (exc Dec 25);
Dec 24
Must book Sat
Meals 12–2, 7.30–9.30

Alc L £2·10 (meal £3·15),
D £6·85 (meal £9·35)

Children's helpings
(under 10)

Seats 32
No dogs
Access, Barclay, Diners,
Euro

FISHGUARD Dyfed   Map 4

Compton House Hotel
The Bistro
Main Street
Fishguard (0348) 873365

Luxton and Horne's hotel basement bistro fell out of the *Guide* for want of support a while back, but travellers through Fishguard have been glad to find it this year, for amiable service of smoked sewin, 'generous and hot chicken and mushroom pancakes as a first course', crisp chicken Kiev with the garlic and herb butter 'safe inside', and 'shaggy mushrooms' among the vegetables. Less has been heard about sweets. Nicolas table wine is £3·95 a litre, and Muscadet '78 was £4·25 in 1979. Recorded music. The rooms seem modestly priced.

Closed L; Sun;
Mon (Dec–Easter);
Dec 25 & 26
Must book
D only, 7–10.30

Alc £7·15 (meal £9·95)

Children's helpings
Seats 48 (parties 26)
Car park (6)

No dogs in public rooms
Barclaycard
5 rooms
B&B £8
Fire cert

Prices of meals underlined are those which we consider represent unusual value for money. They are not necessarily the cheapest places in the Guide, or in the locality.

Inspections are carried out anonymously. Persons who pretend to be able to secure, arrange or prevent an entry in the Guide are impostors and their names or descriptions should be reported to us

We rewrite every entry each year, and depend on fresh, detailed reports to confirm the old, as well as to include the new. The further from London you are, the more important this is.

See p. 441 for pubs and p. 491 for wine bars.

Maesllwch Arms
Glasbury (049 74) 226

Ronnie Williamson's passion is cooking and the Fwlty Twrs rough edges suggest that upkeep and renewal are seen merely as a diversion. But people seem ready to oil their own creaky doors and think the food reads well and tastes almost as good. Peach in curried cream sauce, pear with tarragon cream, and baked avocado with walnut butter exemplify the house style: clever, creamy and sweet. The dinner menu is too long for consistency ('overcooked roast lamb', 'tough guinea-fowl', curdled sauce for a mushy fish course, 'drab' cabbage) but, at the price, Wye salmon, 'juicy' duck, chocolate and chestnut turinois and orange sorbet disarm critics. Well-annotated wine list, strong on Rhône and Loire. Lunchtime bar snacks, and John Smith's bitter (pump). Children welcome. Car park.

Closed L (exc bar)	Service 10%	Access, Barclay, Diners
Must book	Children's helpings	13 rooms (6 with bath,
Meals 12–2 (bar), 7.15–9	(under 10)	1 with shower)
	Seats 30	B&B £8·05–£10·90
Tdh D £6 (meal £9·05)	No dogs in d/r	Fire cert

Cwmllechwedd Fawr
off A483
on road to Knighton
Llandrindod Wells
(0597) 83267

Closed Chr–Easter
Must book
Meals by arrangement

Tdh D £5·95 (meal £7·40)

Service inc
Seats 10
Car park
No dogs
6 rooms
D, B&B from £15

'What bliss: after a hectic summer in the Great Wen, the Barnes family has restored my faith in human nature.' Another London visitor also reports 'young ladies of humour and charm who could sustain discussion with people twice their age': lucky rural Wales, to be spared a youth culture. With Geraldine Barnes's consciously Welsh dinners, the only problem is arriving on time for them – 'Llanbister is only a beginning: take the Knighton road, and after two miles a left-hand U-turn, and later right, up a ridged track.' The remoteness may leave cook and barman out of lemons, but 'a bowl of prawn paste, still warm brown rolls, Welsh butter and home-made oat biscuits' were followed by 'a baked leg of lamb, marinated in cider, smeared with honey, and served with an onion and potato cake, and buttery French beans. Even better was to come: a vigorously risen apple sponge which we ate with huge spoonsful of syllabub.' Another visitor was equally delighted with 'giblet and fennel soup, a whole chicken with rosemary, delicious root vegetables, and apple and bilberry pie. Even so, the porridge, bacon and egg next morning took pride of place.' There is a choice of wine – red or white – at £2·70 in 1979. 'No children, and very definitely no dogs,' says Mrs Barnes. Expect Welsh evenings in a nearby barn once a week, and book at least 24 hours ahead. 'Welsh dances on record' and harp music sometimes. Details approximate. (GHG)

App: D. A. Cresswell, Mrs B. Jeeves, R.J.

LLANDEWI SKIRRID Gwent   Map 4

Walnut Tree Inn

on B4521
3 m NE of Abergavenny
Abergavenny (0873) 2797

Closed Sun; Dec 25 & 26
Must book D (d/r)
Meals 12.15–2.30 (bistro),
7.30–10.30

Alc £10 (meal £14·55)

Cover 50p D
Seats 46 (d/r), 60 (bar)
♿ rest
Air-conditioning
Car park
No dogs

Recipe in *Second Dinner
Party Book*: granita di
fragole

After the year's diet of forgettable trattorias, *Guide* inspectors are apt to say that real Italian cooking exists nowhere outside the covers of Elizabeth David and the doors of Franco Taruschio's stone-flagged, whitewashed inn in the other world at the end of the M4. Neither success, admiration nor even the throng of serious and unserious eaters at the cramped tables have spoilt the owners, and even Franco's spring holiday did not seem to upset anyone – though no doubt the challenging repertoire was tactfully pruned. 'In fourteen years I have never had a bad meal,' says a local who has eaten brodetto (fish stew) for the last three visits, finding the setting not quite relaxed enough for the plateau de fruits de mer. Clams Madras (£2·49 – plus VAT – 'unrounded prices must be an old Italian custom') were oversalted when tried, but handsomely cooked, as was the seafood pancake and 'an elegant trout with a syrupy vermouth sauce and a julienne of blanched orange zest.' A non-fishy route through the card might include the home-cured beef called bresaola, whose recipe missed a place in the *Guide*'s new cookery book but is treasured by the Editor instead; or 'scalding green lasagne' of course; or 'mouthwatering carpaccio'. Then there are main dishes, of which no more than a couple would suffice for less energetic and creative chefs: kid with Marsala and coriander, duck with kumquats, and superb game in season, from grouse and partridge under £8 to venison pie and quails in potacchio. Vegetables, salads and the dressing are less remarkable. At lunch in the bistro it may be wiser to go straight from first course to sweets, remembering that Mr Taruschio combines two enviable talents: a light and rich Austrian touch with Malakofftorte and other such figure-destroyers; and the nearly-lost Italian genius for ices: 'devastating strawberriness', as someone says of one granita – and in Italy they do not have Welsh blackberries too. Coffee is espresso. Drinking comes easily, perhaps with a red-wine spritzer at first, followed by their own imported Montepulciano red or Verdicchio white at £4·75 a litre; or if (like very few) you manage to get a seat in the formal dining-room for a leisurely evening meal, superior bottles from good merchants. 'The waitress – unlike many in Gwent – did not mind when I wrote my cheque in Welsh.'

App: by too many members to list

When a restaurant says 'must book', the context of the entry usually indicates how much or how little it matters, but a preliminary telephone call averts a wasted journey to a closed door. *Always* telephone if a booking has to be cancelled: a small place (and its other customers) may suffer severely if this is not done.

LLANGADOG Dyfed   Map 4

Plas Glansevin
off A4069
1½ m E of Llangadog
Llangadog (055 03) 238

Closed L (exc Sun in
winter); Dec 24, 25 & 31
Must book
Meals 12.30–1.30 (Sun
in winter), 7.30

Tdh £6·85 (meal £8·90)

Service inc
Seats 20 (parties 60)
 🔳 rest
Car park
No dogs
Access, Am Ex, Barclay,
Diners
7 rooms (3 with bath)
B&B £9·05–£10·40
D, B&B £14·70–£16·90
Fire cert

Horace's (freely rendered) line, 'you may drive out
naturalism with a power tool, but people keep looking
for it', accounts for the affection in people's notes
about William and Gwenda Rees's handsome old
house on the road to Myddfai. The oak and the
copper beech, the log fires and even Mrs Rees's
cooking are coupled with a sense of relaxation that
forgives slow service or a bathroom queue; the
hwyrnos (Welsh singing suppers – enquire when you
book) in the barn would also only be possible in a
district that has kept its language. In detail, the best
dishes (not forgetting the teas and the breakfasts)
may be the 'almost too creamy' soups, the pears in
tarragon mayonnaise, 'Celtic chicken' in a cream
sauce, the lamb 'baked en croûte, with orange and
redcurrant sauce, and generously helped', the
vegetables, and sweets such as blackberry fool or
orange pancakes with Grand Marnier ('lemon soufflé
and chocolate pots are too cornfloury'). Cheeses and
coffee are both adequate. Some visitors point out that
canned music is still canned music even when fed in
by a Welsh harp, and the owners seem to have
abandoned children's helpings during the year – a
serious matter for some, though residents' children
may have grills or fry-ups before dinner. The cask
bitter is Felinfoel, and the wines (not yet listed to us
this year) are strong on both Loires and Rhônes.
Enquire about their off-season weekend prices. (GHG)

*App: Ian Hume, A. F. Gueterbock, Peter Crane,
P. J. Baker, Ian & Kirstie Oswald, and others*

LLANGYNIDR Powys   Map 4

Red Lion
on B4558
10 m NW of Abergavenny
Bwlch (0874) 730223

'Nothing in France compares,' says an enthusiast for
this creeper-clad inn, self-styled *Le Lion Rouge*, but
seasoned campaigners in *le Pays de Galles* are less
poetic: 'After an hour, settled for meal abandoned by
less patient people: beef not bad, but under-cooked
potato, near-raw cabbage, vanilla instead of
blackcurrant ice-cream for "Black Death".' Another
visitor luckily found tender veal, good sauté potatoes
and a rich shortcrust in apple tart. Steak and kidney
(£3·25) also sounds reliable. Same menu in bar. Bass
from the cask is much missed; now only pressurised
beers. 'Passable' French house wine, £4·50 a litre.
'Suitable dress.' Overcrowding is a risk.

Closed L (exc Sun);
Dec 25 & 26
Must book
Meals 12–2 (Sun), 6–11

Alc £6 (meal £9·35)

Service 10%
Seats 60 (parties 30)
 🔳 rest

Car park
No dogs
7 rooms
B&B £6·50

LLANRWST Gwynedd   Map 4

Meadowsweet Hotel
Station Road
Llanrwst (0492) 640732

Closed L Oct–Easter
(exc Dec 25)
Must book D
Meals 12–1.45, 6–9.30

Tdh L £3·25 (meal £5·65)
Alc £7·15 (meal £9·95)

Service 10%
Children's helpings
Seats 36
 ⑤ rest (1 step)
Car park
No dogs in d/r
Access, Am Ex, Barclay
10 rooms (all with shower)
B&B from £8·50
D, B&B from £15
Full board from £95
Fire cert

By buying the property next door, John Evans has been able to make more rooms and interpose a thick stone wall between his clamorous children and his dinner guests. His chief pleasure and preoccupation is cooking, and for an ex-banker he learns fast, say members not easily disposed to love the men who mind their money. There have been mishaps sometimes with veal or spare ribs or mistimed potatoes, and the service is keen rather than sophisticated. But celery and almond soup, onion tart, gratin aux fruits de mer (£1·35) or grilled sardines make good preludes to breast of chicken with a well-balanced onion and cream sauce (£3·15), beef in port and Guinness, accurately grilled steaks, and duck with brandied cherries, all with imaginative vegetables. Lemon cheesecake and other sweets are competent, but cheeses may for once be as good a choice. Coffee has lately improved. Rooms are comfortable, and the Conwy water-meadows opposite 'are stocked like a drover's fair with cows and sheep, goats and donkeys.' Breakfasts may offer black pudding, Finnan haddock and 'for a wonder, kidneys'. The red wines jump straight from Choix du Roy at £2·95 to Côtes du Rhône at £4·20 and neither choices nor prices elsewhere on the list invite further exploration. Mr Evans plans to offer bar lunches from Easter, but neither menus nor beers had been finalised when we went to press. 'Quiet' recorded music.

App: Robert Williamson, D. J. Morton, C. A. Bland, T.S., David Lisbona, J.R.T., and many others

LLANWDDYN Powys   Map 4

Lake Vyrnwy Hotel
on B4393
10 m W of Llanfyllin
Llanwddyn (069 173) 244

Closed Jan 14–Mar 1
Must book
Meals 1, 8.30 (summer),
7.30 (winter)

Tdh L £4 (meal £5·10),
Sun L £4·50 (meal £5·60),
D £5 (meal £6·10)

Service inc
Children's helpings
(under 10)
Seats 60 (parties 30)
 ⑤ rest; w.c.

'This hotel properly belongs in the *Good Hotel Guide* alone', says one member, intending it as a compliment not to Mrs Moir's cooking, but rather to 'chambermaids who actually lay out your nightclothes, and clean shoes if you don't put out too many.' Others also suggest that dinner ought to be too important an event to be served in half an hour flat. Still, the inclusive overnight charges 'make the ever-seedier London hotels look purely extortionate' (as they are), even though 'in damp misty weather outer doors should be shut, as we are not all tough crude Scots in shooting jackets or waders.' In spite of these characteristics – not to mention 'kipper en croûte as a third course' – a majority likes the simple cooking as much as it likes the peaceful surroundings, with 'home-made tomato soup or excellent prawn flan followed by a choice of roast Welsh lamb, or tongue braised with raisin sauce.' 'It was the sort of meal my late headmaster would have greatly enjoyed.' Buffet lunches, perhaps with duck or game in a port

Car park
No dogs
30 rooms (9 with bath,
2 with shower)
B&B £9–£15
Full board £14–£20 p.d.
Fire cert

wine jelly, or cream of Stilton ring, and 'delicious bread-and-butter or rice puddings', are mentioned by others. Coffee is 'help-yourself Cona'. Choix du Roy ordinaires are £1·50 for 50 cl, and Tanners of Shrewsbury supply some good clarets: Ch. Cantemerle '70, c.b., £8·50. Pressurised beers. Wear a tie for dinner. Under-threes must eat in the nursery. 'Stamps and drinks can be had on the honour system, as in an Army mess.' (GHG)

App: S. W. Burdon, D. S. Hunter, D.E., A.S.M.J., Dr & Mrs A. M. Brown, J.S.M., and others

LLANWRTYD WELLS Powys   Map 4

Llwynderw Hotel
Abergwesyn
5 m NW of Llanwrtyd
Wells
off Tregaron Road
Llanwrtyd Wells (059 13)
238

'All that you say is true so why is it still included?' was one comment last time on Michael Yates's isolated Georgian house. True, you pay handsomely to step backwards into *Wuthering Heights*, with a landlord who gives and withholds soap and other services at discretion ('television is available for coronations'), and this year's inspectors suggest that dinner is wiser than a stay. In the district – which means twenty miles around – you would be lucky to find better soups, cheese soufflés, chicken liver pâté, pink fillet of beef, Gorgonzola, and gooseberry fool or tart. Vegetables and sauces are more peccable. Sound claret was under £5 in 1979. No pipes, or children under ten; and dogs, if admitted, pay a hair tax.

Closed L (exc by arrangement); Nov to mid-Mar Must book D only, 7.45

Tdh from £8 (meal from £11)

Service inc
Seats 25

Car park
No dogs in d/r
12 rooms (10 with bath)
D, B&B £25–£30
Fire cert

LLANYCHAER BRIDGE Dyfed   Map 4

Penlan Oleu

off B4313
4½ m SE of Fishguard
Puncheston (034 882) 314

Closed L (exc by arrangement); 10 days Oct; 6 weeks Jan/Feb Must book
Meals L (by arrangement), 8–9.30

Tdh £9 (meal £12·25)

Seats 18 (parties 8)
♿ rest

'High place of light' is the quasi-biblical translation of Penlan Oleu, the simple (but surprisingly spacious) farmhouse where Ann Carr and Martin McKeown settled with their family ten years after their first *Guide* appearance at the Peacock in Islington. Light, yes, 'but no glitter', they say. True, but their County-Down-bred instinct for hospitality, and her five-course dinners so sensitively composed and cooked – there is no choice till the sweet stage – have drawn members like moths to a flame. The owners have their own grazing and bake their own bread, and apart from their coffee – described more than once as 'warm and weak' – there are few criticisms. 'Hardly a dish was repeated in a fortnight's stay and much was memorable: carrot soup; a very hot 'Kashmir' soup; spinach and egg mousse; local grilse; noisettes of local lamb (sometimes their own) with a grainy mustard sauce; salads and vegetables; mocha parfait;

Car park
No dogs
Access, Am Ex, Barclay
4 rooms (3 with bath,
1 with shower)
D, B&B £21

'Imogen's iced peaches'; and Caledonian ice-cream, with oatmeal and whisky. A test meal had a few flaws including an off-colour Stilton, but 'an exquisitely delicate elderflower sorbet' made up for it. Breakfasts are light but genuine, the rooms comfortable, and the service natural without being in any way obtrusive. The wines from Berry Bros are appropriately chosen for a short list, with a generous proportion of half-bottles: Crozes-Hermitage '72, £6·40 and £3·20; halves of Ch. de Rayne-Vigneau '72 (a Sauternes) £3·85. No smoking while food is being served. No children under 12 and 'after a scramble round the coast path or the Preseli hills, people usually change for dinner.' To find the house, take the B4313, and four miles out of Fishguard look for a signpost fragment reading 'Pu' on one side, '⚵' on the other. (GHG)

App: David Lewis, John & Marion Hamlin,
F. & D.N., Deborah Buzan, G. & E.R., J.Y., M.J.,
and others

LLOWES Powys   Map 4

Radnor Arms
on A438
3 m W of Hay-on-Wye
Glasbury (049 74) 460

Closed Sun; Dec 25
Must book weekends
Meals 12–2.30, 7–9.30
(10 weekends)

Alc £6·95 (meal £10·30)

Children's helpings
Seats 25
♿ rest
Car park
No dogs

Personal misfortune and domestic reconstruction left the Whitmarshes feeling that 1980 could only be better than 1979, so it is a tribute to them that most visitors have much enjoyed their visits to this 'crumbly stone house and neat garden in open country'. 'We are a hybrid,' Juliet Whitmarsh says, and experiences range all the way from bar lunches to sit-down dinners. On the whole the former are best, though the food (cooked by Julian Whitmarsh with Lucy Thomas to do the sweets) is similar. Carrot and lentil soup, pâtés of pigeon and walnut or trout and almond (£1·10), 'a lovely crab quiche with good short pastry', tagliatelle not overcooked, with a creamy meat sauce (£1·85), and 'what a ploughman's lunch really ought to be' sound better achieved than duckling with gooseberry sauce, the steak or squab pies, and the vegetables. But 'beefsteak and venison pie (£2·85, with jacket potato and salad) was my best dish in three Welsh days.' Note the rib of pork dijonnaise, and oxtail with tomatoes and basil (£3·05), as specialities. The rich chocolate and chestnut cake and other puddings are admired too. Felinfoel Double Dragon bitter and Whitbread Special in cask kept out the cold while the builders were in, and the Luc Lacerre wine list begins with French table wine at £4 a litre. 'Good coffee too.'

App: M. M. Silver, Richard Graham, N. & L.R.,
D.N., J.R., Adrian Underwood, and others

Wine prices shown are for a 'standard' bottle of the wine concerned, unless another measure is stated (e.g. litre, 50 cl., or pint).

NEWPORT Dyfed   Map 4

Pantry
Market Street
Newport (0239) 820420

Closed L (Sept–May);
Sun; Mon; Dec 25 & 26;
Jan 1
Must book D
Meals 12.15–2 (summer),
7.15–9.30

Alc L £3·60 (meal £5·15),
D £7·35 (meal £9·55)

Service 10%
Children's helpings
Seats 45
Car park
No dogs

Robin Evans was cross last time because attention
had been drawn to shortcomings over a public
holiday when 'everyone wants to eat'; happily,
careful descriptions of meals eaten both in and out of
this estuary town's high season make clear this time
that while Mr Evans's range may be confined, by his
own or his clientele's choice, his skills are extensive.
'The only poor dish was the pâté, friable, bitter, and
coarsely seasoned, saved chiefly by good toast and
even better brown bread.' Hors d'oeuvre (£2·20) might
be wiser. Salmon en croûte (£5·70, including
vegetables) was 'magnificent: firm and juicy, in a short
pastry crust that would have blown away in a draught,
with a subtle wine and herb cream sauce. Leeks and
beans were à point, and gratin dauphinoise (45p
extra) correctly cooked.' Melon balls with curried
prawns, lamb stuffed with onion and pineapple, and
filet de boeuf (also en croûte) 'with a delicious
bordelaise sauce' have figured in other meals. Sweets
are mostly simple, but meringue glacé with hot
chocolate sauce 'seemed all to have been made on the
premises', 'raspberry sorbet is as good as ever' and
coffee, when tried, was good. The wine list is modest,
but modestly priced too, with French ordinaires £2·50
in 1979, and four English-bottled clarets of good years
under £5. Details are approximate.

App: Henry Fawcett, J.R.D., P.O'R.S.

PEMBROKE Dyfed   Map 4

Richmond Coffee House
7 Castle Terrace
Pembroke (064 63) 5460

'High-class tea-shop', popular with holiday-makers
and visitors to the nearby castle, serving 'fresh,
honest food' among antiques and prints. Sandwiches,
cakes (bara brith, 28p) and light meals: 'decent
home-made tomato soup with a bowl of Parmesan
and white roll; three-egg omelette with field
mushrooms (£1·50), lightly done; coffee better than
expected (22p).' Lettuce soup, smoked mackerel and
spiced ham salad (£1·80) also mentioned. 'Small
sun-lounge and superior loos.' 'Briskly and capably
run.' 'No smoking near the cakes.' They may have a
wine licence by the time the *Guide* is published.

Closed Sun & Mon
(Nov–Easter);
Dec 24–26 & 31; Jan 1

Open 10–6 (L 12–3,
HT 3–6)

Alc L £2·50 (meal £2·95)

Children's helpings
Seats 48
No dogs
Unlicensed

Unless otherwise stated, a restaurant is open all week and all year and is licensed.

For the explanation of ⓐ, denoting accessibility for the disabled, see 'How to use
the Guide', p. 4.

PENMAENPOOL Gwynedd   Map 4

George III Hotel
on A493
2 m SW of Dolgellau
Dolgellau (0341) 422525

One visitor who grumbled to John Hall about faults upstairs thought he had met George III in person, but the food is reckoned more gracious, owing perhaps to David Collett's return to the kitchen. 'Noble' prawn salad (£2·20), 'baked sea trout with a challenging mussel sauce' and 'lightly done halibut' with anchovies and capers show good use of resources. 'Mushrooms in stout were mismatched with mild salmon.' Snacks in the bar (except on Sunday). Good wines, from £3·45 for Pierre Ponnelle Réserve. Pressurised beers. 'Prompt, polite service', though the breakfast setting may detract from the diner's peace and pleasure. Tables outside on the balcony.

Closed Sun D; Dec 25;
Jan 1 L
Must book D
Meals 12.30–1.45,
7.30–8.45

Alc L (min £2·50) £5·40
(meal £8·35), D (min £4)
£8·50 (meal £11·75)

Service 10%
Children's helpings
(under 10)
Seats 40
♿ rest
Car park

No dogs in d/r
Access, Am Ex, Barclay
Diners, Euro
12 rooms (7 with bath)
B&B £7
Fire cert

RHYDYMAIN Gwynedd   Map 4

Rossi's Ristorante
on A494
8 m NE of Dolgellau
Rhydymain (034 141)
667 *and* 227

Must book
Meals 12–2, 7–9

Alc £7·45 (meal £9·40)

Service inc
Seats 40
♿ rest; w.c.
Car park
No dogs
Access, Am Ex, Barclay,
Diners, Euro
8 rooms
B&B £11·50
Fire cert

Roberto and Susannah Rossi found their sedate old inn (formerly run by a well-known harpist) by serendipity when they had no thought of settling in Wales, and in the past four years a growing number of members have beaten a path to their door. The flavours of Mrs Rossi's cooking are as decided as her husband's character, and Londoners used to the trattoria round the corner may find this *ristorante con camere* a revelation, from the stone-ground porridge for breakfast ('give the cornflakes a miss: they're soft') to the unusual but excellent minestrone, the delight in local venison, hare and pheasant, and Italianate but still individual sweets. Order cautiously, for helpings are large, but children may have lasagne or ravioli as a main course if they wish – and find their mothers finishing the plateful for pleasure rather than duty. Spicy tomato soup, the 'pink and rich' house pâté, and trout in white wine are other notable first courses (avocado soup, though, is more sceptically received). Fillet steak in mustard and cream sauce (£3·55) was, an inspector says, a model of how to choose and time meat and balance a sauce; vegetables are inventive; and the chilled zabaglione with strawberries, or oranges in Cointreau sound much better than 'a heavy trifle that did duty two days running.' Expect a slow-paced meal at busy times, and dress neatly, though they say there are no rules now. Verona table wine is £3·15 a litre and Mr Rossi also suggests the fizzy red Lambrusco: perhaps he is an Emilian. But the Chianti Classico, Spanna and Barolo at fair prices argue the presence of an affectionate connoisseur. Recorded music. (GHG)

App: Kevin O'Mahoney, L. Leventhal, N. V. Crookdake, Guy Caldwell, J.R., J.M.

ROBESTON WATHEN Dyfed   Map 4

Robeston House
on A40
2 m SW of Narberth &
8 m E of Haverfordwest
Narberth (0834) 860392

Closed L (exc by arrangement); Sun D (exc res); Dec 25 & 26; Jan 1
Must book
Meals L (by arrangement), HT 4–4.30, 7.30–9.15

Tdh £6·95 (meal £11·05)

Service 10%
Children's helpings (by arrangement)
Seats 50
[&] rest; w.c.
Car park
No dogs
Access, Euro
6 rooms (3 with bath)
B&B from £10·50
Fire cert

The Barretts are kind enough to say that the *Guide* sends them more custom than all the others put together, even though there is something about their regime that brings out the backhander in visitors' accounts: 'Moths will get at the stuffed buzzard if they don't mend the hole in the glass case', and 'no use trying for Noel Coward country house suavity with those friendly, dotty Pembrokeshire ladies-in-waiting.' Mrs Barrett is a conscientious cook (and has trained a sound occasional deputy, it seems). 'Mushrooms in a brandied cream, onion and cheese mixture made a good first course', and soups are home-made. Specialities include, alongside diced leg of lamb with cumin and mint, the kind of produce that has to be sought with determination: salmon, sea trout and bass; grouse, partridge and pigeon – 'the pigeon well casseroled in cider and herbs.' 'Meat may be overcooked but not vegetables, which were commendably imaginative at an awkward time of year.' There are usually about eight choices in each course, with too much reliance on creamy sweets, perhaps. Coffee – and the fudge that comes with it – is good. Breakfasts lack variety. They are proud of their own-label house wines from only £2·95, and have also taken great trouble over their Bordeaux list: too many '72s, perhaps, but Ch. Léoville-Lascases '69 in magnum at £18·40 is good value set against the £5·60 that has to be charged for English whites. No children under 14 in the hotel; smoking discouraged; dress conventionally for dinner. (GHG)

App: D. S. Borton, J.R.T., P. J. Baker, S. & N. Goodman, E.B., and others

ST DAVID'S Dyfed   Map 4

Warpool Court Hotel
St David's (043 788) 300

Closed Jan
Must book
Meals 11–3, 7–9.30

Tdh D £6·30 (meal £7·75)
Alc (brunch) £2·30
(meal £3·40)

The 'heraldic pretensions' of the house are not the Lloyds' fault, and although the decor, the grounds, the markedly informal service and (in wet summer weather) the high visibility/audibility of children rob the place of the smoothness to which it aspires, almost everyone reports happily. Mark Napper, formerly patissier, is now chef, and apart from a rather thin period during alterations, 'we had hardly a bad dish in 12 days and many novelties,' writes one guest. 'We liked scallops fécampoise, pears stuffed

Service inc
Seats 120
♿ rest (1 step)
Car park
No dogs in d/r
Access, Am Ex
25 rooms (16 with bath,
9 with shower)
B&B £13·40
D, B&B £18·60
Full board £20·50 p.d.
Fire cert

with salmon pâté, turkey en croûte, simple roast lamb
with vegetables from their own nursery (hot and
crunchy runner beans were a great delight in late
August).' Chicken Myfanwy (£3·85 à la carte) is a
speciality, and Stilton and onion or crab soups, and
cassoulet, are good too. Cheeses are served at the
right temperature, and the cold puddings well varied –
'an incredible chocolate and almond gateau,' adds
another guest; the kitchen suggests hazelnut and
bramble meringue gateau (95p), in season presumably.
They do an 'American brunch' from 11 to 3, complete
with cocktails, in a coffee shop called Dylan's
(Thomas, not Bob) and you can also eat outside. The
wines, from Bordeaux Direct Ltd and the Lloyds' own
travels, began in 1979 at only £2·95 for Nicolas and
included Muscadet '77 (Métaireau) at £5·60,
interesting bottles at similar prices from Bergerac and
elsewhere, and a few fine ones (Ch. Latour '61, £21·05).
There is live music sometimes, with dancing on winter
Saturdays. (GHG)

App: Dr & Mrs A. W. Pendlington,
Dr & Mrs J. G. Edwards, R. J. Bocock, J.M.,
Marquess of Anglesey, and others

SWANSEA West Glamorgan   Map 4

The Drangway

🍷

66 Wind Street
Swansea (0792) 461397

Closed Sun; Mon;
Dec 23–30; Dec 31 L;
Jan 1
Must book
Meals 12.30–2, 7.30–10

Tdh L £3·75 (meal £7·25),
D £5·75 (meal £9·45)
Alc £10·45 (meal £14·65)

Children's helpings
Seats 66 (parties 30)
Air-conditioning
No dogs
Access, Am Ex, Barclay,
Diners, Euro

'There is nowhere comparable within forty miles' of
Colin Pressdee's olive-green basement restaurant, with
pine tables and a glimpse of Swansea castle through
the side windows. He himself is feeling buoyant, with
not only a new kitchen to play with after closure for
alterations, but also three colleagues to help him
in it. Mr Pressdee ranges wide in search of fresh
produce that will support his Welsh and Loire
emphases. His favourite à la carte dishes are baked
scallops au beurre blanc (£3·25) and a hot mousse of
shellfish with Nantais sauce (from £3·45) as first
courses, then baked lobster with seaweed and
Muscadet sauce (£11·50) and fillet of beef en chevreuil
(£13·90 for two). But these prices should not frighten
people off his much more modest but interesting set
meals; perhaps crab pâté or mussels, followed by
couscous or cassoulet, with 'admirably cooked'
vegetables and a home-made sweet (or exotic fruit
sorbet), or cheese. One Surrey visitor found himself
not just eating but enjoying cockles and bacon with
laver bread followed by an 'absolutely beautiful
poached sewin', and other travelled members praise the
'fresh and delicate' turbot au beurre blanc. Apart
from the French table wines at £2·25 for 50 cl, people
drink plenty of Muscadet or Gros Plant, as might be
expected, at £5 or so, and though at least half the
numerous clarets and red burgundies are in double
figures now, they are sound wines of good years: at
the £7 level you may choose, for instance, between

Ch. Vieux Ferrand '71 and Côte de Nuits-Villages '72 (Berry Bros). Ch. Grand-Puy-Ducasse '66 is £13·95. (The list, though, fails to distinguish between British and domaine bottlings.) One of numerous vintage ports is kept decanted. Snack lunches and pop records are to be found in the cellar along with lager.

App: Ellis Blackmore, J.S. & F.W.

TAL-Y-LLYN Gwynedd   Map 4

Minffordd Hotel
at junction of A487 &
B4405
7 m S of Dolgellau
Corris (065 473) 665

Bernard Pickles greets arrivals with tea, and encourages gossip (no compulsion) round the Aga, or tours of the Cader Idris range in the footsteps of Peacock and Faraday. Not for misanthropes, though the kindness and homely cooking make almost everyone benign. 'Enough variety, with apt economy: sole with prawns in wine sauce becomes seafood in scallop shell, as a first course next day.' 'Good gammon, peppered pork chop with grilled pineapple, tangy lemon meringue pie and sound cheeses (fetched from Chester twice weekly) made up for bleak weather.' Vegetables 'good for Wales'; 'free range breakfasts'; 'juicy salmon in the packed lunch.' French carafe wine, £2·20 for 50 cl. No children under five. (GHG)

Closed L; Sun (exc res);	Tdh £6·50 (meal £8·10)	Car park
Sun–Thur (Nov–Easter);		No dogs
Dec 24–26 & 31, Jan 1	Service inc	7 rooms (4 with shower)
(exc res)	Children's helpings	B&B £10·90
Must book	(under 10)	D, B&B £16·90
D only, 7.30–8.30	Seats 30	Fire cert

WOLF'S CASTLE Dyfed   Map 4

Wolfscastle Country Hotel
off A40
7 m N of Haverfordwest
Treffgarne (043 787) 225

Closed Dec 24–26
Must book D & Sun L
Meals 12.30–2, 7–9.30

Alc £6·35 (meal £9·45)

Children's helpings
Seats 45
Car park
No dogs in d/r
Access, Barclay
11 rooms (5 with bath or shower)

Andrew Stirling runs a 'cosy' hotel here, with squash courts and trout fishing for diversion, and with Rosanna Lloyd in the kitchen for evidently good meals. Deep-fried chicken balls with artichoke sauce (£1·10) is her own favourite first course but others report just as happily of spinach and mushroom roulade, 'genuine tomato soup', 'excellent haddock crêpes' and sound pâté. Afterwards, 'I had not seen braised oxtail on a menu since the Connaught Hotel and it was well done here too', and 'we were fortunate that a sturgeon, caught locally, appeared one night. It had a delicious flavour and was cooked with wine and herbs.' Stuffed loin of pork with apricots, almonds and cider (£4·60), curries with side dishes (though rather wet rice) and vegetables are also praised. 'The best sweet is still the hazelnut meringue with raspberries, but the home-made fudge and petits fours should be mentioned.' 'So should the lunchtime bar snacks with home-made soup and a fine coarse

B&B £8·60–£15·50
D, B&B £14·40–£20·70
Fire cert

pâté.' Argentine red or white ordinaires are £3·75 a litre and the Stirling family have always kept good claret: Ch. Tronquoy Lalande '75, £5·70; Ch. Cantemerle '71, £11·05. Pressurised beers. Recorded music. No children under three in the dining-room. Locals 'give the bar and restaurant a congenial atmosphere,' writes the owner but it may feel less congenial late on a summer night if you are trying to sleep with the windows open.

App: R. H. Morgan, David Head, Dr & Mrs V. Miller, D. A. Gilmour, and others

WOLF'S CASTLE see also pub section

SCOTLAND

Le Dodo
15 Crown Street
Aberdeen (0224) 26916

Someone suggests that the menu at this spruce sub-French place is like a Green Paper, distantly related to the meal's final form. 'Much is off', and what is on may be cooked with equal caprice: 'Vichyssoise deputising for leeks vinaigrette, nicely presented on a bed of ice but tasteless'; 'good ox liver, properly prepared, let down by dull peas and potatoes.' 'Fondue de fromage frite was crisp and dry but far from cheesy.' Sauces are coarse, and meat might be more tender. Cheers, though, for salmon, langoustines and tarte Dodo – 'delicious crème pâtissière and almonds.' Côtes du Rhône is £3·25. Recorded music.

Closed Sun L (exc Apr 6);
Sat L
Must book D
Meals 12–2.30, 7–11

Tdh L £2·75 (meal £4)
Alc £9·85 (meal £13·05)

Service 10%
Seats 70

♿ rest (1 step)
Car park
No dogs
Access, Am Ex, Barclay, Diners

ACHILTIBUIE Highland   Map 9

Summer Isles Hotel

NW of Ullapool
16 m off A835
Achiltibuie (085 482) 282

Closed L (exc
Smokehouse); mid-Oct to
Easter

Must book
Meals (Smokehouse)
12–2; 7–9 (May–Sept
only by arrangement);
(rest) D only, 7 for 7.30

Tdh D (rest) £11
(meal £12·90)
Alc (one-course) L
(Smokehouse) £2·50
(meal £4), D £4·70
(meal £7·15)

Service inc
Seats 28
Car park

It is ten years since Robert and Roberta Irvine left the London film world – 'though not show-business,' says a mordant critic – to settle in this necessarily self-sufficient hotel in ruggedly magnificent country, 90 miles away from their source of supply for anything that they cannot themselves grow, shoot, lure or smoke. Vigorous complaints of the decor, the beds, the lounges, the temperatures, and the 'steel-in-velvet' dining-room management are not unknown, especially from south of the Trent where the yield of goat's cheese and wind-tunnel greens is less vital, and where you do not expect to feel like Captain Oates every time you venture across from your chalet room to the main building to be in time for the 7.30 dinner gong. Apart from 'a couple of French barons from the Matignon and the Elysée who ordered Muscadet with their breakfast trout' (by a fellow-guest's account), this year's chief bouquets come from Yorkshiremen, delighted by mostly well-balanced set meals. 'Ours brought outstanding soups – lettuce, soissonnaise, mushroom and carrot; thick slices of tender venison (hinds shot "out of the rutting season", according to the proprietor) with rowan jelly: good veal in vermouth and rabbit in madeira, carefully cooked cauliflower, and excellent Swedish apple cake.' Others who stayed longer report individual shortcomings – dry omelette, bitter courgettes that needed tasting in the kitchen, ill-roast duck, and a poor recipe called

No dogs in public rooms
16 rooms (7 with bath)
B&B £11·50–£20
Fire cert

chocolate syllabub; but also 'in every dinner something typical of the hotel or the area, perhaps trout, salmon or scallops from the bay, or kid, or mutton such as one rarely finds in England. Salads are also imaginative.' Mixed fruit tart, raspberry bavarois and grasshopper pie (featuring chocolate and crème de menthe) are also praised. Breakfasts and packed lunches are good – 'we ate our prawns on An Teallach rather than Quinag this year' – and more casual callers may eat inside or outside the Smokehouse restaurant (which opens in the evening in summer only if there is demand). The wines are serious and gently priced, even if you fall for Mr Irvine's offers of extra glasses of this and that – a white wine with the fish ('Hermitage '75 goes well with salmon') or a Beerenauslese wine with the pudding – on top of Ch. Grand-Puy-Lacoste '67, £8·85, or Aloxe-Corton '73 (Bouchard Père et Fils). Justerini & Brooks' table Rhône or claret is £5. Pressurised beers. No smoking in the dining-room. 'No-one under eight or over eighty' in the hotel: the family friend of the Editor's who celebrated his eightieth birthday on top of Liathach in Torridon would have been properly outraged. (GHG)

App: Doug Miles, Philip & Penelope Plumb, S.S.J., P.F., N. V. Crookdake, L. N. Cartwright, Anthony Kerr, Bruce King, and others

---

ALYTH Tayside   Map 9

Lands of Loyal Hotel
Loyal Road
off A926
Alyth (082 83) 2481

'Food a bit on the solid side, like the customers, but fresh, good quality and well cooked,' says one inspector. Another says much the same, after stuffed avocado, poached salmon with dill, and fresh raspberries. 'Carbonnade was based on good thick slices of Scottish beef.' Smoked mackerel pâté with gooseberry sauce is another favourite of the Billingshursts' chef William McNicoll, as a first course or a lunchtime bar snack. Breakfasts are good, and there is now a fine range of red and white Riojas from £2·75 as well as, for instance, red Chassagne-Montrachet '72 (Pierre Ponnelle) at £8·20. Pressurised beers.

Closed Dec 24–Jan 2
Must book
Meals 12.30–2, 7–8.30

Tdh L from £3·50
(meal £5·95), D from
£5·50 (meal £8·45)

Service 10%
Children's helpings
Seats 40 (parties 12)
Car park
No dogs in public rooms

Am Ex, Diners
14 rooms (6 with bath,
1 with shower)
B&B £8·50–£9·50
D, B&B from £13
Fire cert

Scottish public holidays do not all coincide with English ones.

Prices quoted in entries now include VAT.

Ardentinny Hotel
Loch Long
on A880
13 m N of Dunoon
Ardentinny (036 981) 209

The Harrises try hard to be all things to all visitors in their trim inn on the western shore of Loch Long. Milk with coffee and the odd kitchen time-saver are noted, but many praise what they conceive and achieve at the simple à la carte lunches: 'fine turkey and lasagne with salads on the bench with the view'; and the set dinner with 'good kipper pâté and trout Montrose', 'tasty buck rarebit, cream of onion soup, fish pie, and veal with paprika and yoghourt', 'delicious cranachan and treacle tart'. Porc ardennaise and mille-feuille are other favourites. Good breakfasts. Evening as well as at mid-day snacks, and pressurised beers. 'Ecumenical' wines: try Cape whites under £4 and Australian reds under £5, say. Recorded music. They prefer no babies. Wear a tie to dine.

Closed Mon–Wed (Nov–Mar)	Tdh D £6 (meal £8·30)	No dogs
Must book D	Alc L £2·75 (meal £4·85)	Am Ex card
Meals 12 (12.30 Sun)–2,		10 rooms (4 with bath,
HT 5–6, 7 (7.30 Sun)–8.30	Children's helpings	2 with shower)
	Seats 40 (parties 20)	B&B £8–£12·50
	Car park	Fire cert

Loch Melfort Hotel
on A816
Kilmelford (085 22) 233

Two inspections and numerous other members' reports this year leave little room for doubt about Colin Tindal's motor hotel. The single uncontroversial feature has always been the glorious view – which the recorded music does its best to spoil. Peter Deary's cooking has its good points: the soups, local prawn salad, herrings in oatmeal and sole en goujons, steak béarnaise, the roast joints and the Austrian coffee cake. Regrets include soufflés – 'victims of the service system or lack of it' – 'awful vegetables', 'uncooked pastry', ill-preserved cheeses and an 'evanescent' taste of liquor in whisky flummery. Lamborghini red or white wines from Whigham's were £3·80 in 1979 and Ch. Bonis '71, £6·05. Bar lunches, which you may eat on the terrace; pressurised beers.

Closed late Oct to Easter	Children's helpings	Access, Am Ex
Must book D & Sun L	(HT under 8)	28 rooms (23 with bath)
Meals 12.30–2, 7.15–8.30	Seats 50	B&B from £13·80–20·70
	Car park	Fire cert
Tdh L £5·75 (meal £8·10),	No dogs	
D £8·05 (meal £10·65)		

Numbers are given for private parties only if they can be accommodated in a room separate from the main dining-room; when there are several such rooms, the capacity of the largest is given. Some restaurants will take party bookings at times when they are normally closed.

AUCHTERARDER Tayside   Map 9

Gleneagles Hotel
1 m W of Auchterarder
off A9/A823
Auchterarder (076 46)
2231

Considering it was conceived by a general manager of the Caledonian Railway in 1910, this sporting, golfing and conferring hotel at the £50-a-day-full-board end of the market does well to survive and please members, who think the *Guide* is unkind to it out of 'puritanical fear of luxury'. Not so, but if you wish to taste M Cottet's 'real hors d'oeuvre', superb omelettes, excellent veal Vaucanson (£8·70), suprême de volaille aux cèpes (£7·15), properly prepared vegetables, 'gateau made for a birthday', and soufflé Drambuie (£5·50 for two), you may have to eat à la carte. The BTH wines (from £3·35 for sound French or German) are superb and good value, here as elsewhere. Bar lunches in the Golf Club, and pressurised beers. Wear a jacket and tie at dinner.

Closed Apr 4, 6 & 7;
Oct 26–Apr 2
Must book
Meals 12.45–2.30,
HT 3.30–5.30, 7.30–10

Tdh L £9·50 (meal £11·20),
D £12 (meal £13·70)

Alc (min L £5, D £6)
£19·20 (meal £22·20)

Service inc
Children's helpings
Seats 350 (parties 350)
⟨&⟩ rest
Air-conditioning

Car park
No dogs in d/r
Access, Am Ex, Barclay,
Diners, Euro
209 rooms (204 with bath,
5 with shower)
B&B £32·40–£40·50
Full board £50–£58 p.d.
Fire cert

BALLATER Grampian   Map 9

Tullich Lodge

on A93
1½ m E of Ballater
Ballater (033 82) 406

Closed Jan–Mar
Must book
Meals 1, 7.30–9

Tdh L £6·50 (meal £7·70),
D £7 (meal £8·20)

Service inc
Children's helpings
(L under 7)
Seats 30
⟨&⟩ rest (2 steps)
Am Ex card
10 rooms (8 with bath,
2 with shower)
D, B&B £22
Fire cert

The problem of guide-writing is summed up in Neil Bannister and Hector MacDonald's sub-baronial house, for if it is the first duty of a hotel to be all things to all men, it fails. However, if it is regarded as a private house, furnished in striking but admirable taste, and admitting a paying public to rooms and meals, it succeeds triumphantly – but only with people who are on the right wave-length. Visitors who arrive unpunctually or take against Mr MacDonald's 'jovial but enigmatic' manner, or decide too late that Mr Bannister's choiceless set dinners and restrained helpings are not what they want, or expect Jeeves the sheepdog to be overjoyed at a new canine introduction, may miss the smiles others report. Still, even in Mr Bannister's absence, the cooking lost little of its quality, by accounts of the 'mealy home-made bread', green pea soup, 'superb baked egg and haddock in a cocotte', 'good if unseasonable' silverside of beef with root vegetables, pork cutlet with cranberry sauce, braised leeks and dauphinois potatoes, hazelnut gateau, and fresh cherries in brandy. The best things, the owners think, are their fresh vegetables, game in season, sea trout and lobster, and baked chicken with green herbs and cream cheese. But with so little margin for error, people notice when invention or judgement flags. 'Breakfasts are excellent, notably the oranges for pressing, the croissants and the free newspapers, but the system still does not deliver cooked dishes hot.' Lunch may be eaten outside. Cendré de Jura and one or two other bottles were under £3 in 1979, with Muscat les Amandiers (Dopff & Irion) £5, Ch. de Pez '70, c.b., £8, and halves of dessert Ch. Loupiac-Gaudiet '70, £2. Pressurised beers for the bar meals. No smoking in the dining-room. Children under nine are expected to eat high tea, and adults to wear a jacket and tie at meals. 'Don't forget to make a telephone call from their regal booth.' Car park. No dogs in public rooms. (GHG)

App: P. & P.P., A.M.M.A., Walter Buchanan

CANONBIE Dumfries & Galloway   Map 7

Riverside Inn
Canonbie (054 15) 295

Closed L (exc bar);
Sun D; Dec 26; Jan 1
Must book D
Meals 12.30–1.30 (bar),
7.30–8.30

Alc D £5·65 (meal £8)

Service inc
Seats 30
♿ rest
Car park
No dogs in public rooms
7 rooms (1 with bath)
B&B £7·25
Fire cert

Robert and Susan Phillips are gradually converting a 17th-century family house by the Border Esk into a simple inn of character – but the character also derives from cooking of a quality that astonished an experienced inspector who came upon it unawares. The couple both cook, and must have formidable appetites themselves to offer 10–12 oz steaks with green peppercorns (£4·85) or whole roast guinea-fowl with home-made black cherry and port wine sauce (£4·25). But these and other dishes are not cooked in the usual British superfatted style, and come with 'delectably fresh' potatoes and garden vegetables. (Mallard and roe deer are other specialities, and the river is a salmon one.) So it is not unthinkable to begin with a home-made cream of mushroom soup or a hot vol-au-vent filled with creamy shrimps (75p), and end with gooseberry pie, or the raspberry summer pudding and cream that lingers in the memory of another inspector after a subsequent test meal. The simpler bar menus (which may be eaten outside), with Theakston's bitter on hand pump, also sound worth trying, and people report well of the full Scottish breakfast. Among other wines, Ch. de Terrefort Quancard '74 is £4·35. More reports, please.

CLEISH Tayside   Map 9

Nivingston House
on B9097
4 m SW of Kinross
Cleish Hills (057 75) 216

Closed Mon (exc May 5)
Must book D
Meals 12.15–1.45, 7–9

Tdh L £5 (meal £6·65),
D £11 (meal £12·65)

What with their newly-extended house and their chef William Kerr's triumphs in Glasgow's *salons culinaires*, the Scott-Smiths have reason to feel buoyant about their little hotel, and members – especially refugees from Hull, Australia, and other less-favoured localities – sound content. True 'some of the bedroom decoration and the ceramic work can be recommended to nostalgic film directors' and 'too many dishes we tried tasted either salty or glutamaty.' But the enterprising hors d'oeuvre table 'made selection difficult, and they kindly complied with our request for a little of everything.' 'Carrot and orange

Service inc
Children's helpings
(under 12)
Seats 52 (parties 30)
⑤ rest
Car park
No dogs in public rooms
Am Ex, Barclay
4 rooms
B&B £12
Fire cert

soup was not up to the *Guide* cookery book's standard,' but hot avocado with prawns was 'an excellent concoction, and well followed by duck with apple and brandy sauce.' Huîtres aux laitues tendres sauce vin blanc, and cervelles de veau en coquille are unexpected specialities. 'Venison – perhaps underhung – came with compost-grown vegetables from the garden.' 'Fillet steak with chicken livers was well cooked and juicy.' Sweets are conventional, 'even banal', but at least they cut their Stilton now rather than scoop it. Wines come from a firm unpromisingly named Euroscot, but include a not-yet-Euro Rioja Montecillo at £3·55. Perhaps there is also a cordial called Entente. Bar lunches (except on Sundays); pressurised beers. Dress smartly for dinner. To find the place, take exit 5 from the M90 and follow Crook of Devon, then Cleish, signs.

App: A. P. & D. R. Barker, Hector Maclean, W.H.R., J.S.S., Philip and Penelope Plumb, and others

---

DALBEATTIE Dumfries & Galloway   Map 7

Granary
Barend,
Sandyhills
off A710
7 m SE of Dalbeattie
Southwick (038 778) 663

Small restaurant in a converted cowshed amid holiday chalets overlooking a trout loch. 'Dinner party' cooking is the Gourlays' description of their limited choice dinners: pipérade or trout pâté, perhaps, then Armenian lamb pilaff or boeuf bourguignonne, vegetables, sweets and cheese. Lunch is limited to soup and filled rolls in the adjoining Tack Room bar. 'Cheery' service by the owners. Greenmantle ('my brother-in-law's brew') on hand pump; Spanish and Hungarian house wines (£2·90).

Closed L (exc bar); Sun–Thur (early Nov to Chr); early Jan–Easter
Must book
Meals 11.30–2.30 (summer), 12.30–2.30 (winter), 7.30–9

Tdh D £5·20 (meal £7·75)

Children's helpings
Seats 40

⑤ rest (1 step)
Car park
No dogs

DUMFRIES Dumfries & Galloway   Map 7

Bruno's
3 Balmoral Road
Dumfries (0387) 5757

An attractive little Italian restaurant in a quiet street, offering generous portions of carefully prepared dishes: cannelloni, lasagne, veal either pizzaiola or saltimbocca alla romana (£3·50), with hot brown rolls and fresh vegetables. 'Slightly dry chocolate gateau'; reasonable selection of cheeses. Service attentive – too much so in the constant refilling of wine glasses. Uninformative list; house wine £4·40 the litre. Recorded ballads. No dogs. More reports, please.

Closed L (exc Dec 25); Tue; Jan 1
Must book weekends

D only, 6–9.30

Alc £6·20 (meal £9·20)

Seats 70
⑤ rest
Air-conditioning

Gunga-Din
99c–101 Perth Road
Dundee (0382) 65672

The ape at the door may be out of the *Jungle Book* but the cooking at this bright, busy place is much less Kipling-esque than its namesake. Despite the white-on-black menu broken down into 'classical', 'colonial' and 'English', people note authentic shami kebabs, 'first-class' tandoori dishes, good lamb in the biriani, and 'fragrant' peshawari nan stuffed with nuts and sultanas (60p). Pursindah (lamb or other meat with poppy-seeds, aniseed, orris water and cream, £2·10) and vegetarian thalis are specialities. 'Variable' service. 'The Indian music of 1979 has gone British.'

Closed Sun L (exc Apr 6);
Dec 25 & 26
Must book D & weekends
Meals 12–2.15, 6–11.30

Tdh £7
Alc £3·15 (meal £4·10)

Children's helpings
(under 10)

Seats 46
♿ rest (1 step)
No dogs
Diners card

Kippen House
Dunning (076 484) 447

Closed Mon L
Must book D & weekends
Meals 12.30–2, 7.30–9

Tdh L £5 (meal £8·15),
D £8 (meal £11·45)
Alc £11·35 (meal £15·15)

Children's helpings
(under 6)
Seats 40 (parties 35)
Car park
No dogs in public rooms
Access, Am Ex, Barclay,
Diners, Euro
8 rooms (5 with bath,
3 with shower)
B&B £15–£22·50
D, B&B £20–£25
Full board £23–£30 p.d.
Fire cert

Picts, Celts, Jacobites and other gentry have given this ground a good going over in a couple of millennia, but the latest invasion is Dutch. Albert Roebersen took over this Victorian baronial house in 1978 and turned its ballroom into a restaurant, confessing to religious zeal for haute cuisine *and well-spaced tables. His French chef Philippe Mattioni may be finding both staff and customers slow off the mark to appreciate the* bourgeois *and* minceur *menus that are promised for this year, let alone champignons à l'escargot (£4), feuilleté de côte de veau aux épinards (£6·75), sole Gastiglione and gourmandise Prince Murat (both over £10) on the carte. But regular visitors report good value set lunches, with 'creamy vegetable soup, omelette à la turque with rich chicken livers, and deliciously tender escalope de veau au paprika.' Vegetables are kept hot in copper dishes at the tableside for second helpings. Crème caramel was 'relatively disappointing', pineapple Chantilly better. The wines have the air of having been bought in Scotland and priced in Paris (Ch. Haut-Brion '66, £56·50) but in fact Minervois and Corbières are under £5, and '76 Beaujolais under £8. Recorded classical music. 'Tenue de ville', they say for dress, but at least you can take your children. More reports, please.*

Scottish public holidays do not all coincide with English ones.

PLEASE keep sending in reports, as soon as possible after each meal. The cut-off date for the 1981 Guide is September 30, 1980, but reports are even more useful earlier in the year, especially for the remoter areas and new places. Late autumn reports can also affect corrections at proof stage.

EDDLESTON Borders   Map 9

Cringletie House Hotel

♥

on A703
2½ m N of Peebles
Eddleston (072 13) 233

Closed Jan; Feb;
early March
Must book
Meals 1–1.45, 7.30–8.30

Tdh L £4·50 (meal £7),
D £7·50 (meal £10·30)

Children's helpings
Seats 55 (parties 24)
Car park
No dogs in public rooms
16 rooms (9 with bath,
1 with shower)
B&B from £12·50
Fire cert

'It is my practice to cast an eye on the kitchen garden, if any, of any country hotel I visit,' writes one member: no wonder the *Guide*'s collective sleuthery inspires dread here and there. But the Maguires' 'superb walled garden' easily passed this test, and there are also lawns for croquet and putting. Most people also enjoy their meals and stays in the well-kept, peaceful red-stone house, and wonder how Mrs Maguire has time over from the kitchen to arrange flowers so discreetly. Her bread rolls are baked on the spot too. True, the cooking is flawed from time to time: dry joints for a cold lunch, new potatoes gone hard on the surface, and poor boeuf bourguignonne are lapses mentioned, but they are outweighed by, for instance, corn and asparagus Mornay, avocado with tomato water-ice, Stilton and port pâté, interesting soups of cucumber, beetroot or spinach, duckling with apricot in white wine sauce, casseroled aubergine and tomato, rich sweets such as praline vacherin, and mint sorbet. The wines are lovingly chosen and reasonably priced: two '71s, Ch. Beausite at £6·25 and Santenay Les Gravières (Amance) at £9·50 are examples, and drinking starts at around £3. Pressurised beers. No smoking in the dining-room, and no dress rules, though in a fairly sober – indeed 'taciturn' – company, 'an American's short-sleeved scarlet pyjama suit provided a passing *frisson*, and made it hard to look in any other direction.'

App: M. J. & C.I. Robertson, J. S. Scott, W.F., S.J., Iris Willett-Bakke, D. J. I. Garstin, and others

EDDLESTON see also pub section

EDINBURGH   Map 9

(1) Anatolian
13 Dalry Road
031-346 0204

Closed L (exc by
arrangement); Sun; Jan 1
Must book
Meals L (by arrangement),
6.30–11.30

Alc £5·30 (meal £9·40)

Service 10%
Cover 20p
Seats 38

This is not just another Turkish kebab house, for the decor is sub-Scandinavian, the food makes few compromises, and you may be able to admire Anatolian arts and crafts on exhibit. Mr and Mrs Karadeniz and their chef Mr Cicisci have won new friends since last year's provisional entry. Greedy ones begin with either hot or cold mezeler, or indeed a mixture of the two. 'Börek pastries filled with cheese were very good, and müjver were outstanding: rissoles of shredded courgette and carrot in a seasoned batter.' 'There's a pervasive, fascinating flavour that I meet nowhere else. You can't range all that far beyond aubergine, pepper and lamb, but who wants to? And the pitta bread is really good and always served very hot.' Other individual dishes

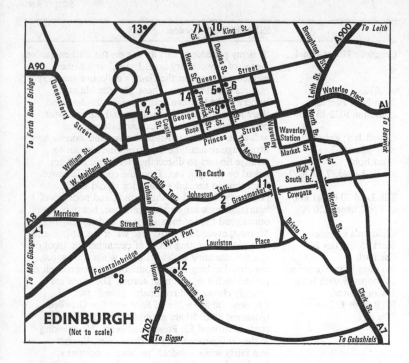

EDINBURGH
(Not to scale)

♿ rest
No dogs
Am Ex, Barclay, Diners

praised include a sandwich of aubergine, veal and
brains (£5·25, when it's on) and eyüp kebab (an
aubergine nest with lamb, £6·50 for two), but note
also the specialities balik bugulama (steamed sole in
wine sauce with vegetables, £3) and spinach tart as a
vegetarian main course. One long wait for oversalted
food is reported. The baklava is a revelation to
southerners who meet only the stale peanutty
confections bought in from mediocre bakers. Turkish
coffee is strong, if not always hot. People differ about
the 'slightly resinous' Trakya white and Buzbag or
Papaskarasi Turkish wines (from £3·90), but Chianti
at £3·20 is an alternative. Raki is 75p a glass. No
children under seven. Recorded Turkish music – live
for occasional folk evenings.

*App: A. M. M. Adam, J. Stephenson, J. & K.L.,
C. J. Richardson, M.R.A.M., and others*

Since each restaurant has a separate file in the Guide office, please use a separate
form or sheet of paper for each report. Additional forms may be obtained free (no
stamp required) from The Good Food Guide, Freepost, 14 Buckingham Street,
London WC2N 6BR (unfortunately Freepost facilities are not available from the
Channel Islands or the Republic of Ireland).

Meal times refer to first and last orders.

(2) **Beehive Inn**
The Steak Experience
18–28 Grassmarket
031-225 7171

Closed Sun; Dec 25 & 26;
Jan 1
Must book
Meals 12.30–2, 7.30–10

Alc (min £5·75) £9·70
(meal £14·35)

Cover 50p
Seats 40
No dogs
Access, Am Ex, Barclay,
Diners, Euro

Clive and Anne Davidson, eager young South Africans, have made this ancient inn into a chop-house on the ground where Edinburgh used to chop heads. As well as steaks, kebabs or chops, the charcoal-grill in the restaurant also yields prawns piri-piri (£9·25 for six), crayfish or king klip ('a delicately flavoured fish found only in South African waters', £5·85) for non-carnivores. Start with expense-account smoked salmon or asparagus, help yourself to crisp salad from the iced buffet, then choose, say, between a half pope's eye (10 oz 'from the heart of the rump', £4·85), a double-sided lamb chop (12–16 oz, £5·10) or 'old man steak', sirloin in a creamy mustard-flavoured sauce with mushrooms (£6·25). Garlic bread and French fries fill any available corners – the sweets are unexciting. (Note the dozen pottery jars of exotic mustards.) Almost half of the fifty wines are South African, all reasonably priced, from Steen '78 (a dry white) at £4·50 to Allesverloren Tinta das Barocca '75 (a 'powerful and mellow' red) at £6·50; house wine, also South African, is £4·50 the bottle. 'Smiling service from friendly girls.' 'Vocalised schmaltz' on record, the Guardian *critic says. No children under ten. More reports, please, of the Steak Experience and also the Drones bar, at ground level, which serves lunchtime snacks (cold buffet with a hot dish in winter) with an impressive range of hand-pumped ales: Theakston's, Belhaven, Samuel Smith's, Bateman's and Jennings.*

---

(3) **Cosmo's**
58a North Castle Street
031-226 6743

A member who 'only has eyes for the seafood' spares a word of praise for Cosmo's new decor before diving into her element: 'enormous dish of mussels, carefully seasoned; antipasto frutti di mare (£2·50) worthy of its name; two new scallop dishes, fried and thermidor, incomparable.' Pasta is left with some bite (agnellotti, layered with spinach and cheese, £1·35, is a speciality) and saltimbocca (£4·20) has satisfied. 'My limp salad was quickly replaced.' Sorbets and testina di negro for those who get to sweets. But negligent, insolent, and time-wasting service has been noted more than once. Valpolicella and Soave are £3·80 a litre. Snacks may be eaten at the bar. No children under four. Recorded classical music.

Closed Sun; Mon; Sat L;
July 1–15; Dec 25; Jan 1
Must book

Meals 12.30–2.15,
6.30–10.15

Alc (min L £3, D £3·50)
£8·65 (meal £11·95)

Seats 62
 ♿ rest
No dogs
Access, Barclay, Euro

---

(4) Denzler's
80 Queen Street
031-226 5467

Closed Sun; May 5, 19 &
20; Sept 15; Dec 25 & 26;
Jan 1
Must book (ground floor)
Meals 12–1.55, 6.30–9.45

Alc (min D £3·10) £5·80
(meal £8·50)

Service 10%
Children's helpings
Seats 130
& rest (1 step)
Air-conditioning
(ground floor)
No dogs

As Londoners also know, Swiss professionalism is
always apt to o'erleap itself, and there have been signs
in these suave but far from atmospheric rooms (the
ground floor has the bookable no-smoking section)
that Sämi Denzler and his seven assistants in the
kitchen cannot control as many meals as they now
serve: 'ratatouille overcooked and short of aubergine',
'very fatty goose with similar potatoes', 'cure-all
cherry garnishes'. However, these lapses remain the
exceptions to very capable avocado with white
crab-meat and a yoghourt dressing, 'skilfully cooked'
escalope of pork stuffed with pâté, or suprême de
volaille Alfio in a crisp batter of herbs and cheese,
served with berrichonne potatoes. Bündnerfleisch
called 'cold and dank' by one man, was 'very
impressive' when an inspector tried the 'grainy beef,
moist ham and slightly fat pork'. Toast Norwegian
(£1·55) is a speciality and they make their own Spätzli
and parfaits. Fondue bourguignonne is good too,
with 'super sauces and endless brown bread', and
Apfelstrudel or Black Forest gateau live up to
expectation of a Swiss place. The service, though
basically amiable, can be imperious and *agitato* by
turns – 'perhaps too tolerant of noisy children.'
L'Alliance French red or German Altdorfer
Trappenberg white are the house wines at £3·80 and
£4 a litre respectively, but you may also try here
Swiss Fendant white at £5·20 or Dôle red at £5·40,
among others; or drink apple juice at £1·10 a bottle.

App: J. Freebairn, D. E. Westoby, I.H.D.J.,
V. Westerman, J. & K.L., E.M.A., and others

(5) Henderson's Salad
Table
94 Hanover Street
031-225 3400

Closed Sun; D Dec 24 &
31; Dec 25 L; Dec 26;
Jan 1
Open 8 a.m.–10.45 p.m.
(L 11.30–2.30,
D 4.30–10.45)

Alc £2·20 (meal £4·35)

Seats 200
Air-conditioning (partial)
Access, Am Ex, Barclay,
Diners

'The only place in Edinburgh where we felt we were
being honestly charged.' Good butter, bread and
eggy mayonnaise are the beginning of it. With hot
dishes, you can eat well if you have shut meat out of
your mind first, and do not expect 'paella', 'moussaka'
and 'chop suey' to resemble the originals too closely.
But 'vegetable curry, cauliflower cheese and courgette
bake made choices worth queuing for', and brava
astouriana (£1·20), leek and potato pie, and
mushroom savoury (£1) are also advocated. The dried
fruit salad with sour cream and stem ginger is
preferred to the confected sweets, though they do
know how to make wholemeal pastry light. On the
sensible wine list (from £1·80 for 50 cl of Quinson red
or white) the Yugoslav grape-varietal wines at £2·75
are notable; so is Ch. Lascombes '73, c.b., at £7.
Pressurised beers. If there is music, it will be from a
live guitar. The non-smoking section sometimes has
to be policed by customers, though one member who
tried was told by the smoker who invaded her space

that prostitution and drink were just as anti-social:
'How could he tell in one quick glance?' *(Alas, a turn-of-the-year meal was so poor, says a normally admiring inspector, that judgement must be suspended as we go to press: please tell us if the 'appalling' mushroom savoury and lasagne were merely a seasonal aberration.)*

Recipe in *Second Dinner Party Book:* dried fruit salad with sour cream

App: H. D. & A. L. Rose, R. A. Bailey, Stephen Coverly, D. Westoby, W.F., I. & K.C., and others

---

(6) Laigh Kitchen
117a Hanover Street
031-225 1552

The Spicers are sprung from the Laigh Bakery next door, and this place also has much in common with the old Laigh (now in other hands, as the Cairn) which was Edinburgh's first 1950's coffee house. That is, unassuming relaxation at comfortable chairs and tables 'with an old range blazing in winter'; and a menu of home-made soups, filled potatoes, and unusual salads (bean sprout and pimento, pears and blue cheese) as well as the expected baked goods, from 'beautifully light' rolls and scones to empire biscuits and hazelnut meringue cake. Some traditional Scots hot favourites like stovies 'to line the ribs' are served in cold months. Unlicensed, 'but strong coffee'. As we went to press there was still no sign outside, so find the bakery and count basements, and report, please.

Closed D; Sun;
Dec 25 & 26; Jan 1

Open 9–5 (2.30 Mon & Sat), L 11–3

Alc L £2·15 (meal £2·40)

Seats 50

---

(7) Loon Fung
2 Warriston Place
031-556 1781

'Not the Canton of the North', it seems, and though dim-sum hold an exotic appeal, veterans will shy from padded paper prawn and turnip cake fried in stale oil. Siu mai at least 'had a nice flavour', and main courses may have suffered less from a chef's departure. Black-bean sauce is commended (though an inspector could have done with more beans and queried the bony ribs); scallops, lemon chicken (now £3·45 and blushing red) and mixed vegetables evoke some praise, and decor is cheerier. Jasmine tea is 'good and weak' and you can pick up Chinese wine at their supermarket across the way. Couples must queue rather than book. No licence: take your own if you wish.

Closed Sun (exc summer);
L Fri & Sat; Dec 25
Must book weekends
Open 12.30 p.m.–
12.15 a.m. (Fri, Sat & Sun
2–12.30 a.m.)

Tdh from £4 (meal £4·45)
Alc £5·70 (meal £6·15)

Service inc

Seats 35 (parties 50)
No dogs
Unlicensed

Scottish public holidays do not all coincide with English ones.

(8) **Lorenzo**
109 Fountainbridge
031-229 2747

Closed L; Sun; Tue;
Dec 25; Jan 1
Must book weekends
D only, 6–11

Alc (min £2·50) £7·20
(meal £10·05)

Service 10%
Seats 35
Access, Am Ex, Barclay,
Euro

With luck, nothing has changed but the name, since Lorenzo Crolla was in charge here last year even though brother Vito had his name on the plate. 'We return again and again,' says one visitor, 'for on a detailed comparison with the Crolla family's other place (q.v. under Vito's), the lasagne is lighter, the scaloppine Montiff with brandy sauce and cherries an irresistible veal dish, and their affocata di Amaretto ice-cream superior in both cream and liquor.' Fritto misto with good tartare, frutte di mare gran pescatora, saltimbocca, and Mr Crolla's own suggestions (scampi Lorenzo, and bistecca pizzaiola) are also worth considering; and as for crêpes Suzette, 'I order it for two and eat the lot myself.' Valpolicella or Frascati are £3·10, and for a step up, try the white Frecciarossa or the Chianti Bessi. They will provide smaller helpings for children. No dogs. More reports, please.

---

(9) **Madogs**
38a George Street
031-225 3408

Lacking midday sun, Scots (and Yanks and, it is said, royalty) retire to this 'semi-American semi-basement' for a glass of bottled sunshine and a B.L.T. Some think the pulsating *son et lumière* cancels out the flip and friendly service. Lunch is complex soup-and-sandwich fare: clam chowder, pastrami, tuna 'in a crisp, hollowed Vienna roll' and eggs Benedict with home-made hollandaise. Guacamole (£1·50), crisp, glazed duck (£4·60) with baked courgettes, and the ever-gooey chocolate cake impressed at dinner. Try teriyaki steak and grouper amandine (both £2·90). Cocktails, American beer, and house wine (£2·90).

Closed Sun; Dec 25; Jan 1   Tdh L £3·50 (meal £5·45),   Seats 75
Must book D   D £6·50 (meal £8·75)   Air-conditioning
Meals 12–3, 6.30–11.30   Alc £7·15 (meal £9·80)   Barclaycard

---

(10) **Mermans**
8–10 Eyre Place
031-556 1177

Closed Mon (exc Apr 21
& May 19); L Sun & Sat;
Sun D (exc Apr to end of
Festival); Apr 22;
May 20; Dec 25, 26 & 31;
Jan 1
Must book
Meals 12–1.30 (2 Festival)
7–10.15 (11.15 Festival)

Tdh L £2·75 (meal £5·35)
Alc (min £3·75) £9
(meal £12·25)

Nothing to do with Ethel, but with two male fish-fanciers, Brian Miller (who cooks) and Alan Alexander, who have done up a little shop off Dundas Street in red, white, and blue, with good linen and cutlery, to serve '99 per cent fresh fish, with oysters and mussels from Loch Sween, Dublin Bay prawns from Oban, lobsters and scallops from Skye, salmon smoked to our own prescription, and white fish from Newhaven market.' Early nominators reported 'delicious fish soup and really fresh plaice lightly grilled, with a taste of fennel in the salad', or seafood Merman and sound poached skate. Inspectors in 1979 happily confirmed these findings with an orgy of 'delectably sweet little mussels in a huge casserole (£2·65 – though perhaps the cream-based sauce was overdoing it)', delicate prawn mousse ('but with turned butter on the good brown bread'), and fresh scampi thermidor ('more like à la crème'). Sweets included 'a delicious meringue with fresh and boozy pineapple'. But there were also faults to be remedied: a bland provençale sauce, 'unspeakable cauliflower', and boiled coffee. Wines begin with French Libertine at £3·45, and include good sparkling Saumur (Gratien & Meyer) at £6, and halves of Barsac (n.v.) at £2·75. There is usually a radio in the background. A seafood bar is planned for 1980. More reports of this and of the restaurant, please.

---

(11) Ristorante Milano
7 Victoria Street
031-226 5260

Aesthetically Italian Primitive, Signor Ferrari's airy, rough-cut grotto gets more mannerist in the kitchen. Chiaroscuro reports this year, and one woman at a second visit regretted earlier praise for 'delicious mussels and two helpings of melting osso buco, with bone marrow specially sought out.' First-course servings of pasta ('good lasagne, solid gnocchi in chilli and tomato sauce') may be meagre for the price. But crème brûlée is 'good enough'. Wines mostly Italian, including Orvieto Abboccato (£4).

Closed Sun; Dec 25; Jan 1
Must book D & weekends
Meals 12–2.30, 6.30–10.55

Alc £7·25 (meal £10·60)
Service 10%
Cover 40p

Seats 65
♿ rest; w.c.
No dogs
Am Ex, Barclay, Diners

---

(12) Shamiana
14 Brougham Street
031-229 5578

Closed L; Sun; Dec 25; Jan 1
Must book
D only, 5.45–10.30

Alc £4·90 (meal £6·55)

Service 12½%
Children's helpings
Seats 42
♿ rest
No dogs
Access, Am Ex, Barclay, Diners, Euro

Scots – with the exception of one sceptic from Tillicoultry – have rejected the last edition's hint that Mr Jogee's handsomely furnished and suavely served restaurant needed more competition or Indian custom to scale the heights. 'I find the chicken tikka particularly good, and shahi korma was a huge dish of first-grade, well-trimmed lamb in a delicious sauce. When I inquired about the black pod in the fragrant rice, the waiter brought me both black and white cardamoms on a saucer so that I would be able to identify them in future.' The chefs, S. K. Maharjan and Jan Mohammed, think their own best dishes are makni chooza (£3·45), murgh masallam (£2·25), lamb pasanda (£2·25), shashlik kebab (£2·25), and Kashmiri chasni tikka (£3·45). Nan and masala poppadums are liked too, but temperatures of main dishes need watching, and vegetables seem dear to those unwilling to make a meal of them. The member disappointed by the halva (£1·05) might have preferred by other accounts sevian zarda (a vermicelli pudding), or 'the best mango I have ever had.' The coffee is said to be coffee, as it should be at 40p. There is a fair choice of wines, from £3·05 for Yugoslav Riesling, besides lager. Recorded ragas.

App: Ian Sims, Nial Brannigan, E. Davies, Lawrence Brown, A. J. R. Stephenson, M.R.A.M.

Service 10%
Children's helpings
Seats 24 (parties 30)
♿ rest (1 step)
No dogs

Scottish public holidays do not all coincide with English ones.

(13) Snobs
1 Dean Bank Lane,
Stockbridge
031-332 0003

Once people have got over *le rouge, le noir et le mauve,* they mostly enjoy the Italian cooking here. Courgettes parmigiana (baked with tomatoes) is a popular choice, then as main course (from £3·50) perhaps trota al cartoccio ('the flavour of the trout not drowned by the clams, mussels, prawns and herbs in the foil packet') or plain roast veal. Good vegetables and salads too. Iced soufflé milanese and a pancake stuffed with cream cheese and candied peel make interesting sweets. Adequate service and 'thudding Beatles records'. Italian carafe £3·60 the litre, 50p the glass.

Closed Sun; Dec 25;
Jan 1
Must book D
Meals 12.30–2.30, 6.30–11

Alc (min £3·50) £7·60
(meal £9·90)

Service inc

Seats 24
No dogs
Access, Am Ex

---

(14) Vito's
55a Frederick Street
031-225 5052

Closed Sun; Dec 25 & 26;
Jan 1
Must book D & weekends
Meals 12–2, 6.30–11

Alc £8·20 (meal £11·55)

Service 10%
Seats 70
No dogs
Am Ex, Barclay

There is something about Scots docility that brings out the Caesar or at best the *largo al factotum* complex in Italians, and Vito Crolla's sunnily decorated New Town restaurant is a conspicuous example. In the kitchen, Frank Fusco has a talent for everything except accuracy and day-to-day consistency, to judge by inspectors' accounts of 'slackly composed' hors d'oeuvre, 'inedibly salt' scampi thermidor, and even (in high summer) tinned green beans along with, on more auspicious occasions, 'well-cooked lasagne and fettuccine with garlic and herbs', 'much-praised hot avocado with generous seafood sauce,' 'an enormous chunk of turbot for £5·50' and 'correct zuppa pavese'. 'Chicken Kiev is fine too if you have tamed your nearest and dearest not to mind the garlic.' 'We found both steaks and service excellent', and 'my Italian friend quelled the waiters by calling "Carissimo" when he wanted attention.' Salad is probably better than vegetables, and testina di negro – though here too the flavours are not always correctly balanced – is the favourite sweet. Most wines look or taste the same out of the pottery goblets so you might as well drink Velletri ordinaires at £3·80 a litre, though there are better bottles at about £5.

*App: D. N. Whyte, Marilyn Bruce, A.J.R.S.,
J. & K.L., J. Freebairn, and others*

Prices quoted in entries now include VAT.

Towns shown in black on our maps contain at least one recommended restaurant, pub or wine bar (see map key). The dot denotes the location of the town or village, not the establishment. Where necessary, we give directions to it in the entry. If you can, help us to improve them.

ERISKA Strathclyde   Map 9

Isle of Eriska Hotel
12 m N of Oban
4 m W of A828
Ledaig (063 172) 371

Closed end Nov to Mar
Must book
Meals 1–1.30, HT 5.45,
7.30–8.30

Tdh L £5·75 (meal £7·30),
D £12·50 (meal £14·05)

Service inc
Seats 45 (parties 12)
♿ rest
Car park
No dogs in public rooms
Cheques by prior
arrangement only
Am Ex card
24 rooms (all with bath)
D, B&B from £31
Full board £190
Fire cert

Recipe in *Second Dinner
Party Book:* chestnut and
orange roulade

The bridge across the water to the Hon. Robin
Buchanan-Smith's Victorian-baronial pile leads,
people say, to bygone manners and assumptions, a
sense of teeming wildlife in earth, air and water, and
(for the Western Highlands) uncommonly good food.
You will naturally not expect much choice, and there
was a sad slip, by one account, when Mrs Buchanan-
Smith was away in May. At these prices, lapses are
hard to excuse. But when all goes well, the soups of
tomato or mushroom or chicken, the lunchtime cold
joints of 'rare and tender' beef or 'succulent' ham, the
interesting and subtly dressed salads and home-made
pickles, and salmon hollandaise (perhaps as a
centre-piece at dinner) satisfy all comers. Pibroch of
chicken and haddock Montrose are kitchen favourites.
Sally Collier's greengage mousse, ginger pudding with
pears, orange and chestnut roulade, and other sweets
are popular too, and the cheeses are not scamped.
'Self-service fried eggs are inadvisable at breakfast.'
'Bread is home-made.' The wines remind you that the
Kirk (in which the owner formerly ministered) is not
lumbered with an over-strong teetotal tradition.
They graduate from Bardolino at just over £3 to Ch.
Calon-Ségur '61, c.b., at ten times as much, with
plenty of halts on the way. 'Their Taylor's Quinta
Vargellas '65 port (£1·35 a glass) compared well with
my own Gonzales-Byass of the same year; a '63 would
have been too heavy after lunch.' Dress for dinner
with suitable reverence, and shed under-twelves at the
dining-room door (they have high tea instead). (GHG)

*App: J. W. A. Forbes, K.S.T., P. H. Johnston,
M.A.P., and others*

FALKIRK Central   Map 9

Pierre's
140 Grahams Road
Falkirk (0324) 35843

Short cuts are discouraged, if not curtailed, since the
kitchen in Pierre and Ellen Renjard's resonant place
is open to view. Prawn cocktail and steak distract
local men of affairs but the set dinners (£6·50 for three
courses) revived an outsider: 'pinkly cooked duck
with duck liver sauce, garlicky terrine, and creamy
eclairs among various items of patisserie.' An inspector
was more cautious about the cheaper lunch, but
frogs' legs and suprême de volaille from the dearer
carte passed muster. 'Tough crêpes, no sign of
flambé.' French wines from £3·60. 'Charming' service.

Closed Sun; Mon (exc
public hols); Sat L;
May 5 & 6; June 30–
July 19; Dec 25 D;
Dec 26; Jan 1
Must book D

Meals 12–2.15, 7–9.30

Tdh L £3·10 (meal £5·70),
D £6·50 (meal £9·45)
Alc (min £3·10) £8·30
(meal £11·45)

Children's helpings
(under 10)
Seats 35
♿ rest
No dogs

383

Strathmore Arms
off A94
4 m S of Forfar
Glamis (030 784) 248

An inn hard by the castle of the Earls of Strathmore, and suddenly popular with local diners who find the McMillans helpful and generous hosts. The cross-cultural menu leans towards guy-wired pastry swans filled with prawns, custard or what-have-you. But guinea-fowl in ham, tongue and wine sauce, veal with mushrooms and peppers, 'bloody' steaks and ratatouille all please. The kitchen suggests smoked fish (£1·80) and nasigoreng (£4·75) but appears willing and able to adjust and improvise. Wines (45p the glass for generic Italian) and children well treated. Bar snacks and pressurised beers. Wear a jacket. Taped music. More reports, please.

Closed Sun; Mon (mid-Oct to Easter);
Dec 25 D; Dec 26; Jan 1
Must book weekends
Meals 12.30–1.45, 7.30–9

Tdh L £3·50 (meal £5·50)
Alc £7·20 (meal £10)

Children's helpings
(under 8)

Seats 60 (parties 40)
 ⅃ rest; w.c.
Air-conditioning
Car park
No dogs

La Bavarde
9 New Kirk Road,
Bearsden
041-942 2202

Closed Sun; Mon;
3 weeks July; Dec 31;
1st week Jan
Must book
Meals 12–1.30, 6.30–9.30

Tdh L £2·50 (meal £5·35)
Alc £6·30 (meal £9·50)

Children's helpings
Seats 50
 ⅃ rest (2 steps)
No dogs
Access, Am Ex, Diners,
Euro

Armenio Trevisan's little restaurant is so busy that he and his young chef Peter Bannister are left wishing they had more time *pour bavarder* with their customers about what they would like to eat. But members seem happy enough for the time being with what they are given: 'a rich and meaty game liver croûte, with light pastry and a hint of orange in the gravy', crab quiche – an impressive sight if you have ordered a whole one for a large party – paw-paws with Stilton and cream, tongue with salsa verde (£1·15) and goujon of smoked haddock – and those are merely first courses, many of which can be bought to take away at the restaurant's shop at 76 Hyndland Road. Thereafter, a regular visitor is not too keen about the rabbit dishes and wishes tomato puree were more effectively disguised, but admires lamb, venison, duck, and pigeon unreservedly – 'especially pigeon and plum pie' (£4). Dover sole in lime juice and mallard in ginger wine are other creations. Sweets are simple, prudently enough, though 'tarts are very reliable and the Stilton usually good.' The waiting is polite even if not always expert. Italian table wines are £3·90 a litre. Choice beyond that is modest (except in price) and also mostly Italian.

App: Mr & Mrs David V. Thomas, David A. Murdoch, R. L., E. Davies

---

1980 prices are as estimated by restaurateurs in the autumn of 1979 (including VAT).

See p. 441 for pubs and p. 491 for wine bars.

Beacons Hotel
La Bonne Auberge
7a Park Terrace
041-332 9438

One expects less of an auberge than of a château but when the original is in Cannes and prices reach Festival heights the critic's eye is beadier. '*Assez bon*' is the consensus, with plaudits for mushroom stuffed with crab (£1·85) or baked in cream, and haddock mousse to start, duckling in cider and sole in flaky pastry to follow. Goat's cheese is preferred to chocolate mousse and 'over-delicate' sorbets. Small portions of vegetables, though 'weeping' ratatouille deserves no more. French Gamay, £3·95 for 75 cl. 'French songs too sentimental for Art Nouveau style.'

Closed Sun; Sat L;
public hols (exc Apr 4;
Dec 25 D)
Must book
Meals 12.30–2.30,
6.30–10.45

Tdh L £4·60 (meal £6·55)
Alc £8·75 (meal £11·10)

Service inc
Seats 72 (parties 60)
Air-conditioning

No dogs
Access, Am Ex, Barclay,
Diners
27 rooms (26 with bath,
1 with shower)
B&B from £13·25

Central Hotel
Malmaison Restaurant

▲

Hope Street/Gordon Street
041-221 9680

Closed Sun; Sat L;
public hols (exc May 26
& Aug 25)
Must book
Meals 12.30–2.30, 7–10.15

Tdh £8·40 (meal £10·40)
Alc £13·90 (meal £17·05)

Service inc
Seats 70 (parties 600)
No dogs in public rooms
Access, Am Ex, Barclay,
Diners, Euro
221 rooms (150 with bath,
20 with shower)
B&B from £22·50

The *bonne table* of the Malmaison over the years has brought it serious customers and a touch of animation, even at night in central Glasgow. The liner's engine-room stutters sometimes, but if everything were to the level of Stuart Cameron's best, a pestle distinction would be deserved, for he is a first-rate *saucier*. 'We'd go again just for the hollandaise on broccoli at a table d'hôte lunch.' 'Langoustines provençale had a very fresh-tasting tomato sauce sadly short of herbs and garlic, but the quail than followed, admirably cooked and barded with apple slices, had a light and expertly seasoned sauce normande.' 'Surprise de sole primeur (a speciality, £6·55) brought two fillets of lemon sole wrapped round a grass-green puree of mange-tout peas, with a very rich egg-and-cream white wine sauce: lovely.' All this bodes well for other specialities such as truite au vinaigre (£5), ris de veau Jacoulet and also the alarming côte de veau aux fraises. Even in these hasty times the larder preserves its own ducks. Hors d'oeuvre are generous with fish and other primary tastes – 'the first time I have been served with a whole avocado, peeled'; 'prawn cocktail sauce was very different from the usual rubbish' – and double sirloin and other red meat joints live up to expectation. 'Suprême de volaille Lady Curzon, with its curry sauce and vegetable *obbligati*, was a splendid dish for two.' Alas, a test meal revealed one fault previously mentioned – niggardly helpings of high-priced vegetables – and added more: 'a bland, tasteless omelette aux foies de volailles', a depleted trolley of sweets that cannot have been all that inviting even at the start of the evening, and cheeses 'ruined by time, warmth, and lack of understanding.' Coffee was poor too, and a request for Laphroaig or any other single malt whisky ought not to tie Glasgow's leading hotel in knots – 'though it was worth it to hear the Gaelic in an Italian accent.' The BTH wines are excellent, and a glance at the Malmaison Wine Club retail list shows that mark-ups are low for the better bottles. The claret is famous, with remarkable '61 bin-ends surviving in 1979, but this is a safe place for burgundy at prices 'still within reach of a working woman's expense account', and the Mosel and Alsace sections deserve a glance – or try Ch. Laville-Haut-Brion '75 (£10·25) with the hors d'oeuvre. The service by 'brushed and muted cherubs' is willing but often inexperienced – 'with so many trolleys, sometimes there is pandemonium à la Paddington.' The 'pianist left at 11 p.m. and he is indispensable to the atmosphere.'

App: Dr G. Davies, S. J. Monkcom, S.L., Peter Carnes, Esme Walker, I. & K. Oswald, and others

---

GLASGOW   Map 9

Ubiquitous Chip

♟

12 Ashton Lane
041-334 5007

Closed Sun; Dec 31 D;
Jan 1
Must book
Meals 12–2.30, 5.30–11

Tdh L £2·15 (meal £4·50)
Alc L £4·35 (meal £7·60),
D £7·30 (meal £9·80)

Children's helpings
Seats 135 (parties 50)
⑤ rest
No dogs

This signal example of technology catching up with a restaurant name (Glaswegians and Californians must interpret it quite differently) still gives pleasure to most of those who manage to find Brydon and Clydesdale's inviting courtyard and fan-noisy dining-room – 'elusive is the word rather than ubiquitous, even if you ask the Byres Road locals.' Mr Clydesdale hopes that when the cooking falls from grace it falls like Lucifer, from a height. Some think the chef has yet to learn the arts of seasoning, herbing, and sauce reduction, and value the place chiefly for the wine, but others report more heavenly (but spicy) fish bisque, asparagus hollandaise, pâté of belly pork and spinach, half a chicken in 'a rich cinnamon and tomato sauce', 'really fresh' Lochinver salmon baked in cream, tasty civet of hare (£2·80), and among sweets, baked plums in vanilla sugar with cream cheese. 'Vegetables are variable, and salads better.' 'I can seldom finish the vast three-course set lunch, but it is usually inventive.' 'We do try to cook our lamb pink and think the combination with mussels a good one,' the owners say. The wines are generously priced and 'matter-of-factly served', add members, with Yugoslav Cabernet or Riesling £2·70, good Riojas and non-European wines under £4·50, and a range of claret and burgundy, hock and moselle that one woman calls 'an Aladdin's cave': Ch. Cos d'Estournel and Ch. Gloria '70, both under £11; Dhronhofberger Auslese '71, £5·25; Mettenheimer Schlossberg Beerenauslese '71, £9·50. (The sweet '76 Beerenauslese wine should not be listed so soon.) More half-bottles would be welcome. Belhaven ale on hand pump. 'We try to curb smoking in one section': please support them.

App: Agnes Williams, Christine Stewart, Bruce Pettie, Paul Gambaccini, and others

La Potinière

Gullane (0620) 843214

Closed D (exc Sat); Wed;
Sat L; Oct; Dec 25 & 26
Must book
Meals 12.45 for 1,
7.30 for 8 (Sat)

Tdh L £4·75 (meal £6·15),
Sat D £7 (meal £8·40)

Service inc
Seats 34
♿ rest
Car park (3)
No dogs

Recipe in *Second Dinner
Party Book:* soufflés aux
courgettes

Many people are surprised to see the *Guide*'s most
sought-after distinctions draped on a place as
unassuming, in all senses, as David and Hilary
Brown's. But no-one disputes the accuracy of last
year's description – 'as you say, the same serious,
efficient, slightly impersonal approach you expect of a
restaurant in France, whether it is a weekday lunch
surrounded by local people, or a large dinner-party
booked months ahead.' France, too, speaks in the
soups, 'by far the best we have had in a restaurant':
pea or cauliflower or cucumber or carrot and orange.
Typically, the second course is a soufflé, or a
mousseline of sole, 'smooth and creamy and tasting of
fresh fish, topped with a cluster of caviare. For main
course, perhaps a classic poulet Mère Michel, or au
vinaigre, or turkey breast with green peppercorn
cream sauce 'garnished with a fresh, *peeled* tomato
section.' Plainly cooked potatoes and a salad are the
likeliest accompaniments. Then there will be a wedge
of ripe Brie and a slice of apple, or a pudding
which might again be a soufflé, or chocolate mousse,
or fresh fruit brûlée. (At dinner, you are offered both
cheese and fruit.) The repertoire is not vast, and it is
possible that the set meal without choice imposes
restrained flavours. But – apart from a hard oeuf en
cocotte at a test meal – technique is impeccable. So
is the taste, prescience, care and morality with which
Mr Brown chooses, buys, serves and prices his wines.
Carafino at £2·85 is an unambitious basic, but
consider that among his clarets (listed by commune)
under £7 appear Chx. Grand-Puy-Lacoste '66,
Lynch-Moussas '61, Gruaud-Larose '66, Brane-
Cantenac '67, Pape-Clément '67 and Pavie '66, to
name but a few. Burgundies are as good: 'velvet,'
says someone of her decanted half-bottle (one of
several) of Corton '71 (Jadot) at £3·50. Superb whites
of contrasted sweetness and character include Muscat
les Amandiers '75 (Dopff & Irion), Ch. Laville-Haut-
Brion '74, a dozen Chablis, Hermitage '73 (Gambert
de Loche) and Ch. Suduiraut '70, all under £6.
Aperitifs and vintage ports are judicious too. No
smoking until the coffee stage.

*App: John H. Duffus, David & Melanie Worrall,
E.M.A., E. M. Duncan, A. P. & D. R. Barker,
and others*

Scottish public holidays do not all coincide with English ones.

**Entries for places with distinctions carry symbols (pestle, tureen, bottle, glass).
Credits are fully written entries, with approvers' names below the text. Passes are
telegraphic entries (useful in the area) with details under the text. Provisional
entries are in italics (see 'How to use the Guide', p. 4).**

Scarista House
Scarista
on A859
15 m SW of Tarbert
Scarista (085 985) 238

Once over-run by sheep, which still encroach, this erstwhile manse has been reclaimed for mankind, or at least for the minority whose wellies carry them to Scarista beach. Reports are few – no wonder – but glowing. From the set menu, an August visitor approves courgettes with cheese, herrings in white wine, fried scallops, civet of venison, crown roast of lamb, lobster ('killed electrically'), pear salad and apricot praline tart. Walkers and bird-watchers are rewarded, and there is a well-stocked library for stay-at-homes. 'The elders still forbid a licence' but exact no corkage charge. No children under 12, and dogs must be controlled. Detailed reports welcome.

Closed L; Sun; Dec 25
Must book
D only, 7.30–8.30

Tdh £7·50 (meal £8·25)

Seats 12
 ⅃ rest (2 steps)
Car park
No dogs in public rooms
Unlicensed

4 rooms (2 with bath)
B&B £9–£13
D, B&B £15–£20
Fire cert

Dunain Park

on A82
2¼ m SW of Inverness
Inverness (0463) 30512

Closed Nov–Mar
Must book
Meals 12.30–1.30
(snacks), 7.30–9

Tdh D £10·75 (meal £12·70)

Service inc
Seats 20 (parties 6)
 ⅃ rest
Car park
No dogs in d/r
6 rooms (4 with bath)
B&B £13·30–£21·50
Fire cert

Judith Bulger writes a good letter and the *Guide* has a soft heart (believe it or not), like her visitors who 'wept at chicken on the menu after seeing me chase a pansy-eating cockerel round the garden,' and 'declined to eat lobster on meeting one taking the air and realising it was purple, not pink.' (The goat is one of nature's survivors – a member fed him oatcakes.) Happily, with one exception who characterises the cooking as 'chives with everything', and another who finds the atmosphere 'slightly stilted', everyone has sighed with relief to relax into a Highland hotel that actually does what it promises, with a peaceful night's sleep and scrupulous breakfasts, snack lunches (which may be eaten in the garden) and afternoon teas (with home preserves) as come-ons for the carefully composed dinner menus. These often feature simply poached salmon or pink-grilled meat but are capable on demand (new Aga permitting) of 'memorable' pigeon casserole, salmon in pastry with ginger and raisins, or baked chicken with limes. 'Soups – lentil, mushroom, carrot and others – were very obviously home-made, and scallops in bacon with a creamy sauce were tenderer than any I remember.' 'Perhaps a few more potato variations would be welcome, but Mrs Bulger's superb chicken curry comes with equally well-cooked rice.' 'Marinated mushrooms tasted deliciously fresh, with a bite to them.' 'A light and tangy lemon mousse made a fine contrast to rich and sweet, but also light, walnut pie.' 'Cheeses were limited in number, but prime in condition.' 'Coffee is good.' Carafino is a comparatively modest £3·90 a litre but those who can afford it may wish to venture beyond to Mr Bulger's

Ch. Chasse-Spleen '71, c.b., at £8·10 or one of the '72 burgundies: the food deserves it. 'No smoking until others in the dining-room consent.' As for children, 'we do banish squawkers and food-mashers, but in general still prefer five-year old continentals to American teenagers': amen, say some Americans.

Recipe in *Second Dinner Party Book:* chicken and almond curry

App: Henrietta & Alastair Munro, P. J. Marshall, Marcia Macleod, L. F. Leech, A. Tomlinson, Bel & Kevin Horlock, N.V.C., and others

---

ISLE ORNSAY Skye, Highland   Map 9

Kinloch Lodge Hotel
off A851
6 m S of Broadford
Isle Ornsay (047 13) 214

Closed Nov–Feb
Must book D
Meals 12–2 (bar),
HT 6, 8

Tdh D £8·05 (meal £10·70)

Children's helpings
(under 12)
Seats 36
♿ rest; w.c.
Car park
No dogs in public rooms
12 rooms (6 with bath)
B&B £12·10–£13·80
Fire cert

New babies (one of them Lady Macdonald's own) mean new cooks, and new decoration means more contented guests recently at this shooting-lodge on the Sleat peninsula, a fine refuge for otherwise inaccessible parts of the Black Cuillin, and 'very quiet if you screen out the cuckoos by day and the owls by night.' Lord Macdonald, the thoroughly modern laird, whose assertion of ancient 'feu superior' rights to get control of a gift-shop interested reporters in 1979, has 'ditched his hacking-jacket in favour of a red sweater', and all goes more or less swimmingly, it seems, though misprisions over bookings (not easy to put right once you have ventured this far) and mishaps in the kitchen do occur. 'Dishes we liked very much included scallops Cordon Bleu, sardine and mushroom pâté, cold courgette and mint soup, honey-roast gammon and chicken sauté au paprika. Pheasant casserole, though, was disappointing and hare braised in port was tough.' However, most others have been lucky even with game dishes like these, and the kitchen is also proud of its venison in orange, port and chestnut sauce. The sweets are generally popular, and well-varied between a speciality carrot cake with cream cheese and butter cream, banana fudge pie, salambô à l'orange, 'trifle with proper egg custard', and blackberry mousse. Breakfasts and packed lunches are also praised. There were still a few wines around £3 in 1979 and some good clarets too: Ch. de Pez '71, c.b., £7·40. Pressurised beers, and at lunchtime, home-made bar snacks. No children under five; older ones have enjoyed their high teas. 'No ashtrays on tables', though 'die-hard or American smokers are not above fetching them from the lounge.' (GHG)

App: I. P. Gordon, Anthea & Douglas Craig, H.R., C. J. Uncles, and others

---

If you think you are suffering from food-poisoning after eating in a restaurant, report this immediately to the local Public Health Authority (and write to us).

See p. 508 for the restaurant-goer's legal rights, and p. 510 for information on hygiene in restaurants.

Taychreggan Hotel
Lochaweside
7 m from Taynuilt
on B845
Kilchrenan (086 63) 211

A converted and extended drovers' inn, Danishly modernised, beside Loch Awe. Mrs Tove Taylor's influence embraces the cold table at lunch and a good use of seafood at dinner. Smoked mackerel pâté when tried was 'soft and smooth', and grilled sole, with home-made tartare sauce, 'faultless'. Others like the mixed grill, local salmon, fresh 'if repetitious' vegetables, and the cheese board. Some neglect of detail ('bottled mint sauce', 'barely thawed crab in avocado'). 'Atholl brose and Danish apple cake are among the cooks' favourite puddings.' House Bordeaux Blanc is £3·45. No under-eights at dinner. You pay £5 a day for their ghillie and 50p for your dog. (GHG – see under Lochaweside).

Closed Oct 14–Apr 1	Children's helpings	Access, Am Ex, Barclay,
Must book	(under 8)	Diners, Euro
Meals 1–2.15, 7.30–9	Seats 48	22 rooms (10 with bath,
	🔊 rest	1 with shower)
Tdh L £3·50 (meal £6.30),	Car park	B&B £13–£16
D £7 (meal £9·60)	No dogs in d/r	Fire cert

The Cairn
on A816
8 m NW of Lochgilphead
Kilmartin (054 65) 254

Closed Sun D; Nov 1–14;
Dec 24 D; Dec 25; Jan 1;
Feb
Must book D
Meals 12.30–2.30,
7.30–9.30

Alc (min £4) £5·10
(meal £7·65)

Children's helpings
(under 10 L)
Seats 60
Car park
No dogs in d/r
Am Ex, Barclay, Diners

'Underrated last time,' says one missive about the Thomsons' 'light and airy' restaurant upstairs from their craft shop and informal coffee room. Both rooms deserve a visit, and Mrs Thomson must work hard to bake 'gorgeous buttery shortbread and fresh apricot pie' for tea, as well as supply produce for restaurant lunches and dinners – 'real French onion soup' (35p), 'deep-fried scallops the like of which I never expect to see again', and 'outstanding chicken Kiev, spurting butter with just the right amount of garlic.' A slightly sceptical inspector confirms the warmth of this praise for much of the cooking – 'a delicious, very large Loch Awe trout with a crisp, and buttery skin' (£2·20), thick entrecôte, cooked rare as requested (a rarity indeed in Scotland), and a properly ethnic cloutie dumpling – 'a cross between Christmas cake and gingerbread, hot.' Pavlova with brambles is another popular sweet. The Alabama sauce for prawns and the combination of dry sherry and tinned peach in sherry trifle seemed less judicious. Coffee is 'very good strong Cona, upstairs and downstairs'. There is a modest wine list, knowledgeably served: 'Mr Thomson keeps Bourgogne Aligoté (R. Félix) '77 at both cellar and refrigerator temperatures, and it is a pleasure to see and taste Asbach brandy here.' Pressurised beers. 'Alas, Abba for an hour through loudspeakers isn't my choice as an accompaniment to a good meal.'

App: Michael and Lelia Popham, A.J.H.,
Paul L. Joslin, M. J. & A. J. Prendergast, and others

KINROSS Tayside   Map 9

Windlestrae Hotel
The Muirs
off M90 at junction 6
Kinross (0577) 63217

Closed Tue; 1st week Oct;
Jan; Dec 26
Must book
Meals 12.30–1.45,
7.30–8.45

Tdh L £4·95 (meal £6·65)
Alc £8 (meal £10·20)

Service inc
Children's helpings
(under 10 L)
Seats 45
Air-conditioning
Car park
No dogs
Access, Am Ex, Barclay,
Diners
4 rooms (all with bath)
B&B £11–£16
Fire cert

The hotel is an adjunct to the restaurant at this sprawling suburban villa, set in four acres of carefully cultivated gardens and ponds near the golf-course. 'Plush' is the byword, at least in the spacious bar, once an indoor swimming-pool. One member prefers to make directly for the dining-room 'where the wait is shorter, though you risk hearing the taped music twice.' Synthetics stop short of the kitchen, which sets high standards for itself and tries hard to meet them in spite of surface pretensions. Duty called an inspector to crêpes St Serf whose 'mushy' turkey and broccoli filling suggested demotion from the Calendar, and tournedos béarnaise in a 'blender' sauce was 'very un-blue'. But 'tangy' devilled whitebait (£1·40), 'spirituous' chicken liver pâté, pork Cordon Bleu, entrecôte in a creamy mushroom sauce (£4·70), and 'better scampi provençale than usual' turned business into pleasure. Crisp duckling with honey, nuts, cherries and pineapple pleased a sweet-toothed teenager, as did the Black Forest gateau. 'Lovely jacket potatoes were neatly cut to reveal a pat of butter.' Wines seem good value: Rioja Montecillo Cosecha '71, £3·65, Ch. Terrefort '74, £5·10. Lunchtime bar snacks; pressurised beers. Service is mostly pleasant but can be inefficient. No children under ten at dinner. 'Smart appearance very important', to them if not to you. More reports, please.

LAMLASH Arran, Strathclyde   Map 7

Carraig Mhor
Lamlash (077 06) 453

A spotless converted house ('outstanding ladies' loo') overlooking a lovely bay and homely at heart. Cramped and bustling 'when first sitting migrates to coffee lounge' and the late shift must choose wisely: 'Duck, last portion, *had* been good' but 'frozen raspberries on frothy Norwegian cream were a collapsed mush.' Lunchtime omelettes (£1·10), cream soups (lettuce, tomato, carrot), seafood pancake, and salmon (grilled or mayonnaise) are approved, and vegetables are hot and fresh, though unrefined, and 'presented in sequence like gifts of the Magi.' Italian house wine is 40p the glass. Children welcome. A few tables outside.

Closed Sun; Mon; Jan 1
Must book D
Meals 12.15–1.45, 7–9

Tdh D £6·50 (meal £8·80)
Alc L about £2·85

Seats 26

Children's helpings
(under 9)
♿ rest (1 step)
No dogs

The Guide News Supplement will be sent out as usual, in June, to everyone who buys the book directly from Consumers' Association and to all bookshop purchasers who return the card interleaved with their copy. Let us know of any changes that affect entries in the book, or of any new places you think should be looked at.

Inverlounin House
Lochgoilhead (030 13) 211

Must book
Meals 12.30–2, 7.30–9.30

Tdh L £6·50 (meal £9·30),
D £9 (meal £12·05)

Seats 16
 ⅊ rest
Car park
No dogs
4 rooms (1 with bath)
D, B&B £17·50
Fire cert

Hugh and Annie Pitt's rugged individualism, nurtured in the media, is luckily deployed against local planners rather than against guests of their lochside house, on which they have worked hard. They have had nearly two years now to settle in, modelling themselves on the *logis de France* concept, and they care enough about food – French, Italian, and British – to make a dispirited inspector fall with joy on their omelette with chicken livers (chopped and done in port), 'convincing' lamb Shrewsbury, and English Walmer pudding ('a very light apricot sponge'). Others over the past twelve months have expressed similar pleasure in fondue aux fruits de mer, feuilletés de crabe, côtelette de chevreuil, and the home-made ices; the Pitts themselves are proud of their gougère, coulibiac, gâteau de crêpes normande, and chocolate fudge pudding. Breakfasts and packed lunches also stand out, it seems, and visitors find the owners friendly, even though firm enough to ban dining-room smoking while others are eating, and to prefer holiday-makers to change for dinner. (Nor are children under 14 encouraged.) You may eat outside on the covered terrace. The wines are personally chosen: you may begin dinner with a Kir (or Myr) and continue with Gamay de l'Ardèche or Jurançon under £5, or Corton '69 or Ch. Lyonnat '67 at £6·75. Let us hope they have got their sums right, since the paddle-steamer no longer brings wealthy Glasgow commuters to peaceful Lochgoilhead. (GHG)

App: M. H. Buchanan, M.A.P., Jonathan Hoyle,
E. J. Bragg, and others

Lochmaddy Hotel
Lochmaddy (087 63) 331

'Whitewashed walls, panelled hall, and a parrot – just what a Hebridean fishing hotel should be, on the edge of a higgledy-piggledy shoreline "township".' Modestly composed four-course dinners, but avocado and prawns have reached Uist, and were good when tried, like Mrs Fraser's 'creamy and tasty' potato and leek soup, 'delicately poached' local salmon, tender sirloin, and 'surely home-made' coffee ice. Hirondelle £3·50. Pressurised beers. (GHG)

Closed Dec 25; Jan 1
Must book D
Meals 12.45–1.45, 7–8.45

Tdh L £3 (meal £5·10),
D £5·50 (meal £7·95)

Service 10%
Children's helpings
(under 12)
Seats 60 (parties 20)
 ⅊ rest (1 step)

Car park
No dogs in d/r
16 rooms (1 with bath)
B&B from £10·80
Fire cert

1980 prices are as estimated by restaurateurs in the autumn of 1979 (including VAT).

LYBSTER Highland   Map 9

Bay View Hotel
Russell Street
on A9
Lybster (059 32) 346

Thirty miles south of John O'Groats 'one is happy to survive and ecstatic to eat so well.' After confirming a bill of £1·45 for a bar lunch of soup, chicken casserole with fresh vegetables, cheese ('no choice, therefore in good shape') and coffee, a member decided that the Huttons cooked for their own pleasure as well as his. 'Seven of us enjoyed every dish at dinner: mushroom quiche and salmon mayonnaise, cream of cauliflower soup, peppery sirloin with mustard sauce, green beans and leeks au gratin, fresh peaches in brandy syrup, and coffee.' 'Everything fresh and a daily-changing menu.' Good Peter Thomson wines, 'none too cheap'. Over a hundred malt whiskies. More reports, please, of Highland hedonism.

Closed Sun; Jan 1
Must book D
Meals 12.30–2, 7.30–11

Tdh D £7 (meal £9·75)

Children's helpings
Seats 22
Car park
No dogs in d/r

3 rooms
B&B £5–£6
D, B&B £11·50–£12·50
Fire cert

MOFFAT Dumfries & Galloway   Map 7

Beechwood Country House Hotel
Moffat (0683) 20210

Must book D & weekends
Meals 12.45–1.45,
7.30–9.30

Tdh L £3·20 (meal £5·45),
D £5·35 (meal £8·05)

Seats 24
♿ rest (2 steps)
Car park
No dogs
Access, Barclay
8 rooms (3 with bath,
1 with shower)
B&B £8–£11
D, B&B £15·50–£20·50
Fire cert

'We were living dangerously in a hotel dropped by the *Guide* this year, but dinner was a very pleasant surprise.' It is good to know that this house – a comfortable place to stay except in the coldest weather – is still contributing to the Lowlands renaissance after its change of hands (Mr and Mrs McIlwrick took over late in 1978). Several others have written to confirm the claims of the set meals, mentioning in particular curried apple and beetroot soups, garlic bread, Snaffles mousse and a good chicken liver pâté among first courses, then sound casseroles of chicken or venison, tasty pommes lyonnaise, a lemony soufflé, and good Orkney among the cheeses. When the garden or other local connections get into their stride no doubt frozen peas will 'softly and suddenly vanish away'. Buffet lunches, breakfasts, and 'a sumptuous afternoon tea on arrival such as I have not seen in years' are also mentioned (children are given high tea). The wines (from £1·75 for 50 cl of ordinaire) are modest, but modestly priced too, with Ch. Chasse-Spleen '73, c.b., £6·85 in 1979. No smoking in the dining-room. Wear a tie to dinner. (To find the hotel, drive north up Academy Road in Moffat, turn right up Harthope Place, then left at the top.)

App: David Harcus, H.T., G.W.D., J.R.T., H.J.W., Linda Page, F. M. Halle, and others

Meal times refer to first and last orders.

Clifton Hotel

Viewfield Street
Nairn (0667) 53119

Closed mid–Nov to Mar
Must book D & weekends
Meals 12–1.30 (bar),
7–9.30

Tdh £8 (meal £10·40)

Seats 60 (parties 30)
🔥 rest (3 steps)
Car park
No dogs in d/r
19 rooms (15 with bath)
B&B £12·50
D, B&B £20
Fire cert

'A veritable magpie's hotel, with Sanderson and Vymura flowers now rampaging over every surface not occupied by *objets d'art*,' is one description, and with *Hedda Gabler* and *The Provok'd Wife* figuring in the winter play and recital season it is natural to wonder who (besides the *Guide*'s chief inspector) is watching while you eat. The answer is Gordon Macintyre, whose dining-room production is 'apt to be over-paced, reminding staff of things before they have been forgotten.' The 'colossal labour,' as he understandably puts it, 'of preparing up to thirty hors d'oeuvre for the warmly spotlit display every evening' may be reduced this year, since many would like to pay less for less choice. But 'good materials will still be used, and we still make our own bread, soups, muesli and marmalade.' Some flavours are on the bland side for current English (as opposed to Scottish) taste, but 'langoustines meunière and chicken in cream sauce were excellent of their kind', and 'we thoroughly enjoyed Sunday evening roast beef cut from a 15 lb rib.' Soupe de poissons, crème de tomates à la bressane, sauté de coquilles St Jacques sauce vierge, and escalope de veau à la crème are good dishes, Mr Macintyre thinks. 'They should learn to keep sauces apart from batter-coated things till the moment of serving.' 'Cheeses looked sad, but cinnamon apple pie was nice.' There are 120 bins in the wine cellar, beginning with J&B house claret and moselle at £3·50 in 1979 (a few wines are cheaper than this). The Loire, Rhône, Jura and Provence sections are enterprising, and for the most part under £5, and with such clarets as Ch. Gloria '67, Ch. Pape-Clément '69, and Ch. Siran '70 well under £10, drinking comes easily here. But some of the '64s should probably be drunk up now at reduced prices. 'No smoking in the main restaurant' – though regular visitors report no enforcement. Bar snacks at lunch-time. Recorded classical music.

App: Arthur Kerr, Philip & Penelope Plumb,
R.H.M.S., Duncan Wright, M.J.C., and others

Peat Inn
6 m SW of St Andrews
at junction of B940 &
B941
Peat Inn (033 484) 206

Closed Mon; Dec 25 & 26;
Jan 1
Must book D

As well as standing up for the *Guide* ('it appears some people only accept flattery'), David Wilson tries to stir local interest in much-criticised aspects of Scottish catering, bar snacks for instance. Too bad that a traveller who sought out this 18th-century inn (which gave its name to the village) found the cupboard bare while the owner was spending a sabbatical at the German Wine Academy as a prize for his fine list. But unless the Australians reward his definitive Pavlova with a ticket for a Sydney Opera House

Meals 12.30–1.45,
7.30–9.30

Alc £6·80 (meal £9·45)

Service 10%
Children's helpings
(under 10)
Seats 46
 ⅃ rest
Car park
No dogs
Am Ex, Euro

Swan Lake, his voice can be heard most nights and his presence deduced from the inventive cooking, marked by a fondness for fruit and liquor. Stilton and port quiche, mushroom tartlets in sherry sauce, and a green salad with grapes might precede 'tender roast quails on toast soaked with brandy, garnished with apple chunks and pitted grapes' (£3·45) or his own recommendations, salmon in pastry with dill, Chambéry and cream sauce (£4·15) and lamb noisettes topped with onion puree and cassis. But crudités with 'perspiring' Arbroath smokie are noted, although pastry for a prawn and tomato dish and for an 'excellent' game pie has been buttery, and Bonnie Prince Charlie bombe (85p) was laced with enough Drambuie to survive freezing. Local gardeners 'are urged to grow mange-touts and calabrese rather than turnip and cabbage', with little success as yet. No matter, for Parmentier potatoes and buttered cabbage with garlic were 'perfect' (though someone spoilt the courgettes one night). Wines are well priced if not always well treated: red or white Château de Fonscolombe '76 (from Provence), £3·20; Ch. Cantenac-Brown '71 (c.b.) £7·60; Hallgartener Schoenhell (Riesling Kabinett) '76, £4·70; Ruppertsberger Hoheburg Spätlese '71 (Bürklin-Wolf) £4·80. Bar lunches and pressurised beers. Smoking is discouraged but clearly not forbidden.

App: G. J. Barton, Dr C. Alison, E.M.A., and others

PEEBLES see EDDLESTON

PERTH Tayside   Map 9

Station Hotel
Leonard Street
Perth (0738) 24141

The Victorian grandeur is the antithesis of Timothy's (*q.v.*), but several members this year have found a good and well-served meal when they had not expected a feast between trains. 'Generous prawn cocktail, kitchen-made soup, fresh Tay salmon on the set dinner, veal escalope, mercifully cooked sprouts, and saturated sherry trifle' have figured; chef Podmore's specialities include crépinette pêcheur (£4·60) and tournedos Chambertin which a member found 'good but too heavily sauced.' French table wines are £3·15; not all the fine BTH list reaches Perth but £6 or so buys excellent Spanish or Rhône wines, or *cru bourgeois* claret or Georges Duboeuf burgundies. Bar lunches and pressurised beers. Recorded music.

Closed Dec 26; Jan 1
Must book
Meals 12.30–2, 7–9

Tdh L £6 (meal £7·55),
D £7 (meal £8·55)
Alc £8·90 (meal £11)

Service inc
Children's helpings
(under 7)
Seats 150 (parties 250)
 ⅃ rest
Car park
No dogs

Access, Am Ex, Barclay,
Diners, Euro
53 rooms (37 with bath,
3 with shower)
B&B £15–£23·50
Fire cert

Timothy's

♥

24 St John Street
Perth (0738) 26641

Closed Sun; Mon;
Dec 25 & 26; Jan 1
Must book
Meals 12–2.30, 7–10.15

Alc (min £3·50 after
9.30 p.m.) £3·55
(meal £6·45)

Cover 25p D
Children's helpings
Seats 50
♿ rest

The Major (Timothy Norman) is conducting a strategic withdrawal from his much-loved smørrebrød restaurant, but no serious change is expected since his Cupar partner, Athole Laing, has taken over. Indeed, after ten years' absence an inspector found everything familiar, from the decor to the menu. The style means that if you are ravenous it will cost you, but most Perth appetites seem very happy with, say, crab Koenig (£1·30), roast fillet of beef with salad and mayonnaise (£1·40), a jacket potato (25p) and Tia Maria ice-cream (65p); or pickled herrings, cream of chicken soup, Andrea's hamful and Danish fruit flan. Flavours of everything were true when tested, and the atmosphere is relaxed, with the help of Bonatello red or French Pintail white at £1·85 a pint, and carefully chosen wines thereafter: Chénas '70 and Châteauneuf-du-Pape '73 in the £5 range, Fixin Clos Napoléon '72 or Ch. La Tour Calon '61 at £8 or so. Pressurised beers. No children under six.

App: Jennifer Bone, D. N. Whyte, E.M.A., E.C.K., R.G.A., H. Wilson, and others

---

Airds Hotel
2 m off A828
Appin (063 173) 236

At this old ferry inn on Loch Linnhe, Elizabeth Allen's cooking shows flair, according to admirers of courgette and rosemary, carrot and orange, pea and lemon, or game soups; apple with tarragon cream; and Atholl brose, cloutie dumpling or fruit-and-nutty Airds flan. But at a test meal an inspector thought fried trout with boiled vegetables 'ordinary', gnocchi heavy and carelessly sauced, and profiteroles 'humdrum'. The kitchen promotes Cullen skink, pork fillets in whisky cream, and prawns in cheese and pineapple sauce. Good breakfasts. Peter Thomson wines. 'Poorly informed on whiskies.' Bar snacks and pressurised beers. No smoking in the restaurant (though cigars are sold).

Closed Dec 24–26 & 31;
Jan 1
Must book D
Meals 12–2, 7–8.15

Tdh L £2·50 (meal £4·35),
D £7 (meal £9·30)

Children's helpings
(under 10)
Seats 42

Car park
No dogs
14 rooms (5 with bath)
B&B £10
Full board £19 p.d.
Fire cert

Prices of meals underlined are those which we consider represent unusual value for money. They are not necessarily the cheapest places in the Guide, or in the locality.

Inspections are carried out anonymously. Persons who pretend to be able to secure, arrange or prevent an entry in the Guide are impostors and their names or descriptions should be reported to us.

PORT ELLEN Islay, Strathclyde Map 9

Machrie Hotel
4 m from Port Ellen
on road to Bowmore
Port Ellen (0496) 2310

Whisky-lovers worship Islay as the source of Laphroaig. Rod Walker's converted farm, with a byre restaurant and a golf-course built in 1891, allows them and others more civilised stays than they might expect, though Mr Walker, 'a refugee from London's Athenaeum Hotel', is his own cook and mate too, so do not expect too much of his scallops Kintyre (£4·70), salmis of duck 'very rich and full of flavour', 'thickish' seafood pancake, and sirloin Balmoral (£5·20). 'Tolerable cheesecake and coffee, unusually good house Beaujolais or white Mâcon at £2·35 for 50 cl.' Recorded music. Wear a jacket and tie. Grill room (where your small children also eat), and tables outside. Bar snacks (12–6). Pressurised beers. You can taste a range of Islay malts in the bar.

Must book	Children's helpings	Access, Am Ex, Barclay,
Meals 1, 7.30–9.30	Seats 72 (parties 186)	Diners
	Air-conditioning	20 rooms (10 with bath)
Tdh D £7 (meal £10·30)	Car park	B&B £15·60
Alc £7·70 (meal £11·55)	No dogs in public rooms	Fire cert

ST ANDREWS Fife Map 9

Pepita's
11–13 Crails Lane
between South Street and
Market Street
St Andrews (0334) 74084

No hint of frugality at lunch when 'students crowd in to eke out their grants' on carrot soup, blanquette de veau (£1), venison stew, pinchpenny pie, salads and pastries (18p–40p). The gold damask is seen to better effect at night bearing Peter Hood's 'traditional French dishes' in more sedate company. Roast wild goose with liver sauce, roast duck with seafood risotto and pancake, and scallops have been praised. Less enthusiasm for 'misjudged courgette and lemon sauce with lamb, redundant crêpe folded Chinese-style beside game in wine and bilberry sauce'. 'Delicious' gratin dauphinoise potatoes. Helpful wine list (Ch. Landon '71, £4·60).

Closed Sun; Mon D;	Alc L £2·75 (meal £4·90),	Seats 60 (parties 20)
Dec 24–Jan 8	D £7·35 (meal £9·50)	♿ rest; w.c.
Must book D		No dogs
Open 10–5 (D 7–9.30	Service inc	Access card
[10 Fri & Sat])	Children's helpings	
	(under 12 D)	

Most places will accept cheques only when they are accompanied by a cheque card or adequate identification. Information about which credit cards are accepted is correct when printed, but restaurants may add to or subtract from the list without notice.

When a restaurant says 'must book', the context of the entry usually indicates how much or how little it matters, but a preliminary telephone call averts a wasted journey to a closed door. *Always* telephone if a booking has to be cancelled: a small place (and its other customers) may suffer severely if this is not done.

Dunmor House
15 m SW of Oban
½ m E of Easdale Village
Balvicar (085 23) 203

Closed L (exc bar);
Oct 14–May 1
Must book D
Meals 12.45–2 (bar), 8–9

Tdh D from £7
(meal £9·55)

Children's helpings
Seats 34
🔥 rest (2 steps)
Car park
No dogs in d/r
11 rooms (3 with bath,
6 with shower)
B&B £11
Fire cert

'Seil has a quietness all its own', and whether in daffodil or autumn leaf time, Dunmor House with its thousand-acre hill farm and sublime views looks inviting. Even in human terms, 'the election result must have mollified Lt Cdr Campbell-Gibson: I was quite disappointed not to feel my hackles rise'; and with the family helpful, and Jackie Morris in the kitchen seldom failing to produce a good dinner, discontent is confined to occasional chills in the built-out dining-room, and 'a slight dearth of fresh vegetables.' 'Our most memorable dinner began with local mussels gathered by Mrs Campbell-Gibson, and went on to a delicious game pie, and unmistakable murmurs of pleasure in the dining-room.' Easdale salmon arrives sometimes, and visitors praise cheese and ham pignatelle, kipper soufflé, lettuce soup, roast lamb and duck, home-made garlic cream cheese, profiteroles, 'lovely apricot, honey and nut ice-cream', and hazelnut meringue gateau. The wine list (from £3·40) is rudimentary, apart from Ch. Gazin '71 at £5·80, perhaps. There are quiches and other bar snacks at lunch-time and early evening but no beer on tap, it seems. No children under eight at dinner. Wear a jacket and tie. (GHG)

App: P. H. Johnston, A.P. & D.R.B., R. G. Evans, D. M. Dossor, Paul Butler, and others

Skeabost House Hotel
6 m NW of Portree
Skeabost Bridge (047 032)
202

The Victorians could choose a site and impose an edifice on it but it took the Stuart-McNab team to bring a taste of Scotland back to Loch Snizort. More than a taste these days, for smoked trout with horseradish, kidney and celery broth, 'ethereal' Skye scallops in lemon sauce, beef in 'subtle' whisky sauce, stovies ('stewed potato and onion') and 'tipsy laird with farm cream' now outnumber this-Véronique and that-Biarritz. They feed seventy between 7 and 8 o'clock sharp so stragglers may be rushed, but a relaxing calm takes over and lasts into the coffee lounge. Justerini's house claret is £4·55, Ch. Lanessan '64 only £1·50 more. Lunchtime bar snacks and pressurised beers. Jacket and tie preferred. Angling coach in residence. (GHG)

Closed end Oct to Apr
Must book
Meals 1–1.30, 7–8

Tdh L £3·15 (meal £5·15),
D £5·75 (meal £8·05)

Service 10%
Children's helpings
(under 10)
Seats 72
🔥 rest

Car park
No dogs in public rooms
28 rooms (12 with bath)
B&B £10·55
Full board £115
Fire cert

STRATHCARRON Highland   Map 9

Carron Restaurant
Cam-Allt
on A890
1 m S of Strathcarron
station
Lochcarron (052 02) 488

This attractive grill 'in early Attadale schoolhouse style' is more than just an outlet for the related pottery next door, and draws tourists and locals alike with sound, simple cooking. Rob Teago 'knows what he's about' at the charcoal grill (venison, salmon, beef steaks, £4·90 to £7·35, with chips and fresh salads), and waiting by local lasses adds to the charm. Praise for rice salad and puddings, especially lemon cheesecake (75p). Good coffee. French Carillon is £3·85 a litre. They were not sure about their winter closures as we went to press. Car park. No dogs. More reports, please.

Closed Sun; Dec 25
Must book D
Meals 12–2.30,
HT 5–6.30, 6–9.30

Alc £8·20 (meal £10·75)

Service inc

Children's helpings
(under 12)
Seats 45
♿ rest (1 step)

TOBERMORY Mull, Strathclyde   Map 9

Macdonald Arms
Tobermory (0688) 2011

'A solid, traditional hotel' with open fireplaces, real porridge for breakfast, coffee and 'relays of fresh toast' (*all* other hotels please copy). The set dinners are admired too: grilled grapefruit, 'delectable' pâté, or 'savourous onion soup with hot croûtons'; followed by roast lamb or duck, or poached salmon, perhaps, with vegetables 'a surprise in the Highlands and Islands' ('nice floury potatoes'; 'cauliflower and sprouts both *al dente* and carefully drained'). More run-of-the-mill cheeses and sweets. Over a hundred single malts, and various wines, from Yugoslav Riesling at £2·45. Lunches and bar snacks are 'by arrangement'; pressurised beers.

Closed L (exc bar by
arrangement); Jan 1
Must book
D only, 7

Tdh £6 (meal £7·20)

Service inc
Seats 40 (parties 18)

No dogs in public rooms
8 rooms (1 with shower)
B&B £16·70
Fire cert

TYNDRUM Central   Map 9

Clifton Coffee House
Tyndrum (083 84) 271
and 242

Weather or history may depress the spirit in Glencoe, but in summer this complex of coffee shop, craft centre, food shop, and 'whisky library' cheers one up. 'Well-organised self-service' offers ghillie's lunch (bannocks, cheese and apple), home-made soups ('superb carrot'), salads with honeyed ham or local salmon (from £1·20), and a daily hot dish. Sandwiches, and treacle scones for odd times or corners. 'No chips.' Wine by the glass, 48p. No-smoking area.

Closed D;
Oct 29–Mar 28
Open 8.30–5.30
(L 11.30–2.30)

Alc meal about £3·95

Seats 220
♿ rest (3 steps)

Car park
No dogs
Access, Am Ex, Barclay,
Diners, Euro

Ceilidh Place
West Argyle Street
Ullapool (0854) 2103

A picturesque and practical landscape delivers up prawns, salmon, scallops and lobsters as well as good views. Robert Urquhart's whitewashed cottages and small boat-shed round a courtyard (where you may eat) belie their origins with airy, chalet-like rooms and promising cooking. 'Tasty prawns provençale in an over-rich garlic and tomato sauce,' says a member who was content with haddock pâté, verdant (dried) herb bread and apple crumble, but found moussaka bland and home-made ice-cream 'nothing special'. Egg mayonnaise, pâté and peach gateau are liked in the coffee shop. House wine (£3·40) may 'even run out'. Service stutters; the brochure gushes. Baroque music on records.

Closed Nov–Apr 1
Must book D
Open (buffet)
8 a.m.–9 p.m.;
(rest) D only, 7–10

Tdh (rest) £5·90 (meal £8·90)

Alc £7·50 (meal £10·70)

Children's helpings
Seats 40
♻ rest
Car park

No dogs in public rooms
Diners card
26 rooms (8 with bath)
B&B £8·50–£11
D, B&B £12–£16·90
Fire cert

Houstoun House

off A8/M8
1½ m W of Broxburn
(turn N at only traffic lights on A8 between Edinburgh & Glasgow)
Broxburn (0506) 853831

Must book
Meals 12.30–2, 7.30–9

Tdh L £5·50 (meal £7·40),
D £8·50 (meal £10·40)

Service inc
Children's helpings (L)
Seats 75 (parties 40)
Car park
No dogs in d/r
29 rooms (26 with bath, 3 with shower)
B&B £15–£24
Fire cert

The problem basic to Keith Knight's hotel and restaurant, in a solid 16th-century laird's house on the way from Edinburgh to Glasgow, may be his belief that a system and culinary method that originated in his modest house in Comrie in 1962 works equally well when cannily tailored for this major trade route in 1980: hence the poor dishes ('raw chicken, bovrilly pork cutlets'), under-briefed staff ('our brusque tartan-skirted waitress described oeufs en meurette as pears in red wine, twice') and wines either unavailable or late-delivered from the famous cellar. The set meals with little choice make people unforgiving of bland or exaggerated flavours (and both occur). Still, wiser inspectors shrewd enough to order their wine in the bar beforehand considered themselves lucky to lunch off 'light, soft, smooth, cold and jellied' haddock mousse crowned with prawns, 'creamy white turnip soup' with croûtons, crusty bread, 'runny' Spanish omelette, lamb chops with aubergine in a good tomato sauce, broccoli hollandaise, pear in wine with cream, and good Brie; moreover, 'the meal became a banquet with a bottle of Quincy '73 at a modest £3, and a half of Ch. Cheval-Blanc '66 at an unrepeatable £6.' Others have been equally happy with, for instance, smoked trout and mustard sauce, duck with orange, roast stuffed loin of pork, 'foamy witches' cream with Kümmel', baked egg custard with apricots, and again, superb wines: 'Gewürztraminer Les Maquisards '75 (Dopff & Irion) at £6·90, and Fixin La Mazière '69 at £7·80. One member says it is hard to find any but sweet German wines (the character of recent vintages is partly to blame). But virtually everything else that matters (including, with notice, claret of the early 1900s and bottles, 'though not glasses', of vintage port) is there at a fair price; Ch. Palmer '71 or Ch. Figeac '66, both c.b., at £12·80; Loires, Rhônes and '78 Beaujolais at half this figure. (Perhaps a silicon chip would help with retrieving what you want from the 24,000 bottles stocked?) Pressurised beers and lunchtime sandwiches. No pipes, they say, but 'they encourage other smokers by providing ashtrays and advertising matches, and the result ruined my dinner.' The rooms are comfortable and the breakfasts good.

App: Patrick Bromley, J. M. Ragg, Alasdair Adam, T. V. Stanley, G.M. McI., G.R.C., and others

---

WEEM Tayside   Map 9

Ailean Chraggan Hotel
on B846
¾ m N of Aberfeldy
Aberfeldy (088 72) 346

A comfortable and welcoming little family-run hotel. Set dinners (priced according to the main course) might offer prawn cocktail, boeuf bourguignonne (£5·85), Tay salmon hollandaise (£6·20) or a steak cooked as requested, with creamy sweets to finish. Bar meals are served at lunch-time and in the evening except between 7.30 and 9 p.m. (soup, burgers, toasted sandwiches, salads, fish and chips and omelettes, with pressurised beers). About twenty wines (house wine 55p the glass) and over fifty tongue-twisting single malts. A few tables outside.

Closed Dec 24–26 & 31; Jan 1	Tdh D from £5 (meal £6·95)	Car park No dogs in d/r
Must book D & weekends Meals 12.30–1.45 (bar), 7.30–8.30	Children's helpings Seats 45 ⑆ rest (2 steps)	4 rooms B&B £8·05–£9·20 Fire cert

---

Scottish public holidays do not all coincide with English ones.

We rewrite every entry each year, and depend on fresh, detailed reports to confirm the old, as well as to include the new. The further from London you are, the more important this is.

The Guide accepts no advertising. Nor does it allow restaurateurs to use its name on brochures, menus, or in any form of advertisement. If you see any instances of this, please report them to us.

When a restaurant says 'must book', the context of the entry usually indicates how much or how little it matters, but a preliminary telephone call averts a wasted journey to a closed door. *Always* telephone if a booking has to be cancelled: a small place (and its other customers) may suffer severely if this is not done.

Old Howgate Inn
on B7026
10 m S of Edinburgh
Penicuik (0968) 74244

Closed Sun; Dec 25;
Jan 1 & 2
Must book
Meals 12–2, 6.30–10

Alc £3·85 (meal £7·45)

Cover 40p
Seats 50
♿ rest; w.c.
Car park
No dogs

The *Guide* would hardly be the *Guide* without this whitewashed inn at the first coaching stage on the Dumfries road, and though now owned by the Di Rollos, it has changed little since the Garrads' quarter-century. The specialities remain the fresh Scottish half-lobsters in summer, buttered or with mayonnaise, and the fondue bourguignonne (£4·05 a head). But many more people choose the spinach soup with cream (50p) – 'better than ever', followed by one of the forty smørrebrød items: ox's eye (raw egg yolk, onion and anchovy, 45p); king prawns in mayonnaise (£1·50), stuffed collared beef with creamed mushrooms (80p), boeuf tartare (from £1·50) and others. Cheeses, Very Cheering ice-cream and coffee are also usually on the programme. The wines, too, are good, with about a hundred bins, beginning with Catalan at £3·90 a litre (the current list is not to hand). 'Service is apt to be slow with the bill.' The Belhaven 70/- or 80/- ales – or, if you prefer, specific gravities 1033 or 1045 – are in cask, and they keep akvavit for devoted smørrebrød fanciers.

App: Ian Oswald, K.M., W. Frankland, M.R.A.M., J. & K.L., and others

CHANNEL ISLANDS

GUERNSEY

ST PETER PORT   Map 1

Le Français
Market Street
Guernsey (0481) 20963

Closed Sun; Sat L;
Apr 7; May 26; Dec 25 &
26; Jan 1; Feb
Must book D
Meals 12.30–1.45,
7.30–9.45

Tdh L £3·65 (meal £5·45)
Alc £6·80 (meal £9·25)

Service 10%
Seats 40 (parties 20)
No dogs
Access, Am Ex, Barclay,
Diners, Euro

Peter Schmid's upstairs restaurant in a row of shops dropped out of the book for want of support last time, but this year visitors have confirmed the local popularity of Jean Bertran's French regional repertoire. (Both men worked for London's Le Français in its palmy days.) 'We were impressed with onion soup, done with vinegar and egg, and also a very light sole terrine. Hake with mushrooms was more ordinary.' Fish soup (£1·35) 'tasted very fresh, even on a Monday.' Carbonnade de boeuf (£3·75 on the day's regional menu) had become rather salt in reduction, but 'it was a relief on Guernsey to find some beef that had not been grilled.' They tend to use cream and butter as substitutes for real skill and timing in cooking vegetables; thus lemon sorbet (90p) may be the best finale. Mâcon or Muscadet is £2·60, and there are some fine wines: Ch. Langoa-Barton '66, £9·25. You may have to enquire for the set lunch. Dress smartly. Expect alterations early in 1980, which will improve comfort, Mr Schmid says.

App: N. Hayter, Dr & Mrs D. L. Cohen, M.H.N.

La Frégate
Les Cotils
Guernsey (0481) 24624

Must book
Meals 12.30–1.30, 7–9.30
(Sun 9)

Tdh L £4·50 (meal £6·60),
D £6 (meal £8·20)
Alc £7·45 (meal £9·80)

Service 10%
Seats 50 (parties 14)
Car park
No dogs
Access, Am Ex, Barclay,
Diners
13 rooms (all with bath)
B&B £14–£19·50
Full board £24·50–£30
p.d.
Fire cert

The view of castle, islands and harbour from this 18th-century manor high above the town is heavenly, and even radio and TV are banished to help keep guests clean and unspotted from the world. The service has a good memory and Konrad Holleis in the kitchen a good technique. Early in the season a party reported a mediocre meal poorly served, and a test meal later included 'very puddingy' crème caramel, but there is general content with both set and à la carte meals (the former modestly priced for a place of this kind). 'Soups are obviously genuine' and combinations often adventurous – garlic and anchovies with lemon sole, smoked scallops and cashew nuts with fillet steak (£5·75): an inspector 'would have been happier with just the nuts but some people like a smoky taste to steak.' Other specialities include délice de turbot grillé au genièvre et au poivre vert (£4·75) and carrelet pêcheur (£3·95). 'Fried aubergines could be heard rustling on the serving table.' The creamy sweets might pall in a long stay. The wines (from £2·75 for house burgundy or Loire) include useful half-bottles of red burgundy (Côtes de Nuits-Villages '75, £3) and adequate fine claret (Ch. Léoville-Barton

'71, c.b., £9), but the German wines are very limited. Wear a jacket and tie for dinner. You may eat outside on the terrace. To stay, you will have to book many months ahead. No children under 14 in the hotel or under eight to dine.

Recipe in *Second Dinner Party Book*: limande Monte Carlo

App: Dr & Mrs D. L. Cohen, Jonathan Mason, H.M., and others

ST PETER PORT   Map 1

La Nautique
Quay Steps
Guernsey (0481) 21714

Closed Sun (Nov–Mar);
Dec 25 D; Dec 26;
3 weeks Jan
Must book
Meals 12–2, 7–10

Alc £9·15 (meal £11·55)

Service 10%
Seats 60 (parties 25)
No dogs
Access, Am Ex, Barclay,
Diners, Euro

This 'romantic restaurant in a converted warehouse overlooking the harbour' has been in and out of the Guide for the past fifteen years, but sounds as if it is on an upswing under Messrs Diverio and Klebert in the kitchen, and Mr Graziani as manager. It would be foolish not to eat the fish, such as moules à la crème and langoustines à l'ail – 'simple, memorable and delicious' – to start with, and thereafter, perhaps filet de barbue en papillote (£4·60): 'an outstanding treatment of an unusual fish, with fresh mussels and scallops in the parcel as well as chunks of brill.' Turbot poché sauce hollandaise (£4·50) and loup de mer au beurre blanc are other kitchen favourites. 'Rock-hard meringues' are criticised, but raspberry soufflé glacé and 'light profiteroles with Guernsey cream and good chocolate sauce' sound more encouraging. House Muscadet is £2·15 and Ungsteiner Honigsäckel Sylvaner Spätlese '71, £5·45, and there are adequate half-bottles. Recorded music. More reports, please.

Whistlers Bistro
Hauteville
Guernsey (0481) 25809

Whistler's mother would find the climb to Hauteville stiff and the foreground music disturbing. But people young enough to enjoy an animated bistro will feel at ease in these dark smoky recesses where more of their own kind serve. Too much of the long menu is routine or bought-in, but among the escargots and grilled steaks an inspector found 'creamy cauliflower soup' and 'a Denby bowl of plump scallops, shrimps, prawns and other fish in an enhancing béchamel', £2·50. 'Rice appeared reheated.' 'Delicious' garlic bread (30p) 'surpassed by mushrooms and croûtons in garlic' (85p). ' "Nearly mousse" (50p) was barely mousse, and just dandy for the under-fives.' Red Rhône and white Loire house wines, £2·60 a litre.

Closed L; Mon;
Dec 25 & 26
Must book
D only, 7–10.30

Alc £5·95 (meal £8·35)

Service 10%
Seats 48

♿ rest
Air-conditioning
No dogs
Access, Am Ex, Barclay,
Euro

VAT is not levied in the Channel Islands.

JERSEY

ST AUBIN Map 1

Portofino
Jersey (0534) 42100

Closed Wed; Dec 25 & 26
Must book D
Meals 12–2.30, 7–10.30

Tdh L from £2·50
(meal £4·45), D from £4
(meal £6·10)
Alc £7·60 (meal £10·05)

Service 10%
Children's helpings
Seats 70 (parties 35)
[] rest (2 steps)
Car park
No dogs
Access, Barclay

Fino beforehand and porto afterwards in the upstairs
bar, and a taste of Pasquale Fuschetto's food, are all
intoxicating, but stay sober for the spiral staircase. A
level-headed inspector was persuaded over sherry and
olives to confront the seafood platter and wisely asked
for a small one. Even so the quantity astounded:
a crab, prawns, shrimps, cockles, and whelks ringed
by scallops, oysters and mussels in shells.' Fegato alla
veneziana was underdone by request, and fault was
hard to find. 'In a mosaic of liqueurish, precisely cut
apples, strawberries, halved orange segments and
melon balls, there were three orange pips.' The
restaurant has on occasion even turned stale coffee to
its credit: 'Distress was spotted and special Mocha
took its place.' Please report on Brian Skelley and
Renzo Acronzio's 'sparkling, sincere and unfussy'
enterprise, and also their new menu. Expect
nothing Ligurian except minestrone with basil and an
appreciation of the sea. They suggest cacciucco
livornese (£4·80), anitra con ciliegie and piccata
calvados (£3·20). Italian house wines are £2·40 a
litre; Frascati from Monte Porzio Catone is £3·60.
Recorded music and live guitar.

App: Helen Macintosh, K.B.G.

ST BRELADE Map 1

Château Valeuse
St Brelade's Bay
Jersey (0534) 43476

Closed Dec 31; Jan 1 to
mid-Feb
Must book weekends
Meals 1–2, 7–9.45

Tdh L £3 (meal £5),
D £4·50 (meal £6·65)
Alc £6·60 (meal £9)

Service 10%
Seats 80
Car park
No dogs
Barclaycard
26 rooms (23 with bath,
2 with shower)
B&B £10·50–£12·50
D, B&B £13·50–£15

The connection with Manzi's in London (*q.v.*) may
not enthral Soho buffs but has done wonders for the
food, value, and general morale of this imposing
hotel, inspectors say. The accent of the food is on the
sea; visitors note the lobster bisque and the surprising
oyster pâté, 'light and full of flavour.' Main dishes
praised include sole Colbert, halibut and large scampi,
both grilled, and at a test meal the hot crab Clarence
in a good curry sauce with well-cooked rice made 'an
outstanding dish for the price, carefully served.'
Escalope Cordon Bleu also stood out for the use of
of real ham and Gruyère in a dish so often travestied.
Chateaubriand (£7 for two) is another speciality.
Vegetables and sweets are less remarkable: finish with
pears in wine, perhaps, or gâteau St Honoré.
Valgardello ordinaires are £2·40; other 1980 wine
prices are not to hand. Recorded music. No children
under five. A full credit entry is earned, but please
report: we know little as yet about the set meals.

App: M. H. Peers, J.G.K., and others

La Capannina
67 Halkett Place
Jersey (0534) 34602

This fairly formal and clubby businessmen's place was Jersey's Italian *duce* for some time, and Luigi's pasta (£1·60), fish hors d'oeuvre and seasonal local fish, and the saddle of lamb roasted daily (£3·40) are dependable orders. Lobster bisque is praised too. But at a test meal the main dish and its accompanying vegetable were very carelessly cooked, and the sweets looked dreary. Chianti red or Tocai white are £2·80. Recorded music.

Closed Sun; public hols (exc Apr 4 & May 5)
Must book
Meals 12–2, 7–10

Alc £5·90 (meal £8·50)

Service 10%
Seats 65 (parties 18)

Air-conditioning
No dogs
Access, Am Ex, Barclay, Diners

Mauro's
37 La Motte Street
Jersey (0534) 20147

Closed Sun; public hols (exc May 5)
Must book
Meals 12.30–2.15, 7–10.15

Alc £8 (meal £10·75)

Seats 50
♿ rest
Air-conditioning
No dogs

After a year's trial separation from the Guide, *mainly for want of enough reliable information about his epic-length international menu, dimly lit outside the restaurant at the wrong end of a dark street, Mauro Mori bounces back, as buoyant and effusive as ever. In 1979, 'perfect' asparagus (an unlisted special) with melted butter served separately was worth hunting for, and coquilles St Jacques provençale (£2·75) bring praise: 'There were ten firm scallops, and they wisely held back the tomato, let go on the garlic, and reduced the sauce without yielding to sieve or blender.' Scampi done similarly are liked, and tagliatelle verde bolognese (£1·75) and risotto ai frutti di mare are possible choices before Dover sole or steak and veal in any of a dozen ways (rognons de veau aux champignons, £2·95). Flambées take pride of place for sweet; a member's zabaglione (done for one) 'tasted more of vanilla than Marsala.' The lengthy wine list, at least, leads with two dozen Italian; house wine is £2·75 a bottle. 'Smoke and music drift in from the bar.'*

SARK

Aval du Creux

Harbour Hill
Sark (0481 83) 2036

Closed Oct 5–May 1
Must book
Meals 12.30–1.30,
7.30–8.30

Tdh L £3 (meal £4·70),
D £4 (meal £5·80)
Alc £6·50 (meal £8·55)

Service 10%
Children's helpings
Seats 50 (parties 16)
♿ rest (3 steps)
No dogs
10 rooms (all with shower)
D, B&B £12–£15

Lucky Sark, that for all its tiny population possesses three hotels of merit. Peter Hauser's stone-built Elizabethan house, run by his wife and her sister while he minds the stove, has recently become a pace-maker to the other two, to judge by numerous detailed descriptions of food and service received. If the art of the *chef-patron* in a place like this is to steer a judicious course between dishes that evoke his own creativity and those that appeal to more conventional tastes, Mr Hauser has evidently set his compass correctly. He would be happy, he says, to do away with the *carte* altogether, for most of his favourite dishes (some borrowed from Parisian *nouvelle cuisine*) appear sooner or later on the set menus: for instance, filet de plie au beurre de tomates parfumé à l'estragon, and côtelettes d'agneau farcies des gourmets – 'that is,' says a guest, 'a veal stuffing cooked with cranberries, and an accompaniment of creamed carrots and little sweetcorn pancakes – delicious.' Hors d'oeuvre and soups (one person even praises peanut and banana) are also imaginative, and another visitor picks out from a fortnight's menus one that began with smoked duckling galantine and crab bisque, followed by poularde sautée Noilly Prat (stuffed with chicken livers and herbs), with 'such a spread of freshly made gateaux, cheesecake, pies, strudel and fruit meringues at the end that there is always a murmur in the room as the trolley appears.' Simple trout, lobster, and hot veal and ham pie with a rich and golden crust are praised no less highly. Italian ordinaires are under £1 for 50 cl, and though the wine list is not the island's chief, Ch. Canon-la-Gaffelière '67 and Ch. Gruaud-Larose '73, both under £7 in 1979, are not to be despised. You should dress for dinner. No cigars or pipes in the dining-room.

App: Ian Culley, K.G., M. Vierstraete,
Mrs R. Le Marchand, James Todd, and others

Dixcart Hotel
Sark (0481 83) 2015

Closed mid-Oct to Easter
Must book
Meals 12.30–1.15,
7.30–8.30

Tdh L £3·75 (meal £5·05),
D £5 (meal £6·45)

Peggy Ravenshaw – almost a deputy Dame of Sark by her own unmentionably long reign at Swinburne's favourite hotel – can still turn her hand to a tournebroche or a typewriter, and since her former chef's departure to the 'still-vexed Bermoothes', she has been helping his lieutenant and successor evolve new dishes in the intervals between commissioning overdue hotel improvements. Cheese cutlets, salmon in puff pastry with fish duxelles, and deep-fried billiard balls of carrot and ham (why not turnip and chicken too?) are examples, but more conservative visitors have

Service 10%
Children's helpings
Seats 70
♿ rest (1 step)
No dogs in d/r
17 rooms (6 with bath,
3 with shower)
Full board £15·50–£19·50
p.d. (min 3 days)

contented themselves with the Sark mackerel, the ever-present crabs 'both spiders and chankers', the profusion of Sark cream, and locally produced pork, beef, veal, and, more lately, kid. 'Spring chicken Rossini and caneton bigarade were both successes,' an inspector says – a welcome verdict after an awkward gear-change at Easter when the vegetables were overboiled and the Alaska, like the service of it, half-baked. The Sunday curry lunches are mostly still liked, though 'seasoning may get out of hand.' They provide weekday bar lunches too (which may be eaten outside), and children's lunches (£2). The wines are odd bins rather than Oddbins, with bargains here and there: half-bottles of Ch. Langoa-Barton '67 at £2·75 or Ch. Boyd-Cantenac '70 at £2·70. Ties for dinner are appreciated. More reports, please. (GHG)

SARK Map 1

Hotel Petit Champ
Sark (0481 83) 2046

Closed Oct–Easter
Must book
Meals 12.30–1, 7.30–8.15

Tdh L £2·50 (meal £4·10),
D from £4·75 (meal £5·95)

Service 10%
Children's helpings
Seats 50 (parties 20)
No dogs
Access, Barclay, Diners
16 rooms (7 with bath,
4 with shower)
Full board £13·75–£17·40
p.d.

In the case of Terry and Janie Scott's long and deservedly loved hotel, this year's italic type represents no more than a small cloud in a clear sky, for though their chef of recent years, Brian Rolls, is planning his own business in England, the sous-chef Leslie Duffen is poised to succeed, and with luck the differences will suffice only to encourage progress reports from visitors who are understandably lazy over writing to us about a place they return to year after year. The hotel, which is constantly being upgraded during the winter months with a new suite here or a new window there, is run with unremitting yet unobtrusive attention to detail from the moment the horse and carriage meets you at the harbour. The set dinners now usually present some choice of main course as well as at the cheese and dessert stage: lucky he or she who must choose between rheinische Sauerbraten and homard chaud chinoise, or between escalope of Sark veal and carré d'agneau en chemise sauce poivre. On Sunday evening too you may normally take a hot or cold lobster alternative to the buffet of cold meats. Sweets, mercifully, normally stress fruit rather than cream. Packed lunches seem better than ever, especially if you specify the wholemeal rolls: 'There are always two different fruits.' The wines are excellent, and very modestly marked up, even bearing in mind the Channel Islands' comparatively low wholesale prices after tax: in 1979, a sound Petit Chablis at £3·80, and fine '70 clarets, including Ch. Calon-Ségur under £5. Côtes du Rhône red and Bergerac white are £1·80 a litre, and the rule against smoking in the dining-room is generally observed 'except by a few Frenchmen who can usually be tucked away in a separate room.' Children, if they are to stay, must be old enough to sit up to dinner. Jackets and ties are preferred. More reports, please.

ISLE OF MAN

BALLASALLA   Map 7

Coach House
Silverburn Bridge
Castletown (062 482) 2343

Closed Sun; Dec 25; Jan 1
Must book weekends
Meals 12–2.30, 7–10.30

Alc £8·75 (meal £12·05)

Seats (rest) 70,
(Saddle Room) 35
♿ rest
Car park
No dogs
Am Ex, Barclay

'Restaurants such as the Coach House are at a premium on the Isle of Man,' writes a member who was glad he had booked before sailing over to Port St Mary – and his yachting clothes 'put the other diners off, perhaps, but not the staff.' Terry Croft of Bonaventure Foods has what the jargon calls a vertically integrated operation: it does not make the lobsters, queenies and Dublin Bay prawns that his boats catch any cheaper but it does make them better, locals say. 'A tasty and ample helping of scallops with bacon', 'delicious Dover sole and skate with Pernod', and turbot Mornay, are examples of chef Windsor's specialities; he also suggests entrecôte Patti Melba (£5·50) among his meat dishes: it features peaches, but the two song-thrushes in juxtaposition suggest that the dish must be at war with itself. Trolley sweets are £1·40, crêpes Suzette £2·40. Snacks can be had in the adjoining Saddle Room. A standard wine list (from £3·20) includes Ch. Meyney '67 at £9·20. Pressurised beer. Recorded music.

App: R. J. S. Marsh, C.C., T.M.H., and others

DOUGLAS   Map 7

Crows Nest
Sea Terminal
Douglas (0624) 5009
and 5454

Vistas of harbour and hills are more spectacular than the Italo-Manx dishes (on an over-long menu) competently cooked at the top of the 'lemon squeezer' sea terminal. They use good materials, though, and know how to make creamy tortellini (£1·40) 'delicately flavoured with marjoram.' Praise too for 'tender' roast beef, plump lemon sole (local queenies are also offered, Mornay, provençale and deep fried), potatoes sautéed lightly with onion, and fruit salad. They fail to say whether rumpsteak Ladykiller (£4·05) has a waxed moustache, garlic breath, or what. Italian wines are best buy (Lambrusco and so on, £3·10). Quiet recorded music.

Closed Sun; Jan 1
Must book D
Meals 12–2, 7–9.45

Tdh L £2·70 (meal £4·70)

Alc (min £3·20) £5·80
(meal £8·50)

Service 10%

Seats 90
♿ rest
Car park
No dogs
Access, Diners

Do not risk using an out-of-date Guide. A new edition will appear early in 1981.

For the explanation of ♿, denoting accessibility for the disabled, see 'How to use the Guide', p. 4.

Grosvenor
on A9
5 m N of Ramsey
Kirk Andreas (062 488)
576

'Highly popular among tax fugitives,' reports a man with no price on his head but a plaice on his mind – 'the fish was big, but it failed to live up to the menu blurb, and vegetables were soft too.' However, a Sunday party starting with strawberries in melons and ending with a topping of berries on every cold trolley sweet made no bones about 'succulent' duckling legs. Bernard Hamer suggests queenies in garlic butter and scampi Lord Darling. Fair wines in the £4 range. Bar lunches with Okell's XXX on pump.

Closed Tue; Sun D;
D Apr 4 & 7; Oct; Dec 25;
Must book D & Sun L
Meals 12–2, 7.30–9

Alc L £4 (meal £6·75),
D (min £2·30) £6·15
(meal £9·35)

Service 10%

Seats 48
  rest
Car park
No dogs

The Barn
The Quay
Port St Mary (0624) 2064

Closed Sun; Mon (exc
May 5 & 26, & Aug 25);
Apr 4; Dec 24–26 & 31;
Jan 1
Must book
Meals 12.30–1.30, 7.30–9

Tdh D £6 (meal £6·60)

Alc L (min £2) £3·50

(meal £4·10)

Seats 39
Air-conditioning

'About the best value on the island,' says a local inspector of this candle-lit barn with church pew seating, for Gastone Quaglio and his Manx wife Sue not only cook well but invite customers to bring their own wines which 'we chill or warm for them.' There are usually over twenty hors d'oeuvre, 'many of them our own making', and always a fish dish, 'usually poached or cold salmon in season, or a sole, at about £2, including simple but well-treated vegetables.' 'Gastone takes good care of his avocados.' The stock main dishes are joints of beef, lamb and ham, with a house sauce of mushrooms, peppers, wine and cream for the cut called beef à la Barn. Sweets (60p) depend mostly on cream or buying. Recorded music. No jeans. No dogs. Unlicensed.

App: Henry Fawcett, C.C., T.E., A. P. B. Harston, R. Y. Keers

Harbour Bistro
5 East Street
Ramsey (0624) 814182

Harbour bistro too admired by locals to leave much space for casual visitors. Amid fishing nets, tiled tables, white walls and exposed beams people find 'tasty' fried chicken and bacon, chicken casserole, and sirloin steak as ordered. Fish pie is the kitchen's pride, queenies are cooked in the traditional Ben-my-chree style (bacon, cucumber, Pernod and cream) and they will point chicken 'blunderbust' at you if you ask. French house wines, £3·15 a litre. Background music.

Closed Sun; Dec 25;
Dec 26 L; Jan 1
Must book D
Meals 12–2.30, 6–10.30

Alc £5 (meal £7·55)

Service 10%

Seats 40 (parties 30)
  rest (1 step)
No dogs

IRELAND

From plaice to pigs' trotters

Every traveller to Ireland expects to encounter paradoxes – if no worse – and no national tourist board anywhere in the world is as candid as Bord Fáilte in enumerating and explaining the absurdities that enchant or madden their visitors: for instance, a spirit-prone people who are apt to forbid the consumption of spirits where food is served; islanders who go to great trouble to avoid eating salt-water fish . . . As Ireland develops – and in various ways (inflation included) the country is developing rather fast – further oddities may well emerge. Readers of these pages will already notice that in the kitchens of Irish restaurants and hotels, high talent and well-trained technique can be found co-existing with food marketing systems and popular attitudes to cooking and service that would seem unacceptably primitive in some of Europe's remotest valleys.

It is therefore a serious problem – for Ireland, not just for the individual – at what level the foreign tourist is going to pitch his or her expectation. It is possible, even wise if funds permit, to come to Ireland determined to eat little but smoked salmon, black soles and grilled lobster, set off by some of the world's best bread and potatoes, and by good French wine if the licensing laws or personal preference rule out Guinness and whiskey under the same roof. There are many kitchens that can cope with a demand of this kind even though they could not make a béchamel sauce to save their lives. But as far as the development of real cooking in Ireland is concerned, this type of trade is an aristocratic backwater: the materials are scarce, the price is high, and the connection with real life, as it is experienced by most cooks and most eaters in these islands, is remote. One is pleased to find the speciality sea-food restaurants, often run by immigrant continentals, that have sprung up in recent years on the southern and western coasts, but they are not capable of infinite multiplication. The same is naturally also true of the select band of places run by geniuses who have married French craft to Irish traditions and made something wholly admirable: it is no use pretending, under Irish conditions, that the exceptional can suddenly become the typical and every other country hotel transform itself into an Arbutus Lodge or a Ballymaloe. Yet in one respect places such as these are often much more humble than their descriptions in these pages make them appear: like the French, the owners care about cookery and the teaching of cookery, and about the best use of natural and homely things, from plaice to pigs' trotters. It is on this aspect of Irish catering for tourists that Bord Fáilte and the restaurant trade associations ought to build in their information services for foreign visitors, many of whom also use and report to this book.

Ireland is still a small enough country for much of all this to happen by word of mouth – luckily, since the cookery books written for the British market are seldom attuned to what is possible in Ireland and what is not. However, there is at least one book (published in 1979) that deserves to be in the hands of anyone who cooks and eats for pleasure on this and other north Atlantic seaboards. This is Alan Davidson's *North Atlantic Seafood* (Macmillan, £12·75; paperback edition due in the autumn). It takes its readers into a world that few but professional ichthyologists know – and even they are seldom as well informed as Mr Davidson about different national ways of cooking the fish they study.

Ireland's own contribution to this lore is comparatively modest – and though I shall be trying the Dublin Sea Fisheries Board's recipe for mackerel with rhubarb in due season, I shall be doing it with butter (of which Ireland has more than it can use) not the margarine that the authors permit. But the point of mentioning Mr Davidson's book here is not to commend individual species to fishermen and fish traders or individual recipes to cooks, but to enrich everybody's experience by widening the range of what they are prepared to try. We are talking, after all, of a country whose own fishing industry lets Frenchmen take some of the best species home to Brittany; of a country that possesses all the materials for a north Atlantic matelote, but hardly anyone with the courage to assemble, cook, or eat one. What Irish catering needs – and not only in the context of fish – is well summed up in a compliment Mr Davidson pays to a recipe of Elizabeth David's which 'deftly transports us back through the age of culinary ostentation to a simple dish which was made by normal people, and which both reflects a proper respect for the sole itself and demonstrates the appropriate use of other ingredients.'

REPUBLIC OF IRELAND

ANNAMOE Co Wicklow   Map 10

Armstrong's Barn
Wicklow 5194

Closed L; Sun; Mon;
Tue (late autumn);
public hols
Must book
D only, 7.30–10

Tdh from £10
(meal £12·95)

Seats 56 (parties 14)
♿ rest
Car park
No dogs
Am Ex, Barclay

It is unusual for a chef to survive very long a
restaurant's change of ownership from one
individualist to another, but Humphrey Weightman,
who served Peter Robinson at this far-outlying but
Dublin-urbane restaurant in the Wicklow hills, has
ideas that clearly chime with Paul Tullio's too. There
is a report of one miscarried dinner, and the
combination of decided flavours with restricted
choice (about five dishes in each course) may deter as
many Irishmen as it attracts. But most members are
made of more adventurous stuff, and fall with delight
on Mr Weightman's offal and other specialities: crab
with fresh dill in puff pastry, lambs' hearts stuffed with
apricots, lamb's liver done with hyssop, oregano and
lovage, and pork fillet with slices of green ginger in
the Marsala juices. Brains are another possibility.
There will also be a 'fish of the day', and perhaps fillet
of beef with herb butter. 'They had gone to the
trouble of finding and preparing small potatoes, and
cauliflower *nature* had a splendid bite to it.' 'Even
squid was tender, and the treacle bread to mop up
sauces is a further pleasure.' You may begin with
trout mousse or beetroot soup, perhaps, and finish
with blackcurrant and mint tart, or coffee and
cardamom mousse. Italian Merlot is £3·50 a litre, and
there are other carefully chosen Italian wines as a
relief from the fine but mostly double-figure clarets
and burgundies (however, Ch. Branaire-Ducru '73,
c.b., is just under £10, and sometimes there are
bin-ends). A few tables outside. There may be
'unsolicited touches such as a complimentary glass of
port, and perfume for the ladies.'

App: Henry Fawcett, A.C., J.G.R.

BALLYCONNEELY Co Galway   Map 10

The Fishery
Doohulla
2½ m SE of Ballyconneely
on L102
9 m SE of Clifden
Ballyconneely 31

Closed Oct–May
Must book D
Meals 12.30–2.30,
7.30–9.30

The last *Guide* overstated the involvement of Nick
Tinne of Snaffles (*q.v.* under Dublin) in this
timber-built summer restaurant, which has Edward
O'Brien ('a direct descendant of Brian Boru') as
chef-manager. The Tinnes, it seems, have a majority
financial interest and lend a hand at the skillet from
time to time, no more. Anyway, there are warm
accounts of meals here this year: 'We did not care for
the lobster bisque but the other two soups, lettuce and
tarragon with a handsome deep green colour and a
delicious taste, and fish soup with rouille, more than
made up for this.' Brawn vinaigrette is another first

413

Alc £9·65 (meal £12·55)

Service 10%
Cover 20p
Children's helpings
Seats 36
Car park
No dogs
Am Ex card

course. Baked crab (£3·50) or turbot hollandaise are possibilities if purse or sentiment forbids the lobsters in the tank, which gave one woman 'the most thrilling taste since my childhood on the Canadian seaboard, when we caught lobsters as our daily bread.' 'Lobster in whiskey sauce with rice was also well cooked, though more modest in quantity.' There are steaks too. Finish with négresse en chemise or orange and lemon sorbet, perhaps. Vieux Ceps or Soave are £2·75 and Ch. Pontet-Canet '73, £13·75. Recorded classical music.

App: M. O'Reilly, Joan Taylor, G.H., Seamus Corballis, Louise Wheeley

---

BALLYDEHOB Co Cork   Map 10

Audley House Hotel
Ballydehob 74

The Konigs' hotel overlooking Roaring Water Bay and the Calf Islands (the origin of surf'n'turf?) is described by owners and visitors alike as unusual. Horses that wander into the dining-room can be sent away in Dutch, German or French but humans are given 'personal care', though 'few of them want their shoes shined any more.' Those who dine out may be quizzed on return. Most who stay for 'hearty' dinners of smoked salmon, smoked eel on toast, 'excellent' soups, John Dory, satay pork, entrecôte bretonne and 'Dutch delight', made with yoghourt, cream and advocaat, feel no urge to leave. 'Breakfast lacked conviction.' No word on rijsttaffel. A litre of Pedrotti ordinaire is £4·25. Pressurised beers for snacks. Recorded music. (GHG)

Closed Feb
Must book
Meals 1–2.15, 7.30–10

Tdh L from £4·50
(meal £6·65), D from £9
(meal £11·15)

Alc £6·70 (meal £9·15)

Service inc
Children's helpings
Seats 50

⚀ rest
Car park
No dogs in d/r
10 rooms (all with bath)
B&B £9–£11
Fire cert

Basil Bush
Main Street
Ballydehob 10

Closed Sun; L public hols;
Dec 24–26 & 31; Jan 1
Must book
Meals 12.30–2, 7–10

Alc £5·80 (meal £8·35)

Service 10%
Seats 24
No dogs

'The place wraps itself round you, and you wrap yourself round their food,' says an inspector, basking in the way Shirley Foster and Alfie Lyons cook for their neatly converted stone-flagged cottage, with its wooden furniture, good pottery, checked napkins and salt and pepper mills. 'Still no telephone of our own, despite the advocacy of the tourist board and the local MP,' they say, so by the time you have got through to the pub across the street and waited for your individually cooked food, you will be hungry. This means you will be bound to eat a loaf of sour-dough bread with butter before you even reach the gravadlax, the cold cream of cucumber soup with fresh mint, or the dolmades from their own vine leaves. After these, inspectors report 'Bally de Bouillabaisse: exquisitely fresh mussels, prawns and other fish in their own essences, with something to deepen the flavour'; 'unexpectedly flavoured' stuffed sole, done, it seems, with a brunoise of aromatic vegetables and sauce suprême; Pernod-flavoured suprême de volaille with duxelles stuffing; and other delights. On the side, there may be mange-tout peas and a salad including mung beans, and rhubarb ice-cream or blackberry mousse for pudding. ('Brandied peach ice-cream was too assertive and heavy.') 'Wednesday night is Chinese night,' Mr Lyons says, pointing readers to his Szechuan chicken, hot and spicy, at £3·50, and 'with any encouragement' he will set aside evenings for other regional dinners. Captain red or Blanc de Blancs are £3, and there are about a dozen other wines, sensibly chosen and priced, with California varietals this year at £5–£6. Recorded chamber music, and a merciful absence of rules about children, dress and so on.

App: Henry Fawcett, M.J.M., C.H.

BALTIMORE Co Cork   Map 10

Chez Youen
Baltimore 36

Oct–Apr: closed L;
Sun; Mon; Dec 25
Meals 12.30–3.30, 6–11
(summer), 7.30–10 (winter)

Tdh from £6 (meal from £7·90)
Alc £7·80 (meal £10·10)

Service inc
Children's helpings
(under 12)
Seats 36
♿ rest (1 step)
No dogs
Barclay, Euro

The 'untouched' quayside cafe decor and appointments signal a Frenchman who cares about food and little else. Youen Jacob, a Breton married to an O'Neill, does his own cooking during the winter and hires a chef for the summer. Either way the cooking as reported in 1979 has been good, 'indeed, just as good or better on the cheapest as on the dearest menu.' A test £7 dinner produced 'giant crab claws with firm and moist meat inside, and a salty home-made mayonnaise; then scallops in a rather sweet cream and brandy sauce. Tarte Tatin was also well-made.' Other specialities include palourdes farcies (one wonders faintly whether M Jacob has to go to Cherbourg to buy back Ireland's own clams), oysters grilled or fresh, sea trout with cream and basil, and lobster grilled or armoricaine. Other visitors report 'very good onion soup and monk-fish with onions and tomatoes on the menu touristique'; there is also a menu enfantine at £2. Loire red or white wines are £3·80 a litre and Saumur '78 is £5·50. Clarets (including a run of Ch. Sociando-Mallet) are dear: Ch. Lynch-Bages '73, £15. Music – live sometimes – is 'classic and Irish'. More reports, please.

In the Republic of Ireland some restaurants are licensed to sell wines only (not spirits or beer).

Irish public holidays do not all coincide with English ones.

Entries for places with distinctions carry symbols (pestle, tureen, bottle, glass). Credits are fully written entries, with approvers' names below the text. Passes are telegraphic entries (useful in the area) with details under the text. Provisional entries are in italics (see 'How to use the Guide', p. 4).

BEARNA PIER Co Galway   Map 10

Ty Ar Mor
Sea Point
3 m W of Galway
Bearna 65031

Hervé Mahé and his Breton chef run a 'hit or miss' place on the edge of the sea, and this season people will miss the 'pretty Galway student who made heavy pancakes but lightened other kinds of lumpishness.' With fair luck, garlicky fish soup (80p), seafood crêpe, tomates antiboise (stuffed with fish and mayonnaise), scallops bretonne and turbot are good choices, but langoustines in shell coated with sauce were 'hard to eat decently' and sweets, service and coffee are liable to be poor. A few meat dishes. French white or red wine £3. Set lunch in July and August. Recorded 'classical jazz'.

Closed L (exc July & Aug); Sun (exc summer); Jan	Meals 12–2 (July & Aug), 7–11	Alc £6·90 (meal £9·70)
Must book D	Tdh L £3 (meal £4·95)	Seats 45 ⟨⟩ rest (1 step)

CAHIR Co Tipperary   Map 10

Earl of Glengall
The Square
Cahir 205 *and* 644

Closed Sun; Apr 4;
Dec 24 & 25
Must book D & weekends
Meals 12.30–2.30, 7–10

Tdh L £5 (meal £6·90),
D £9·95 (meal £12·30)
Alc £8·95 (meal £11·65)

Service 10%
Seats 50
No dogs
Access, Am Ex, Barclay,
Diners

The restaurant in Cahir's handsome square is called 'cosily Tudor', and a picture in the bar 'shows a knight discussing with his lady the possibility of slaying a dragon.' A member who queried the date on his wine bottle felt he had met the dragon in person, but it makes a change from sloppy Irish restaurant management, and Wolfgang Stroms' cooking is pretty good, in the continental professional tradition. From the large table d'hôte menu inspectors report 'delicious aubergines algérienne, with minced meat, tomato and garlic stuffing and a cheesy sauce, fresh cream of mushroom soup, and roast duckling in honey with ginger and apricot sauce'; or 'double the amount of plaice one would get in England, very fresh fish, coated in fine breadcrumbs and fried just right.' Mr Stroms has a vivier for lobsters, and other dishes he thinks worth commending include scallops à l'ail, prawns thermidor, fillet of turbot grand-duc (£5·50), escalope de veau zingara and venison cutlets Baden-Baden (£5·75). French ordinaire is £2·50 and there is a standard Grants of Ireland list with about fifty bins. Oysters, cutlets, sandwiches and other snacks can be had in the bar at lunch-time. Recorded music. Dress conventionally for dinner. More reports, please.

Since each restaurant has a separate file in the Guide office, please use a separate form or sheet of paper for each report. Additional forms may be obtained free (no stamp required) from The Good Food Guide, Freepost, 14 Buckingham Street, London WC2N 6BR (unfortunately Freepost facilities are not available from the Channel Islands or the Republic of Ireland).

Please report to us on atmosphere, decor and – if you stayed – standard of accommodation, as well as on food, drink and prices (send bill if possible).

CARRIGBYRNE Co Wexford   Map 10

Cedar Lodge
on N25
14 m W of Wexford
Waterford 24386 *and*
24436

Conflicting reports on this smart motel half an hour from the Rosslare ferry, but inspection after complaints of frozen vegetables, bottled mint sauce, stale bread and other 'cut corners' happily yielded marinated tomatoes ('good tomato salad, really'), tender beef Stroganoff (£5), lamb chops 'with home-made mint sauce' (£3·50), 'giant' croquette potatoes and tinned pineapple 'on a super sponge' (75p). Trout with almonds was enjoyed to Schubert's *Trout*. French ordinaire is £3·25 for 50 cl. Snacks ('lovely smoked salmon sandwiches') all day in the bar, which you may also eat outside.

Closed L (exc summer or by arrangement); Apr 4; Dec 25
Meals 12.30–2, 6–10

Tdh L £4·50 (meal £6·75), D £7·50 (meal £10·05)

Alc £7·75 (meal £10·60)

Service 10%
Children's helpings (under 13)
Seats 46 (parties 84)
🔲 rest; w.c.

Car park
No dogs
Access card
6 rooms (5 with shower)
B&B £8–£9
Fire cert

CASTLEBAR Co Mayo   Map 10

La Petite France
Castle Street
Castlebar 22709

Closed L (winter);
2 weeks Mar;
3rd week Oct
Must book D
Meals 12.30–2, 7.15–10
(9 Sun in winter)

Tdh L £3·50 (meal £6·15)
Alc £8·75 (meal £12)

Children's helpings
Seats 35
Car park
No dogs
Barclay, Diners

A Frenchman cooking the characteristic dishes of his native Alsace in a tastefully converted warehouse fronting on Castlebar's car park can hardly have been surprised by 'a slow start'. But Gérard Morice (late of Newport House Hotel) and his Irish wife Imelda are already being rewarded by frequent return visits from early customers who know a good thing when they find it. The set lunch sounds especially good value, and this being Ireland rather than Alsace, there is plenty of fish on the menu, with hure de saumon au poivre vert (£1·95) and ragoût de fruits de mer (£14·50 for two, including scallops, prawns, turbot and langoustines, some stewed and some grilled) among M Morice's favourite dishes. Others to look out for include médaillons de porc vallée d'Auge (£5·70, including vegetables) and charcoal-grilled côte de boeuf – 'absolutely delicious, sliced at the table by the chef.' But a much-travelled Irish eater also reports happily on the smoked haddock timbale and the boned saddle of lamb vert-pré, 'pink in the middle, with a coating of garlicky breadcrumbs.' Note, too, that the restaurant won the Irish National Dairy Council's competition in 1979 for its array of French and Irish cheeses – though it would be a pity to miss the crêpe Grand Marnier too, not to mention open fruit tarts in the Alsace manner, and Michel Guérard's recipe for granité au vin de St Emilion (£1·40). Mommessin red or white burgundy is £3·60, and dry white Ch. Olivier '75 is £7·50. They record their own classical music, they say, and discourage small children from eating after 9 p.m. More reports, please.

Arbutus Lodge

St Luke's Cross,
Montenotte
Cork 501237

Closed Sun L (exc bar);
Sun D (exc res);
Dec 24–26
Must book
Meals 1–2, 7–9.30

Tdh L £7·95 (meal £9·90),
D £10·65 (meal £12·60)
Alc £12·95 (meal £15·40)

Service inc
Seats 65 (parties 30)
 rest
Air-conditioning
Car park
No dogs
Am Ex, Barclay, Diners
20 rooms (16 with bath,
4 with shower)
B&B £16·25–£23·50

Recipe in *Second Dinner
Party Book:* nettle soup

'The Roux brothers would be happy to eat here,' says
one Home Counties visitor, and the compliment to
Declan Ryan and his hotel perched high above
Cork's river is confirmed by *Guide* inspectors who
would at least as soon eat here as chez Roux. For, in
this 'small, cared-for dining-room', French
professionalism (the Ryans have had family
exchanges with the Troisgros in Roanne) is lightened
by Irish amiability. 'Sauces tend to be reductions
without flour. The locals may regard them as short
change' – says an Irishwoman – 'but French diners
were sighing with pleasure.' A Dutchwoman adds 'the
drisheen (blood sausage) is in a class apart.' (It is
served with traditional tansy which 'some think would
be better in a handkerchief drawer than in a béchamel.')
Nettle soup is another possibility, and other first
courses noted include spinach salad with lardons still
hot from the pan, moules farcies, and mosaïque de
légumes – 'a very light mousse of ham cut through
by lines of exquisitely prepared vegetables, lightly
blanched.' ('Declan's herb and vegetable garden is a
sight to see.') A test meal began with tourte Forezien,
'a game flan with the wisp-like pastry that this
kitchen achieves', and the crumbed pig's trotter that
unites Irish tradition with *cuisine bourgeoise*. Then
came the house speciality chicken Hibernia, with
nutmeggy spinach and sauté potatoes 'for once just
as they should be', and wild duck 'hung and cooked
just right, with a sauce of enriched pan juices.' Even
all this omits the dishes that the seven-strong team in
the kitchen themselves pick out this year: salade de
ris de veau, cassolette of fresh prawns, côte de boeuf
sauce Beaujolais à la moelle, and escalope of salmon
with sorrel sauce. 'The Arbutus cheeseboard, offered
with walnut bread, outdoes any other in Ireland. Mrs
Allen at Shanagarry (*q.v.*) also serves Veronica Steele's
remarkable new Irish cheese called Milleens, but for
the Ryans someone brings in French goat cheeses,
Gaperon and Epoisses which can hardly be bought in
Ireland.' Strawberry mille-feuille was 'lovely, right
down to the jam at the bottom; but bilberry fool was
too sweet.' The wines are equally fine, and
knowledgeably treated. There is an interesting new
consignment of California wines under £10, and in
higher reaches, £25 is generous for Ch. Pape-Clément
'61 and £20 for the '60 and '69 vintages of Ch.
d'Yquem. The run of Ch. Latour goes back to 1942
(£62). For £5 wines, look first at the German list. No
pipes. Breakfasts, and bar lunches (which you may
eat on the terrace) are good too.

*App: Geoffrey & Jenifer Rowntree, Val Watson,
Peter Hood, Leo J. Murphy, J. R. Williams,
and many others*

Lovetts
Churchyard Lane,
Well Road, Douglas
Cork 294909

Closed Sun; Sat L;
public hols; Mar 31–Apr 5
Must book
Meals 12.30–1.45,
7.30–9.45

Tdh L from £5
(meal £6·70)
Alc £10·10 (meal £12·30)

Service inc
Seats 30 (parties 20)
🔗 rest (1 step)
Car park
No dogs
Access, Am Ex, Barclay,
Diners

*Dermod Lovett, a former hotel manager, has set up in a
'century-old, odd-shaped house and run-down grounds'
on the outskirts of Cork. His integrity and enthusiasm
in honouring a solitary booking when all his neighbours
had shut up shop to see the Pope were rewarded by a
member's warm account of crème portugaise,
'wonderful salmon that had kept its flavour in its
papillote' (£5·50), and 'soufflé glacé au Bailey's Irish
Cream'. This Irish surprise was consummated by
Cafetière coffee. Mr Lovett's chef Manuel Las Heras is
especially keen on fish, and his mousseline of fresh
turbot sauce cardinal (£2·25), escalopes de saumon
nantaise (£2 as a first course or £5 as a main) and
stuffed sole should be noted. Inspectors report equal
contentment with an unexpected salmon soup – 'there
was real eating and drinking in it' – and veal cutlet
persillé on a set lunch. Rack of lamb, and noisettes of
veal with lemon sauce, are other good meat dishes.
Vegetables are carefully cooked, and served on a
separate plate. With more time, Mr Lovett hopes to
improve the house, grow vegetables as well as herbs,
and provide a wider range of sweets, but he has evidently
made a good start in this 'calm' dining-room. The house
wines are Loire white and Portuguese Serradayres '74
red at £3·50. The list of Latour and Jadot white
burgundies, and the chance to drink Ch. Léoville-Barton
or Ch. Cos d'Estournel '73, both c.b., under £10, is also
promising. No pipes, and a non-smoking alcove to
protect you from the rest. No children under 12.
More reports, please.*

COURTMACSHERRY Co Cork   Map 10

Courtmacsherry Hotel
12 m S of Bandon
Bandon 46198

Visitors may contemplate picking wild garlic in the
woods behind the Adams' 'handsome and friendly
house in an adorable village' to give some life to the
vegetables and erratic sauces that find their way on to
good salmon and prawns. But salmon is smoked locally
and seafood cocktail combines it with mackerel,
prawns and crab. Whitebait is 'perfect' and the light
touch with brill and steak ('good value') is also
praised. Improved sweets but 'the pastry deserves
better than tinned filling.' A member who was rushed
into a noisy coffee lounge would have paid more to
stay at her table. Italian and German house wine,
£1·80 for 50 cl. Bar snacks.

Closed L (exc Sun &
Apr 7); Oct–Easter
Must book weekends
Meals 12.45–2 (Sun),
7.30–9.15

Tdh Sun L £4
(meal £6·05), D from £6·50
(meal £8·80)

Service 10%
Children's helpings

Seats 70 (parties 30)
🔗 rest
Car park
No dogs in public rooms
17 rooms (6 with bath)
B&B £9–£12·50

Irish public holidays do not all coincide with English ones.

CROOKHAVEN Co Cork   Map 10

Journey's End
12 m SW of Schull
Skibbereen 35183

A remote fishing village (include Skibbereen in the address if you write) houses Ina Manahan's informal little place where even a screaming baby was absorbed (though she tends to discourage children under ten). The menu changes little, but people enjoy scallops in garlic butter (£3), avocado and prawns vinaigrette, chicken breasts with a whiskey cream sauce, fillet steak béarnaise ('if the wind is in the wrong direction, *you* feel charcoal-broiled') with 'adequate rather than inspired' vegetables, and fresh peach Pavlova for sweet. 'Everything is home-made.' The wines (from £3) will be curtailed in 1980 'to protect people who already have trouble making decisions.' 'Guitar by the turf fire' occasionally, and visitors choose records at other times. Dress is still 'oilskins to mink'.

Closed L; Mon; Sept–May
Must book

D only, 7.30–9

Alc £8·30 (meal £11·25)

Service 10%
Seats 22
♿ rest

CURRAGH Co Kildare   Map 10

Jockey Hall
2 m E of Kildare
Naas 41416 *and* 41401

Closed L; Sun; Apr 4;
Dec 24 & 25
Must book
D only, 6.30–10

Tdh £6·25 (meal £8·60)
Alc £10·70 (meal £13·05)

Service inc
Children's helpings
Seats 65 (parties
L 90, D 50)
♿ rest
Car park
No dogs
Access, Am Ex, Barclay

The flaky ceiling, dreary bar, and – on Curragh race days – two sittings, with waitresses at the double, do not bode well even for a chef as well certificated as Paul McCluskey (who works in the kitchen with four assistants). These and other misjudgments of service evidently deter from repeat visits many who warmly admire the actual food. 'Potato and onion soup was delicious, and onion tart, served warm, was also good. We had a long wait for excellent grilled salmon béarnaise and chicken Michel, but it was foolish to serve all the superb vegetables onto the same plate: tasty mushrooms in port, hot cucumber à la crème, and gratin dauphinoise potatoes, as well as carrots and cabbage. Praline ice-cream afterwards was mouthwatering – but it was the only sweet left by then.' A test meal confirmed most of this, and the kitchen by its own account is 'always experimenting with new recipes', including this year raw mushroom salad (£1·25), sole with chives (£6·95), lambs' kidneys with mustard and parsley (£4·75), game in various ways, and rack of lamb diable (£6·75). Chocolate roulade and gâteau St Honoré may be offered, but the inspector was more impressed to find a fine tart made with marzipan-stuffed prunes. Chianti or Orvieto are £3·90 for just under a litre. Marqués de Riscal '73 is £5·75.

App: D. J. Hogan, J. Kenneth O'Brien, J.B. McG., H.L.

For Irish pubs, see p. 488.

DINGLE Co Kerry   Map 10

Doyle's Seafood Bar
John Street
Dingle 144

Closed Sun; Nov–Feb
No bookings
Meals 12.30–2.15, 6–9

Alc £5·75 (meal £8·20)

Service 10%
Seats 24
♿ rest (1 step); w.c.
No dogs
Am Ex, Barclay

Recipe in *Second Dinner Party Book:* mussels and garlic stuffing

'John and Stella Doyle have got it right. Their modest bar is simple and clean without descending to folksy-country level, and the owner circulated easily, advising German, Dutch, French, South African, American, Irish and us two English on what to eat.' In their six *Guide* years the Doyles have steadily sought improvement through French and English wine and cookery courses, and their reward is contented accounts of their 'sweet, nutty' mussel soup and 'rich, thick, and brown' crab bisque with a sea tang. 'We were pleased to be offered brown trout instead of tasteless rainbow, and the highly flavoured mushroom sauce did not disguise the taste of the superb pink flesh.' Chicken and scallop pie is a 'delicate and unusual' speciality, though the luck of the slice determines which you get most of. Taramosalata, sweet marinated herrings, mussels, 'thick, sharp and yellow' mayonnaise and other salad dressings also have admirers, but 'crayfish salad outdid everything, the beast split open and served with about half a pint of melted garlic butter and a green salad.' Sweets may include blackberry fool, 'featherlight' almond meringue, and well-made chocolate choux. Valpolicella or Soave are £3·90 a litre, but the most suitable wines will be the Muscadets, Saumur or white Viña Sol under £5 for the plainer fishes, and Rhône whites at various prices for more assertive dishes. International customers' assertive cigars are not amenable to vinous solutions. 'We have a lot of fun with our guests,' says Mr Doyle. Bar meals all day may be offered in 1980.

App: Gill & Peter Wooldridge, H.C., K.F.W., David Horkan

Half Door
John Street
Dingle 300

Celeste Slye, who cooks, makes free with exclamation marks and her guests are quick to catch the habit. 'For adventure, go elsewhere!', but scallops in wine sauce (£4·30) are called 'better than my own!' and moules provençale (£1) 'marketable in St Malo'. A 'satisfactory' dinner of potato soup, grilled turbot, jacket potato and scones held up well to the end with apricot sorbet and good coffee with cream. Mrs Slye commends her own crab quiche, poached salmon (£4·75), and moist chocolate cake. Courteous service. French house wine, £3 the litre. Patio dining. 'Neat dress essential.'

Closed Tue; Nov–Mar; Apr 4
Must book D
Meals 12.30–2.15, 6–9

Tdh L £3 (meal £4·50)

Alc £6·65 (meal £8·50)

Service inc
Children's helpings
Seats 36 (parties 16)

♿ rest
Air-conditioning
No dogs
Am Ex, Barclay, Diners, Euro

DUBLIN   Map 10

(1) Le Coq Hardi
29 Pembroke Road.
Ballsbridge
Dublin 689070

Closed Sun; Sat L;
public hols; Dec 24;
2 weeks Jan
Must book
Meals 12.30–2.30, 7–11

Tdh L £6·50 (meal £9·45)
Alc £11·75 (meal £15·90)

Service 12½%
Seats 40
rest (3 steps); w.c.
Air-conditioning
Car park
No dogs
Am Ex, Barclay, Euro

John Howard, as *chef-patron*, with Jimmy Sullivan's help, has built up this restaurant in the basement of the Lansdowne Hotel into one of Dublin's favourite business venues – with some of the entailed penalties (notably tobacco smoke that clings to the curtains, and to the noses of people who forget to book early meals). The set meal at midday, when tried, was nevertheless enjoyed, and carefully cooked. 'Perhaps both the crêpe de fruits de mer and the baked potatoes had suffered somewhat from being kept warm, and a finger-bowl should have been provided for chicken winglets' (crumbed and fried, served over tomato and garlic sauce). But roast beef came rare as ordered, with featherlight Yorkshire pudding, cabbage lightly cooked with lardons of bacon, and home-made horseradish sauce. At dinner, aubergine provençale (£1·75) – 'though surely the smallest aubergine in Ireland that day' – pâté, Dublin Bay prawns, veal escalope Marquise de Sévigny (£7·10), jugged hare (£6) and filets au poivre vert et au cognac (£8·50) should be considered. 'Mange-tout peas were buttery and peppery and good' – indeed, the vegetable-cooking far surpasses Dublin norm. The same is true of the ice-cream, perhaps with rum-soaked raisins and walnuts folded into it. But cheesecake is called by an inspector 'one of those mediocre gelatine-set ones.' 'Cheeses are cling-wrapped as though they don't seriously expect people to eat them.' French ordinaires are £3·80 ('the red is preferable to the white') but the names and prices of most other wines reflect the character of the clientele all too accurately. At about £8, consider Ch. Camensac '73 or Fleurie '78 (Louis Jadot) perhaps. If circumstances demand £50 and '61 *grands crus*, they are there. Service of wine is professional, of food less reliably so, but it was good at a test meal. 'Wear a suit and tie.'

App: D. C. Arnold, E.K.R., L.O'B.

---

(2) Kilkenny Kitchen
Kilkenny Shop
Nassau Street
Dublin 777066

'Good design in all but the lunch-hour queue up the spiral staircase.' The captive audience is at least distracted by pottery and elegant furniture (sold in the crafts shop downstairs) and by a view of Trinity's priveted green. A refugee from the National Library found ham with fresh pineapple, mushrooms in home-made mayonnaise (40p), 'a healthy slice of mild Brie' (30p) and aromatic filter coffee (25p). Soups (carrot, pumpkin), salads and cakes ('walnut slice with a crunchy demerara base') appeal to weary shoppers, travellers and students, as do the large tables and clean surroundings. A few hot dishes (Irish stew, £1·80). French house wine is 55p a glass.

Closed D; Sun;
public hols; Dec 24
Open 9.30–5.30
(L 12–2.30)

Alc L (min 75p) £3·70
(meal £5·45)

Service inc
Seats 80
No dogs

---

(3) Snaffles
47 Lower Leeson Street
Dublin 760790 *and* 762227

Closed Sun; Mon D;
Sat L; 10 days Chr;
public hols
Must book
Meals 12.30–2.30, 7–11

Alc £10 (meal £13·55)

Service 12½%
Cover 25p
Children's helpings
Seats 40 (parties 12)
No dogs
Am Ex, Barclay, Diners

'I think the food here is very good, and probably better when Jack Williams is cooking than when I am,' says Nick Tinne disarmingly, and though it was left without a prize in last year's distribution of *Guide* distinctions, this flavoury Georgian basement with the unobtrusive approach still has its nose ahead of the Dublin field. 'Snaffles mousse still intrigues even when you know the trick, carré d'agneau was a lovely piece of meat simply and well cooked, the salad well dressed, and the pudding, a sort of crème brûlée with seedless green grapes buried within, extraordinary. When the waiter had finished serving our excellent coffee he returned to the kitchen saying, "Well, that's it", but we didn't mind because the service from both men had been deft, friendly and helpful.' Not everyone is as taken by grape pud these days, and a San Franciscan is properly indignant about 'tough, flavourless scallops meunière with ill-matched vegetables.' But note that their best dishes are seldom the dearest (unless it be golden plover at £8·95), for lambs' kidneys in mustard sauce and ox-tongue vinaigrette, both £3·25, are mentioned by Mr Tinne and also in reports. Robust potato and bacon soup, 'spinach beyond reproach', and other rustic delights are reported. Valpolicella or Soave are

423

a modest £3 a bottle. Prices rise less sharply thereafter than used to be the case, relative to other places, with Muscadet '77, Marqués de Riscal red '74, and a '73 Côtes de Blaye under £5, and Ch. Phélan-Ségur '71 or sweet white Ch. Filhot '75 under £10. Nor is £50 now a bad price for magnums of Ch. Léoville-Barton or Léoville-Poyferré '61 (Berry Bros bottlings). 'I abhor smoking myself but for too many a cigar rounds off their meal,' Mr Tinne says.

App: Rita Erlich Pryor, Edward & Primrose Wilson, H.W., James Doherty, and others

---

DUBLIN   Map 10

---

(4) Tandoori Rooms
Golden Orient
27 Lower Leeson Street
Dublin 762286

Closed L; Sun;
public hols (exc May 5)
Must book
D only, 7–12.15

Tdh £8·50 (meal £12·05)
Alc £11·05 (meal £14·80)

Service 12½%
Cover 20p
Children's helpings
(under 12)
Seats 60 (parties 26)
Air-conditioning
No dogs
Access, Am Ex, Diners

Strength through joy, variety through spice, and other maxims are Mike Butt's secret, and he is imparting them (along with the secrets of Kenyan-Asian cuisine applied to Irish materials) to the Swiss this spring. Dubliners have been mostly too hesitant (or is it blasé?) to describe the style this year but an inspector found both the tastes and the bonhomie of the basement restaurant unchanged. Mr Butt shares the cooking with Mohamad Yusuf and Kevin Pigot. Whoever was responsible, the deep-fried pakoras (with strips of different green vegetables and fresh coriander) and cumin-flavoured minced lamb samosas, both served with yoghourt, mint and lemon, tasted very promising, and the promise was fulfilled by the mild boned chicken chillifry and lambs' sweetbreads fenugreek – 'not attractive to the eye, but subtle and distinctive, far superior to most French sauced versions of this rich delicacy.' Pulao rice had clearly sat in a warming-oven too long. Specialities to note include the platter of Dublin seafood with shorba or garlic butter (£4·75), Peshawari lamb pot roast, sole on the bone Lahori (from £8·50) and individual rib of beef Rickshawboy (£8·95). There is also a wholly vegetarian menu (£5·60). 'Crème caramel was unmemorable but the mango sorbet, though too crystalline, had a marvellous flavour.' Corbières or Limoux Blanc de Blancs are £3·65, Gewürztraminer (Dopff) is £7·75, and there are several fine wines best ignored in this context. 'Why don't they offer a good cider as an alternative, since the law forbids beer and the food needs copious draughts?' Dress reasonably.

App: Henry Fawcett, E.K., L.O'B.

DUBLIN see also pub and wine bar sections

'Meal' indicates the cost of a meal for one, including food, coffee, a half-bottle of one of the cheapest wines listed, cover, service, and VAT (see 'How to use the Guide', p. 4).

DUNDERRY Co Meath   Map 10

Dunderry Lodge

♥

5 m SW of Navan
on L23
Navan 31671

Closed L; Sun; Mon;
most public hols
Must book
D only, 7.30–10.30

Tdh £4·95 (meal £7·15)

Alc £7·65 (meal £10·35)

Seats 36
🔄 rest (1 step); w.c.
Car park
No dogs
Access, Am Ex

A normally fierce inspector was 'bowled over by the excellence' of Nicholas and Catherine Healy's converted barn and cowhouse (ask for directions when you book). Unpretentious enthusiasm for fresh food, and determination to keep prices down are the Healys' secret, and as the spelling of their name promises, wine-lovers are stayed with admirable flagons.
Summer set dinners reported seem well balanced as well as carefully cooked, with tasty vegetable soup, and stuffed peppers and aubergines, Mexican pork 'hot with chilli' or local veal provençale, 'delicious turbot in tarragon sauce', inexpensive but well-kept cheeses, and chocolate roulade. A test meal produced among other dishes 'a somewhat too rich and sloppy' smoked mackerel mousse, 'tender and moist pigeon breasts in red wine, the rich sauce very gamey', and for pudding 'damsons in red wine which tasted very good after the pigeon.' Other à la carte favourites from Mrs Healy's often-changed menus include paupiettes of ham with prawns (£2·10), dressed crab, moules marinière (£1·80), and roast wild duck with plum and madeira sauce (£5·05). Mommessin white table wine is £3·25 and La Table du Roy red Rhône £3·10. Other Jaboulet Rhônes, and Riojas under £5, are sound too; even Aloxe-Corton '73 (Louis Latour) only just touches £11, Muscat de Beaumes de Venise by the glass. Dress neatly. There is a courtyard where you may eat on one of Co Meath's fine days.

App: Jan Verstraten, E.K., C.H.

DUNGARVAN Co Waterford   Map 10

Seanachie
5 m from Dungarvan
on N25
Dungarvan 41738

'Seanachie' means old storyteller and there are some stories to tell about this barn, 'reeking of character and charred peat'. Laurann Casey's set dinner menus read well: pâté or pizza, soup, deep-fried monk-fish provençale or roast beef béarnaise, with rum bombe to finish. But inspectors' experience was of 'cream with everything': pork kebabs in cream sauce (faintly sweet and curried), melon and ginger with cream, spinach, cabbage and beetroot, all à la crème. Others prefer stuffed pancakes, carrot soup, fresh salmon or turbot, Irish stew and 'huge' meringues. Bar lunches – in the courtyard if it's fine; Smithwick's and Guinness. Pleasant and capable service. Reasonably priced wines; carafe Valpolicella £3·30 the litre. Dancing at weekends. More reports, please.

Closed Sun; Apr 4; Dec 25
Must book weekends
Meals 11–2.30, 7–10

Tdh L £3 (meal £5·20),
D £8 (meal £10·80)
Alc £9·30 (meal £12·75)

Service 12½%

Children's helpings
(under 10)
Seats 50
Air-conditioning
Am Ex card

DUN LAOGHAIRE Co Dublin Map 10

Trudi's
107 Lower George's Street
Dublin 805318

Closed L; Sun; Apr 4 & 7; Dec 25 & 26; Jan 1
Must book
D only, 7.30–11

Alc £8·70 (meal £11·90)

Seats 55
♿ rest
No dogs
Am Ex, Barclay

Finding the front door bell on a dark night can be a problem, and 'service at first was brisk in every sense', but both customer and staff thawed after that, and the local popularity of Trudi's (now run by Johnny Robinson, with his Swiss-trained brother Patrick in the kitchen) is evident. Fresh crab in the shell (£2·50) may vary somewhat with the season and the crab, but was good when tried in the summer. Tomato and orange soup, or avocado with prawn mayonnaise, are other opening possibilities. Thereafter, trout with almonds, 'a very large chicken Kiev, lightly garlicked, and not armour-plated in breadcrumbs', fillet of pork with apples and cider, and lambs' kidneys in a 'rich and sharp' brandy, cream and mustard sauce are praised by various visitors; note also roast pigeon breasts with raisin and cream sauce (£4·95) and roast rack of lamb, the Robinsons say. Ratatouille 'had not been cooked too much' but potatoes might be better without a coating of red Cheddar. 'Caramel fudge ice-cream tasted of coffee, actually, but was agreeable.' So was a bottle of Viña Pomal, good value at £4·10 in 1979. 'Beaujolais white or red as house wine is £4·50 a litre, and Ruster Neusiedlersee Beerenauslese (of unspecified year) is an unusual dessert offering at £7·95. Recorded jazz.

App: J. D. Mitchell, A. J. R. Stephenson, J.G.R.

GOREY Co Wexford Map 10

Marlfield House

on Courtown Road
1 m SE of Gorey
Courtown Harbour 21124

Closed Dec 24–26 & 31; Jan 1
Must book
Meals 1–2.30, 7.30–8.30

Tdh L from £3 (meal from £4·95), D £8·50 (meal £10·45)

Seats 66 (parties 34)
♿ rest
Euro card
11 rooms (10 with bath, 1 with shower)
B&B £11·50–£15
Fire cert

Mary Bowe's finely furnished Regency dower house, on the wooded Courtown estate, has been heavily reported on this year by several old readers and correspondents of the *Guide* and by an alarming number of new ones, all in the same month. Their compliments sound sincere enough, though, and may be attributed partly to the house itself, but principally to the food (now cooked by Patricia Hoyle). Some have found the atmosphere of the place vaguely impersonal (though one party was generously treated by the owner in the absence of her staff). 'Fish and vegetable cookery stand out,' says one regular Irish visitor. Other more occasional members and inspectors describe set meals in affectionate detail: 'prawns Alabama with peppers, much better than the usual prawn cocktail, crisp and light mushrooms in batter with garlic sauce, very good cream of mushroom soup, magnificent grilled turbot meunière with creamed celery and aubergines, and further good sauces (chocolate and butterscotch) with profiteroles and ice-cream.' At a test meal, the crab salad had an 'item-by-item freshness that reveals a well-run kitchen, and mayonnaise and vinaigrette were both oily rather than vinegary.' Tomato soup was milky and thin on this occasion but filet de porc crumbed and fried with a suspicion of ginger in the coating, and a dollop of béarnaise with roughly chopped tarragon, restored hopes. Pear cake 'which tasted much better than it looked' confirmed them. 'What a breakfast, if only one could eat it,' a visitor adds, noting the offer of early morning French onion soup for 'a Marlfield hangover'. A wide range of the dinner dishes, including salmon and plaice, and the trolley sweets as well as the more obvious pâté and soup, can be had in the bar at lunch-time. La Tourelle and La Gravette ordinaires are £3, and though wines in the £5–£7 range are mostly unexciting (the Germans are very poor), purses that can stretch to Ch. Pontet-Canet or Ch. Croizet-Bages '70, c.b., at £12 or so, may be content. 'Consideration' is expected of smokers, at least until everyone has finished eating. No children under seven, and no children's helpings or prices. Dress conventionally. You may eat outdoors in summer. Car park. No dogs.

App: Ann Kierans, Ann Murphy, J. L. Morton, H. & L.L., Mr & Mrs P. Hegarty, and others

HOWTH Co Dublin   Map 10

King Sitric
East Pier,
Harbour Road
Dublin 325235 *and* 326729

Closed L; Sun; Mar 17;
Apr 4 & 7; June 2;
Aug 4; Oct 27;
10 days Chr
Must book
D only, 6.30–11.15

Alc £10·50 (meal £14·35)

Cover 20p
Seats 82 (parties 20)
♿ rest (1 step)
No dogs
Access, Am Ex, Barclay,
Diners, Euro

Aidan MacManus, king of Howth, and his chef John Houraghan had some rebellious subjects among members last year, and though most meals reported this time have been better the throne is still rocking slightly, to judge by accounts of compulsory waits in the bar, 'cardboard pastry for blackberry tart', and as usual 'shameless selling of cigars while other wretched customers are still eating.' The service, which one member finds chilly, was attentive and good at a test meal – 'a fingerbowl was at my elbow when I picked up a bone to chew.' Cervelles au beurre noir (£1·50) was lightly fried with a lemony black butter – 'a good version of an uncommon dish in Ireland.' Herring roe pâté (£2·25) was delicate, served with sauce maltaise, 'a good idea, though it would have been better with Seville orange or the zest of a sweet one.' Other dishes mentioned are mainly – though not exclusively – fish: monk-fish thermidor (£4·95), fillet of brill au beurre Pernod, prawns provençale, and black soles meunière or Colbert. Plaice portugaise had enough innate freshness to win through a sauce with capers in it, and widgeon Beaulieu with a glossy red sauce was 'as tender as widgeon can be expected to be.' Cheeses are generally in good condition, and more advisable than the sweets, perhaps. Cafetière coffee can be had – at a premium – for the asking. Sometimes they seem to economise on quantities of expensive fish, and a sharp-eyed member noticed a waitress filling a glass from two differently labelled sherry bottles. The wines (from £4) include plenty of excellent white burgundies

427

for the fish if you can stay the course, with Chablis Montmains '77 at £8 and a run of le Montrachet (mostly Barton & Guestier) from '67 to '73 at £20–£30; the colour and taste of the older ones should be assessed critically in the glass. Recorded classical music.

App: James Doherty, H.C., T.N.

KILLARNEY Co Kerry   Map 10

Gaby's Seafood Restaurant
17 High Street
Killarney 32519

Closed Sun; Mon L (exc
July & Aug);
Nov 15–Mar 17
Open 12.30–8
(L 12.30–3, D 6–8)

Alc £7·35 (meal £10·70)

Service 10%
Seats 45
♿ rest
No dogs

Ireen Maes and his wife Gaby are Flemings, which explains a lot in this bistro-like, pine-and-tile restaurant, including the patience needed to get a seat. That is, Mrs Maes and her assistant Eric Claerhoudt cook fresh seafood 'the way we always did at home, undercooked and without mass production, unspoiled by heavy sauces or spices. Canned products, margarine, garlic and curry are banned.' In 1979 they 'hosted 28 nationalities', including a perspicacious German who searched for the non-existent English equivalent of al dente *to describe the texture of his lobster. 'The fish salad platters, hot smoked trout, black sole on the bone, grilled salmon steak, and "four fish Ivernia" (£5·20) were also unforgettable, and the waiting period passes quickly for you can watch lobsters in the* vivier. *Service during the meal itself is efficient but not hectic, and everything looks very clean and fresh.' Irish visitors also agree that 'the hors d'oeuvre seems to display fish of every possible variety', and that the cream sauce for sole is tasty and well made. Haddock in wine (£4) is another speciality. They provide cold meals all afternoon. 'Wine is our hobby,' Mr Maes writes, but he also thoughtfully serves French fruit juices as well as Pinot Chardonnay from Poitou (£3·80), young Sancerre (£8), good Alsace wines at £6 or so, and Corton-Charlemagne '76 (Louis Latour) at £16. Recorded music. More reports, please.*

KINSALE Co Cork   Map 10

Man Friday
Scilly
Cork 72260

Closed L; Sun; Apr 4;
Dec 25 & 26
Must book
D only, 7.30–10

Alc £8 (meal £10)

Service inc
Children's helpings
Seats 70
Air-conditioning

The decor looks as though Man Friday put it together from shipwrecked cargoes without any very obvious guiding principle, but perhaps Philip Horgan's first ideas went up in smoke when local labour had the disastrous idea of 'burning off the thatch' to prepare for alterations. Anyway, the cottage now makes an attractive restaurant, and people who know Mr Horgan has worked with Myrtle Allen at Shanagarry and with Peter Robinson in his Annamoe days (both q.v.) have been beating a path to the door. Inspectors who have followed suit praise his soups (onion, celery and others), plaice stuffed with prawns, mushrooms in cream sauce, cauliflower in cheese sauce and other simple vegetables. Fillet of beef marinated in soy sauce and garlic, and cooked with stir-fried vegetables, also

No dogs
Am Ex, Barclay

*had admirable rice – 'if only the Chinese would cook
like this I'd eat more Chinese food than I do.'
Buttered mussels (£1·95) or prawns au gratin as first
courses, grilled turbot with prawn sauce (£5·50)
and veal zurichoise are other dishes in favour.
Profiteroles, 'just slightly bland' lemon syllabub, and
grape pudding are mentioned among sweets. Coffee is
also praised. Pedrotti carafes are £3 a litre, and among
several fine if dear clarets, Clos l'Eglise '66, c.b., is
£12·50. Recorded music. More reports, please.*

The Vintage
Main Street
off N71
Cork 72502

Rough stone walls, 'beam-to-beam plastic vines' and
– if wind, sea and rain are lashing the harbour – a
glowing stove sum up the look of the Galvins'
restaurant. When tried, their fresh stuffed peach, 'light
and delicate salmon quenelles' in a gentle pink sauce,
good potatoes with cream and onion, spiced
cabbage, and well-risen banana soufflé supported
other accounts of good curried apple soup, coquilles
en brochette and other dishes. Wines from £2·50 (in
1979); Muscadet Domaine du Cléray '78, £6; Ch.
Latour '67, £20. Recorded music. Details are
approximate.

Closed L; Tue;
Wed (Oct–May);
Dec 25 & 26; Jan; Feb
D only, 7–10.30

Alc £7·05 (meal £9·95)

Service 10%

Seats 40
♿ rest (1 step)
No dogs

KINSALE see also wine bar section

KNOCKFERRY Co Galway   Map 10

Knockferry Lodge
Roscahill
off T71
6 m N of Moycullen
Galway 80122

'Dusty' accommodation on the shores of Lough
Corrib, spartan in tone, but food more sybaritic.
Salmon is from Corrib and smoked locally, prawns
and sole are from Galway Bay, lamb from Connemara
and gazpacho Des Moran from the owner's garden.
'Well-planned and competent cooking', though first
courses and sweets are limited. After a year's testing,
Des seems to have settled on vanilla for his home-
made ice-cream except in blackberry season.
Watercress and sorrel graced soups in June. Smoked
pike is recommended by the kitchen. Italian house wine,
£3 the litre. 'Incidental' Irish music. One long table
for patio eating.

Closed L; Nov–Easter
Must book
D only, 7–9

Tdh £5·75 (meal £7·95)

Service 10%
Children's helpings
Seats 39 (parties 60)
Car park

No dogs (exc bar)
10 rooms (2 with bath)
B&B £6
D, B&B £11 (min 3 days)

Meal times refer to first and last orders.

Rosleague Manor
8½ m NE of
Clifden
Moyard 7

Closed Nov–Easter
Must book D & weekends
Meals 1–2.30,
HT 6.30–7.30, 8–9.30

Tdh D £7 (meal £9·50)
Alc (bar) L about £3

Service 10%
Children's helpings
(under 12)
Seats 70
 ▣ rest
Car park
No dogs
16 rooms (14 with bath)
B&B £9–£12
D, B&B £15–£17·50
Fire cert

Recipe in *Second
Dinner Party Book*:
simple gazpacho

'It is a risk to commit yourselves to 14 meals from the same kitchen, but at the end of a fortnight we felt we would entrust our digestions to Paddy Foyle and Nigel Rush for as long as they would have us.' This (English) compliment to the Foyles' Regency house in Connemara, with gardens running down to the water's edge, is qualified when it comes to the sweets, but 'all soups were delicious, with seafood chowder and lobster bisque notable; also claret consommé, gazpacho, and chilled beetroot.' Smoked salmon is generously helped, and another visitor praises the smoked salmon mousse. 'Dressed crab is fresh and tasty, Stilton and other quiches are quite good, and one day there was a commendable shot at pizza.' Fish, naturally, is the forte – 'a huge sea trout cooked the day it was caught proved unforgettable' – and the kitchen is proud of its sauces for skate, prawns provençale, sole, and escalopes of salmon with sorrel and vermouth. Beef and lamb are well hung, and they know how to make béarnaise and horseradish sauces; 'liver was lightly sautéed in wafer-thin slices, exquisite.' Vegetables are of an un-Irish crunchiness, and they seldom fall back on plain boiled when it comes to potatoes. It is a pity – though in the light of all this understandable – that puddings show signs of haste: little variation, poor pastry, ice crystals in rum ice, and bought-in Swiss roll for trifle. Brie may be a better choice, and the French red or Mosel white wines at £2·50 for 50 cl are drinkable: Ch. Pontet-Canet '73 is £9·60 and Mâcon Lugny '78 (Louis Latour) £6·30. Breakfasts and bar snacks are praised – 'the creamy scrambled eggs often need seasoning, though.' Service is amiable and the house 'a pleasure to stay in', though they are not alert to minor faults: 'sheets still too small for the double bed', 'no side knife for buttering their excellent bread at dinner', and so on. No pipes in the dining-room.

App: Joan Taylor, A.W., and others

MALLOW Co Cork   Map 10

Longueville House

 ✓ ♢ ♟

3 m W of Mallow
Mallow 27156

Closed L, Sun, Mon
(exc res); mid-Oct
to Easter
Must book
D only, 7–9

'Not in the same league as —,' one man says. But Mrs O'Callaghan has added a pestle to her tureen by unremitting attention to detail in that fast-vanishing *genre* of cooking known as 'Irish country house'. Unlike most Irish caterers, she seems to have known when she started that her own best was not quite good enough, which is why that same critical inspector is now able to salute such rarities as 'tiny home-grown artichoke hearts dripping with *maître d'hotel* butter, served with red roast beef, and a chocolate roulade filled with coffee cream, cracked and oozing deliciously: surely she learnt that from John Tovey at

Tdh from £9·40
(meal from £10·90)

Service inc
Seats 50
♿ rest (3 steps)
Car park
No dogs
20 rooms (18 with bath,
2 with shower)
B&B from £10·50
D, B&B from £112 p.w.
Fire cert

Windermere?' (q.v.) Fresh orange juice for breakfast and respectable coffee are no less exceptional for the country (alas). The rest of the family do almost as much as the cooks to smooth and cheer a stay in this mellow mansion and park above the Blackwater river. 'Michael O'Callaghan describes himself as "basically a farmer" so the lamb, beef, pork and even veal are as dependable as the salmon and the garden vegetables.' But he also finds time to talk and buy good wine too; and 'even young Donagh and his friend saw that my Daimler was spotlessly cleaned.' Another long-stayer, thinking back to his meals, mentions among other dishes the salmon mousse, the flaky pastry for hot mushroom flan, 'meaty scallops in a subtle wine sauce', 'tasty and varied' cream soups, pickled ox tongue and mustard sauce 'a rare treat', lovingly prepared and cooked vegetables, 'even creamed nettles', and uniformly excellent sweets including (in April) a Christmas pudding. A more temperate admirer scolds an 'assisted' gravy for lamb and 'freezing Sancerre', but on the whole the service of wine does justice to a formidable list. Mr O'Callaghan's own Müller-Thurgau vines are too young as yet to match the English Chilsdown he stocks at £4 or so, but those who can afford it – and are given time at table to browse properly – will not pass easily beyond the six '66 clarets – four of them classed growths – under £10 in 1979, and he is now buying burgundies at source. Bar lunches are for residents only, perhaps in the conservatory. No pipes; no children under 10; wear a tie. (GHG)

App: P. B. Heffernan, P. J. Scherer, K. J. Vaughan, Adrian Scott, K. W. Daley, and others

---

MOYARD Co Galway   Map 10

Crocnaraw
6 m N of Clifden
Moyard 9

Closed Sun D; Mon L;
Apr 4 & 6;
Dec 24–26 & 31; Jan 1
Must book D
Meals 1–2.15, 8–9.30

Tdh L £4·75 (meal £6·90),
D £8 (meal £10·50)

Service 12%
Seats 36
10 rooms (6 with bath)
B&B £12
D, B&B £16
Full board £18 p.d.

Joanne Fretwell is her own cook at this comfortable, informally run hotel by the sea, and since her attitude to salmon is 'you just have to look at it and it's cooked', fish-lovers are pleased with it. Bouquet of seafood, smoked trout, and turbot with crab sauce are other favourite dishes, and 'I recall dressed crab one evening and a superb salmon mousse the other.' Much produce comes from garden, orchard and home farm too, for praiseworthy soups and stuffed lamb; there are also home-baked bread and cakes for afternoon tea. 'They will occasionally feed non-residents on a Sunday evening if the hotel is not full.' Wines (from £2·80) include some sound Dopff Alsace wines and '75 clarets around £5. No provision is made for children under 12 or for dogs. Car park. You may eat in the garden. Am Ex card.

App: Joan Taylor, J. Kenneth and Mary O'Brien, and others

Currarevagh House

4 m N of Oughterard
on lake shore road
Galway 82313

Closed early Oct to Easter
Must book
Meals 1.15, 8

Tdh L £3·50 (meal £5·40),
D £7 (meal £9·25)

Service 10%
Seats 30
♿ rest
Car park
No dogs in d/r
15 rooms (5 with bath)
B&B £11·50
Full board £123·50

You could describe Currarevagh – a Victorian house in 150 acres on the shores of Lough Corrib, now in its fifth generation of Hodgsons – as an anti-hotel which all its guests are pro. In other words, it is a place where you pay to stay – and mostly, must stay in order to eat – but where there is no choice at dinner (with punctuality 'requested and observed as from one good cook to another'), and where the service can only be compared with 'old-fashioned butlering'. Alas, it is also a place where some guests who will surely not be invited again have lit cigarettes between courses (cigars, at least, are banned till coffee). But otherwise there is nothing but pleasure in June Hodgson and Bridie Molloy's soups, devilled eggs, mousses of tomato or smoked salmon, 'fresh lake trout', generously helped roast lamb and beef 'with good roast potatoes too', and perhaps coffee mousse, chocolate Maire, caramelised oranges or 'a superb baked Alaska' for pudding. 'Our friends were amazed at the afternoon teas with drop scones and two cakes.' 'Breakfasts are as good as ever, and are still served beneath John the Baptist's head (silver service).' Some even attempt packed or in-house lunches too. Harry Hodgson is a good guide to his own modestly priced wines (from £2·80) – 'we had Ch. Beaumont '70 (£5·80) twice because it was so nice the first time.' They prefer ties at dinner, and 'at best tolerate children', but a baby who shared his parents' room was royally treated. (GHG)

*App: Joan Taylor, Valerie Yorke, Val Watson,
D. Lisbona, K. W. Daley, and others*

Killakee House
Killakee Road
Dublin 906645 *and* 906917

Josef Frei's hospitable house and capable cooking 'just below the Hell Fire Club on the Glencree Road' would be in the credit category but for slips and confusions hard to excuse at the price. Home-made ravioli (£1·80), veal forestière (£5·40) and soufflé glacé au Pernod (£1·20) made an excellent test meal, but beignets de fromage and avocado mousse with Grand Marnier showed inferior execution or judgement, and vegetables were also erratic. Sole farcie (£6·50) and chicken Kiev are other dishes to try. La Tourelle or La Gravette wines are £3; Ch. Brane-Cantenac '70, £16 on a sound if dear list. Under-sevens are not encouraged. 'Unrelieved James Galway on tape.'

Closed L (exc parties);
Sun; Mon; Feb;
most public hols
Must book
D only, 7–11

Alc £10·75 (meal £14·25)

Service 12½%
Seats 50 (parties 25)

Car park
No dogs
Am Ex, Barclay, Diners

ROSSLARE Co Wexford   Map 10

Strand Hotel
Wexford 32114

'I haven't seen so many satisfied sleepers spread round the lounges since I last trod a luxury liner', and Breda Kelly's hotel, with its numerous diversions and year-round custom, does indeed feel like a beached cruise. The cooking is workmanlike but not what it was, some say, and a test set meal with good green lasagne, mutton hot-pot, buttered swede, and rice pudding, but 'pale, bland' game pâté and 'tinned peach' meringue, tends to support this verdict. Over a hundred wines survive from the late Billy Kelly's collection: prices are still fair, even though Ch. Latour '64 in magnum has gone from £18 to £29 in a year. Car park. No dogs. Details approximate.

Closed mid-Dec to
mid-Feb
Must book
Meals 1–2.15, 7.30–9.15

Tdh L £4·65 (meal £6·55),
D £7·40 (meal £9·55)

Service 10%
Seats 200

 ⅋ rest
Air-conditioning
99 rooms (87 with bath,
12 with shower)
B&B £10–£12

SANDYCOVE Co Dublin   Map 10

Mirabeau
Marine Parade
Dublin 809873

Closed L; Sun; public hols
Must book
D only, 7.30–11.30

Alc £14·60 (meal £20·30)

Service 12½%
Seats 50 (parties 25)
⅋ rest; w.c.
Air-conditioning
No dogs
Am Ex, Barclay, Diners

Sean Kinsella's sea-front restaurant behind a New Orleans wrought iron façade is one from which Irish legends are made, some of them even true. He lives in the style to which his P & O and Paris Ritz training, and his vintage Rolls Royce, have accustomed him. Prices are never mentioned, and some find them unmentionable. He practises – against the grain of today's would-be-French Irish cuisine – the principle that the best food round Dublin is the least interfered with. As a result, says a foreign correspondent after a day in pursuit of the Pope, 'it is one of the very few places that I have dared to visit, late and tired, and simply say, "feed me".' Anyone else who tries this experiment may be offered 'magnificent fresh prawns in garlic butter' followed by well-chosen, plainly cooked escalopes of veal, or lamb cutlets, or chateaubriand (for two), duck or sole. An inspector's dogged attempt to try dishes that might have exploited Mr Kinsella's skill further yielded excellent lobster bisque and 'very possibly the only edible chicken Maryland in the British Isles'. (The kitchen even commits a worthy banana split, if pressed.) Vegetables, 'only so-so' at a test meal, are normally 'lightly cooked and full of flavour'. The bread is superb. Service is good if you like an atmosphere of complimentary drinks and contrived panache. There are about thirty wines (Ch. le Menaudat '75, £9 in 1979). As for price, £50 for two ought to see you through to 1981, if you need or wish to know. Recorded music.

App: Barry J. Edgar, S.S., J.D.M., R.W.A., and others

433

Ballymaloe House

 ▼ ♀

Cork 62531 *and* 62506

Closed Dec 24–26
Must book
Meals 1–1.30, 7–9.30

Tdh buffet L £3·75 (meal
£6·05), D £9·50 (meal
£12·35)

Service 10%
Children's helpings
(under 8, L & HT)
Seats 80 (parties 25)
⟐ rest (1 step)
Car park
No dogs
23 rooms (14 with bath,
3 with shower)
B&B from £7·20

There is only one Ballymaloe in members' affections.
Fourteen years after the *Guide* first heard about this
family mansion and farm that is also medieval castle
and park, and about Myrtle Allen's gradual
transformation of it from an occasional guest-house
into one of Ireland's best-known eating places, it is
showing its age. A test meal towards the end of the
season argued the absence – admitted, on two nights
a week – of the owner's guiding, supervising hand,
with kitchen smells noticeable, a 'leftover' impression
from the hors d'oeuvre and mediocre tastes in the
carrot soup and the orange soufflé. 'Both main
courses – roast pork, and turkey in tarragon cream
sauce – and their vegetables were better, but the
coffee was full of grounds and the wine full of
sediment.' Happily, at other dates other visitors found
the usual scattiness sometimes – 'they lost our dinner
order and we had to re-order just when we were
expecting our first courses' – but also the usual feasts:
at dinner, 'a scallop shell with lobster, salmon and
crab, baked with breadcrumbs', 'delicious Ballycotton
salmon with hollandaise', 'plaice fresher than I have
ever had it, and I live in a good town for fish', 'superb
côte de boeuf, good soups and sauces, and original,
natural-tasting puddings.' 'Cheeses (including Irish
Milleens) were in fine condition and served with little
home-made wheaten biscuits.' The various breads that
also emerge from this kitchen make breakfasts and
the famous buffet meals for residents (notably Sunday
dinner) seem even better. 'Packed lunches easily
stretch to two days.' The girls who serve are friendly
and do their best with a clientele that needs all that
space and informality to achieve the biblical miracle
of lion lying down with lamb: American millionaires
and creative artists have to contend in high summer
with tribes of children needing to get lost (and
usually succeeding). The young are offered high tea
rather than dinner. The wines – which only Ivan
Allen himself understands and serves well – are very
fine, especially in claret, and fairly priced: Ch.
Léoville-Poyferré '73, £7; Ch. Branaire '66, £14.
Rhônes, Beaujolais, and white burgundies are sound
too. Smoking is now barred in the dining-room: a
daring reform which they may need all your
encouragement to enforce. 'Saturday evening folk
music is great fun.' (GHG)

*App: Hilary Murray, D. S. Borton, Louis Kentner,
A. J. R. Stephenson, C.H., and others*

**We rewrite every entry each year, and depend on fresh, detailed reports to confirm
the old, as well as to include the new. The further from London you are, the more
important this is.**

SLANE Co Meath   Map 10

Slane Castle
Drogheda 24207 *and* 24163

Closed L; Sun; Mon;
public hols
Must book
D only, 7–10.30

Tdh £4·50 (meal £7·30)
Alc £9 (meal £12·35)

Service 12½%
Seats 60 (parties 110)
🔄 rest; w.c.
Air-conditioning
Car park
No dogs
Am Ex card

An Irishman entertaining a dozen overseas guests felt a plot was afoot as 'more dishes were off than on, wines ran out, soups and sauces were spilled and draughts raced through the converted servants' hall.' An inspector, too, found the Earl of Mount Charles clearly pained by his trivial questions about how things were prepared and cooked. However, Tommy Fitzherbert's cooking 'uses good ingredients, and is well-meaning and fairly priced.' First courses 'combine talents of smart buying, tasteful garnishing and honest cooking' in smoked mackerel and pineapple mousse, marinated herring fillets and 'undercooked' cheese and bacon quiche. Most game and seafood dishes are outside the set menu ('good roast duck with orange salad, and pheasant with redcurrant jelly, £3·75 extra') and a member wondered how tough casseroled ('née sautéed') pigeon had found its way on. Tarragon chicken arrived as paprika but was otherwise faultless, though rather nakedly presented. Vegetables 'from the castle garden' are lightly cooked. 'Chocolate mousse was the gelatine kind.' Wines, to judge from the 1978 list, are extensive but costly. Mommessin carafes are £3·25 when available, and may suit the cigars sold. Recorded music.

App: Marise Gordon, Linn Morton, K.R.

SNEEM Co Kerry   Map 10

Casey's Seafood Restaurant
New Street
Killarney 45147

G.B.S., Princess Grace and General de Gaulle all passed through Sneem, but it is the boxing, rowing, and fishing Caseys who are enshrined here against a backdrop of rough plaster, hanging pots, turf fires, local timber tables and 'light fittings made from buoys'. 'Very friendly,' all agree, most in a belated rush of reports. Seafood chowder, brown bread and 'fresh dabs coated in brown breadcrumbs served with hot, thick aïoli' are singled out. Michael Casey suggests codling in mustard and cream sauce, scallops in wine, lobster from the *vivier* in brandy sauce (£7), and fish bisque or smoked salmon in the bar. Adequate wines (Ch. Chanteloiseau Graves Sec £3·20). Traditional Irish music.

Closed Oct 21–Easter
Must book D
Meals 12.30–2.30,
6.30–10

Tdh L £3·50 (meal £6·15)
Alc £5·35 (meal £8·20)

Service 10%
Children's helpings
(under 14)

Seats 26
Air-conditioning
Car park (3)
No dogs

VAT is, by law, included in Irish restaurant and hotel prices.

Barberstown Castle
Dublin 288206 *and* 288020

More a home than a castle but well restored 'as far as we could tell through the dim lighting.' Irish speculators and others with a fortune to risk on a Kenmare laureate chef have done well with nettle soup, baked stuffed mussels, and prawns provençale – and 'garlic comes in chunks.' But at a test meal sole Lafayette (filled with dull prawns, £7·95) was unboned and very overcooked, and 'competent' veal Cordon Bleu (£7) was marred by the wrong cheese and sodden vegetables. Sweets and cheeses are a half-way stage on the descent to 'vile' coffee. French house wine is £3·50 a bottle. Recorded music. No children at dinner. (GHG)

Closed Apr 4; Dec 24–26	Service 12½%	Car park
Must book	Children's helpings L	No dogs
Meals 12.30–2.30, 7–10	(under 8)	Am Ex, Barclay, Diners,
	Seats 60 (parties 30)	Euro
Alc £13·10 (meal £17·05)	🔾 rest	12 rooms (3 with bath)
	Air-conditioning	B&B £17·50
		Fire cert

Oyster Tavern
Spa
on Fenit Road
4½ m W of Tralee
Tralee 36102

Closed Sun L; Apr 4;
Dec 25
Meals 1–2.30, 7–10.30

Alc £5·80 (meal £7·30)

Service inc
Children's helpings
Seats 80 (parties 30)
🔾 rest (1 step)
Car park
No dogs

Michael Lynch's world is his oyster, he says, and his vast tavern and its railway waiting-room decor should suit a Russian poet. Of course most people come for the large helpings of seafood, often fresh from Tralee Bay. An inspector's wait for doors to open at 1 p.m. bore fruits de mer, though 'rolled fillets of turbot in delicious Mornay sauce, covered in parsley and Parmesan' bettered the mussels, prawns, salmon and dry crab claws served alongside. Sweets would be wasted (there are none) on diners fresh from combat with 'two complete soles in garlic butter (£4) served with Irish bread and a salad of raw onion rings, red and green peppers, cucumber, lemon, tomato, cabbage and grated carrot in a sweetish vinaigrette.' Three fillets of herring in a 'sharp' sweet-and-sour sauce (£1·75) 'was a rousing alternative to the usual first courses.' Lobster (£10) and salmon (£4·75) come grilled, poached or with mayonnaise, and mussels are served vinaigrette as a main course. 'Bemused wine service', but they let a member drink half of a bottle of Pouilly Fumé for half-price. House wine is £3·75 a litre. Pop music on radio.

App: H. & L.L., C. & T.S.

In the Republic of Ireland some restaurants are licensed to sell wines only (not spirits or beer).

Irish public holidays do not all coincide with English ones.

WICKLOW Co Wicklow   Map 10

Old Rectory
Wicklow 2048

An 'almost-Georgian' rectory rescued by Paul and Linda Saunders and turned into a 'welcoming and relaxing' guest-house. Cuisine is Hibernian-French, 'varied and rethought seasonally.' An inspector in late summer found little seasonal apart from the 'watery' vegetables. But 'admirable' duck livers and savoury pancake, sea trout, and a home-made peppermint meringue were better. Leek soup, duck en croûte, and Champagne Charlie ice-cream also have fans. Saumur-Champigny and Sauvignon ordinaires are £3·50. No pipes or cigars. Tales of summer barbecues (on Thursdays) and Great House dinners welcome.

Closed L; Sun &
Mon (June–Sept exc res);
Sun–Thur (Oct–May exc
res); Dec 24–26 & 31;
Jan; Feb
Must book
D only, 7.30–10

Tdh £7·20 (meal £10·30)
Alc £9·10 (meal £12·45)

Seats 24
♿ rest (3 steps)

Car park
No dogs
6 rooms (1 with bath,
3 with shower)
B&B £11
Fire cert

YOUGHAL Co Cork   Map 10

Aherne's Seafood Bar
163 North Main Street
Youghal 2424

Closed Mon D; Apr 4;
Dec 24
Must book D
Meals 12–2.15, 6.30–10

Alc £7·55 (meal £9·95)

Service 10%
Seats 50 (parties 20)
♿ rest (1 step)
Air-conditioning
Car park
No dogs
Am Ex, Barclay, Diners,
Euro

The neon signs outside the Fitzgibbons' bar and restaurant 'made us apprehensive but we were restored by the sight of the *vivier* for lobsters and oysters, and a bar to sit in. Then we had exquisitely juicy prawns baked in garlic butter and served in specially designed local pottery dishes.' Others too have been struck by the freshness of the fish 'and by the way a hard-pressed member of the family made time to chat to us.' Mussels, scallops, and black sole, on the bone or filleted (£5·95, with vegetables), are other staples, and there is steak if you wish. People have been too dazzled by the fish to tell us about cheeses and sweets this year. Carafino is £2·40; Alsace Riesling £3·50. 'Dress respectably.' Recorded music. As it is a licensed pub (unlike many Irish restaurants, which cannot serve beer or spirits), children under 14 are not admitted. Bar lunches. You may eat outside on the patio.

*App: Philip & Jill Donnellan, Laurence Blackall,
I. Harmer, J. D. Nathan, and others*

NORTHERN IRELAND

BELLANALECK Co Fermanagh Map 10

Sheelin
Bellanaleck
5 m S of Enniskillen
Florencecourt 232

Open L (exc Sun in
winter); Sat; D Wed &
Fri (exc winter)
Closed Apr 6; Dec 25 & 26
Must book D
Open 9 a.m.–9 p.m.
(meals 12.30–2.15,
HT 5–6, 8.30–9)

Tdh buffet £4·50 (meal
6·30), Sat D £8·50 (meal
£10·90)
Alc L £2·65 (meal £4·50)

Service inc L, 10% D
Seats 20

*Three generations of Cathcarts in this pretty thatched
cottage have developed an honourable tradition as a
tea-shop into 'anything from a snack to a substantial
meal at any time of the day.' This may mean coffee
and cakes for tourists, wayfarer's lunches (including
home-made bread – on sale in their supermarket
opposite – and soup as well as cheese, 95p) for hikers,
and inventive dinners for locals and cruise-passengers
on shore-leave. Lunch might include home-baked ham
marinated in honey and fruit (£2, with vegetables),
roast chicken, beef or pork, and an appetising range of
salads. Summer meals are buffet-style (chicken
Elizabeth in curried apricot mayonnaise) except on
Saturday when there is a more elaborate candle-lit
meal: tastes of all hors d'oeuvre and sweets, with a
pre-chosen main course (sole stuffed with prawns,
beef Wellington) and sorbets between courses. As an
inspector says: 'They cater well for purses of varying
size and appetites of varying ambition.' Several wines
(we have not seen the list) from about £2·50.
'Charming service.' Smaller helpings for children.
Car park. No dogs. More reports, please.*

COMBER Co Down Map 10

Old Crow
Glen Road
9 m S of Belfast
Comber 872255

Michel Legrand celebrated this padded room's fifth
birthday and his own arrival with an exotic 'gourmet
dinner'. His *carte* for diners fresh from a day's
commuting is no less ambitious, but too long, as if he
were wary of pruning while grafting on his own
creations (scallops, prawns, mushrooms in champagne
sauce, £4·90; sauté de boeuf Anastasia flamed with
vodka, £7·05). Old Crow entrecôte with its 'pleasing
cream, mushroom and whiskey sauce' has gone, but
sole, tournedos, escalopes (zingara, £5·20) remain.
Note kidneys liégeoise (gin and juniper) from the
chef's homeland. Creamy sweets. Simpler lunches in
bar and dining-room. Hirondelle is 60p a glass.
'Background' music and dancing on Saturdays.
No jeans.

Closed Sun L; July 12; Dec 25	Tdh L £4·60 (meal £8·10)	Seats 65 (parties 115)
Must book D	Alc £10·30 (meal £14·40)	Air-conditioning
Meals 12.30–2.30, 7–9.30		Car park
(Sun 5–8)	Children's helpings (under 12)	No dogs

**Please report to us on atmosphere, decor and – if you stayed – standard of
accommodation, as well as on food, drink and prices (send bill if possible).**

GILFORD Co Armagh   Map 10

Pot Belly
7 m SE of Portadown
Gilford 404

Closed Mon; Sun D
(exc Apr 6); Sat L;
Dec 25 & 26
Must book D
Meals 12.30–2, 7.30–10.30

Alc £8·40 (meal £10·40)

Seats 48 (parties 25)
♿ rest
Air-conditioning
Car park
No dogs

Not a refuge for the corpulent beyond the dieters' pale but an old linen mill (with pottery and leather works adjacent) recreated as an 'intimate' restaurant. The warming pot-belly stove is supported by open fires and candles, and if the mill atmosphere is a reminder that linen's heyday is past, Helen Boyd's cooking is a growth industry. Her reliance on fruit may fool weight-watchers, but an unsparing topping of sliced orange, fresh pineapple and fried banana on a large chunk of pork fillet in wine sauce is hardly *minceur*. An inspector recommends 'tonic' orange and lemon sauce with 'delicate stuffed trout (£2·40 for one fish, £4·70 for two)', as a commentary on restaurant pricing logic. Those who embark on pineapple and prawn gondola (£2·35), 'with mayonnaise and smooth tomato sauce on board the pineapple as well as the prawns', may prefer for main course the relatively conventional kidneys braised in port, honey-roast chicken or mustard rabbit casserole (all £4·35) to 'more-of-same' pineapple stuffed with meat, vegetables and nuts. Chilled avocado soup (90p) was the right colour and thickness but bland and acidic when tried while the Boyds were on holiday. Vegetables, now priced separately, were overcooked at a late meal and the eater wonders if she should have been irked or relieved to find few sweets left at midnight: 'but orange and almond cake shouldn't have been so dry.' French house wines are £4 and vintages are now listed (Ch. St Claude '70, £6·80). Recorded music. Dancing 'by request'.

App: E. & P.W., R.S., J. Ryman

HELEN'S BAY Co Down   Map 10

Carriage Restaurant
Station Square
1 m N of Crawfordsburn
Helen's Bay 852841

Pictures askew and diners asquint in this converted station, dimly lit and 'very quiet except when a train goes by.' Prices are pegged at what they attempt rather than what they achieve, but tomato and orange soup ('a taste of peel'), 'bland' hummus (£1·25), 'crisp and chewy' sucking pig with red wine sauce and fresh fruit (£6), chicory Mornay, fennel, okra and 'good potato latkes' (55p) all show promise. Sauces and stocks may lack finesse and in choosing a sweet do not always go by looks. 'Tinned peaches in gateau, but fresh cream and good macaroons.' Unlicensed, but no corkage. Quiet recorded music.

Closed L; Mon;
Dec 25 & 26; Jan 1
Must book
D only, 7.30–11

Alc £9·05 (meal £12·05)

Seats 30

Car park
No dogs
Unlicensed

Bramley Apple
Old Cope School,
Main Street
Loughgall 318

The village schoolhouse, set in orchards, has been well converted into a rather sombre restaurant with turf fires. Set Sunday lunch (£3·70) or à la carte dinners might offer oeuf champignons à la crème, 'smooth, tasty chef's pâté with redcurrant jelly' (£1·20 à la carte), Swiss pork 'in a creamy sauce with almonds, rather cloying' (£4·15), carefully cooked kidneys, and turbot with lobster sauce (£6·05). Vegetables include crisply fried potatoes and parsnips, 'bland' ratatouille. Apple crumble a better bet than Pavlova. French house wine £3·70 the litre. List includes 'Rolls Royce' Ch. d'Yquem '55 at £21·70 – for the pâté perhaps rather than the crumble. 'Adequate' service. Recorded music. Children for Sunday lunch only. Two or three tables outside. More reports, please.

Closed L (exc Sun); Mon;
July 7–19; Dec 26
Must book
Meals 12.30–2 (Sun),
7.30–10

Tdh Sun L £3·70
(meal £6·35)
Alc £9 (meal £12·30)

Children's helpings
(under 10 Sun L)

Seats 45
 rest; w.c.
Car park
No dogs

The Barn
120 Monlough Road
1¾ m from Saintfield
Saintfield 510396

Closed L; Sun–Tue;
Thur (exc Jan 1)
Must book
D only, 7.30–9.30

Tdh £9·20 (meal £12·65)

Seats 35
 rest (1 step)
Car park
No dogs

Members have responded nobly this year to last year's request for more news of Miss McDonald and Miss Jackson's scrupulously converted barn 'whose excellence we have taken for granted since the early '70s.' True, one couple equally familiar with the place hit an off-night with 'bland' prawn mousseline, 'rather dry' pork medallions and 'raspberry cheesecake of an unfortunate texture.' But even at that meal other favourites were up to standard and, in general, visitors are more than content with Miss McDonald's artichoke or cucumber soups, pâté, stuffed plaice, scallops in cream and wine with savoury rice, flamed kidneys, roast lamb stuffed with lemon and herbs, 'and in season, salmon and venison'. 'Above all there are the rural setting, flowers, and civilised courtesy.' There are a few wines (from £4·60 for a litre of Hirondelle) of no great moment, but Ch. du Mirail '73, a red Graves, is £6·30. Recorded classical music. Please keep us posted on this and other Northern Irish places where eating is a pleasure.

App: Rosemary Cunningham, Ivor Ray, A. P. Webb, E.P.W., and others

PUBS

Criticism of the *Guide* in the trade press last year implied that we must be infrequent visitors to licensed premises because we were bemoaning the poor standard of pub grub when, in fact, there was now more food than ever being served over the bar. Like the publicans they were so stoutly defending, the critics had missed the point, that quantity does not entail quality. You have only to cast an eye over the glossy advertising that affronts the glance of the would-be pub caterer to see what is wrong. It is easy to spend a fortune on misapplied gadgetry. Good Food Club members who have been out and about in town and country pubs over the past year confirm that no machine is proof against lazy or unthinking dependence on it. There are complaints about good steaks being spoiled by interminable frozen peas and chips like impacted sawdust, about the plastic-wrapped cheese that turns a ploughman's lunch into an agrarian operative's in-put, about sandwiches curling up under the heat of illuminated showcases.

The number of pubs recommended by members has fallen this year. This could, of course, mean that members are losing interest or that they are visiting fewer pubs. But it is equally likely that they are becoming more discriminating about what they are offered. This decrease in the number of places recommended is a pity, for those regions where pubs serving decent food were already thin on the ground. The vast majority of pubs in the *Guide* are to be found south of a line drawn between the Wash and the Severn Estuary. Is this a reflection on midland and northern pubs and their masculine, as opposed to family, appeal? Or does it simply reflect the eating and travelling habits of people who buy and use the *Good Food Guide*? There has also been a dearth of recommended pubs in the big cities: London, Birmingham, Manchester, Liverpool, Leeds, Sheffield, Glasgow and Dublin can boast only a handful among them, and *Guide* inspectors in cities usually find better casual food in wine bars than in pubs. Again, why? In neither case can the question be satisfactorily answered without a thorough survey of British pubs and their clienteles. All the *Guide* can do is point to the popularity and profitability of inns that do take trouble, even in localities where they have no serious competitors.

What can a publican do to improve his food? The answer is almost certainly *not* to invest in all the latest machines, spread gingham tablecloths throughout the bar and organise a menu as long as the bar counter. This may be all very well if it is justified by demand and if the pub kitchen and its staff are able to cope. Even so, it is wise to specialise – in pizza, perhaps (one of the fast food trade's best freeze-and-deliver inventions, if trouble is taken to find a good brand), or in soups and salads, or in home-smoked meat and fish. Most pubs, however, would do well to follow a few basic rules, which involve little or no extra work or expense but make for contented regular customers.

First, think genuine. Fresh potatoes and other vegetables, home-cooked ham, and bread from the local baker are always preferable to anything that comes in packets or tins. Second (and this is especially relevant to the smaller pubs), think simple. Too many pubs are now offering pretend-restaurant menus ('snails, £1·80' seen on a bar blackboard the other day) instead of concentrating on what they are good at, even if that means no more than freshly cut sandwiches, or sausages from the butcher round the corner. And third, remember that though pubs can be and are run in many different ways, some responsibilities are inescapable. Restaurants in pubs are all very well – if they measure up to the standard, they are separately listed in the main section of the *Guide*, and even if they do not, their existence is noted in the pub entry. But we are concerned in this section only with food served over the bar, food that can be enjoyed by customers who are also there for the beer or a glass of wine and a chat. At the same time, the customers who are there *only* for a drink and a game of darts must not be forgotten: the fuss and smell that goes with much pub food must surely drive some non-diners to drink – elsewhere.

As for the drink itself, there are some encouraging signs in this direction at least. Virtually every pub listed here now sells wine over the bar, though the actual bottles chosen are seldom any cause for congratulation. And again, a still-growing majority serve unpressurised draught beer, or real ale as it has become known since the advent of CAMRA, the Campaign for Real Ale. We have renewed our liaison with CAMRA, whose annual *Good Beer Guide* lists pubs throughout Britain which serve traditional draught beer of consistently good quality, and we hope that the exchange of information between the two guides will benefit both eaters and drinkers.

Pub entries

The same abbreviations have been used in the pub section as in the rest of the *Guide* (see 'How to use the *Guide*', p. 4) but there are some differences:

The left-hand column of each entry gives the pub's name, its address or location (where necessary), telephone number and weekday opening hours (Sunday hours in England and Wales are universally 12–2, 7–10.30 – except for those Welsh places which do not open on Sundays at all). When food is not served throughout licensing hours, the actual times are shown in the text.

Some pubs, particularly those off the beaten track, do not always serve food during the advertised hours; if in doubt, telephone to check.

Separate restaurants, where they exist, are mentioned only for information and not as recommendations. If pub restaurants are good enough, they are listed in the main section of the *Guide*, with a cross-reference in the pub section.

Rooms, where they exist, are also mentioned for information. People who find the atmosphere of pubs congenial often describe them as much better value than most hotel accommodation.

Beer dispense is described thus:

'from the cask' – drawn by gravity
'pump' – drawn by hand pump (beer engine) or electric pump
'pressurised' – served by, or stored under, carbon dioxide pressure
'air pressure' – served by air compressor

Cider, where listed, is stored and served without carbon dioxide from a cask or similar container.

'Wine' means wine by the glass.

'Children' means they are legally allowed inside the building, but not into a bar where alcohol is served. In England and Wales, children over 14 and under 18 can, at the licensee's discretion, go into any part of a pub but cannot drink alcohol.

The licensee's reply has been accepted without query in many cases, which means that words or phrases such as 'home-made' or 'pump' may not always be accurate: good-quality pies may have been bought in, for instance, and beer served through a hand pump may be pressurised in the cellar.

(CAMRA) at the end of an entry indicates that the pub is listed in the 1980 *Good Beer Guide*, with a reciprocal (GFG) symbol.

ENGLAND

ABBOTSBURY Dorset   Map 2

Ilchester Arms
Market Street (B3157)
Abbotsbury (030 587) 243
and 225
10.30–2.30, 7–10.30
(6–11 Fri, Sat & summer)
Closed Dec 25 evening

'This pub has now promoted itself to a hotel' – an old building in a 'delightful, unspoilt village'. Bar food (L only): scampi £1·60, soup 48p, bubble-and-squeak 25p, home-made pasties 60p, sausage and chips 80p, ham and chips £1·10. Dinner by arrangement only. Devenish bitter and best bitter (pump). Taunton cider. Wine. Children. Fruit machine; bar billiards; darts. Garden. Car park. B&B £8·50. (CAMRA)

AINSWORTH Greater Manchester   Map 5

Duke William
Well Street
Bolton (0204) 24726
11.30–3, 5.30–10.30
(11 Fri, Sat)

A 'country' pub between Bolton and Bury – well patronised by the locals and appreciated for its home-made pies: steak and kidney, chicken, steak and mushroom, all £1·50; braised steak; prawn curry £1·75. Other food includes pâté 65p, grills £1·65–£2·80, and prawn and egg platter £1·50. Food served Mon–Fri, 12–2 only. Whitbread beers. Wine. Juke-box; fruit machine. Bowling-green with seats. Car park.

ALBURY Surrey   Map 3

Drummond Arms
on A248
4 m SE of Guildford
Shere (048 641) 2039
10.30–2.30, 5.30–10.30
(11 Fri, Sat)

A 'fairly simple' pub bounded by a fast-running stream with ducks. A correspondingly simple menu of bar snacks (12–2.30, 7.30–10.30 or 11; not Mon, Sat, Sun D) includes plaice and chips £1·10, chicken curry, sausages 90p, salads, soup, daily special. Ploughman's only Sun L. Separate restaurant (12.15–2.45, 7.30–9.45; closed Sun D, Mon). Range of pressurised beers. Wine. Juke-box; darts; fruit machine. Garden.   B&B £6·50.

ALLERTHORPE Humberside   Map 6

Plough

See main *Guide*

ALMONDSBURY (LOWER) Avon   Map 2

The Bowl
16 Church Road
M5 exit 16
Almondsbury (0454)
612757
11–2.30, 6.30–10.30
(11 Fri, Sat & summer)

An old country pub in a beautiful village (take the third left off A38 towards Gloucester). The service is 'very willing' and the bar food includes home-made pâté 75p, turkey pie 55p, ploughman's 45p–85p, salads 80p–£1·95, things with chips: scampi £2·40, plaice £1·25, steak and kidney pie 75p. Separate restaurant (L only). Courage (Bristol) bitter and Directors (pump). Wine. Juke-box; fruit machine; pool; football machine. Garden. Car park.

ALNWICK Northumberland   Map 8

Market Tavern
Fenkle Street
Alnwick (0665) 2759
11–3, 7–11

Two small bars in a simply decorated but clean hotel. Sue Chapman, the landlord's wife, does the cooking and 'makes a fine job of it' – 'she hates packet and tinned food.' Snacks (from 35p) include soup, toasties and soft, filled rolls. Pressurised Vaux beers. Wine. Children. Juke-box; darts; fruit machine. B&B £4·50.

AMBLESIDE Cumbria   Map 7

Rothay Manor

See main *Guide*

AMERSHAM Buckinghamshire   Map 3

Elephant and Castle
High Street (A413)
Amersham (024 03) 6410
11–2.30, 6–10.30
(11 Fri, Sat)
Closed Dec 25

An Elizabethan house with a pretty façade; full of beams and brasses. Bar food (12–2, 7–9.30; exc Sun): home-made pâté 75p, potted shrimps 85p, ploughman's 70p, smoked mackerel or prawn salad, sandwiches. Separate restaurant (12–2, 7–9; exc Sun). Wethered's special and Trophy (pump). Wine. Garden and patio. (CAMRA)

AMPNEY CRUCIS Gloucestershire   Map 2

Crown of Crucis

See main *Guide*

ANSTY Dorset   Map 2

The Fox
10 m SW of Blandford
Milton Abbas (0258)
880328
11–2.30, 6.30–11
Closed Tue (exc res)

'Everything to all men, in the nicest possible way' – a 200-year-old building in the lee of Bulbarrow with a collection of hundreds of Toby jugs. Bar snacks (60p–£3): ploughman's, choice of 13 meats and 30 salads 'in a stunning array of bowls', and village-made gateaux. Separate restaurant. Hall & Woodhouse bitter and best bitter, Bass (pump), Old Ansty Ale (air pressure). Dorset farmhouse cider. Wine. Children. Juke-box; darts; fruit machine; bar billiards. Lawns. Car park. B&B £7.

ARDLEIGH Essex   Map 3

Wooden Fender
Harwich Road (A137)
Colchester (0206) 230466
11.45–2.30, 6–11
(Sat 11.45–2.30, 7–11)

A wealth of brass and oak beams in this 'excellent' old coaching inn, with 'the best local sausages I've had in England' (70p), according to one appreciative customer. Other bar food (Mon–Fri L) includes gammon £1·40, scampi £1·40, daily dish £1, ploughman's 70p, sandwiches. Cold food only Sat L; none Sun. Adnams' bitter and Tally Ho, Greene King IPA and Abbot ale (pump). Wine. Tables outside. Car park. (CAMRA)

ARRETON see under ISLE OF WIGHT

ASHBURNHAM East Sussex   Map 3

Ash Tree
Brown Bread Street
off B2204
Ninfield (0424) 892104
12–2.30, 7–10.30
(11 Fri, Sat & summer)
Closed Mon

Attractive and popular pub in a pretty and 'hidden' village. Bar lunches only (12–2; 12–1.30 Sun): home-made soup 30p, pâté 70p, salads £1–£2·50, home-made steak and kidney pie £1·05, turkey curry £1·95, grills £1·95–£2·95, ploughman's 75p, quiche 65p; children's dishes 50p–85p. Separate restaurant (12–2, 7–10; closed Mon). Ind Coope Burton ale and Charrington IPA (pump). Wine. Darts; bar billiards. Garden. Car park.

Hours given are opening times. Food may not be served over the whole period.

ASKERSWELL Dorset see SPYWAY

ASTON CREWS Hereford & Worcester   Map 2

White Hart
Lea (098 981) 203
12–2.30, 7–11
Closed Dec 25 evening

A 'real olde worlde country pub in a beautiful location.' Bar food (12–2, 7–10): home-made soup 30p, pâté 65p, steak £3·10, goulash £1·50, turkey and ham pie 65p, cheese and bacon flan 55p. Separate restaurant (12–2, 7.30–10; closed Tue D). Wadworth's pale ale (pump) and 6X from the cask. Wine. Children. Fruit machine. Garden. Car park.

AUSTWICK North Yorkshire   Map 8

Game Cock Inn

See main *Guide*
(CAMRA)

AXMOUTH Devon   Map 2

Ship
S of A3052
5 m W of Lyme Regis
Seaton (0297) 21838
10.30–2.30, 5.30–11
(winter 11–2, 6–10.30;
11 Fri, Sat)

A pleasant pub with 'friendly, obliging and efficient service.' 'Delectable' bar food of 'exceptional value' (12–2, 7.30–10; exc Fri D in winter): mushrooms on toast 80p, crab bisque 45p, home-made pâté 70p, prawns 85p, sirloin steak £2·65, salads from £2·15, sandwiches 50p–75p – but farmhouse soup (35p) was 'transparent, Oxo-style liquid'. Separate restaurant (D only, till 9 p.m.; closed Fri in winter). Devenish bitter and Wessex best bitter from the cask. Taunton cider. Wine. Darts; fruit machine; shove ha'penny. Garden. Car park. (CAMRA)

BANBURY Oxfordshire   Map 2

Unicorn
Market Place
Banbury (0295) 3396
10–2.30, 6–10.30
(11 Fri, Sat)

'Vast expanses of flocked wallpaper more usually found in Indian restaurants' but 'a useful place to know'. Lunchtime bar food only (11–2): ploughman's 60p–70p, basket meals 70p–£1·25, omelettes 75p, sandwiches 40p–50p, beefburger 75p, salads, steaks £2·95. Separate restaurant. Mitchells & Butlers bitter and Bass (pump). Wine. Outside gents'.

BARFORD Warwickshire   Map 2

Glebe Hotel
Church Street
Barford (0926) 624218
10–2.30, 6–10.30
(11 Fri; 7–11 Sat)

'Impressive and well-decorated hotel' which used to be a rectory. Bar food (12.30–2, 7.30–10; exc Sun D): home-made pâté 85p, soup, mackerel, home-made steak and kidney pie £1·95, gammon £1·95, steaks, omelettes, salads from £1·35. Davenports' bitter (pump). Wine. Garden. Car park. B&B £12.

BARNSLEY Gloucestershire   Map 2

The Village Pub
on A433
Bibury (028 574) 421
11.30–2.30, 7–11

Cosy and friendly atmosphere in a popular 17th-century village pub. Bar food (12–2, 7–9; exc Sun D): trout £2·55, plaice £1·85, scampi £2·15, pork chop £1·85, home-made soup 45p, salads £1·85. Wadworth's 6X, Courage Directors from the cask and pump. Wine. Garden. Car park.

BASLOW Derbyshire   Map 5

Cavendish Hotel

See main *Guide*

BASSENTHWAITE LAKE Cumbria   Map 7

Pheasant
off A66
at NW end of lake
Bassenthwaite Lake
(059 681) 234
11–3, 5.30–10.30
(11 Fri, Sat)
Closed Dec 25

An old coaching inn with a 'delightful view' from the lounge and 'courteous and helpful service'. Bar lunches (11–1.45; Sun 12–1.30): soup 35p, smoked salmon £2·35, smoked salmon mousse 90p, eel fillet £2, smoked chicken 90p, prawns with lobster sauce £1·10, Parma ham with melon 95p, cold meats with salad £1. Separate restaurant (12.30–2, 7–8.30). Theakston's bitter and Bass (pump). Wine. Gardens. Car park. B&B from £11.

BATH Avon   Map 2

Park Tavern
3 Park Lane
Bath (0225) 25174
11.30–2.30, 6–10.30
(11 Fri; 6.30–11.30 Sat)

A 'small, ordinary pub' on the west side of Victoria Park, with young barmaids and pleasant service. Bar food (exc Sun; 12–2, 7–9.30; 7–10 Sat) includes soup 30p, pâté 50p, home-made cottage pie 60p, ploughman's 50p–60p, curries 85p, mussels 85p, seafood platter £2·50, salads, rolls, sandwiches, and 'the best pizza in town' £1. 'No chips.' Courage bitter and Directors (pump). Wine. Juke-box; darts; fruit machine; shove ha'penny; dominoes; backgammon. Garden and patio. Car park.

BATH Avon   Map 2

Woods

See main *Guide*

BATH see also wine bar section

BECKHAMPTON Wiltshire   Map 2

Waggon and Horses
at junction of A4 & A361
Avebury (067 23) 262
11.30–2.30, 6.30–10.30
(11 Fri, Sat)
Closed Dec 25

Oak beams and old fire-places in a stone and thatch pub near Avebury Circle. Substantial portions of bar food (until 45 min before closing): steak £3·20, scampi £3, chicken £2·70, salads £1·75, rolls and sandwiches, plus strangely named dishes such as 'one man's meat', 'parson's pâté', 'beefeater's' and 'pig in a poke' (a 'mystery' dish). Wadworth's 6X, IPA and Old Timer (pump). Wine. Fruit machine. Table outside. Car park. (CAMRA)

BEGBROKE Oxfordshire   Map 2

Royal Sun
Woodstock Road (A34)
Kidlington (086 75) 2231
10–2.30, 6–10.30
(11 Fri, Sat)
Closed Dec 25

'Worth going quite a way' to get to this country inn which offers 'superb food at very reasonable prices' (10–2, 6–10), including 'huge and delicious' smoked mackerel, trout £2·10, veal £1·40, home-made pâté £1·10, pizza £1·10, ploughman's 70p–£1·10, 'a really lovely stock soup', sandwiches 50p–75p. Separate lunch and evening menus; more limited choice Sun. Pressurised Ind Coope beers. Wine. Fruit machine. Two gardens. Car park.

BELTHORN Lancashire   Map 5

Grey Mare
on B6232
Blackburn (0254) 53308
11.30–2.30, 7–10.30
(11 Fri, Sat)

A remote moorland pub, which used to brew its own beer when it was a farmhouse. 'Plain, well-presented' bar food (exc Sat L, Mon D; 12–2, 8–10; 8–10.30 Fri, Sat): black pudding 70p, steak muffin 75p, Cumberland sausage 75p, plaice £1·10, cold turkey £1·30, soup 30p (L only), sandwiches 40p–55p; also ploughman's and salads in summer. Thwaites mild and bitter (pump). Wine. Children. Fruit machine. Car park.

BENENDEN Kent   Map 3

King William IV
The Street
Benenden (058 082) 636
11–2.30, 6–11

A 'draughty pub with ingle-nook fire blazing, and clearly popular.' Bar food always available (45p–£1·20): ploughman's, quiche, cottage pie, fish pie, salads, soup. Shepherd Neame bitter and mild (pump), old ale from the cask. Wine. Juke-box; darts; fruit machine; cribbage; skittles. Garden. Car park. (CAMRA)

BIDDENDEN Kent   Map 3

Three Chimneys
on A262
Biddenden (0580) 291472
11–2.30, 6–10.30
(11 Fri, Sat & summer)
Closed Dec 25

A tiny pub, 'over-full of dogs and children.' Bar food chalked on a blackboard (until 30 minutes before closing) likely to include salmon mousse £1, kipper pâté 95p, soup 55p, steak and kidney pie £2·10, quiche £1·95, Hawaiian pork £2·35, chicken and ham loaf £2·15; jugged hare, duck and pheasant casserole in season £2·35. Choice of cask beers, including Whitbread Trophy, Fremlin's Tusker, Adnams' best bitter, Greene King Abbot and Gibbs Mew Bishop's Tipple (winter). Weston's cider. Wine. Darts; shove ha'penny. Garden. Car park.

BIRDLIP Gloucestershire   Map 2

Golden Heart
on A417
1 m E of village
Coberley (024 287) 261
11.30–2.30, 6–10.30
(11 Fri, Sat)
Closed Dec 25

Dating partly from the 16th century, this cosy Cotswold pub specialises in home-made food (12–2.15, 6–9; Sun 12–1.45, 7–9): pâté 85p, ploughman's 85p–95p, sandwiches 45p–55p, stockpot soup 50p, Gloucester sausages and baked potato £1, mushroom casserole £1·20, lasagne £1·20. Wadworth's 6X, Donnington best bitter, Bass, Theakston's bitter and Old Peculier from the cask. Weston's cider. Wine. Darts. Garden. Car park.

BISHOP'S LYDEARD Somerset   Map 2

Rose Cottage

See main *Guide*

BITTESWELL Leicestershire   Map 5

Man at Arms
The Green
Lutterworth (045 55) 2540
12–2.30, 7–11

A Davenports' house offering an 'excellent pub lunch' (Mon–Sat, 12–2): 'huge' ploughman's 90p, soup 35p, ham and chips £1·15, steak and kidney pie 80p, salads 75p–£1·15, chip butty 25p, toasted sandwiches 30p–35p. Davenports' bitter (pump). Wine. Children. Juke-box; darts; fruit machine; skittles. Tables outside. Car park. (CAMRA)

BLEDINGTON Gloucestershire   Map 2

King's Head
3¼ m SE of
Stow-on-the-Wold
Kingham (060 871) 365
10–2.30, 6–10.30
(11 Fri, Sat)

'A really good pub' in a pleasant setting. Lunchtime cold buffet (priced according to what you eat) includes salads, cold meats, pies, quiche, smoked mackerel, cheese. Hot food always available: soup 50p, pâté 85p, savoury pancakes £1·20, steak and wine pie £2·35, rabbit pie £2·15, spare ribs £2·25. Variety of beers, including Hook Norton and Whitbread bitter (pump). Weston's cider. Wine. Darts; fruit-machine; Aunt Sally. Patio and garden. Outside lavatories. Car park.

BLYTHBURGH Suffolk   Map 6

White Hart
on A12
3½ m from Southwold
Blythburgh (050 270)
217
10.30–2.30, 6–11

Built as an ecclesiastical courthouse in 1248 – now 'a lovely place to rest for a while.' Cold food in summer (40p–£2): meats, smoked fish, home-made pasties, 'enormous' salads, plus basket meals from £1·20. Hot food in winter: soup, jacket potatoes, pies, quiche. Separate restaurant (closed D Sun, Mon & Tue). Adnams' bitter and mild, and old ale in winter (pump). Wine. Children (if eating). Seats outside. Car park. (CAMRA)

BODIAM East Sussex   Map 3

Curlew
on A229
Hurst Green (058 086)
272
11–2.30, 6–10.30
(11 Fri, Sat)

17th-century pub in the heart of the old hop-growing region. Self-service buffet (12–2, 7.30–10; £2·45): soup, melon, sweetcorn, chicken curry, hot-pot, fisherman's pie, blanquette of rabbit, cold meats, home-made Scotch eggs, quiche, salads. Separate restaurant (12–2, 7.30–10; closed Mon). Harvey's bitter and old (winter), Whitbread Trophy (pump). Wine. Fruit machine. Garden. Car park.

BOUGHTON Kent   Map 3

White Horse
246 The Street
Boughton (022 775) 343
10.30–3, 6–11

A 15th-century inn on the London/Dover road, with beams, giant bellows as tables, church pews and hops. Bar food includes 'coarse and tasty' home-made pâté 65p, ploughman's 55p, various sandwiches (prawn 75p), lasagne £1·20, treacle tart 55p. Separate restaurant (closed Sat L & Sun). Shepherd Neame bitter and best bitter (pump). Wine. Darts. Children. Covered terrace. Car park. B&B from £6·50.

BOURTON-ON-THE-WATER Gloucestershire
Map 2

Rose Tree

See main *Guide*

BOWLAND BRIDGE Cumbria   Map 7

Masons Arms
Strawberry Bank
Crosthwaite (044 88) 486
10.30–3, 6–10.30
(11 Fri, Sat)

Low ceilings, stone floors and open fires in tiny rooms in a country pub with beautiful views. 'Genuine and wholesome' bar food includes 'delicious' soup 43p, 'gigantic' ploughman's 97p, salads 97p–£1·70, home-made pies £1·07, lasagne, moussaka or cannelloni £1·07. Pressurised Thwaites beers. Wine. Children. Darts; dominoes; cards. Tables outside. Car park.

BRANDON Suffolk Map 6

Great Eastern Hotel
next to the station
Thetford (0842) 810229
11.30–2, 6.30–11

A well-kept old hotel serving bar food at lunch-time and before 9 in the evening: soup, egg mayonnaise, pâté, ploughman's, 'speedy' toasted sandwiches. Separate restaurant. Ind Coope bitter (pump). Wine. Fruit machine; darts; pool table. Car park. B&B. No details from landlord.

BRIDPORT Dorset Map 2

George
4 South Street
Bridport (0308) 23187
10–2.30, 6–10.30
(11 Fri, Sat & summer)
Closed Dec 25 evening

A busy 18th-century pub with low ceilings and open fire. Bar food (12–2, 7.30–10; not Sun L, Thur D): home-made soup 45p, pâté 70p–85p, plaice £1·35, omelettes 65p, chicken curry £1·35, home-made ham, chicken and mushroom pie 95p, steaks £2·50–£3, sandwiches 40p–65p. Palmer's best bitter and IPA (pump). Wine. Children. Darts. B&B £6.

BRIGHTON & HOVE East Sussex Map 3

Cricketers
Black Lion Street
Brighton (0273) 29472
10–2.30, 6–11

A beautiful Victorian pub just off the seafront beside the Old Ship Hotel – 'warm, bright, clean and comfortable.' Bar food always available: home-made cottage pie 60p, chicken and ham or steak and kidney pie 90p, quiche, sausages, sandwiches 35p–55p. Separate Buttery Bar. Watney's fined bitter (pump). Wine. Children. Fruit machine. Seats in stable. Outside gents'.

BRITWELL SALOME Oxfordshire Map 2

Red Lion
on B4009
2½ m off M40
Watlington (049 161) 2304
11–2.30, 6.30–10.30
(11 Fri, Sat)

A country pub near the Icknield Way. Bar food (12–1.45, 7.15–9.45, exc Wed D): sandwiches 30p–40p, ploughmans', pâté 65p, gammon £1·80, fish £1·60, lamb cutlets £1·60, steak £2·80. Brakspear's bitter, special bitter and mild (pump). Wine. Darts; fruit machine. Seats outside. Car park. B&B £5·50.
(CAMRA)

BURHAM Kent Map 3

Toastmaster's Inn

See main *Guide*
(CAMRA)

BURNHAM MARKET Norfolk Map 6

Hoste Arms
The Green
Burnham Market (032 873) 257
10.30–2.30, 6–11

A 'genuinely old' coaching inn with dark panelling and a 'dire flower arrangement in the fireplace.' Lunchtime bar food (80p–£1·50): smoked mackerel, pâté, 'delicious' cod mousse, ham off the bone, cheese, beef, salads. Separate restaurant. Norwich Castle bitter (pump). Wine. Children. Fruit machine; bar billiards; pool table. Car park. B&B £5–£6.

See p. 443 for 'How to use the pub section.'

Do not risk using an out-of-date Guide. A new edition will appear early in 1981.

CALLINGTON Cornwall   Map 1

Coachmakers Arms
N of A390 at junction
with A338
Callington (057 93) 2567
11.30–2.30, 6.30–10.30
(11 Fri, Sat & summer)

A 300-year-old pub, extended to three times its
original size. Bar food (not Sun L) includes
home-made pâté 90p, soup 38p, mackerel 90p,
omelettes £1·65–£1·95, salads £1·95–£3, chicken
£1·85, gammon £2·65. Bass from the cask. Wine.
Fruit machine. B&B £7·50.

CAMBRIDGE Cambridgeshire   Map 3

Fort St George
Midsummer Common
Cambridge (0223) 354327
11–2.30, 6–10.30
(11 Fri, Sat)
Closed Dec 25

An early 16th-century pub, originally on an island in
the Cam, with its own ferry and lock gates. Bar food
(12–2, 6–10; Sun 12–2, 7–10): home-made soup 25p,
cottage pie 80p, macaroni cheese 60p, beef pie 90p,
home-made pâtés 75p, cheese, quiche 60p, salads.
Greene King IPA and Abbot ale (pump). Wine.
Children. Juke-box; fruit machine; Ringing the Bull.
Large garden.

CASTLE ACRE Norfolk   Map 6

The Ostrich
Stocks Green
Castle Acre (076 05) 398
11–2.30, 6.30–11
Closed Dec 25 evening

A 16th-century coaching inn 'where somehow the
landlord manages to find time to cook', including
soup over an open fire at winter lunch-times. Bar
food (not Thur D) includes basket meals 65p–£1·85,
ploughman's 70p, fisherman's lunch 75p, pâté 75p,
'mock caviare' £1·60, smoked trout £1·70, sandwiches
35p–90p. Greene King beers (pump in lounge bar,
otherwise pressurised). Taunton cider. Wine. Children.
Juke-box; darts; fruit machine; pool; dominoes; dice.
Garden. Car park. (CAMRA)

CAVENDISH Suffolk   Map 3

Bull Hotel
High Street
Glemsford (0787) 280245
11–2, 6–11

Dull Victorian façade conceals a 16th-century interior,
with low ceilings and beams. 'Good plain home
cooking' (12–1.45, 6–8.30, exc Sun, Mon D;
90p–£2): steak and kidney pie, Dunmow ham, roasts,
savouries, curries, ploughman's, salads. Adnams'
bitter, mild and old (pump). Wine. Juke-box; darts;
fruit machine; shove ha'penny. Garden and patio.
Car park. B&B £6·50.

CHADDESLEY CORBETT Hereford & Worcester
Map 5

Talbot
High Street
Chaddesley Corbett
(056 283) 388
11–2.30, 6.30–10.30
(11 Fri, Sat)

A 'useful watering place in the desert south of
Birmingham.' 'Excellent' cold buffet (Mon–Sat, 12–2
only; £1·50) includes beef, pork, quiche, veal and ham
pie, Scotch eggs and assorted salads – 'as much as
you can pile on a plate'; hot daily dish £1·50; basket
meals. Separate restaurant. Banks's beers (pump).
Wine. Juke-box; darts. Car park. (CAMRA)

Pubs are represented on the maps by a tankard.

In England and Wales, Sunday opening hours are 12–2, 7–10.30.

CHADDLEWORTH Berkshire   Map 2

The Ibex
Chaddleworth (048 82) 311
10.30–2.30, 6–10.30
(11 Fri, Sat)
Closed Dec 25 evening

An 'uninspiring brick pub' in a pretty village – but
'very pretty' inside. The food is 'magnificent':
stockpot soup 40p, pâté 80p, prawns in garlic butter
£1·50, omelettes 80p, salads £1·10–£1·65, ploughman's
75p–85p, steak sandwich £1·10. Separate restaurant.
Courage best bitter (pump). Wine. Children.
Juke-box; darts; fruit machine; bar billiards; pool
table. Garden. Car park. (CAMRA)

CHICKSGROVE Wiltshire   Map 2

Compasses
2 m SE of Tisbury
Fovant (072 270) 318
12–2.30, 7–10.30
(11 Fri, Sat & summer;
closed Tue L)

An 'unretouched' 16th-century thatched inn with 'a
really enterprising' cold buffet on Sunday. Mon–Sat
bar food (until 10 p.m.; not Tue): ploughman's
60p–70p, soup 35p, pâté 70p, sirloin steak £2·95,
'superb' baked ham £1·35, veal £1·40, trout £1·25,
jumbo sausage 75p, sandwiches from 30p. Separate
restaurant (Thur–Sun, 7–9). Wadworth's 6X, Ind
Coope bitter and Burton ale (pump); Wadworth's
Old Timer from the cask. Bulmer's cider. Wine.
Children. Darts; fruit machine; shove ha'penny; bar
skittles. Garden. Car park. B&B £5. (CAMRA)

CHIPPING Hertfordshire   Map 3

Countryman
on A10
Royston (0763) 72616
11–2.30, 5.30–10.30
(11 Fri, Sat)
Closed Dec 25 evening

A 17th-century pub which has restored one visitor's
faith in landlords, partly because of its 'excellent,
promptly served' bar snacks (35p–£5·50), including
home-made pizza, beefburger, plaice, trout, steaks,
local spicy sausages and chip butties. Greene King
IPA, Adnams' bitter and Marston's Pedigree (pump).
Wine. Children at lunch-time. Cribbage; dominoes.
Donkey rides in summer in the garden. Car park.
(CAMRA)

CHIPPING CAMPDEN Gloucestershire   Map 2

Kings Arms

See main *Guide*

CHUDLEIGH Devon   Map 1

Highwayman's Haunt
Old Exeter Road
Chudleigh (0626) 853250
10.30–2.30, 6.30–11
Closed Sun

Quick and friendly service in a free house more than
600 years old. 'Large menu of bar snacks' (not Sun;
Sat D): sandwiches 75p–£1, home-made soup 43p,
pâté 74p, plaice £1·50, whitebait £1, ploughman's
75p, curried prawns £1·60; daily specials. Separate
restaurant (12.30–2, 7–9; closed Sun). Usher's bitter
(pump). Wine. Children. Terrace. Car park. B&B
promised.

CHURCH KNOWLE Dorset   Map 2

New Inn
Corfe Castle (0929) 480357
10.30–2.30, 6–10.30
(11 Fri, Sat; 11.30 most
public hol weekends &
Chr; supper licence until
midnight)

'Typical country pub' with 'simple and honest' bar
food, including crab sandwiches 60p, pâté 90p,
sausages £1, plaice £1.20, scampi £1.95. Separate
restaurant (D only, 7.30–10; closed Mon). Pressurised
Devenish beers. Taunton cider. Wine. Children.
Fruit machine; darts; shove ha'penny. Garden.
Car park.

CIRENCESTER Gloucestershire Map 2

Plough
Gloucester Road
Cirencester (0285) 3422
10.30–2.30, 6–10.30
(11 Fri, Sat)

Plain and pleasant pub 'with bunches of hops and football photos', popular for its weekday lunchtime cold buffet (12.15–2; from £1): cut a slice from the huge cottage loaf and build your own sandwich (underdone beef, ham, pork, prawns and salad) or try the pies, cheeses or daily hot dish (85p–£1·25). 'Lovely chocolate cake.' Sandwiches and basket meals at weekends and in the evening (8–10). Whitbread pale ale and best bitter (pump). Wine. Darts; fruit machine. Garden. Car park.

CLEOBURY MORTIMER Salop Map 5

Old Lion
High Street
Cleobury Mortimer
(029 95) 395
10.30–2.30, 6–10.30
(11 Fri, Sat)

Pleasant and relatively unspoilt country-town pub with a log fire in the lounge. 'The first pub I've come across,' says one visitor, 'where you make up your own ploughman's . . . with no size restriction.' Other bar snacks (25p–£1·95) include home-made pâté, beef curry, trout, mackerel, cold meats (L only), basket meals, sandwiches, steak. Separate restaurant. Banks's bitter and mild (pump). Bulmer's cider. Wine. Juke-box; darts; fruit machine; dominoes. Seats at front. Car park. B&B £8. (CAMRA)

COBERLEY Gloucestershire see COLESBOURNE

CODICOTE Hertfordshire Map 3

The Goat
High Street (B656)
Stevenage (0438) 820475
10.30–2.30, 6–10.30
(11 Fri, Sat)
Closed Dec 25 & 26
evenings

'The best ploughman's I recall,' reports one visitor to this old pub with beams and low ceilings. Bar lunches (not Sun) also include pâté 70p, and daily specials such as lamb stew and dumplings £1·40, plaice Mornay £1·20, or baked trout £1·60. Sandwiches only in evening (not Tue, Wed, Sun). Ind Coope bitter and mild (pump). Wine. Darts; dominoes; shove ha'penny. Garden. Car park. (CAMRA)

COLESBOURNE Gloucestershire Map 2

Colesbourne Inn
on A435
6 m SE of Cheltenham
Coberley (024 287) 376
10.30–2.30, 6–10.30
(11 Fri, Sat)
Closed Dec 25 evening

An old inn with oak beams and log fires. Bar food available at all times: soup 50p, salads £2, steak £3·50, pâté £1, home-made steak and kidney pie £2·50. Wadworth's 6X, IPA and Old Timer (pump). Wine. Children. Darts; fruit machine; video games. Garden. Car park. (CAMRA)

COMPTON Surrey Map 3

Withies Inn

See main *Guide*

CORNHILL-ON-TWEED Northumberland Map 8

Collingwood Arms

See main *Guide*

(CAMRA) **at the end of an entry indicates that the pub is listed it the 1980 Good Beer Guide.**

CORSE LAWN Gloucestershire   Map 2

Corse Lawn House

See main *Guide*

COWTHORPE North Yorkshire   Map 5

Old Oak
off A1
3 m N of Wetherby
Tockwith (090 15) 272
12–2.30, 6.45–10.30
(11 Fri, Sat)

'All rather modern although meant to be old' – the
victim of a fire early in 1979 but now back in business.
One visitor reports on 'the most attractive cold buffet
I have encountered in England' £2·95 (L only; exc
Mon) with 'a remarkable variety of cold meats, fish
and salads' as well as soup, moussaka, 'excellent' beef
and ham rolls 80p, lasagne £1·35, cottage pie £1·25
and others. Separate restaurant. Tetley's mild and
bitter, Theakston's bitter and Old Peculier, Younger's
bitter (pump). Wine. Children. Garden and patio.
Car park.

CRAWLEY Hampshire   Map 2

Fox and Hounds

See main *Guide*

CRETINGHAM Suffolk   Map 3

New Bell
Earl Soham (072 882) 419
10.30–2.30, 7–11
Closed Dec 25

A 'neat little pub, with some real beams and some
ghastly fakeries' – 'an excellent find for those who can
find it.' Bar food (12.30–2, 7.30–10; 38p–£1·25):
home-made soup, plain and toasted sandwiches,
basket meals, smoked mackerel. Separate restaurant
(12.30–2, 7.30–9.15; closed Sat L; D Sun & Mon).
Adnams' bitter, Tolly Cobbold bitter (pump). Wine.
Darts. Garden. Car park.

CROSBY-ON-EDEN Cumbria   Map 7

Crosby Lodge Hotel

See main *Guide*

CROSSBUSH West Sussex   Map 3

Plough and Sail
on A27
½ m E of Arundel
Arundel (0903) 883118
10.30–2.30, 6–10.30
(11 Fri, Sat)

'An exceptionally pleasant pub – well furnished, very
clean and with cheerful staff.' Bar food (11–2, 6–10;
Sun 12–1.45, 7–10): choice of about 25 hot and cold
dishes, plus lunchtime specials, such as smoked
mackerel £1·65, home-made steak, kidney and
mushroom pie with jacket potatoes £1·75, curry £1·50,
roast chicken £1·70. Separate restaurant (11.45–1.30,
6.45–9.30; closed Sun; Mon D). Pressurised Watney
and Truman beers. Wine. Furnished patio for children.
Car park.

CULLERCOATS Tyne & Wear   Map 8

Piper
Farringdon Road
Whitley Bay (0632)
530272
11–3, 6–10.30
(11 Fri, Sat in summer)

A modern pub on a housing estate near the sea. The
menu changes from day to day (and is limited on
Mondays and weekends) but includes soup 21p,
beefburger 65p, haddock 85p, gammon 88p,
ploughman's 70p–85p, home-made steak and kidney
pie 88p, stottie cakes (Tyneside buns), sandwiches and
salads. Toasted sandwiches (27p) only in the evening.
Bass (pump). Wine. Fruit machine; dominoes; cards.
Tables outside in summer. Car park. (CAMRA)

DEDHAM Essex   Map 3

Marlborough Head
Mill Lane
Colchester (0206) 323124
11–2.30, 6–11

Restored beams and fireplaces in an old pub serving 'cheap and plentiful' bar food: soup, pâtés, salads, 'overflowing' sandwiches. Ind Coope bitter. Wine. Garden. Car park. B&B. No details from landlord.

DEDDINGTON Oxfordshire   Map 2

Holcombe Hotel

See main *Guide*

DENVER Norfolk   Map 6

Jenyns Arms
at Denver Sluice
Downham Market
(036 63) 3366
10.30–2.30, 6–11
Closed Dec 25 evening

Wooden beams in a single 'tastefully furnished' bar. Bar food (until 30 min before closing): scampi and 'masses of good chips' £1·90, ham, egg and chips £1·80, fisherman's platter £1·90, prawn curry and jacket potato £1·10. Separate restaurant (12–2, 7–10.30). Adnams' bitter from the cask. Wine. Children. Juke-box; fruit machine. Riverside garden with peacocks. Car park.

DERBY Derbyshire   Map 5

Ben Bowers

See main *Guide*
(CAMRA)

DEREHAM (EAST) Norfolk   Map 6

Phoenix Hotel

See main *Guide*
(CAMRA)

DORCHESTER Dorset   Map 2

Royal Oak
High West Street
Dorchester (0305) 2423
10–2.30, 6–10.30
(11 Fri, Sat)

'Fast and efficient' service in a town-centre pub offering 'snappy snacks' in the Acorn Bar: soup 26p, home-made quiche 55p, ploughman's 72p–75p, pâté 78p, sandwiches 42p–50p, basket meals £1·05–£1·75, hamburgers £1·45–£1·75, grills 64p–£2·45, salads 82p–£1·75. Separate restaurant (closed Sun). Eldridge Pope Royal Oak and IPA (pump). Wine. Fruit machine. Patio. Outside gents'. Car park.

DRAGONS GREEN West Sussex   Map 3

George & Dragon
on A272
E of Billingshurst
Coolham (040 387) 320
10.30–2.30, 6–10.30
(11 Fri, Sat)
Closed Dec 25 evening

An attractive pub with low ceilings, open fires and 'sensible and appropriate decor'. Bar food (until 20 min before closing) includes ploughman's 65p, sandwiches 35p–60p, salads £1·60, macaroni cheese £1, hot-pot, toad-in-the-hole £1·20. King & Barnes bitter, mild and old (pump). Bulmer's cider. Wine. Children. Darts; fruit machine; bar billiards. Garden. Car park.

EASTBOURNE East Sussex   Map 3

Porthole

See main *Guide*

STD telephone codes are given in brackets. Remember that in some cases, different local codes may apply within the district.

EAST CLANDON Surrey Map 3

Queen's Head
The Street
4 m E of Guildford
Guildford (0483) 222332
11.30–2.30, 6.30–10.30
(11 Fri, Sat)

An early 16th-century inn with ingle-nooks and an often unusual selection of bar snacks (12–2.15, 7–10.15 or 10.45; Sun 12–1.30 only): samosa pie £1·50, Northumberland pan hagarty, Huntingdon fidget pie £1·30, for instance, as well as more conventional food. Separate restaurant (12.30–2, 7.30–10; closed Sun). Ind Coope bitter and Burton ale (pump). Wine. Garden. Car park.

EAST MARTON North Yorkshire Map 5

Cross Keys
on A59
3 m W of Skipton
Earby (028 284) 3485
11–3, 5.30–10.30
(11 Fri, Sat)

A 'cosy' old canalside pub with a friendly atmosphere, but occasional hints of complacency. Bar food includes sandwiches, soup, pâté, cottage pie, basket meals and salads. Theakston's bitter and Old Peculier from the cask or pump. Wine. Separate restaurant. Children. Juke-box; fruit machine; darts. Forecourt. Car park. (CAMRA)

EAST SUTTON Kent Map 3

Prince of Wales
off A274
3¼ m N of Headcorn
Sutton Valence (062 786) 2235
11–2.30, 6.30–10.30
(11 Fri, Sat & summer)

Clean, comfortable and pleasantly furnished bar, which is part of the Shant Hotel. 'Imaginative' list of bar snacks includes 'substantial' lentil soup 50p, chili con carne 65p, rabbit and pork pie – all prepared on the premises, according to a notice. Separate restaurant. Young's special bitter (pump). Wine. Seats outside. Car park. B&B £15·85.

EGGLESTON Durham Map 8

Three Tuns
Church Bank
Teesdale (0833) 50289
11–3, 6.30–10.30 (11 Sat)
Closed Mon (exc public hols) & Dec 25

A village pub on the green. Bar food (12–1.45, 7.30–9.45; not Sun D; 35p–£2·55) includes soup, steaks, pâté, steak pies, salads and home-made bread. Separate restaurant. Pressurised Whitbread beers. Wine. Children ('usually'). Dominoes. Patio and garden. Car park.

ELSWORTH Cambridgeshire Map 3

George and Dragon
41 Boxworth Road
Elsworth (095 47) 236
10.30–2.30, 7–10.30
(11 Fri, Sat)

Old-fashioned, beamed pub with 'lots of things hanging from the roof.' 'Very generous' portions of bar food (until 30 min before closing): soup 60p, pâté 85p, tenderloin of pork £1·90, moussaka £1·65, goulash £1·65, salads £1·35–£1·90, sandwiches 45p–85p (exc Sat D). Separate restaurant (12–2, 7.30–9.30; closed Sun, Mon). Tolly Cobbold bitter, Cantab (pump) and Old Strong from the cask. Wine. Children. Darts; fruit machine. Patio and garden. Car park.

ESSENDON Hertfordshire Map 3

Rose and Crown
22 High Road
Hatfield (070 72) 61229
11–2.30, 6–10.30
(11 Fri, Sat)
Closed Dec 25 evening

A local customer points to the success of the lunchtime food (not Sun) which includes hot-dog with 'enormous' sausages 35p; ploughman's, soup and 'generous portions' of pâté, all 50p. Ind Coope bitter, and Burton ale (pump). Wine. Darts; fruit machine; skittles. Garden. Car park. (CAMRA)

EVERCREECH Somerset   Map 2

Natterjack
Evercreech Junction
on A371
N of Castle Cary
Ditcheat (074 986) 253
11.30–2.30, 6.30–11

An old railway hotel, recently restored with beams, brasses and 'indifferent pictures'. Efficiently served bar food (12–2, 7–10.30): ploughman's ('about the best in the West') 85p, cannelloni £1, cold meat platter £2·95, home-made steak and mushroom pie £1·65, curried beef £1·75, salads, sandwiches, elaborate gateaux. Separate restaurant (D only, Tue–Sat; 7–10.30). Wadworth's 6X, Courage Directors (pump). Wine. Fruit machine. Patio. Car park.

EWHURST GREEN East Sussex   Map 3

White Dog
Village Street
Staplecross (058 083) 264
Summer: 11.30–3, 6.30–11
Winter: 12–3, 7–11
Closed Dec 25 & 26

'A welcoming staff and friendly service' in an attractive pub. 'Excellent' bar food includes soup, 'mouth-watering' prawns in garlic butter 95p, pâté 95p, steak and kidney pie £1·20, shepherd's pie £1·10, seafood pie £1·45. Harvey's bitter, Fremlin's bitter and Bass (pump). Bob Luck's cider. Wine. Children. Darts; snooker; swimming-pool (residents and club members only). Terrace. Car park. B&B from £6·50.

EXETER Devon   Map 1

White Hart
South Street
Exeter (0392) 79897
11–2.30, 5–10.30
(11 Fri, Sat)

An old coaching inn – the only hotel owned by Davy's Wine Bars (*q.v.* in London section) – with snacks in the 'pleasing and old-fashioned' Wine Room: pâté 75p, prawns 85p, soup 25p, steak and oyster pie £2·50, bacon and eggs £1·45, ham or beef £1·60, turkey pie £1·60. Separate restaurant (12.15–2.15, 7–10). Courage bitter (pump). Wine. Children. Garden. Car park. B&B from £10·25.

EXMINSTER Devon   Map 1

Swan's Nest
Station Road (A379)
Exeter (0392) 832371
11–2.30, 5.30–10.30
(11 Fri, Sat)

A converted farmhouse with leather and horse brasses in a dark atmosphere. Bar food (12–2, 6.15–10): salads 96p–£2·10, pâté £1·08, baps or sandwiches 64p–74p (£1·15–£1·25 with salad). Choice of pressurised beers. Wine. Fruit machines. Patio ('not for children'). Car park.

FADMOOR North Yorkshire   Map 8

Plough Inn

See main *Guide*

FALMOUTH Cornwall   Map 1

King's Head
Church Corner
Church Street
Falmouth (0326) 315273
10.30–2.30, 6–10.30
(11 Fri, Sat)

A 400-year-old coaching inn with antique advertising signs. Bar lunches (12–2; not Sun; 85p–£1·20) include home-made cheese and potato pie, quiche, 'traditional English' pies, 'tasty' moussaka, lasagne, home-baked ham and salads. Separate restaurant (7–10.30; closed winter). Devenish bitter and Cornish best bitter (pump). Wine. Fruit machine. (CAMRA)

Do not risk using an out-of-date Guide. A new edition will appear early in 1981.

FARNSFIELD Nottinghamshire Map 5

White Post
off A614
Mansfield (0623) 882215
12.30–2, 7.30–10
(1 a.m. Fri, Sat; closed
Sun evening)

'A real haven of comfort on an otherwise bleak route.'
The bar food (not Sat L, Sun) includes ploughman's
80p, sandwiches 70p, whitebait 90p, 'lavish plate' of
chicken and ham with 'absolutely fresh' salad £2·30,
rabbit pie £1·75, spare ribs £1·75, hot-pot £2·25.
Separate restaurant (closed Sat L; Sun D). Pressurised
Mansfield beers. Wine. Juke-box; fruit machine; bar
billiards. Car park.

FAUGH Cumbria Map 8

String of Horses
5 m E of M6, exit 43
3 m S of A69
Hayton (022 870) 297
11.30–3, 5.30–10.30
(11 Fri, Sat)

An attractive 17th-century pub with beams and
several little alcoves. Friendly service of bar food:
soup 35p, smoked mackerel 85p, grills £1·35–£3·75,
curry £1·85; seafood platter and help-yourself salads
£2·45 (L only); sandwiches and salads (D only). Dish
of the day £1·50. Separate restaurant (D only,
7.30–10.30). Variety of pressurised beers. Wine.
Children. Fruit machine. Patio. Car park. B&B
£14·50–£16·50.

FIDDLEFORD Dorset Map 2

Fiddleford Inn

See main *Guide*

FINDON West Sussex Map 3

Findon Manor

See main *Guide*

FINGEST Buckinghamshire Map 3

Chequers

See main *Guide*

FINGLE BRIDGE Devon Map 1

Anglers' Rest
off A30 & A382
Drewsteignton (064 721)
287
10.30–2.30, 7–10.30
(11 Fri, Sat & summer)

A comfortable, clean and friendly pub in 'a setting of
fantastic beauty'. Bar food (12–2, 7–10): soup 40p,
whitebait 70p, home-made pâté 70p, home-made
steak and kidney pie £1·55, local steaks £3·25–£4·15,
ploughman's 70p–£1, salads £1·95. Separate restaurant
(L only; 12.30–2). Courage bitter, Bass and Wadworth's
6X (pump). Bromell's local cider. Wine. Children.
Riverside terraces. Car park.

FLITTON Bedfordshire Map 3

White Hart

See main *Guide*

FORDCOMBE Kent Map 3

Chafford Arms
4 m W of Tunbridge Wells
N of A264
Fordcombe (089 274) 267
10.30–2.30, 6–10.30
(11 Fri, Sat)

An old stone building clad in creeper: the public bar
is crowded and smoky; the saloon 'far more comfy'.
Cooked bar food (12.30–2, 7.30–9.30) includes
chicken or scampi in the basket £1·65–£1·85, home-
made pies with vegetables £1·35, pâté 80p, bread and
cheese, salads, quiche 50p. Fremlin's bitter (pump).
Bob Luck's cider. Wine. Darts; fruit machine;
video machine. Garden. Car park.

FORTY GREEN Buckinghamshire Map 3

Royal Standard of England
1 m NW of Beaconsfield
Beaconsfield (049 46) 3382
10.30–2.30, 6–10.30
(11 Fri, Sat)

'The place to go with tourists or children' – a famous old inn, surrounded by delightful scenery in the Chilterns. 'Large quantities' of bar food (no prices stated) includes 'good selection of cheeses', cold meats, specially baked local bread, salads; home-made soups and brandy pâté in winter. Marston's Pedigree and Owd Roger, Samuel Smith's bitter (pump). Wine. Garden. Car park. (CAMRA)

FOSSEBRIDGE Gloucestershire Map 2

Fossebridge Inn
on A429
3 m SW of Northleach
Fossebridge (028 572) 310
11–2.30, 6–11
Closed Dec 25 evening

A Georgian riverside inn in the Cotswolds with 'a fine choice of bar food' (12–2, 7–9.30; Sun 12–1.30, 7–9.30): home-made soup 60p, pâté 90p, omelettes £1·20, trout £2·90, home-made cottage pie £1·10, Cotswold pot (stewed beef in beer) £2·40, cold table £2, ploughman's, sandwiches. Some food in Buttery Bar. Usher's best bitter and Mitchells & Butlers bitter (pump); Thomas Usher 1060 from the cask in winter. Wine. Darts; fruit machine. Garden and riverside terrace. Car park. B&B from £7·50.

FOWLMERE Cambridgeshire Map 3

Chequers
on B1368
Fowlmere (076 382) 369
11.30–2.30, 6–10.30
(11 Fri, Sat)
Closed Dec 25 & 26

A 'pleasing atmosphere' and 'excellent value' in an old inn – though opinions on the service vary. Selection of cold meats and seafood £3–£5, plus dishes such as 'delicious' turkey pancake £1·90, steak and kidney pie £2·25, and mushrooms in batter £1·75. Separate restaurant (12.30–2, 7.30–9.30). Tolly Cobbold bitter and Cantab (pump). Wine. Garden. Car park.

FRENCHBEER Devon Map 1

Teignworthy Hotel

See main *Guide*

FYFIELD Oxfordshire Map 2

White Hart
just off A420
Frilford Heath (0865)
390585
10.30–2.30, 6.30–10.30
(11 Fri, Sat)

Originally a chantry house; a pub since the 16th century. Bar food (12–2, 7–10 or 10.30; 45p–£2·95) includes game soup, pigeon and peas, hare, ploughman's, steak and salad, 'excellent' sandwiches. Separate restaurant. Theakston's bitter and Old Peculier from the cask; Bass, Morland's bitter and Wadworth's bitter (pump). Weston's cider. Wine. Children. Darts; fruit machine. Garden. Car park.

GEORGEHAM Devon Map 1

Rock Inn
Rock Hill
Croyde (0271) 890322
Summer: 11–2.30, 5.30–11
Winter: 11.30–2.30,
7–10.30

A 'good example of a Devon pub not designed for and swamped by holiday makers.' Bar food (12–2, 7–10): summer – local crab £1·75, chicken pie £1, ploughman's 60p–65p, rolls 38p; home-made casseroles in the evening; winter – home-made soup 42p, pasty 38p, gammon sandwich 42p. Usher's best bitter from the cask. Taunton cider. Wine. Children. Darts; fruit machine; table skittles; draughts. Garden. Car park.

GITTISHAM Devon Map 2

Combe House

See main *Guide*

GLYNDE East Sussex Map 3

Trevor Arms
off A27
Glynde (079 159) 208
10–2.30, 6–10.30
(11 Fri, Sat)

'A very posh pub, with expensive carpets, velvet furnishings and a prima donna's room upstairs.' Bar food includes 'gorgeous, underdone, tender beef sandwiches' 50p, steak, scampi, plaice, home-made steak and kidney pie, salads, cold platters. Harvey's best bitter and old (pump). Wine. Darts; fruit machine. Garden. Car park. (CAMRA)

GODSTOW Oxfordshire Map 2

Trout Inn
Oxford (0865) 54485
2 m NW of Oxford
11–2.30, 6–10.30
(11 Fri, Sat)
Closed Dec 25 evening

A 'cheery' Bass Charrington house in a 'romantic' riverside setting – 'is it beginning to rest on its laurels?' Bar food (no prices stated) includes sandwiches, pies, quiche, sausages, Scotch eggs, salads. Separate restaurant (12–2, 7–10). Pressurised beers. Wine. Children. Terrace. Car park.

GOOSTREY Cheshire Map 5

Crown
111 Main Road
off A535 & A54
Holmes Chapel (0477)
32128
11.30–3, 5.30–10.30
(11 Fri, Sat)

An old farmhouse near Jodrell Bank – now a friendly pub with 'nicely served' bar food (not Mon): soup, scampi, chicken, toasted sandwiches, pâté, pizza, lunchtime specials. Separate restaurant (7.30–10.30; Wed–Sat). Marston's Pedigree, Burton bitter and mild (pump). Wine. Children. Darts; fruit machine. Tables outside. Car park. (CAMRA)

GREAT BARRINGTON Gloucestershire Map 2

Inn for All Seasons

See main *Guide*

GREAT DUNMOW Essex Map 3

Queen Victoria
on A120
Great Dunmow
(0371) 3330
11–2.30, 6–10.30
(11 Fri, Sat)

A 'quiet, restful pub', built in the 15th century. Bar food includes special lunch (not weekends) £1·40, ravioli 85p, pâté £1·20, soup 65p, spaghetti bolognese £1·20, scampi £1·70, home-made steak and kidney pie £1·70, ploughman's 65p, sandwiches 40p. Separate restaurant. Tolly Cobbold bitter and Original (pump). Wine. Children. Garden. Car park.

GROOMBRIDGE Kent Map 3

Crown
3½ m SW of
Tunbridge Wells
Groombridge (089 276)
361 *and* 742
10.30–2.30, 6–11
Closed Dec 25 evening

A 16th-century free house with beams and ingle-nooks. Bar snacks (12–2, 6–8): soup 40p, ploughman's 60p, pâté 80p, cold meat salads £1·35, home-made beefburgers £1·35, steak and kidney pie £1·10. Separate restaurant (7.45–9.45; closed Sun). Harvey's bitter and old (winter), King & Barnes bitter, Fremlin's Tusker (pump). Bulmer's cider. Children. Garden. Car park. B&B £7·50.

Pubs are represented by a tankard on the maps, wine bars by a wine glass.

HAVANT Hampshire   Map 2

Old House at Home
2 South Street
Havant (0705) 483464
10–2.30, 6–10.30
(11 Fri, Sat & summer)

The 'oldest building in Havant' serves lunchtime bar
food only (12–2; not Sun): sandwiches, filled cottage
rolls, plaice, scampi, meat and fish salads; daily
specials 82p–£1·50. Separate restaurant (closed Sun).
Gale's bitter, HSB, light mild and 5X (pump). Wine.
Darts; fruit machine. (CAMRA)

HELFORD Cornwall   Map 1

Shipwright's Arms
Manaccan (032 623) 235
10.30–2.30, 6–10.30
(11 in summer)

A 'fairly stark' pub with an old-fashioned bar,
wooden chairs, benches and tables. Bar food (12–2,
7–9.30): cold lunchtime buffet, including crab and
prawn salads £2·75, mackerel £1·35, ploughman's 65p,
pasty 36p; steak, scampi, plaice in the evening.
Pressurised Devenish beers. Wine. Children. Riverside
terraces. Car park.

HENNOCK Devon   Map 1

Palk Arms
off B3193
Bovey Tracey (0626)
833027
11–2.30, 6–10.30
(11 Fri, Sat)

A 16th-century inn overlooking the Teign valley. Bar
food (£2·50–£4·50) includes rump steak, gammon,
cold buffet, curry, shepherd's pie; Irish stew in winter.
Usher's bitter (air pressure). Hills' cider. Wine. Darts.
Benches outside.

HINDON Wiltshire   Map 2

The Lamb
2 m S of A303
Hindon (074 789) 225
10–2.30, 6–10.30
(11 Fri, Sat)

Friendly old coaching inn in the centre of a small
village. 'Surprisingly extensive' bar menu (12–2, 7–10):
soup, sandwiches from 30p, bread and cheese 50p,
salads from £1·25, 'excellent' home-made pâté,
'splendid' curry; daily lunch (exc Sun). Separate
restaurant (12.30–1.30, 7.30–9). Wadworth's 6X,
IPA and Old Timer (pump). Wine. Children. Shove
ha'penny. Garden. Car park. D, B&B £12·50.

HOLNE Devon   Map 1

Church House
Poundsgate (036 43) 208
Summer: 11–2.30, 6–11
Winter: 11–2, 7–10.30
(11 Fri, Sat)
Closed Dec 25 evening

An ancient hostelry in the centre of a tiny village on
the edge of Dartmoor. Bar food (until 30 min before
closing, or 10 p.m.): soup 38p, pâté 75p, scampi £1·28,
trout £1·50, chicken £1·50, steak £3·63, chicken curry
£1·60, ploughman's 77p–95p, pasty 43p. Separate
restaurant with same menu. Bass, Blackawton bitter
and Headstrong (winter), all on pump. Hills' cider.
Wine. Children. Darts; fruit machine; dominoes;
cribbage. Patio. Car park. B&B £8·95. (CAMRA)

HOLT Dorset   Map 2

Old Inn
1 m from Wimborne
Wimborne (0202) 883029
11–2.30, 6.30–10.30
(11 Fri, Sat & summer)

'A really nice pub' offering 'attractively laid-out' bar
food in 'plentiful quantity' (not Sun D Oct–Feb):
soup 40p, whitebait 90p, pâté 70p, smoked salmon
£1·65, steaks £2·55–£3·45, 'excellent' home-made
steak and kidney pie £1·70, duckling £3·35, sole £4·55,
plaice £3, hamburger 55p, salads £2·10–£3, sandwiches
65p–80p. Pressurised Hall & Woodhouse beers. Wine.
Garden. Car park.

HOLYWELL Cambridgeshire   Map 6

Old Ferryboat
St Ives (0480) 63227
11–2.30, 6–10.30
(11 Fri, Sat)

'Cars and boats jostle almost for the same space' in front of this old riverside pub, reputedly haunted by a 17-year-old girl who killed herself for the love of a woodcutter 900 years ago. Bar food (Mon–Sat, 12.30–2 only) includes soup 40p, home-made pâté 95p, ploughman's 75p, scampi £1·60; daily special £1·25. Separate restaurant. Greene King Abbot ale from the cask. Wine. Children. Garden and terrace. Car park. B&B £9·20.

HORTON Dorset   Map 2

Horton Inn
off B3078
Witchampton (025 884) 252
11–2.30, 6–10.30
(11 Fri, Sat)
Closed Dec 25 evening

One visitor found the cool atmosphere a delight on a hot day and food being pleasantly served in the bar: 'absolutely delicious' home-made soup 70p, pâtés 95p, sandwiches from 55p, salads from £1·75, cottage pie £1·45, mixed grill £1·75, curries £1·50, daily dishes from £1·70. Separate restaurant. Eldridge Pope Royal Oak and IPA (pump). Wine. Patio and garden. Car park. B&B £15.

HOUGHTON West Sussex   Map 3

George and Dragon
on B2139
Bury (079 881) 225
11–2.30, 6–10.30
(11 Fri, Sat & summer)

Charles II stopped here after his defeat at Worcester in 1651 – a clean, comfortable pub at the foot of the Downs. 'Nicely prepared' bar food: home-made soup 40p, chicken and chips £1·30, pâté 85p, sandwiches 40p–95p,'generous' ploughman's 75p–85p, salads £1·60–£2·10, pan-fried trout from £2·40; L and D menus vary. Separate restaurant (D only 7–9.30; closed Sun). Young's special bitter, King & Barnes bitter (pump). Wine. Garden. Car park. (CAMRA)

HOUGHTON-ON-THE-HILL Leicestershire   Map 5

Rose and Crown
69 Uppingham Road (A47)
Leicester (0533) 412044
10–2, 6–10.30
(11 Fri, Sat)

An old coaching inn, modernised in Georgian style. Buffet lunches only (Mon–Fri), though 'skittle parties catered for.' 'Still the best cold meats I have found anywhere,' says one visitor. 'Excellent value' – £1·65. Sandwiches 40p. Bass and Mitchells & Butlers mild (pump). Wine. Long alley skittles. Car park.

HOVINGHAM North Yorkshire   Map 8

Worsley Arms

See main *Guide*

HULL BRIDGE Humberside   Map 8

Crown and Anchor
2 m NE of Beverley
Leven (0401) 42816
11–3, 6–10.30 (11 Fri, Sat)
Closed Dec 25 evening

'Pretty and unpretentious riverside pub, full of friendly locals', on the Hornsea side of Beverley. Wide range of bar food (12–2, 7.30–10; 25p–£1·40): home-made pies (pigeon, meat and potato), beefburgers, ploughman's, scampi, plaice, sandwiches. Two-course Sunday lunch £1·65. North Country bitter and mild (pump). Wine. Children. Juke-box; darts; fruit machine; pool. Seats outside. Car park.

HUNTINGDON Cambridgeshire   Map 3

Old Bridge Hotel   See main *Guide*

ICKHAM Kent   Map 3

Duke William
The Street
Littlebourne (022 778) 308
10.30–2.30, 6.30–10.30
(11 Fri, Sat & summer)

A 'very pleasant' old coaching inn with a good range of snacks (until 30 min before closing; not Sun), including cold meats 85p, home-made pâté 65p, beefburger 35p, home-made soup 60p, curry £1·35, sandwiches 40p–60p, ploughman's 65p. Young's bitter and Winter Warmer, Courage Directors, Fremlin's bitter, Bass (pump). Wine. Darts; fruit machine; bar billiards; shove ha'penny; table skittles. Terrace and garden. (CAMRA)

IDDESLEIGH Devon   Map 1

Duke of York   See main *Guide*

IDEN GREEN Kent   Map 3

Royal Oak
3¼ m SE of Cranbrook
Benenden (058 082) 585
10.30–2.30, 6–10.30
(11 Fri, Sat)
Closed Mon (exc
public hols)

Difficult to find (take the Sandhurst turning at Benenden crossroads) but 'friendliness is the order of the day' in this free house. 'The proprietor selects food personally on morning visits to market.' Bar food (12–2, 7–9.30) includes prawns in garlic butter ('a delight' at £1·20), smoked trout £1·25 ('substantial and mouth-watering'), home-made steak pies, crab, lobster, sole, soft roes, sausages. Separate restaurant. Range of pressurised beers. Wine. Fruit machine. Garden. Car park.

ISLE OF WIGHT   Map 2

White Lion
Arreton
Arreton (098 377) 230
10.30–2.30, 6–11

'Attractively decorated with copper and brass and always spotlessly clean.' 'Consistently good' bar snacks (25p–£1·50) include cheese, pâté, home-made broth, veal, ham and egg pie. Whitbread Trophy and mild from the cask. Bulmer's cider. Wine. Children. Darts; fruit machine. Garden. Car park. (CAMRA)

KELSALL Cheshire   Map 5

Morris Dancer
Chester Road (A54)
Kelsall (0829) 51291
11.30–3, 5.30–10.30
(11 Fri, Sat)
Closed Dec 25

An old coaching inn which 'appears to be surprisingly unspoiled.' Bar food (until 10 p.m.): soup 20p, ploughman's 60p, pâté 60p, local steak and kidney pie 65p, ham salad 75p, sausage and chips 60p, curry 75p, scouse 70p, sandwiches 30p. Greenall Whitley bitter (pump). Wine. Fruit machine; bar billiards. Tables outside. Car park.

KING'S BROMLEY Staffordshire   Map 5

Royal Oak
at junction of A515 &
A513
Yoxall (0543) 472289
11–2.30, 6.30–10.30
(11 Fri, Sat)

A former farmhouse attached to the manor house. Bar food always available: steak sandwich and chips £1·30, omelette £1, ham 95p, beef 95p, cheese 75p, beef curry £1·05, fried chicken £1·20. Separate restaurant. Pressurised Ansells' beers. Wine. Darts; dominoes. Garden. Car park.

KING'S NEWTON Derbyshire   Map 5

Hardinge Arms
Melbourne (033 16) 2724
10.30–2.30, 6–10.30
(11 Fri, Sat)
Closed Dec 25 evening

An old, beamed pub with open fires but two bars have been modernised 'and rather spoilt'. Bar food (12–2.15, 6–10.15; not Sun) includes half-lobster (when available) £3, smoked salmon £1·80, seafood platter £1·50, beef £1·70, chicken £1·40, ploughman's 65p–70p, soup 25p, sandwiches 40p–55p. Ansells' bitter, Marston's bitter (pump). Wine. Car park.

KINGSTON NEAR LEWES East Sussex   Map 3

The Juggs
The Street
Lewes (079 16) 2523
10–2.30, 6–10.30
(11 Fri, Sat)

'A lovely old pub with a beautiful tranquil atmosphere and plenty of room.' Bar food (12–2, 6–9.30; not Sun D): 'superb' sausages 90p, haddock £1·35, scampi £1·50, spaghetti bolognese 85p, home-made pies 70p, ploughman's 50p, sandwiches 35p–55p, pâté 60p. Martlet's bitter and Bass from the cask. Wine. Children. Video machine; darts. Seats outside. Car park.

KINTBURY Berkshire   Map 2

Dundas Arms

See main *Guide*
(CAMRA)

KIRKBY OVERBLOW North Yorkshire   Map 5

Shoulder of Mutton
1½ m E of A61
Harrogate (0423) 871205
11.30–3 (2 in winter),
5.30–10.30
(11 Fri, Sat)
Closed Dec 25 evening

A 'very congenial' atmosphere in an old stone pub in a pretty village. Bar food includes filled rolls 25p–38p, steak and kidney pie 36p, pâté 65p, soup (winter only) 25p, mixed meat salad (summer) £1·40. Tetley's bitter and mild (pump). Wine. Children. Darts; fruit machine; bar billiards; shove ha'penny. Garden. Car park. Caravan site.

KNOWSTONE Devon   Map 1

Masons Arms
7 m E of South Molton
off A361 & B3221
Anstey Mills (039 84) 231
Summer: 11–2.30, 6–11
Winter: 12–2, 7–10.30
(11 Fri, Sat)
Closed Dec 25 evening

'A lovely thatched and ancient pub in a remote village.' Bar food (until 30 min before closing): soup 50p, ham with pineapple and cheese on toast 80p, pâté 75p, ploughman's 60p, cold platter £1·50, devilled chicken £1·50, pasty 75p, sandwiches 45p; daily special 95p (home-made pies). Separate restaurant (D only, 7.30–9). Hall & Woodhouse best bitter and Cotleigh Tawny bitter from the cask. Wine. Darts; fruit machine; dominoes; draughts; cards. Benches outside. Car park. B&B from £7·50.

KNUTSFORD Cheshire   Map 5

David's Place

See main *Guide*

Some pubs off the beaten track do not always serve food at times notified. Phone to check.

(CAMRA) **at the end of an entry indicates that the pub is listed in the 1980 Good Beer Guide.**

LANCASTER Lancashire   Map 7

Brown Cow
44 Penny Street
Lancaster (0524) 66474
10.45–3, 5.45–10.30
(11 Fri, Sat)

Small, warm pub with friendly atmosphere behind an 'unprepossessing exterior'. Bar food (12–2; Mon–Sat, L only) all served with peas and jacket potato or chips: home-baked chicken and mushroom or steak and kidney pie 85p, chicken £1·10, gammon £1·15, farmhouse grill 95p, savoury flan 85p, pizza 85p. Buns in the evening. Yates & Jackson bitter and mild (pump). Wine. Juke-box; darts; fruit machine; cards; dominoes.

LANGTON HERRING Dorset   Map 2

Elm Tree
on B3157
Abbotsbury (030 587) 257
11–2.30, 6–10.30
(11 Fri, Sat)

'Lots of brass' in this cosy 16th-century inn with log fires. Bar menu chalked on blackboard (11.30–2, 7–10; Sun 12–1.30, 7–10): soup 25p, ploughman's 80p–£1, home-baked gammon £1·20, meat platter £1·50, slimmer's special £1·40, basket meals, sandwiches. Devenish Wessex bitter (pump). Wine. Patio and garden. Car park.

LAPWORTH West Midlands   Map 5

Boot Inn
Old Warwick Road
Lapworth (056 43) 2464
11–2.30, 6–10.30
(11 Fri, Sat)

This canal-side pub 'makes a relief from the prawn cocktails and over-cooked steak the district seems to prefer.' The food includes pâté 65p, soup 40p, smoked salmon £2·20, steak £2·75, omelettes £1·65, cold meats and shellfish. Whitbread bitter (pump). Wine. Darts; fruit machine. Garden. Car park.

LECHLADE Gloucestershire   Map 2

Crown
High Street
Lechlade (0367) 52218
11–2.30, 6–10.30
(11 Fri, Sat & summer)

A 17th-century coaching inn – 'rather crude and basic and reminiscent of a French bar, but food and service are excellent.' Bar snacks: home-made hamburgers 80p–£1·50, roast chicken £1·45, home-made pâté 90p, ploughman's 65p–75p, cold buffet £1·20–£1·60; range of hot meals changes daily – home-made soup 45p, saddle of lamb £1·95, steak £2·95, beef provençale £1·85, trout £2·20, and many others. Separate restaurant. Large range of beers, including Morland's bitter, Wadworth's 6X, Hook Norton bitter and mild (pump) and Wadworth's Old Timer from the cask. Weston's cider. Wine. Juke-box; darts; fruit machine. Live music Tue (no food late that evening). Garden and yard. B&B £5·75. (CAMRA)

LEOMINSTER Hereford & Worcester   Map 4

Baron's Cross Inn
Baron's Cross Road
Leominster (0568) 2098
11–2.30, 6–10.30
(11 Fri, Sat)

A barman told one visitor sampling the 'excellent, help-yourself buffet': 'If you don't get enough, it's your own fault.' Lunch-times only (12–2; Sun 12–1.30; £1·40): beef, pork, ham, chicken, turkey, pork pie, quiche, salads, cheeses, fruit; curry 90p, ploughman's, sandwiches. Evenings: sandwiches only. Whitbread beers. Wine. Children. Darts; dominoes. Car park.

LEWES East Sussex   Map 3

Pelham Arms

See main *Guide*

LEYBURN North Yorkshire   Map 8

Bolton Arms

See main *Guide*

LINCOLN Lincolnshire   Map 6

Wig and Mitre
29 Steep Hill
Lincoln (0522) 35190
11–3, 5.30–10.30
(11 Fri, Sat)
Closed Dec 25; Jan 1

'All beams and plaster, tapestry and wood chairs'; a
14th-century building with bars up and down stairs.
Bar food (until 30 min before closing): egg cocotte
with garlic bread 80p, salads £1·05–£1·35, ploughman's
70p–80p, six pâtés 70p–75p, sandwiches 35p–70p; hot
dishes chalked on blackboards 85p–£2·65. Samuel
Smith's bitter (pump). Wine. Fruit machine. Seats
outside. (CAMRA)

LITTLE WASHBOURNE Gloucestershire   Map 2

Hobnails Inn
on A438
4 m off M5, junction 9
Alderton (024 262) 237
and 458
10.30–2.30, 6–10.30
(11 Fri, Sat)

'This is what I call a good country pub – no
pretensions.' Dating in part from 1474 and run by the
same family since 1743. 'First-class' bar food (exc
Dec 25; 30p–96p): forty kinds of Scottish baps with
'plenty of filling', pâté, soup, large variety of sweets.
Separate restaurant (12–2, 7–10; closed D Sun & Mon).
Pressurised Whitbread beers. Bulmer's cider. Wine.
Juke-box; fruit machine; skittles. Patio and lawn.
Car park.

LIVERPOOL Merseyside   Map 5

Everyman Bistro

See main *Guide*

LONG MELFORD Suffolk   Map 3

Crown Inn
Hall Street
Sudbury (0787) 77666
11–2, 6–11

A listed building, dating back to 1620 or before. Bar
food includes soup 30p, game pie £1·35 and pâté 60p,
all home-made; scampi £1·75, quiche £1, ploughman's
75p. Separate restaurant (12–1.45, 7–9.30). Greene
King IPA and Abbot ale, Courage Directors, Adnams'
bitter (pump). Wine. Darts; fruit machine. Garden.
Outside gents'. Car park. B&B from £9·50.

LONGPARISH Hampshire   Map 2

Plough
Longparish (026 472) 358
10.30–2.30, 6–10.30
(11 Fri, Sat)

A village pub with ducks in 'an exceptionally large
and pleasant garden.' Bar food (12–2, 7–10 or 10.30,
exc Mon D): home-made soup 50p, pâté 80p, salads
£1·30–£2·75, savouries on toast 45p–£1, daily hot dish
£1·50–£2·85. Separate restaurant (Tue–Sat D only).
Pressurised Whitbread beers. Wine. Fruit machine.
Patio and garden. Car park.

LOWER SWELL Gloucestershire   Map 2

Old Farmhouse

See main *Guide*

Wine bars are represented by a wine glass on the maps, pubs by a tankard.

LYDFORD Devon   Map 1

Castle
Lydford (082 282) 242
11–2.30, 7–10.30
(11 Fri, Sat & summer)
Closed Dec 25

A 16th-century free house next to Lydford Castle and providing attentive and friendly service of bar snacks (until 30 min before closing): home-made soups 45p–55p, home-made pâté 75p, crab sandwiches 78p, jacket potatoes 65p, ploughman's 55p–70p, scampi £2; cold buffet (12–2 – 'excellent value if you're there early'). Separate restaurant (12–2, 7.30 & 9.30). Courage bitter (pump). Hills' cider. Wine. Darts; fruit machine. Verandah and garden. Car park. B&B £8. (CAMRA)

LYMPSTONE Devon   Map 1

Globe
The Strand
Exmouth (039 52) 3166
10.30–2.30, 5.30–10.30
(11 Fri, Sat)

One visitor reckons this old village inn on the Exe estuary is 'the best pub I've ever entered.' Bar food (12–1.30, 7–10.15; Sun 12–1.15, 7–10.15): soup 25p, salads 90p–£5·50 (fresh lobster or crawfish as available), salmon or crab £1·50, sandwiches 50p–55p, ploughman's 45p. Home-made curries and cottage pies in winter. Selection of pressurised beers. Hills' cider. Wine. Darts; fruit machine; cards; dominoes.

MAIDENSGROVE Oxfordshire   Map 2

Five Horseshoes
4½ m NW of Henley
Nettlebed (0491) 641282
11–2.30, 6–10.30
(11 Fri, Sat)
Closed Dec 25 evening

'Wellies are much in evidence' at this 'nice little pub.' Bar food (not Mon): pâté, soup, ploughman's, toasted sandwiches; daily dish, including country meat pie, smoked salmon and prawn quiche, curries, around £1·35; warm suppers in winter (Tue–Thur, Oct–Mar; must book) including venison stew, rabbit casserole, oxtail hot-pot. Brakspear's bitter and special (pump), old ale (winter) from the cask. Gaymer's cider. Wine. Darts. Garden. Car park. (CAMRA)

MALHAM North Yorkshire   Map 8

The Buck
5 m E of Settle
Airton (072 93) 317
11.30–2.30, 6–10.30
(11 Fri, Sat & summer)

Stone-built inn in centre of village – one of the few with a bar especially for walkers; 'an oasis in a wilderness.' 'Good' bar food includes ploughman's £1, pie and peas 60p, fish and chips £1·15, sandwiches 45p, smoked mackerel salad £1, home-made soup 35p, home-made steak and kidney pie 75p. Theakston's bitter and Younger's XXPS bitter from the cask. Wine. Cider. Children. Juke-box; darts; football machine. Garden. Car park. B&B £7 (in 1979).

Most places will accept cheques only when they are accompanied by a cheque card or adequate identification. Information about which credit cards are accepted is correct when printed, but restaurants may add to or subtract from the list without notice.

Inspections are carried out anonymously. Persons who pretend to be able to secure, arrange or prevent an entry in the Guide are impostors and their names or descriptions should be reported to us.

MANACCAN Cornwall Map 1

New Inn
off B3293
S of Helford
Manaccan (032 623) 323
11–2.30, 6–10.30
(11 Fri, Sat & summer)

A small pub of 'two rooms knocked into one' – 'unpretentious, attractive and very friendly.' Bar food (11–2, 7.30–10; Sun 12–1.30, 7.30–10): home-made soup 30p, crab soup 50p, home-made pâté 65p, ham and onion pie 50p, ploughman's 65p, sandwiches from 40p; salads in summer £1·30; home-made fish or cottage pie in winter. Devenish Cornish bitter from the cask. Taunton cider. Wine. Darts; shove ha'penny; dominoes; cards. Beer garden. Outside lavatories. Car park. (CAMRA)

MARKET LAVINGTON Wiltshire Map 2

Green Dragon
High Street
Lavington (038 081) 3235
10–2.30, 6–10.30
(11 Fri, Sat)

A 'friendly, unaffected 18th-century pub in a nice village' offering 'excellent' bar snacks (12.30–2.15, 7–10.15): sandwiches 33p–75p, home-made soup 35p, ploughman's 65p, salads £1·25–£1·70, sausages and chips 95p, scampi £1·55, mixed grill £1·85. Separate restaurant. Wadworth's 6X, IPA and Old Timer (winter) on hand-pump. Wine. Darts; bar billiards; shove ha'penny; dominoes. Garden. Car park. B&B £5·75.

MARSTON TRUSSELL Northamptonshire Map 5

Sun Inn

See main *Guide*

MAYFIELD East Sussex Map 3

Rose and Crown

See main *Guide*

MENTMORE Buckinghamshire Map 3

Stag Inn

See main *Guide*

MIDHURST West Sussex Map 3

Royal Oak
Chichester Road
Midhurst (073 081) 4611
Summer: 10.30–2.30, 6–11
Winter: 11–2.30, 6–10.30

A pleasant olde-worlde pub with low ceilings and two acres of grounds overlooking the South Downs. Bar food (usually until 9 p.m.; not Sun D): 'excellent' home-made pâté 95p, soup 50p, chicken and chips £1·50, pancake rolls £1, grills £2·95–£4·25, sandwiches 45p–75p, salads £2·25–£2·55. Separate restaurant (12–1.45, 7–9; closed Sun; Mon in winter). King & Barnes bitter and old ale (winter), Whitbread Pompey Royal and Trophy (pump). Wine. Darts; fruit machine; dominoes; chess. Garden. Car park. (CAMRA)

Towns shown in black on our maps contain at least one recommended restaurant, pub or wine bar (see map key). The dot denotes the location of the town or village, not the establishment. Where necessary, we give directions to it in the entry. If you can, help us to improve them.

Please report to us on atmosphere, decor and – if you stayed – standard of accommodation, as well as on food, drink and prices (send bill if possible).

MILBORNE PORT Dorset   Map 2

Queens Head
on A30
2 m E of Sherborne
Milborne Port (0963)
250314
11.30–2.30, 6.30–10.30
(11 Fri, Sat & summer)

A Georgian stone pub with an unattractive exterior but a friendly welcome – 'they could not have done more for us.' Bar food (L only; Fri, Sat D promised): 'superb' home-made pizza 60p, 'excellent' pâté 65p, hot Somerset smokie (haddock in cheese and cider) 70p, 'very wide range' of sandwiches 30p–60p; daily specials £1·10–£1·30. Separate bistro-type restaurant opening this spring. Courage Directors, Wadworth's 6X and IPA, Hook Norton bitter (pump), Wadworth's Old Timer from the cask. Wine. Darts; fruit machine; bar skittles. Enclosed courtyard. Car park. B&B £6.

MILLTHORPE Derbyshire   Map 5

Royal Oak
Sheffield (0742) 890870
11.30–3, 5.30–10.30
(11 Fri, Sat)

Friendly, relaxed atmosphere in a small pub with an open fire and beams. 'Richly varied' selection of bar food (Mon–Sat, 12–2 only; not public hols): sandwiches 45p–70p, Royal Oak Special (bacon and black pudding in a bap) 65p, cheeses 70p–85p, pâté 80p, smoked mackerel 90p, ploughman's £1·10–£1·20. Ward's Sheffield best bitter, Darley's bitter (pump). Wine. Tables outside. Car park.

MILTON STREET East Sussex   Map 3

Sussex Ox
off A27
Alfriston (0323) 870840
Winter: 11–2.30, 7–10.30
(11 Fri, Sat)
Summer: 10.30–2.30, 6–11

A country pub with an adventure playground for children – 'a super place to take the family.' Bar food (12–2, 6 or 7–9.30; 80p–£1·25): home-made soups, casseroles and other hot meals in winter; cold buffet, home-baked bread, pâté, quiche, mackerel in summer. Harvey's bitter, mild and old (pump). Wine. Children. Darts; shove ha'penny; Devil among the Tailors. Garden. Car park.

MORPETH Northumberland   Map 8

Gourmet

See main *Guide*

MOULTON North Yorkshire   Map 8

Black Bull

See main *Guide*

MURCOTT Oxfordshire   Map 2

Nut Tree
Charlton-on-Otmoor
(086 733) 253
11–2.30, 6.30–10.30
(11 Fri, Sat)
Closed Dec 25 evening

A well-kept old thatched pub, serving 'excellent' bar food (not Sun, Mon D): fish platter, 'tender' gammon, fish £3·10, steaks £4·50, lunchtime snacks and special meals 'generally under £1', and 'a large selection of cold food'. Ind Coope bitter and Burton ale from the cask. Cider. Wine. Draughts; cards. Patio. Car park.

NEEDHAM MARKET Suffolk   Map 3

The Swan
9 High Street
Needham Market (0449)
720280
11–2.30, 6.30–11
Closed Dec 25 evening

'A nice pubby pub' with bar food from 12 to 2 and until 10: home-made soup 32p, home-baked rolls, pâté 60p, ploughman's 54p, omelettes 60p; daily dish £1·10. Separate restaurant (12.30–2, 7.30–9.30; closed Sun D). Tolly Cobbold bitter and Original (pump). Wine. Children. Fruit machine. Car park.

NETHER WALLOP Hampshire   Map 2

Five Bells
Wallop (026 478) 572
11–2.30, 6–10.30
(11 Fri, Sat)

A pleasant old pub 'with a fair sprinkling of well-off country types'. Bar food (11–2, 6–9.45; not Wed D, Sun): pâté 80p, home-made soup 30p, ploughman's 65p–75p, 'very tasty' sausages and bread 65p, salads 80p–£1·10, toasted sandwiches 55p–80p, daily specials 'always less than £1'. Marston's Burton bitter, Pedigree and mild (pump). Wine. Darts; fruit machine; bar billiards. Garden. Car park.

NEWBOLD-ON-AVON Warwickshire   Map 5

Barley Mow
64 Main Street (B4112)
¾ m from M6, junction 1
Rugby (0788) 4174
11–2.30, 6.30–10.30
(7–11 Fri, Sat)

An old canal-side building, now completely renovated – 'not a pretty pub at all.' Bar food (Mon–Sat L only): soup 26p, pâté 55p, ploughman's 70p, home-made pie and vegetables £1·15, gammon £1·60, cold meat platter 95p, rolls 25p. Separate restaurant. Mitchells & Butlers bitter and mild, Bass (pump). Wine. Children. Dominoes; cards. Car park.

NEWLANDS VALLEY Cumbria   Map 7

Swinside Inn
1½ m S of Portinscale
Braithwaite (059 682) 253
11–3, 5.30–10.30
(11 Fri, Sat)

A large, whitewashed pub with magnificent views and 'good, hefty helpings' of bar food (12–1.45, 6–8.45; Sun 7–8.45; not Mon D): basket meals 90p–£1·60, rolls 35p, pâté 80p, steaks £3–£4, pork chop £2·60, Swiss pancakes £2·20, trout £2·40, local salmon £3·30. Jennings' bitter (pump). Wine. Children. Juke-box; darts; fruit machine; bar billiards; dominoes. Garden and verandah. Car park. B&B from £6·50.

NEWTON Cambridgeshire   Map 3

Queen's Head
on B1368
1 m off A10 at Harston
Cambridge (0223) 870436
11.30–2.30, 6–10.30
(11 Fri, Sat)
Closed Dec 25

A mixture of building styles – the earliest part being Elizabethan – but 'sadly needing a coat of paint.' Bar food includes home-made soup 45p, sandwiches 40p–45p, stuffed baked potatoes in winter 40p. Adnams' bitter and old from the cask. Bulmer's cider. Wine. Darts; fruit machine; bar skittles; dominoes. Tables outside in summer. Car park. (CAMRA)

NORTHREPPS Norfolk   Map 6

Church Barn

See main *Guide*

ODIHAM Hampshire   Map 2

The George
High Street
Odiham (025 671) 2081
10.30–2.30, 5.30–10.30
(11 Fri, Sat)
Closed Dec 25 evening

'Eat fish and stay thin' is the motto of this old hotel – and visitors confirm that the fish is the main attraction: 'beautifully cooked' cod, plaice, haddock, mackerel. There are also home-made chicken pie, curries, salads, sandwiches and bowls of shellfish (49p–£1·60). Courage bitter, mild and Directors (pump). Wine. Fruit machine. Garden. B&B £9·20.

Hours given are opening times. Food may not be served over the whole period.

OLDBURY-ON-SEVERN Avon   Map 2

Anchor
Thornbury (0454) 413331
11.30–2.30, 6.30–10.30
(11 Fri, Sat)

A mill house until 1620 – now a clean and simple country pub with good service of bar snacks (exc Sun L): cheese 34p–44p, roast beef £1·16, home-made pâté 52p, turkey pie 74p, smoked spare ribs 60p; hot lunches, including rabbit pie 85p, prawn and mussel chowder £1, lamb pilaff 95p. Theakston's bitter, Marston's Pedigree (pump), Robinson's bitter, Bass, Theakston's Old Peculier from the cask. Bulmer's cider. Wine. Fruit machine; darts. Large garden. Car park. (CAMRA)

OLD SODBURY Avon   Map 2

Dog Inn
Badminton Road
M4, junction 18
Chipping Sodbury
(0454) 312006 *and* 317053
10.30–2.30, 6–10.30
(11 Fri, Sat)
Closed Dec 25 evening

Poor external appearance belies the character and atmosphere of the beamed interior of this 400-year-old pub on the village green. Bar food always available: moussaka 75p, ploughman's 80p, snails £1·40, seafood cocktail £1·20, mackerel £1, pork kebab 95p, fried mussels 65p, curries, crab £1·50. Daily lunches 80p. Separate restaurant (12–2.30; 7–10.30 or 11). Pressurised Whitbread beers, though pumps promised. Children. Juke-box; darts; fruit machine; skittles. Garden. Car park.

ONECOTE Staffordshire   Map 5

Jervis Arms
4 m E of Leek
Onecote (053 88) 206
12–2.30, 7–10.30
(11 Fri, Sat)
Closed (Oct–Apr)
Tue & L Wed

Pleasant, quiet pub at the bottom of a pretty valley. All the bar food is home-made (12–2, 7–10.30): ploughman's with 'marvellous' cottage loaf 65p, shepherd's pie 40p, pizza 70p, steak £2·60, chicken £1·10, scampi £1·25, 'super' soft rolls 20p–24p. McEwan's 70/- and 80/-, Winkle's Saxon Cross bitter, Ansells' bitter and Marston's Pedigree (pump). Bulmer's cider. Wine. Children. Juke-box; darts; fruit machine. Garden. Car park. (CAMRA)

PATTISWICK Essex   Map 3

Compasses
off A120 between
Braintree and Coggeshall
Coggeshall (0376) 61322
10.30–2.30, 6–11

'Beautiful, peaceful surroundings' in a little pub where bar food is always available: ploughman's 'for a mere 60p', pâté, basket meals 75p–£1·45, sandwiches 30p–40p. Separate restaurant (12–2, 7–10.30; closed Mon L; Sun). Greene King IPA and Abbot ale, Adnams' bitter, Courage Directors (pump). Wine. Children. Darts; fruit machine. Garden. Car park.

PETER TAVY Devon   Map 1

Peter Tavy Inn
off A386
3 m NE of Tavistock
Mary Tavy (082 281) 348
11.30–2.30, 5.30–10.30
(11 Fri, Sat & summer)

'Efficient and friendly' service in this 15th-century pub, not to be confused with the nearby Mary Tavy Inn. Bar food (12–2, 7–10): sandwiches 55p–81p, ploughman's 71p–82p, pâté 82p, smoked salmon flan £1·25, salads £1·50–£1·65, soup 49p–71p, hot daily dish £1·65, steak buns £1·82–£2·20. Large range of beers from the cask, including Charles Wells bitter, Usher's best bitter, Bass, Courage Directors, Gibbs Mew Bishop's Tipple. Three ciders. Wine. Large beer garden. Outside lavatories. Car park.

PIDDLEHINTON Dorset   Map 2

Thimble
Piddletrenthide (030 04)
270
11–2.30, 6–10.30
(11 Fri, Sat)

A tiny, thatched pub with low ceilings and log fires. Bar food (50p–£2·50) includes pâté, chicken or scampi in the basket, quiche, ploughman's, prawns. Separate restaurant (Wed–Sat D only; 7.30–9.30). Pressurised Hall & Woodhouse beers. Wine. Garden. Car park. B&B £8.

POOLE Dorset   Map 2

Dolphin Hotel

See main *Guide*

PORLOCK WEIR Somerset   Map 1

Ship Inn

See main *Guide*
(CAMRA)

PORTINSCALE Cumbria see
NEWLANDS VALLEY

PRIORS HARDWICK Warwickshire   Map 2

Butchers Arms

See main *Guide*

RAMSBURY Wiltshire   Map 2

The Bell at Ramsbury

See main *Guide*

RAVENGLASS Cumbria   Map 7

Ratty Arms
Ravenglass (065 77) 676
11–3, 6–11
Closed Dec 25

A former railway station, at one end of the Ravenglass-Eskdale miniature steam railway. Bar snacks (12–2, 7–9.30): ploughman's 70p, mackerel £1·25, baked potato with cheese 60p, hot Cumberland sausage, home-baked ham £1·80; scampi £1·60 and steak £1·75 in the evening. Jennings' bitter (pump). Wine. Children. Juke-box; darts; fruit machine; pool table in winter. Seats on forecourt. Car park.

RIPLEY Surrey   Map 3

Anchor
High Street
Ripley (048 643) 2120
11–2.30, 6–10.30
(11 Fri, Sat)

Built around 1252 – a long low-gabled building with beams, low ceilings and ingle-nook. Bar food (12.15–2.15, Mon–Sat only; 60p–£1·20): home-made pies (turkey and ham, steak and kidney, and shepherd's), curries, haddock, mackerel, pâtés, ploughman's, salads, soup. Ind Coope Burton ale (pump). Wine. Children. Darts. Patio. Car park.

ROMALDKIRK Durham   Map 8

Rose and Crown
on B6277
Teesdale (0833) 50213
11–3, 6–10.30
(11 Sat)
Closed Dec 25

An 'attractive old stone-built pub' with a friendly welcome and log fires. Bar food (35p–£5·40): 'excellent home-made pea and ham soup', home-made pâté, mackerel, scampi, 'outstandingly good' meat and potato pie, grills, salads. Separate restaurant. Theakston's bitter (pump). Wine. Children. Dominoes. Car park. B&B £9·85. (CAMRA)

ROWSLEY Derbyshire   Map 5

Peacock Hotel

See main *Guide*

ST IVES Cambridgeshire   Map 6

Slepe Hall   See main *Guide*

ST MAWES Cornwall   Map 1

Rising Sun   See main *Guide*

SEAVINGTON ST MARY Somerset   Map 2

The Pheasant   See main *Guide*

SEIGHFORD Staffordshire   Map 5

Holly Bush
near M6, exit 14
Seighford (078 575) 280
12–2.30, 7–10.30
(11 Fri, Sat)
Closed Dec 25

'A real gem' – lots of silver coins and little alcoves, and friendly service. Bar food: ploughman's, 'delicious' French onion soup 45p, 'substantial' seafood platter £1·45, plaice and chips £1·50, whitebait 95p. Pressurised Ansells' beers. Wine. Children. Darts; fruit machine. Garden. Car park.

SELLACK Hereford & Worcester   Map 2

Lovepool Inn   See main *Guide*
(CAMRA)

SELMESTON East Sussex   Map 3

Barley Mow
on A27
Ripe (032 183) 322
10.30–2.30, 6–10.30
(11 Fri, Sat & summer)
Closed Dec 25

A well-patronised old coaching inn, midway between Lewes and Polegate. Bar food (12–2.15, 7–10.15) includes steak and kidney pie, plaice, sandwiches and ploughman's, but food from the restaurant can also be eaten in the bars (exc Mon, Sun L): soup 45p, mackerel 55p, steaks £3–£4·30, trout £2·50, sole from £3·75, salads. Cold food only Sun L. Pressurised Bass Charrington beers. Wine. Fruit machine. Garden. Car park.

SHAFTESBURY Dorset   Map 2

Ship
Bleke Street
(opposite main car park)
Shaftesbury (0747) 3219
10.30–2.30, 6.30–10.30
(11 Fri, Sat)

A well-preserved 17th-century building with the original oak staircase, open fires, and 'a cheerful atmosphere'. Bar food (until 45 min before closing): soup 25p, sandwiches, steak and kidney pie £1·05, various other hot dishes from 95p, and help-yourself salads from £1·50. Hall & Woodhouse bitter and best bitter (pump). Wine. Fruit machine; darts; dominoes and other games. Tables outside. (CAMRA)

SHEPTON MONTAGUE Somerset   Map 2

Montague Inn
2 m S of Bruton
Bruton (074 981) 3213
10.30–2.30, 5.30–10.30
(11 Fri, Sat & summer)
Closed Mon Oct–Apr;
Mon L May–Sept;
Dec 25 evening

A small out-of-the-way pub with a friendly atmosphere – 'most pleasant and uncommercial.' Bar food (Tue–Sat until 1.45 and 9.15; Sun until 1.30 and 9.15): steak £2·80, ploughman's 60p, home-made soup (winter only) 30p, buck rarebit 80p, omelettes 55p–65p, toasted sandwiches 35p. Wadworth's 6X, IPA, Old Timer (winter) and Butcombe bitter from the cask. Wine. Darts; fruit machine; shove ha'penny; cribbage. Garden. Car park. B&B £4·50.

SHERE Surrey   Map 3

Prince of Wales
off A25
Shere (048 641) 2313
10.30–2.30, 5.30–10.30
(11 Fri, Sat)

A 'real local' just above the village square. Bar food
(65p–£1·75) includes 'delicious' home-made pizza,
daily specials and, in summer, a cold buffet; sandwiches
35p–50p. Young's bitter and special bitter (pump),
Winter Warmer from the cask. Wine. Children.
Juke-box; darts; fruit machine; pool table. Garden.
Car park. (CAMRA)

SHIPSTON ON STOUR Warwickshire   Map 2

White Bear

See main *Guide*

SICKLINGHALL North Yorkshire   Map 5

Scotts Arms
Main Street
Wetherby (0937) 62100
11–3, 5.30–10.30
(11 Fri, Sat)

An old free house, with log fires, offering 'simple pub
food at a standard well above the average': soup 60p,
steakburger 90p, haddock £1·20, scampi £1·65, chip
butties 30p, ploughman's 90p, salads, sandwiches.
Separate restaurant. Tetley's, Theakston's and
Younger's beers (pump). Wine. Children. Juke-box;
darts; fruit machine. Garden. Car park. (CAMRA)

SIDMOUTH Devon   Map 2

Bowd Inn
on A3052
2 m N of the town
Sidmouth (039 55) 3328
11–2.30, 6.30–10.30
(11 Fri, Sat)

A 12th-century thatched inn with brass and copper.
Bar food (12–2, 7–10): steak and kidney pie £1·40,
scampi £1·75, trout £2·25, quiche £1·20, steak £3·20,
duckling £3, lamb chops £2·50, 'very good'
sandwiches from 60p, salads £1·45. Devenish bitter
and Wessex best bitter (pump). Taunton cider. Wine.
Garden. Car park. B&B £10.

SIZEWELL Suffolk   Map 3

Vulcan
6 m E of Saxmundham
Leiston (0728) 830748
11–2.30, 6.30–11

Oak beams and open fires in a 17th-century pub,
once a blacksmith's shop. Bar food includes
selection of home-made pies £1·10, home-boiled ham
from £1·15, sausages, scampi, omelettes £1–£1·10.
Separate restaurant. Adnams' bitter and mild
(pump), old ale from the cask. Wine. Darts. Garden.
Car park.

SMARDEN Kent   Map 3

The Bell
¾ m NW of Smarden
Smarden (023 377) 283
11–2.30, 6–10.30
(11 Fri, Sat)
Closed Dec 25

'Full marks for English pub atmosphere' in this old
inn with beams and ingle-nooks. Bar food (until 30
min before closing): rump steak £3·25, sole £2·25,
basket meals 90p–£1·50, ploughman's 60p, pizza 60p,
sandwiches, 'enormous portions of crisp and crunchy
chips.' Range of real ales includes Fremlin's bitter,
Bass, Shepherd Neame bitter (pump), Whitbread
Tusker, Theakston's Old Peculier from the cask. Bob
Luck's cider. Wine. Juke-box; darts; fruit machine;
bar billiards. Garden. Car park. B&B £6·50. (CAMRA)

See p. 443 for 'How to use the pub section.'

SNAPE Suffolk   Map 3

Crown
Snape (072 888) 324
10.30–2.30, 5.30–11
Closed Dec 25

A 15th-century pub with beams and log fires – and a 'very unusual lay-out'. The emphasis is on food: stock-pot soup 45p, home-made steak and kidney pie £1·65, poached bass £2·65, country casserole £1·55, jugged hare £2·45, crab £2·30, smoked local eel £2·45, local garlic sausage 95p. Adnams' bitter, mild and old (pump). Wine. Garden. Car park. B&B £7·50.

SOUTHILL Bedfordshire   Map 3

White Horse
Hitchin (0462) 813364
11–2.30, 6–10.30
(11 Fri, Sat)
Closed Dec 25 & 26

A country pub with beams and three open fires. Bar food (12–1.45, 7.30–9; not Sun): prawns £1·40, smoked trout £1·40, smoked salmon £2·10, grills £2·50–£4·50, salads £2–£2·90, home-made steak and kidney or chicken, ham and egg pie £1·90, 'something from the pot' £1·90. Separate restaurant (closed Sun). Wethered's bitter (pump). Wine. Darts; fruit machine. Garden. Car park.

SOUTHSEA Hampshire   Map 2

Eldon Arms
13–17 Eldon Street
Portsmouth (0705) 24140
10–2.30, 6–10.30
(11 Fri, Sat)

'Congratulations to the nominators' of this 150-year-old pub, says one grateful diner. Bar food includes meat platter £1·75, ploughman's 65p–80p, fisherman's lunch 90p, 'splendid' seafood salads £2·30–£4·50, seafood sandwiches 70p, beefburger, pizza, cottage pie. Separate restaurant. Eldridge Pope beers (pump). Wine. Juke-box; darts; fruit machine. Garden.

SOUTHWOLD Suffolk   Map 6

King's Head
23–25 High Street
Southwold (0502) 723829
10.30–2.30, 6–11
 Closed Dec 25 evening

A 'first-class pub, well-run when the manager is there', though one visitor found it scruffy. Bar food (11.45–2.15, 6–9; Sun 12–1.45 only): shepherd's pie 80p, 'excellent' hamburger 80p, omelettes 80p, toasted sandwiches 35p–70p, pizza £1·30. Separate restaurant (exc Sun D). Adnams' bitter, mild and old (pump). Wine. Juke-box; darts; fruit machine; pool table. B&B £5. (CAMRA)

Red Lion
South Green
Southwold (0502) 722385
10.30–2.30, 6–11

An old fishermen's pub overlooking a beautiful green. Bar food (12–2 only; £1·20–£1·40) includes cold buffet, fowl, meats, pâté, smoked fish, 'delicious' pork pie, all with salads. Adnams' bitter, mild and old (pump). Wine. Children. Tables outside. Car park. B&B £5·50.

SOUTH ZEAL Devon   Map 1

Oxenham Arms
off A30 in centre of village
Sticklepath (083 784) 244
11–2.30, 6–11
Closed Dec 25 evening

An ancient building 'furnished with splendid antiques' and offering the best ploughman's (85p) one visitor has ever had. Other bar food (12–2, 6.30–9.30; not Fri, Sat D) includes seafood basket £1·65, home-made steak, kidney and mushroom pie £1·15, pâté 85p, soup 35p, salads £1·15–£1·65, sandwiches 55p–65p. Separate restaurant. Whitbread bitter from the cask. Tom Bray's cider. Wine. Children. Darts; shove ha'penny. Garden. Car park. B&B from £10·70.

SPELDHURST Kent   Map 3

George and Dragon
Langton (089 286) 3125
10–2.30, 6–10.30
(11 Fri, Sat & summer)

Restored 13th-century building; 'would be lovely as a house – pity it's a pub.' Bar food (25p–£1·25): pâté, cold meats, hot local sausage, salads, smoked mackerel, soup, open sandwiches, quiche, hot daily dishes. Separate restaurant (12–2, 7–10; closed Sat L, Sun). Bass, Harvey's bitter, best bitter and mild, King & Barnes bitter and old (pump). Bob Luck's cider. Wine. Children. Darts. Garden. Car park.

SPYWAY Dorset   Map 2

Spyway Inn
½ m off A35
5 m E of Bridport
Powerstock (030 885) 250
10–2.30, 6–10.30
(11 Fri, Sat)
Closed Dec 25 evening

'A very comfortable inn,' formerly a smugglers' look-out on the approaches to Eggardon Hill near Askerswell. Bar food (27p–£1·20) includes 'good, solid' vegetable soup, home-made pies and pasties, sausages, pâté, sandwiches and salads. Separate restaurant (D Tue–Sat; 7.30–9). Bass, Whitbread bitter and Eldridge Pope Dorchester bitter from the cask. Wine. Darts. Garden. Car park. B&B £6. (CAMRA)

STAMFORD Lincolnshire   Map 6

George of Stamford
High Street St Martins
Stamford (0780) 2101
10.30–2.30, 6–11
Closed Dec 25

'Gorgeously warm, comfortable and welcoming'; 'every sign of being run with a great deal of care and attention.' Bar food: minestrone 75p, gammon £1·95, turkey and mushroom pie £1·55, fried mushrooms in beer batter £1·20, trout £2·10, home-made pâté £1·20, bread and cheese 90p. 'Substantial' buffet at lunch-time. Separate restaurant. Pressurised beers. Wine. Children. Courtyard/garden lounge. Car park. B&B £16·75–£20·75. (GHG)

STAPLE FITZPAINE Somerset   Map 2

Greyhound
4½ m SE of Taunton
Hatch Beauchamp (0823) 480227
10.30–2.30, 5.30–11
(6 Fri, Sat)
Closed Dec 25 evening

Mixed opinions on this former hunting lodge, from complaints about the standards of hygiene to praise for the 'excellent, wholesome food' – 'the best value I have found in Somerset.' Bar food (11.30–2, 6.30–10; Sun 12–1.45, 7–10) includes cold buffet £2, chicken curry, scrumpy chicken, pâté, home-made soup, vegetarian flans, smoked mackerel, ploughman's 75p–£1·50. Separate restaurant (D & Sun L only; 12–1, 7.30–9.30). Eldridge Pope Royal Oak and Dorchester bitter (pump), Theakston's bitter and (occasionally) Old Peculier from the cask. Taunton cider. Wine. Children. Darts; fruit machine; skittles. Courtyard. Car park. B&B £4·50. (CAMRA)

STEEP Hampshire   Map 3

Harrow
off A272
1½ m NW of Petersfield
Petersfield (0730) 2685
10.30–2.30, 6–10.30
(11 Fri, Sat)

One visitor to this lovely old pub suggests you should 'get there early as the locals know it well.' 'Very generous helpings' of bar food, including vegetable soup ('a meal in itself') 50p, ploughman's ('best ever') 70p, rare roast beef salad £2·20. Whitbread bitter, Pompey Royal and mild from the cask. Cider. Garden. Lavatories over the road. Car park. No details from landlord. (CAMRA)

STEEPLE ASTON Oxfordshire   Map 2

Red Lion

See main *Guide*
(CAMRA)

STOCKBRIDGE Hampshire   Map 2

Vine Inn
High Street
Stockbridge (026 481) 652
10–2.30, 6–10.30
(11 Fri, Sat)
Closed Dec 25

An old coaching house with 'a fairy grotto for a fire-place' and a stream stocked with trout for eventual consumption by the customers. Bar food: pâté 90p, ploughman's 75p, sandwiches 45p–75p, salads £1·15–£1·65, soup 45p, lasagne £2·50, trout and prawn Mornay £1·75, spiced liver hot-pot £1·65, stuffed jacket potatoes 65p–70p. Ploughman's and sandwiches only Sat D, Sun. Whitbread Trophy and Pompey Royal (pump). Wine. Darts; fruit machine. Garden. Car park. B&B £6·25.

STUDHAM Bedfordshire   Map 3

The Bell
Dunstable Road
Whipsnade (0582) 872460
11–2.30, 6.30–10.30
(11 Fri, Sat)
Closed Dec 25 evening

An 'agreeable' old village pub offering 'excellent' bar snacks: whitebait 90p, pâté platter 75p, soup 40p, salads £1·10–£1·65, cheese 50p–60p, crab £1·65, trout £2·50, seafood platter £1·75, chicken and ham pie 85p, duck £4·35, steaks £3·50–£4, sausages 95p. Ind Coope bitter and Burton ale (pump). Wine. Darts; fruit machine; dominoes. Garden. Car park. (CAMRA)

SUMMER BRIDGE North Yorkshire   Map 8

Knox Manor

See main *Guide*

SWINTON Greater Manchester   Map 5

White Swan
186 Worsley Road
off A580
061-794 1504
11.30–3, 7–10.30
(11 Fri, Sat)

This 'quite typical, virtually untouched period piece' from the turn of the century offers lunchtime bar food only (12–2; Mon–Fri), including 'large barm cakes' with beef, turkey or sausage 45p–55p, meat and potato pie 90p, steak £1·15, sausage and egg 90p, plaice £1·20; menu changes daily. Holt's bitter and mild (pump). Children (L only). Juke-box; darts; fruit machine; bar billiards; pool table; dominoes. (CAMRA)

TADCASTER North Yorkshire   Map 5

Angel & White Horse
Bridge Street
Tadcaster (0937) 835470
10.30–3, 6–10.30
(11 Fri, Sat)

A 'nice, light atmosphere' in a Samuel Smith's house with views from the bar to the brewery stables and shire horses. Bar food available at all times: soup 45p, Yorkshire pudding and onion gravy 45p, hot daily dish £1·70, meat salads £2, pâté salad £1·10, sandwiches 45p. Separate restaurant. Samuel Smith's bitter (pump). Wine. Children. Darts.

Towns shown in black on our maps contain at least one recommended restaurant, pub or wine bar (see map key). The dot denotes the location of the town or village, not the establishment. Where necessary, we give directions to it in the entry. If you can, help us to improve them.

THAMES DITTON Surrey Map 3

Crown
Summer Road
01-398 2376
10.30–2.30, 5.30–10.30
(11 Fri, Sat)

A mock-Tudor building of the 1920s – 'lots of regulars and everyone eating' from the lengthy menu (12.15–2, 7–9.45): soup 30p, home-made pâté 90p, daily specials around £1·40, grills £1·85–£3·40, scampi £2·20, prawn curry £1·50, steak sandwich 90p, salads £1·40–£2·40. Home-made soup and ploughman's Sun L. Watney's Stag and London bitters (pump). Wine. Children. Juke-box; darts; fruit machine; video games. Patio. Car park.

TIMPERLEY Greater Manchester Map 5

Bon Viveur

See main *Guide*
(CAMRA)

TIPTON ST JOHN Devon Map 2

Golden Lion
Ottery St Mary (040 481)
2881
10.30–2.30, 6–10.30
(11 Fri, Sat; opens
7 p.m. Nov–Feb)

A village pub with a 'superbly calm atmosphere and freshly prepared snacks' (12–2, 7–9.45 or 10.15; Sun 12–1.15, 7–9.45): ploughman's from 71p, sandwiches 46p–99p, smoked mackerel 75p, pâté 62p, crab soup 45p 'a house speciality', salads £1·32–£3·20; hot daily dish in winter. Bass and Whitbread Trophy (pump). Inch's cider. Wine. Darts; fruit machine. Garden. Car park. B&B £7·45.

TOCKHOLES Lancashire Map 5

Victoria
Blackburn (0254) 71622
12–2, 7–11

'Pleasant and prompt' service in a pub originally believed to have been a mill. 'Good, straightforward' bar food (12–2, 8–10): pie and peas 32p, sandwiches 32p, plaice 95p, steak £1·20, chicken pie 60p. Separate restaurant. Range of pressurised beers. Wine. Children. Fruit machine. Car park.

TORMARTON Avon Map 2

Compass
M4, junction 18
E of A46
Badminton (045 421) 242
10–2.30, 6–10.30
(11 Fri, Sat)

An enclosed orangery in this Cotswold-stone pub makes a 'delightful setting' for the bar snacks (until 30 min before closing): sandwiches 45p–£1, home-made Scotch egg 70p, pâté 95p, 'excellent' cheese flan 75p, salads 95p–£2·10; hot dishes chalked on a blackboard in the Vittles Bar, but can be eaten anywhere. Wadworth's 6X and Bass (pump), Wadworth's Old Timer from the cask. Wine. Darts; fruit machine; dominoes. Garden. Car park. B&B from £9·60.

TREGREHAN Cornwall Map 1

Britannia
on A390
Par (072 681) 2889
11–2.30, 6–10.30
(11 Fri, Sat & summer)

An 18th-century free house, rebuilt after a fire. Bar food includes cold buffet 70p–£1·50, scampi £1·95, chicken £1·50, chef's specials. Separate restaurant. Bass, St Austell best bitter and mild (pump). Wine. Juke-box; fruit machine; darts (winter). Large garden with swings. Car park.

See p. 443 for 'How to use the pub section.'

TROTTON West Sussex Map 3

Keepers Arms
on A272
Midhurst (073 081) 3724
10.30–2.30, 6–10.30
(11 Fri, Sat & summer)
Closed Mon

Pleasant atmosphere, despite the extension work – 'a lovely view on top of a hill.' Bar food in 'generous quantities' includes sandwiches from 35p, basket meals from 75p, home-made onion soup and pâté, salads from £1·70, jacket potatoes, 'excellent' chips. Separate restaurant (12–2, 7–9.45; closed Sun D, Mon). Hall & Woodhouse bitter, Whitbread Pompey Royal, Courage Directors (pump). Wine. Patio. Car park.

TUNBRIDGE WELLS Kent Map 3

Hole in the Wall
9 High Street
Tunbridge Wells (0892)
26550
10–2.30, 6–11
Closed Sun

Velvet, mirrors and friendly service in this crowded pub, opposite Central station. Bar food (12–2.15, 7–10): home-made pies, flans, pasta and rice dishes, salads £1·20, pâté 80p, ploughman's 70p, soup 45p. Separate restaurant (12–2, 7–10). Young's bitter, Samuel Smith's bitter, Whitbread Trophy (pump). Wine. Children. Garden.

UPPER DICKER East Sussex Map 3

Plough
on B2108
2½ m W of Hailsham
Hailsham (0323) 844859
10.30–2.30, 6–10.30
(11 Fri, Sat)
Closed Dec 25 evening

'Pleasant staff' in a 17th-century pub, recently altered. Excellent range of bar food (from 12 and 7) includes grills £1·05–£2·70, soup 35p, pâté 65p, salads £1·20–£1·35, turkey kebab £1·25, pizza 95p, steaks £2·05–£2·70, ploughman's 50p, sandwiches 35p–40p. Pressurised Watneys beers. Wine. Darts; dominoes. Garden and forecourt. Outside gents'. Car park.

UPTON-UPON-SEVERN Hereford & Worcester
Map 2

Swan
Riverside
Upton-upon-Severn
(068 46) 2601
11.30–2.30, 6–10.30
(11 Fri, Sat)
Closed Dec 25

A 'chintzy place in a clean, cosy and appealing way' – a 17th-century riverside inn with private moorings. 'Attractively served' bar food (12–2, 7.30–9; exc Sun; Mon D; no prices stated): home-made soup, 'excellent' quiche, lasagne, smoked mackerel pâté, moussaka, ploughman's; cold table offering lobster, crab, oysters, salmon. Separate restaurant opening Easter 1980. Wadworth's 6X (pump) and Old Timer (winter) from the cask. Wine. Walled garden.

WAREHAM Dorset Map 2

Priory

See main *Guide*

WARNINGLID West Sussex Map 3

Half Moon
The Street (B2115)
Warninglid (044 485) 227
10.45–2.30, 6–10.30
(11 Fri, Sat)

A 'plain, small house' built in 1680 with 'brasses, beams, settles and the usual clutter.' Bar food (35p–£1·25): 'generous' sandwiches, 'very good' pasties, ploughman's, pizzas, salads, 'tip-top' home-made soup and pâté. Whitbread Trophy and Pompey Royal from the cask. Wine. Darts; shove ha'penny. Garden. Car park.

WARWICK Warwickshire   Map 2

Roebuck
Smith Street
Warwick (0926) 41072
10.30–2.30, 6–10.30
(11 Fri, Sat)
Closed Dec 25 evening

Beams and brass in a 16th-century half-timbered inn
on the main street. Bar food (12–2, 7–10) revolves
around 'huge' plates of salad with roast beef £1·90,
pork £1·80, chicken and ham pie £1·40, salami £1·30,
smoked mackerel £1·30. There are also sandwiches
70p–75p, cheese 50p and soup 35p. Pressurised
Watney Mann & Truman beers. Wine. Fruit machine.
Courtyard. Outside loos. B&B £5·75.

Zetland Arms
11 Church Street
Warwick (0926) 41974
10–2.30, 6–10.30
(11 Fri, Sat)
Closed Dec 25 evening

'Packed and noisy' old pub with comfortable
furnishings. Bar food (L only): soup 25p, pizza 45p,
home-made steak and kidney pie 45p, ploughman's
60p, faggots and vegetables 65p. Davenports' bitter
(pump). Wine. Garden. B&B £5·75. (CAMRA)

WATFORD GAP Northamptonshire   Map 5

Stag's Head
Daventry (032 72) 3621
10–2, 6–10.30
(11 Fri, Sat)

'A welcome refuge from motorway food.' Bar snacks
(12–2, 7–10; Sun 7–9): sandwiches 40p–90p, sausages
90p, 'well-flavoured' steak and kidney pie £1·85,
steak £3·50 ('prices are going up all the time' says the
landlord, and are higher in the evening). Separate
restaurant (12.30–2, 7–10; closed Sun D). Variety of
pressurised beers. Wine. Children. Fruit machine.
Canal-side gardens. Car park.

WELLESBOURNE Warwickshire   Map 2

King's Head
on A429
5 m E of Stratford
Stratford-upon-Avon
(0789) 840206
10–2.30, 6–10.30
(11 Fri, Sat)

'Exceptionally good value' in this 'basic' 16th-century
inn. Bar food (12–2, 6.30–9.30; Sun, Mon 7–8.30):
home-made soup 40p, pâté 90p, hot daily dish £1·50,
scampi £1·90, steak £3·50, home-made pizza 75p,
cold meat and salad £1·50, ploughman's 60p–75p,
beefburger 45p. Separate restaurant (12–2, 7.30–9.30;
Mon 7–8.30; closed Sun D). Mitchells & Butlers
bitter and Bass (pump). Wine. Children. Juke-box;
darts; fruit machine. Garden. Car park. B&B
from £8.

WESTLETON Suffolk   Map 6

Crown
Westleton (072 873) 273
and 239
10.30–2.30, 6–11
Closed Dec 25 &
26 evenings

An old, red-brick building in the centre of a pretty
village; 'pictures of ships, and ex-P&O landlord of
massive proportions.' Bar snacks (L only; from 25p)
include jacket potatoes and sandwiches. Separate
restaurant (7.30–9.30). Adnams' bitter (pump) and old
ale (winter) from the cask. Wine. Ornamental yard.
Car park. B&B £8·35.

**Some pubs off the beaten track do not always serve food at times notified.
Phone to check.**

In England and Wales, Sunday opening hours are 12–2, 7–10.30.

WESTON Northamptonshire Map 2

Crown
off A43
Sulgrave (029 576) 328
11–2.30, 6–10.30
(11 Fri, Sat)
Closed Dec 25 evening

An old coaching inn with beams and log fires. 'Music accosts you from all directions' but service is 'friendly and efficient'. Bar food: home-made soup 43p, ploughman's 85p, chicken £1·25, lasagne £1·50, pizza 96p, omelettes 90p, spare ribs £2·35. Large range of beers, including Hook Norton bitter, Marston's Pedigree, Fuller's ESB (pump). Bulmer's cider. Wine. Children. Juke-box; darts; fruit machine; bar billiards; skittles; shove ha'penny. Garden. Outdoor gents'. Car park. B&B £7.

WHATCOTE Warwickshire Map 2

Royal Oak
Tysoe (029 588) 319
10.30–2.30, 6–10.30
(11 Fri, Sat)

A 12th-century ale house 'with olde worlde suburban' decor, 'bustling with trade' though in an out-of-the-way village. The 'quality and variety of the accompanying salads' impressed one Sunday snacker: pâté 60p, soup 35p, veal £2·35, plaice £1·10, seafood platter £1·70, freshly baked pork sausage 95p, cold meats. Hook Norton bitter (pump or pressure). Wine. Fruit machine. Garden. Car park.

WHITEWELL Lancashire Map 5

The Inn at Whitewell

See main *Guide*

WHITNEY-ON-WYE Hereford & Worcester Map 4

Rhydspence Inn
on A438
Clifford (049 73) 262
12–2.30, 7–10.30
(11 Fri, Sat)
Closed Dec 25

'A beautiful half-timbered inn in lovely country' with 'competently cooked' bar food (until 45 min before closing): home-made stock-pot soup 45p, pâté 70p, steak and kidney pie £1·50, lasagne £1·25, 'landlord's favourite' (a concoction of eggs and cheese) £1·25, haddock and mushroom pancakes £1·25, sandwiches 50p–65p, steak £3·70, roast duckling £2·75. Robinson's bitter, Penrhos bitter (pump), Robinson's Old Tom from the cask. Fleming's cider. Wine. Children (L only). Darts; fruit machine; quoits; dominoes. Garden. Car park. B&B £7·50. (CAMRA)

WINKLEIGH Devon Map 1

King's Arms
in village square
Winkleigh (083 783) 384
10–2.30, 6–10.30
(11 Fri, Sat & summer)
Closed Mon (exc public hols)

'Characterful', whitewashed pub with pleasant hosts. Bar food: soup 40p, home-made pasties, pies and flans 40p–45p, salads £1·60, basket meals £1·75–£2·75 (exc Sun); 3-course Sun lunch £2·50. Separate restaurant (Tue–Sat, from 8 p.m.). Pressurised beers. Inch's cider. Wine. Children (L only). Garden. Holiday flat to let.

WOODS CORNER East Sussex Map 3

Swan
on B2096
Brightling (042 482) 242
11–2.30, 6–10.30
(11 Fri, Sat)
Closed Dec 25

'A pretty pub with fantastic views.' The bar is decorated with international car number plates. Bar food (12–2, 7–10; not Sun L): avocado and prawns £1, snails £1·60, pâté 95p, soup 40p, beef salad £2·50, plaice £2, lasagne £1·50, home-made pie from £2. Beard's bitter and old (pump). Wine. Children. Fruit machine; bar billiards. Garden. Car park.

WRECCLESHAM Surrey   Map 3

Bear and Ragged Staff
on A325
Farnham (0252) 716389
10.30–2.30, 6–10.30
(11 Fri, Sat)

A 17th-century inn with low beams. Bar food includes 15 kinds of sandwiches 33p–65p, ploughman's 50p, soup 50p, pâté 85p, pizza £1·25, chicken curry £1·25, plaice £1·50, seafood platter £2. Cold food only Sun. Courage bitter and Directors (pump). Wine. Fruit machine. Tables on forecourt. Car park.

WRELTON North Yorkshire   Map 8

Huntsman

See main *Guide*

WYTHAM Oxfordshire   Map 2

White Hart
1 m N of Botley
Oxford (0865) 44372
11–2.30, 6–10.30
(11 Fri, Sat)
Closed Dec 25

A 'delightful pub in a beautiful village', offering 'extensive, imaginative cold buffet' (12–2, 7–9.30; Sun 12–1.45; not Sun, Mon D). Hot food includes steaks, gammon, chicken Kiev, mixed grill (£1·50–£3·75). Ind Coope bitter and Burton ale (pump). Wine. Children. Fruit machine. Garden. Car park.

YORK North Yorkshire   Map 5

Lew's Place

See main *Guide*

WALES

BABELL Clwyd   Map 4

Black Lion
Caerwys (035 282) 239
11.30–3.30, 5.30–10.30
(11 Fri, Sat)

A low-beamed hotel with 'better than average' bar food: 'delicious' leek soup 50p, roast duckling £1·50, plate of four cheeses 70p, minute steak £2·35, gammon £1·85, beefburger £1·20. Wine. Details approximate.

BROAD HAVEN Dyfed   Map 4

Druidstone Hotel

See main *Guide*

CRICKHOWELL Powys   Map 4

Nantyffin Cider Mill

See main *Guide*

CROSS INN Dyfed   Map 4

Rhos-yr-Hafod Inn

See main *Guide*
(CAMRA)

DINAS Dyfed   Map 4

Ship Aground
Dinas Cross
off A487
Dinas Cross (034 86) 261
11–3, 5.30–10.30
(11 Fri, Sat & summer)

A 'warren of comfortable bars, with nautical gear'. Bar lunches (12–2; 40p–£1·75): sandwiches, pizza, potted shrimps, ploughman's, home-made pâté, crab salad. Grills (£1·20–£3·30) and salads in the evening (7–9.30). Cold buffet £2 Sun (12–2). No food Sun D. Felinfoel Double Dragon (pump). Wine. Children. Darts; fruit machine. Car park.

Within parts of these old county boundaries, alcohol is not served on Sunday, except to hotel residents: Anglesey, Cardigan, Carmarthen, Merioneth.

GLASBURY-ON-WYE Powys   Map 4

Maesllwch Arms

See main *Guide*

HAY-ON-WYE Powys   Map 4

Old Black Lion
on B4350
Hay-on-Wye (0497)
820841
11–2.30, 7–11
Closed Dec 25 evening

Rest your feet between bookshops in this sprawling old pub 'with no great charm or tastelessness.' Bar food (12–2, 7–9): soup 55p, pâtés £1·05, home-pickled salmon £3·95, cheese and home-made bread 70p, Welsh prawn paste £1·70, risotto £1·20, cheese flan £1·20. Separate restaurant. Pressurised beers. Wine. Children 'by arrangement'. Darts; cards; dominoes. Car park. B&B £7·30–£8·60.

LLANDEWI SKIRRID Gwent   Map 4

Walnut Tree Inn

See main *Guide*

LLANDUDNO Gwynedd   Map 4

King's Head
Old Road
Llandudno (0492) 77993
11–3, 5.30–10.30
(11 summer)

The emphasis is on food in this old pub near the Great Orme tramway. There is praise for the special hot meals (sole in cream sauce £1·10, on one occasion), crab salad £1·50, beef salad £1·20 and 'excellent' home-made soup 40p. Ind Coope bitter (pump). Wine. Car park. No details from landlord.

LLANDYSILIO Dyfed   Map 4

Bush Inn
on A478
Clunderwen (099 12) 239
11–3, 5.30–10.30
(11 summer)

'A no-nonsense pub with cottage-type, comfy lounge.' The landlord does not want to appear in the *Guide*, but his bar food pleases customers: 'excellent salad selection', duck, turkey pie, chicken and 'heaps of chips', soup, scampi, lasagne. Worthington best bitter from the cask. Garden. Car park. (CAMRA)

LLANGYNIDR Powys   Map 4

Red Lion

See main *Guide*

LLANWDDYN Powys   Map 4

Lake Vyrnwy Hotel

See main *Guide*

LLOWES Powys   Map 4

Radnor Arms

See main *Guide*

PEMBROKE FERRY Dyfed   Map 4

Ferry House
off A477 at S end of
Cleddau Bridge
Pembroke (064 63) 2947
11.30–2.30, 6–11
(7–10.30 winter;
11 Fri, Sat)
Closed Mon in winter

A cosy little riverside bar, 'inoffensively nautical'. 'Good fresh food' with a strong leaning towards fish, served at the bar at lunch-times only (12.15–1.45; not Sun): there might be soup 38p–65p, 'honest, home-made' pâté 65p–75p, smoked mackerel 70p–80p, plaice 75p, prawns 80p, rump steak £2·85, 'meal in one' fish pie £1·30, cold beef £1·25. Must book for the 'consistently good' self-service carvery Sun L: 'all you can eat for £2·80.' Separate restaurant (not D Sun, Mon, Tue). Felinfoel Double Dragon and bitter (pump). Wine. Patio. Car park. (CAMRA)

PENMAENPOOL Gwynedd   Map 4

George III Hotel

See main *Guide*

PONTARGOTHI Dyfed   Map 4

Cothi Bridge Hotel
on A40
5 m E of Carmarthen
Nantgaredig (026 788) 251
11–3, 5.30–12
Sun: 12–2, 7–11

A well-kept riverside hotel with 'willing' service. Bar
snacks (not Sun L): home-made soup 45p, chicken
and chips £1·60, sausages and chips 75p, scampi
£1·90, pizza 75p–£1·50, sandwiches 40p–70p, salmon
salad £2·40. Separate restaurant. 'Bar food is only
available when the kitchen is not too busy.' Felinfoel
Double Dragon and mild (pump). Garden. Car park.
(CAMRA)

RAGLAN Gwent   Map 4

Beaufort Arms Hotel
on A472
Raglan (0291) 690412
11–2.30, 5.30–11

A pretty pub which one visitor thought was 'a
welcome spot in a rather barren area.' Bar food
(12–2.15, 7–10.30) includes 'very good' ploughman's,
pie, chips and peas. Separate restaurant (12–2, 7–10).
Selection of pressurised beers. Wine. Darts; fruit
machine; pool; video machine. Garden. Car park.
B&B £9·80.

ST FAGANS South Glamorgan   Map 4

Plymouth Arms
Cardiff (0222) 569130
11–3, 5.30–10.30

A large, busy house with a stately Victorian façade,
near the Welsh National Folk Museum. Bar food
(12–2.30; Mon–Sat L only; up to £1·70): 'two or three
hot dishes and two or three cold,' including lasagne,
beef Wellington, Vienna steak, mackerel, chicken
casserole. Separate restaurant. Bass (pump). Wine.
Darts; fruit machine. Large patio. Car park.

WOLF'S CASTLE Dyfed   Map 4

Wolfe Inn
on A40
7 m N of Haverfordwest
Treffgarne (043 787) 662
11–3, 6–10.30
(11 Fri, Sat & summer)
Closed Dec 25

A solid stone house with rather bare public bar and a
'posher' saloon. 'Attractively presented' bar food
(12–2 Tue–Sat; 7–10 Tue–Sun): home-made soup 35p,
'gorgeous' home-made pâtés 75p–£1·05, scampi £1·75,
plaice £1·20, sausage and chips 75p, nine different
salads, including lobster in season. Separate restaurant
(Tue–Sat L; Tue–Sun D; must book). Felinfoel
Double Dragon (pump). Wine. Children. Darts;
fruit machine. Garden and patio. Car park. B&B £5.

Wolfscastle Country Hotel

See main *Guide*

SCOTLAND

ACHILTIBUIE Highland   Map 9

Summer Isles Hotel

See main *Guide*

ALYTH Tayside   Map 9

Lands of Loyal Hotel

See main *Guide*

ARDENTINNY Strathclyde   Map 9

Ardentinny Hotel   See main *Guide*

ARDUAINE Strathclyde   Map 9

Loch Melfort Hotel   See main *Guide*

AUCHTERARDER Tayside   Map 9

Gleneagles Hotel   See main *Guide*

BALLATER Grampian   Map 9

Tullich Lodge   See main *Guide*

CABRACH Grampian   Map 9

Grouse Inn
on A941
Cabrach (046 689) 200
Summer: 11 a.m.–11 p.m.
(Sun 12.30–11 p.m.)
Winter: 11–2.30, 5–11
(Sun 12.30–2.30, 6.30–11)

A wayside inn run by the same family for forty years and boasting more than a hundred different whiskies. Bar food (25p–£2·80) includes soup, sandwiches, ploughman's, fish, chicken, salads, scampi, steaks. Separate restaurant. Pressurised McEwan's beers. Wine. Children. Fruit machine. Car park. B&B £4·50.

CANONBIE Dumfries & Galloway   Map 7

Riverside Inn   See main *Guide*
(CAMRA)

CARBOST Skye, Highland   Map 9

Old Inn
Carbost (047 842) 205
11–2.30, 5–11
Closed Sun

A Victorian pub, a contemporary of the nearby distillery, but recently renovated. In summer food is available from 11 a.m. to 11 p.m., including the unlicensed afternoon session: home-made soup 35p, pâté 50p, basket meals 95p–£1·90, pizza and chips £1·20, sandwiches and rolls 25p–30p; daily specials £1·50–£2·50. Pressurised beers only. Wine. Children. Darts; dominoes. Car park. B&B from £4.

CLEISH Tayside   Map 9

Nivingston House   See main *Guide*

DALBEATTIE Dumfries & Galloway   Map 7

Granary   See main *Guide*

EDDLESTON Borders   Map 9

Horse Shoe
on A703
Eddleston (072 13) 225
and 306
11.30–2.30, 6–10.30
(11 Fri, Sat)
Closed Dec 25; Jan 1

Spruce white roadside inn, a blacksmith's shop until 1968. 'Over-decorated but charmingly served'. Bar menu chalked on a blackboard (12–2, 6.30–10; Sun 12.30–2.15; 85p–£2·75): lasagne, local bread, salads, ploughman's, pizzas, coq au vin, beef olives. Separate restaurant (12–2, 7–10). Belhaven 70/- and 60/- (air pressure). Children. Car park. (CAMRA)

EDINBURGH   Map 9

Beehive Inn   See main *Guide*

GLAMIS Tayside   Map 9

Strathmore Arms   See main *Guide*

ISLE ORNSAY Skye, Highland   Map 9

Kinloch Lodge Hotel   See main *Guide*

KINROSS Tayside   Map 9

Windlestrae Hotel   See main *Guide*

LATHERON Highland   Map 9

Latheronwheel Hotel
17 m S of Wick
on A9
Latheron (059 34) 209
11–2.30, 5–11
Sun: 12.30–2.30, 6.30–11

Colin Sutherland, the licensee, occasionally plays the bagpipes in this old coaching inn. Bar lunches: 'tasty' soup 30p, pork chop and onions, roast lamb, haddock, gammon and pineapple £1·60, cold meat salads £1·40. Separate restaurant. Pressurised Scottish & Newcastle beers. Children. Darts; pool. Car park. B&B £6·50.

LOCHMADDY North Uist, Highland   Map 9

Lochmaddy Hotel   See main *Guide*

MELROSE Borders   Map 8

Burts Hotel
Market Square
Melrose (089 682) 2285
11–2.30, 5–11
(Sun 12.30–2.30, 6.30–11)

A busy old hotel with beams, copper and brass. Wide range of 'good, simple' bar food (12–2, 6–10.30; menu changes daily): broth 35p, haddock £1·10, navarin of lamb, cold meat salad, curried beef, sweet-and-sour pork £1·20, sandwiches, basket meals. Separate restaurant (12.30–2, 7–9). Belhaven 80/- (pump). Wine. Children. Car park. B&B £8·75–£10·25.

NAIRN Highland   Map 9

Clifton Hotel   See main *Guide*

PEAT INN Fife   Map 9

Peat Inn   See main *Guide*

PERTH Tayside   Map 9

Station Hotel   See main *Guide*

PORT APPIN Strathclyde   Map 9

Airds Hotel   See main *Guide*

PORT ELLEN Islay, Strathclyde   Map 9

Machrie Hotel   See main *Guide*

Pubs are represented on the maps by a tankard.

ST BOSWELLS Borders   Map 8

Buccleuch Arms
on A68
St Boswells (083 52) 2243
11–2.30, 5–11
Sun: 12.30–2.30, 6.30–11

'Pleasant and willing service' in an 18th-century coaching inn surrounded by beautiful countryside. Bar lunches (12–2): 'excellent' home-made soup 30p, pâté 75p, hot dishes 65p–£2. Suppers (6–9): scampi £1·90, chicken £1·45, steak sandwich £1·75, mixed grill £2·75, steak platter £3·50. Separate restaurant (D only, 7–9). Pressurised beers. Wine. Children. Darts; fruit machine. Seats outside. Car park. B&B from £8·50.

SEIL Strathclyde   Map 9

Dunmor House

See main *Guide*

SELKIRK Borders   Map 8

Queen's Head
West Port
Selkirk (0750) 21782
11 a.m.–11 p.m.
Sun: 12.30–2.30, 6.30–11

A 'welcoming, pleasant' old coaching-inn in a beautiful town. Robert Burns visited it as an exciseman. Bar food (not Sun): 'particularly good' home-made soup 25p, haddock £1·30, chicken £1·30, jumbo sausage £1, scampi £1·55, omelettes £1, toasted sandwiches. Pressurised Ind Coope beers. Wine. Children. Juke-box; darts; fruit machine; dominoes; cards; video machine.

SKEABOST BRIDGE Skye, Highland   Map 9

Skeabost House Hotel

See main *Guide*

STRACHUR Strathclyde   Map 9

Creggans Inn
on A815
Strachur (036 986) 279
11–2.30, 5–11
Sun: 12.30–2.30, 6.30–11

'Paintings of Bonnie Prince Charlie and comrades all around walls' of one bar. Bar food (11–2 only): 'hot and filling' soup 35p, home-made pâté with oatcakes 80p, local trout, haddock £1·95, 'delicious' bacon roll 60p, toasted sandwiches 65p, omelettes £1·40, lamb cutlets £3. Separate restaurant (closed L exc Sun). Pressurised Scottish & Newcastle beers. Wine. Children. Darts; fruit machine. Garden. Car park. B&B £14–£20.

THORNHILL Dumfries & Galloway   Map 7

Buccleuch and Queensberry Hotel
Drumlanrig Street (A76)
Thornhill (0848) 30215
11–2.30, 5–11
(Sun 12.30–2.30, 6.30–11)

A sandstone hotel, 'marred by show-cases of dreadful Scottish souvenirs.' Extensive bar menu (12–2 only): home-made soup 25p, scampi £2·50, salads 95p–£2·10, steak and kidney pie £1·30, home-made minced meat tart and chips 90p, braised steak 95p, local smoked trout £2·50. Sandwiches only in evening. Separate restaurant (high tea 5–6, dinner 7–8). Pressurised Scottish & Newcastle beers. Wine. Children. Darts; fruit machine; dominoes. Car park. B&B from £10.

WEEM Tayside   Map 9

Ailean Chraggan Hotel

See main *Guide*

WESTER HOWGATE Lothian   Map 9

Old Howgate Inn

See main *Guide*
(CAMRA)

ISLE OF MAN

KIRK ANDREAS   Map 7

Grosvenor

See main *Guide*
(CAMRA)

IRELAND

BALLYDEHOB Co Cork   Map 10

Audley House Hotel

See main *Guide*

BUNRATTY Co Clare   Map 10

Durty Nellys
next to the castle
Limerick 61194 *and* 62953
10.30 a.m. to 11.30 p.m.
Sun: 12–2, 4–10
Closed Apr 4 & Dec 25

'One of the oldest pubs in Ireland', 'all nooks, crannies and winding, narrow stairs.' Some reckon it 'the only place to eat really good fish in the Limerick area', though the bar menu is limited to 'tasty' home-made soup 50p, toasted sandwiches 60p–£1·10, smoked salmon on soda bread £1·10, grilled brill, and similar snacks (available all day). Separate restaurant (12–2.30, 6–10.30) may be worth trying for oysters, smoked trout, scallops, lobster, crayfish and steaks. Pressurised beers and stout. Wine. Children. Cards. Seats outside.

CAHIR Co Tipperary   Map 10

Earl of Glengall

See main *Guide*

CARRIGBYRNE Co Wexford   Map 10

Cedar Lodge

See main *Guide*

CLARINBRIDGE Co Galway   Map 10

Paddy Burke's
11 m S of Galway
on Limerick road
Galway 86107
10.30 a.m.–11 p.m.
(11.30 p.m. in summer)
Sun 12–2, 4–10
Closed Apr 4; Dec 25

Several small rooms make up this pub, the home of the Galway Oyster Festival. Oysters (of course), but also 'excellent' chowder, chicken, salmon, prawns, pâté, soup, Irish stew, lasagne, and cold meat salads. Separate restaurant (closed Sun, Mon in winter). Range of pressurised beers. Wine. Children. Garden. Car park.

COURTMACSHERRY Co Cork   Map 10

Courtmacsherry Hotel

See main *Guide*

Some pubs off the beaten track do not always serve food at times notified. Phone to check.

DUBLIN   Map 10

(5) The 51
51 Haddington Road,
Ballsbridge
Dublin 600150
10.30–2.30, 3.30–11
Sun: 12.30–2, 4–10

Licensed for over 120 years and 'thronged by office people' who appreciate the lunchtime bar food (Mon–Fri only): soup 30p, cottage pie £1, quiche 75p, sandwiches and rolls 35p–40p, 'light and generously filled' pasties, open sandwiches 75p; salads with ham £1·75, prawns £2, smoked mackerel £1·60. Sandwiches and rolls in the evening. Variety of pressurised beers. Wine. Bar billiards. Tables outside in summer.

DUBLIN see also wine bar section, and city plan on p.422

GOREY Co Wexford   Map 10

Marlfield House

See main *Guide*

KILCOLGAN Co Galway   Map 10

Moran's Oyster Cottage
The Weir
Galway 86113
10.30 a.m.–11 p.m.

A small, thatched pub on the coast with turf fires in winter and 'feeding cubicles' seating up to eight people. The food includes mussel soup 60p, 'big, juicy' crab claws £1·80, 'superb' prawn cocktail £1·65, oysters £3·10 a dozen, 'generous helpings of delicious smoked salmon' £2·35; fresh salmon, mackerel and trout in summer. Choice of pressurised beers and stout. Wine. Children. Seats outside.

LETTERFRACK Co Galway   Map 10

Rosleague Manor

See main *Guide*

YOUGHAL Co Cork   Map 10

Aherne's

See main *Guide*

NORTHERN IRELAND

COMBER Co Down   Map 10

Old Crow

See main *Guide*

HILLSBOROUGH Co Down   Map 10

Hillside Bar
21 Main Street
Hillsborough 682765
12.30 p.m.–11.30 p.m.
Closed Sun

Renovated and enlarged old pub offering lunchtime home-cooked bar food (12.30–2.30, Mon–Sat): soup 35p, hot dishes £1–£1·50, filled jacket potatoes £1·10, ('a satisfying meal'), ploughman's 90p, pâté 95p, 'delicious' hot bread 15p; 'excellent' salads only in summer £1–£1·60. Separate restaurant. Range of pressurised beers. Wine. Darts; bar billiards; draughts. Tables outside in summer. Car park.

No children under 18 are allowed in bars in Northern Ireland.

Daft Eddy's Sketrick Bar
Sketrick Island,
Whiterock
Killinchy 541615
11.30 a.m.–11 p.m.
Closed Sun; Dec 25

Daft Eddy was an 18th-century pirate who played hide-and-seek with the excisemen among the islands in the lough. Modern law-abiders arrive by yacht or causeway at this converted farmhouse near the ruined castle. The food (12.30–3, 6.30–8.30; not Mon) includes mushroom soup 40p, spicy sausage £1·90, chicken in lemon sauce £1·25, and an appealing cold table of meats, pâté, quiche and salads (beef £1·80). Separate restaurant (12.30–2, 7–9.30; closed Mon). Selection of pressurised beers. Wine. Children. Darts. Patio. Car park. Self-catering chalets from £10.

WINE BARS

ENGLAND

AMERSHAM-ON-THE-HILL Bucks Map 3

Annie's
16 Hill Avenue
Amersham (024 03) 22713
10.30–2.30, 6–10.30
(11 Fri, Sat; 7–10.30 Sun)
Closed Sun L; Dec 25;
L public hols

'Cross between an up-market snack-bar and a disco' fits the Robinsons' wine bar, where food, wine and music change constantly. At present they do only one hot dish each day (boeuf bourguignonne and rice, £1·90; macaroni, cheese and ham, 75p) to supplement the extensive cold snacks: taramosalata (70p), quiches (65p), smoked mackerel, home-made Scotch eggs (40p) and toasted sandwiches. All wines have a flat-rate mark-up 'so the most expensive are the best bargains', and there are free tasters before you buy. Pasquier-Desvignes Mâcon Blanc (£4·70 the bottle, 80p a glass) remains popular; other good buys include Amarone (£4·50) and Argentine Los Hermanos (£2·90). Old Peculier, Tequila Sunrise, Perrier and His Eminence port (55p) 'for a change'. All kinds of live music, from 'outrageous new wave' to Paraguayan complete with harp. Smoking discouraged 'generally', though they sell cigars at lunch-time.

AYLSHAM Norfolk Map 6

D'Accord
Bank Street
Aylsham (026 373) 3582
9–5 (9–2 Wed; 9–6 Sat),
7.30–11
Closed Sun; Wed D

Robin Barnes' 'wine and pâté bar' adjoins his first-floor delicatessen 'with over forty Eurocheeses in stock' as well as pâtés and sausages. In the wine bar, choose these or the generous cold pies rather than the hot food: venison and claret pâté with salad (£1·40), ham and egg pie (£1·30), cheese (45p with biscuits, £1·20 with salad). 'Good pastry on the apple pie too.' (Note the opening hours: morning coffee and afternoon tea are also served.) French house wine £2·40 the bottle, 36p the glass; Châteauneuf-du-Pape '73 (Jaboulet-Vercherre) £6·60. Taped music. Plans for outdoor eating in 1980.

BATH Avon Map 2

Clarets
6–7 Kingsmead Square
Bath (0225) 310072
10–2.30, 6.30–11
(11.30 Sat; 7–10.30 Sun)
Closed Sun L; Dec 25 & 26

'Remarkably smoke-free cellar', with slate-and-pine decor. Crowded, but polite service and (mostly) interesting food: mushrooms burgundian (deep fried, with Béarnaise sauce, 75p), potted crab (£1·20), casseroles of lamb and aubergine or pork and cucumber or vegetables and cheese (from £1·95), as well as soups, salads and sweets. Some would prefer larger helpings or lower prices. Wine by the glass from 50p; other French bottles from £4·35 (Corbières or Averys Ronsac). Failing that, try Argentine, Rumanian or Australian wines. Taped music. No children under 14. No dogs. A few tables in the square under the plane tree.

La Vendange
11 Margaret's Buildings,
Brock Street
Bath (0225) 21251
10.30–2.30, 5.30–10.30
(11 Fri & Sat)
Closed Sun; public hols

Small and cheerfully crowded place 'on the tourist route'. Pine indoors, wrought-iron outside in summer. Home-made soups ('straightforward and honest tomato', 35p), pâtés, quiches (70p–80p), salads, and casseroles (lamb and courgette, £1·30), as well as cauliflower cheese with bacon (90p) or 'aubergines stuffed with chicken and cream – a delight.' Sweets and coffee too. (Food is served from 12 and 7.) French house wine, £3·45 the litre, 45p the glass. Other wines include the local Roughtons from Dunkerton (£3·30) and Gevrey-Chambertin '69 (Averys) at £9·60. 'Quiet' taped music in one room.

BATH see also pub section

BEACONSFIELD Buckinghamshire   Map 3

Buck's Fizz
3 Warwick Road
Beaconsfield (049 46)
71582
12–2.30, 7.15–10.30
(Sat 11.30)
Closed Sun

Homely red and stripped pine place where you choose food at the counter and relax into 'efficient and interested' service thereafter. Blackboard menu might offer chicken liver and pistachio pâté (95p), seafood quiche (£1·10), 'lasagne as good as my wife's' (£1·50), smoked fish, imaginative salads, frangipane flan or blackberry and apple crumble. Buck's Fizz, of course (£1·20 the half-pint); French house wines £2·65 the bottle, 50p a glass; other modestly priced bottles; sherry, port, madeira (from 55p the glass). Piped music, live at weekends. A few outdoor tables.

BIRMINGHAM West Midlands   Map 5

Hawkins Café-Bar
King Edward Building,
205–219 Corporation
Street
021-236 2001
8.30 a.m.–11 p.m.
(Sat from 10 a.m.;
Sun from 5 p.m.)
(L 12–2; D 6–10)
Closed Sun L; Dec 25;
Jan 1

Enterprising two-floor cafe-cum-wine bar, popular with the neighbouring Law Courts, hospital and police station. Drop in any time from breakfast to supper (last orders 10 p.m.) for chef-made croissants, pizzas (Four Seasons, £2·15), hamburgers ('even the bun is home-made', £1·95), stuffed baked potatoes (£1·15), salads, pies, pâté and sweets. House wine £2·65 the bottle, 50p the glass; Vouvray '77, £3·95; Chianti £3·15. Also sherries, port, Lillet, sangria and fruit juices. Efficient and charming service. Tables bookable at lunch-time. Entertainment 'from time to time': from dry wit (George Melly) to Dry Ice.

BRISTOL Avon   Map 2

Arnolfini Gallery
Narrow Quay
Bristol (0272) 299191
11–10.30 (Sun from 7)
Meals 12.30–2.30, 5–8
(not Sun)
Closed Sun L; Mon;
public hols; Dec 24–Jan 2

A plain but attractive self-service wine bar in the dockside arts warehouse opposite the Trade Centre. Crowded, even hectic, with loosely supervised service sometimes. Queue up for inventive salads ('all fresh, seasonal ingredients'), cold meats and fish, as well as soup, quiches and a hot daily dish (curries, casseroles, pastas). Home-made cakes and pastries too. Queue again at the wine counter for French house wine (£3·45 the litre, 44p the glass) and other good bottles, many from Harvey's (Crozes-Hermitage '76, £4); or Smiles best bitter on tap and some unusual bottled beers. Picnic tables on the quay.

CHELTENHAM Gloucestershire   Map 2

Montpellier
Bayshill Lodge,
Montpellier Street
Cheltenham (0242) 27774
12–2.30, 6–10.30
(Sun 12–2)
Closed Sun D;
Dec 25 & 26

A two-level wine bar with food in the cosy cellar.
Choose from home-made soup (30p), the extensive
cold buffet ('good meats and imaginative salads', from
£1·30) and appealing gateaux and Stilton. One hot
dish daily. Twelve wines by glass or goblet (from
45p); several more in bottle and half-bottle (Côtes du
Rhône, n.v., £3·05). Sherries, ports, sangria, 'speciality
cocktails and punches'. Background music. A few
tables on the 'rotunda terrace'.

EXETER Devon   Map 1

White Hart

See pub section

FOLKESTONE Kent   Map 3

The Pullman
7 Church Street
Folkestone (0303) 52524
11–2.30, 7–11
(Sun 12–2, 7.30–10.30)
Closed Mon; Dec 25–28;
Jan 30–Mar 1

The Pardoes, popular in previous *Guide*s for their
generous buffet at the George and Dragon, Fordwich,
justify the name of their new wine bar with railway
memorabilia, as well as 'Tudor front, medieval
cellars.' Help-yourself without restraint to hot or cold
displays (£2·30), with home-made soup, sweets and
cheese as extras for the insatiable. Chili, poulet
niçoise, and a half-lobster for a birthday treat have
pleased members, as have the salads. (Sunday snacks
are limited.) Fifty wines, all bottled in their country
of origin, from 45p a glass for French house wine.
Ch. Cheval Blanc '70, £8·95. Sherries, ports,
aperitifs and liqueurs. Various beers on tap. Walled
garden. No dogs. Taped 'popular' music. Season-
ticket-holders commute happily.

GLOUCESTER Gloucestershire   Map 2

Tasters
22 London Road
Gloucester (0452) 417556
12–2.30, 7–10.30
Closed Sun; Dec 25–Jan 3;
one week Easter;
public hols and day after

A comfortable wine bar 'with generally civil service'
of home-made food ('we don't buy in pies or puds;
nor do we do chips and veg,' says the owner, whose
wife cooks). The blackboard menu might offer Snaffles
mousse, Mexican hot soup (60p), smoked salmon and
asparagus quiche, hot Salcombe smokies (£1·20),
'delicious' raised pies. Fresh and imaginative salads,
and attractive sweets: lemon bombe (£1), cranberry
cream tart (80p), chocolate pots. French house wine
£3·30 the litre, 55p the glass; Manzanilla (60p),
Muscat de Beaumes de Venise (for the sweets) 90p,
Gamay de l'Ardèche (Yapp) £4·50; English Three
Choirs '77, £4·95. 'No beer or fags' on sale, and no
smoking at the food counters. Taped music.

GUILDFORD Surrey   Map 3

Rowley's
Tunsgate,
124 High Street
Guildford (0483) 63277

'The second oldest building in Guildford High Street',
complete with oak beams and open fires, makes a
relaxed and comfortable wine bar ('opposite the
clock'). Cold meats and salad ('excellent game pie
with fresh and crisp salad', £2·35), a dozen cheeses
(from 65p with French bread), pâtés, and a hot dish

12–2.30 (Sat 11.30–2.30),
6.30–11
Closed Sun; Mon evening;
public hols

in winter: quiche, lasagne, boeuf bourguignonne.
Finish with a home-made sweet (fruit pies, Bakewell
tart, cheesecake from 65p). About thirty wines, most
by glass as well as bottle: house French £2·65 (48p
the glass); Coteaux du Tricastin £3·60 (65p);
Rüdesheimer Rosengarten £3·60. Live entertainment
mid-week, taped light music otherwise.

HERTFORD Hertfordsh:re   Map 3

Bottles
11 Old Cross
Hertford (0992) 50405
12–2.30, 6.30–10.30
(11 Fri, Sat)
Closed Sun

'Fresh food, freshly cooked' is the aim in this
ambitious health-shop-cum-wine-bar-cum-carvery. It
is crowded, and 'the pianist thinks a silent bar would
be a confession of failure', so it is not a place for a
quiet drink. But the blackboard lists inviting dishes:
avocado and tuna mayonnaise ('home-made', 90p),
quiche, mushrooms provençale (50p), cold joints and
chicken sections, with a choice of about a dozen
salads ('lovely' coconut and banana, creole with chilli
and nuts, Waldorf, beetroot and yoghourt, all 40p a
portion). The daily hot dish might be shredded
chicken with almonds and fresh pineapple (£2·30) or
cassoulet or devilled ribs of beef or . . . To say
nothing of passion cake and raisin pie. Carvery
operates at weekday lunches (£2·75). Tables bookable
in the conservatory. Mostly routine wines, from 45p
the glass; Bordeaux Sauvignon £3·20; Valpolicella
£2·85. Amateurish but pleasant service.

KINGSBRIDGE Devon   Map 1

Woosters
The Quay
Kingsbridge (0548) 3434
11.30–2.30 (Sun 12–2),
7–1 a.m.

Former fishermen's hut (when the estuary reached the
Salcombe road), now well situated at the head of the
river. Ambitious menu (with light snacks also at
lunch-time) offering soup (plain or seafood),
'delicious' smoked fish pâté (80p), various local fishes,
barbecues and hot-pots (spare ribs £2·25). Only house
wines by the glass (48p); Marqués de Riscal £4·90;
Muscadet Domaine du Cléray '76, £4·95. Tables on
the patio. Recorded music. No food after 11 p.m.

LEAMINGTON SPA Warwickshire   Map 2

Alastair's
40 Warwick Street
Leamington Spa (0926)
22550
12.15–2.30, 7–11.30
Closed Sun evening;
Mon L

Attractive basement wine bar with 'rather rudimentary
seating' and a courtyard for summer wining and
dining. You buy a ticket at the bar (£2·85 for boeuf
bourguignonne, for example) and are served in the
kitchen, which 'glistens with a marvellous display of
food.' Lunch is soup (50p), pâtés, quiches, salads and
sweets, with one hot dish as well as steaks (£3·95).
Candle-lit evenings bring 'scrupulously prepared'
moules marinière, boeuf en daube, whole fresh plaice
(with hot vegetables or salads, £2·50), moussaka
(£1·95) and chocolate trifle or home-made meringues
(half-portions on request). Traditional Sunday roast
(£2·50, including vegetables). Own-label wines from
£2·75 the bottle (45p the glass) for French table wine;
house champagne £7·95. No dogs. Recorded music.

MORETON-IN-MARSH Gloucestershire   Map 2

Lamb's

See main *Guide*

NORWICH Norfolk   Map 6

Skippers Wine Cellar Bar
18 Bedford Street
Norwich (0603) 22836
10.30–2.30, 6–11
Closed Sun; public hols

After thirty years in the wine trade Bernard Skipper knows how to choose wine, and members suggest that a visit to the cellar bar is primarily for what's in the glass, not for what's on the plate. That said, you will enjoy the olives with the Manzanilla or Fino (38p) and the Madeira cake with the Rutherford's Bual (43p). In between, choose carefully: various pâtés (rock lobster, 91p), cheese with French bread, 'good' lasagne (£1·10), Lancashire hot-pot, or daily dish. Salads are 'unorthodox' (baked beans, pickles, no dressing). More elaborate dinners in the ground-floor restaurant. About fifty wines, all by glass as well as bottle: house wine £2·05 for 50 cl, 41p the glass; Ch. des Carmes '75, £3·75 (65p); Viña Real £3·60 (60p); Fressingfield, n.v., £3·50 (60p). Attractive retail prices too. Light background music. (If you need an excuse, Skippers is opposite Hovells, 'the finest basket shop in the country', and near the Mustard Shop and the Bridewell Museum.)

Wine Press
Woburn Court,
8 Guildhall Hill
Norwich (0603) 612874
10–3
Closed evening; Sun;
public hols

Norfolk Vintners' 'attractive but stuffy cellar' no longer opens in the evenings, but is so popular 'lunchers spill over into the bar.' Appetising cold display: good chicken and ham pie (75p), crab pâté (55p), baked ham (£1·05); conventional salads (70p). Daily hot dish (£1·10): chicken curry with almonds, lasagne, beef risotto. 'Moist and delicious' chocolate gateau (50p). Coffee 10–11 a.m. Four wines by the glass ('rather inky Bordeaux', 48p), about ten more by bottle only (Muscadet '78, £5·22). Taped music.

NOTTINGHAM Nottinghamshire   Map 5

Ben Bowers

See main *Guide*

OXFORD Oxfordshire   Map 2

Emperors'
22 Broad Street
Oxford (0865) 42253
10.30–2.30 (Sun 12–2),
6–10.30 (exc Sun; 11 Fri
& Sat)
Closed Sun evening;
2 days Chr & Easter

Atmospheric little three-tier wine bar in a 17th-century house, with a garden ('welcome in summer') backed by the old City wall. Start the day, if you wish, with coffee and croissants, move on to lunch, and even return for supper – and free Angostura bitters brûlés, should that be necessary. Warm praise for steak and kidney pie (£1·50), quiche with salad (£1·05) and the cheeses. Impressive range of wines, from 'cheap and cheerful' house wine, called French Quaff, at £2·55, through Tricastin at £3·10 (55p the glass) and Saumur Blanc at £3·70 (65p the glass) to Ch. Mouton-Rothschild '61 at £64 (£32 the half, if you are counting pennies). Fine sherries, ports and madeiras too; hock and seltzer, Kir or sangria in the summer; Bishop (mulled port) in the winter. No dogs.

POOLE Dorset   Map 2

Dolphin Hotel   See main *Guide*

ST ALBANS Hertfordshire   Map 3

Aspelia   See main *Guide*

WINCHESTER Hampshire   Map 2

Mr Pitkin's
4 Jewry Street
Winchester (0962) 69630
11–2.30, 6–10.30
(11 Fri & Sat); Sun 12–2,
7–10.30

The first-floor 'eating house' offers two- or three-course set lunches (from £3·45) and four-course dinners (£5·50). At ground level, the Edwardian-style wine bar has a blackboard menu: ploughman's (60p), quiche and salad (£1·25), cold meats (including 'excellent rare sirloin'), smoked trout or mackerel, cheese and biscuits (55p). 'All fresh and clean and friendly.' Wide range of wines by glass and bottle from £2·50 (48p the glass) for the French house wines. Loire Gamay £2·95, Ch. Fourcas-Hosten '66, c.b., £8·45, Perlé d'Alsace £3·95. Sherries, ports and madeiras too. Taped and live music ('on a fully-restored 1896 Bechstein').

WALES

LLANGOLLEN Clwyd   Map 4

Gales
18 Bridge Street
Llangollen (0978) 860089
12–2, 6–10.30
(7–10.30 Sun)
Closed Sun & Mon
(Nov–May);
Dec 25 & 26; Jan 1;
2 weeks Nov; 2 weeks Feb

'Over the bridge and turn left' to find this popular family-run wine bar with its chapel pews. Some find the proprietor 'rather overpowering' and the helpings small, but most are well pleased with the competent service and interesting food: 'creamy and nutmeggy' onion soup (50p), 'very palatable' prawn fricassee, apple and prawn curry, quiche, various salads (smoked salmon £1·70), 'lovely home-made almond ice-cream' and raspberry cheesecake. Granary bread is good, salads 'rather ordinary'. Impressive wines, only seven available by the glass (French house wines, 45p). California Chenin Blanc £3·90, Rioja Cvne '74, £3·95, Chianti Classico '75, £2·95. Taped music. B&B £5.

SCOTLAND

EDINBURGH   Map 9

Henderson's Salad Table   See main *Guide*

Wine bars are represented by a wine glass on the maps, pubs by a tankard.

PLEASE keep sending in reports, as soon as possible after each meal. The cut-off date for the 1981 Guide is September 30, 1980, but reports are even more useful earlier in the year, especially for the remoter areas and new places. Late autumn reports can also affect corrections at proof stage.

IRELAND

DUBLIN   Map 10

(6) Shrimps
1 Anne's Lane
Dublin 713143
noon–11
Closed Sun; public hols
Service 10%

Shrimps will have room for scampi people with the upper-floor extension to this comfortable wine bar (Dublin's first), used by shoppers as well as chess and backgammon players. The short menu changes frequently and offers a few hot dishes as well as pâtés and salads. 'Reasonable prices for Dublin.' 'Delicious cream of spinach soup' or seafood chowder, perhaps, stuffed aubergine, rabbit and prune terrine (£1·75), dressed crab (£2), smoked salmon (£2·85), apple tart or 'superb fresh strawberries with a huge bowl of cream.' French house wine £3·25 (60p the glass), Beau Rivage '75, £3·75, Puligny-Montrachet '70 (whose?) £6·95. Sherries, port and Perrier. 'We were smoked out by the next-door table.' Taped music. (Note the £1 minimum between 12 and 2.30.)

DUBLIN see also pub section, and city plan on p. 422

KINSALE Co Cork   Map 10

Max's
Main Street
Kinsale 72443
12.30–2.30, 7.30–11
Closed Tue; mid-Oct to
early Dec;
mid-Jan to Mar 1

Main Street is not the main street (which runs parallel) and Max (a Dobermann Pinscher) does not actually own the wine bar though he may behave as if he does. Otherwise all is plain sailing in this spruce modern place 'where the posh locals go to sober up from the night before.' 'Excellent' moules farcies (£1·05), good home-made tomato soup, 'delicate' salmon mousse (£2·05), 'amateurish but tasty' lasagne (in the winter), crab claws (in the summer), pâté, salads and steak (£4·90). Soave or Valpolicella 50p the glass, £2·30 the jug (six glasses); Vinho Verde £3·25; Rioja, Marqués de Riscal (red) £4·10. One table on the patio. Taped music. If you eat at a table, rather than prop up the bar, there seems to be a 10 per cent service charge.

SCHULL Co Cork   Map 10

Lucullus Wine Tavern
Main Street
Schull 28230
12–3, 6–10
Closed Sun

Lars and Brigitta Säflund, ex-restaurateurs, now run this informal wine bar and the adjacent delicatessen, 'so if you order ham salad, Lars cuts it from the bone and passes it through.' Wines too may travel from the shop stock if you fancy something esoteric. Warm praise for Brigitta's 'rich, sharp and lovely' tomato soup (70p), 'exceptionally good' quiche, generous rare beef salad (£1·70), butler's pie (hot or cold, £1·20), pâté, salamis and cheeses. House wine 50p the glass (£2·50 the litre), Vacqueyras (Côtes du Rhône) £3·45. 'Friendly and capable service.' Stone tables in the courtyard. Light classical music on tape. 'This is where all the iron artefacts that look so fake in Surrey pubs look utterly at home.'

Restaurants with air-conditioning

London

L'Amico, SW1
Arirang, W1
Arlecchino, W8
Averof, W1
Beotys, WC2
Bloom's, E1
Brinkley's, SW10
Bumbles, SW1
Il Camino, New Malden
Canaletto, W2
Capital Hotel Restaurant, SW3
Carlo's Place, SW6
Carlton Tower, SW1
Carrier's, N1
Carroll's, W1
Chez Moi, W11
Daphne's, SW3
Drury Lane Hotel, Maudie's, WC2
Fogareiro, N3
Food for Thought, WC2
Gatamelata, W8
Gay Hussar, W1
Granary, W1
The Grange, WC2
Les Halles, WC1
Hathaways, SW11
Joe Allen, WC2
Justin de Blank, W1
Kerzenstüberl, W1
Kew Rendezvous, Richmond
Langan's Brasserie, W1
Lebanese Restaurant, W2
Leith's, W11
Lockets, SW1
Lok Ho Fook, W1
Mata Hari, NW1
Maxim, W13
Monte Grappa, WC1
Oslo Court, NW8
Poissonnerie de l'Avenue, SW3
Red Lion Chinese, Richmond
San Frediano, SW3
Satay House, W2
Siena, N5
Sweetings, EC4
Swiss Centre Restaurant, W1
Tate Gallery Restaurant, SW1
Throgmorton Restaurant, EC2
Upper Crust, SW1
Walton's, SW3
Wei Hai Wei, SW13
Wolfe's, W1

England

Ambleside, Cumbria
Rothay Manor

Bath, Avon
Priory Hotel

Beaminster, Dorset
Pickwick's

Belper, Derbys
Rémy's

Birmingham, W. Midlands
Dionysos

Blackpool, Lancs
Danish Kitchen

Bridgnorth, Salop
Bambers

Brighton & Hove, E. Sussex
Bannister's
Chez Moi
Hove Manor Restaurant
Oats

Burnham Market, Norfolk
Fishes'

Cambridge, Cambs
Peking

Cheltenham, Glos
Food for Thought

Chichester, W. Sussex
Christophers

Derby, Derbys
Ben Bowers

Eastbourne, E. Sussex
Porthole

East Looe, Cornwall
Runnelstone Restaurant

Elland, W. Yorks
Bertie's Bistro

Folkestone, Kent
Emilio's

Framfield, E. Sussex
Coach House

Halsetown, Cornwall
Chef's Kitchen

Harrogate, N. Yorks
Oliver Restaurant

Heckfield, Hants
Andwell's

Hemel Hempstead, Herts
Casanova

Huddersfield, W. Yorks
Shabab

Ivinghoe, Bucks
King's Head

Keswick, Cumbria
Yan . . . Tyan . . . Tethera

Leeds, W. Yorks
Shabab

Lewes, E. Sussex
Pelham Arms, Sussex Kitchen

Liverpool, Merseyside
Oriel

Lytham St Anne's, Lancs
Lidun Cottage

Maidenhead, Berks
Maidenhead Chinese Restaurant

Manchester
Hotel Armenia Shish Kebab House
Danish Food Centre
Isola Bella
Kwok Man
Midland Hotel French Restaurant
Royal Exchange
Woo Sang
Yang Sing

Nottingham, Notts
Ben Bowers

Oxford, Oxon
Opium Den
Les Quat' Saisons
La Sorbonne

Poole-in-Wharfedale, W. Yorks
Pool Court

Ramsbury, Wilts
Bell Inn

Rugby, Warwicks
Andalucia

St Albans, Herts
Aspelia

St Mawes, Cornwall
Rising Sun

Salisbury, Wilts
Le Provençal

Sellack, Hereford & Worcs
Lovepool Inn

Sheffield, S. Yorks
Just Cooking

Southport, Merseyside
Squires

Tiverton, Devon
Henderson's

Weybridge, Surrey
Casa Romana

Whitstable, Kent
Giovanni's

Windermere, Cumbria
Miller Howe
Postern Gate

Wolverhampton, W. Midlands
Tandoor

Wales

Cardiff, S. Glamorgan
Harvesters
Riverside

Llandewi Skirrid, Gwent
Walnut Tree Inn

Swansea, W. Glamorgan
Drangway

Scotland

Auchterarder, Tayside
Gleneagles Hotel

Dumfries, Dumfries & Galloway
Bruno's

Edinburgh
Denzler's
Henderson's Salad Table
Madogs

Glamis, Tayside
Strathmore Arms

Glasgow
Beacons Hotel, La Bonne Auberge

Kinross, Tayside
Windlestrae Hotel

Port Ellen, Islay, Strathclyde
Machrie Hotel

Channel Islands

Guernsey, St Peter Port
Whistlers Bistro

Jersey, St Helier
La Capannina

Isle of Man

Port St Mary
The Barn

Republic of Ireland

Cork, Co Cork
Arbutus Lodge

Dingle, Co Kerry
Half Door

Dublin
Le Coq Hardi
Tandoori Rooms

Dungarvan, Co Wexford
Seanachie

Kinsale, Co Cork
Man Friday

Sandycove, Co Dublin
Mirabeau

Slane, Co Meath
Slane Castle

Straffan, Co Kildare
Barberstown Castle

Youghal, Co Cork
Aherne's Sea Food Bar

Northern Ireland

Comber, Co Down
Old Crow

Gilford, Co Down
Pot Belly

Where to dine and dance

London

Cervantes, Coulsdon (Fri & Sat)
Kerzenstüberl, W1 (Mon–Sat)
Mata Hari, NW1

England

Birmingham, W. Midlands
Dionysos

Branston, Staffs
Riverside Inn (Wed & Fri)

Chittlehamholt, Devon
Highbullen Hotel

Dereham (East), Norfolk
Phoenix Hotel (Sat Sept–Apr)

Farnham, Surrey
Latour (Fri & Sat)

Limpley Stoke, Wilts
Danielle (occasionally)

Lyme Regis, Dorset
Toni

Manchester
Hotel Armenia, Shish Kebab House

Milford-on-Sea, Hants
Westover Hall (Fri & Sat)

Oundle, Northants
Tyrrells

Torquay, Devon
Toorak Hotel (Wed & Sat in season)

Yarm, Cleveland
Santoro

Wales

Abersoch, Gwynedd
Porth Tocyn Hotel

St David's, Dyfed
Warpool Court Hotel

Scotland

Auchterarder, Tayside
Gleneagles Hotel

Republic of Ireland

Dungarvan, Co Waterford
Seanachie (weekends)

Northern Ireland

Comber, Co Down
Old Crow (Sat)

Restaurants where smoking is restricted

Refer to the restaurant's entry to find out exactly what the restrictions are

London

Balzac Bistro, W12
Le Bressan, W8
Bunny's, NW3
Il Camino, New Malden
Capital Hotel Restaurant, SW3
Connaught Hotel, W1
Food for Thought, WC2
The Grange, WC2
Lockets, SW1
Ma Cuisine, SW3
Oven d'Or, Orpington
Oslo Court, NW8
Simpsons, SW15
Swiss Centre, W1
Tate Gallery Restaurant, SW1

England

Ambleside, Cumbria
Harvest
Rothay Manor
Sheila's Cottage

Bath, Avon
The Laden Table
Priory Hotel

Beaminster, Dorset
Pickwick's

Berwick St John, Dorset
Michelmersh Grange

Billingshurst, W. Sussex
Jennie Wren

Bourton-on-the-Water, Glos
Rose Tree

Brighton & Hove, E. Sussex
Eaton Restaurant

Bristol, Avon
Michael's

Broadway, Hereford & Worcs
Collin House Hotel

Burford, Oxon
Bay Tree

Burham, Kent
Toastmaster's Inn

Caldbeck, Cumbria
Parkend Restaurant

Cauldon Lowe, Staffs
Jean-Pierre

Chagford, Devon
Gidleigh Park

Cheltenham, Glos
Food for Thought

Chesterton, Oxon
Kinchs

Chichester, W. Sussex
Little London Restaurant

Chittlehamholt, Devon
Highbullen Hotel

Coatham Mundeville, Durham
Hall Garth Hotel

Colyton, Devon
Old Bakehouse

Dartington, Devon
Cranks

Drewsteignton, Devon
Castle Drogo

Eastbourne, E. Sussex
Bistro Byron
Porthole

East Grinstead, W. Sussex
Gravetye Manor

Findon, W. Sussex
Darlings Bistro
Findon Manor

Flitton, Beds
White Hart

Framfield, E. Sussex
Coach House

Frenchbeer, Devon
Teignworthy Hotel

Glastonbury, Somerset
No 3 Dining Rooms

Grasmere, Cumbria
White Moss House

Guildford, Surrey
Cranks

Halesworth, Suffolk
Bassett's

Hertford, Herts
Dimsdales

Hunstrete, Avon
Hunstrete House

Iddesleigh, Devon
Duke of York

Ipswich, Suffolk
Rosie's Place

Jevington, E. Sussex
Hungry Monk

Kintbury, Berks
Dundas Arms

Knutsford, Cheshire
David's Place

Lewes, E. Sussex
Bull House

Lower Swell, Glos
Old Farmhouse

Malvern Wells, Hereford & Worcs
Croque-en-Bouche

Manchester,
On the Eighth Day

Montacute, Somerset
Milk House

Nantwich, Cheshire
Churche's Mansion

Nottingham, Notts
Ben Bowers

Ottery St Mary, Devon
The Lodge
Wheelhouse

Parkham, Devon
Foxdown Manor

Porlock Weir, Somerset
Ship Inn

Priddy, Somerset
Miners' Arms

Ramsbury, Wilts
The Bell

Rushlake Green, E. Sussex
The Priory

St Martin in Meneage, Cornwall
Boskenna

Sheffield, S. Yorks
Just Cooking

Shepton Mallet, Somerset
Bowlish House

South Petherton, Somerset
Oaklands

Stratford-upon-Avon, Warwicks
Ashburton House

Talkin, Cumbria
Tarn End

Temple Sowerby, Cumbria
Temple Sowerby House

Tunbridge Wells, Kent
Mount Edgcumbe Hotel

Ullswater, Cumbria
Sharrow Bay

Underbarrow, Cumbria
Greenriggs Country House

West Stoughton, Somerset
Eethuys

Windermere, Cumbria
Miller Howe

Woodstock, Oxon
Luis

Wootton, Wilts
Loaves and Fishes

York, N. Yorks
St William's Restaurant

Wales

Cardiff, S. Glamorgan
Harvesters

Cricieth, Gwynedd
Moelwyn Restaurant

Crickhowell, Powys
Gliffaes Country House

Llanwrtyd Wells, Powys
Llwynderw Hotel

Llanychaer Bridge, Dyfed
Penlan Oleu

Pembroke, Dyfed
Richmond Coffee House

502

Scotland

Achiltibuie, Highland
Summer Isles Hotel

Ballater, Grampian
Tullich Lodge

Eddleston, Borders
Cringletie House Hotel

Edinburgh
Denzler's
Henderson's Salad Table

Glasgow
Ubiquitous Chip

Gullane, Lothian
La Potinière

Inverness, Highland
Dunain Park

Isle Ornsay, Skye
Kinloch Lodge Hotel

Lochgoilhead, Strathclyde
Inverlounin House

Moffat, Dumfries & Galloway
Beechwood Country House Hotel

Nairn, Highland
Clifton Hotel

Peat Inn, Fife
Peat Inn

Port Appin, Strathclyde
Airds Hotel

Tyndrum, Central
Clifton Coffee House

Ullapool, Highland
Ceilidh Place

Uphall, Lothian
Houstoun House

Channel Islands

Sark
Aval du Creux
Hotel Petit Champ

Republic of Ireland

Annamoe, Co Wicklow
Armstrong's Barn

Cork, Co Cork
Arbutus Lodge
Lovetts

Gorey, Co Wexford
Marlfield House

Letterfrack, Co Galway
Rosleague Manor

Mallow, Co Cork
Longueville House

Oughterard, Co Galway
Currarevagh House

Shanagarry, Co Cork
Ballymaloe House

Wicklow, Co Wicklow
Old Rectory

Entries for places with distinctions carry symbols (pestle, tureen, bottle, glass).
Credits are fully written entries, with approvers' names below the text. Passes are
telegraphic entries (useful in the area) with details under the text. Provisional
entries are in italics (see 'How to use the Guide', p. 4).

If you think you are suffering from food-poisoning after eating in a restaurant, report
this immediately to the local Public Health Authority (and write to us).

'Meal' indicates the cost of a meal for one, including food, coffee, a half-bottle of
one of the cheapest wines listed, cover, service, and VAT (see 'How to use the
Guide', p. 4).

Wine prices shown are for a 'standard' bottle of the wine concerned, unless another
measure is stated (e.g. litre, 50 cl., or pint).

Where to eat out of doors (*4 or more tables*)

London

Bagatelle, SW10
Brinkley's, SW10
Le Chef, W2
Down by the Riverside, Kingston
Fingal's, SW6
Gino's, Richmond
Il Girasole, SW3
Hard Rock Cafe, W1
Oslo Court, NW8
Poissonnerie de l'Avenue, SW3
The Refectory, Richmond
Le Routier, NW1 (L)
San Lorenzo Fuoriporta, SW19
Simpsons, SW15

England

Allerthorpe, Humberside
Plough Inn

Alresford, Hants
O'Rorkes

Birmingham, W. Midlands
Jonathans'

Bishop's Lydeard, Somerset
Rose Cottage

Bourton-on-the-Water, Glos
Rose Tree

Brentwood, Essex
Moat House

Brighton & Hove, E. Sussex
Al Forno

Broadstairs, Kent
Marchesi Restaurant

Broadway, Hereford & Worcs
Collin House Hotel
Hunter's Lodge

Caldbeck, Cumbria
Parkend

Cheltenham, Glos
Aubergine

Chichester, W. Sussex
Little London Restaurant

Chipping Campden, Glos
Kings Arms

Clanfield, Oxon
The Plough

Colchester, Essex
The Barn

Compton, Surrey
Withies Inn

Corse Lawn, Glos
Corse Lawn House

Dartington, Devon
Cranks

Farnham, Surrey
Latour

Findon, W. Sussex
Findon Manor

Fingest, Bucks
Chequers Inn

Flitton, Beds
White Hart

Guist, Norfolk
Tollbridge Restaurant

Helford, Cornwall
Riverside

Herstmonceux, E. Sussex
The Sundial

Honiton, Devon
Knights

Hunstrete, Avon
Hunstrete House (L)

Huntingdon, Cambs
Old Bridge Hotel

Iddesleigh, Devon
Duke of York

Lower Swell, Glos
Old Farmhouse

Monkleigh, Devon
Beaconside (L)

Nayland, Suffolk
The Bear

Northallerton, N. Yorks
Romanby Court

Parkham, Devon
Foxdown Manor

Poundisford, Somerset
Well House

Prior's Hardwick, Warwicks
Butcher's Arms

St Albans, Herts
Aspelia

St Ives, Cambs
Slepe Hall, Rugeley's Restaurant

Shepton Mallet, Somerset
Bowlish House

Skipton, N. Yorks
Oats

South Molton, Devon
Stumbles

South Petherton, Somerset
Oaklands

Wareham, Dorset
Priory Hotel

York, N. Yorks
St William's Restaurant

Wales

Abersoch, Gwynedd
Porth Tocyn Hotel (L)

Broad Haven, Dyfed
Druidstone Hotel

Colwyn Bay, Clwyd
Holland Arms (L)

Crickhowell, Powys
Nantyffin Cider Mill

Llandewi Skirrid, Gwent
Walnut Tree Inn

Penmaenpool, Gwynedd
George III Hotel

St David's, Dyfed
Warpool Court Hotel

Scotland

Achiltibuie, Highland
Summer Isles Hotel (L)

Ardentinny, Strathclyde
Ardentinny Hotel

Ballater, Grampian
Tullich Lodge (L)

Kilchrenan, Strathclyde
Taychreggan Hotel (L)

Lochgoilhead, Strathclyde
Inverlounin House

Port Ellen, Islay, Strathclyde
Machrie Hotel

Ullapool, Highland
Ceilidh Place

Weem, Tayside
Ailean Chraggan Hotel

Channel Islands

Guernsey, St Peter Port
La Frégate

Republic of Ireland

Annamoe, Co Wicklow
Armstrong's Barn

Carrigbyrne, Co Wexford
Cedar Lodge

Dunderry, Co Meath
Dunderry Lodge

Dungarvan, Co Wexford
Seanachie

Gorey, Co Wexford
Marlfield House

Mallow, Co Cork
Longueville House

Shanagarry, Co Cork
Ballymaloe House

Tralee, Co Kerry
Oyster Tavern

See p. 508 for the restaurant-goer's legal rights, and p. 510 for information on
hygiene in restaurants.

Unless otherwise stated, a restaurant is open all week and all year and is licensed.

Value for money

We list here restaurants and hotels whose prices are underlined in the text to indicate (in the *Guide*'s opinion) good value for money. Please consult individual entries carefully: such meals may not be offered every day, or at all times of day. Restaurants awarded a pestle-and-mortar distinction are automatically considered to offer good value for money.

London

Alonso's, SW8
Aziz, W6
Bloom's, E1
Bubb's, EC1
Le Chef, W2 (tdh)
Eatons, SW1
Efes Kebab House, W1
Ganpath, WC1
Geeta, NW6
The Grange, WC2
Hathaways, SW11
Standard Indian, W2

England

Alresford, Hants
O'Rorkes (tdh D)

Banbury, Oxon
Peppermill (tdh L)

Biddenden, Kent
Ye Maydes (tdh L)

Bishop's Cleeve, Glos
Cleeveway House

Botallack, Cornwall
Count House (tdh Sun L)

Brampton, Cumbria
Farlam Hall

Burnham Market, Norfolk
Fishes' (tdh weekday)

Caldbeck, Cumbria
Parkend

Chichester, W. Sussex
Little London (tdh L)

Chittlehamholt, Devon
Highbullen Hotel

Deddington, Oxon
Holcombe Hotel (tdh L)

Fadmoor, N. Yorks
Plough

Folkestone, Kent
Emilio's (tdh L)

Frenchbeer, Devon
Teignworthy Hotel (tdh Sun L)

Great Witley, Hereford & Worcs
Hundred House (tdh buffet L)

Guist, Norfolk
Tollbridge Restaurant

Heald Green, Gtr Manchester
La Bonne Auberge (tdh L)

Hemel Hempstead, Herts
Lautrec

Husbands Bosworth, Leics
Fernie Lodge

Manchester, Gtr Manchester
Kwok Man
Woo Sang
Yang Sing

Nantwich, Cheshire
Churche's Mansion

Newcastle upon Tyne, Tyne & Wear
Black Gate Restaurant (tdh L)

Parkham, Devon
Foxdown Manor

Porlock Weir, Somerset
Ship Inn

Poynings, W. Sussex
Au Petit Normand (tdh Sun L)

Pulborough, W. Sussex
Stane Street Hollow

Ramsbury, Wilts
The Bell (tdh)

Rugby, Warwicks
Andalucia

St Martin in Meneage, Cornwall
Boskenna

Shipston on Stour, Warwicks
White Bear

South Petherton, Somerset
Oaklands

Storrington, W. Sussex
Manleys (tdh Sun L)

Stratford-upon-Avon, Warwicks
Ashburton House

Talkin, Cumbria
Tarn End Hotel (tdh)

Tregony, Cornwall
Kea House

Underbarrow, Cumbria
Tullythwaite House

Uppingham, Leics
Lake Isle

Westerham, Kent
Alison Burt's

West Runton, Norfolk
Mirabelle (tdh)

Weybourne, Norfolk
Gasché's (tdh)

Wrelton, N. Yorks
Huntsman

Wales

Llanbister, Powys
Cwmllechwedd Fawr

Llanwddyn, Powys
Lake Vyrnwy Hotel (tdh L)

Swansea, W. Glamorgan
The Drangway (tdh L)

Scotland

Kilmartin, Strathclyde
The Cairn

Lochgoilhead, Strathclyde
Inverlounin House

Moffat, Dumfries & Galloway
Beechwood Country House Hotel (tdh)

Nairn, Highland
Clifton Hotel

Perth, Tayside
Timothy's

Channel Islands

Sark
Aval du Creux (tdh)

Isle of Man

Port St Mary
The Barn (alc L)

Ireland

Ballydehob, Co Cork
Basil Bush

Dingle, Co Kerry
Doyle's

Dunderry, Co Meath
Dunderry Lodge (tdh)

Gorey, Co Wexford
Marlfield House (tdh L)

Oughterard, Co Galway
Currarevagh House (tdh L)

Shanagarry, Co Cork
Ballymaloe House (tdh buffet L)

DINERS' GUIDE
to restaurant law

A restaurant does not have to accept your booking, or serve you, even if there is obviously space. But it is illegal for them to refuse to serve you on the grounds of your colour, sex, race, or ethnic origin. And if a restaurant which is part of a hotel (not a private hotel) refuses food and drink to a traveller, the proprietor could be prosecuted and made to pay damages.

Booking a table at a restaurant obliges you to turn up and obliges them to provide a table. Either side may sue for breach of contract if the booking is not honoured. Strictly speaking, even if you later telephone to cancel the booking (as you certainly should if you change your plans) you can be made to pay something, though most restaurateurs will be grateful just to be told. If you fail to show up altogether, the restaurateur can ask for compensation for his expense in keeping your table, and for his business loss.

You have no redress in respect of items which are on the menu, but which turn out to be 'off' when you come to order.

The menu must be accurate in describing the food and drink served. Any wrong description should be reported to the Trading Standards Department of the local authority (as well as being taken up with the manager), with a view to action under the Trade Descriptions Act. If a restaurant is convicted under this Act, the court may award compensation to anyone who suffered from the misdescription.

Restaurants are now obliged to display their food and drink prices (or a spread of their prices if the menu is long) at or near the entrance to their premises, and these prices must include VAT at the current rate. By an anomaly, the requirement to include VAT in prices does not extend to menus inside the restaurant, so you should still make sure whether the menu given you at table includes VAT or not.

The quantity specified in what you are invited to order must be provided (so oeufs en cocotte should mean at least two). This also applies to wine sold in carafes (see 'How to use the *Guide*', page 4).

The meals served in a restaurant must be edible and composed of ingredients which conform to strict and well-defined standards. Failure in this regard is a criminal offence under the Food and Drugs Act. The local Environmental Health Officer deals with this. If you are ill through eating bad food, the restaurant could be fined for infringing the Food and Drugs Act, and must compensate you for the pain, suffering, loss of earnings and other expenses you incur. Smoking by staff in the kitchen, breaches of the rules about hygiene, and failures in kitchen cleanliness, are also forbidden. (See also our hygiene article on page 510.)

The food, drink and service provided by a restaurant must be reasonable, according to the standards you might expect from the type of place it is. A serious disparity between what you reasonably expected and what you actually received entitles you to compensation for breach of contract. In theory you are entitled to recover this compensation by deducting a fair sum from the restaurant's bill for food or service. If *in extremis* you do this, do not be put off by any threat to call the police, or even by any contrary advice that a policeman who is called may give. Deducting from the bill is a civil matter, and so has nothing to do with the police, unless a breach of the peace is involved. This you will naturally do your best to avoid, for instance, by providing a verifiable name and address, but you are entitled to quote, and to stand fast on, your rights in this situation. If things look very difficult, you could pay up, making it clear that you do so 'under protest' and 'without prejudice'. You would then have to sue to get the money back.

Always check a restaurant bill for accuracy. If it is correct, you must pay it there and then, in cash. The restaurant is not obliged to accept a cheque or payment by credit card, although it can, of course, do so if it wants to.

If a service charge is prominently mentioned on the menu, you must pay it, if the service was satisfactory. You may assume that it is imposed in lieu of expecting a tip. If the service is seriously deficient, you can recoup the compensation you are entitled to for this by refusing to pay some or all of the service charge. You are never obliged to leave a tip, as such – don't feel pressured by social niceties into paying one. What happens if you withhold it is not a matter of law. Not unless you are actually assaulted. But that is another matter.

David Tench

DINERS' GUIDE
to catering hygiene

Restaurants, and the food they produce, must be clean. A restaurant kitchen handles such a lot of food in a year that there is bound to be a risk of some cross-contamination. Sound practice cannot always be relied upon, and because, unfortunately, good food and clean food cannot always be equated, even in these pages restaurants sometimes appear whose conduct is open to criticism on public health grounds. *Guide* inspectors are not trained as Environmental Health Officers, and, to preserve their own anonymity, they usually ask to see kitchens only if other customers are also invited to do so. But an alert consumer can often sense what is happening behind the scenes by knowing what to look for elsewhere. For instance:

1. How does the place look from outside? Is the menu grubby, are the windows and curtains uncleaned? Is there refuse about, or food deliveries waiting for attention? Is the ventilator grille greasy and dirty? Inside, are there tell-tale signs of rodents about – a gnawed food packet, or holes in the skirting-board?

2. What are the table-cloths and settings like? Does the restaurant smell clean? Is the dining-room floor clean at the approaches to the kitchen? If they do not bother with what the customer sees, would you expect them to bother with what he does not see?

3. Notice the lavatories. Provision for the staff is unlikely to be better than it is for customers, and negligence in this area probably indicates the management's attitude to hygiene in general.

4. Watch the personal habits of the staff. Are cuts and sores covered with waterproof dressings? Incidentally, smoking while handling open food (including drinks) is a legal as well as a social offence.

5. Is open food exposed for long at room temperature, or where it can be breathed over? Do the cooked meat and fish on an hors d'oeuvre table, or the creamy puddings on a sweets trolley, look as though they had lasted the weekend? Is reheated food hot through? (Poor temperature control is a principal cause of food-poisoning, because it encourages organisms to multiply.)

If conclusions so far are unfavourable, you are not – unless you are a *Guide* inspector – obliged to take the risk of eating a meal. Just drop us a line. But if, in spite of favourable appearances, you still decide afterwards that you have been poisoned, you should if possible take the following steps:

1. Whether or not you have been to a doctor, get in touch promptly with the Environmental Health Department of the restaurant's Local Authority (or your own Department if you ate in a distant town – they will pass the information on). If you can provide a specimen of the food or its after-effects, so much the better.

2. Check with other members of the party, if any, to pin down the source of the trouble (which items on the menu did everyone affected eat?) and the time at which symptoms appeared.

3. If you feel strong enough, tell the restaurant proprietor and, in any event, the *Guide*.

4. Remember that the meal to blame may not be the last one you ate. Some forms of food-poisoning wreak their vengeance quickly, but most organisms take anything from a few hours to two days or more.

5. Be particularly careful for a few days afterwards about the way you prepare food for other people: consult your doctor.

Remember that Environmental Health Officers (who can close a restaurant at very short notice if there is a risk to health) are just as concerned to advise and educate restaurateurs as to prosecute them and that by reporting a case of suspected food-poisoning you may spare many others from similar suffering.

(For your civil rights as a restaurant customer, see the Diners' Guide to restaurant law, p. 508.)

REPORT FORMS
for the use of members

Please use a separate report form (or sheet of paper if you prefer) for each restaurant or hotel, so that we can file each report separately in its own restaurant file. Forms for reporting on restaurants, pubs or wine bars follow.

Tell us, if you can, exactly what you ate and drank, what it cost and whether or not it was good, and what the service was like. Mention the surroundings, the decor, the music. Was the place friendly? Clean? Quiet? Was it good value for money?

If you report on a hotel you have stayed at, tell us also something about the standard of accommodation – whether or not it was comfortable and pleasant, and if it was good value for money. But please: food first and foremost; comfort and hotel facilities second.

Let us have your report as soon as you can after your meal or stay, and in no case later than September 30, 1980.

Write – and sign – as clearly as possible: we hate misprinting names.

Ask us for more forms, which we will send free from Freepost, The Good Food Guide, 14 Buckingham Street, London WC2N 6BR (unfortunately Freepost facilities are available only within the United Kingdom).

And above all, please do report to us. Do not let the villain who half-poisoned you get away unmarked; do not deprive the excellent people who served you so well of the reputation and custom they deserve.

The Good Food Guide REPORT FORM (I.80)

To the Editor, *The Good Food Guide,* Freepost,
14 Buckingham Street, London WC2N 6BR

From my personal experience I CONFIRM that _____

_____

on page ____ deserves its place in the list.

I stayed/had lunch/dined there on _____ 19____

I am not connected directly or indirectly with management or proprietors.

You may/may not print my name.

Signed _____

Name and address (BLOCK CAPITALS) _____

_____

Report (please describe anything you think relevant – style, comfort,
accommodation if any, sounds and smells, as well as food, drink and service.)

☐ *please tick if you would like
this report acknowledged*

☐ *please tick if you would like
more report forms*

please continue overleaf

My meal for . . . . people		
cost: food	£	
drink	£	
service	£	
(if added on)		
total	£	
Attach bill where possible		

To the Editor, *The Good Food Guide,* Freepost,
14 Buckingham Street, London WC2N 6BR

From my personal experience I CONFIRM that ————————

————————————————————————————

on page ——— deserves its place in the list.

I stayed/had lunch/dined there on ———————————— 19——

I am not connected directly or indirectly with management or proprietors.

You may/may not print my name.

Signed ——————————————————————————

Name and address (BLOCK CAPITALS) ————————————

————————————————————————————

Report (please describe anything you think relevant – style, comfort,
accommodation if any, sounds and smells, as well as food, drink and service.)

☐ *please tick if you would like
this report acknowledged*

☐ *please tick if you would like
more report forms*

please continue overleaf

My meal for . . . . people
cost: food £
drink £
service £
(if added on)
total £
Attach bill where possible

To the Editor, *The Good Food Guide,* Freepost,
14 Buckingham Street, London WC2N 6BR

From my personal experience I CONFIRM that _____

_____

on page _____ deserves its place in the list.

I stayed/had lunch/dined there on _____ 19____

I am not connected directly or indirectly with management or proprietors.

You may/may not print my name.

Signed _____

Name and address (BLOCK CAPITALS) _____

_____

Report (please describe anything you think relevant – style, comfort,
accommodation if any, sounds and smells, as well as food, drink and service.)

☐ *please tick if you would like
this report acknowledged*

☐ *please tick if you would like
more report forms*

please continue overleaf

My meal for . . . . people	
cost: food	£
drink	£
service	£
(if added on)	
total	£

Attach bill where possible

To the Editor, *The Good Food Guide*, Freepost,
14 Buckingham Street, London WC2N 6BR

From my personal experience I NOMINATE for inclusion in your list the
following restaurant, hotel, pub or wine bar

_____

_____

Telephone: _____

I stayed/had lunch/dined there on _____ 19____

I am not connected directly or indirectly with management or proprietors.

You may/may not print my name.

Signed _____

Name and address (BLOCK CAPITALS) _____

_____

Report (please describe anything you think relevant – style, comfort,
accommodation if any, sounds and smells, as well as food, drink and service.)

☐ *please tick if you would like
this report acknowledged*

☐ *please tick if you would like
more report forms*

please continue overleaf

My meal for . . . . people		
cost: food	£	
drink	£	
service	£	
(if added on)		
total	£	
Attach bill where possible		

To the Editor, *The Good Food Guide*, Freepost,
14 Buckingham Street, London WC2N 6BR

From my personal experience I NOMINATE for inclusion in your list the
following restaurant, hotel, pub or wine bar

_____

_____

Telephone: _____

I stayed/had lunch/dined there on _____ 19____

I am not connected directly or indirectly with management or proprietors.

You may/may not print my name.

Signed _____

Name and address (BLOCK CAPITALS) _____

_____

Report (please describe anything you think relevant – style, comfort,
accommodation if any, sounds and smells, as well as food, drink and service.)

☐ *please tick if you would like
this report acknowledged*

☐ *please tick if you would like
more report forms*

please continue overleaf

My meal for . . . . people		
cost:	food	£
	drink	£
	service	£
(if added on)		
	total	£

Attach bill where possible

To the Editor, *The Good Food Guide*, Freepost,
14 Buckingham Street, London WC2N 6BR

From my personal experience I DO NOT/WOULD NOT APPROVE of the inclusion in your list of the following establishment

_____

_____ on page _____

for the reasons given below.

I stayed/had lunch/dined there on _____ 19____

I am not connected directly or indirectly with management or proprietors.

This communication is confidential and my name is not to be disclosed.

Signed _____

Name and address (BLOCK CAPITALS) _____

_____

Report

☐ *please tick if you would like
this report acknowledged*

☐ *please tick if you would like
more report forms*

please continue overleaf

My meal for . . . . people
cost:　　food　£
　　　　drink　£
　　　service　£
(if added on)　──────
　　　　total　£　──────
Attach bill where possible

The Good Food Guide REPORT FORM (III.80)

To the Editor, *The Good Food Guide*, Freepost,
14 Buckingham Street, London WC2N 6BR

From my personal experience I DO NOT/WOULD NOT APPROVE of the inclusion in your list of the following establishment

_____

_____ on page _____
for the reasons given below.

I stayed/had lunch/dined there on _____ 19____

I am not connected directly or indirectly with management or proprietors.

This communication is confidential and my name is not to be disclosed.

Signed _____

Name and address (BLOCK CAPITALS) _____

_____

Report

please continue overleaf

please tick if you would like
this report acknowledged

please tick if you would like
more report forms

My meal for . . . . people
cost: food £
       drink £
       service £
(if added on)   _____
       total £
Attach bill where possible

To the Editor, *The Good Food Guide*, Freepost,
14 Buckingham Street, London WC2N 6BR

From my personal experience **I DO NOT/WOULD NOT APPROVE** of the inclusion in your list of the following establishment

_____

_____ on page _____

for the reasons given below.

I stayed/had lunch/dined there on _____ 19____

I am not connected directly or indirectly with management or proprietors.

This communication is confidential and my name is not to be disclosed.

Signed _____

Name and address (BLOCK CAPITALS) _____

_____

Report

*please tick if you would like
this report acknowledged*

*please tick if you would like
more report forms*

please continue overleaf

My meal for . . . . people
cost: food   £
         drink   £
         service £
(if added on)
         total   £
Attach bill where possible

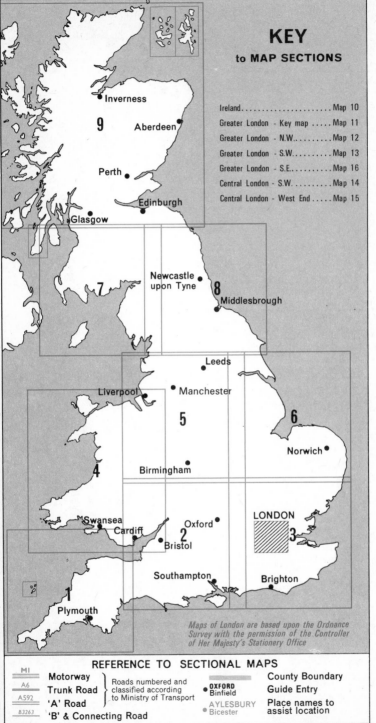

KEY
to MAP SECTIONS

Inverness

Aberdeen

9

Perth

Edinburgh

Glasgow

Newcastle
upon Tyne

7   8

Middlesbrough

Leeds

Liverpool   Manchester

5   6

Norwich

4

Birmingham

Swansea   Oxford

Cardiff   2

Bristol   LONDON

Southampton   3

Brighton

1

Plymouth

*Maps of London are based upon the Ordnance
Survey with the permission of the Controller
of Her Majesty's Stationery Office*

REFERENCE TO SECTIONAL MAPS

M1 Motorway	Roads numbered and classified according to Ministry of Transport
A6 Trunk Road	
A592 'A' Road	
B3263 'B' & Connecting Road	

County Boundary

OXFORD Binfield — Guide Entry

AYLESBURY Bicester — Place names to assist location

Cartographic Services (Cirencester) Ltd.

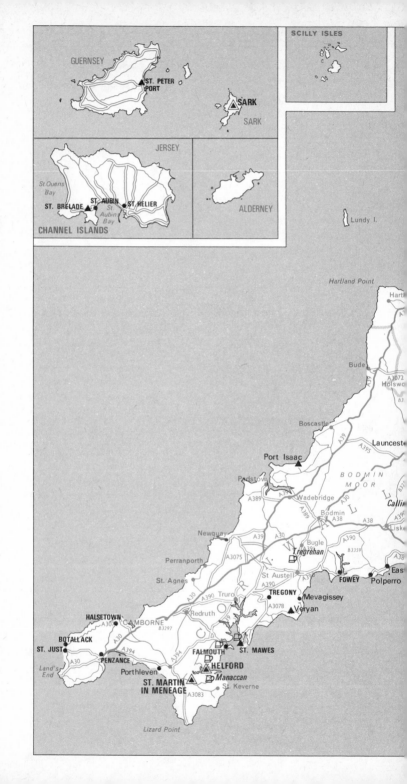

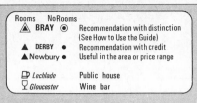

1

SOUTH-WEST ENGLAND

SCILLY ISLES

CHANNEL ISLANDS

Rooms   NoRooms
△ **BRAY**   ◉   Recommendation with distinction
                            (See How to Use the Guide)
▲ **DERBY**   ●   Recommendation with credit
▲ Newbury   ●   Useful in the area or price range

🍺 Lechlade   Public house
🍷 Gloucester   Wine bar

BRISTOL   CHANNEL

Lynton
Ilfracombe   **PORLOCK WEIR**
Ilfracombe   MINEHEAD
acombe   Watchet
🍺 Georgeham   E X M O O R   **WILLITON**
raunton
Wrafton   Bishop's
BARNSTAPLE East Buckland   Lydeard
                    SOUTH   **DULVERTON**
Bideford   **MOLTON**   Milverton
PARKHAM **CHITTLEHAMHOLT**   🍺 Knowstone   Bampton
388▲   Great   A361
KLEIGH Torrington   Chulmleigh
                                                        2
IDDESLEIGH 🍺🍺 🍺 Winkleigh   Honiton
A3072   **GITTISHAM**
          D   E   V   O   N   **OTTERY**
Okehampton   Exeter   **ST MARY**
          South   🍺 A3052   **Tipton**
          Zeal ● Drewsteignton   St John
CHAGFORD 🍺 Fingle   **NEWTON** ▲
FRENCHBEER ▲ Bridge   Exminster **POPPLEFORD** Sidmouth
Lydford 🍺   **LUSTLEIGH** ● Hennock   🍺 Lympstone
          D A R T M O O R   A379   Budleigh
          🍺 Peter Tavy   **EXMOUTH** Salterton
                    B3357   🍺 Chudleigh   Dawlish
          ●**GULWORTHY**   Combeinteignhead
St Dominick   Holne 🍺   Newton
          Buckfastleigh   Abbot   ▲
388▲   A381   **Torquay**
Crown Hill   ● Dartington   PAIGNTON
PLYMOUTH   ● Totnes
          Plympton   **BRIXHAM**
                              A381   F
                    Modbury   Kingswear
                                        DARTMOUTH
                    🍺 Kingsbridge
                              Start Point
SALCOMBE

10   0   Miles   10   20

Cartographic Services (Cirencester) Ltd.

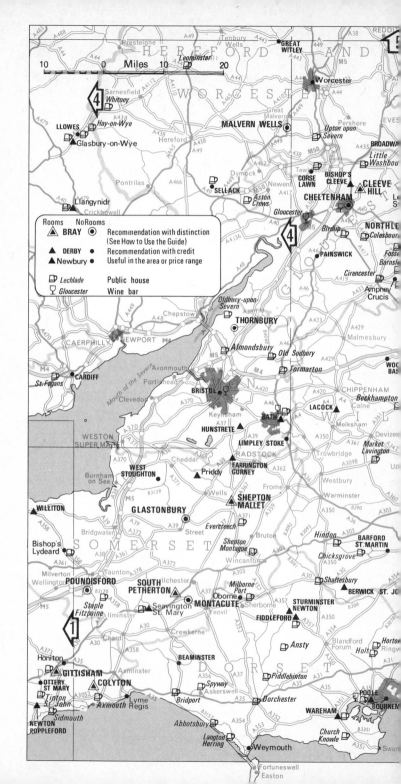

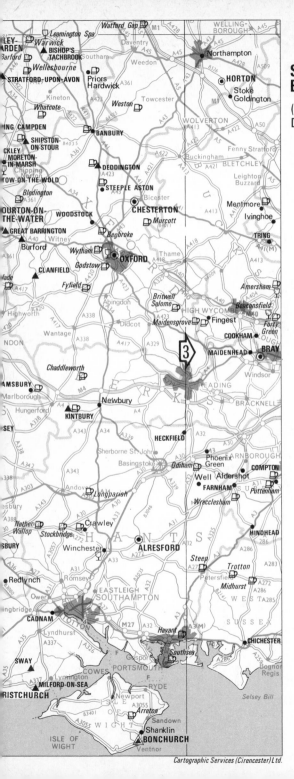

SOUTH-WEST ENGLAND

(see map 1 for
Devon and Cornwall)

Cartographic Services (Cirencester) Ltd.

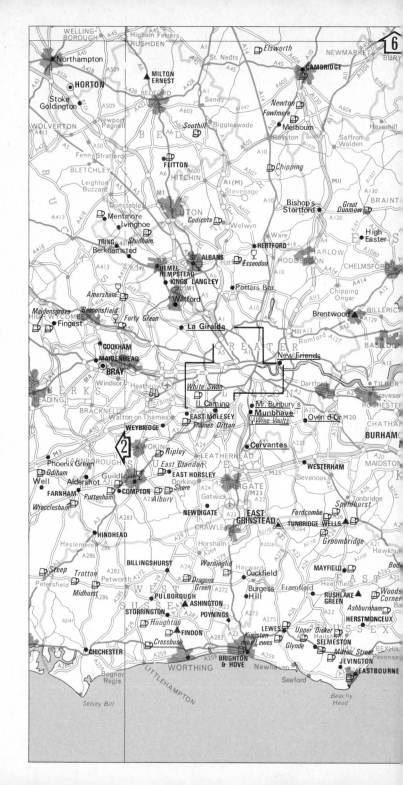

3

SOUTH-EAST
ENGLAND and
THE HOME
COUNTIES

Westleton

Saxmundham
Sizewell
Leiston

Cretingham
Snape

Stowmarket

ORFORD

Needham
Market
Bildeston

Woodbridge

Orford Ness

Cavendish
Long Melford Kersey

HADLEIGH
HINTLESHAM

IPSWICH

NAYLAND

FELIXSTOWE

DEDHAM
Ardleigh

HARWICH

Halstead
Earls
Colne

COLCHESTER

The Naze

Pattiswick

Walton-on-the-Naze

Frinton

CLACTON-ON-SEA

West Mersea

BURNHAM-ON-CROUCH

ayleigh

SOUTHEND
Shoeburyness

River Thames

SHEERNESS

Leysdown-on-Sea

MARGATE

North Foreland
BROADSTAIRS

Herne Bay

Whitstable

RAMSGATE

SITTINGBOURNE

FAVERSHAM

Boughton

Ickham
Sandwich

CANTERBURY

Chilham

EASTRY

Deal

East Sutton

WYE

Walmer

Ashford

BIDDENDEN
Tenterden

South Foreland

Dover

FOLKESTONE

Hythe

whurst
een

RYE

Lydd

Winchelsea

Dungeness

S T R A I T

O F   D O V E R

ASTINGS

10   0   Miles   10   20

Rooms   NoRooms
△ BRAY ⊙   Recommendation with distinction
               (See How to Use the Guide)
▲ DERBY ●   Recommendation with credit
▲ Newbury •   Useful in the area or price range

🏠 Lechlade   Public house
🍷 Gloucester   Wine bar

Restaurants which appear
on the London pages are
underlined.

Cartographic Services (Cirencester) Ltd.

WALES

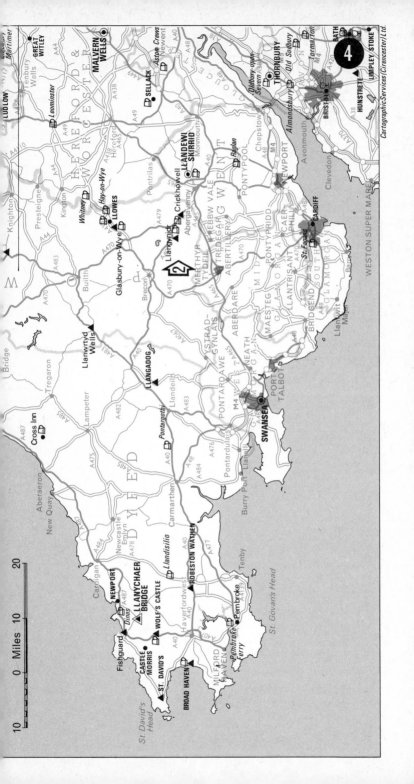

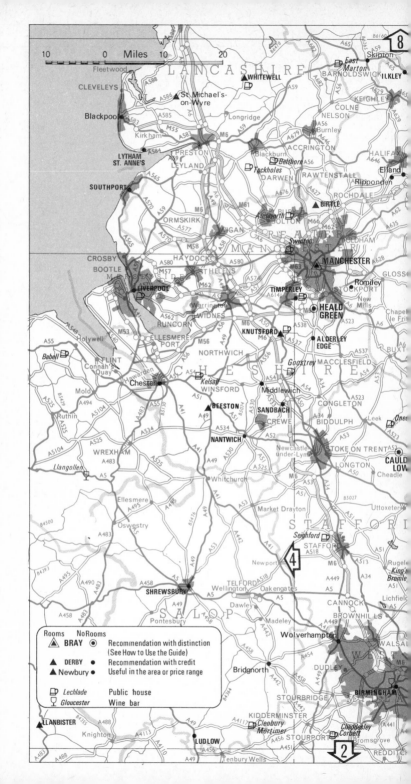

**THE MIDLANDS
and
NORTH-WEST
ENGLAND**

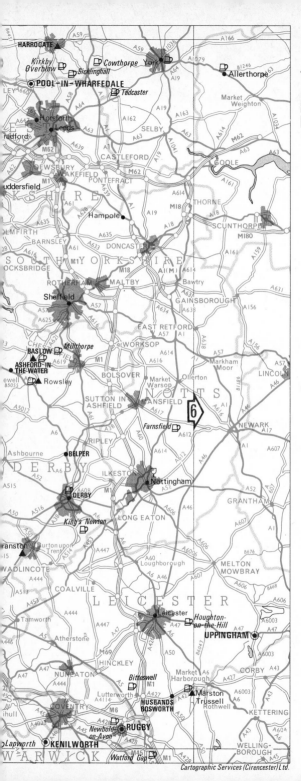

HARROGATE

A59

*Kirkby
Overblow*
Sicklinghall
Cowthorpe
York
A1036
A166
A1079
Allerthorpe
B1246

POOL-IN-WHARFEDALE
Tadcaster
A64
A19

Market
Weighton

LEY
A660
A58
A162
A19
A163
A1034

Horsforth
A64
SELBY
A63
A63
A614
M62

Leeds
A639
A1
A63
A1041

radford
A642

A62

M62
CASTLEFORD
A19
GOOLE

DEWSBURY
WAKEFIELD
PONTEFRACT
M62
A161

uddersfield
M1
A61
A614
THORNE
A18

KS·HIRE
A628
A19
M18
SCUNTHORPE
M180

Hampole
A1
A18

LMFIRTH
A635
A635

BARNSLEY
A61
A633
DONCASTER
A161
A159
A631

28
A616
M1
YORKSHIRE
A614
A156

OCKSBRIDGE
SOUTH
M18
A1(M)
Bawtry

ROTHERHAM
MALTBY
A631

Sheffield
A57
GAINSBOROUGH
A156

A57
A634
A638

A625
A616
EAST RETFORD
A57 A1
A638
A156

BASLOW
CHES
Millthorpe
WORKSOP
A57

ASHFORD-IN-
THE-WATER
A619
M1
A614
A616
Markham
Moor
A57
LINCOLN
A46

ewell
B5055
Rowsley
BOLSOVER
Market
Warsop
Ollerton
B1188

A5012
SUTTON IN
ASHFIELD
MANSFIELD
NOTTS
A1
A46

A61
A617
6
A614
A612
A1
NEWARK
A17

Ashbourne
A6
Farnsfield
A60
A607

BELPER
RIPLEY
A614
A612
A46
A1

DERBY
A515
A52
ILKESTON
Nottingham
A52
A607

DERBY
A608
M1
A51
GRANTHAM

A50
A516
A46
A1

King's Newton
LONG EATON
A606
A607

ranston
Burton upon
Trent
A453
A606
B676

A447
A60
MELTON
MOWBRAY

ADLINCOTE
A444
Loughborough
A607
A606
B668

A513
COALVILLE
A46
A606

Tamworth
A444
LEICESTER
Leicester
A47
*Houghton-
on-the-Hill*
A6003

A447
A426
A47
A47

Atherstone
A5
M69
UPPINGHAM

A446
A5
HINCKLEY
A50
B6047
A6003

NUNEATON
Bitteswell
Market
Harborough
A6
CORBY
A43

A47
A444
M1
A427
A6003
A43

A5
Lutterworth
A427
*Marston
Trussell*
A6
A6003

ihull
A4114
**HUSBANDS
BOSWORTH**
A50
Rothwell
KETTERING

COVENTRY
M6
A43
A604

A4023
A426
*Newbold-
on-Avon*
RUGBY
A43

Lapworth
KENILWORTH
A45
A428
WELLING-
BOROUGH

WARWICK
Watford Gap
A45
M1
A428

Cartographic Services (Cirencester) Ltd.

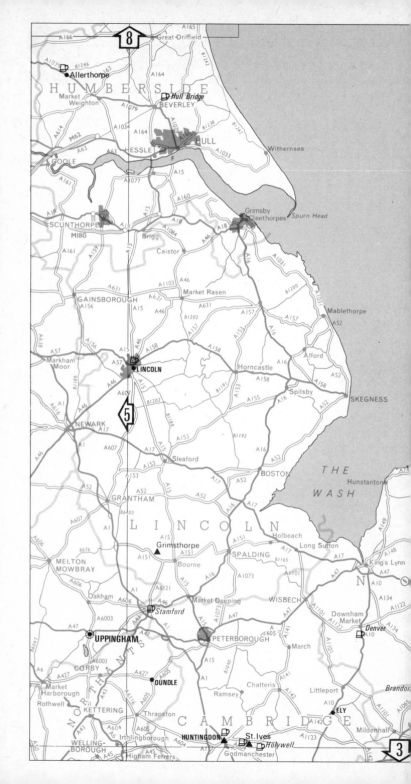

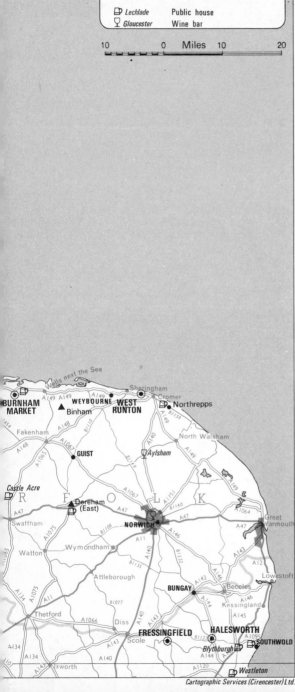

Rooms   NoRooms
△ **BRAY** ◉   Recommendation with distinction
(See How to Use the Guide)
▲ **DERBY** ●   Recommendation with credit
▲ Newbury ●   Useful in the area or price range

◿ *Lechlade*   Public house
� *Gloucester*   Wine bar

10   0   Miles   10   20

Wells next the Sea
Sheringham
Cromer
BURNHAM ◿   **WEYBOURNE** **WEST** ◿ Northrepps
MARKET   ▲ Binham   **RUNTON**
A149 A149
A454 Fakenham   A148
A148 B1110
A1067   A148 B110
GUIST ◿ *Aylsham*
North Walsham
A1067 A149
Castle Acre
◿ R   F   O   L A1151   K
A47 ◿ Dereham   A1067 B1140
Swaffham (East)   A47   A47
A1075   B1108 A1064   Great
Watton   **NORWICH**   A146   Yarmouth
A11 A140 Wymondham   A47
A1075   B1135   A12
Attleborough   B1332   Lowestoft
A1075   B1077   A143   Beccles
A134 A11   **BUNGAY** ● A144   Kessingland
Thetford   A1066 Diss   A140 A143   A146
FRESSINGFIELD   **HALESWORTH**
A134   A143   Scole   B1123   A1095
A134   ◉   *Blythburgh* ◿ ◿ **SOUTHWOLD**
Ixworth   A144
A10   A140   A1120   ◿ *Westleton*

Cartographic Services (Cirencester) Ltd.

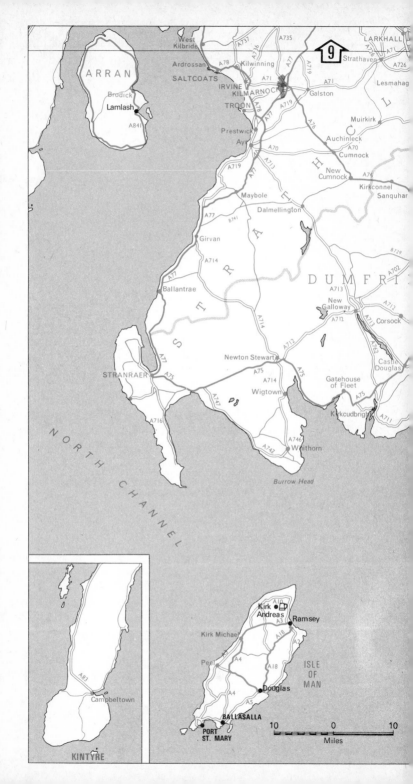

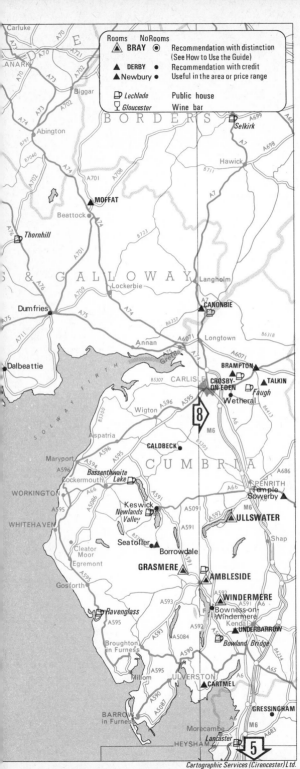

7

NORTH-WEST ENGLAND
ISLE OF MAN
SOUTH-WEST SCOTLAND

Rooms	NoRooms	
△ **BRAY**	⊙	Recommendation with distinction (See How to Use the Guide)
▲ **DERBY**	●	Recommendation with credit
▲ Newbury	●	Useful in the area or price range
⊡ *Lechlade*		Public house
⟁ *Gloucester*		Wine bar

Cartographic Services (Cirencester) Ltd.

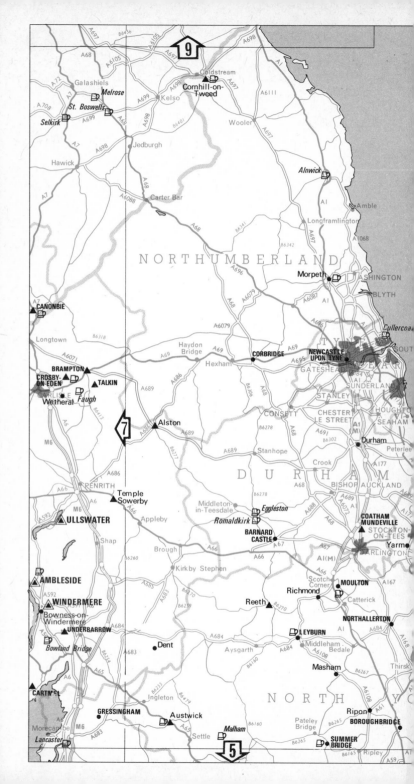

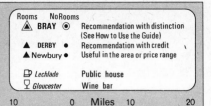

	Rooms	NoRooms	
△	**BRAY**	⊙	Recommendation with distinction (See How to Use the Guide)
▲	**DERBY**	●	Recommendation with credit
▲	Newbury	●	Useful in the area or price range
⌂	*Lechlade*		Public house
⌁	*Gloucester*		Wine bar

10   0   Miles   10   20

8

NORTH-EAST ENGLAND and SOUTH-EAST SCOTLAND

HIELDS

SPRING

HARTLEPOOL

REDCAR

ENGLAND

Middlesbrough
Loftus

Guisborough

A171 WHITBY

Stokesley

A169

FADMOOR
Kirby
Moorside
WRELTON
AISLABY
Pickering
A170 Thornton-le-Dale
SCARBOROUGH
Seamer
Filey

Hovingham

ORKSHIRE

Easingwold Malton

BRIDLINGTON

A166
A165

6

Cartographic Services (Cirencester) Ltd.

SCOTLAND (see also maps 7 & 8)

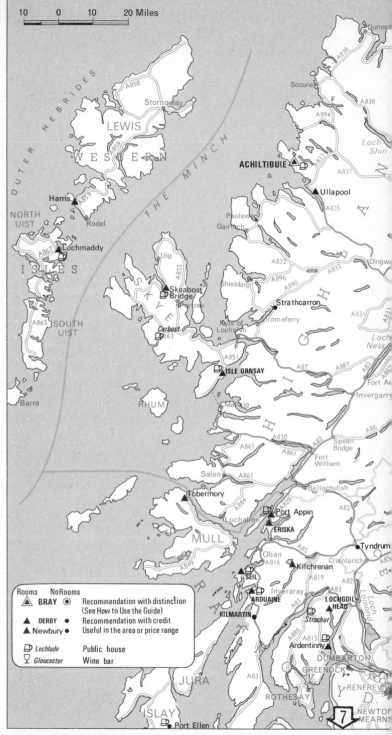

10 0 10   20 Miles

Durness

Scourie

F

Stornoway

LEWIS

OUTER HEBRIDES

WESTERN

THE MINCH

Loch Shin

A838

A838

A894

A858

A859

A837

A835

ACHILTIBUIE

Ullapool

Harris

Rodel

NORTH UIST

Lochmaddy

A867

ISLES

SOUTH UIST

Barra

A865

Uig

A855

Skeabost Bridge

Portree

Carbost
A863

SKYE

RHUM

Poolewe

Gairloch

Shieldaig

Strathcarron

Stromeferry

Kyle of Lochalsh

A832

A896

A890

Dingwall

A832

A831

A831

Loch Ness

A851

ISLE ORNSAY

F

Mallaig

F

A87

A887

Fort A

Invergarry

HIGH

A830

A861

A861

A86

Spean Bridge

Fort William

Ballachulish

A82

Salen

A861

Tobermory

Lochaline

Port Appin

ERISKA

A828

MULL

Oban

A816

Kilchrenan

Crianlarich

Tyndrum

A85

A85

SEIL

A849

A819

A82

Inveraray

ARDUAINE

A83

Strachur

LOCHGOIL HEAD

KILMARTIN

A83

A886

A815

Ardentinny

DUMBARTON

GREENOCK

RENFREW

D

NEWTON MEARNS

ROTHESAY

JURA

ISLAY

Port Ellen

7

Legend

Rooms	NoRooms	
▲ **BRAY**	⊙	Recommendation with distinction (See How to Use the Guide)
▲ **DERBY**	●	Recommendation with credit
▲ Newbury	●	Useful in the area or price range
🏠 *Lechlade*		Public house
🍷 *Gloucester*		Wine bar

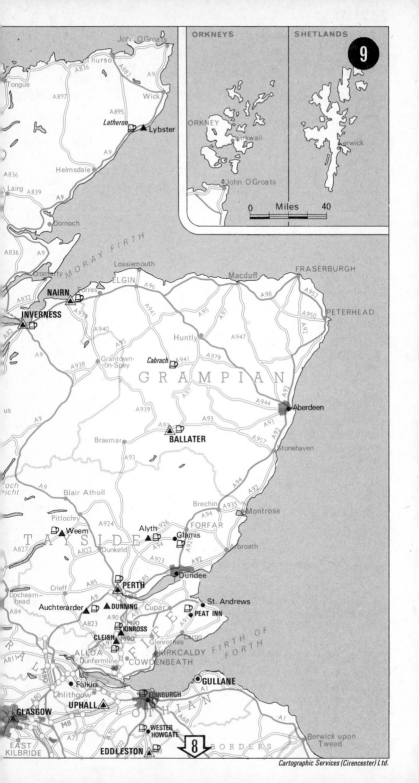

IRELAND

ANTRIM

LONDONDERRY

TYRONE

DONEGAL

FERMANAGH

ARMAGH

DOWN

MONAGHAN

CAVAN

LEITRIM

SLIGO

MAYO

ROSCOMMON

LONGFORD

COMMON

LOUTH

MEATH

WESTMEATH

BELFAST

Helen's Bay

Newtownards

Kilkinchy

SAINTFIELD

Comber

Lisburn

Hillsborough

Downpatrick

GILFORD

Portadown

Loughall

Armagh

NEWRY

Monaghan

SLANE

DUNDERRY

Drogheda

Mullingar

Longford

Roscommon

Cavan

Enniskillen

BELLANALECK

Ballysadare

Sligo

Ballina

CASTLEBAR

Newport

Westport

LETTERFRACK

MOYARD

BALLYCONNEELY

Achill Island

Omagh

Dungannon

Strabane

Londonderry

Coleraine

Portrush

Ballymena

Aldergrove

Larne

50 Miles

0   25   50

Cartographic Services (Cirencester) Ltd.

GREATER LONDON
Key Map

SEE
MAP
14

SEE MAP 13

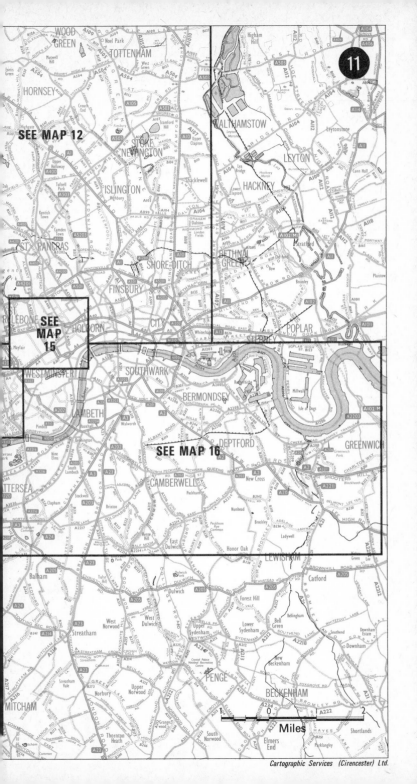

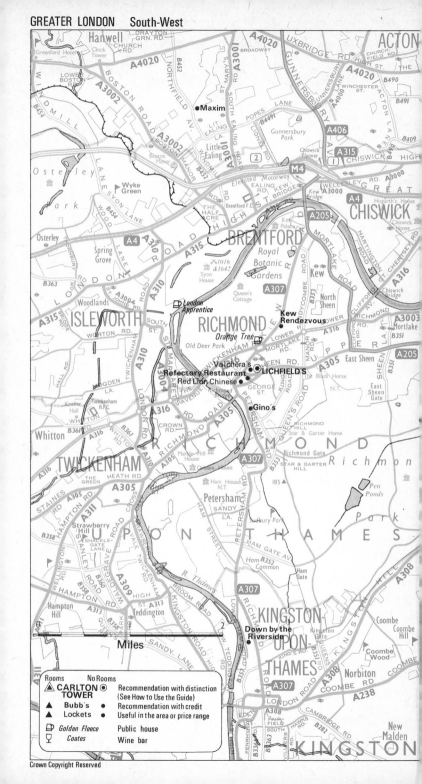

GREATER LONDON   South-West

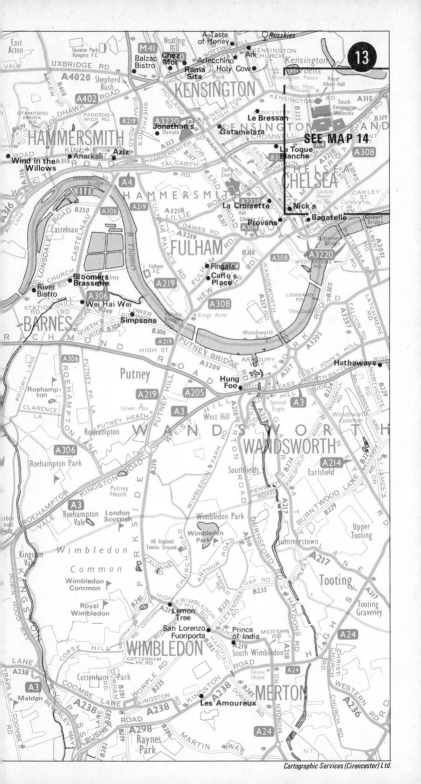

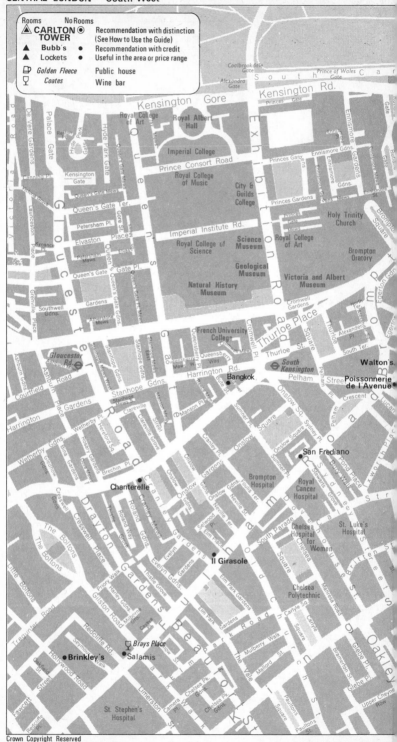

CENTRAL LONDON   South-West

Crown Copyright Reserved

CENTRAL LONDON West End

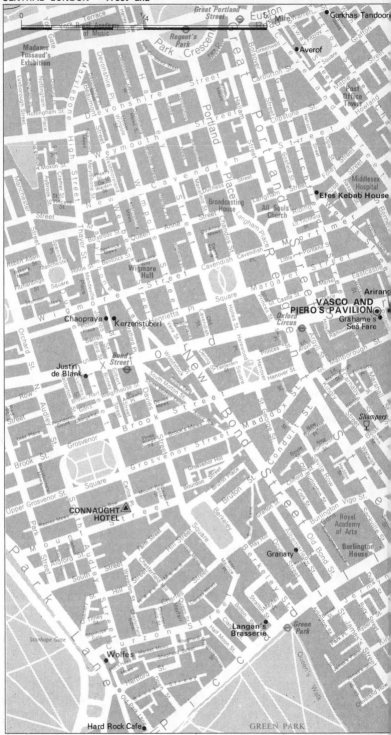

Crown Copyright Reserved

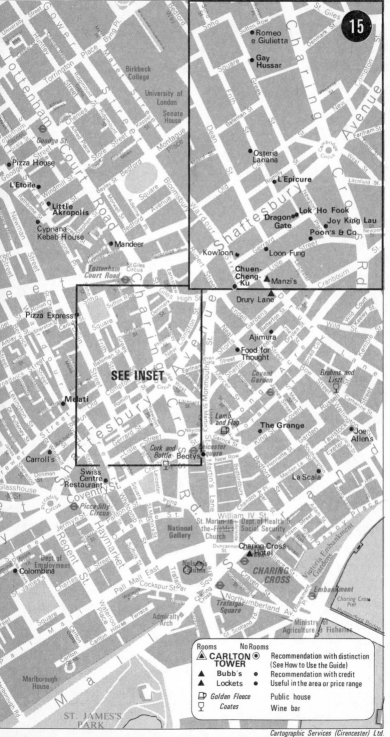

15

Romeo e Giulietta

Gay Hussar

Birkbeck College

University of London
Senate House

Osteria Lariana

L'Epicure

Pizza House

L'Etoile

Little Akropolis

Cypriana Kebab House

Mandeer

Lok Ho Fook

Dragon Gate

Joy King Lau

Poon's & Co.

Kowloon

Loon Fung

Chuen-Cheng-Ku

Manzi's

Tottenham Court Road

Drury Lane

Pizza Express

Ajimura

Food for Thought

SEE INSET

Covent Garden

Brahms and Liszt

Melati

Lamb and Flag

The Grange

Joe Allen's

Carroll's

Cork and Bottle

Beotys

La Scala

Swiss Centre Restaurant

Piccadilly Circus

National Gallery

St. Martin-in-the-Fields Church

Dept. of Health & Social Security

Dept. of Employment

Colombina

Charing Cross Hotel

Nelson's Column

CHARING CROSS

Embankment

Charing Cross Pier

Trafalgar Square

Admiralty Arch

Ministry of Agriculture & Fisheries

Marlborough House

ST. JAMES'S PARK

Rooms	No Rooms	
△ **CARLTON TOWER**	⊙	Recommendation with distinction (See How to Use the Guide)
▲ *Bubb's*	●	Recommendation with credit
▲ Lockets	●	Useful in the area or price range
🏠 *Golden Fleece*		Public house
♈ Coates		Wine bar

Cartographic Services (Cirencester) Ltd.

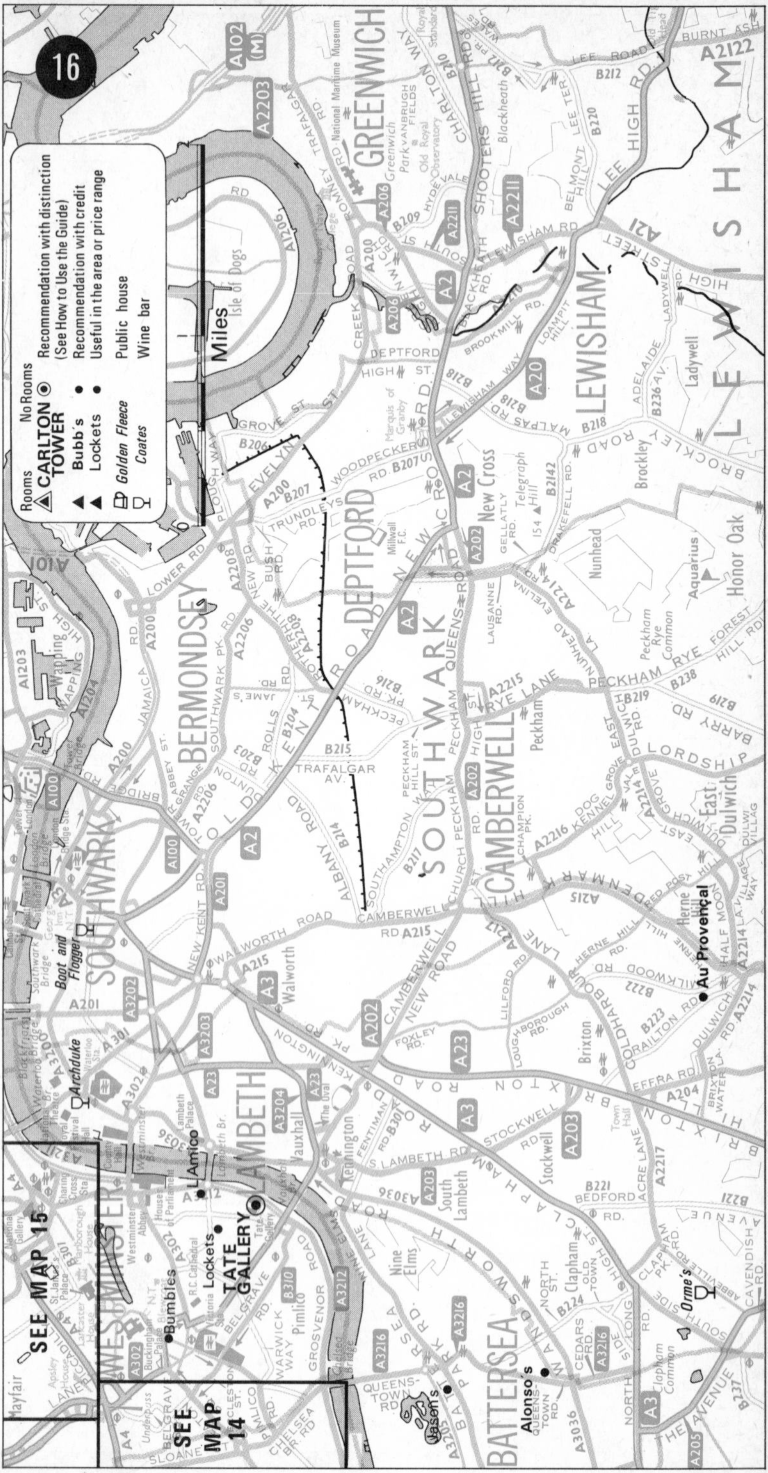
16
Rooms
No Rooms
CARLTON TOWER
Recommendation with distinction (See How to Use the Guide)
Bubb's
Recommendation with credit
Lockets
Useful in the area or price range
Golden Fleece
Public house
Coates
Wine bar
Miles
SEE MAP 15
SEE MAP 14
GREENWICH
DEPTFORD
BERMONDSEY
SOUTHWARK
CAMBERWELL
LEWISHAM
LAMBETH
WESTMINSTER
BATTERSEA
Isle of Dogs
Wapping
Blackheath
New Cross
Peckham
Nunhead
Brockley
Honor Oak
East Dulwich
Herne Hill
Brixton
Stockwell
Clapham
Kennington
Vauxhall
Walworth
Pimlico
Nine Elms
South Lambeth
Ladywell
Boot and Flogger
Archduke
L'Amico
Bumbles
Lockets
TATE GALLERY
Au Provençal
Orme's
Alonso's
Jason's
Aquarius